中国翻译研究院“中国特色话语对外翻译标准化术语库”项目成果

中国民俗文化词典

A Dictionary of Chinese Folk Culture (Illustrated)

插图本（汉英对照）

《中国民俗文化词典》编写组 著

SinolinguA
华语教学出版社

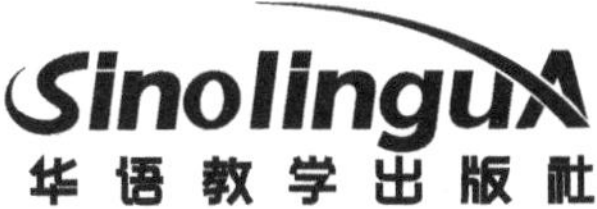

First Edition 2023
Second Printing 2024

ISBN 978-7-5138-2457-6

Published by Sinolingua Co., Ltd
24 Baiwanzhuang Street, Beijing 100037, China
Tel: (86) 10-68320585 68997826
Fax: (86) 10-68997826 68326333
https://www.sinolingua.com.cn
E-mail:hyjx@sinolingua.com.cn
Printed by Beijing Zhongke Printing Co., Ltd

Printed in the People's Republic of China

目　录
Contents

出版前言

习近平主席在文化传承发展座谈会上指出，中华优秀传统文化有很多重要元素，共同塑造出中华文明的突出特性。中国民俗文化是民间智慧的结晶，是中国传统文化的重要组成部分，不仅广泛存在于我国各族人民的日常生活、生产和各种社会组织当中，也广受对中国文化感兴趣的外国受众关注。做好民俗文化的翻译和对外传播对于弘扬中华传统文化、增进文明交流互鉴具有重要意义。由于民俗文化中国特色鲜明，很多专业术语在对外翻译传播过程中难以找到对应的外文表述，或者外文表述很不统一，成为中外文化交流中的一个难点。为解决这一问题，当代中国与世界研究院联合华语教学出版社共同组织中外专家编撰并翻译了我国第一本较为系统的民俗文化双语辞书—《中国民俗文化词典·插图本》（汉英对照）。

《词典》从岁时节令、人生仪礼、衣食住行和信仰崇拜等四个极具代表性的民俗领域精选了相关民俗术语 700 余条，在广泛查阅权威文献的基础上提炼出简明扼要、适合国际传播的术语释义，涵盖术语的历史演变、现状、地域特点等，并配以精美插图，通过具体的民俗事象展现中华文明源远流长的历史变迁，多元统一的文化传统，以及新时代中国人民日新月异的生活风貌。词条的英文译文充分考虑到海外受众的特点，力求准确达意，且易于海外读者理解，充分展现中华文化的魅力。

为方便读者较为直观地了解全书收词情况，并根据类别查阅所需了解的词条内容，本词典设有词目表，在书末还根据词条汉语拼音音序，提供音序索引。本词典附录部分还提供了朝代表、二十四节气表、中国各民族分布表、中国民间重要节日等相关内容。

《词典》可供从事文化对外传播工作的翻译业务部门、专业翻译出版机构以及各行各业涉外交流人员参考使用，也可为学习中文或对中国文化感兴趣的外国读者提供参考。

《词典》在编写过程中参考了国内外出版的有关民俗文化的文献，征求了民俗和对外文化传播领域众多专家学者的意见和建议。西安外国语大学高级翻译学院部分师生参与了词典内容的编撰。在此，谨向参与《词典》研制编写的学者同仁表示诚挚感谢和崇高敬意！

民俗文化是一个博大精深的领域，限于时间、精力和能力等因素制约，《词典》涵盖的范围还比较有限，内容也难免存在不当和疏漏之处，欢迎广大读者批评指正，我们将在后续修订版中逐步完善。

Preface

President Xi Jinping pointed out at a meeting on cultural inheritance and development that traditional Chinese culture, with its rich and essential elements, contributes to the formation of the unique Chinese civilization. As an integral part of traditional Chinese culture representing the wisdom of the Chinese people, Chinese folk culture is present everywhere—in our daily life, work, and various social organizations. It is also of great use to international audiences interested in Chinese culture, hence the need to translate it into other languages. However, the lack of unified and standardized translation for folk cultural terms makes it difficult to present our folk culture accurately and effectively to the outside world. Therefore, the Academy of Contemporary China and World Studies and Sinolingua have worked jointly to compile *A Dictionary of Chinese Folk Culture (Illustrated) (the Dictionary)*, the country's first bilingual dictionary of Chinese folk culture.

The *Dictionary* contains over 700 folk terms selected from four areas: solar terms and festivals; rites of passage; food, clothing, shelter, and transportation; and beliefs and worship. Based on an extensive review of authoritative literature, the *Dictionary* provides a concise yet informative bilingual interpretation for each entry, covering its historical evolution, current practice, geographical features, and more. Illustrations are provided for some entries to facilitate understanding. Together, these specific folk events and phenomena reflect the evolution of the Chinese culture over time, the tradition of diversity in unity, and the ever-changing lifestyle of the Chinese people in the new era.

To help readers understand all the terms included and for easy reference, the *Dictionary* has a keywords list and a Chinese phonetic order index, namely the pinyin index, at the end of the book. The appendices include a dynasties list, the list of twenty-four solar terms, the distribution of Chinese ethnic groups, and important Chinese folk festivals.

The *Dictionary* can serve as a reference book for translators and other professionals engaged in international cultural communications. It also hopes to be of help to international readers who are studying Chinese or are interested in learning more about Chinese culture.

During the compilation process, we have done thorough research on literature concerning Chinese folk culture and consulted many experts and scholars in the fields of folklore and cross-cultural communication. A team of teachers and graduate students from the School of Translation Studies, Xi'an International Studies University (XISU) participated in this project. We would like to express our sincere gratitude to all for their contribution to this project.

You are welcome to provide us with feedback so that future editions can be improved.

词目表
Keywords List

岁时节令
Solar Terms and Festivals

人生仪礼
Rites of Passage

		arrange for a proper burial	
叫魂	*jiao hun*	soul calling; calling back one's soul	308
喊魂	*han hun*	calling souls	308
招魂	*zhao hun*	soul summoning	309
灵堂	*lingtang*	mourning hall; funeral hall	309
报丧	*bao sang*	announcing the death	310
戴孝	*dai xiao*	wearing mourning clothes; be in mourning	311
守灵	*shou ling*	keep vigil beside the coffin; hold a wake	312
守丧	*shou sang*	observing the conventions of mourning; be in mourning	313
丁忧	*dingyou*	be in bereavement	314
接三	*jie san*	receiving the returning soul on the third	314
送三	*song san*	bidding farewell to the soul on the third	315
吊丧	*diao sang*	(pay) a condolence visit	316
吊孝	*diao xiao*	(pay) a condolence visit	316
谢孝	*xie xiao*	thank friends and relatives for offering condolences	317
发丧	*fa sang*	announce the death of a family member; arrange funeral affairs	318
小殓	*xiaolian*	dress a dead body	319
大殓	*dalian*	enconffin	319
入殓	*ru lian*	enconffin	320
出殡	*chu bin*	funeral procession	320
摔老盆	*shuai laopen*	breaking an old pot	322
纸扎	*zhizha*	paper offerings	323
纸活	*zhihuo*	paper work	324
买路钱	*mai lu qian*	money for passing the road	324
祭坟	*ji fen*	offering sacrifices at the	325

衣食住行
Food, Clothing, Shelter and Transportation

信仰崇拜
Beliefs and Worship

		accidents (usually refers to death)	
六六大顺	*liuliu dashun*	lucky double six; double six makes for good luck	654
好事成双	*haoshi chengshuang*	Good things come in pairs	655
寡妇年	*guafu nian*	widow year	655
左眼跳财，右眼跳灾	*zuoyan tiao cai, youyan tiao zai*	twitching left eye foretells fortune, twitching right eye foretells disaster	657

XXXVI

岁时节令

SOLAR TERMS AND FESTIVALS

岁 *sui;* year; age

中国传统的时间观念，指两个冬至日之间的时间间隔。古人以木星所在的位置来纪年，把木星每年行一个星次称为一岁，因而木星又称岁星。岁与现代天文学的回归年一致。岁还可泛指时间、光阴，年岁，年龄及一年的收成、年景等。

Chinese traditional concept of time, namely the time span between two winter solstices. Ancient Chinese recorded the year according to the position of Jupiter in the sky. The orbit of Jupiter was divided into twelve parts, with one part called one *xingci*. The time span for Jupiter to orbit one *xingci* (the twelve Jupiter stations on the ecliptic) is called one *sui* (year), therefore ancient Chinese people also referred to Jupiter as *suixing* (literally, "the planet for marking the year"). *Sui* is equal to the length of a tropical year in modern astronomy. The term can also refer to time in general, age, the harvest of a year and so on.

例句：

新春佳节之际，中国人常说"辞旧**岁**，迎新年"。

Example Sentence:

On the occasion of the Spring Festival, the Chinese people often say, "Let's ring out the old year (*sui*) and ring in the new one."

时 *shi;* two-hour time span; season

中国传统的时间观念，指季节或时辰。古代称春、夏、秋、

Chinese traditional concept of time originally referring to seasons and also the two-hour time span. In ancient times, the four seasons of

冬四季为四时，四时成岁。也用来指更小的时间单位时辰，古人分一昼夜为十二时辰（一个时辰为两小时），与十二地支相配来计时，如子时便指十二时辰中的第一个时辰（夜里 11 时至次日 1 时）。现在也用来泛指光阴、岁月等。

spring, summer, autumn, and winter were called *sishi* (four seasons). But *shi* was also used to refer to the smaller time unit *shichen*, which is equivalent to two hours. Ancient Chinese traditionally divided the day into twelve *shichen* and calculated the time by corresponding *shichen* with the twelve Earthly Branches. For instance, *zishi* (the period from 11:00 p.m. to 1:00 a.m.) is the first *shichen* of the day. Nowadays, it is also common for *shi* to refer to time and years in general.

例句：

"时不我待"是劝解人们珍惜时间的成语。

Example Sentence:

Time and tide wait for no man (shíbùwǒdài) is a Chinese idiom that urges people to cherish time.

节

jie;
festival; solar term

中国传统的时间观念，指节气、节日，是人们为适应生产和生活需要依照岁时次序创造出的一种民俗文化。一年有二十四节气：冬至、小寒、大寒、立春、雨水、惊蛰、春分、清明、谷雨、立夏、小满、芒种、夏至、小暑、大暑、立秋、处暑、白露、

Chinese traditional concept of time, referring to solar terms and also festivals, created to help people adapt to the needs of agricultural production and daily life. There are 24 solar terms in a year, namely: the Winter Solstice, Slight Cold, Great Cold, Beginning of Spring, Rain Water, Waking of Insects, Spring Equinox, Pure Brightness, Grain

秋分、寒露、霜降、立冬、小雪、大雪。二十四节气比较准确地反映了季节变化的规律，是指导农业生产和人们日常生活的指南针，并由之衍生出了丰富的岁时节令文化（如清明踏青、中秋赏月等），是中国传统文化的瑰宝。

Rain, Beginning of Summer, Grain Full, Grain in Ear, Summer Solstice, Slight Heat, Great Heat, Beginning of Autumn, Limit of Heat, White Dew, Autumn Equinox, Cold Dew, Frost's Descent, Beginning of Winter, Slight Snow, and Great Snow. These 24 terms reflected the seasonal variations and also lead to multitudes of festive activities such as spring outings during the Qingming (Pure Brightness) Festival, appreciating the moon during the Mid-Autumn Festival, and more. These festivals are treasures of traditional Chinese culture.

例句：

如今，中国越来越重视中华民族传统**节**日的传承与发展。

Example Sentence:

Now Chinese people pay greater attention to maintaining and celebrating traditional festivals.

令 *ling;* season; seasonal decree

中国传统的时间观念，指时节、法令。古人将按季节制定的政令称为时令，如夏令，冬令；并且以十二个月份分别记述应当实施的政令，叫作月令。节令还可指某个节气的气候和物候，人们会按照季节次序举行

Chinese traditional concept of time, namely a season or a decree released at a certain season. In ancient China, certain decrees were formulated by the government to guide agricultural production and other activities. The decrees were formulated according to the season, such as the summer and

不同的仪式和节庆活动来加以庆祝。

winter decrees, while the monthly recordings of the degrees to be executed in the 12 months *yueling*. *Ling* can also refer to the climate and phenology during a specific solar term. People would celebrate this time by holding different ceremonies and festivals based on the season.

例句：

中国古时制定的时**令**主要与农事有关，以期指导农业生产。

Example Sentence:

Seasonal decrees formulated in ancient China were mainly related to farming and intended to guide agricultural production.

四时八节 *sishi bajie;* four seasons and eight solar terms; all seasons and solar terms

汉族岁时风俗，流行于中国各地。古代称春、夏、秋、冬为四时或四季；称四立（立春、立夏、立秋、立冬）、两至（夏至、冬至）、两分（春分、秋分）八个节气为八节，可泛指一年四季各个节气。

Terminology used by the Han ethnic group to describe different seasonal periods throughout the year. The four seasons are spring, summer, autumn, and winter. The eight solar terms are: Beginning of Spring, Beginning of Summer, Beginning of Autumn, Beginning of Winter, Summer Solstice, Winter Solstice, Spring Equinox, and Autumn Equinox. This expression is also used to refer to all seasons and solar terms in general.

例句：

二十四节气是在四时八节的基础上发展起来的。殷、周之交已分**四时**，春秋战国时代已有**八节**，西汉初期，《淮南子》中就出现了完整的二十四节气名称。

Example Sentence:

The 24 solar terms evolved on the basis of the four seasons and the eight solar terms. The term "four seasons" appeared around the Shang Dynasty (1600-1046 BC), while the "eight solar terms" came into being during the Spring and Autumn Period (770-476 BC) and Warring States Period (475-221BC). A complete set of 24 solar terms first appeared in the book *Huainanzi* in the early Han Dynasty (206 BC-AD 220).

阳历 *yangli;* solar calendar;

历法的一种，全称"太阳历"，以地球绕太阳公转的运动周期为基础制定，平均历年为一个回归年。阳历的月数和日数是人为规定的，与月相盈亏无关。每年 12 个月，一年 365 天，每四年有一个闰年，闰年是 366 天。目前世界通行的格里历（公历）就是一种典型的阳历。

A yearly calendar based on the time it takes the earth to make one revolution around the sun. The number of months and days of a solar calendar are artificially determined and have nothing to do with the waxing and waning of the moon. There are 12 months encompassing roughly 365 days each year, but an extra day is added every four years to account for leap years. The current Gregorian calendar is a typical solar calendar.

例句：

罗马的儒略历和古埃及的科普特历为世界上最古老的几种**阳历**之一。

Example Sentence:

The oldest solar calendars include the Julian Calendar and the Coptic Calendar.

阴历 *yinli;* lunar calendar

历法的一种，全称“太阴历”，指按照月亮的月相周期来安排的历法，与阳历对应。一年有12个朔望月（即月亮相继具有相同的月相），约354或355日，以月亮绕地球运行一周的时间为一个月（约29.5天），大月30日，小月29日。因月相变化是人们最容易观察到的天象，所以在大多数国家阴历的出现都早于阳历。目前只有少数国家和地区仍在使用阴历，其他国家大都已不再使用。

A yearly calendar which contrasts with the solar calendar in that it is based on the cycles of the phases of the moon. There are 12 synodic months (complete cycles of phases of the moon), which encompass around 354 to 355 days a year. The time it takes the moon to go around the earth is about 29.5 days, so there are 29 or 30 days per month in the lunar calendar. Since changes in lunar phases are the most easily observed astronomical phenomena, it is no surprise that the lunar calendar appeared earlier than the solar calendar in most countries. Today, only a few countries and regions still use the lunar calendar.

例句：

中国民间人们常说的**阴历**是指中国的传统历法农历。

Example Sentence:

The traditional Chinese calendar is often referred to as the "lunar" calendar.

阴阳历 *yinyangli;* lunisolar calendar

历法的一种，兼具阳历和阴历的性质，同时考虑到月亮和太阳的运行周期（即朔望月和回归年）。阴阳历以月亮绕地球一周为1个月，但每隔3年设置一个闰月。闰年13个月，全年383或384天；没有闰月的平年为354或355天，这样阴阳历的年平均天数为365，约等于回归年。中国现在仍在使用的农历就是一种阴阳历。

A calendar that takes into account both the cycles of the moon and the sun. The time the moon takes to go around the earth is one month in the lunisolar calendar, but a leap month is added every three years. In a lunisolar calendar, there are 13 months and 383 or 384 days in leap years; in regular years there are 12 months and 354 or 355 days in the year. This averages to 365 days (the length of a solar year). The Chinese calendar still in use today is a lunisolar calendar.

例句：

阴阳历既可反映月亮的圆缺，还可体现四季寒暑往复变化。

Example Sentence:

The lunisolar calendar can reflect both the waxing and waning of the moon and the cycles of the four seasons.

农历 *nongli;* the Chinese calendar

中国传统历法，相传创始于夏代并一直沿用至今，又名夏历、旧历。农历设置二十四节气指导农业生产活动，主要在农村中使用，因此得名。农历兼具阳历和阴历的性质，是一种阴阳合历。它根据朔望月周期来定月，平年十二个月，有六个大月各三十天，六个小月各二十九天，全年共354天；又用大约每隔三年设置一个闰月的置闰法使历年的平均长度大约等于一个太阳年（回归年）。农历纪年用天干地支搭配，六十年为一个周期，周而复始。

The ancient Chinese calendar which is still in popular use today. It was believed to have been created during the Xia Dynasty (c. 2070-1600 BC), so it was also called the Xia Calendar or the Old Calendar. The calendar sets 24 solar terms to guide agricultural production, and has been widely used in rural areas. It is a lunisolar calendar, its year consisting of 12 months of alternately 29 and 30 days, equal to 354 days, or approximately 12 full lunar cycles. Intercalary months have been inserted to keep the average calendar year in step with the solar year of about 365 days. The calendar records the year through the combination of a Heavenly Stem and an Earthly Branch which repeat itself on a 60-year cycle.

例句：

至今，几乎全世界所有华人及朝鲜、韩国和越南等国家仍使用**农历**来推算传统节日，如春节、中秋节、端午节等。

Example Sentence:

Chinese people and people of Chinese origin across the world, as well as people in the Democratic People's Republic of Korea, the Republic of Korea, Vietnam, etc. still use the Chinese calendar to determine dates of traditional festivals such as the Spring Festival, the Mid-Autumn Festival, and the Dragon Boat Festival.

夏历 *xiali;* the Xia Calendar

参见"农历"。夏历与黄帝历、颛顼历、殷历、周历、鲁历合称古六历。

See *nongli* (the Chinese calendar). It is one of the six ancient Chinese calendars, the other five being the Yellow Emperor Calendar, the Zhuanxu Calendar, the Yin Calendar, the Zhou Calendar, and the Lu Calendar.

例句：

夏历是中国最早的历法之一，并一直被广泛采用。

Example Sentence:

The Xia Calendar is one of the earliest calendars in China, and has been used extensively till today.

旧历 *jiuli;* the Old Calendar

参见"农历"。

See *nongli* (the Chinese calendar).

例句：

旧历又称夏历，是中国最早的历法之一，并一直被广泛采用。

Example Sentence:

The Old Calendar, also known as the Xia Calendar, is one of the earliest calendars in China, and has been used extensively till today.

万年历 *wannianli;* perpetual calendar

中国古代传说中最古老的一部太阳历，以该历法的编撰者万年的名字命名，记录一定时间段内的具体阳历和阴历的日期。现代的万年历指包括若干年或适用于若干年的历书，可同时显示农历、公历等多套历法，还可包含黄历相关吉凶宜忌、节假日、提醒等多种功能信息；其形式也更丰富多样，包括出版物、电脑软件、手机应用等，十分便捷。

The oldest solar calendar according to ancient Chinese legend, named after its compiler, *Wan Nian* which literally translates to "ten thousand years". It records specific dates of solar and lunar calendars over a certain period of time. The modern perpetual calendar refers to a kind of almanac that includes many years or can be used for many years. It can now display the contents of multiple calendars, like the Chinese calendar and the Gregorian calendar. It also includes information about good and bad luck as well as recommendations for auspicious and inauspicious activities typical of the yellow calendar, festivals and holidays, and reminders. It is convenient and available through publications, computer software, and mobile APPs.

例句：

万年历可适用于许多年，可计算出未来具体的某天是周几。

Example Sentence:

A perpetual calendar is a calendar which can be used for many years, designed to figure out what day is a given date in the future.

黄历 *huangli;* Chinese almanac; yellow calendar

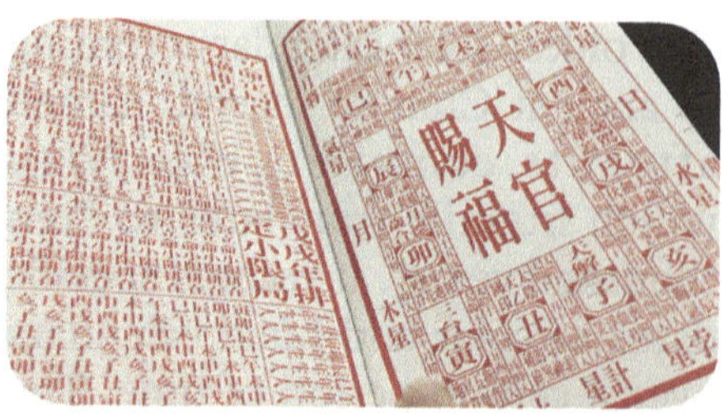

相传是由黄帝创制的历法，故称为“黄历”。黄历是在中国农历基础上产生出来的，包括二十四节气等指导农民耕种的农时节气并带有每天的宜忌凶煞的一种历法。因古时由皇室、朝廷颁发，因此也称“皇历”。

A kind of almanac, allegedly created by the Yellow Emperor and thus called yellow calendar. It was derived from the Chinese calendar, and includes 24 solar terms to help guide farmers in agricultural production and in avoiding daily taboos. Since it was officially issued by the imperial court in ancient times, it is also known as the imperial calendar.

例句：

中国一直以来都是农业大国，因而**黄历**以为广大农民提供信息和农耕知识为主。

Example Sentence:

China has long been an agricultural country. Therefore, the Chinese almanac was mainly designed to provide agricultural information to farmers.

皇历 *huangli;* imperial calendar

参见“黄历”。

See *huangli* (Chinese almanac).

二十八宿 *ershiba xiu;* twenty-eight mansions

中国古代天文学术语，指星空区划中的二十八组恒星，又称“二十八舍”或“二十八星”。“宿”或“舍”，有“停留”的意思，指位置相对固定的恒星。二十八宿分东南西北四方各七宿，合称二十八宿，主要用于测定太阳、月亮等在星空中的位置，从而确定季节、方位和制定历法等。古代的印度和阿拉伯民族也有自己的二十八宿体系。

An ancient Chinese astronomical term. It refers to 28 groups of stars which have relatively fixed positions in the ecliptic — the path in the earth's sky which the sun follows over the course of one year. The mansions are divided into four groups according to the four directions of east, west, south, and north, each group containing seven constellations, totaling 28 constellations, which were used to measure the locations of the sun and the moon on the ecliptic so that different seasons, locations, calendars and others could be determined. Ancient India and the Arab nations had similar astronomical systems.

例句：

二十八宿是中国古代星空区划体系的重要组成部分，与西方天文学上的星座颇为相似。

Example Sentence:

The ancient Chinese system of twenty-eight mansions divides the stars in the sky in an organized manner, and is similar to the modern zodiac constellations in Western astronomy.

二十八舍 *ershiba she;* twenty-eight mansions

参见“二十八宿”。

See *ershiba xiu* (twenty-eight mansions).

二十八星 *ershiba xing;* twenty-eight constellations

参见“二十八宿”。

See *ershiba xiu* (twenty-eight mansions).

十二生肖 *shi'er shengxiao;* twelve zodiac animals

中国用于记录人的出生年的十二种动物，生肖又称“属相”。用十二种动物配十二地支，即子（鼠）、丑（牛）、寅（虎）、卯（兔）、辰（龙）、巳（蛇）、午（马）、未（羊）、申（猴）、酉（鸡）、戌（狗）、亥（猪）。人们认为人生在

An ancient Chinese system for designating each year with one of the 12 zodiac animals representing the 12 Earthly Branches and associated with a 12-year cycle. Each year corresponds to an "earthly branch," which is represented by an animal believed to entail the characteristics of people born in that year. These 12 Earthly Branches

某年就肖某种动物，如子年生的肖鼠，丑年生的肖牛。人们还用这十二种动物来直接纪年，十二年一个循环，周而复始。在东汉的文献中就有与如今相同的十二生肖的记载。随着历史的发展，生肖逐渐成为民间信仰，如婚配属相、庙会祈祷、本命年等。生肖作为悠久的民俗文化符号，历代留下了许多描绘生肖形象和象征意义的诗歌、春联、绘画、书画和民间工艺品。中国和世界其他一些国家会在春节期间发行生肖邮票，以表达对中国新年的祝福。

and corresponding animals are: *zi* (the Rat), *chou* (the Ox), *yin* (the Tiger), *mao* (the Rabbit), *chen* (the Dragon), *si* (the Snake), *wu* (the Horse), *wei* (the Sheep), *shen* (the Monkey), *you* (the Rooster), *xu* (the Dog) and *hai* (the Pig). For example, a person born in the year of the rat or in the year of the ox is said to have the characteristics of a rat or an ox respectively. This complete set of zodiac animals can be found in documents from the Eastern Han Dynasty (25-220), and eventually the concept of zodiac animals became ingrained into folk beliefs such as marriage pairing and temple worship. It also became the subject of zodiac-themed poems, couplets, paintings, calligraphic works, and other handicrafts through the ages. During the Spring Festival, China and other countries issue zodiac animal stamps to express best wishes for the Chinese lunar New Year.

例句：

中国人现在用公历纪年和计算年龄的同时，仍然习惯用**十二生肖**来纪年和计算年龄，并能够根据人的属相推算出其年龄。

Example Sentence:

Although the Gregorian calendar has been adopted to designate a year and a person's age, zodiac animals can also be used in this way. A person's age can be deduced according to his/her zodiac animal.

属相 *shuxiang;* birth sign

参见"十二生肖"。

See *shi'er shengxiao* (twelve zodiac animals).

天干 *Tiangan;* Heavenly Stems

中国古代用来表示次序或类别的符号，又称"十干"。中国古人选取十种天象名称来确定这些符号，即甲、乙、丙、丁、戊、己、庚、辛、壬、癸。除用于表示次序外，还常与地支相配合用以纪年和日。

An ancient Chinese numerical system, also called "ten stems." The Heavenly Stems are symbols used to indicate sequence or classification. Ancient Chinese selected ten celestial phenomena to determine the names of Heavenly Stems, namely, *jia, yi, bing, ding, wu, ji, geng, xin, ren, gui*. They are usually used in combination with 12 Earthly Branches to indicate the date and year.

例句：

天干是中华祖先创造的一种事物顺序记录方式。

Example Sentence:

The Heavenly Stems were created by ancient Chinese to indicate sequence.

十干 *shigan;* ten stems

参见"天干"。

See *Tiangan* (Heavenly Stems).

地支 *Dizhi;* Earthly Branches

中国古代用来记数或表示顺序、类别的符号，又称“十二支”。中国古人根据木星围绕太阳公转的轨道划分确定这些符号，轨道分成十二个部分，分别用十二个汉字代表，即子、丑、寅、卯、辰、巳、午、未、申、酉、戌、亥。地支常与天干相配合，用以纪年和日，也可单独用于纪月、纪时。

An ancient Chinese numerical system, also called the "12 branches." They are 12 symbols which were used to designate numbers, sequence, or classification. Ancient Chinese divided the orbit of Jupiter around the sun into 12 parts which determined the names of the 12 branches, which are represented by the 12 Chinese characters: *zi, chou, yin, mao, chen, si, wu, wei, shen, you, xu, hai*. The Earthly Branches are used either in combination with the Heavenly Stems to designate days and years, or singularly to denote months and hours.

例句：

地支计时就是将一日均分为十二个时段，分别以十二地支表示，称为十二时辰。

Example Sentence:

Using Earthly Branches to designate time means that a day is equally divided into 12 periods (called 12 *shichen* in Chinese), which is symbolized by the 12 Earthly Branches.

十二支 *shi'erzhi;* twelve branches

参见“地支”。

See *Dizhi* (Earthly Branches).

干支 *ganzhi;* stems and branches

天干和地支的合称；中国古代用来记录年、月、日和时的一种方式。用十个天干和十二个地支搭配成六十组，通称“六十甲子”。干支为周期的表示次序。纪年从甲子开始，以癸亥结束，周而复始。殷商时开始用干支纪日，春秋战国时流行用干支纪年。中国数千年文明史的所有年代和月、日都可以用干支法准确地记录或推算出来。人们至今仍在历法、计算、命名等方面使用干支。

An ancient Chinese system for designating hours, days, months, and years, known as the 10 Heavenly Stems and 12 Earthly Branches. Together, they form a cycle of 60 pairs which can be used to designate dates and years. This system dates back to the Shang Dynasty (1600-1046 BC), and became popular during the Spring and Autumn and the Warring States Periods (770-221BC). All years, months, and days in Chinese history can be accurately determined according to this system. The system is still used in such fields as calendar records, mathematics, and naming.

例句：

干支纪年法是中国历法上自古以来就一直使用的纪年方法。

Example Sentence:

The system for designating years by stems and branches has been adopted in China since ancient times.

二十四节气 *Ershisi Jieqi;* the 24 Solar Terms

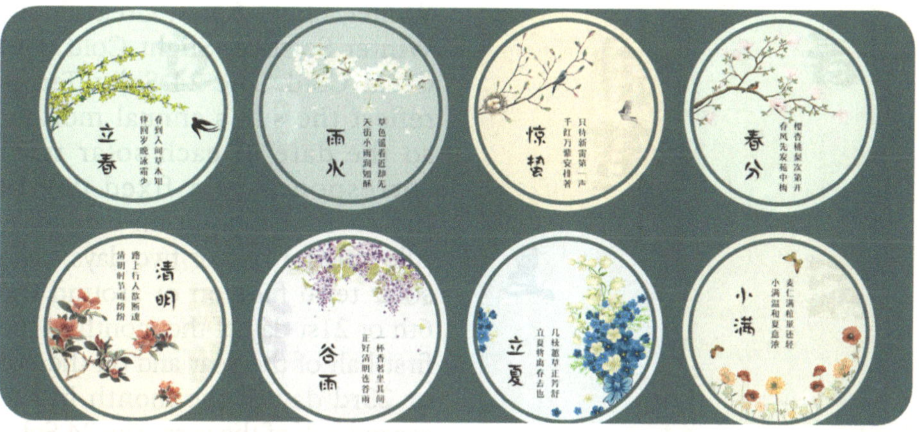

中国人通过观察太阳周年运动而形成的对时间体系的认识，即将太阳周年运动轨迹或地球绕太阳公转的轨迹（即黄道）划分为二十四等份，每一等份为一个节气，统称“二十四节气”。远在春秋时期，中国古人就已经通过测量太阳影子的长短确定出夏至、冬至、春分、秋分四个节气。到秦汉年间，二十四节气已完全确立，分别是：立春、雨水、惊蛰、春分、清明、谷雨、立夏、小满、芒种、夏至、小暑、大暑、立秋、处暑、白露、秋分、寒露、霜降、立冬、小雪、大雪、冬至、小寒和大寒。二十四节气反映了太阳的周年运动，所以各节气

A system of knowledge and practices about time formed by observing the sun's annual motion. Ancient Chinese divided the sun's annual motion into 24 segments, each called a specific "Solar Term" with its own unique name. As early as the Spring and Autumn Period (770-476 BC), ancient Chinese determined the Summer Solstice, the Winter Solstice, the Spring Equinox, and the Autumnal Equinox according to the length of the sun's shadow. During the Qin (221-206 BC) and Han (206 BC-AD 220) dynasties, the 24 Solar Terms were determined, which include Beginning of Spring, Rain Water, Waking of Insects, Spring Equinox, Pure Brightness, Grain Rain, Beginning of Summer, Grain Full, Grain in Ear, Summer Solstice, Slight Heat, Great Heat, Beginning

在现行公历中的日期基本固定，上半年在每月6日、21日左右，下半年在每月8日、23日左右，前后相差不超过一两天，每个节气大约15天。二十四个节气作为一套完整的农业气候历，几千年来在指导中国农业生产上发挥了较大作用，并被周边的一些国家采用，沿用至今。2016年，二十四节气被列入联合国教科文组织人类非物质文化遗产代表作名录。

of Autumn, Limit of Heat, White Dew, Autumn Equinox, Cold Dew, Frost's Descent, Beginning of Winter, Slight Snow, Great Snow, Winter Solstice, Slight Cold, and Great Cold. The 24 Solar Terms reflect the sun's annual motion, so the date of each solar term corresponds to a fixed day in the current Gregorian calendar. Allowing for one or two days, each solar term falls on or around the 6th or 21st day of the month in the first half of the year and on the 8th or 23rd day of the month in the second half of the year. The 24 Solar Terms form a complete climatic calendar that has provided guidance to agricultural production in China for thousands of years. It has also been adopted and used by some neighboring countries. In 2016, the UN Educational, Scientific, and Cultural Organization (UNESCO) included China's "24 Solar Terms" on its Representative List of the Intangible Cultural Heritage of Humanity.

例句：

二十四节气起源于中国黄河流域，主要反映黄河中下游地区的季节、气候与农事活动规律，逐步为全国各地所采用。

Example Sentence:

The 24 Solar Terms originated from China's Yellow River Basin. They reflect seasons, climate, and farming guidelines. Over time, they came to be used all over China.

立春 *Lichun;* Beginning of Spring

二十四节气中的第一个节气，公历2月4日前后太阳到达黄经315°时开始。立春即春季的开始，此时天气逐渐回暖，农民应抓紧进行春耕准备和越冬作物田间管理。立春这天，民间有“鞭春”的习俗，就是鞭打泥或纸做的牛，意在催耕，体现了人们对丰收的美好期盼。立春这天，人们习惯吃春饼、春卷等食品，称为“咬春”。民间有句谚语“一年之计在于春”，强调春天对于全年的重要性。

The first of the 24 solar terms. It refers to the time when the sun's ecliptic longitude reaches 315° around February 4. During the *Lichun* (which means the beginning of spring), the weather gradually warms up again, and farmers should lose no time in preparing to plow and manage their fields with crops that have made it through the winter. On the day of *Lichun*, there is a folk custom of "whipping spring oxen," that is, whipping fake oxen made of mud or paper. The purpose of the custom is to urge farmers to begin plowing in order to achieve a good harvest. On the day of *Lichun*, people eat such foods as spring pancakes and spring rolls, referred to as "nipping the spring." There is a folk proverb that goes, "the whole year must be planned in the spring."

例句：

“立”是“开始”的意思，中国自古为农业国，春种秋收，关键在春，自秦代以来，就一直以**立春**作为农历正月的开始，所谓“一年之计在于春”。

Example Sentence:

"*Li*" means "to start." From time immemorial, China has been an agricultural nation. Crops are planted in the spring and harvested in the fall, but the crucial point is the spring. Since the Qin Dynasty (221-206 BC), *Lichun* has always marked the start of the first month of spring, hence the saying, "The whole year must be planned in the spring."

雨水 *Yushui;* Rain Water

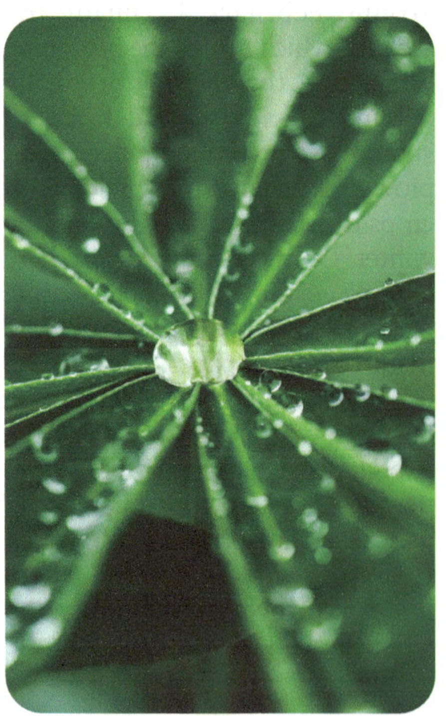

The second of the 24 solar terms. It refers to the time when the sun's ecliptic longitude reaches 330° around February 19. With the exception of northwest and northeast China and some areas on plateaus in southwest China which are still experiencing winter, temperatures rise in most parts of the country. Ice and snow melt as rainfall increases. Farmers have already started plowing the fields, as reflected in the saying "The days are getting warmer when *Lichun* arrives, and farmers are busy fertilizing the land when *Yushui* comes." A popular custom on the day of *Yushui* among Han people in western Sichuan is for married women to return to their maiden

二十四节气中的第二个节气，公历2月19日前后太阳到达黄经330°时开始。此时除中国西北、东北、西南高原的部分地区仍是寒冬之外，大部分地区气温回升，冰雪融化，雨水增多，农民已开始春耕，民间有"立春天渐暖，雨水送肥忙"的说法。"雨水节回娘家"是流行于川西一带的汉族习俗：雨水这天，出嫁的女儿纷纷带上礼物回娘家看望父母。

homes with gifts to see their parents.

例句：

雨水后天气转暖，但风多物燥，早晚较冷，故民间多吃新鲜蔬菜、多汁水果以补充身体水分。

Example Sentence:

The weather gradually warms after *Yushui*, but the winds leave the land dry and it is rather cold during mornings and nights. As a result, people often eat more fresh vegetables and juicy fruits to replenish the moisture in their bodies.

惊蛰 *Jingzhe;* Insects Awakening

The third of the 24 solar terms, referred to as *Qizhe* (waking from hibernation) in ancient times. It refers to the time when the sun's ecliptic longitude reaches 345° around March 6. Temperatures rise further at this time and rainfall increases. Spring thunder will become more likely, rousing

二十四节气中的第三个节气，古称“启蛰”，公历3月6日前后太阳运行到黄经345°时开始。此时气温进一步回升，雨水增多，渐有春雷，惊醒了蛰藏在土中的冬眠动物。中国大部分地区春耕开始，民间有“过了惊蛰节，春耕不能歇”的谚语。此时温暖的气候条件可能导致病虫害蔓延，田间杂草也相继萌发，所以要注意防治病虫害，常中耕除草。惊蛰这天，民间有祭雷神、祭白虎（化解口舌之争）、吃梨（调理身体）等习俗。

hibernating animals to awaken. In most parts of China, plowing fields for the spring will begin during this time, as the folk proverb goes, "With the coming of *Jingzhe*, fields are plowed without stop." At this time, the warm climate causes diseases and pests to spread, and weeds in the fields will successively sprout as well. As a result, attention must be paid to preventing pests and curing disease. On the day of *Jingzhe*, besides tilling and weeding the fields, people will make offerings to the God of Thunder as well as the white tiger (said to be able to diffuse verbal disputes), and eat pears (to nourish their bodies).

例句：

惊蛰意味着桃花盛开、黄鹂鸣叫、布谷鸟飞来的时节到了。

Example Sentence:

The arrival of *Jingzhe* is signified by blooming peach blossoms, singing yellow orioles, and flying cuckoos.

春分 *Chunfen;* Spring Equinox

二十四节气的第四个节气，公历3月21日前后太阳位于黄经0°（春分点）时开始。春分这天，阳光直射赤道，昼夜平分；之后阳光直射位置逐渐北移，北半球开始昼长夜短，中国大部分地区的越冬作物进入春季生长阶段。“一场春雨一场暖，春雨过后忙耕田”，春分过后，农忙季节就要开始了。春分这天，民间有祭日、祭祖、放风筝、吃春菜等习俗。

The fourth of the 24 solar terms. It begins around March 21 when the sun's ecliptic longitude reaches 0° (the Spring Equinox). On *Chunfen*, the sun shines directly on the equator, where day and night are evenly divided. Afterwards, it gradually shifts northwards, causing days in the northern hemisphere to grow longer and nights to grow shorter. In most parts of China, the crops that made it through the winter enter their next phase of growth in spring. "Each spring rain brings more warmth, and all hands are busy tilling the fields." After *Chunfen*, the busy period of the farming season begins. On the day of *Chunfen*, people make offerings to the sun and their ancestors, fly kites, and eat spring dishes.

例句：

古代有**春分**祭日、夏至祭地、秋分祭月、冬至祭天的习俗，其祭祀场所分别称为日坛、地坛、月坛、天坛。

Example Sentence:

In ancient times, offerings were made to the sun on *Chunfen*, to the earth during *Xiazhi* (Summer Solstice), to the moon on *Qiufen* (Autumn Equinox), and to heaven on *Dongzhi* (Winter Solstice). The names of the sites where these offerings were made were referred to as the sun altar, earth altar, moon altar, and heaven altar respectively.

清明 *Qingming;* Pure Brightness; Fresh Green

二十四节气的第五个节气，公历4月5日前后太阳到达黄经15°时开始。清明时节，气候转暖，草木萌动，除东北与西北地区外，中国大部分地区的日平均气温都升到12°C以上，长江南北直至长城内外，到处是一片繁忙的春耕春种景象。民间有俗语称"清明前后，种瓜点豆。""种树造林，莫过清明。"清明是唯一一个既是节气又是节日的节气，也是最重要的祭祀日之一，是传统的扫墓祭祖的日子。清明时节，民间有踏青、荡秋千、蹋球、打马球、植树、放风筝等习俗。

The fifth of the 24 solar terms. It refers to the time when the sun's ecliptic longitude reaches 15° around April 5. During *Qingming*, the climate grows warmer. Except for northeast and northwest China, plants sprout and daytime temperatures in most parts of China rise to above 12°C. From the north and the south of the Yangtze River to both sides of the Great Wall, the whole country is a scene of farmers busily plowing fields and planting seeds. A popular folk proverb goes, "Around *Qingming*, plant melons and beans." Another goes, "Plant trees to make a forest no later than *Qingming*." *Qingming* is a solar term that falls on the same day as a holiday, known as the Qingming Festival, also known as the Tomb Sweeping Day. This is one of the most important days for offering sacrifices to ancestors, and it is also the day when the tombs of ancestors are traditionally swept. During *Qingming*, it is customary for people to go on hikes, plant trees, fly kites, play soccer or polo, and leisurely rock on a swing.

例句：

清明与其他传统节日不同，是融合了“节气”与“节俗”的综合节日，几乎是所有春季节日的综合与升华，清明节俗也具有更加丰富的文化内涵。

Example Sentence:

Qingming is different from other traditional festivals in that it is a combination of a “solar term” and a “folk festival.” It is essentially a combined, refined version of all the springtime festivals, and the customs associated with it contains richer cultural connotations.

谷雨 *Guyu;* Grain Rain

二十四节气的第六个节气，也是春季的最后一个节气，公历4月20日前后太阳到达黄经30°时开始。谷雨，意为雨生百谷。谷雨节气天气温和，降雨增多，有利于谷类农作物的生长，是中国北方春作物播种、出苗的重要季节。传说谷雨与远古时期的圣人仓颉有关。仓

The sixth of the 24 solar terms. It refers to the time when the sun’s ecliptic longitude reaches 30° around April 20. *Guyu* means that rain facilitates the growth of all crops. Temperatures rise during this solar term as precipitation increases, benefitting the growth of cereal crops. This is an important time for the sowing of seeds and the sprouting of buds in northern China. Legend has it that *Guyu* is related to the ancient sage Cangjie who is attributed to having created written Chinese characters, which greatly promoted social progress. To reward him, the Jade Emperor had crops rain from the sky into the human realm. As a result, offerings are made to Cangjie every year during *Guyu*. Other popular customs include drinking

颉造字成功，大大推进了社会的进步，为此玉皇大帝专门为人间下了一场谷子雨。因此每年谷雨节都要举行祭祀仓颉的活动。此外，民间还有喝谷雨茶、食香椿、赏牡丹、禁蝎（消灭虫害）等习俗；中国北方沿海一带的渔民要在谷雨这天举行渔民节并祭海。

Guyu tea, eating Chinese toon, enjoying peonies, and eradicating pests such as scorpions. Along northern coastal regions of China people hold the Fisherman Festival in which they make offerings to the sea.

例句：

谷雨茶就是人们常说的雨前茶，谷雨时节采制的春茶。

Example Sentence:

Guyu tea refers to fresh spring tea harvested and made before this solar term.

立夏 *Lixia;* Beginning of Summer

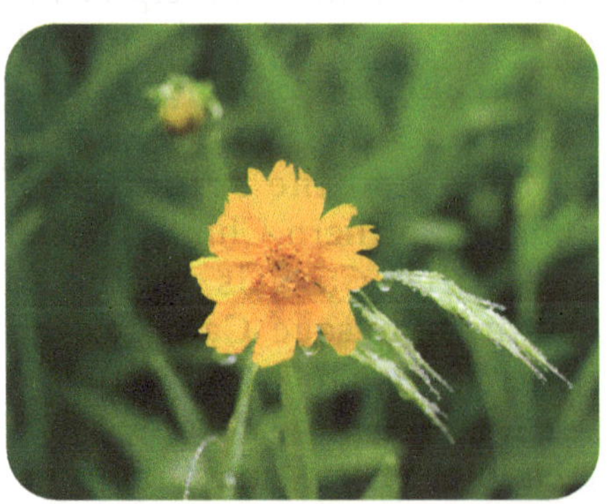

二十四节气的第七个节气，公历5月6日前后太阳到达黄经45°时开始。立夏即夏天的开

The seventh of the 24 solar terms. It refers to the time when the sun's ecliptic longitude reaches 45° around May 6. *Lixia* marks the start of the summer. Temperatures rise during this time as summertime heat approaches, and thunderstorms become more frequent. In most parts of the country, average temperatures hover around 18-20°C. Warm-season crops enter their final stage of growth, and field management grows busier with each passing day. In ancient times, emperors led civil and military officials to the southern suburbs of the capital on this day to welcome the summer and express wishes for a

始。此时温度升高，暑热将至，雷雨增多，中国大部分地区的平均气温在18°C~20°C上下，夏收作物进入生长后期，田间管理日益繁忙。古代帝王在这一天要率文武百官到京城南郊去迎夏，表达期待丰收的愿望。民间有尝新、吃蛋、斗蛋、称人等习俗，南方一些地方用五种豆子和白粳米一起煮"五色饭"，称为吃"立夏饭"。

bumper harvest. Folk customs include eating fresh rice, eating eggs, playing with eggs (fighting eggs), and weighing people. In some parts of southern China, people boil "five-colored rice" with five kinds of beans and white rice, which they call "*Lixia* Rice."

例句：

中国南方**立夏**日有"称人"习俗，据说人在这一天称了体重之后夏天就不会消瘦，否则会有病灾缠身。

Example Sentence:

One custom of *Lixia* in southern China is "weighing people." It is said that if people are weighed on this day, they won't grow thin during the summer and they'll be free from diseases and disasters.

小满 *Xiaoman;* Grain Full

二十四节气的第八个节气，公历5月21日前后太阳到达黄经60°时开始。此时夏熟作物的籽粒开始灌浆饱满，但还未成熟，因此称“小满”。从小满到芒种，中国各地相继入夏，南北温差进一步缩小，降水进一步增多，南方进入夏收夏种季节。小满这天，民间有抢水、祭车神、祭蚕等习俗；吃苦菜也是小满的独特食俗，苦菜清凉嫩香，富含维生素，夏季可清热解毒。

The eighth of the 24 solar terms. It refers to the time when the sun's ecliptic longitude reaches 60° around May 21. At this time, warm-season crops begin to grow out, though they are not yet ripe. As a result, they are referred to as "*Xiaoman*," which means "little full." From *Xiaoman* to *Mangzhong*, every part of the country enters summer, and temperature differences between the north and the south gradually lessen as precipitation increases in the south, which enters its summertime harvest season. On the day of *Xiaoman*, folk customs include water fights and making offerings to the god of wheels and silkworms. Another unique custom of the day is eating sowthistle as it is refreshing, tender, and fragrant. The sowthistle is full of vitamins and able to alleviate summertime diseases.

例句：

小满相传为蚕神诞辰日，所以在这一天，中国以养蚕著称的江浙一带有给蚕神过生日的习俗。

Example Sentence:

Xiaoman is the birthday of the God of the Silkworm, according to legend. On this day in Jiangsu and Zhejiang, two provinces famous for their sericultural tradition, there is the custom of celebrating the birthday of the God of the Silkworm.

芒种 *Mangzhong;* Grain in Ear

二十四节气的第九个节气，也称“忙种”，公历6月6日前后太阳到达黄经75°时开始。“芒”字指收获麦类作物，“种”字指播种谷黍类作物，“芒种”二字表明这是农事最为繁忙的时节，中国从南到北都在忙着夏收夏种，中国长江中下游地区先后进入梅雨季节。芒种时节，民间有送花神、安苗、打泥巴仗、煮梅等习俗。

The ninth of the 24 solar terms. It refers to the time when the sun's ecliptic longitude reaches 75° around June 6. In this solar term's name, "*mang*" refers to harvesting certain rice or wheat crops, while "*zhong*" refers to sowing the seeds for crops like corn and millet. "*Mangzhong*" indicates that this is the busiest season for farming. During this time, the country is busy harvesting summer crops and planting summertime seeds. It is also during this time that the middle and lower reaches of the Yangtze River begin entering the monsoon season. During *Mangzhong*, folk customs include saying farewell to the gods or goddesses of flowers, safeguarding sprouts, playing in the mud, and boiling plums.

例句：

民间过去有在**芒种**节“送花神”的习俗，将农历二月十二“花朝节”上迎来的花神送回归位，并期待来年再会。

Example Sentence:

In the past, folks had the custom of "saying farewell to the gods or goddesses of flowers" during *Mangzhong*. According to folklore, these gods or goddesses are welcomed to the earth during the "Huazhao Festival", which is on the twelfth day of the second lunar month. After "saying farewell", they return to their celestial palace and will not come back until a year later.

夏至 *Xiazhi*; Summer Solstice

二十四节气的第十个节气，又称“夏节”，公历6月22日前后太阳位于黄经90°（夏至点）时开始。夏至表示夏季已经来到，这一天太阳直射

The tenth of the 24 solar terms. It refers to the time when the sun's ecliptic longitude reaches 90° around June 22, also called "*Xiajie* (the summer festival)." *Xiazhi* means the arrival of summer. On this day, the sun shines directly on the Tropic of Cancer, and the day is the longest in the Northern Hemisphere. During the Summer Solstice, temperatures in most parts of China rise a little higher. There is abundant sunshine, and crops grow very quickly. Weeds and pests quickly spread, so more attention needs to be paid to managing fields. At this time, precipitation has an enormous effect on agricultural output. Eating noodles is a folk custom

北回归线，是北半球白昼最长的一天。夏至期间，大部分地区气温较高，日照充足，作物生长很快，杂草、病虫迅速滋生蔓延，应加强田间管理，此时的降水对农业产量影响很大。民间在夏至这天有吃面的习俗。

during the Summer Solstice.

例句：

夏至时节，江淮一带正值梅雨天气，空气潮湿，阴雨连绵。

Example Sentence:

During *Xiazhi*, the region around the Yangtze and Huaihe rivers is at the height of monsoon weather, and moist air, overcast weather, and rains are constant during this time.

夏节 *Xiajie;* Summer Festival

参见“夏至”。

See *Xiazhi* (Summer Solstice).

小暑 *Xiaoshu:* Lesser Heat

The eleventh of the 24 solar terms. It refers to the time when the sun's ecliptic longitude reaches 105° around July 7. *Xiaoshu* comes before the hottest solar term *Dashu* (Greater Heat). As the hottest periods of the year begin, crops across China enter a stage of robust maturity,

二十四节气中的第十一个节气，公历7月7日前后太阳到达黄经105°时开始。小暑虽不是一年中最炎热的时节，但紧接着就是最热的大暑节气。此时伏天开始，中国的农作物都进入茁壮成长的阶段，需加强田间管理，南方应注意抗旱，北方须注意防涝。民间有小暑"食新"的习俗，如尝新米，用新磨的面粉包饺子或做面条等。民间还有吃藕、鳝鱼的食俗。

meaning more efforts are needed in field management. Those in the south should be on guard against drought while those in the north must be on guard against floods. During *Xiaoshu*, it is a folk custom to "eat the new and fresh," which includes eating new rice or using freshly ground flour to make dumplings or noodles. It is also customary for people to eat lotus roots and eel during this time.

例句：

小暑、大暑到立秋之间的这段时间是中国大部分地区最热的时节，称为"三伏"。

Example Sentence:

The three periods of *Xiaoshu*, *Dashu*, and *Liqiu* are the hottest in most parts of China, and this is referred to as "*sanfu* (three hottest periods of the year)."

大暑 *Dashu*; Greater Heat

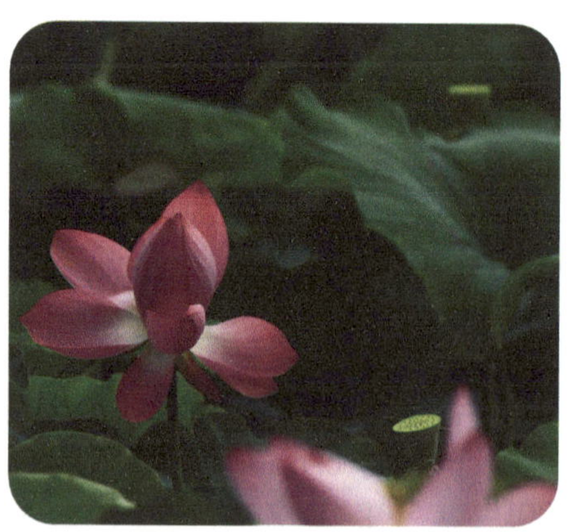

The twelfth of the 24 solar terms. It refers to the time when the sun's ecliptic longitude reaches 120° around July 23. It is the hottest time of the year. Temperatures reach their climax and crops grow the quickest. At the same time, it is also the season when natural disasters such as droughts, floods, and windstorms occur most

二十四节气中的第十二个节气，公历7月23日前后太阳到达黄经120°时开始。大暑正值二伏前后，是一年中最热的时节，气温最高，农作物生长最快，同时，很多地区的旱、涝、风灾等各种气象灾害也最为频繁。大暑期间，民间有饮伏茶、晒伏姜、烧伏香等习俗，浙江沿海地区有送大暑船的习俗。

frequently. During *Dashu*, people customarily drink a special herbal tea to cool down, dry ginger under the sun to make ginger tea, and burn incense to pray for a good harvest. In the coastal regions of Zhejiang, there is a custom to hold a parade of a ceremonial *Dashu* ship and launch it out to sea as an offering to the Five Gods of Plagues.

例句：

大暑是消化道疾病多发的季节，需注意饮食调理与卫生。

Example Sentence:

During *Dashu*, diseases of the digestive tract occur quite frequently, so people need to pay more attention to their food and personal hygiene.

立秋 *Liqiu;* Beginning of Autumn

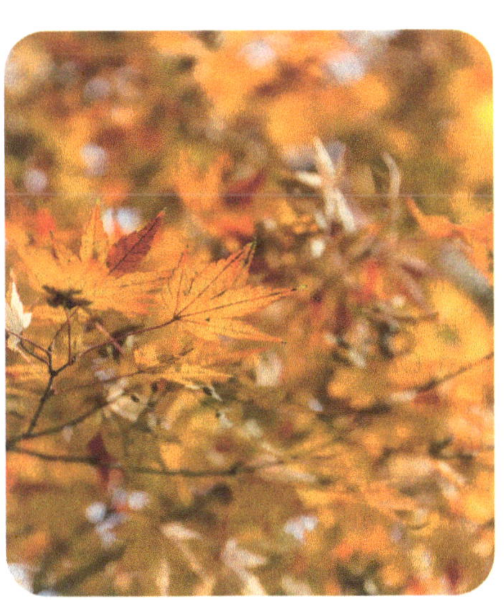

The thirteenth of the 24 solar terms. It refers to the time when the sun's ecliptic longitude reaches 135° around August 8. *Liqiu* marks the start of autumn. It is still part of the hot season, and scorching hot weather will persist for about another half month. As a result, the time is called the "fall tiger." After *Liqiu*, the temperatures gradually drop, especially in the morning and at night. People need to frequently change the amount

二十四节气的第十三个节气，公历8月8日太阳到达黄经135°时开始。立秋是秋天的开始，此时仍在伏天，炎热的天气将持续半个月左右，所以有“秋老虎”之说。不过立秋后气温会逐渐下降，特别是早晚渐凉，应及时加减衣物，避免由于贪“凉”致病。立秋之后，谷物成熟，农民迎来丰收。民间有秋忙会、贴秋膘、食秋桃、啃秋等习俗。

of clothing they wear to adapt to the temperature and avoid getting sick. After *Liqiu*, grains are mature and farmers welcome the harvest season. Folk customs during this time include attending the Fall Trade Fair, gaining fall weight, eating fall peaches, and “gnawing” on the fall harvest.

例句：

立秋时节，不少地方流行“贴秋膘”的食俗，就是多吃肉类食物，以弥补夏天食欲不振造成的消瘦。

Example Sentence:

During *Liqiu*, people tend to “gain fall weight.” By eating a lot of meat, people make up for losing weight during summer.

处暑 *Chushu; Limit of Heat*

The fourteenth of the 24 solar terms. It refers to the time when the sun’s ecliptic longitude reaches 150° around August 23. *Chu* means to stop or hide away, and *Chushu* indicates the days of blistering heat are coming to an end. This is the time when temperatures in most parts of China begin to drop and the differences between daytime

二十四节气的第十四个节气，公历8月23日前后太阳到达黄经150°时开始。"处"是终止、躲藏的意思，处暑表示炎热的暑天结束了。这时中国大部分地区气温逐渐下降，昼夜温差较大，不时有秋雨降临，人们常用"一场秋雨一场寒"来形容处暑时逐渐转凉的天气。处暑期间气候干燥，人的皮肤会因此变得紧绷，甚至起皮脱屑，嘴唇干燥，嗓子发干。处暑时节，民间有祭祖、出游迎秋、放河灯、吃鸭子、举行开渔节等习俗。

and nighttime temperatures grow more pronounced. Autumn rains are frequent during this time, and people use the saying "with each autumn rain comes the cold" to describe the cooling weather during *Chushu*. Also, less moisture in the air causes people's skin to get dry and even crack. Lips are chapped and voices are hoarse. Folk customs include making sacrifices to ancestors, going on autumn outings, releasing lamps on the river, eating duck, and celebrating the start of the fishing season.

例句：

处暑之后，秋意渐浓，正是外出秋游的好时节。

Example Sentence:

Outdoor outings are popular after *Chushu* as the weather cools and leaves begin to change to autumn colors.

白露 *Bailu; White Dew*

The fifteenth of the 24 solar terms. It refers to the time when the sun's ecliptic longitude reaches 165° around September 8. The weather is cool and refreshing during this time as fall winds from the north blow down southward across China. After entering *Bailu*, water

二十四节气中的第十五个节气，公历9月8日前后太阳到达黄经165°时开始。此时凉爽的秋风自北向南已吹遍中国大地。进入白露后，夜间水汽凝结在叶子上面，清晨时分结成露珠。此时中国大部分地区天气逐渐转凉，温差大。民间有喝白露茶、酿米酒等习俗，人们常食梨、柑橘等水果润燥。

condenses on leaves during the night, forming dew early in the morning. In most parts of China it gradually grows colder during this time, and temperatures will vary considerably throughout the day. Folk customs during this time include drinking *Bailu* tea and brewing rice wine. People often eat pears, oranges, and other fruits to gain more moisture.

例句：

进入**白露**后，随着气温降低，人们会明显地感觉到秋天的到来。

Example Sentence:

After entering *Bailu*, a drop in temperature will cause people to begin to sense that autumn has arrived.

秋分 *Qiufen;* Autumn Equinox

The sixteenth of the 24 solar terms. It refers to the time when the sun's ecliptic longitude reaches 180° around September 23. On this day, the sun shines directly on the Earth's equator where there is an equal division between day and night. There are no occurrences of a polar day or night anywhere on the globe during this day. Afterwards, daytime in the northern hemisphere grows shorter as nights grow longer. Most parts of China gradually

二十四节气中的第十六个节气，公历9月23日前后太阳到达黄经180°（秋分点）时开始。此日阳光直射地球赤道，这一天昼夜均分，全球无极昼极夜现象。此后，阳光直射的位置便继续向南推移，北半球昼更短、夜更长。此时中国大部分地区逐渐进入秋季，南下的冷空气与逐渐衰减的暖湿空气相遇，产生降水，气温下降。中国北方开始秋收、秋种。民间有秋分祭月、送秋牛、吃秋菜等习俗。

enter autumn at this time. Cold air moves southward, producing precipitation and lowering temperatures. In northern China, farmers begin the autumn harvest and plant fall crops. Folk customs during this time include making offerings to the moon, selling printed pictures of "fall cows," and eating wild herbs.

例句：

秋分至寒露这半个月是秋熟作物收获前田间管理的关键期。

Example Sentence:

The half month from *Qiufen* to *Hanlu* is just before crops have ripened and can be harvested, and it is a crucial time for field management.

寒露 *Hanlu;* Cold Dew

The seventeenth of the 24 solar terms. It refers to the time when the sun's ecliptic longitude reaches 195° around October 8. At this time, temperatures drop rapidly, and average temperatures throughout the country vary greatly. Most parts of China are already in the midst of autumn at this time, and the weather

二十四节气的第十七个节气，公历 10 月 8 日前后太阳到达黄经 195° 时开始。此时，气温快速下降，平均气温分布差异较大，中国大部分地区已进入秋季，天气凉爽，适合进行秋收、秋种。此时人体会出现秋燥症状，饮食调养应以滋阴润燥为宜。民间有登高赏菊、斗蟋蟀、秋钓、饮菊花酒、喝寒露茶等习俗。

is cool and refreshing during autumn harvests and planting. People begin to experience autumn dryness at this time. As a result, diets should provide extra moisture. Folk customs during this time include hiking mountains, appreciating chrysanthemum flowers, cricket fights, fishing, enjoying chrysanthemum wine, and drinking *Hanlu* tea.

例句：

寒露节气到来时，人们需要随着气温的早晚变化逐渐增添衣服。

Example Sentence:

When *Hanlu* arrives, people need to change the amount of clothes they wear throughout the day to adjust to temperature changes.

霜降 *Shuangjiang;* First Frost

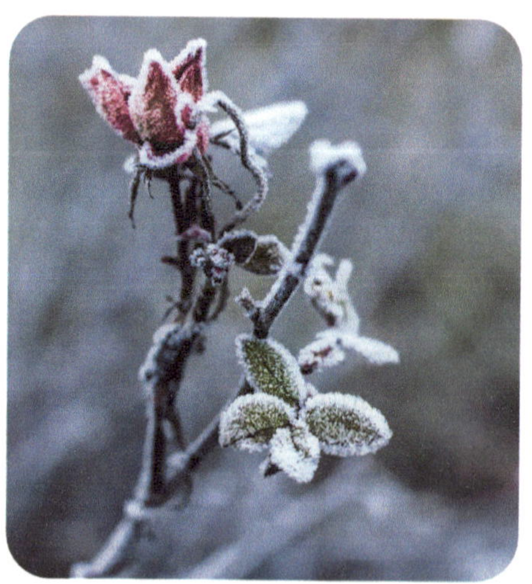

The eighteenth of the 24 solar terms. It refers to the time when the sun's ecliptic longitude reaches 210° around October 24. *Shuangjiang* is the solar term signifying that winter is about to come. Temperatures become colder, abruptly dropping down below zero at night in northern China. This can produce early frosts which can cause great harm to crops. Insects hide and prepare for hibernation. Folk customs

二十四节气的第十八个节气，每年公历10月24日前后太阳位于黄经210°时开始。霜降是秋季到冬季的过渡节气，意味着冬天即将开始。此时天气渐冷，北方晚上温度骤然下降到0度以下，产生初霜，对农作物会造成危害。昆虫蛰伏起来，预备开始冬眠。民间有吃柿子、赏菊等习俗。

include eating persimmon and appreciating chrysanthemums.

例句：

霜降时节秋菊盛开，很多地方此时举行菊花会。

Example Sentence:

Autumn chrysanthemums bloom during *Shuangjiang*, and many places hold chrysanthemum exhibitions during this time.

立冬 *Lidong;* Beginning of Winter

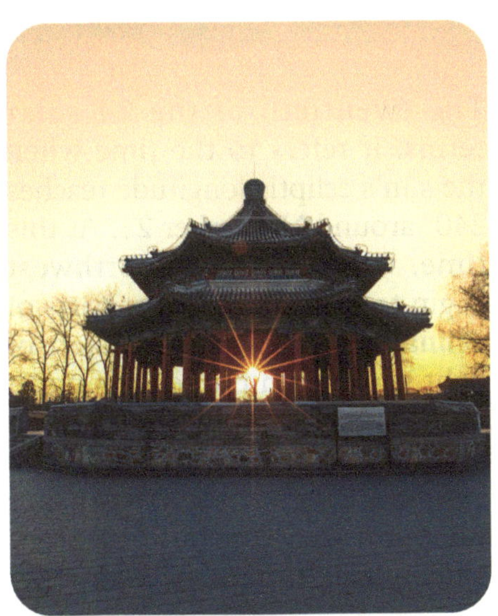

The nineteenth of the 24 solar terms. It refers to the time when the sun's ecliptic longitude reaches 225° around November 8. *Lidong* marks the beginning of winter. It was an important holiday in ancient China, when kings and emperors led civil and military officials to set up an offering altar. Around this time there is a significant reduction in precipitation in most parts of the country. Northern China freezes over, and crops and other plants go dormant. Forested regions need

二十四节气的第十九个节气，公历11月8日前后太阳位于黄经225°时开始。立冬是冬季的开始。立冬在中国古代是一个重要节日，这一天，古代帝王会率领文武百官设坛祭祀。立冬前后，中国大部分地区降水显著减少，北方大地封冻，农林作物进入越冬期，林区要注重防火。民间有迎冬、补冬等习俗；北方人在这一天吃饺子，南方人吃鸡、鸭、鱼等肉食。

to be vigilant against fires. Folk customs during this time include welcoming the winter and holding a winter feast. People in northern China eat dumplings on this day while those in southern China eat such meats as chicken, duck, and fish.

例句：

立冬是冬季的开始，万物收藏，规避寒冷。

Example Sentence:

Lidong is the start of winter. All manner of things are collected and sheltered to avoid the cold.

小雪 *Xiaoxue;* Light Snow

The twentieth of the 24 solar terms. It refers to the time when the sun's ecliptic longitude reaches 240° around November 23. At this time, winds from the northwest begin to blow across most parts of China, which leads to the start of light snowfall in the regions north of the Yellow River. Regions in the middle and lower reaches of the Yangtze River enter winter and temperatures continue to drop. During this time it is customary

二十四节气的第二十个节气，公历11月23日前后太阳到达黄经240°时开始。此时中国广大地区刮起西北风，黄河以北地区开始降雪，雪量不大；长江中下游地区陆续进入冬季，气温持续走低。民间有吃糍粑、做香肠、晒鱼干等习俗。

for people to eat sticky rice cakes, make sausages, and dry fish under the sun.

例句：

在中国北方，**小雪**时节人们喜欢吃涮羊肉。

Example Sentence:

In northern China during *Xiaoxue*, people like to eat mutton hot pot.

大雪 *Daxue;* Heavy Snow

二十四节气的第二十一个节气。公历12月7日前后太阳到达黄经255°时开始。此时天气更加寒冷，中国大部分地区的最低温度都降到了0℃或

The twenty-first of the 24 solar terms. It refers to the time when the sun's ecliptic longitude reaches 255° around December 7. At this time, temperatures grow even colder, dropping to 0°C or below freezing in most parts of China. Large snowfalls

以下，通常会降大雪，甚至暴雪。降雪有利于缓解冬旱，消除农田病虫，为冬作物创造良好的越冬环境。此时民间有腌肉、腌雪菜、观赏封河、捕鱼等习俗。

and even snow storms are common during this time. Snowfalls bring relief from wintertime droughts and eradicate farmland pests, creating favorable conditions for the crops to make it through the winter. Folk customs during this time include making cured meat and pickled vegetables, appreciating frozen rivers, and fishing.

例句：

大雪是“进补”的好时节，素有“冬天进补，开春打虎”的说法。

Example Sentence:

Daxue is the good season to “have nourishing food.” There is an ancient saying that goes, “have nourishing food in the winter so you can become strong enough to fight a tiger in the spring.”

Dongzhi; Winter Solstice

二十四节气的第二十二个节气，公历12月22日前后太阳到达黄经270°（冬至点）时开始，俗称“冬节”。此时太阳直射地面的位置到达一年的最南端，几乎直射南回归线，这一天北半球的白昼最短。冬至既是中国农历中的一个重要节气，也是一个传统节日。在古代民间有“冬至大如年”的说法，现在不少地方仍有过冬至年的习俗。民间有祭拜祖先、祭冬、玩九九消寒图等习俗；人们喝冬酿酒、红豆粥，吃饺子、馄饨、汤圆、黍米糕等。

The twenty-second of the 24 solar terms. It refers to the time when the sun's ecliptic longitude reaches 270° around December 22. At this time, the point at which the sun shines directly on the earth reaches its most southern position, shining almost directly upon the Tropic of Capricorn. This is the time during which the day is the shortest in the Northern Hemisphere. The Winter Solstice is not only an important solar term in the Chinese calendar, but also a traditional holiday. There is the saying that "*Dongzhi* is as important as the Spring Festival," and there are still a good number of places that still celebrate the Winter Solstice as the start of a new year. Folk customs during this time include making offerings to ancestors, winter sacrifices, and starting to paint a picture or write a calligraphy work which counts down to the end of the coldest period of winter. People drink winter wine and eat red bean porridge, dumplings, wontons, *tangyuans*, and millet rice cakes during this solar term.

例句：

冬至日中国大部分地区将进入隆冬时期，常遭强冷空气，甚至寒潮袭击。

Example Sentence:

Dongzhi is the day when most parts of China enter the depth of winter and suffer from especially cold weather and even cold waves.

冬节 Dongjie; Winter Festival

参见“冬至”。

See *Dongzhi* (Winter Solstice).

小寒 Xiaohan; Lesser Cold

二十四节气的第二十三个节气，公历1月6日前后太阳到达黄经285°时开始。根据中国气象资料记载，小寒是气温最低的节气，只有少数年份的大寒气温低于小寒。此时中国大部分地区进入严寒时期。小寒日，民间有溜冰、探梅，吃黄芽菜、菜饭、糯米饭等习俗。此时人们开始忙着写春联，剪窗花，买年画、彩灯、香火等，开始筹备春节。

The twenty-third of the 24 solar terms. It refers to the time when the sun's ecliptic longitude reaches 285° around January 6. According to meteorological records in China, *Xiaohan* is the solar term with the lowest temperatures. There are only very few years on record that the temperatures during *Dahan* were colder than those during *Xiaohan*, and accordingly most parts of China enter a period of extreme cold during this time. On this day, folk customs include ice skating, appreciating plum blossoms, and eating yellow cabbage dishes, vegetarian dishes, and glutinous rice. During this time, people begin to busy themselves making preparations for the Spring Festival by writing Spring Festival couplets, making paper-cuts, and buying New Year pictures, colorful lights, and incense.

例句：

小寒节气的到来，说明一年中最寒冷的时节来了。

Example Sentence:

The arrival of *Xiaohan* signifies that people have entered the coldest period of the year.

大寒 *Dahan;* Greater Cold

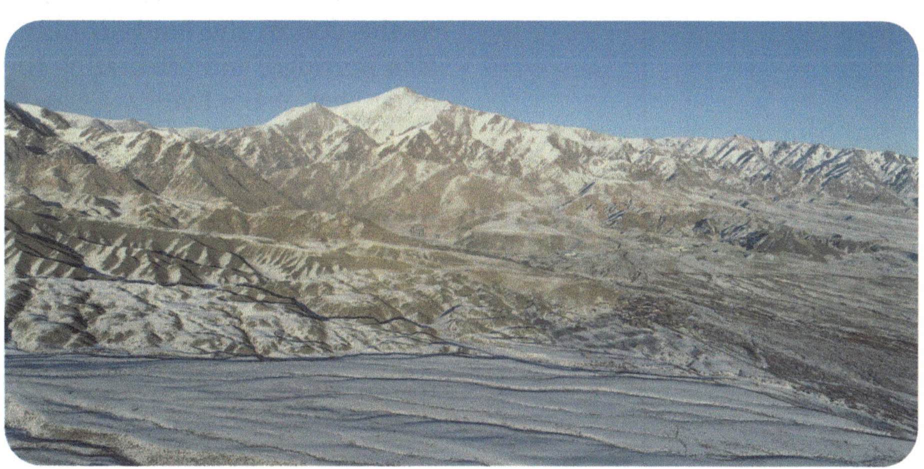

二十四节气中的第二十四个节气，公历1月20日前后太阳到达黄经300°时开始。此时寒潮南下频繁，是中国部分地区一年中的最寒冷时期。中国北方地区多忙于积肥堆肥，为开春耕种做准备，或者加强牲畜的防寒防冻；南方地区则仍加强小麦及其他作物的田间管理。从大寒到立春的这段时间，人们开始忙着除旧布新，准备祭祀供品，扫尘洁物，准备年货；

The twenty-fourth of the 24 solar terms. It refers to the time when the sun's ecliptic longitude reaches 300° around January 20. Cold waves frequently head to the south during this time, which is the coldest period in some parts of China. In northern China, people are both busy amassing manure and compost to prepare for spring farming or bolstering their efforts to protect their livestock from freezing. In southern China, people are still managing farmlands with wheat

还有一些重要的民俗和节庆，如祭灶、打尾牙祭、喝腊八粥、和过除夕等。

and other crops. During the period from *Dahan* to *Lichun*, people start busying themselves by preparing offerings, cleaning away dust, and preparing for the Chinese New Year. There are also a few important popular customs and festivals during this time such as offering sacrifices to the God of the Kitchen, offering a meal to the god of the land, drinking *laba* porridge, and celebrating the lunar New Year's Eve.

例句：

大寒节气风大气温低，地面积雪不化，呈现出天寒地冻的严寒景象。

Example Sentence:

During *Dahan*, the wind is strong and the temperature is low, so the snow will not melt, presenting a frozen winter scene.

春节

Chunjie;
Spring Festival; Chinese New Year

中华民族最重要的传统节日，又称“旧历新年”。春节的正日是农历每年的正月初一，但传统民俗中从腊月二十三（祭灶）到正月十五（元宵节）的一段时间都可称为“春节”，包括辞旧和迎新两大主题。从腊月二十三祭灶起，人们就开始为除夕和正月初一进行一系列准备，包括扫尘、置办年货和新衣、张贴春联和年画、理发沐浴等。除夕守岁，吃团圆饭，发压岁钱；正月初一起，人们身着新衣，燃放爆竹迎接新年，走亲访友互相拜年。春节期间各地还举办庙会和其他丰富多彩的娱乐活动。海外华人及受中华文化影响的部分周边国家也有庆祝春节的习俗。

The most important traditional festival in China, also called Chinese New Year. The Spring Festival falls on the first day of the first lunar month, but according to traditional customs it refers to the period from the twenty-third day of the twelfth lunar month (worshipping the Kitchen God) to the fifteenth day of the first lunar month (the Lantern Festival). The Spring Festival is when people ring out the old year and ring in the new. Beginning on the twenty-third day of the twelfth lunar month, people start preparing for New Year's Eve by cleaning the house, making special purchases for the Spring Festival, and pasting New Year pictures and couplets on the walls. They usually stay up all night on New Year's Eve, which is called *shousui*. On this day, family members eat dinner together and give one another a *hongbao*—a traditional red envelope containing money. On the first day of the first lunar month, they wear new clothes and set off firecrackers to welcome the New Year. They also deliver New Year's greetings to relatives and friends. During the Spring Festival, temple fairs and other activities are held. The Spring Festival is also celebrated by overseas Chinese and those living in neighboring countries influenced by Chinese culture.

例句：

春节是个欢乐祥和的节日，也是亲人团聚的日子，离家在外的孩子在过春节时都要回家欢聚。

Example Sentence:

The Spring Festival is full of happiness and harmony. On this day, children who are away from home return for a holiday family reunion.

腊祭 *Laji;* Winter Sacrifice

中国古代祭祀祖先和天地神灵的活动在农历十二月举行，因此十二月就叫“腊月”。腊祭是春、夏、秋、冬四次大祀中规模最大、最为隆重的冬祀，古人用猎获的禽兽祭祀众神，感谢神灵一年的庇佑和恩赐，祈求来年吉祥安康。腊祭的时间最初不固定，到南北朝时期才固定在腊月初八，称为“腊八”。参见“腊八节”。

An ancient rite of offering sacrifices to ancestors, heaven and earth, and deities observed during the twelfth lunar month. This was one of the four major sacrificial rites of the year, the other three were the spring, summer, and autumn sacrifices. Compared with the other three, the Winter Sacrifice is the largest and also the grandest. Ancient Chinese offered sacrifices to the deities to express their gratitude for the blessings they received over the year and pray for good luck in the coming one. The exact date for the Winter Sacrifice was not set until the Southern and Northern Dynasties (420-589). From that point on, the sacrifice was held on the eighth day of the twelfth lunar month, which is also known as *laba*. See “Laba Festival.”

例句：

腊八节起源于古代的“**腊祭**”，到南北朝时才成为固定的节日，至今已有 1000 多年的历史。

Example Sentence:

The Laba Festival, which has a history of over 1,000 years, originated from the ancient Winter Sacrifice. It has been designated as a festival ever since the Southern and Northern Dynasties (420-589).

腊月忙年

layue mangnian;
preparation for the coming Chinese New Year during the twelfth lunar month

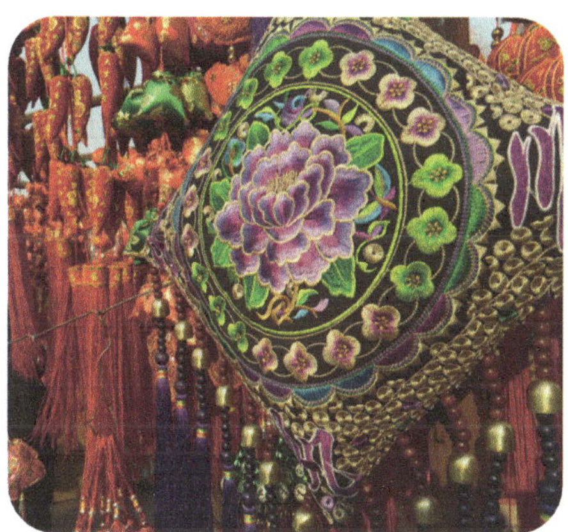

在农历年岁末人们忙碌筹备过年的一系列民俗活动。忙年一般从腊月（农历十二月）二十三祭灶开始到除夕，也有的地方从腊月初八开始计算。腊八节照例要喝腊八粥，以求来年丰收。传统上，北方在腊月二十三、南方在腊月二十四举行祭灶仪式，送

A series of folk activities conducted at the end of the lunar year to prepare for the coming Chinese New Year. It typically lasts from the worshipping of the Kitchen God (twenty-third day of the twelfth lunar month) to the lunar New Year's Eve. It may also start from the eighth day of the twelfth lunar month in some localities. People eat *laba* porridge during the Laba Festival to pray for a good harvest in the coming year. Traditionally, the ceremony of worshipping the Kitchen God is held on the twenty-third day of the twelfth lunar month in northern China and the twenty-fourth day in southern China. After that, people are busy almost every day. Women make new clothes for family members, make paper-cuts to decorate windows and lanterns, and prepare New Year sticky rice

灶神上天，之后几乎天天都有各种活动：妇女给家人缝新衣、剪窗花、糊灯笼、蒸年糕、炸供果，男人们忙着清扫庭院、房屋，裱糊窗户，粉刷墙壁，上街置办年货等。能歌善舞的姑娘、小伙子在村中空地广场打锣鼓、扭秧歌、耍狮、舞龙，为节日期间村社的拜年和元宵节的社火活动做准备。

cakes. Men clean the yards and houses, paste window decorations, paint the walls, and do Spring Festival shopping. Young people may play gongs and drums, do the *yangge* dance, perform the Lion and Dragon Dance, prepare for New Year visits and performance of *shehuo* (Land God and Fire God Worship) during the Lantern Festival.

例句：

腊月忙年虽然事情很多很杂，但处处洋溢着欢快的气氛，因为最隆重的节日春节即将来临。

Example Sentence:

People are busy with many activities during the twelfth lunar month because of the upcoming Spring Festival.

过小年 *guo Xiaonian;* celebrating *Xiaonian* (Minor Chinese New Year)

中国传统年节习俗，标志着春节的开始。许多地方有祭灶、扫尘、剪窗花等习俗。由于各地风俗不同，过小年的时间也不尽相同，北方一般在腊月二十三日，南方一般在腊月二十四日。小年意味着人们开始为新年做好准备，表示新年要有新气象。

A traditional Chinese custom that celebrates the start of the week-long Spring Festival. In many localities there are the customs of offering sacrifices to the Kitchen God, sweeping the dust from the house, and making window paper-cuts. Since the customs vary in different localities, the time to celebrate the "Minor Chinese New Year" also varies. In northern China, it is typically celebrated on the twenty-third day of the twelfth lunar month, and in southern China it is held one day later on the twenty-fourth. The custom implies that people are beginning to make preparations for the coming new year and that this new year will be a fresh start.

例句：

中国民间传说**过小年**这一天，灶王爷要升天向玉皇大帝汇报家家功过，民间也在这一天举行祭灶活动。

Example Sentence:

Legend has it that on the day of the Minor Chinese New Year, the Kitchen God ascends to heaven and reports to the Jade Emperor on the merits and demerits of all the homes, so on this day people hold a ceremony to give offerings to the Kitchen God.

祭灶 *ji zao;* worshipping the Kitchen God

An ancient Chinese folk custom. Worshipping the Kitchen God originated from the ancient worship of the God of Fire in primitive times. Nearly 2,000 years ago, during the Eastern Han Dynasty (25-220) and the Three Kingdoms Period (220-280), pantheism and Daoism prevailed across the country. During this period the Kitchen God became known as the representative of heaven and the master of a house. It was believed he observed a family's behavior and then determined their fate. At the

中国民间流传极广的传统习俗，起源于远古先民对火神的崇拜。距今千余年的汉魏时期，神仙思想和道教流行，灶神逐步变成监察一家善恶和掌握兴衰荣辱的命运之神，成为上天派到人间的一家之主。据称，灶神在年底要上天汇报一家的功过，因此每年农历腊月二十三或二十四，各家都要焚香设供，祈求他到天庭后隐恶扬善。北方祭灶必用饴糖粘灶神之嘴，使其“好话多讲，坏话少说”，因而形成富有情趣的民俗活动。

end of the year, the Kitchen God would return to heaven to report on the family's deeds. On the day of his departure (the twenty-third or twenty-fourth day of the twelfth lunar month), joss sticks would be burnt and sacrifices were offered to him so that he would reward good people and punish the evil. In northern China, there is an interesting custom of smearing malt sugar onto the mouth of an image of the Kitchen God because this made him speak favorably of the family when he reported their deeds in heaven.

例句：

旧时过春节从腊八喝腊八粥开始，二十三**祭灶**过小年，而后是大扫除，进入腊月忙年，一直到正月十五闹元宵，前前后后要一个多月的时间。

Example Sentence:

In ancient times, Chinese New Year celebrations would last for more than a month: starting from the eighth day of the twelfth lunar month of the previous year when *laba* porridge was cooked and enjoyed by every household, to the twenty-third day known as the *Xiaonian* (Minor Chinese New Year) when, people worshipped the Kitchen God and cleaned their houses thoroughly, to a week of busy preparations for New Year celebrations, till the Yuanxiao Fesitval (Lantern Festival) which was celebrated on the fifteenth day of the first lunar month.

扫尘 *sao chen;* sweeping the dust

传统年节习俗，春节前夕举行的大扫除活动，也称“扫年”“打扬尘”。扫尘一般在腊月二十三到除夕之间，多在腊月二十三、二十四日。届时，家家户户都会打扫房屋庭院，清洗器物，拆洗被褥，干干净净迎接新年。因为“尘”与“陈”同音，因而扫尘也有“除陈布新”的涵义，意指把一切穷运、晦气扫地出门。这一习俗表达了人们辞旧迎新、希望美好事物到来的愿望。

A traditional custom of the Spring Festival. Before the Spring Festival, people thoroughly clean their homes, which is also referred to as "*sao nian*, sweeping the year" or "*da yangchen*, removing the dust." Sweeping the dust typically happens between the twenty-third day of the twelfth lunar month and the lunar New Year's Eve, but more often than not it is held on the twenty-third or twenty-fourth of the twelfth lunar month. At that time, every household clears their home, tidies their courtyard, and washes utensils and beddings to welcome the new year on a clean note. Since the Chinese word for dust (尘) is a homophone for 陈 (which means "old" in Chinese), sweeping the dust also has the implication of "removing the old to usher in the new." This implies sweeping all the poverty and bad luck out of the door, a custom reflecting the desire to ring out the old and ring in the new, hoping for good fortune in the coming year.

例句：

土家人**扫尘**后，会把粘满扬尘与蛛网的扫帚扔到屋后山上，据说这样屋里就会一年太平。

Example Sentence:

After the Tujia people sweep the dust from their homes, they will throw away the brooms with the dust and cobwebs onto the mountain or hillsides behind their houses with the belief that peace for the new year will descend upon their house.

对联 *duilian;* rhyming couplet

张贴或悬挂在大门两旁或楹柱上的对偶式联语，又称楹联、对子，对仗工整，平仄相间，结构、字数相同，是一种独特的汉语言文学形式。

A pair of lines of verse written vertically on scrolls that are typically pasted or hung on either side of a door or pillars of a house, also called *yinglian* (pillar couplets) or *duizi* (couplets) in Chinese. It is a unique Chinese

一般以两行文句为一副，并列竖排展示，自上而下读，先右后左，右边为上联，左边为下联。对联无字数限制，少则一两字，多至百千言。相传对联始于五代时期，宋代以后蔚然成风，明、清最为盛行。对联应用范围广泛，根据所用时间、场合不同可分为春节时张贴的春联、婚庆时张贴的喜联、哀悼逝者时张贴的挽联等。对联是中国民族文化的瑰宝，至今仍受到全球华人的广泛欢迎。

literary genre with a one-to-one correspondence in terms of length, structure, level, and oblique tones. Rhyming couplets typically include two phrases or sentences that are aligned vertically with the first line on the right and the second line on the left. They are read from top to bottom and right to left and can be long or short. The shortest ones contain one or two characters, while the longest are comprised of several hundred characters. Legend has it that rhyming couplets originated from the Five Dynasties Period (907-960), thrived in the Song Dynasty (960-1279), and were most popular in the Ming and Qing dynasties (1368-1911). Rhyming couplets are widely used and can be divided into Spring Festival couplets for the Chinese New Year, wedding couplets hung on walls at weddings, elegiac couplets for condolences, among others. As a treasure of traditional Chinese culture, rhyming couplets are still very popular among people of Chinese origin all over the world.

例句：

2005 年，**对联**被列入中国第一批国家非物质文化遗产名录。

Example Sentence:

In 2005, rhyming couplets were among the first group to be included in the National Intangible Cultural Heritage List of China.

春联 *chunlian;* Spring Festival couplet; New Year scroll

对联的一种，春节期间张贴在大门或楹柱上的联语。春联内容喜庆、吉祥，寄托了一家人对新一年的美好愿望，多用大红纸书写，增添新年喜庆氛围；但庙宇用黄纸，守制（服孝未满）用白、绿、黄三色，守制第一年用白纸，第二年用绿纸，第三年用黄纸，第四年服丧期满才恢复用红纸。贴春联是全球华人过春节的重要标志。时至今

A kind of rhyming couplet pasted on both sides of the doors or pillars of a home during Spring Festival. They generally feature black or gold characters written on red paper and festive and auspicious content that expresses the family's best wishes for the coming New Year and enlivens the festive atmosphere. Couplets for temples are written on yellow paper, those for families in mourning are written on white paper in the first year after death, green paper in the second year, yellow paper in the third year, and red paper again in the fourth year. Hanging up Spring Festival couplets is one of the most important customs when celebrating Chinese New Year. Today, every Chinese family carefully chooses Spring Festival couplets to ring out the old year and ring in the new, and pray for happiness and auspiciousness.

日，每逢春节，家家户户都要精选春联贴于门上，辞旧迎新、迎祥纳福。

例句：

春联起源于桃符——周代悬挂在大门两旁的桃木板，上有题辞。

Example Sentence:

Spring Festival couplets originated from *taofu*, a Zhou Dynasty (1046-256 BC) practice in which inscriptions are engraved on boards made from peach trees.

jianzhi;
paper-cutting

中国最古老的民间艺术之一，用剪刀或刻刀在纸上剪刻花纹，用于装点生活。该艺术源于民间，历史悠久，是各种民俗活动的重要组成部分。剪纸颜色美丽鲜艳，多为红、绿、紫，题材广泛，包括花卉、虫鱼、鸟兽、人物、图案等，构图简洁，线条明快，形式优美，兼具审美价值及实用价值。中国北方的剪纸多粗犷豪爽，江南的剪纸多精细俏丽，风格不一，地域特色鲜明，较为著名的有河北蔚县的民间剪纸，江苏扬州、南京剪纸，广东佛山剪纸，广西桂林剪纸等。

One of the oldest folk art forms in China. Artisans use scissors or engraving knives to cut paper into various patterns to be used as decorations. Paper-cutting has a long history and plays an important part in folk culture. Paper-cutting is usually made with colored paper such as red, green, or purple. It is neat and exquisite in terms of design and form, and has aesthetic and practical value. Its patterns include flowers, insects, fish, birds, animals, and figures. Paper-cutting styles vary in different regions. In northern China, paper-cuts are usually bold and considered unconstrained. The paper-cuts of Yuxian County, Hebei Province are a typical example of northern style paper-cutting. In southern China, paper-cuts are more exquisite and delicate. Such examples can be found in Yangzhou and Nanjing of Jiangsu Province, Foshan in Guangdong Province, and Guilin in Guangxi Zhuang Autonomous Region.

例句：

2006 年，**剪纸**艺术遗产经国务院批准列入中国第一批国家级非物质文化遗产名录；2009 年入选联合国教科文组织“人类非物质文化遗产代表作名录”。

Example Sentence:

In 2006, paper-cutting was ranked among the first batch of China's National Intangible Cultural Heritage List approved by the State Council, and it was included on the UNESCO Intangible Cultural Heritage List in 2009.

窗花

chuanghua;
paper-cut as a window decoration; window paper-cut

民间剪纸艺术的一种，因用于装饰窗户而得名。逢年过节，人们喜欢在窗户上张贴各种剪纸窗花，既烘托喜庆的节日氛围，也表达人们追求幸福的美好愿景。窗花内容多为象征吉祥富贵的动物、花卉，如“五谷丰登”“六畜兴旺”“龙凤呈祥”等，还有神话传说、戏曲故事等题材，多用红、绿纸剪成，极富生活气息和艺术感染力，深受人们喜爱。其中河北蔚县窗花尤为著名。

Folk paper-cutting artworks used to decorate windows. During the Chinese New Year and other holidays, people enjoy pasting paper-cuts on their windows for decoration which creates a festive atmosphere and shows people's aspiration for happiness. Paper-cuts used as window decorations are usually made of red and green paper, and they contain rich patterns such as animals and flowers that symbolize auspiciousness and prosperity, myths and legends, and stories from traditional operas. The art form is widely popular and adored by most Chinese people. The paper-cuts from Yuxian County, Hebei Province, perhaps are among the best-known in China.

例句：

窗花目前已成为中国一种独特的室内装饰艺术品。

Example Sentence:

Window paper-cuts have become a unique form of interior decoration in China.

纸塑窗花 *zhisu chuanghua;* embossed window paper-cut

一种类似浮雕的彩色窗花剪纸，多见于陕西省合阳县。这种剪纸把纸扎、彩绘、剪纸的手法结合起来，材料除了各种色纸外，还有布、绸、轻纱等。纸塑窗花一般用于装点春节居室和结婚的新房，色彩鲜艳，立体感强。表现内容多为戏曲故事和花卉。

A kind of color paper-cut with raised patterns, very popular in Heyang County of Shaanxi Province. Such paper-cuts are made through paper folding, painting, and paper-cutting techniques. Apart from colored paper, materials like cloth, silk, and gauze are also used. Colorful and three-dimensional, embossed window paper-cuts are mainly used to decorate rooms during the Spring Festival or rooms in a couple's bedroom on their wedding night. Opera stories and flowers are common subjects of the artwork.

例句：

纸塑窗花贴在窗格上迎风舞动，铮铮作响，栩栩如生。

Example Sentence:

Embossed window paper-cuts are usually placed in windows, where they gently sway in the wind while making a soft flipping sound, as if the figures on the paper-cuts have come to life.

点染剪纸 *dianran jianzhi;* dyed paper-cut

一种彩色剪纸。采用易吸水又很薄的连史纸，二三十张纸叠成一叠，用尖刀刻好，然后用白酒调和不含胶、矾不带粉质的"品色"一次染出，色彩强烈、明艳。题材有戏曲人物、花卉瓜果、鸟兽鱼虫和吉祥图案。

A kind of colorful paper-cut. To make a dyed paper-cut, artisans use *lianshi* paper (fine paper made of bamboo), because the paper is thin and highly absorbent. Usually, 20 to 30 sheets of paper are placed in a pile. After engraving patterns on the pile of paper, artisans mix liquor with special watercolor paints and dye all the cutouts at the same time. The dyed paper-cuts are bright and colorful. Common subjects of this genre include flowers, melons, fruits, birds, animals, fish, insects, figures from traditional operas, and auspicious patterns.

例句：

河北省蔚县的**点染剪纸**最为著名，相传已有200多年的历史。

Example Sentence:

Yuxian County of Hebei Province is best-known for its dyed paper-cuts. It is said to have a history of more than 200 years.

熏烟剪纸 *xunyan jianzhi;* soot-blackened paper-cut

一种通过传统的"翻样"复制的方法制作的剪纸，也称"熏花"。将剪纸放在纸上面，用水喷湿，然后放在油灯上用油烟熏黑，便留下了清晰的底样。陕西省延安市富县剪纸将底样施以颜色点染，形成虚实相接、黑白对比鲜明的艺术风貌。

A kind of paper-cut made through a traditional reproduction technique, also known as soot-blackened flowers. The artist puts the cutout on a sheet of white paper and sprays water on it. Then, the two sheets of paper are placed above an oil lamp so that soot can blacken the patterns. In Fuxian County near Yan'an City, Shaanxi Province, there is another step afterwards. The cutout is dyed with different colors, thus creating sharp contrasts between the solid base and the delicately cut shapes, as well as between the blackened part and the clean part of the work.

例句：

熏烟剪纸多见于陕西省境内。

Example Sentence:

Soot-blackened paper-cuts are mostly found in Shaanxi Province.

熏花 *xunhua;* soot-blackened flower

参见"熏烟剪纸"。

See *xunyan jianzhi* (soot-blackend paper-cut).

贴福字 *tie fu zi;* mounting character *fu* (blessings)

中国传统年俗。每逢新春佳节，许多中国人要在门上、墙上或是家具上贴上大大小小的纸“福”字。福字象征着幸福、福气。贴福字体现了人们希望生活幸福的美好愿望。有的人家还会将福字倒贴，讨个“福到”的口彩。

A traditional Chinese New Year custom. As the Chinese New Year approaches, people mount pieces of paper in various sizes with the character *fu* (blessings) on doors, walls and furniture. *Fu* means good luck and blessings, and pasting this character is a way to express people's hope for a happy life. Some people paste the character *fu* upside down, as the words for "upside-down" (倒) and "to arrive" (到) are homophonous. Therefore, the phrase an "upside-down *fu*" sounds nearly identical to the phrase "Good luck arrives."

例句:

旧俗中，倒**贴福字**主要用于以下几个地方：水缸、垃圾箱或是屋内的柜子上。

Example Sentence:

The upside-down character *fu* was traditionally pasted on water vats, dustbins or cupboards.

年画

nianhua;
New Year picture; Spring Festival painting

中国民间特有的美术形式。始于古代的“门神画”，大都用于新年时张贴，装饰环境，含有祝福新年吉祥喜庆之意。早期年画多为人工绘制，随着木版印刷技术的发展，木版印刷的年画逐渐成为主流。明清时代，年画成为过年不可缺少的民俗艺术品，“有钱无钱，买张画儿过年。”上自宫廷王公大臣，下至民间贩夫走卒，新年均买年画张贴。近现代则出现了石印、胶版年画。

A unique style of Chinese folk painting, with door-god pictures as its earliest form. They are usually hung during the Chinese New Year as decorations and as hopes for an auspicious new year. The earliest New Year pictures were painted, but with the development of printing techniques, woodblock New Year pictures became mainstream. During the Ming (1368-1644) and Qing (1616-1911) dynasties, New Year pictures gradually became an indispensable form of artwork during festivals. As an old saying goes, “Rich or not, one has to buy a picture to celebrate the New Year.” From court ministers down to street peddlers, people from all walks of life buy the New Year pictures to decorate their homes during the Lunar New Year holiday.

例句：

各地的**年画**作者多为民间画师，他们熟悉民众生活，创作出的年画内容和形式各具特色。

Example Sentence:

Most New Year pictures are made by folk artists who are familiar with the daily lives of common people. Their works have distinctive local features in subject and form.

桃花坞年画

taohuawu nianhua;
Taohuawu New Year picture

中国民间木版年画品种之一，因盛产于苏州城内的桃花坞一带而得名。桃花坞年画为木版水印年画，约始于明代后期，盛行于清乾隆之后，最盛时年产年画数百万张，主要行销江浙一带。年画多表现当地风俗、戏文故事等，趣味性强，色彩鲜艳柔和。现在由于印刷技术的迅猛发展，桃花坞年画已日趋衰微。2006年，该年画批准列入第一批国家级非物质文化遗产名录。

A type of Chinese folk woodblock New Year picture made in Taohuawu (Peach Blossom Dock) in Suzhou, Jiangsu Province. The Taohuawu New Year picture is produced with woodblocks and bears watermarks. Production of Taohuawu New Year pictures first began in the late Ming Dynasty, and was popular after the reign of Emperor Qianlong (1711-1799) of the Qing Dynasty. During this period, several million copies were produced every year, and they were primarily sold in Jiangsu and Zhejiang provinces. The pictures express local customs, stories of dramas and literature and so on. They are fun, colorful, and exquisite. Their color schemes are bright and mild. With the rapid development of modern printing techniques, however, the Taohuawu New Year pictures have been on the decline. In 2006, it was included in the first batch of National Intangible Cultural Heritage List.

例句：

桃花坞年画作者多为民间画师，因此很多人已经不可考。

Example Sentence:

Those who created the Taohuawu New Year pictures were mostly folk artists, many of whom cannot be identified now.

chuxi; Chinese New Year's Eve

中国传统节日春节中最重要的组成部分，指农历岁末最后一天的夜晚，俗称“大年三十”“大年夜”。除夕是除旧迎新的重要时间界点，也是中国人最为看重的家庭团圆之夜。除夕这天人们无论身在何处，都要想办法赶回家，与全家人一起吃团年饭——一年中最丰盛、隆重的一顿饭。饭后，长辈要给家中的小孩子发压岁钱。压岁钱一般用红纸包好，称为红包，据说能够护佑孩童岁岁平安。除夕夜家家户户灯火通明，燃放鞭炮，传说这是为了吓走一个叫“夕”的吃人怪兽，这就是“除夕”的来历。这天夜里，全家人围坐在一起聊天，通宵不眠，迎接新年的到来，称为守岁。新岁降临时，人们纷纷燃放鞭炮迎接新年。虽然除夕的一些习俗已经随着社会的发展而发生了变化，但除夕在中国人心目中的重要地位仍然没有改变。

A Chinese holiday which is the key part of the Spring Festival celebrations. Also known as *danian* ye or *danian sanshi* (Chinese New Year's Eve). *Chuxi* is the last day of the calendar, and is the time when people ring out the old and ring in the new. It is the most anticipated holiday in Chinese culture, with family members all gathering together—some from very far—especially for the New Year's Eve meal, usually the most sumptuous meal of the year. After dinner, senior family members give *hongbao* (red packets) to children, which is money wrapped in red paper, believed to bring peace to the children during the coming year. The whole family stays up all night to welcome the New Year, and people light firecrackers as midnight arrives to scare away Xi—a human-eating demon—which is the origin of *chuxi* (literally: to get rid of Xi). Although some *chuxi* customs have changed due to societal development, the importance of *chuxi* in Chinese culture has never changed.

例句：

除夕一般为农历十二月三十日，如果当月没有三十日，则为二十九日，但人们习惯上仍然称之为“大年三十”。

Example Sentence:

Chuxi is usually on the thirtieth day of the twelfth lunar month. If the last lunar month has only 29 days, then *chuxi* will fall on the twenty-ninth.

爆竹 *baozhu; firecracker*

节庆用品，亦称“炮仗”“鞭炮”。放鞭炮庆贺新春这一传统民俗在中国已有两千多年的历史，相传最初是为了在除夕驱赶山臊恶鬼。最早的爆竹是把竹节丢进火堆，使之在火堆中爆烈发出很响的声音。随着火药的发明，唐时人们开始把火药装在竹筒里燃放，响声更大。北宋民间出现了用纸包卷火药制成的炮仗和专门生产炮仗的作坊，还出现了连响、双响等各式各样的花炮。在其后很长一段历史时期中，放鞭炮成为一种有民族特色的庆祝节日的娱乐活动，也是民间举行婚礼等庆典仪式的重要组成部分。由

An item used during festivals, also called *paozhang* or *bianpao* in Chinese. The traditional custom of setting off firecrackers to celebrate the Lunar New Year has a history of over 2,000 years. These firecrackers are said to drive away a monster on New Year's Eve. The earliest firecrackers were created by throwing bamboo into a bonfire to produce a large noise like a loud bang. With the invention of gunpowder, people began putting gunpowder into thick bamboo tubes to produce a louder noise during the Tang Dynasty (618-907). Later in the Northern Song Dynasty (960-1127), special workshops emerged that produced firecrackers by wrapping gunpowder with paper. Later on, various continuous-bang and double-bang firecrackers were created. Setting off firecrackers has become a unique way of celebrating festivals. This important national custom is an important component of weddings and other folk celebrations. However,

于放鞭炮会造成严重的空气污染、噪音污染，还具有很大的危险性，如今中国的有些地方已禁止燃放鞭炮。

as it may cause severe air and sound pollution and harm people, nowadays some places in China have banned setting off firecrackers.

例句：

在大年初一，中国民间家家户户开门的第一件事就是燃放**爆竹**，以噼里啪啦的爆竹声除旧迎新。

Example Sentence:

On the Lunar New Year's Day, the first thing Chinese people do is to open the door and set off firecrackers to ring out the old year and ring in the new one.

年夜饭

nianye fan;
New Year's Eve dinner; Chinese New Year reunion dinner

中国传统年节习俗之一，指除夕夜阖家团圆，共进丰盛的晚餐。年夜饭一般包括鸡、鱼、饺子及各种肉类、瓜果蔬菜。"鸡"和"吉"谐音，象征吉利、吉祥；"鱼"和"余"谐音，象征年年有余。吃饭前需先祭神拜祖，吃饭时要多说吉祥语以讨吉利。

Traditional family reunion dinner held at the Chinese New Year's Eve. Dishes commonly served include chicken, fish, dumplings, meat, fruits, and vegetables. Chicken, which is pronounced jī in Chinese, is a homophone for "auspiciousness" and fish (yú) is a homophone for "surplus" indicating abundance for each year. Before dinner, family members worship the gods and their ancestors. When they begin to eat, they say lots of auspicious things, hoping for good luck. A seat is saved for anyone who can't make it to the dinner, symbolizing that he or she is present with the family. Family reunion dinners mark the most

如若家中有人在外地不能出席，也会留出他的位置和碗筷，象征其已回家、全家团圆。年夜饭是中国人最重要的一顿晚餐，是家庭和睦的象征，充分体现了中华民族对于家庭的重视。

important gatherings for Chinese people. They also symbolize family harmony and fully demonstrate that Chinese people highly value their families.

例句：

中国人把**年夜饭**又称为“团圆饭”，既是一顿饭，更是一种仪式。一家人在饭桌上推杯换盏，聊着山南海北，叙着友爱亲情。

Example Sentence:

The New Years Eve dinner, also called family reunion dinner, is both a meal and a celebration. Family members help one another fill the wine cups, chat on a wide host of topics, and enjoy the intimate atmosphere.

年糕 *niangao;* Chinese New Year cake; Spring Festival cake

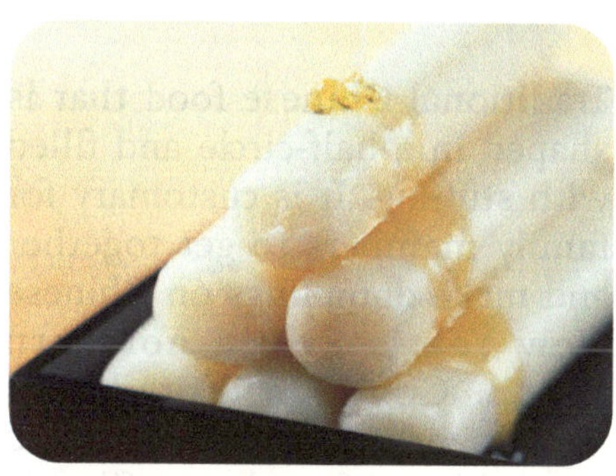

中国农历春节传统食品，是一种用有黏性的米或米粉做成的糕点。有红、白、黄三色，口味因地区而异。北方的年糕以甜为主，南方则甜

Traditional food served during the Spring Festival. *Niangao* is a kind of cake made of glutinous rice or rice flour. It comes in three different decorative colors, namely red, white, and yellow. Its taste varies in different regions. It is mainly sweet in northern China while it is both sweet and salty in southern China. It is produced in different ways according to the regions. Generally speaking, it is prepared by steaming, deep-frying, stir-frying, or boiling in a soup. *Niangao* indicates that one will be “higher” in the New Year (this is the result of a homonym

咸兼具。在做法上，有蒸、炸、炒或煮汤，各地制法不一。年糕谐音“年高”，有一年更比一年好、年年高升的吉祥含义，几乎中国各地都有春节吃年糕的风俗。

in Chinese). This implies that one may, for example, be promoted to a better or higher post in the coming new year, which is undoubtedly an auspicious event. Accordingly, people eat *niangao* all over China.

例句：

年糕象征成长、进步和高升，经常可作为假日走亲访友、拜访长辈的礼品。

Example Sentence:

The Chinese New Year cakes symbolize growth, progress, and promotion, and are commonly used as gifts for visiting friends and family elders during festivals and holidays.

饺子 *jiaozi;* Chinese dumpling

Traditional Chinese food that is shaped in a half-circle and filled with stuffing. It is customary for family members to get together and make dumplings on Chinese New Year's Eve in northern China. Common ingredients include meat, eggs, seafood, and vegetables. After the stuffing is prepared, the dough is kneaded to form the dumpling skin. Then, small circles of skin are laid out and small amounts of stuffing are placed in each circle. They are then rolled over and bound to form the dumplings. When they

中国传统特色面食，有馅，半圆形。中国北方地区，除夕夜有全家人围坐在一起包饺子过年的传统。包饺子首先要和面做成饺子皮，再用皮包上馅，用清水煮熟，捞起后可蘸着醋、蒜末、香油一起吃。饺子馅可荤可素，可咸可甜，各种肉、蛋、海鲜、蔬菜均可入馅。同时还有炸饺子、烙饺子（锅贴）等吃法。饺子的形状像元宝，因此饺子具有团圆相聚、招财进宝的吉祥含义。过年人们包饺子时还会在其中一两个内放糖、枣、硬币等，寓意吃到这些饺子的人来年会有好运气。现在，饺子已是中国人的日常食物，不只是在春节时才吃。

are all prepared, they are usually boiled though they can also be fried (called pot stickers). After they are cooked, people eat them by first dipping them into a sauce consisting of vinegar, soy sauce, minced garlic, and sesame oil. Dumplings are shaped like ancient Chinese gold ingots, symbolizing auspicious reunion and good fortune. People may also put sugar, dates, and coins in one or two of the dumplings as a game, believed that whoever chooses to eat these dumplings will have good luck in the coming year. Dumplings have since become a common food in China, and are not exclusively eaten during the Spring Festival.

例句：

饺子是中国传统食物的代表，是北方人许多节假日如春节、冬至的必备食物。

Example Sentence:

Chinese dumpling is a typical, traditional food that is a must-have for festivals and holidays such as the Spring Festival and the Winter Solstice in northern China.

辞旧岁

ci jiusui;
bidding farewell to the old year

中国年节习俗，亦称辞年、别岁。农历除夕，人们会准备祭品祭祀祖先、叩拜尊长以辞别旧岁、迎接新年。辞岁习俗在中国南北方均十分流行，且自宋代以来流传至今，晚辈向长辈行礼请安，长辈会给晚辈发压岁钱，反映了人们辞旧迎新、迎祥纳福的美好希冀。

A Chinese Spring Festival custom that is also known as *cisui* or *biesui* in short. On lunar New Year's Eve, Chinese people make offerings to their ancestors and honor elders. They do this to bid farewell to the old year and usher in the new one. Since the Song Dynasty (960-1279), this custom has been very popular in both northern and southern China. Children pay tribute to their elders, and in turn receive red envelopes filled with money to express good wishes for happiness and auspiciousness.

例句：

春节人们经常以不同的方式来**辞旧岁**、迎新年，祈求来年五谷丰登，国泰民安。

Example Sentence:

Chinese people often bid farewell to the old year and usher in the new one in various ways during the Spring Festival. They also express hopes for a good harvest, that the country will enjoy prosperity, and they will live in peace during the coming year.

shousui; staying up all night on Chinese New Year's Eve

中国民间除夕习俗。除夕夜，全家人吃过年夜饭后，围炉夜话，通宵不眠，灯火不灭，等待旧年过去，迎接新年到来。守岁有两种含义：年长者守岁为珍惜光阴；年轻人守岁是为父母延寿。

A folk custom on Chinese New Year's Eve. On the evening after the New Year's Eve dinner, the whole family gathers together to talk and stay up all night to usher in the New Year and see off the old one. *Shousui* has two meanings: for the elderly, it means to cherish each moment; for the young, *shousui* means to elongate the life of their parents.

例句：

守岁既有对逝去的岁月惜别留恋之情，又有对新年的美好希望。

Example Sentence:

Shousui is a nostalgic event when people reminisce over the past, and it is also a time when they set their hopes on having an even better new year.

大年初一 *danian chuyi;* Chinese New Year's Day

正月初一，农历新年的第一天。大年初一早晨，家家户户开门第一件事便是燃放红皮爆竹，象征新一年的日子红红火火。接下来会贴春联、走亲访友相互拜年，长辈还会给晚辈发压岁钱，祈求新年大吉大利。民间

The Chinese New Year falls on the first day of the first lunar month. On the morning of New Year's Day, Chinese people open their doors and set off red firecrackers, symbolizing hopes for good luck in the New Year. Next, people paste Spring Festival couplets and visit relatives and friends. Elders also give red envelopes filled

认为人们在大年初一做的事情会影响一整年的运气，因此有许多禁忌，如不扫地、不倒垃圾、不往外倒水，以免好运气流失。

with money to their children as a symbol of good fortune in the coming new year. It is believed that what one does on New Year's Day will affect one's luck throughout the rest of the year. Therefore, there are many taboos during this time. For example, one should not sweep the floor, dump out garbage, or pour out water on this day to avoid losing out on good luck.

例句：

大年初一是中国法定节假日，学校及大多数商店等关门歇业，庆祝春节。

Example Sentence:

The Chinese New Year's Day is a legal holiday. The general public gets this day off, and most schools and businesses are closed to celebrate the Spring Festival.

拜年 *bai nian;* paying a New Year visit

中国春节传统习俗之一，又称"贺岁"。春节期间人们拜访长辈、亲戚、朋友，祝贺新年的到来并互致新年祝福，称为"拜年"。拜年一般从正月初一起持续到正月十五。拜年一般先家人后亲朋。按照旧习俗，给家族中年长者拜年，要带拜年礼并行跪拜礼。随着科技的发展，通过手机微信拜年已成为新时尚。

A traditional Chinese Spring Festival custom. It is also referred to as *hesui*—extending a New Year's greeting. During the Spring Festival, people visit their elders, relatives, and friends to congratulate the arrival of the new year and also to bestow good wishes. This custom usually begins on New Year's Day and continues to the fifteenth day of the first lunar month. People usually first visit their closer family members and then their relatives and friends. According to old customs, when visiting a middle-aged or senior relative, one should bring a present and perform a kowtow. With the development of modern technology, people enjoy using the mobile app WeChat to practice this custom.

例句：

拜年是一种联络亲情、乡情、友情的节日活动。

Example Sentence:

New Year visits are festive activities which help strengthen ties between relatives, neighbors, and friends.

压岁钱

yasui qian;
money given to children as new year present; new year's gift money

中国民间年俗的节物之一。“岁”与“祟”谐音，“祟”指鬼神带来的灾祸。人们认为小孩容易受鬼祟的侵害，因此除夕团年饭后，长辈要将事先准备好、用红纸包着的压岁钱分发给晚辈，寓意辟邪驱鬼，保佑他们在新的一年里健康吉利，平平安安。这一习俗至今仍盛行不衰，不过时间不严格局限在除夕夜，也可以在春节期间拜年的时候给。

Money given to children for good luck during the New Year. 岁(year, age), pronounced suì, sounds the same as 祟 (the disasters that evil spirits can bring). Chinese people believe that children are prone to getting harmed by evil spirits. After the New Year's Eve dinner, seniors of the family would gift the children red envelopes filled with money called *yasui qian*, hoping that it would ward off evil forces and bring them good luck and health in the year to come. This remains a popular custom till this day, but the occasion for giving *yasui qian* is no longer limited to the New Year's Eve; it can also be given at the first few days of the new year when children come with their parents for a visit.

例句：

压岁钱既是喜庆的贺岁之礼，也是长辈给予儿童的保护力量。

Example Sentence:

Yasui qian is both a way to extend a new year greeting and a symbolic expression of the notion that older generations should help protect the young members of the family.

祭财神 *ji caishen;* worship of the God of Wealth

中国民间传统祭祀习俗，时间因地区而异，南方为正月初五，北方为正月初二。人们在该日会打开大门和窗户，燃香，点爆竹，放烟花，供奉鱼肉、羊肉、鸡肉等，迎接财神，保佑来年财源广进，大富大贵。有的地方人们还会到寺庙烧香求财。

A traditional Chinese folk worship custom. It is observed at different times in different regions. In southern China, it is held on the fifth day of the first lunar month, and in northern China it is held on the second day of the first lunar month. On this day, Chinese people open their doors and windows, light incense, set off firecrackers, and offer such sacrifices as fish, lamb, and chicken to the God of Wealth, who they hope will bless them with great fortune and good luck over the next year. In some localities, people go to temples to burn incense and pray for wealth.

例句：

中国的有些地方还保留着春节期间举行**祭财神**活动的习俗。

Example Sentence:

People in some regions of China still worship the God of Wealth during the Spring Festival celebration.

破五 *powu;* lifting prohibitions on the fifth of the first lunar month

中国民间称正月初五为“破五”。人们认为除夕以来的

Chinese folk custom during the Spring Festival. Chinese people believe that many taboos—such as prohibiting women from going

诸多禁忌如禁止妇女出门、不向屋外倒垃圾等过此日皆可破，因此得名。正月初五也被当作财神生日，人们在这一天送穷、迎财神、开市贸易。破五也有送年的意思，人们黎明即起，放鞭炮、打扫卫生，寓意将一切不吉利的东西都赶走。很多地方在初五这天吃饺子，叫“食元宝”，以表达人们渴望招财进宝、迎祥纳福的心情。

outside or dumping garbage outside—should be observed during the New Year holiday, beginning on New Year's Eve. However, on the fifth day of the first lunar month, these prohibitions can be lifted. This day is also regarded as the birthday of the God of Wealth. On this day, people pray to the God of Wealth and begin doing business again. This day in Chinese also means bidding farewell to the previous year. People get up at dawn, set off firecrackers, and clean their houses to drive away what is inauspicious. In many localities, eating dumplings on this day is dubbed "eating golden ingots," which symbolizes hope for wealth and good luck.

例句：

一般认为**破五**之后春节就结束了，人们的生活会慢慢恢复常态。

Example Sentence:

People generally consider the the fifth day of the first lunar month as the end of the Spring Festival holiday, and life gradually returns to normal after that.

开市 *kaishi;* resuming business

旧时中国春节期间所有店铺从大年初一起关门，年后择

As shops were all closed on the New Year's Day to celebrate the occasion in olden days, they would choose an auspicious day after the holiday

吉日（正月初五、初六）重新开张，称为“开市”。民间习俗认为初五是财神生日，店铺此日开张便可财源广进发大财。目前也有很多商家不再遵循此旧俗，春节期间照常开门做生意。

to reopen their businesses. Usually this falls on the fifth or sixth day of the first lunar month. People widely believe that the fifth day of the first lunar month marks the birthday of the God of Wealth. Accordingly, if stores open on this day, people believe they will be able to make a great fortune. Nowadays, many merchants no longer follow this old custom and do business as usual during the Spring Festival.

例句：

旧时民俗**开市**时店铺会燃放鞭炮、贴红对联以求吉利。

Example Sentence:

In the past, when businesses resumed after the Spring Festival holiday, shops would light fireworks and paste red rhyming couplets for blessings.

miaohui;
temple fair

中国传统岁时节令活动，又称“庙市”，一般在春节、元宵节、二月二龙抬头等节日举行。南北朝时期佛教盛行，寺庙殿宇众多，每逢举行盛大宗教活动，人们都聚集到寺庙周围，小商贩们为了给游人和信徒提供货物，在寺庙道路两边摆起小摊，形成了集市，因起源于寺庙周围，所以称为“庙会”。久而久之，“庙会”演变成了如今节日期间，特别是春节期间的商贸、娱乐活动。现在的庙会除了商业活动外，还有手工艺展，杂耍、曲艺等休闲娱乐活动。

Traditional Chinese event usually held during the Spring Festival, the Lantern Festival, and the Dragon Head-Raising Festival. During the Southern and Northern Dynasties (420-589), Buddhism flourished and many temples were built. During religious festivals, people would gather at the temples. This prompted vendors to set up booths along the temple roads, which gradually transformed into a market. Because of their location, people referred to them as "temple fairs." The markets gradually expanded to include entertainment and other activities such as arts and crafts exhibitions, variety shows, and recreational events of all kinds. These fairs are especially popular during the Spring Festival.

例句：

庙会在中国南北各地均很流行，有些地方的庙会被列入国家级非物质文化遗产名录。

Example Sentence:

Temple fairs are popular in both the northern and southern parts of China. Some of them are included on the National Intangible Cultural Heritage List.

庙市 *miaoshi;* temple market

参见“庙会”。

See *miaohui* (temple fair).

面人 *mianren;* dough figure; dough figurine; dough modeling

中国传统手工艺品，以面粉、糯米粉为主要原料捏制而成。艺人用彩色面团捏塑出各种人物和飞禽走兽、花卉果品形象。面人制作一般先采用捏、搓、揉、掀等手法塑造大体形制，再用竹刀灵巧地点、切、刻、划，丰富手脚、面部等局部细节。面人既可以作为儿童的玩具，也可以成为陈设的艺术品。北京、上海、山东等地的面人比较知名。

A traditional folk handicraft in China. Using colorful rice dough, craftsmen make vivid figures of humans, animals, flowers, and vegetables. They first model the dough using techniques such as pinching, rubbing, kneading, and twisting. Then they use a small pointed bamboo stick to carve the details in the figure's hands, feet, and on its face. The dough figurines can be used as toys for children or as artistic decorations. This art form is quite popular in Beijing, Shanghai, and Shandong Province.

例句：

北京**面人**以塑造各种戏曲舞台人物形象和表现老北京生活场景见长。

Example Sentence:

Beijing's dough figures are known for their lively portrayal of traditional opera figures and the everyday lives of people who lived in Beijing in olden times.

毛猴 *mao hou;* hairy monkey; woolly monkey

北京特有的传统手工艺品。艺人巧用带有绒毛的玉兰花蒂、蝉蜕的头和爪子做成毛茸茸的小猴，故名“毛猴”。毛猴常摹拟人们劳作和生活神态，令人忍俊不禁。

A folk handicraft unique to Beijing. Using fluffy magnolia buds and cicada shells, craftsmen make all sorts of miniature scenes with monkey-like figures, hence the name "hairy monkey." The humourous scenes consist of monkeys performing daily tasks of work and life normally performed by humans.

例句：

相传在清同治年间北京城南的一家药铺里，一个小伙计为了发泄对账房的不满，用一些中药材做出了第一个以尖嘴猴腮的账房为原形的**毛猴**。

Example Sentence:

It is said that some time during the reign of Emperor Tongzhi (1862-1874) of the Qing Dynasty (1616-1911), a salesclerk of a drugstore in the south of Beijing was discontented with the shop accountant, so he fiddled around with some Chinese herbs and made the very first hairy monkey to mimic this accountant with a thin, angular face.

鬃人 *zongren; bristle figure*

A traditional folk toy usually sold at temple fairs in Beijing. Glue mud is used to make the head and base, while sorghum stalks are used to make the body frame. Colorful paper can be made into clothes, and cotton is wadded into the figures. After the basic parts are prepared, facial makeup is drawn, and details of the clothes are added. Each figure is secured to the base with a circle of bristles and then placed on a copper plate. When a little bit of force is applied, the figures move and appear to fight due to the bristles' flexibility.

北京庙会的民间传统玩具。手工艺人用胶泥胎做人物的头和底座，秫秸做身架，外裹彩衣，内絮棉花，然后勾画脸谱，描绘服饰，然后将人物固定在沿周粘有一圈猪鬃毛的底座上，并置于铜盘之中，借助鬃毛的弹力，稍受震动鬃人便会自动转动或表演打斗、厮拼等动作。

例句：

北京民间玩意儿种类很多，有脸谱、面塑、风筝、**鬃人**、草编、毛猴、刀马人等。

Example Sentence:

There are a wide variety of folk handicrafts in Beijing, including opera masks, dough figures, kites, bristle figures, straw figures, hairy monkeys, and clay figures of generals.

草编

caobian;
straw figure; straw plaited article

庙会常见的传统民间工艺品。艺人以嫩软的草叶为原料，运用编扣、打结、穿插等工艺手法，编结出青蛙、乌龟、蝉等各种动物，栩栩如生。

A folk handicraft often seen at temple fairs. Using techniques like weaving, knotting and plaiting, craftsmen turn soft straw into frogs, turtles, cicadas, and other animals.

例句：

草编也可以用来指利用各地所产的草编成的各种生活用品，如提篮、帽子和杯垫等。

Example Sentence:

In a broader sense, the term *caobian* can also be used to refer to local straw-plaited daily items such as baskets, hats, and coasters.

老鼠嫁女 *Laoshu Jia Nü;* Mouse Marries Off His Daughter

中国民间传说，讲的是一对老鼠夫妇为鼠女寻找最佳女婿的故事。因地区和民族不同，故事有多个版本，“嫁女”的时间和民俗活动也有差别，但都发生在春节之后老鼠繁殖期开始的时候。民间对“老鼠嫁女”有两种矛盾的心态：一种是将老鼠视为一种灵性动物加以崇拜，如有些地方在老鼠嫁女日炒芝麻糖给老鼠当喜糖，或早早就寝以免打扰老鼠娶亲；另一种是将老鼠视为祸害，催促其快快“嫁娶”离家，消除鼠害。

A Chinese folk story. Different regions and ethnic groups produced different versions of the story. In summary, a mouse father and mother search for the best husband for their mouse daughter. They ask the sun, who says the clouds are stronger. They ask the clouds, who reply the wind is stronger. The wind says that a wall is stronger, and the wall replies that a mouse is stronger because the mouse's teeth can eat away at the wall. In the end, the mouse couple realize that a mouse would make an adequate husband for their daughter. The marriage is said to be after the Spring Festival, when mice begin to breed. The Chinese people have two conflicting views towards the mouse: it is regarded as an intelligent and divine animal to be worshipped, but it is also regarded as a pest that should be eradicated. To reflect this contradiction, some common practices include frying sesame candy to be given to mice as a kind of candy for the mouse daughter's wedding, wishing for the wedding to go smoothly so that the mice will go away. People will also go to bed early so as not to disturb the mouse's wedding plans.

例句：

老鼠嫁女常见于年画、剪纸等民间艺术作品中，画面一般包含花轿、彩旗、灯笼、鼓乐、仪仗等，类似于中国古代结婚的场景。

Example Sentence:

Chinese New Year pictures and paper-cuts often feature this story with a scene similar to a wedding ceremony in ancient China, which usually includes a bridal chair, colorful flags, lanterns, musical instruments, and a procession.

元宵节 *Yuanxiao Jie;* Yuanxiao Festival; Lantern Festival

中国传统民俗大节，时在正月十五。“元”指元月，即一年之始；“宵”即夜晚，“元宵”意为一年中第一个月圆之夜。因历代元宵节有观灯的习俗，故元宵节又称“灯节”。相传元宵节起源于汉代：西汉时期，吕后专制，诸吕作乱，汉文帝在大臣周勃的帮助下平定战乱后即位，那天恰逢正月十五；此后每

A traditional Chinese festival celebrated on the fifteenth day of the first lunar month. *Yuan* means “the first lunar month” and *xiao* means “night.” Hence they are brought together to form “the first night with a full moon of the year.” The Yuanxiao Festival is also known as the Lantern Festival as people appreciate lanterns during this time. According to legend, it was during the Western Han Dynasty (206 BC-AD 25) that Emperor Wendi

逢正月十五夜晚，汉文帝都会出宫游玩，与民同乐，并将这一天定为元宵节。另说元宵节起源于对上元天官的祭祀活动，故元宵节又名“上元节”。随着历史的发展，中国元宵节逐渐形成了吃元宵、赏花灯、踩高跷、舞龙、舞狮等习俗。

seized power from Empress Lü. The day he ascended the throne was the fifteenth day of the first lunar month. He declared this day the Lantern Festival, and would often spend time outside his royal palace with ordinary people on this day. Another story attributes its inception to sacrifices made to Shangyuan, a Heavenly Official, which is why it is also known as the Shangyuan Festival. Throughout history, customs like eating *yuanxiao*, appreciating lanterns, and walking on stilts, performing dragon and lion dances have become popular, thus forming the traditions of the Lantern Festival.

例句：

唐代**元宵节**庆贺以正月十四、十五、十六共三天为限，至宋代增加十七、十八两天，明代朱元璋又规定正月初八张灯至十七日落灯，共有十天庆贺。

Example Sentence:

During the Tang Dynasty (618-907), Lantern Festival celebrations were limited to three days—the fourteenth, fifteenth and sixteenth days of the first lunar month. During the Song Dynasty (960-1279), the seventeenth and eighteenth days were added. During the Ming Dynasty (1368-1644), Emperor Zhu Yuanzhang stipulated that the celebration should span from the eighth to the seventeenth of the first lunar month, making the celebration last for 10 days.

元宵 *yuanxiao;* glutinous rice ball (northern style)

中国传统节日元宵节的节令小吃，是中国历史最悠久的小吃之一。元宵的做法是将芝麻、杏仁、核桃、玫瑰、豆沙等制成馅，然后把馅块放入箩筐、筛子之类的传统容器或现代化的机器里，倒上糯米粉，不断地洒水滚动或摇动起来，使馅料沾上糯米粉变成球状，就成了元宵。正月十五元宵节中国北方普遍吃元宵，表示"团圆如月"的意思，表达了一家团聚的美好愿望。中国南方则习惯吃另一种做法的"汤圆"。

Traditional snack of the Lantern Festival, and one of the oldest festival foods still prevalent throughout China. They are made of sesame seeds, almonds, walnuts, roses, bean paste, and other ingredients. The filling ingredients are divided into small cubes or rolled into balls, and then placed onto glutinous rice flour and continually sprinkled with water before being rolled into glutinous rice balls. Eating glutinous rice balls during the Lantern Festival is fairly widespread in the north, expressing "family reunions as consummate as the moon is round" and wishes for happy family gatherings. In southern China, it's customary for people to use different cooking techniques to produce this, which is called *tangyuan* (汤圆).

例句：

元宵节的应节食品是**元宵**，元宵以其圆形象征团圆和幸福。

Example Sentence:

The food most-associated with the Lantern Festival is *yuanxiao* (glutinous rice balls). The round shape of these rice balls symbolizes family reunion and happiness.

 汤圆 *tangyuan;* glutinous rice ball (southern style)

中国传统节日元宵节的节令小吃，与“元宵”形状类似，但制作方法和口感不同，多见于南方。汤圆的做法是将糯米粉加水和好切成小块做成皮，将水果、芝麻、豆沙或肉丁等制成馅，然后用糯米皮包上馅料，用开水煮熟后即可食用。有些地方还流行将汤圆放在锅里油炸后食用。元宵节吃汤圆同样表达了与家人团聚的美好愿望。

A snack often seen in southern China during the Lantern Festival. Despite looking similar to *yuanxiao*, it is actually prepared and tastes differently. This snack is made by adding water to glutinous rice before cutting the dough into small pieces. Each piece is rolled into a smooth ball, and a cube of fillings is pushed into the center of each. The fillings are made of fruit, sesame, bean paste, or diced meat. In some places, it is also popular to fry them. Eating *tangyuans* during China's Lantern Festival is also an expression of "family reunions like the moon" and wishes for happy family gatherings.

例句：

一般说来，北方“滚”或“摇”元宵，南方“包”**汤圆**。

Example Sentence:

Generally speaking, in the north the glutinous rice dough is rolled over the filling while in the south the filling is pushed into the dough. Both *yuanxiao* and *tangyuan* are translated as glutinous rice balls.

闹元宵 *nao yuanxiao; celebrating the Lantern Festival*

庆祝元宵节的民间说法。元宵节是春节之后的第一个重要节日。这一天从早到晚，一切活动的主题都围绕“闹”开展，各地举办丰富多彩的娱乐活动，民众举家出动看花灯、猜灯谜、观社火、放烟花、踩高跷、扭秧歌、唱大戏等，热闹非凡，是春节期间娱乐庆祝活动的高潮。

A colloquial expression of celebrating the Lantern Festival. Lantern Festival is the first important holiday to follow the Spring Festival, and there are lively celebrations on this day from morning to night. Vibrant entertainment can be found everywhere, and entire families will set out to see the festive lanterns, guess lantern riddles, watch traditional *shehuo* festivities, set off fireworks, see people walking on stilts, do the *yangge* dance, and enjoy traditional operas. The festival is exceptionally lively, representing the climax of entertainment and celebration during the Spring Festival.

例句：

闹过**元宵**，新年才算正式结束。

Example Sentence:

The Chinese New Year comes to an end after the lively celebration of the Lantern Festival.

灯会 *denghui;* lantern fair

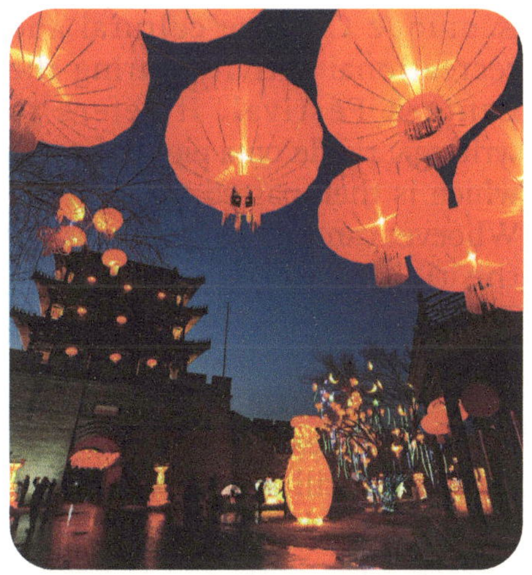

元宵节诸多节庆活动之一。按照传统习俗，正月十五月圆之夜，家家门口都要张挂和燃点各式各样的彩灯，同时举行观灯、赏灯、赛灯等庆祝活动，以祈阖家团圆，人寿年丰，因此“元宵节”也称“灯节”。以灯会为中心，各地形成了猜灯谜、吃元宵、走百病等一系列富有特色的元宵节俗。

One of the many activities during the Lantern Festival. According to traditional customs, all homes should light and hang up all manner of colorful lanterns on the fifteenth day of the first lunar month. On that night, people admire the lanterns, hold contests to determine which are the best, and engage in other such celebratory activities. These activities are a kind of wish for family unity, longevity, and prosperity. Accordingly, the festival is called the "Lantern Festival." Centered around the lantern, a number of unique customs have emerged such as guessing lantern riddles, eating glutinous rice balls, and taking long walks in the hope of dispersing disease.

例句：

南京花灯名闻遐迩，秦淮河畔的**灯会**万紫千红，流光溢彩。规模宏大的四川自贡恐龙灯会负有盛名，大型彩灯制作精美，颇具气势。

Example Sentence:

Lanterns in Nanjing are well-known throughout China, and lantern fairs held along the Qinhuai River are renowned for their dazzling spectacles. The dinosaur lantern fair held in Zigong, Sichuan Province is also an impressive sight. The delicately-made lanterns there are imposing and magnificent.

猜灯谜 *cai dengmi;* guessing lantern riddles

中国独有的元宵节特色文娱活动，也是中国古代谜语与元宵节赏灯习俗的巧妙结合。猜灯谜，即将写有谜语的纸条贴在元宵花灯之上，供人猜度，猜对者可扯下纸条领取谜赠。猜灯谜约起源于宋代，盛行于明清，近来也见于农历新年活动。

A unique Chinese cultural and recreational activity during the Lantern Festival. It refers to writing a riddle on a piece of paper which is then pasted to a lantern. Whoever can first correctly answer the riddle is awarded a prize. This custom originated during the Song Dynasty (960-1279) and thrived during the Ming and Qing dynasties (1368-1911). The custom is still a part of Chinese New Year celebrations today.

例句：

猜灯谜不仅增添了节日气氛，而且是中国古人聪明才智的体现。

Example Sentence:

The custom of “guessing the lantern riddles” not only enlivens the festive atmosphere, but also reflects the ancient wisdom of Chinese people.

社火 *shehuo;* festival entertainment

春节期间的民间庆典狂欢活动。起源于土地和火神崇拜，“社”即土地神，“火”为火神。土地和火种自古以来都是人类生存发展的物质基础，因此远古时候中国就产生了祭

Celebratory folk activities held during the Spring Festival derived from ancient worship of the *She* (Land God) and the *Huo* (Fire God). Sacrificial offerings to the earth and fire developed early in human history. As society and science developed, however, such

祀社与火的风俗。随着社会的发展和人们认识能力的提高，这种祭祀仪式中逐渐加入了娱乐的成分，最终形成规模宏大、内容繁复的民间娱乐活动。中国各地社火种类数以百计，主要以民间传说和戏剧故事为题材，以一个或一组人物展现一个故事，一个故事即为一转社火。人物要画社火脸谱，穿社火服装，持社火把杖。社火按表演形式可分为列队游演形式的造型社火和现场打斗形式的表演社火两大类。

sacrificial ceremonies evolved into entertaining celebrations which ultimately formed large-scale folk activities of rich content. There are hundreds of different *shehuo* customs across China. Folklore and dramas are usually the main themes of such activities, and one person or a group of people play out the stories. Each performance tells one *shehuo* story. *Shehuo* performances include face makeup, costumes, and canes. The performance types can be divided into two categories: parade form and fight form.

例句：

社火常见的表演有开路、狮子、龙灯、高跷、秧歌、五虎棍、少林拳、中幡、旱船、竹马、芯子、腰鼓、太平鼓等等。

Example Sentence:

There are many kinds of performances in a *shehuo* event, including the opening performance, the lion dance, the dragon dance, walking on stilts, *yangge* dance, cudgel fighting, Shaolin boxing, flagpole juggling, land boat dance, bamboo horse dance, *Xinzi* performance (standing on a wooden or iron frame), and performances of waist drums and *Taiping* (peace) drums.

踩高跷 *cai gaoqiao;* walking on stilts; stilt walking

汉族和部分少数民族传统民俗活动之一，又称"踏高跷"。高跷通常由十余人演出，舞蹈者身着戏装，浓妆艳抹，脚上绑着长木跷进行表演。木跷根据角色造型而高低不一。高跷分文跷、武跷，文跷注重舞步及演唱，武跷则注重表演惊险动作；也分双跷、单跷，双跷多绑扎在小腿上，以便展示技艺，单跷则以双手持木跷的顶端，便于上下跳跃，动作风趣。

A traditional folk custom among the Han people and some other ethnic groups, also called *ta gaoqiao* (stepping on stilts). Stilt performances are often performed by over ten people. Dancers wear festive costumes, apply copious amounts of makeup, and tie long stilts of wood to their feet. The length of the stilts varies according to the performers' roles. Stilt performers are divided into cultured stilts and martial stilts. Cultured stilts focus on dance steps and singing, while martial stilts exhibit thrilling movements. Performers can also be divided into dual stilts and single stilts. The dual stilts are generally bound to the lower leg to display the performer's skill. A single stilt is held by both of the performer's hands, so it is easy for them to go up and down and make humorous movements.

例句：

雷州南门高跷龙舞将**踩高跷**和舞龙两者合二为一，是富有地方特色的传统舞蹈形式。

Example Sentence:

Leizhou Nanmen Dragon Stilt Dance combines stilt performances with the traditional dragon dance. It is a traditional dance performance with unique local characteristics.

秧歌 *yangge; yangge dance*

广泛流行于中国北方地区的民间群体性舞蹈，因源于农民劳动、生活中所唱的歌而得名，有“高跷秧歌”和“地秧歌”之分。秧歌中的“丑角”活泼诙谐，深受群众喜爱。现各地的秧歌一般以秧歌队为主要组织形态，少则数十人，多时达上百人共同表演，表演者根据角色的需要手持相应的手绢、伞等道具，在唢呐、锣鼓等吹打乐器的伴奏下尽情舞蹈。

A group folk dance popular in northern China. *Yangge* means "songs from the field" in Chinese, which tells the origin of this performing art form. There are two major types of *yangge* dance: one is *yangge* stilt dance, which is performed on stilts, and the other is ground *yangge*, which is performed without stilts. The role of the *chou* (clown) in *yangge* dance is vivacious and humorous, and very popular with the spectators. Most performances are organized by local *yangge* troupes consisting from a dozen up to a hundred dancers. Performers will dance merrily while holding handkerchiefs, umbrellas, or other props to the accompaniment of wind and percussion instruments such as suona horns, gongs and drums.

例句：

大年初一，**秧歌**队会到村里各户家中拜年。

Example Sentence:

On Chinese New Year's Day, the *yangge* dance troupe would visit all the households in the village.

皮影戏 *piying xi;* Chinese shadow puppetry

中国民间传统戏曲形式之一，傀儡戏的一种，又称“灯影戏”。艺人将驴皮或牛皮、羊皮、纸板雕镂做成各种人物形象和布景、道具。皮影人物一般高一尺左右，身有若干关节，根据动作需要安有三五根操纵细杆。演出时，通过灯光照射，将皮影人物投影到帷幕上，艺人在幕后边操纵边唱念，“一口述说千古事，双手对打百万兵”，表演民众喜爱的神话传说、历史演义的剧目。

A traditional form of theatre in China using colorful silhouette figures made from leather or paper and accompanied by music and singing. The puppet figures are about thirty centimeters tall and have many movable joints. Manipulated by puppeteers using rods, the figures create the illusion of moving images illuminated from behind onto a translucent cloth screen. Shadow puppet shows depict popular myths and historical stories. Typically to begin the show, the puppeteers will chant, "A shadow play performer operates millions of soldiers and tells age-old stories with the use of only two hands."

例句：

皮影戏起源于汉代，经过历代演变，到宋代已成为民间常见的表演艺术。

Example Sentence:

Chinese shadow puppetry is said to date back to the Han Dynasty (206 BC-AD 220), but it was not until the Song Dynasty (960-1279) that the art form became popular.

灯影戏 *dengying xi;* lantern shadow puppetry

参见“皮影戏”。

See *piying xi* (Chinese shadow puppetry).

木偶戏 *mu'ou xi;* puppetry

表演者在幕后操纵木偶来表演的戏剧形式。木偶，又称“傀儡”，起源于远古用作殉葬的“俑”。据说两千年前便有木偶制作，北齐（550–577 年）出现了“傀儡子”演“郭秃”故事的木偶戏。唐宋时木偶戏进一步发展，至明清时已在各地广泛流行。傀儡戏与巫文化关系密切，民间名目繁多的神佛庆诞、迎神赛会等，使木偶艺术如鱼得水，异常活跃。木

A form of theatre in which the performer manipulates the puppet from behind or beneath the scene. Chinese puppetry is said to have originated from the ancient practice of constructing human figurines to be buried with the dead. It is said that people started to make puppets 2,000 years ago. The earliest puppet show is thought to be "Guo, the Bald," which emerged during the Northern Qi Dynasty (550-577). Puppetry developed during the Tang and Song dynasties

偶演出与民俗生活关系密切，如四川乡间常随节令变化而演出不同内容的木偶戏：正月为求一年清吉演清醮戏；二月九月为求观音佑安演观音戏；三月四月为祈庄稼不受虫害演秧苗戏等。木偶戏演出剧目多为历史演义、神话传说和民间故事，形式活泼，表演生动，颇受民众尤其是少年儿童的欢迎。

but became popular across the country during the Ming and Qing dynasties. Closely related to shamanism, puppet shows were often performed on special occasions such as birthdays of the many gods and Buddhas or other religious ceremonies, through which the art form thrived. In the countryside of Sichuan Province, puppet shows offer different programs according to the season. In the first lunar month, the program is about praying for a peaceful and auspicious year; in the second and ninth lunar months, it is about seeking blessings from Guanyin (the Goddess of Mercy); in the third and fourth lunar months, it is about praying to prevent insects from damaging crops. Puppet shows mostly tell stories from history, legends, or folk tales. Owing to their vivid and vigorous performances, puppet shows are very popular among the general public, especially children.

例句：

根据木偶形体和操纵技术不同，**木偶戏**主要分布袋木偶、提线木偶、杖头木偶、铁线木偶等种类，表演各具特色。

Example Sentence:

Based on different figure models and manipulative skills, puppet shows fall into several categories featuring different puppets, such as glove, string, rod, and wire puppets, each having its own unique characteristics.

咬春 *yao chun;* biting the Spring

立春节气的习俗，即尝新活动，表示迎接春天之意。立春之时，春回大地，万物复苏，各种蔬菜发出嫩芽，为了尝鲜，古人就用面皮包着时令蔬菜卷成卷蒸熟（即“春饼”）或者油炸（即“春卷”），放在盘子里互赠亲友，称为“春盘”。立春之日还讲究吃辛辣的萝卜等，据说能解春困和祛病。咬春的风俗自唐宋以来盛行于民间，特别是北方，至今不衰。

A folk custom observed during *lichun* (the Beginning of Spring, which is the first of 24 solar terms falling on the third, fourth, or fifth of February) wherein people eat seasonal food while ushering in the spring. During this time of year, spring returns to the earth and everything comes back to life. Various types of vegetables sprout new buds. To get a taste of such delicacies, ancient Chinese put seasonal vegetables into wrappers and roll them up. They then steam or fry them, producing either spring pancakes or spring rolls, which they often give on plates to relatives and friends, referred to as “spring plates.” When the Beginning of Spring comes around, people also eat spicy radishes as they believe the radishes will help relieve spring fever and cure diseases. Ever since the Tang (618-907) and Song (960-1279) dynasties, the custom of “biting the spring” has been observed throughout northern China.

例句：

吃春饼时也有讲究，要先咬在嘴里，停三到五秒后再吃，这才是真正的“**咬春**”，寓意留住百花齐放的春天，留住春耕时间。

Example Sentence:

Eating a spring pancake requires skill. First, one should bite into it for three to five seconds, which is symbolic of “biting (into) the spring.” It implies letting the beautiful spring and farming season last longer.

花灯 *huadeng;* festive lantern

灯笼是一种起源于中国的传统民间工艺品，古时主要用于照明，由纸或者绢作外皮，竹或木条作骨架，中间放上蜡烛或灯泡，成为照明工具。中国元宵节有张挂各色灯笼的习俗，为佳节喜日增光添彩，祈求平安；因其五彩斑斓、如花似锦，故称“花灯”。唐宋以来元宵花灯取得长足发展，开始出现各式花灯，更有所谓灯楼、灯树、灯山。时至今日，花灯在元宵节仍十分常见，且出现了利用现代声光效果的新型花灯。

A traditional Chinese folk handicraft mainly used for lighting in ancient times. It is made with paper or silk as a cover and bamboo or wood as a frame. The *huadeng* light is lit with candles or light bulbs that are placed inside. Chinese people often hang colorful festive lanterns during the Lantern Festival to celebrate and enliven the festive atmosphere and pray for peace. Due to its colorful and flower-like appearance, festive lanterns were called “*huadeng*,” which literally translates to “flower lantern.” They can be made in many shapes such as buildings, trees, and mountains. People have been making these festive lanterns since the Tang (618-907) and Song (960-1279) dynasties. Currently, they are still widely used during the Lantern Festival, and new lanterns with modern acousto-optic special effects are also made.

例句：

由于赏**花灯**活动广受欢迎，十分普遍，唐宋以后的小说中有关赏灯活动的描绘甚多。

Example Sentence:

Ever since the Tang (618-907) and Song (960-1279) dynasties, the “festive lantern fair” has been a popular scene commonly depicted in novels.

舞狮子 *wu shizi;* lion dance; performing lion dance

中国传统舞蹈形式之一。每头狮子有两个人合作表演，一人舞头，一人舞尾，舞时配以鼓、钹、锣演奏的音乐。表演者在音乐伴奏下装扮成狮子的样子，做出狮子跌扑、翻滚、跳跃、搔痒、滚绣球等形态动作，非常富有阳刚之气。舞狮子是中国元宵节、新年等节令和各种庆典期间的重要娱乐活动。狮子是中

A traditional Chinese dance in which two dancers wear a lion costume. One holds the lion's head while the other holds its tail, and they perform this dance together by mimicking a lion's movements such as swooping, tumbling, jumping, scratching, and rolling. The dance is performed to the musical accompaniment of the drum, cymbal, and gong. Lion dances are a typical form of entertainment during the Lantern Festival, Chinese New Year, and other festivals and

国人心中的瑞兽，代表吉祥如意，因此人们借由舞狮来祈求五谷丰登，消除灾祸。近现代舞狮有南北之分：北方狮外形与真狮相似，娇憨可爱，多以嬉戏玩耍为主；南方狮则主要为广东狮，起源于南北朝，神态矫健凶猛。舞狮子根据动作风格又有文武之别。文狮注重表情，动作诙谐细腻，表现狮子温柔可爱的一面，动作多为打滚、搔痒、舐毛、相互依偎等；武狮动作幅度大，力度强，动作多为跳跃、跌扑、腾转，充分表现狮子勇猛威武的一面。

special celebrations. As the lion is considered an auspicious animal and a symbol of good fortune, the lion dance is usually performed as a way of praying for a bumper harvest and averting disasters. There are two forms of the Chinese lion dance in modern times: the Northern Lion and the Southern Lion. The Northern Lion Dance is centered on the lion's charming and lovely disposition, mainly focusing on its playful behavior. The Southern Lion Dance originates from the Northern and Southern Dynasties (420-589), and typically depicts the Guangdong Lion, which tends to be vigorous and ferocious. The lion dance can also be divided into civil and martial lions according to the performance style. The civil lion emphasizes the lion's gentleness and loveliness through delicate and humorous movements, such as rolling, scratching, licking, and cuddling. The martial lion is focused on vigorous and energetic movements, aiming to fully display the might and boldness of a lion's movements, like jumping, swooping, and writhing.

例句：

舞狮子至今仍盛行于中国各地，为观众所喜闻乐见。

Example Sentence:

The lion dance continues to be popular across China.

舞龙

wu long;
dragon dance; performing dragon dance

中国民间的一种舞蹈形式，始于汉代，是元宵节或重大庆典活动的传统节目。舞龙源于中国人对龙的崇拜，古人认为龙可以呼风唤雨，消灾除疫，保佑风调雨顺，四季平安，由此用舞龙的方式祈求平安和丰收。最初的舞龙是作为祀神、娱神活动出现的。唐宋以后，舞龙逐渐演化为一种民间喜庆节日的娱乐活动。每条龙由11人至13人组成，最长的由百人组成，表演时都有锣鼓在旁边按照龙舞步姿助威。比较流行的舞龙有两种：一种是"火龙"，用篾竹扎成龙的样子，糊上纸，画上色彩，龙身有节，节数可多可少，为单数，如九

A Chinese folk dance. Originating during the Han Dynasty (206 BC-AD 220), the dragon lantern dance is a traditional performance during the Lantern Festival and other major festive celebrations. It stemmed from the ancient worship of dragons when ancient Chinese believed that the dragon could eliminate disasters and epidemics as well as endow people with peace and favorable weather. Ancient legends spoke of dragons being the rulers of rain and wind. The dragon dance was therefore performed as a way of praying for peace and a good harvest, and also as an activity for worshipping and entertaining the gods. The dragon lantern dance gradually evolved into a festival activity that has been performed since the Tang (618-907)

节、十一节、十三节，每节长五尺许，每节当中点上蜡烛或是别的燃料；还有一种是“布龙”，龙节中没有蜡烛，主要在白天表演。此外，舞龙又有文龙和武龙之别；文龙主要表现龙的气质和神态，动作稳健；武龙重于技巧，以表现龙的雄伟气魄，矫健灵活。

and Song (960-1279) dynasties. Dragon dances are performed by a team of dancers that usually include 11 to 13 people, but which might even include as many as 100. The dancers mimic the movements of the dragon, which are accompanied by the sounds of gongs and drums. The "fire dragon dance" and "cloth dragon dance" are two popular versions. The former uses bamboo as a frame that is wrapped with colorful paper and painted to look like a dragon. It can be divided into varying odd-numbered sections, such as 9, 11, or 13. Each section roughly measures 5 *chi* (1/3 meter) long and a candle or another form of lighting is placed inside. The cloth dragon dance is performed without candles and is typically during the daytime. The dragon dance is also divided into the civil and martial dragon dances. The civil dragon features a robust performance style while the martial dragon highlights acrobatic skills. It displays the dragon's majestic nature with nimble, vigorous movements.

例句：

舞龙起源甚早，汉代画像砖中即已有舞龙场面的描绘。

Example Sentence:

The dragon lantern dance originated very early in history; it was even depicted in brick portraits from the Han Dynasty (206 BC-AD 220).

划旱船 *hua hanchuan;* land boat dancing

中国传统民间岁节娱乐活动，是一种模拟水中行船的民间舞蹈，常见于正月十五元宵节等节日。“旱船”即陆地上的船，多由竹竿、木棍作架子，扎裹成船形，围缀上绘有水纹的棉布裙或是海蓝色的棉布裙，并装饰有红绸、纸花、彩灯等装饰物。乘船者一般是一个人，也有双人、四人甚至七人共乘一船的，乘船者多为姑娘、媳妇。跑旱船时，一般使用锣、鼓、钹等打击乐器伴奏，有的地方会加上一至两支唢呐，气氛热烈，情绪活跃，具有浓郁的地方风情和民族色彩。

A traditional Chinese festival entertainment event commonly seen during festivals like the Lantern Festival. It refers to a folk dance that simulates the movements of a boat in a river. A small, boat-like structure is made with bamboo or wooden sticks wrapped into a boat-like shape and carried by one person, usually a girl or a married woman. Painted water-ripple patterns or marine blue cotton cloths serve as a covering, and decorations are made with red silk, paper flowers, and colored lanterns. Other performers may help guide the boat with sticks, and percussion instruments like gongs, drums, and cymbals are used as accompaniments, along with one or two *suona* horns. Land boat dancing is a very festive activity with local and ethnic characteristics.

例句：

划旱船历史悠久，在唐代已经流行，不仅在民间表演，还经过改造成为宫廷舞蹈。

Example Sentence:

Land boat dancing has a long history, and was popular during the Tang Dynasty (618-907). It was adapted into a dance for the imperial court.

天穿节 *Tianchuan Jie;* Tianchuan Festival; Sky-Patching Festival

中国传统纪念节日，有正月初十、二十、二十三、二十五等几种说法，以正月二十居多。该节起源于女娲炼石补天的传说。据说在远古时代，共工和颛顼两位天神争夺天帝位，共工战败，一怒之下撞断了擎天柱不周山，导致苍天倾塌，大雨不止，洪水泛滥。女娲炼出五色石，补住了天的漏洞。该日民间做薄饼放在屋顶上，效法女娲补天，以示纪念。如今该传统节日仍流行于山西、陕西、河南等北方地区及客家地区。

A traditional Chinese festival commemorating a day from legend, which is held on the tenth, twentieth, twenty-third, or twenty-fifth day of the first lunar month. According to Chinese legend, the ancient god Gonggong defeated Zhuanxu in a battle for the throne of heaven, and bashed Zhuanxu's head against Mount Buzhou, which was one of the four pillars supporting the sky. This tilted the sky and a torrential rain poured down, flooding the land. Nüwa, a goddess in Chinese mythology, was greatly distressed and patched up the sky with five-colored stones. Later generations declared the day she patched up the sky to be the Tianchuan Festival. People commemorate that day by placing pancakes on their roofs, which is an imitation of Nüwa repairing the sky. Currently, the festival is still popular across Hakka areas and in northern China's Shanxi, Shaanxi, and Henan provinces.

例句：

天穿节既是中国民间关于女娲补天从而拯救万物的纪念日，也是古人表达对风调雨顺、五谷丰登之期盼的节日。

Example Sentence:

Besides serving as a commemorative day for Nüwa patching up the sky to save the world, the Tianchuan Festival is also an expression of hope by ancient Chinese people for favorable weather and a bumper harvest.

填仓节 *Tiancang Jie;* Tiancang Festival; Granary-Filling Festival

旧时民间传统节日，又称“天仓节”，时在农历正月二十五，主要流行于中国北方农村。其起源有两种说法。一说是中国古时北方连年大旱，赤地千里，颗粒无收，可是皇家无视灾情，照样征缴皇粮，导致饿殍遍野。看守皇粮的一个仓官目睹此景，毅然开仓济贫，让农民把皇粮搬运一空。事后他无法向皇上交差，就在正月二十五这天放火烧仓，连同自己一起烧死。人们为了纪念他，重补被烧坏的“天仓”，定这一天为填仓节。另一说法为农历正月二十五是谷仓神诞辰，民间在此日祭祀该神。填仓节习俗因地区不同有所差异，多为用灰等圈出仓的形状，在其中放些粮食以示仓满，以此祈求风调雨顺，五谷丰登。

A traditional Chinese festival mainly celebrated in northern China on the twenty-fifth day of the first lunar month in the past also called Imperial Granary Festival. There are two origin stories about this festival. One tells of how a devastating famine once caused a severe drought, but the cruel imperial family still ordered all scarce grain to be collected, resulting in mass starvation of the region. An upright official who was tasked with guarding the imperial grain decided to open up the warehouse, allowing poor people and farmers to take the government-owned grain. But because of this, he was unable to deliver the grain to the emperor. On the twenty-fifth day of the first lunar month, he burned the warehouse to the ground with himself inside. People restored the burnt warehouse and commemorated the day as the Granary-Filling Festival. Another origin story claims that the twenty-fifth day of the first lunar month marks the birthday of the Granary God. Customs vary in different regions, but most include making a barn-like circle out of ashes and then placing grain inside as a representation of a packed barn. This is also considered a way of praying for favorable weather and a bumper harvest.

例句：

填仓节有小填仓与大填仓之分，时间分别在农历正月二十和二十五。

Example Sentence:

There are two "Tiancang Festivals," a minor one and a greater one, which are celebrated on the twentieth and twenty-fifth days of the first lunar month respectively.

龙抬头 *Long Tai Tou;* Dragon Head-Raising Day

汉族传统节日，时在农历二月初二。传说冬眠的龙在该日会被春雷唤醒，抬头而起，故称"龙抬头"。该节起源很早，明代已见此俗，本由农业生产与某种天象的联系而起，后逐渐演化为祈求龙神赐福的活动。届时，民间有扶龙、挑龙头、剃龙头、吃龙须面等习俗，还有停针、忌磨等禁忌，有些地区在这一天还要耍龙灯以示庆贺。中国人对龙的崇拜和古代农业生产在中国的重要地位是该节产生的主要原因：中华民族自古以来就以龙为图腾，把龙视为带神秘色彩的吉祥物。龙抬头意味着云兴雨作，而天地交泰、云兴雨作是万物生长的条件，"二月二"是龙抬头的日子，又正值春回大地、农事开始之时，就自然而然地成为民间一个重

A traditional festival of the Han ethnic group that is celebrated on the second day of the second lunar month. Legend has it that the hibernating dragon is awakened by spring thunder on this day and raises its head up, hence the name meaning "dragon looking up." The festival dates back to the Ming Dynasty (1368-1644), originating from the connection between agricultural production and celestial phenomena, and over time it became an activity aimed at praying for blessings from the Dragon God. Various customs are practiced on this day such as "helping the dragon," "picking up and shaving the dragon head," and eating very fine noodles shaped like dragon whiskers. There are also taboos on this day such as prohibiting needlework and milling. The dragon lantern dance is also performed in some areas. Since ancient times, Chinese

要的节日。龙抬头日的许多节俗活动流传至今，带有一定迷信色彩。

people have revered the dragon as an auspicious and mysterious creature. The festival marks the advent of rainfall, which is a requirement for the reproduction of all things on earth. The day also marks the beginning of spring and the start of farming, so the Dragon-Head Raising Day has naturally become an influential folk festival. There are many customs and celebratory activities of this festival that have been passed down to the present day.

例句：

“二月二，**龙抬头**，大仓满，小仓流”，这首广为流传的民谣体现了人们对五谷丰登的希冀。

Example Sentence:

“On the second day of the second lunar month, the Dragon Head-Raising Day, big granaries are filled and small ones spilled.” This popular ballad reflects people’s wishes for a bumper harvest.

龙须面 *longxu mian; longxu* noodles

A traditional Chinese noodle dish that is named after its appearance—thin and long like a dragon’s whiskers. It is typically eaten on Dragon Head-Raising Day. It’s said that such a noodle, which has a history of over 300 years, evolved from the hand-pulled noodle style of Shandong

中国传统面食，因又细又长、形似龙须而得名。中国有在“龙抬头日”吃龙须面的习俗。据说龙须面由山东抻面演变而来，已有300多年的历史。今已为居民普通食品，常年食用。

Province. Nowadays it is a common food eaten by people throughout the year.

例句：

随着面食文化的发展，如今的餐饮业已将**龙须面**的标准定义为14扣（即16384根）。

Example Sentence:

With the development of pasta culture, today's catering industry has defined the standard quantity of *longxu* noodles as 14 bands, or 16,384 strands.

接姑奶奶 *jie gunainai;* welcoming a married daughter back for a visit

满族习俗，指娘家人出面，将已出嫁的女儿(被称为姑奶奶)接回娘家小住一段时日，多于农历二月二进行。辽宁、吉林的满族人一般避开灯节，在正月十六日、十八、二十等双日接姑奶奶。是日，娘家接姑奶奶的人应带上礼品，向婿家的尊亲长辈说明来意，得到后者许可后，姑奶奶方能收拾衣物，带着孩子回娘家。被接回娘家的日子里，姑奶奶除了吃喝就是串门聊天儿，生活惬意。

A Manchu custom that involves escorting a married daughter back to her parents' home for a short stay. The custom is commonly practiced on the second day of the second lunar month. Manchurians in Liaoning and Jilin provinces (located in northeast China) usually pick up their married daughters on even-numbered days like the sixteenth, eighteenth, or twentieth day of the first lunar month, after the Lantern Festival. On that day, those who are supposed to pick up their married daughter should bring gifts and must obtain permission from the husband's family before escorting the married daughter back home. After being taken back, the married daughter is not given any chores to do and spends her time eating, drinking, and chatting.

例句：

流行于北京的童谣《拉大锯》唱的就是“**接姑奶奶**”的习俗。

Example Sentence:

The nursery rhyme “drawing a saw,” which is popular in Beijing, is centered on the custom of “welcoming a married daughter back for a visit.”

清明节

Qingming Jie;
Qingming Festival; Tomb-Sweeping Day

中国传统节日，时在阳历四月五日前后。清明节有祭扫坟墓、踏青春游、戴柳插柳、植树等习俗，还流行放风筝、玩蹴鞠、荡秋千等活动。此节与寒食节时间相近，节俗活动亦有交叉。清明节在遥远的周代已经流行，许多少数民族也过此节，风俗相似。清明也是二十四节气中的第五个节气。参见“清明”。

A traditional Chinese festival celebrated around the fifth day of April. Various customs are practiced on this day such as tomb sweeping, spring outings, wearing soft willow branches, planting branches in front of doors, and planting trees. People also like to fly kites, play *cuju* (ancient Chinese football), and play on swings during the festival. The Cold Food Festival, another festival in China, often overlaps with the Qingming Festival, and involves similar activities. The Qingming Festival has been popular since the Zhou Dynasty (1046-256 BC), and is also celebrated by many ethnic minorities who share similar customs on this day. Qingming is also the fifth solar term of the 24 solar terms. See Qingming.

例句：

诸多民俗节日中，**清明节**因是唯一一个节气兼节日的大节，最具独特性。

Example Sentence:

Among the many folk festivals, the Qingming Festival is a unique festival as it is both a solar term and a festival.

寒食节 *Hanshi Jie;* Hanshi Festival; Cold Food Festival

中国古代传统节日，在清明节前一两日。节日期间禁烟火，只吃寒食。据传说，寒食节源于春秋时期晋国大臣介子推的故事。忠心耿耿的介子推曾割下自己的肉献给流亡中的晋国公子重耳。重耳当上国君后，介子推归隐山林，不愿出来接受封赏。重耳为寻介子推以火烧山，没想到介子推宁死不出，与老母一起烧死在山中。为了纪念介子推，重耳令百姓五天不得生火，只吃寒食，是为寒食节。由于寒食节与清明节日期接近，唐朝以后逐渐纳入清明节。

An ancient traditional Chinese festival held one or two days before the Qingming Festival. All fire and smoke is prohibited, and people must only eat cold food. The festival is derived from a story regarding Jie Zitui, a loyal chancellor of the State of Jin during the Spring and Autumn Period (770-476 BC). While lost and starving in the wilderness with exiled Prince Chong'er, loyal and devoted Jie Zitui secretly cut off a portion of himself to give the Prince to eat. Years later Chong'er became ruler and wanted to reward Jie Zitui, but Jie Zitui was living in seclusion in the mountains. Chong'er then set fire to the mountain forests in order to flush him out, but this unexpectedly led to the death of Jie Zitui and his mother. In order to commemorate him, Chong'er ordered that for the next five days people were not to light any fires and were only to eat cold food. Cold food is pronounced "Hanshi" in Chinese, so the holiday was named the "Hanshi Festival." Since the Hanshi and Qingming festivals fall very close to one another, the former gradually merged with the Qingming Festival during the Tang Dynasty (618-907).

例句：

寒食节是中国传统节日中为数不多的以饮食习俗来命名的节日。

Example Sentence:

The Hanshi Festival is one of the few Chinese traditional festivals whose name is derived from food and drinking customs.

扫墓 *sao mu; sweeping tombs*

祭扫坟墓、祭祀死者的活动，以示对死者的缅怀、崇敬之情。这一风俗起于秦代，至隋唐时才开始盛行。上坟祭扫包括挂纸烧钱和培修坟墓两项内容。届时，扫墓人前往墓地，剪除杂草，培上新土，致祷词，并

An ancient folk custom of paying respects to the deceased which originated in the Qin Dynasty (221-206 BC) and became popular during the Sui and Tang dynasties (581-907). It includes the two primary activities of burning paper money and filling graves with fresh earth. People go to graveyards to clear the weeds, add fresh earth, pay tribute to the deceased, offer wreaths and oblations, and burn paper money on this day. Presently, tombs can be swept by groups, families, or individuals. People pay tribute to renowned heroes and leaders, and mourn deceased family members and friends.

献上花圈、花束或摆上祭品，烧化纸钱。如今扫墓一般可分为集体或家庭、个人的扫墓，前者多为祭奠英雄、领袖，后者多为悼念家人亲友。

例句：

扫墓表达了祭祀者的孝道和对已故亲人的思念之情。

Example Sentence:

Sweeping tombs refers to worshipping deceased ancestors or family members to express filial piety and honor their memory.

吃坟会 *chifen hui;* banquet after tomb sweeping

中国旧时部分地区的祭祖风俗，一般在清明节期间进行。大姓人家在举行祭祀祖先仪式后将祭品分给参加祭祀的族人，或者设宴大吃一顿作为祖先的恩赐，无论贫富，来者有份，以示祖宗没有偏心。

An old custom observed during the Qingming Festival (Tomb-Sweeping Day) in some parts of China in the past. After an influential family finished offering sacrifices to their ancestors, they shared the sacrificed food with the people who attended the ceremony, or held a banquet to express gratitude to their ancestors. Family members, rich or poor, would get a fair share to show that their ancestors were impartial to them.

例句：

吃坟会的风俗在 1949 年建国以后就很少见了。

Example Sentence:

It is rare now to see the custom of holding a banquet after sweeping the tomb since the founding of the People's Republic of China in 1949.

踏青 *taqing*; a nature walk; spring outing

一种节令性的民俗活动，又叫“春游”，指在花草返青的春季结伴到郊外原野远足。踏青源于远古农耕祭祀的迎春习俗，汉代以后逐渐演变成为游春访胜的一项活动。魏晋时，每到农历三月三日上巳节，人们便到风景优美之地嬉乐，或席地野餐，或在河边“曲水流觞”相与为乐。唐宋时，踏青活动更为盛行，人们特别是妇女以盛服靓妆结伴踏青，尽情地赏春嬉戏，开展玩蹴鞠、荡秋千、放风筝等各种活动。后来由于上巳节并入清明节，而清明节祭祖活动往往在郊外进行，人们便把祭祖扫墓和郊游踏青结合起来，既追思先人，又健康身心。因此踏青便成为清明节前后的一项重要民俗活动，代代流传。

A seasonal folk custom in which people go hiking with friends in the countryside when flowers are in bloom and plants are turning green. *Taqing* originated from ancient rituals when farmers walked in the countryside in the spring to pray for good harvests, and following the Han Dynasty (206 BC–AD 220) it gradually evolved into outing and sightseeing. During the Wei-Jin Period (220-420), it was customary for people to have a picnic together or drink, write, and read poems by the riverside during the Shangsi Festival (the third day of the third lunar month). The practice became very popular with women during the Tang (618-907) and Song (960–1279) dynasties where they dressed up, wore makeup, and went on outings with friends in the spring. Popular activities during outings were playing *cuju* (ancient Chinese football), playing on swings, and flying kites. Later, the Shangsi Festival was incorporated into the Qingming Festival (Tomb-Sweeping Day), and people combined ancestor worship and tomb-sweeping into *taqing* so that they could honor the memory of their ancestors while also spending time outdoors to maintain physical and mental health. Since then, *taqing* has become an important folk custom held around the Qingming Festival, and has been passed down from generation to generation.

例句：

清明前后，春回大地，人们纷纷结伴走出居室来到户外郊游**踏青**。

Example Sentence:

Around the Qingming Festival, with the coming of spring, people often go on outings in the countryside with their friends.

chunyou;
spring outing

参见“踏青”。

See *taqing* (a nature walk).

荡秋千

dang qiuqian;
playing on a swing

一种清明节传统娱乐活动。据传秋千为春秋时齐桓公由山戎（北方一个古老部族）引入，后在中原地区逐渐流传开来，成为每年清明前后的一种游戏，唐宋时期更是风靡一时。清明节荡秋千的主要是女孩子。古人认为荡秋千可"摆疥"，除掉疾病，可释闺闷，使深闺女子得到消遣。

A traditional form of entertainment during the Qingming Festival. The *qiuqian*, a type of swing, was supposedly introduced from Shanrong (an ancient tribe in northern China) by Duke Huan of Qi during the Spring and Autumn Period (770-476 BC). It gradually became popular throughout China's central plains, and became a traditional activity during the Qingming Festival. Playing on swings gained popularity during the Tang (618-907) and Song (960-1279) dynasties. Ancient Chinese believed that playing on swings could help get rid of illnesses and relieve girls of depression.

例句：

在中国大部分地区，**荡秋千**已成为儿童的专项活动。

Example Sentence:

Nowadays, playing on swings has become an activity widely enjoyed by children in China.

蹴鞠 *cuju*; kick the ball

中国古代的一种足球运动，清明节民俗活动之一。"蹴"有用脚蹴、蹋、踢的含义，"鞠"最早为外包皮革、内实米糠的球。因而"蹴鞠"即古人以脚蹴、蹋、踢皮球

A kind of football game played in ancient China that is also a custom of the Qingming Festival. Since *cu* means "kicking some object" and *ju* means "chaff-filled ball using leather as its surface," the phrase *cuju* collectively refers to kicking a ball, which is similar to

的活动，类似今天的足球。早在战国时期中国民间就流行娱乐性的蹴鞠游戏；唐代这项运动更加盛行，允许女子参加，且鞠球制作也很精致，已接近于当今的皮球；宋代出现了蹴鞠组织与蹴鞠艺人；明代将其分为有球门和无球门两项运动，前者称“蹴球”，后者称“蹴鞠”；清代开始流行冰上蹴鞠。

the modern sport of football. As early as the Warring States Period (475-221 BC), *cuju* was already a popular recreational game among the general public. It thrived during the Tang Dynasty (618-907), with the balls more delicate and similar to modern rubber balls. In the Song Dynasty (960-1279) special *cuju* organizations and practitioners emerged. During the Ming Dynasty (1368-1644), *cuju* was divided into two kinds of sports based on whether or not the game used a goal. The version with a goal was called *cuqiu* while the version without was called *cuju*. Playing *cuju* on ice came into being during the Qing Dynasty (1616-1911).

例句：

经国务院批准，**蹴鞠**已于2006年5月20日被列入第一批国家级非物质文化遗产名录。

Example Sentence:

Through the approval of the State Council, *cuju* was included in the first batch of the National Intangible Cultural Heritage List on May 20, 2006.

放风筝 *fang fengzheng; flying kites*

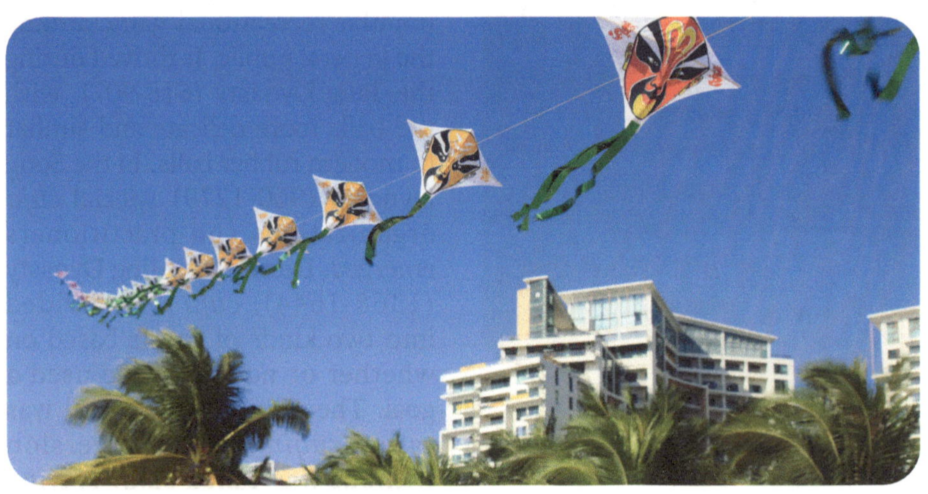

中国民间传统娱乐活动，多在春季清明时节进行。风筝，旧名纸鸢，是中国古代的一项发明，也是民间工艺品、玩具。放风筝的活动在中国流传久远，初期被用于军事，约从唐代开始，风筝成为娱乐品。到了宋代，民间放风筝逐渐风行，明清之际达到鼎盛。近代以来，放风筝仍是中国城乡春季的风俗。

A traditional Chinese leisure activity, commonly seen during the Qingming Festival. Flying kites, which used to be called flying a "*zhiyuan* (paper eagle)", is an ancient Chinese folk invention. Flying kites was initially used for military purposes but became a form of entertainment during the Tang Dynasty (618-907). It became popular during the Song Dynasty (960-1279) and thrived in the Ming (1368-1644) and Qing (1616-1911) dynasties. Flying kites is a popular springtime custom across all of China.

例句：

宋代时，民间**放风筝**逐渐风行，已有专营风筝的买卖人出现。

Example Sentence:

Vendors selling kites first emerged during the Song Dynasty (960-1279) as flying kites became increasingly popular.

清明柳 *Qingming liu;* Qingming willow; pure brightness willow

春秋晋文公赐名的一棵柳树。晋文公在做国君前曾流亡在外，饥寒交迫之时其属臣介子推割自己的肉用以煮汤，晋文公因此得救。晋文公即位后封赏有恩于他的人，只有介子推不愿接受，与其母归隐绵山。晋文公便命人放火烧山，逼出介子推。结果后者与其母被烧死在一棵老柳树下。晋文公悔不当初，此后将这棵老柳树命名为“清明柳”，又把这天定为寒食节。参见“寒食节”。

A willow tree named by Duke Wen of Jin (697-628 BC) to commemorate the sacrifice made by a loyal minister. During the time Duke Wen was in exile he was known as Chong'er, and was a scion of the Jin royal family during the Spring and Autumn Period. While he suffered from freezing cold and starvation, one of his faithful ministers named Jie Zitui made a soup with his own flesh which he'd secretly cut from his own leg. After Chong'er ascended to power, he wanted to reward this man who had saved his life, but Jie Zitui had since gone deep into Mianshan Mountain with his mother to live in seclusion. Chong'er ordered a fire be set to the mountain forest to compel Jie out of hiding so that he could reward him, but Jie Zitui was instead killed by the fire along with his mother, their bodies found beside an old willow tree. Overwhelmed by grief, Chong'er named the old willow tree the "pure brightness willow" and he named the day when Jie Zitui died the Hanshi Festival (Cold Food Festival). See Hanshi Festival.

例句：

“**清明柳**”的起源与春秋五霸之一的晋文公有关。

Example Sentence:

The origin of the pure brightness willow is related to Duke Wen of Jin, one of the five overlords of the Spring and Autumn Period.

插柳 *chaliu; planting soft willow branches*

中国年节风俗，亦称“戴柳”。在清明节或寒食节，人们在门口或檐前插柳枝，或于头上戴柳圈，女子头上簪柳，男子身上佩柳，相传此俗最初是为了纪念“教民稼穑”的神农氏。另一说插柳戴柳之俗可能与柳树的强大生命力有关——随便插在什么地方，它都能成活下来并生长得很快，人们觉得柳树有灵，由此形成插柳的习俗。唐代以后，插柳戴柳之风盛行。

A Chinese custom observed during festivals, usually during the Qingming Festival or Cold Food Festival. People attach willow sticks to the front of doors or eaves, or wear willow wreaths on their heads. Women wear willow sticks as hairpins and men wear them as pendants. It is said that this custom is to commemorate Shennong, a mythical sage ruler of ancient China who taught ancient Chinese people how to farm. It is also said that this custom may be related to the strong vitality of the willow,

人们还通过插柳预测天气及收成好坏。此外，南北朝时还盛行元宵节插杨柳于门以祀门神的习俗。

which can survive and grow very quickly wherever it is planted. People believed that the willow had a spirit, which led to the custom of wearing willows, which has has been popular since the Tang Dynasty. It is said that ancient Chinese could predict the weather and the outcome of harvests by wearing willows. In addition, during the Southern and Northern Dynasties (420-589), Chinese people had the custom of pinning willow sticks on doors to worship the God of Doors to dispel evil spirits.

例句：

清明节有**插柳**戴柳之俗。

Example Sentence:

Chinese people have the custom of planting and wearing willow branches during the Qingming Festival.

dailiu;
wearing soft willow branches

参见“插柳”。

See *chaliu* (planting soft willow branches).

折柳赠别

zheliu zengbie;
picking up willow branches as departure gifts

古代赠别方式，将柳树枝条折下赠送远行亲友从而表达

An ancient custom of presenting willow branches as gifts to relatives and friends when bidding farewell. The Chinese pronunciation of “willow” (liǔ)

惜别之情。因中文“柳”与“留”读音相似，而“留”可表示留别、恋恋不舍之情，后以“折柳”为赠别的代称。此习俗盛于唐代，据说，当时灞桥两岸种满杨柳，春天到来时，柳絮便会像雪花一样随风飘飞。灞桥边设有驿站，人们往往于此处折柳送别客人。

and “stay” (liú) are similar, therefore it became a custom to present willow branches to friends when parting. This custom was popular during the Tang Dynasty (618-907) when the banks of the Bahe River (located in Xi’an, Shaanxi Province) were full of willows. When spring came, the catkins would fly in the wind like snowflakes. There was a courier station on the side of Baqiao Bridge where people gave willow branches to friends as parting gifts.

例句：

折柳赠别与古人重视离别的心理有关，柳条细长柔软易绕，因此古人借柳来表达柔情萦绕和感情绵长之意。

Example Sentence:

Giving gifts of willow branches to relatives and friends when they depart may be related to ancient beliefs about parting. As wickers are slender and pliant, they were associated with tenderness and longevity, and thus symbolized deep emotions for parting friends.

都江堰放水节

Dujiangyan Fangshui Jie;
Water Discharge Day at Dujiangyan

中国四川省都江堰市清明节期间的传统节日。都江堰是公元前256年秦国蜀郡守李冰带领民工修筑的至今还在沿用的水利枢纽工程，每年冬天断水维修，清明放水灌溉。为了纪念李冰，公元978年，北宋政府正式将清明节这一天定为放水节。二千多年来，每年都江堰放水时都要依俗举行盛大活动，祭祀古蜀国先王和蜀郡守李冰，祈求五谷丰登，祭毕在礼炮声中放水灌田。如今此节日是当地最盛大的文化活动之一，2006年列入第一批国家级非物质文化遗产名录。

A traditional Chinese festival in Dujiangyan City, Sichuan Province, that falls on the same day with the Qingming Festival. Dujiangyan is a water conservancy project that was constructed around 256 BC under the leadership of Li Bing, the governor of the Shu Prefecture (part of present-day Sichuan Province) that was part of the State of Qin during the Warring States Period (475-221 BC). It has been used for irrigation and flood control for more than 2,000 years. Every winter, the river water is dammed for maintenance, and during the Qingming Festival the water is discharged for irrigation. To commemorate Li Bing, the government of the Northern Song Dynasty (960-1127) announced in 978 that the Qingming Festival would be Water Discharge Day in Dujiangyan. Every year for more than 2,000 years, a grand ceremony has been held on this day in memory of Li Bing and the kings of the ancient State of Shu (part of present-day Sichuan Province). People also use the occasion to pray for a bumper harvest. The water is discharged into the fields amid a cannon salute. The festival has become one of the largest cultural events in the region. In 2006, it was included in the first batch of National Intangible Cultural Heritage List.

例句：

都江堰放水节反映了在两千年后继续发挥作用的古代灌溉工程的成功。

Example Sentence:

Water Discharge Day at Dujiangyan celebrates the success of the ancient irrigation system which has continued to function two millennia later.

斗鸡 *dou ji;* cockfighting

中国古代一种传统的娱乐形式，以鸡相斗决胜负。历史上曾被人们视为消遣解闲的方式。斗鸡起源于先秦，且多在寒食节进行。斗鸡所用的鸡是一种身高体壮且好斗的良种鸡。进行斗鸡活动时，参斗双方商定好规则后即可比赛，一般采用三战二胜制。比赛时，主人各捧一只鸡相对而立，比赛开始，主人松手，斗鸡扑向对手，互相厮打，整个比赛一般是以一方已完全无力反击方才结束，场面激烈。这种斗鸡的爱好和习俗流传至今。

A traditional form of entertainment in ancient China in which roosters are pitted against each other and made to fight. Cockfighting originated before the Qin Dynasty (221-206 BC) and usually occurred during the Cold Food Festival. Strong and aggressive roosters are raised and trained to fight. Roosters are placed on opposite sides of the match ring and released when the match begins. They rush forward and fight, and the fierce match ends when one is completely unable to fight back. The custom of cockfighting is still practiced nowadays.

Example Sentence:

Cockfighting originated in Asia. China is one of the oldest countries in the world to tame game fowl.

例句：

斗鸡游戏起源于亚洲。中国是世界上驯养斗鸡的古老国家之一。民间有中原斗鸡、漳州斗鸡、吐鲁番斗鸡、西双版纳斗鸡等“中国四大斗鸡”之说。

People often speak of “China's four big cockfighting contests” which refer to those held in the Central Plains, Zhangzhou, Turpan, and Xishuangbanna.

斗蛋 *dou dan; egg competition*

立夏节气的习俗之一。立夏这天，大人把煮熟的鸡蛋装入丝线制成的蛋套中，然后将其挂在小孩子的脖子上，孩子们会互相比较所持蛋壳硬度，进行鸡蛋碰鸡蛋的比赛，鸡蛋相撞直到一方撞破壳为止，蛋壳完好的一方胜出，胜出者被尊为“蛋王”。古人认为，鸡蛋的圆形象征着生活的圆满，立夏吃鸡蛋能祈祷夏日平安。

A custom practiced on the day of the Beginning of Summer. People put a boiled egg into a silk case and hang the case around a child's neck. The child holds the hard-boiled egg and knocks it against the egg of another player until one egg breaks. The one whose egg remains intact is declared the winner and hailed as the “egg king.” Ancient Chinese believed that the round shape of an egg symbolized the completeness and happiness of life, and eating eggs on the Beginning of Summer is symbolic of blessings for peace in the summer.

例句：

斗蛋没有规则，但多数人在斗蛋之前都有口头协定，即输方会当场把斗输的蛋吃掉。

Example Sentence:

There are no established rules for the egg competition, but most players would reach a verbal agreement before the event that the loser must eat his egg on the spot.

长命缕 *changming lü;* longevity thread braid

古代端午节结成各种形状用以避邪的五彩带。农历五月初五时，妇女们用红、黄、蓝、白、黑五色丝线或绒线编成线绳拴在儿童手臂、手腕等处；或悬挂于儿童胸前、蚊帐、摇篮之中。据说五色丝象征五色龙，可以免除瘟病，使人健康长寿。这一习俗至今在民间流行。

Five-colored silk-threaded braid used to dispel evil spirits during the Dragon Boat Festival in ancient China. On the fifth day of the fifth lunar month, women use red, yellow, blue, white, and black silk or woolen threads to make a braid which is tied around a child's arms and wrists. It is sometimes hung around the neck or in a mosquito net or cradle. It is said that the five-colored, silk-threaded braid symbolizes the five-colored dragon, which was believed to protect people from plagues and ensure good health and longevity. This custom is still popular among people today.

例句：

长命缕是端午节吉祥物兼饰物。唐代长安每逢端午，宫中常以长命缕赐各位大臣。

Example Sentence:

The longevity thread braid was an important accessory given to ministers during the Dragon Boat Festival in Chang'an, which was the capital of the Tang Dynasty (618-907), now present-day Xi'an, Shaanxi Province.

称人 *cheng ren; summer weighing*

立夏节气风俗。立夏时家家都会用大称称人体重，立秋日时则再称一次体重，从而观察夏季体重的变化。相传该习俗起源于三国时代，诸葛亮将刘备儿子刘禅委托给吴国孙夫人抚养，孙夫人每年立夏都为其称一次体重，再告知诸葛亮，表明刘禅身体健康。后来该风俗传入民间，主要流行于南方地区。

An ancient Chinese tradition of checking one's weight on the day of the Beginning of Summer. People weigh themselves on this day as well as the day of the Beginning of Autumn to see how their weight changed during the summer. According to legend, this custom originated from the Three Kingdoms Period (220-280). Zhuge Liang (the famous adviser to Liu Bei, founding emperor of Shu) entrusted Liu Bei's son Liu Shan to Lady Sun of the Kingdom of Wu. Lady Sun weighed Liu Shan on the day of the Beginning of Summer every year to show Zhuge Liang that he was healthy and strong. Later, this custom became popular among people, especially in southern China.

例句：

立夏**称人**的习俗虽然故事版本很多，甚至与史实有异，不过终归源于三国，与刘禅有关。

Example Sentence:

The custom of weighing people on the day of the Beginning of Summer varies greatly among different groups of people. It is even different from how it was historically recorded. It is considered to be derived from the Three Kingdoms Period, and inextricably related to Liu Shan (Liu Bei's eldest son and successor).

端午节 *Duanwu Jie*; Duanwu Festival; Dragon Boat Festival; Double Fifth Festival

中国最重要的传统节日之一，时在农历五月初五，也称“端阳节”“龙舟节”。端午节始于中国的春秋战国时期。关于端午节的来历有多种传说，其中纪念爱国诗人屈原之说影响最广最深，占据主流地位。屈原是战国时期楚国的大臣、著名诗人，因遭谗言被流放。他得知楚国都城被秦国攻破的消息后悲愤不已，于五月五日抱石投汨罗江自尽。当地百姓闻讯纷纷赶来，划船打捞；由于找不到，大家纷纷将饭团等食物投进河里喂鱼，以免它们伤害屈原的身体。以后每年五月初五民间就用龙舟竞渡、吃粽子等来纪念屈原，这一天逐渐成为一个重要节日。农历五月，夏至到来，天气开始变得炎热潮湿，容易时疫流行，因此端午节也用喝雄黄酒，挂艾草、菖蒲等方式驱毒强体，远离疫病。

One of the most important traditional festival in China which falls on the fifth day of the fifth lunar month, also called *Duanyang Jie* (Duanyang Festival), *Longzhou Jie* (Dragon Boat Festival). It started in the Warring States Period (475-221 BC) with a history of over 2,000 years. Legends vary at different places and during different historical times, but the most influential story is associated with the great poet Qu Yuan. Qu Yuan, a wise and honest minister of the State of Chu was sent into exile due to false accusations. When he heard the fall of the capital of his home state to the hands of the strong State of Qin, he was in such despair that he flung himself into the Miluo River. Local people, upon learning the sad news, raced in boats out to try to save him. As his body was nowhere to be found, they dropped balls of sticky rice into the river so that the fish would eat the rice instead of Qu's body. This is said to be the origin of dragon boat race and eating *zongzi* (sticky rice dumpling) during the festival. The fifth lunar month is the beginning of summer, characterized by hot and humid weather which is congenial for the spread of epidemic diseases. So people also drank or sprayed realgar wine and hang calamus and mugwort leaves to drive away diseases and other evil things.

例句：

端午节是中国传统三大节日之一，流传至今已逾两千年。东亚很多国家和地区受中华文化影响也有过端午的习俗，并融入了本民族的元素。

Example Sentence:

The Dragon Boat Festival is one of the three major traditional Chinese festivals. It has a history of more than 2,000 years. Under the influence of Chinese culture, quite a number of East Asian countries have also celebrated the Dragon Boat Festival, adding to it their own national features.

Duanyang Jie;
Duanyang Festival

参见“端午节”。

See *Duanwu Jie* (Duanwu Festival).

龙舟节 *Longzhou Jie;* Dragon Boat Festival

参见“端午节”。

See *Duanwu Jie* (Duanwu Festival).

赛龙舟 *sai longzhou;* dragon boat race

中国端午节重要的民俗活动。据说赛龙舟是为了纪念被流放后愤懑投江自尽的爱国诗人屈原而举行。龙舟饰有龙头龙尾，一般长约20余米。登舟比赛队员为23人，包括舵手、锣手、鼓手各1人，划手20人。比赛是在规定距离内同时起航，以到达终点先后决定名次。后来赛龙舟传到其他国家。赛龙舟被列

An important custom observed during the Dragon Boat Festival. It is believed that the race is held to commemorate the death of Qu Yuan, a famous poet of the Warring States Period (475-221 BC) who was exiled by a corrupt king and, in his sorrow, drowned himself in a river. Dragon boats are decorated with the head and tail of a dragon and are generally over 20 meters long. Each boat has a crew of around 23 people,

入第三批国家级非物质文化遗产名录。

including a person to steer, a gong striker, a drummer, and 20 paddlers. Very popular in China, the race has spread to other countries. The dragon boat race was included in the third batch of China's National Intangible Cultural Heritage List.

例句:

赛龙舟在中国南方地区更为流行。

Example Sentence:

The dragon boat race is more popular in southern China.

粽子 *zongzi;* sticky rice dumpling

A traditional food of the Chinese Dragon Boat Festival. It is made by boiling glutinous rice that is wrapped in (reed) leaves. People have been eating *zongzi* for roughly 2,000 years, and during the Eastern Han Dynasty, eating *zongzi* was associated with making an offering to the great poet Qu Yuan. Legend has it that Qu Yuan committed suicide by hurling himself into a river on the fifth day of the fifth lunar month after learning that his home state of Chu had been conquered. People filled bamboo poles with rice to feed the fish, and shrimps so that they wouldn't get hungry

中国传统节日端午节的节令食品，用粽叶包糯米煮熟而成。两千多年前民间已开始食粽。东汉时将食粽与祭祀爱国诗人屈原联系起来。传说屈原因其祖国楚国灭亡于农历五月五日投江而死。人们用竹筒装米投入河中以饲蛟龙鱼虾，以免它们伤害屈原的身体，后来演变成为用粽叶包裹。粽子品种多样，形状多为锥角形，也有包成三角形、四角形、方形的。南北各地的粽子风味不同，北方多为红枣糯米粽，江浙地区粽子包火腿、猪肉等，广东粽子有以鸡、鸭、猪肉和各种配料包成的什锦粽。

and consume Qu Yuan's body. Later, this practice evolved into using (reed) leaves to wrap up the rice. There are many different types of *zongzi*. The most prevalent has a pyramid shape, but there are also others that have triangular, quadrilateral, and square shapes. Across the country, the customs pertaining to *zongzi* differ. In the north, red date glutinous rice *zongzi* is common; in Jiangsu and Zhejiang, ham and pork are wrapped in the *zongzi*; in Guangdong, chicken, duck, pork, and all manner of other ingredients are mixed in with the *zongzi*.

例句：

粽子原称"角黍"，即用黍（即黄黏米）制作的角形的食物，是祭祀神灵和祖先的祭品。

Example Sentence:

Zongzi was originally called "cornered sticky rice" because it is yellow sticky rice molded together in a shape with distinct corners. It is a kind of offering for spirits and ancestors.

毒五月 *du wuyue;* evil fifth lunar month

农历五月的民间称谓，又被称为"毒月"或"恶月"。此说法可追溯到先秦时代。进入

A folk name for the fifth lunar month. The term "evil fifth month" can be traced back to the Pre-Qin Period (before 221 BC). In the fifth lunar month, the

农历五月后气温升高，降雨量也随之增加，空气变得潮湿，容易造成传染病的爆发和流行。人们会在这个月举办喝雄黄酒、插菖蒲等活动来辟邪驱毒。这些习俗后来都成为端午节的习俗。参见“端午节”。

temperature rises, the rainfall increases, and the air becomes damp. These are all factors that increase the likelihood of an outbreak of infectious diseases. The fifth lunar month, therefore, was regarded as an evil month. To dispel evil spirits, people wear calamus and drink realgar wine during the month. These practices later became part of the Duanwu Festival activities. See *Duanwu Jie* (Dragon Boat Festival).

例句：

古代人为了不生病，在所谓的**“毒五月”**通过各种方式，比如饮食清淡、益肝补肾、节制欲望、平心静气等来养生。

Example Sentence:

To avoid disease during the evil fifth lunar month, ancient Chinese tried many methods to keep healthy, such as maintaining a light diet, tonifying the liver and kidneys, restraining desire, and maintaining a good state of mind.

五毒 *wudu;* five poisonous creatures

民间指五种有毒的动物，即蜈蚣、蝎子、壁虎、癞蛤蟆、蛇。中国民间认为五月气温升高，降水增加，是五毒出没之时，于是在端午节当日在屋内撒石灰，喷雄黄酒，并张贴五毒图案剪纸。端午节驱五毒

The five poisonous creatures in folk beliefs include the centipede, scorpion, house lizard, toad, and viper. As the temperature and precipitation increase in the fifth lunar month, worms and insects become active. During this time, people take measures to protect themselves such as scattering

是为了提醒人们要防害防病。

lime and sprinkling realgar wine around the house on the day of the Dragon Boat Festival. At the same time, people hang paper-cuts with images of the five poisonous creatures, meant to protect people from these threats. These activities are performed during the Dragon Boat Festival with the intent of reminding people to take steps to prevent the spread of disease.

例句：

中国民间认为，每年夏历五月端午日午时**五毒**开始孳生，应于此日午前在屋角及各阴暗处洒石灰、喷雄黄酒、燃药烟，以灭五毒，驱秽气。

Example Sentence:

Chinese people believe that the five poisonous creatures become rampant at noon on the day of the Dragon Boat Festival. On the morning of that day, people take preventive measures to get rid of the five poisonous creatures and dispel evil spirits. Measures include scattering lime, sprinkling realgar wine, and burning medicinal incense around the corners of the house and in the shade.

斗百草 *dou baicao; tugging grass*

中国民间端午节期间流行的一种游戏，亦称“斗草”。

A popular game played in China during the Dragon Boat Festival, also known as *dou cao* in Chinese. Two players each hold the stem

斗草时，两人将手中草相互勾搭在一起，并用力往自己方向拉，谁手中的草茎断了就算输。斗草的游戏起源于先秦时期，后融入民间风俗，如今该习俗仍在中国部分地区流传。

of a piece of grass intertwined with the opponent's grass. The opponents tug with force in their direction. The player with the stem of grass that breaks is the loser. Tugging grass originated in the Pre-Qin Period (before 221 BC) and later merged with folk customs. The game is popular in some parts of China.

例句：

在唐代，**斗百草**不仅仅受妇女儿童的欢迎，成年男子也对此颇为喜欢。

Example Sentence:

During the Tang Dynasty (618-907), tugging grass was not only a popular game played among women and children, but was also popular among adult men as well.

挂艾叶

gua ai'ye;
hanging mugwort leaves

中国民间端午节传统习俗之一。农历五月夏天开始，天气湿热，容易生病，古人称此月为"毒月"或者"恶月"，其中农历五月初五（端午节）这天毒气最重。届时，天降瘟疫，蛇、蜈蚣等有毒动物也会出来害人。艾叶和菖蒲等多年生草本植物含有挥发性芳香油，可杀虫灭菌，净

A traditional custom during China's Dragon Boat Festival. Beginning in the fifth lunar month, the weather grows hot and humid, and it is easy to get sick. As a result, people often call this month the "month of poison" or the "evil month." When the Dragon Boat Festival is held on the fifth day of the month, it is considered the most poisonous day of the month when all manner of poisonous beasts and insects are the most dangerous. It was believed that

化空气，因此人们会摘来挂在房门上、窗前辟邪驱虫，杀菌防病，祈愿身体健康。

demons and ghosts utilized many poisons to cause harm in people. Chinese mugwort and calamus are both perennial herbaceous plants containing an aromatic, volatile oil. This oil can both serve as an insecticide and air purifier. As a result, people hang such herbal medicines as Chinese mugwort leaves and calamus from their doors and in front of their windows to ward off evil spirits, drive away insects, kill germs, and prevent disease.

例句：

端午节甚至整个五月**挂艾叶**和菖蒲的习俗至今仍在中国民间广为流传。

Example Sentence:

The tradition of hanging mugwort leaves and calamus during the Dragon Boat Festival or during the whole month is still observed by many people.

悬菖蒲 *xuan changpu;* hanging calamus

中国民间端午节传统习俗之一。参见“挂艾叶”。

A traditional custom during China's Dragon Boat Festival. See *gua ai'ye* (hanging mugwort leaves).

例句：

菖蒲的叶子形状似剑，民间称之为“水剑”，说它可“斩千邪”，于是**悬菖蒲**以驱邪避害成了人们过端午节时的一大风俗。

Example Sentence:

Calamus leaves are shaped like a sword, and are called "water swords" by ancient Chinese.

Because of this shape, it was believed that they could "chop" any evil spirit. Therefore, hanging calamus developed into a tradition during the Dragon Boat Festival.

雄黄酒 *xionghuang jiu;* realgar wine

中国旧时民间端午节的一种饮品。雄黄也称为"鸡冠石"，中医常用作解毒杀虫药，尤其可以驱逐蜈蚣、毒蛇之类的毒虫。在古代，人们认为喝雄黄酒可以治病解毒，祛除灾难。端午节时，人们会喝雄黄酒或用雄黄酒涂于小儿额头与鼻尖以驱赶毒虫，消除疾病。现在，人们了解了雄黄酒的毒性后不再饮用，只是打扫屋子时洒一些雄黄酒以杀虫消毒。

A traditional beverage consumed during China's Dragon Boat Festival. Realgar, which is also called *jiguanshi* (cockscomb stone), is considered by Chinese TCM as a universal antidote against poison delivered by such poisonous insects as centipedes and vipers. In ancient times, people believed that drinking realgar wine could detoxify and treat disease. During the Dragon Boat Festival, people either drank realgar wine or applied it like an insecticide to the foreheads and noses of children to repel poisonous insects and prevent disease. These days, people understand that realgar wine is toxic and no longer drink it; they do, however, sprinkle some realgar wine around the home to disinfect and guard the home against bugs.

例句：

经典民间故事《白蛇传》中，白娘子在端午节被迫喝下**雄黄酒**后现出蛇形，吓死了她的丈夫许仙。

Example Sentence:

In the classical Chinese folklore *The Legend of the White Snake*, Madame White is persuaded to drink some realgar wine which reveals her true form as a white snake, which shocks her husband Xu Xian to death.

戴香包 *dai xiangbao; wearing a perfume pouch*

中国民间端午节传统习俗之一。香包是一种传统的佩饰物，又叫香袋、香囊、荷包等。用丝绸、碎布缝制或用五色丝线缠成老虎、葫芦、梅花、鸡、兔和蝙蝠等形状的绣花包，内装雄黄或者中药香料。佩戴香包既可以作为美丽的饰品，又有驱虫防病的作用。

A custom during the Chinese Dragon Boat Festival. It is a kind of traditional clothing accessory, also called a "*xiangdai* (perfume bag)" "*xiangnang* (spice bag)," and "*hebao* (embroidered pouch)." People use either silk or other fabric to sew images of tigers, gourds, plum blossoms, chickens, rabbits, or bats onto an embroidered bag. They also make shapes of these animals by tying together multi-colored threads. Realgar or other kinds of Chinese medicine is placed inside the bag. The perfume pouch is an ornate accessory that also has the function of repelling insects and preventing disease.

例句：

小孩子夏季**戴香包**可防蚊虫叮咬。

Example Sentence:

Wearing a perfume pouch in summer can protect children from mosquito bites.

缠百索 *chan baisuo; tying a multi-colored thread braid*

中国民间端午节传统习俗之一。百索又称"端午索"或"长寿线"。古时，人们在端午节将五色丝系于手臂，用于避兵灾、辟邪，防病。后世民间多把五色线系在小孩儿手腕上，保佑孩子不被病瘟纠缠。

A traditional custom of the Chinese Dragon Boat Festival, also referred to as the "*duanwu suo* (Duanwu braid)" or "*changshou xian* (longevity threads)." In ancient times, people wrapped multi-colored threads around their arms to symbolize protection against war, evil spirits, and disease. Later it became more common to tie multi-colored strings around the wrists of children to symbolize protection against disease.

例句：

如今北方一些地区尚有在孩童的脖颈、手腕和脚腕**缠百索**的习俗。

Example Sentence:

The custom is still observed in some areas of northern China where people tie multi-colored braids around children's necks, wrists, and ankles.

端午索 *Duanwu suo;* Duanwu braid

也称"长寿线"。参见"缠百索"。

See *chan baisuo* (tying the multi-colored thread braid).

例句：

端午索常系于小孩子的手腕上。

Example Sentence:

Duanwu braids are often tied to the wrists of children.

长寿线 *changshou xian;* longevity threads

参见"端午索"。

See *Duanwu suo* (Duanwu braid).

赠扇 *zengshan;* giving fans; granting fans

A custom observed during the Dragon Boat Festival. The custom was supposedly started by Emperor Taizong (598-649) of the Tang Dynasty (618-907) who, during the Dragon Boat Festival, wrote inscriptions on two fans and gave them to Minister Zhangsun Wuji and Grand Councilor Yang

端午节习俗之一。流行于唐朝，唐太宗曾于端午亲书扇面赠于重臣长孙无忌和杨师道。于是唐代长安市民在端阳时也多互相馈赠扇子，包括羽毛扇、绸缎扇、檀香扇等。扇子为夏季人们常用之物，端午赠扇正当时节，且暗含辟邪、凉快之意。后来发展为未婚青年男子在送“端阳礼”时将最宝贵的扇子送给情人。

Shidao as gifts. Soon afterwards, people of Chang'an (present-day Xi'an, Shaanxi Province) began giving each other fans made of feathers, satin, and sandalwood during the Dragon Boat Festival. Fans are used to stay cool during the summer and to ward off evil spirits. Later the custom evolved into a romantic gesture in which an unmarried young man would give his most precious fan to the woman he loved during the Dragon Boat Festival as a token of his affection.

例句：

端午**赠扇**的习俗在中国长江中游部分地区流传较广。

Example Sentence:

The custom of giving fans during the Dragon Boat Festival is still popular on the middle reaches of the Yangtze River.

簪榴花 *zan liuhua; wearing pomegranate blossoms with hairpins*

中国北方一种民俗。明代端午节时，从五月初一至初五，北方家家户户的母亲都给女儿佩戴榴花于鬓发两旁作为装饰，以衬托女孩子的明媚鲜妍。

A folk custom in northern China. During the Dragon Boat Festival in the Ming Dynasty (1368-1644) in northern China, mothers would stick pomegranate blossoms in the hair of their daughters, which they believed would make them more attractive.

例句：

端午“**簪榴花**”，是人们爱美、追求美的一种表现。

Example Sentence:

Girls all wearing pomegranate blossoms with hairpins were eye-pleasing, expressing people's love for beauty.

姑姑节 *Gugu Jie; Married Daughter's Home Visit Day*

汉族传统节日。每年农历六月初六，各家各户请回已出嫁的老少姑娘和女婿，精心招待一天，故又名“六月六”或“回娘家节”。此时正值多雨的盛夏季节，这一天人们还会晾晒衣物和书籍以防虫蛀和霉变、取井水收藏用以制造酱醋及腌瓜茄等。如今，该节日的相关民俗活动已渐渐被人们遗忘，只在个别地方有所保留。

A traditional Chinese festival observed by the Han ethnic group. Every year on the sixth day of the sixth lunar month, parents invite their married daughters and their husbands to return home, where they will be entertained for one day. As it is usually during the summer rainy season, people will often dry their clothes or books on sunny days to avoid insect bites and mildew, and store extra water from the well for making vinegar and soy sauce as well as preserving melons and eggplants. Although the folk activities related to this festival have largely been forgotten, they are still popular in certain places today.

例句：

农历六月六日不仅是**姑姑节**，还是古代另外一个节日——天贶节，系宋真宗假造“天书”之后设立的。

Example Sentence:

The sixth day of the sixth lunar month is not only Married Daughter's Home Visit Day, but also the *Tiankuang* (heavenly blessed)

Festivial which was established by Emperor Zhenzong (968-1022) of the Song Dynasty (960-1279) after the fabricated "Book from Heaven" was produced.

六月六 *liuyueliu;* Double Sixth Day

参见"姑姑节"。

See *Gugu Jie* (Married Daughter's Home Visit Day).

回娘家节 *Huiniangjia Jie;* Festival of Returning to Maiden Home

参见"姑姑节"。

See *Gugu Jie* (Married Daughter's Home Visit Day).

七夕节 *Qixi Jie;* Qixi Festival; Double Seventh Festival

中国传统节日，又称“乞巧节”或“女儿节”，时间为农历七月初七。七夕节起源于牛郎织女爱情传说故事，现在被视为中国的情人节。传说织女是天帝的女儿，她到人间游玩时与牛郎相识相爱并结为夫妻，生一儿一女，生活美满。天帝得知后非常愤怒，派天兵将织女押回天庭。牛郎带着孩子苦苦追赶。快要追上时，王母用头上金钗在天空划出一道银河将两人分开，牛郎和织女只能在银河两岸对望。天上的喜鹊被他们的真情感动，飞到一起给他们搭了一座鹊桥。以后每年七月七日，喜鹊都会在银河上搭桥帮他们团聚。民间主要民俗活动有拜祭织女、乞巧、食巧果等。

A Chinese traditional holiday, also called *Qiqiao Jie* (literally, Praying for Domestic Skills Festival) or the *Nü'er Jie* (literally, Girl's Festival). It is held on the seventh day of the seventh lunar month. The festival originated from the classic folk tale "The Cowherd and the Weaver Girl", and is widely considered the Chinese Valentine's Day. In the story, Weaver Girl is the daughter of the Celestial Ruler. One day while taking a stroll through the human world, she meets Cowherd. They fall in love, get married, and live a happy life with their son and daughter. Hearing that his daughter has fallen in love with a human, the Celestial Ruler is furious and sends his troops to escort Weaver Girl back to the skies. Cowherd chases after them through the sky with their children, but just as he begins to catch up the Queen Mother uses her hairpin to stretch out the Milky Way between them, separating the two lovers. Separated forever, they can only gaze at each other from opposite sides of the silver river known as the Milky Way. Moved by their love, magpies decide to fly together to form a bridge with their wings every year on the seventh day of the seventh lunar month so that the two can be reunited. There are many customs during Qixi, such as worshipping the Weaver Girl, praying for sewing and needlework skills (*qiqiao*), and eating *qiaoguo*—a special food for the festival.

例句：

七夕节是中国最具浪漫色彩的传统节日。

Example Sentence:

The Double Seventh Festival is the most romantic traditional festival in China.

乞巧节 *Qiqiao Jie;* Praying for Domestic Skills Festival

参见“七夕”。

See *Qixi Jie* (Qixi Festival).

女儿节 *Nü'er Jie;* Girl's Festival

参见“七夕”。

See *Qixi Jie* (Qixi Festival).

拜祭织女 *baiji zhinü;* worshipping Weaver Girl

七夕节活动之一。只有女子才能参与。七夕之夜，女子们相约女性亲友，在月光下摆上供桌，放置茶、酒、水果等祭品，点上蜡烛和香炉，

One of the activities of the Qixi Festival. Only girls and young women can participate in worshipping Weaver Girl, the heroine of the famous Chinese legend "The Cowherd and the Weaver Girl." On the evening of

一同祭拜织女。之后大家一起围坐在桌前享用美食，并朝着织女星座默念自己的心事。因织女代表着对爱情忠贞不渝的追求，故女子们以此活动来期盼自己嫁得如意郎君或早生贵子。

the seventh day of the seventh lunar month, young women would invite female friends and relatives to their home. They would set a table with offerings including tea, alcohol, fruit, and light candles and incense to worship Weaver Girl together. After that, they would sit around the table eating snacks while looking at the Weaver Girl Star (Vega), making their own silent wishes. The Weaver Girl represents the pursuit of love and loyalty, so by worshipping her, women usually hope to marry a good husband or pray to have children soon.

例句：

拜祭织女实际上源于古代对星辰的崇拜，牛郎织女传说也源于此。

Example Sentence:

Worship of Weaver Girl actually stems from ancient worship of the stars, upon which the legend "The Cowherd and the Weaver Girl" is based.

乞巧 *qiqiao; praying for sewing and needle-work skills*

One of the main folk customs of the Qixi Festival. On the night of the seventh day of the seventh lunar month, girls and young women gather together to have a competition on needle threading, praying for sewing and needlework skills to Weaver Girl. They each

中国民间风俗，七夕节的主要活动。七月七日夜为牛郎织女相会之期，是夜，姑娘们一起进行穿针比赛，祈求像织女一样心灵手巧。乞巧时，姑娘们每人拿一根针和一根线，在月光下同时穿引，最先把线穿入针孔的人被认为是“得巧”，意味着她得到了灵巧和智慧，晚穿上针的人被认为是“输巧”，需要把事先准备的小礼物赠给巧者。由于各地文化、习俗不同，故乞巧的方式也不同。根据记载，七夕乞巧起源于汉代，在中国民间代代延续，经久不衰。

get a needle and some thread and start to thread their needles at the same time in the moonlight. The girl who threads her needle first is considered a skilled sewer or embroiderer, which means she has been endowed with sewing and embroidery skills and wisdom. The other girls are considered the losers without such skills and wisdom, and they must give gifts to the winner. Ways of praying to Weaver Girl for sewing and embroidery skills are different according to the different cultures and customs of different localities. The custom originated in the Han Dynasty (206 BC-AD 220), and it has continued in China for generations.

例句：

七夕时女孩子们祭织女，拜巧神，穿针**乞巧**，祈求爱情，是女孩子最为喜欢的节日之一。

Example Sentence:

The Qixi Festival was one of the most popular festivals in ancient times. On this day, girls pray to Weaver Girl for sewing and needle-work skills and also pray for romantic love.

鹊桥相会

queqiao xianghui;
meeting on the magpie bridge

The famed meeting from the Chinese legend "The Cowherd and the Weaver Girl." On the seventh night of the seventh lunar month each year, a flock of magpies form a bridge to reunite Zhinü (Weaver Girl, symbolized by the star Vega) and Niulang (Cowherd, symbolized by the star Altair). The phrase has come to symbolize the reunion of lovers or couples who have stayed loyal and faithful to each other despite long years of separation.

中国民间传说农历七月初七晚上喜鹊会在银河上搭桥，让长期分离的牛郎、织女夫妇在鹊桥上相会。常用来比喻情人或夫妻久别之后的团聚。

Example Sentence:

Mr. Zhang can only reunite with his wife during the summer and winter vacations, much like meeting on the magpie bridge from thousands of miles away.

例句：

张老师只有在寒暑假才能与千里外的夫人**鹊桥相会**。

为牛庆生

wei niu qingsheng;
celebrating the birthday of the ox

七夕节民俗之一。民间传说中织女被天兵抓走后，牛郎放养的具有神性的老牛让牛郎将自己的皮剥下，驾着牛皮飞入天宫追赶织女。为了纪念老牛这种无私奉献的精神，这一天儿童会采摘野花挂在牛角上，祝愿它获得重生。

A custom during the Qixi Festival. According to the folklore of "The Cowherd and the Weaver Girl," when Weaver Girl was caught by the celestrial soldiers and taken back to the Heavenly Palace, the divine Old Ox that Cowherd raised told him to use its hide after its death as a magic cape which would enable Cowherd and his children to fly up to Heaven to meet Weaver Girl. To commemorate Old Ox's selfless dedication, children would pick wild flowers and hang them on the horns of oxen on that particular day to wish him a rebirth.

例句：

为牛庆生由来的另一种说法是农历七月七日是老牛的生日，将花挂到牛角上以示祝贺。

Example Sentence:

Another version of the origin of "celebrating the birthday of the ox" is that the seventh day of the seventh lunar month is the birthday of the Old Ox. People hang flowers on the horns of oxen to celebrate the occasion.

巧果 *qiaoguo;* fried thin pastry

七夕节特有的节庆食品，品种极多，主要原料是油、面、糖、蜜。具体做法为将发面团放入具有梨、茄、石榴、小猪、小狮子、金鱼、虾等各种花形图案的木模中，将成形后的小饼油炸或烙食。

A unique food eaten during the Qixi Festival. There are many varieties of *qiaoguo*, but the main materials are oil, flour, sugar, and honey. The dough is placed in wooden molds in the shapes of pears, eggplants, pomegranates, piglets, lions, goldfish, shrimp, etc. and then fried or baked.

例句：

上海地区**巧果**做法不同，面和糖、芝麻制成竖条片状，在竖条上切三刀后油炸至金黄。这样做出来的巧果甜脆可口。

Example Sentence:

In Shanghai, *qiaoguo* is prepared in a different way. The dough is made of flour, sugar, and sesame and is cut into small pieces and then made into very flat strips. Next, a knife is used to make three cuts in each strip. Finally the strips are fried in hot oil until they become golden. This kind of *qiaoguo* is sweet and crisp.

拜魁星 *bai kuixing; worshipping the Kuixing star*

中国古代民俗之一。魁星就是魁斗星，为北斗七星的第一颗星，也称“魁首”。俗传七月七日是魁星的生日。魁星主文事，掌考运，古时想求取功名的读书人崇敬魁星，所以会在七夕这天祭拜，祈求魁星保佑自己考运亨通，高中状元。这一风俗在闽东地区尤其盛行，有时与七夕拜祭织女一同举行。

An ancient Chinese folk custom. The seventh day of the seventh lunar month is known as the birthday of the Kuixing star, the first star of the Big Dipper, known in Western countries as the North Star. Kuixing is regarded as the star in charge of literacy and exams. Ancient scholars aspiring to success in exams and higher social status would worship the star on this day to pray for good luck in exams and for career success. This practice was particularly popular in east Fujian Province, and sometimes was held with the worship for Weaver Girl at the same time.

例句：

七月七日是魁星的生日，旧时每逢这一天，读书人都会祭**拜魁星**。

Example Sentence:

Scholars worship Kuixing on the seventh day of the seventh lunar month, which is regarded as the birthday of the star.

晒衣书 *shai yishu;* sunning books and clothing

中国民间农历六月六的传统活动。这一天既是"晒衣节"也是"晒书节"，人们都拿出藏书、衣物及装饰用具进行晾晒，晒过的物品不易起霉、遭虫蛀。

A traditional folk activity on the sixth day of the sixth lunar month. This day is known as *Shaiyi Jie* (Sunning Clothing Festival) and *Shaishu Jie* (Sunning Books Festival). On this day, people take out books, clothes, decorative articles, books, and other things and place them in the sun to dry and get rid of mold and insects.

例句：

晒衣书的习俗历史悠久。

Example Sentence:

The custom of sunning books and clothing has a long history.

晒衣节 *Shaiyi Jie;* Sunning Clothing Festival

参见"晒衣书"。

See *shai yishu* (sunning books and clothing).

晒书节 *Shaishu Jie;* Sunning Books Festival

参见"晒衣书"。

See *shai yishu* (sunning books and clothing).

中元节 *Zhongyuan Jie; Zhongyuan Festival; Ghost Festival*

中国传统节日，时间是每年农历的七月十五日，又名"鬼节""七月半"，主要是为了祭祀亡灵，祈祷平安。传说这一天鬼魂会从阴间来到人间，寻找食物和娱乐，逃脱地狱折磨，人们需为他们备好食物和供品，并烧纸以便鬼魂在阴间使用。中元节来源有两种说法。一说始于道教。道教认为，七月十五日为中元日，地官下降，定人间善恶，赦免亡魂的罪孽，道观乃做斋醮荐福。一说始

A traditional Chinese festival held on the fifteenth day of the seventh lunar month to offer sacrifices to the deceased and pray for safety, also called *Guijie* (Ghost Festival), and *qiyue ban* (Mid-July Festival). This day is believed to be the time when spirits of the netherworld roam freely among the living, seeking food and entertainment as a relief from the tortures of Hell. People need to prepare food and offerings as well as burn joss paper, which is believed to have value in the netherworld. There are two stories explaining the origin of the Zhongyuan Festival.

于佛教。佛经说，释迦牟尼的弟子目连曾供养十方僧众，救母于倒悬之中，佛教于是兴起盂兰盆会，后演变为民间祭祖日，家家追荐祖先亡灵。

One story derives from Daoism, holding that on this day Diguan (the Official of Earth) decends to the human world to determine good and evil, and to remit the sins of ghosts. The other story stems from Buddhism, in which this day is known as Ullambana (the Yulanpen Festival), based on the story of a pious Buddhist monk who offered food to other monks on this day for their aid in freeing the suffering of his deceased mother, starving in Hell. For Chinese people, it is the day to pay respects to ancestors and deceased family members.

例句：

中元节送祖时，纸钱冥财烧得很多，以便祖先享用。

Example Sentence:

When paying respects to ancestors during the Zhongyuan Festival, people will burn much paper money.

Guijie;
Ghost Festival; Hungry Ghosts Festival

参见“中元节”。

See *Zhongyuan Jie* (Zhongyuan Festival).

qiyue ban; Mid-July Festival

参见“中元节”。

See *Zhongyuan Jie* (Zhongyuan Festival).

盂兰盆节 *Yulanpen Jie;* Ullambana; Yulanpen Festival

佛教纪念日，时间是每年农历七月十五日，人们在这一天供佛祀祖。该节日得名于目连救母的故事，参见“中元节”。因该节日提倡的是报答父母之恩，与传统儒家的孝道思想不谋而合，因而中国民间也有盂兰盆节祭先人的传统。

A festival in Buddhism on the fifteenth day of the seventh lunar month to offer sacrifice to monks and pay respects to one's ancestors. It is believed the festival originated from the story of a monk named Maudgalyayana who liberated his mother from the sufferings in Hell. See the entry "Zhongyuan Festival". The story coincided with the Confucian concept of filial piety, which has long made the festival popular among common people who offer sacrifices to ancestors on this festival.

例句：

盂兰盆节最早起源于印度的一个节日。

Example Sentence:

The Yulanpen Festival originated from a festival in India.

祭祖

jizu;
worshipping one's ancestors; ancestor worship

一种祭祀先祖的民俗活动。各地礼俗不同，故祭祖形式也不同。祭祖时，先把先人的牌位请出来，恭恭敬敬地放到专门做祭拜用的供桌上，插上香，每日晨、午、昏供三次茶饭，直到中元节结束为止。祭拜时依照辈份和长幼次序给每位先人磕头，默默祷告，向先人汇报这一年

A traditional Chinese folk custom. Different places have different rites concerning worship of ancestors. Tablets memorializing ancestors are taken out and placed on a worship table. Incense is lit, and tea and meals are offered in the morning, afternoon, and evening until the end of the festival. When worshipping ancestors, family members kowtow to each tablet and pray silently, telling of deeds

的言行，并请先人保佑全家平安幸福，后烧纸钱等。祭祖民俗相沿数千年，具有深刻意义，时至今日仍为中国民众广泛重视。

over the past year and begging for safety and happiness for the family. They burn paper money and other items. Ancestor worship has a history of several thousand years in China and is a significant element of Chinese culture. It is still popular among Chinese people today.

例句：

祭祖是一项隆重的民俗活动。除夕、清明节、重阳节、中元节是中国传统节日里祭祖的四大节日，中国人过节总不会忘记祭拜祖先。

Example Sentence:

Ancestor worship is a solemn folk custom of China. The four major festivals to worship ancestors are New Year's Eve, the Qingming Festival, Double Ninth Festival, and the Ghost Festival. Chinese people maintain the tradition of worshipping their ancestors during festivals.

放焰口 *fang yankou; feeding hungry ghosts*

佛教仪式，属于汉族丧葬风俗，也是中元节活动之一。焰口，又称“面燃”，指佛教所谓地狱中渴望饮食，口吐火焰的饿鬼。放焰口则是对饿鬼施舍食物与水，解其饥渴之苦，该仪式一般在人死后举行。日落黄昏之后，法师敲响引钟，带领座下众僧

A Buddhist ritual and funeral custom of the Han ethnic group, also one of the activities of the Ghost Festival. Yankou refers to starving ghosts in Hell who breathe fire and aspire for food and drink. The ritual is held to give food and water to the hungry ghosts so as to alleviate their hunger and thirst. It is usually performed after a person's death. After sunset, a

一边念咒诵经一边施舍食物，将一盘盘桃子和大米撒向四方，反复三次，让恶鬼食之，并死者免于沦为饿鬼。

senior monk rings a bell and leads a crowd of monks to chant sutras while spreading out plates of peaches and rice to all directions for hungry ghosts to eat. The ritual would be repeated for three times. This is also meant to help the deceased from becoming a hungry ghost.

例句：

在佛事活动中凡重大法会圆满之日或举办追荐亡灵活动中，都有**放焰口**施食仪式。

Example Sentence:

The ritual of feeding hungry ghosts is performed on important Buddhist events or on occasions to commemorate the dead.

放河灯 *fang hedeng; floating a river lantern; launching a lotus lantern*

A traditional custom of the Han ethnic group, usually held on the evening of the Ghost Festival on the fifteenth day of the seventh lunar month. At this time, people light lanterns which are decorated with colored paper of different shapes, and are delicate and exquisite. The lanterns are placed on boards or other floating structures and placed in a river. The lanterns then float with the water on the river, like stars in the sky. It is believed that the river lanterns can illuminate the darkness in hell to relieve the

传统汉族岁时风俗。又称“放水灯”，一般在农历七月十五日中元节晚上举行，晚间沿河燃灯，谓之“放河灯”。河灯用彩纸糊成，精巧玲珑，形状各异，装上蜡烛，置于木板或所制作的船形物上，将其浮于河水之上，任其随波逐流。河灯浮满水面，灿如繁星。民间以为河灯可照亮九幽黑暗地狱，解脱鬼魂痛苦。又有传说河灯可为孤魂野鬼引路。如今这个风俗依然可见，而且不拘于农历七月十五日，很多都是纯粹的娱乐活动。

agony and sadness of spirits who dwell there. It is also said that the lanterns will light the way for earth-bound wandering spirits to return to the netherworld. Nowadays, the custom of floating water lanterns is also obvserved on other holidays.

例句：

布依族也有**放河灯**的习俗，布依族的少女们用放河灯来预测自己未来的运气。河灯亮的时间长、飘得远则预示着好运，河灯很快熄灭或者在水中沉没，则预示着厄运。

Example Sentence:

The Bouyei people also have the custom of floating river lanterns. For them, it is a way to foretell a young woman's fate. If a woman's lantern floats far and its light lasts a long time, it means she will have good luck. If the lantern sinks or its light goes off in a short time, it signifies bad luck.

放水灯 *fang shuideng; floating a lantern*

参见“放河灯”。

See *fang hedeng* (floating a river lantern).

烧包衣

shao baoyi;
burning joss paper and paper clothing for the deceased

中国祭祀习俗。包衣是将纸钱和纸衣装在白纸封里，并在白纸封上庄重地写上已故亲人的名字。夕阳西下之后，家人带上酒菜和包衣来到河边，在地上插上香，按照故亲的辈份大小和离世时间顺序摆好包衣，而后焚烧，使每位故亲都收到各自的礼品。

A sacrificial custom in China. Joss paper money and paper clothing are placed into a white envelope with the name of each deceased family member written solemnly on it. After sunset, each family prepares food, joss paper and clothing in envelopes. Then the family go to a river bank, stick in the incense, place the envelopes in the order of seniority and time of departure of the deceased. They then burn the envelopes in the hope that each of the beloved ones would receive its share for use in their afterlife.

例句：

每年农历七月十五日是祭祖节，人们**烧包衣**敬祖，以寄托对亲人的无限思念之情。

Example Sentence:

On the fifteenth day of the seventh lunar month, the festival for worshipping ancestors, people would burn joss paper and paper clothing in envelopes for their deceased family members.

 *qianggu;* offerings-grabbing competition

一种流行于中国福建和台湾的中元节庙会活动。民间在中元普渡后，会将祭祀的供品提供给民众抢夺，称为"抢孤"。"抢孤"通常在每年的夏季举行，在普渡的广场上搭起约13层楼高的台子，上置饭食及各种人、鸟造型的面制食品供民众抢夺。参赛者踩在队员肩上向上攀登台子，夺得台顶祭品的队获胜。得到奖励并寓意全年受到庇护。来自世界各地的队员都可以参加比赛。一种说法认为"抢孤"是为了与孤魂野鬼抢夺祭品；另有说法认为"抢孤"是为了吓退流连忘返的鬼魂。

An event during the Ghost Festival, popular in China's Taiwan and Fujian. A huge structure is built thirteen stories high consisting of various pillars which contain food offerings in the shapes of humans and birds. Team members help one another race up the pillars in order to get the offerings on top. The winning team receives a prize which means they will receive a blessing for the whole year. Teams from all over the world may come to participate. The origins of the festival are said to represent how "hungry" ghosts rush to grab offerings. Others believe it is an event to scare away lingering ghosts.

例句：

抢孤活动是中国台湾宜兰县头城镇在农历七月举办的最重要的活动之一。

Example Sentence:

The offerings-grabbing competition is one of the most important events held in the town of Toucheng in Yilan County of China's Taiwan during the seventh lunar month.

地藏王节 *Dizangwang Jie;* Birthday of Ksitigarbha Bodhisattva

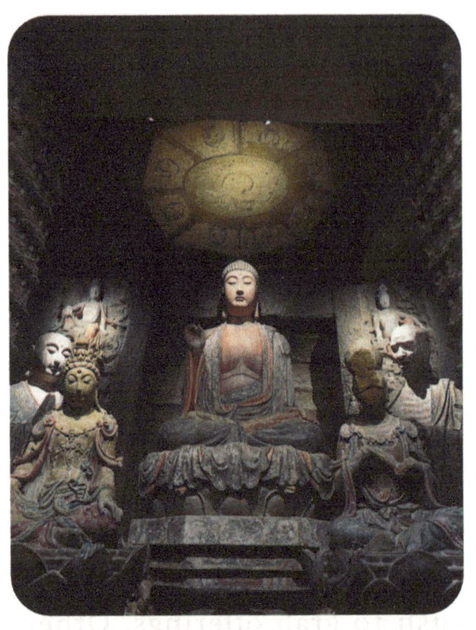

中国汉传佛教传统节日。农历七月三十日为地藏王节，相传是地藏王的生日。佛教传说地藏菩萨主宰阴司，他现身于天上、人间、地狱三界，救苦救难，普渡众生。节日期间，善男信女们前往供奉地藏王的寺庙焚香祝祷，顶礼膜拜。

Traditional festival of the Han Buddhism. The thirtieth day of the seventh lunar month is celebrated as the birthday of Ksitigarbha Bodhisattva, who reigns over the netherworld according to Buddhist legend, and who vowed to rescue all sentient beings from the netherworld and save them from suffering. He travels between heaven, the human world, and the underground world. On this day, pilgrims go to Ksitigarbha Bodhisattva's temple to burn incense and pray for good fortune.

例句：

农历七月三十日中国佛教信徒庆祝**地藏王节**，他们会去地藏王圣殿朝圣，诵念地藏王的名字。

Example Sentence:

On the thirtieth day of the seventh lunar month, Chinese Buddhists celebrate the birthday of Ksitigarbha Bodhisattva. Pilgrims usually travel to the Shrine of Ksitigarbha Bodhisattva and chant his name.

中秋节 *Zhongqiu Jie;* Mid-Autumn Festival; Moon Festival

中国传统节日，又称“仲秋节”“团圆节”等。依据中国古历法，农历八月在秋季中间，叫仲秋；八月十五日又在仲秋之中，称中秋，定八月十五为节，故名为“中秋节”。中秋节成为节日可追溯到唐朝，到宋朝时达到鼎盛。中秋节的起源有多种说法：一种说法是起源于周代祭祀秋月。还有一种说法是起源于农业生产，庆贺秋收来临。明清时，中秋节成为国家传统节日之一。自2008年起，中秋节成为国家法定节日。各地中秋节俗甚

A traditional Chinese festival, celebrated on the fifteenth day of the eighth lunar month. The Mid-Autumn Festival can be traced back to the Tang Dynasty (618-907), and flourished during the Song Dynasty (960-1279). There are many claims on origin of the Mid-Autumn Festival. Some say it started as early as the Zhou Dynasty (c.1046-256 BC) when emperors made sacrifices to the autumn full moon. Others attribute it to agricultural production when the time for harvest had come, which called for celebration. By the time of the Ming (1368-1644) and Qing (1616-1911) dynasties, it had become

为隆重，民间以此日为家人欢聚团圆之期，探亲访友，月下团聚，赏月、吃月饼，共享天伦之乐。

one of China's traditional holiday festivals. Since 2008, it has been listed as a national legal holiday. It is a time when families reunite, visit friends and relatives, admire the full autumn moon, eat moon cakes, and share the joy of family reunions.

例句：

因为古代中国文化的影响，**中秋节**已传到东南亚的其他地区。

Example Sentence:

Due to ancient Chinese cultural influence, many people in Southeast Asia also celebrate the Mid-Autumn Festival.

月宫 *Yuegong;* Moon Palace

中国古代神话中月神居住的宫殿，也称“广寒宫”“蟾宫”。传说射日英雄后羿从西王母处得来不死之药，其妻嫦娥食后成仙，飞入月宫并从此

The palace inhabited by the Moon Goddess in Chinese tales, also called the Guanghan Palace or Chan Palace. It is said that Houyi (the hero who shot the nine suns) obtained a pill from the Queen Mother of the West that could grant immortality. His wife Chang'e ate it and became a celestial being. She flew to the moon and became the Moon Goddess, and has lived there ever since. According to the tale, other celestial beings also live on the moon including the Moonlight Goddess (also called

定居下来，被奉为月神。根据传说，月宫里还住有月神太阴星君(也称“月光娘娘”)、伐树不止的吴刚和一只玉兔。这些神话意象也渐渐渗入人们的生活，民间习俗、文学作品、艺术品等都有月宫、嫦娥、玉兔这些意象，北京航空航天大学建立的“月宫一号”实验装置也是取名于此。

the Moonlight Empress), a jade hare, and a man named Wu Gang who was banished to the moon to chop trees for eternity. These tales have become popular folklore, and the images of Chang'e, the jade hare, and the Moon Palace exist in many folk customs as well as in literature and artworks. The artificial life support space ecosystem known as "Moon Palace 1," which was created by Beijing University of Aeronautics and Astronautics, was named after the tale.

例句:

唐明皇游**月宫**的故事流传极广，唐代多部笔记小说都有记载，后世还被搬演为戏曲。

Example Sentence:

There is a popular story about Emperor Tang Xuanzong visiting the Moon Palace which was mentioned in several diary novels written during the Tang Dynasty (618-907), and later became adapted into traditional Chinese operas.

广寒宫 *Guanghan Gong;* Guanghan Palace

参见“月宫”。

See *Yuegong* (Moon Palace).

蟾宫 *Chan Gong;* Toad Palace

汉族神话传说中月宫有一只三条腿的蟾蜍，而后人也用蟾宫指月宫。参见“月宫”。

Legend of the Han ethnic group has it that there is a three-leg toad on the moon. So the moon is also called the Chan (Toad) Palace. See *Yuegong* (Moon Palace).

兔儿爷 *Tu'r Ye;* Rabbit God

北京中秋节传统手工艺品。兔儿爷的形象来源于月宫里的玉兔，据说有一年京城闹瘟疫，嫦娥仙子派玉兔下凡帮助人们治病。玉兔化成人形，挨家挨户帮助很多人治好了病。为了感谢玉兔，人们用泥塑造了可爱的玉兔形象并施彩饰，尊称为“兔儿爷”。每到农历八月十五中秋节那一天，北京家家都要供奉他，给他摆上

A popular handicraft from Beijing for the Mid-Autumn Festival. The Tu'r Ye figure comes from the folk tale about the Jade Rabbit in the Moon Palace. Legend has it that a plague struck Beijing one year, and Chang'e (the Moon Goddess) sent the Jade Rabbit down to the human world to cure the disease. The Jade Rabbit transformed itself into a human shape and went from door to door helping the sick. The people were so grateful to the Jade Rabbit that they made colored clay figurines of the rabbit. The figurines come in a variety of adorable postures, and people respectfully call them "Tu'r Ye." Every year on the fifteenth day of the eighth lunar month (the Mid-Autumn Festival), Tu'r Ye used to be worshipped in each household in Beijing. He is offered fruits and vegetables for the peace and

好吃的瓜果菜豆，用来酬谢他给人间带来的吉祥和幸福。兔儿爷是北京最具代表性的非物质文化遗产之一。

happiness he brought to the world. Tu'r Ye is one of Beijing's most well-known intangible cultural heritage characters.

例句：

兔儿爷已经成为北京中秋节形象大使，一则因为它是最具地域代表性的民俗符号，二则它具备玩赏趣味，可以为节日增添喜庆祥和的气氛。

Example Sentence:

Tu'r Ye has become the icon of Beijing's Mid-Autumn Festival, as it is a representative of the city's folk customs and adds a fun touch to the festival.

祭月 *jiyue;* moon worship

汉族中秋节习俗之一，又称"拜月"。有一种说法起源于周朝的祭月活动。中秋节夜晚，在月亮未升起时，人们先朝月初的方向把月神图像贴好，摆好祭品；待到月亮升起时，便烧香恭祀神灵享用，以求月神保佑。

One of the traditional customs believed to be the origin of the Mid-Autumn Festival of the Han ethnic group. Worshipping the moon could be dated back to the Zhou Dynasty (1046-256 BC). Common customs of moon worship on the night of the Mid-Autumn Festival entail hanging paintings of the Moon Goddess in the direction where the moon will rise, and prepare offerings. When the moon rises, people burn incense to worship the Moon Goddess for protection.

例句：

月亮的神秘性和生命及宇宙的韵律紧密挂钩。**祭月**这种在不同时期分布广泛的文化，产生了大量的象征及神话。

Example Sentence:

The mystery and beauty of the moon has enthralled mankind since ancient times, and moon worship has produced rich symbolism and mythology in many different cultures around the world.

赏月 *shangyue;* appreciating the moon

中国民间中秋节习俗，指在中秋之夜欣赏当空之月，以及在月下宴饮吟诗等活动。俗传赏月始于汉代，至宋代赏月之风最盛。每逢中秋佳节，

A folk custom observed during the Mid-Autumn Festival. It includes a series of activities such as dining, drinking wine, and reciting poetry in the moonlight. The custom of appreciating the moon is believed to take shape in the Han Dynasty

天高气爽，明月高悬，千家万户便于庭院中、楼台上，摆上月饼、水果、花生等，合家团圆，饮酒赏月。月圆象征着人间的团圆和生活的圆满如意。

(206 BC-AD 220), and became quite popular during the Song Dynasty (960-1279). During this time, families usually come together and eat moon cakes, fruit, and peanuts in the courtyards or pavilions and also drink alcohol while they appreciate the moon. For Chinese people the full moon symbolizes family reunions and happiness.

例句：

中秋之夜，我们仰望天空如玉如盘的朗朗明月，期盼远在他乡的亲人能够一起**赏月**。

Example Sentence:

During the Mid-Autumn Festival, we gaze up at the round, silver moon and hope to reunite with our kinsfolk from afar and appreciate the moon with them together.

博饼 *bobing; moon cake dice game*

中国闽南及台湾地区特有的中秋节习俗。相传，中秋“博状元饼”是郑成功屯兵鼓浪屿时为解士兵的中秋相思之情、鼓舞士气而让人发明的一种游戏。博饼游戏用六粒骰子投掷结果组合来决定参与者的奖品，传统的奖品为大小不同的月饼，设状元奖和其他奖项。博饼后来演变成一种娱乐活

A dice game played during the Mid-Autumn Festival in southern Fujian Province and Taiwan region of China. Legend has it that the game was created thanks to Zheng Chenggong (1624-1662), a famous general who retook Taiwan from foreign occupation in 1661. While stationed at Gulangyu Island off the coast of Fujian Province, he had the game invented to help relieve his soldiers of their

动，代代流传下来，形成了如今闽南和台湾地区独具特色的民间习俗。

homesickness during the Mid-Autumn Festival and build up their morale. The game determines the prizes of mooncakes of different sizes according to the results of the dice. Later, the game became popular and has been handed down from generation to generation, forming a unique folk custom in southern Fujian and Taiwan.

例句：

中秋佳节之际，闽南人都喜欢邀亲朋好友或者同事聚在一起，围桌"**博饼**"，无论博到什么等级都能赢取奖品，热闹非凡。

Example Sentence:

People from southern Fujian would invite family members or colleagues to play moon cake dice game during the Mid-Autumn Festival. It's a very joyous occasion where all participants would end up with some rewards.

嫦娥奔月 *Chang'e Benyue;* Chang' e Flying to the Moon

中国古代神话。传说的版本很多，其中之一为嫦娥本是后羿之妻，后羿射下九个太阳后西王母赐其不老仙药，但后羿不舍得吃下，就交于嫦娥保管。后羿门徒逢蒙觊觎仙药，逼迫嫦娥交出仙药，嫦娥情急之下吞下仙药，便向天上飞去。当日正是八月十五，月亮又大又亮，因不舍后羿，嫦娥就停在了离地球最近的月亮，从此长居广寒宫。后羿回家后心痛不止，于是每年八月十五便摆下宴席对着月亮与嫦娥团聚。这个爱情悲剧代代相传至今。

An ancient Chinese folk tale. There are many versions of the tale. One of them goes that a long time ago the earth had ten suns. It was very hot and people could not live. One day, a man named Houyi—who was considered the world's best archer—shot down nine suns so it would not be so hot. As a reward, the Queen Mother of the West gave him a pill of everlasting life. Houyi entrusted the pill to his wife Chang'e. One of his evil apprentices named Pang Meng wanted to take away the pill. To stop him, Chang'e swallowed the pill, and immediately her body floated up to the sky. It was the fifteenth day of the eighth lunar month and the moon was full and bright. Chang'e decided to stop at the moon where she was fated to stay forever. From that time on, on the evening of that day each year, Houyi would prepare a delicious meal under the moon to remember her. The tragic love story has been passed down from generation to generation.

例句：

“**嫦娥奔月**”的神话源自古人对星辰的崇拜。

Example Sentence:

The myth of Chang'e flying to the moon is derived from the worship of the stars by ancient Chinese.

吴刚伐桂

Wu Gang fa gui;
Wu Gang chopping the osmanthus tree

中国古代神话。相传汉代有一人姓吴名刚，因为醉心修炼仙道而不专心学习，被天帝遣送到月宫砍伐桂树。宫中月桂高五百丈，树创随合，因此吴刚只好永无休止地砍树。吴刚伐桂比喻劳役、工作无休无止，无法摆脱。

An ancient Chinese myth related to the Mid-Autumn Festival. Legend has it that a woodcutter named Wu Gang lived during the Han Dynasty (206 BC-AD 220) and wanted to be immortal. However, Wu Gang was very lazy and did not like to work, so the Heavenly Emperor decided to teach him a lesson. He planted an immortal osmanthus tree on the moon, and told Wu Gang he could become immortal if he could cut down the tree. However, after each cut of his axe, the tree healed itself, leaving Wu Gang never able to finish the task. The phrase of "Wu Gang chopping the osmanthus tree" is used to refer to a laborer whose work is endless and can never be completed.

例句：

恶毒的继母天天都让女孩儿干活，从早干到晚，真是**吴刚伐桂**，永无出头之日。

Example Sentence:

The evil stepmother forced the girl to work from dawn till dusk, much like Wu Gang chopping the osmanthus tree, a task which had no end.

月饼 *yuebing;* moon cake

中国中秋节的节令食品，中式烘焙糕点之一。中国有中秋祭月的古老习俗，明代开始，圆圆的月饼成为中秋不可缺少的祭品，也成为人们互相赠送的节令食品。月饼呈圆形，中秋节时全家分吃，象征着团圆和睦，因此也称“团圆饼”。清代以后，月饼的制作工艺和质量有了较大提高，品种也不断增加，与各地饮食习俗相融合，发展出广式、京式、苏式等各种口味的月饼，饼皮有的酥脆，有的绵软，馅料有甜有咸，成为四季常备的精美糕点。

A traditional Chinese pastry eaten during the Mid-Autumn Festival. During the Ming Dynasty (1368-1644), moon cakes became a part of ancient traditions of worshipping the moon. People made moon cakes and gave them as gifts during the festival period. Moon cakes are round and symbolize reunion (*tuanyuan*), so they are also known as "*tuanyuan* cakes." After the Qing Dynasty (1616-1911), the process of making moon cakes greatly improved, and new recipes were added to suit the tastes of people all around China, such as Cantonese, Beijing style, and Jiangsu style. The moon cake crust can be crispy or soft, and the flavors

现在祭月的风俗已经慢慢消失，但中秋全家团圆分享月饼和以月饼馈赠亲友的习俗仍很盛行。

can be sweet or salty. Now, the moon cake has become a regular pastry enjoyed all year round. Moon-worshipping traditions have gradually disappeared, but families gathering for the Mid-Autumn Festival still give each other moon cakes and enjoy eating them during the holiday.

例句：

秋收季节，瓜果飘香，亲朋好友之间馈赠**月饼**，阖家团圆，共赏明月，增加了中秋的人情之美。

Example Sentence:

In the fall harvest season, the air is filled with the fragrance of ripe fruits. Friends give each other moon cakes, gather with their families, and enjoy each other's company with a view of the full moon.

团圆饼 *tuanyuan bing;* tuanyuan cake; family reunion cake

参见“月饼”。

See *Yuebing* (moon cake).

例句：

月饼也被称为**团圆饼**。

Example Sentence:

Moon cakes are also known as family reunion cakes.

重阳节 *Chongyang Jie; Chongyang Festival; the Double Ninth Festival*

中国民间传统节日之一，即农历九月九日。“九”这个数字被人们认为是“阳数”。9月9日这天，月和日都逢九，两个阳数重叠起来，所以这一天被称为“重阳”。重阳节有很多习俗，如游玩、登高、插茱萸、赏菊花、饮菊花酒等。数字九还有长寿之意，因此重阳节也被视为老年节。过重阳节的许多风俗始于战国时代，相沿至今。该节日于2006年被列入第一批国家级非物质文化遗产代表性项目名录。

A traditional Chinese folk festival which falls on the ninth day of the ninth lunar month. According to the *Book of Changes*, the number 9 is considered a "yang" number. Therefore, the ninth day of the ninth lunar month is called *chong yang* (double *yang*). There are many customs during the Double Ninth Festival such as outdoor excursions, climbing, wearing cornel, appreciating chrysanthemum flowers, and drinking chrysanthemum wine since the ninth lunar month is traditionally known as the month to appreciate chrysanthemums. The number 9 also has the meaning of longevity, so it is also regarded as the elderly's day. Many customs of the Double Ninth Festival date back to the Warring States Period (475-221 BC), and some are still observed today. In 2006, the festival was included in the first batch of National Intangible Cultural Heritage List.

例句：

重阳节是关注健康和长寿的传统民间节日，也是拜访老人和亲朋好友、出门享受好天气的好机会。

Example Sentence:

The Double Ninth Festival is a traditional folk holiday with an emphasis on health and longevity. It's a great opportunity to visit the elderly, relatives, and friends and go outside to enjoy the good weather.

重阳糕 *Chongyang gao; Chongyang cake*

汉族节日糕点食品，俗称“花糕”。以米粉蒸成，面上撒有肉丝果脯。如今重阳节吃重阳糕的风俗仍十分盛行，年轻人都以此糕赠送老人以示敬老。

A cake traditionally eaten by the Han people during the Double Ninth Festival in China, also known as *huagao* (flowery cake). It is steamed with ground rice and topped with a layer of bean paste, candied fruits, and red and green fruits. Nowadays, the custom of eating the cake remains popular, and young people often give this cake to the elderly as a gift to show respect.

例句：

吃**重阳糕**是重阳节重要的活动，但是中国北部和南部的做法差异很大。

Example Sentence:

Eating Chongyang cake is an important part of the celebration of the Chongyang Festival throughout China. Customs on preparing the cake, however, differ substantially in northern and southern China.

插茱萸 *cha zhuyu:* picking and wearing cornel

汉族民间节日风俗。茱萸是中国一种特有的树木，其果实和根常入中药。插茱萸是重阳节的一项重要内容，指将采来的新鲜茱萸戴在头上。也有用茱萸制囊佩于身的，认为能驱邪治病，寄托离情别意，又有祝颂延年益寿的含义。

A folk custom observed by the Han people during the Double Ninth Festival. Cornel is a tree native to China, and its fruit and root bark are often used in traditional Chinese medicine. During the festival, people often go out and pick fresh cornel and wear it in their hair. Also, a scented sachet stuffed with cornel can be worn on clothing. It is believed that the scented sachet can exorcise evil spirits and treat various diseases. It also can be given as a gift, expressing friendship and love in separation, and wishing someone longevity.

例句：

在秋天的农历九月初九重阳节，人们举行各种活动来庆祝，如登高和**插茱萸**。

Example Sentence:

The Double Ninth Festival falls on the ninth day of the ninth lunar month. There are various interesting activities to celebrate the festival such as climbing and picking and wearing fresh cornel.

赏菊花 *shang juhua;* appreciating chrysanthemums

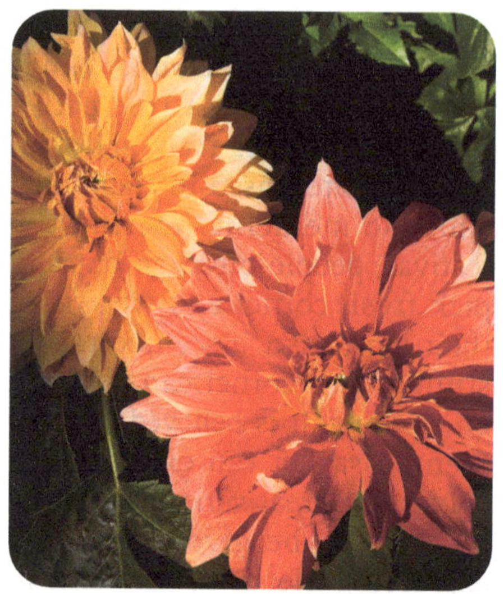

汉族民间节日风俗。在中国民俗中，菊花象征长寿，从三国魏晋以来，重阳聚会饮酒、赏菊赋诗流传很久，赏菊也就成了重阳节习俗的重要组成部分。因此，重阳节又称“菊花节”。

A popular folk custom observed by the Han people during the Double Ninth Festival. In Chinese culture, chrysanthemums symbolize longevity. Since the Three Kingdoms Period (220-280), appreciating chrysanthemums, drinking chrysanthemum wine, and composing poetry have been a fashionable pastime during the Double Ninth Festival as chrysanthemums are in bloom during this time. Therefore, the Double Ninth Festival is also called the Chrysanthemum Festival.

例句:

因为重阳节处在秋天中期，恰逢菊花盛开，因此**赏菊**和饮菊花酒特别盛行。

Example Sentence:

Because chrysanthemums are in full bloom during the autumn Double Ninth Festival, appreciating chrysanthemums and drinking chrysanthemum wine are popular during this time.

祭海神 *ji haishen;* worshipping the Sea God

旧时汉族渔民祭祀风俗，流行于中国沿海地区。新船下水，渔民在船舱中点香烛、焚纸锭、供祭品，面向大海磕头，祈求太平。该习俗自唐朝便有文字记载，各地区习俗亦有所差别。

A folk custom observed by fishermen of the Han ethnic group, which was popular in the coastal areas of China in olden days. When a new ship was about to set sail on the sea, fishermen prepared incense sticks, paper ingots, and sacrificial offerings. They then kowtowed to the sea, praying for a peaceful voyage. This custom has been recorded in the Tang Dynasty (618-907) and varies from region to region.

例句：

祭海神的故事在诗人、哲学家、历史学家和人类学家的作品中都有提及。

Example Sentence:

Stories about worshipping the Sea God appear in the works of poets and philosophers, historians, and anthropologists.

寒衣节 *Hanyi Jie;* Hanyi Festival; Winter Clothing Festival

中国北方民间传统节俗。该节日在农历十月一日，象征冬天的第一天，意为天气冷了，给去世的亲人送些纸钱买衣服过冬。这一天，家家户户都要备好供品、香火、纸钱等，到先祖坟上给死去的亲人烧纸

A folk traditional festival in northern China. The Winter Clothing Festival falls on the first day of the tenth lunar month, and symbolizes the first day of winter when the weather is getting cold. On this day, people burn incense and prepare sacrificial offerings such as paper clothing and joss

衣和纸钱，故又俗称“寒衣节”。各地习俗略有差异。

paper, which is burned and sent to the deceased. The custom has slight differences between regions.

例句：

寒衣节是怀念逝者和先祖的一个历史悠久的传统节日。

Example Sentence:

The Winter Clothing Festival is a traditional holiday with a long history when Chinese people cherish the memory of and pay respects to the deceased and their ancestors.

烧纸钱 *shao zhiqian; burning joss paper*

民间传统祭祀风俗，起源于汉代。人们相信纸钱就是死者所去的另一个世界里的钱，烧纸钱可以让死者在那个世界里有钱使用。该习俗其实是一种对死者的悼念，如今在民间依然盛行。烧纸钱还用于祭祀各种神灵的仪礼上。

An ancient folk sacrificial custom which dates back to the Han Dynasty (206 BC-AD 220). People believed that paper money could be used by the deceased in the netherworld, but it needed to be burned in order to be sent to them. Instead of burning real money, joss paper was used to represent the money instead. The custom is also a way of mourning the deceased, and is still popular today. Burning joss paper is also used in rituals to worship various gods.

例句：

烧纸钱是中国传统道家习俗，将纸钱等供给神和逝者在阴间使用。

Example Sentence:

Burning joss paper is a traditional Chinese Daoist custom that "sends money" to gods and the deceased in the afterlife.

冬至节

Dongzhi Jie;
Dongzhi Festival; Winter Solstice

汉族传统节日，源于汉朝，兴起于唐宋。冬至是二十四节气之一，一般在每年农历的十二月二十二日。冬至日最短，此后日子一天天长起来。这天，家人会团聚，祭祀先祖，如同过节一般。东北、河北、河南等地则有冬至吃饺子的习俗。相传汉朝医生张仲景还乡时看到百姓受冻，便以羊肉和一些祛寒药材为馅，用面皮包成像耳朵的样子，做成寒耳汤施舍给百姓吃。百姓吃完后果然治好了冻伤。冬至吃饺子习俗一直流传至今。

A traditional festival of the Han ethnic group, originating in the Han Dynasty (206 BC–AD 220) but flourishing during the Tang and Song dynasties. The Winter Solstice is one of the 24 solar terms, and it usually falls on the twenty-second day of December. The day of the Winter Solstice is the shortest of the year, and the days afterwards grow longer. Family members reunite and worship their ancestors, just like other festivals. There is also the custom of eating dumplings in northeast China, and Hebei and Henan provinces. Legend tells the story of the renowned Han Dynasty doctor Zhang Zhongjing who, upon returning home and seeing cold villagers with ear frostbite, made a hot soup with mutton and herbs. He made flour dumplings in the shapes of ears with the ingredients, and gave the dumplings to the villagers. After eating, they became warm, and their frostbite was cured. The custom of eating dumplings during the Winter Solstice is still popular today.

例句：

二十四节气之一的**冬至节**是中国的传统节日，通常在 12 月 21、22 或者 23 日，而非固定的一天。

Example Sentence:

The Winter Solstice is one of the 24 solar terms, and is a traditional Chinese festival. It usually falls on the twenty-first, twenty-second, or twenty-third day of December.

三门祭冬

Sanmen jidong;
Sanmen winter worship

浙江省三门县各乡镇在冬至节举行的拜冬祭祖的民俗活动。其内容包括祭天、拜祖、祝寿、老人宴等在内的多种仪式。三门祭冬是保存至今冬至节气民俗活动的代表，表达了对天地自然与祖先的感恩之情。2014 年 12 月，三门祭冬被列入国家非物质文化遗产代表性项目名录。

A folk custom observed during the Winter Solstice in townships of Sanmen County, Zhejiang Province. There are various ceremonies such as offering sacrifices to heaven, worshipping ancestors, offering birthday greetings, and holding banquets for the elderly. The custom encompasses traditional folk activities during the Winter Solstice by Chinese to express gratitude for nature and ancestors. In December 2014, the custom was included on the National Intangible Cultural Heritage List.

例句：

三门祭冬具有鲜明的地方文色彩。

Example Sentence:

The Sanmen winter worship is a distinctive local tradition.

数九歌

Shu Jiu Ge;
the "Nines of Winter Song"; "9 Nines Song"

民间记述冬季寒冷变化的歌谣，亦称"九九歌"。"数九寒天"是从冬至逢壬日算起，每九天算一"九"，一直数到"九九"八十一天。流传比较广泛的一首数九歌是："头九二九，闭门抄手；三九四九，冻破石头；五九六九，河岸看柳；七九河开，八九雁来；九九寒尽，春暖花开。"每"九"的内容根据生活生产实践反映天气变化规律和农事活动而定。据说人们创作数九歌是为了提振度过漫长严冬的信心，并记录冬季的节令。

An ancient Chinese folk song describing the weather changes every nine days beginning from the Winter Solstice for nine consecutive periods, also called *Jiu Jiu Ge* (the 9 Nines Song). One popular 9 Nines Song goes, "In the first and second nine days, people keep doors closed and keep their hands in pockets/in the third and fourth nine days, even stones can be frozen off/in the fifth and sixth nine days, willows on the banks start to sprout/in the seventh and eighth nine days, the swallows come back/and after the ninth nine days, spring has come and all the flowers are in bloom." The content of each nine days may differ as determined by weather patterns and farming activities in different regions. It is believed people created the song to lift their spirits during the long and harsh winter period, and also to keep track of winter's progress.

例句：

数九歌是记录冬至之后九段时间里每九天的气候变化的民谣。

Example Sentence:

The "Nines of Winter Song" is a popular folk song tracking weather changes for the nine periods of nine days following the Winter Solstice.

九九消寒图 *jiu jiu xiaohan tu;* The 9 Nines Drawing for Winter

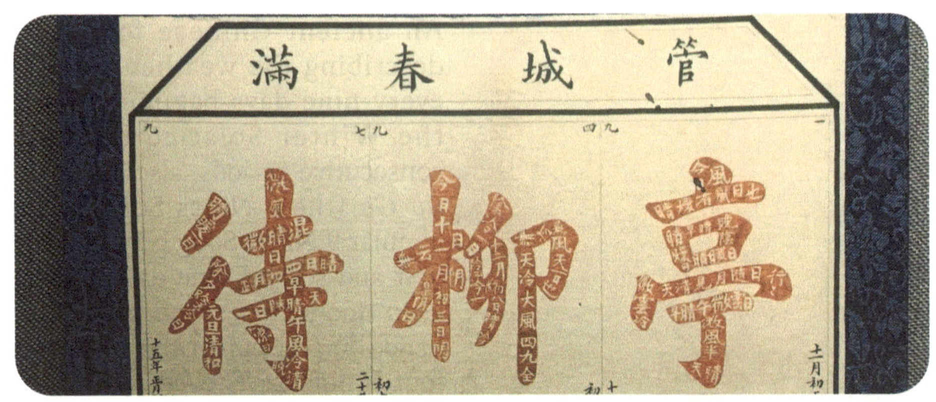

旧俗冬至后计算春暖日期的图，亦称“九九消寒画”。古代汉族一种以九计日的方法，旧俗以冬至为“入九”，九九八十一天后，天气转暖，寒意消除，故名。其方法是以画梅、画圆圈、填影格字等多种形式来记载“数九”日期和预测气温，直至寒尽。

A drawing, painting, or calligraphy work used to calculate the coming of spring after the Winter Solstice. In ancient times, the Han people used to count winter days in periods of 9 days which would begin with the Winter Solstice and continue for 9 terms. After the subsequent 81 days, spring will have arrived, and the weather will be warm. The dates of 9 nine-day periods and corresponding temperatures estimated would be recorded till the end of winter by way of drawing a plum or a circle, or filling in a grid.

例句：

如今，人们不再画“**九九消寒图**”来计算冬日的余日，只是将其作为一种民间习俗和文化遗产来保存和挖掘。

Example Sentence:

Nowadays, people no longer make the 9 nines drawings to count the remaining days of winter, but still maintain it as a folk custom and cultural heritage.

赤豆粥 *chidou zhou;* red bean porridge

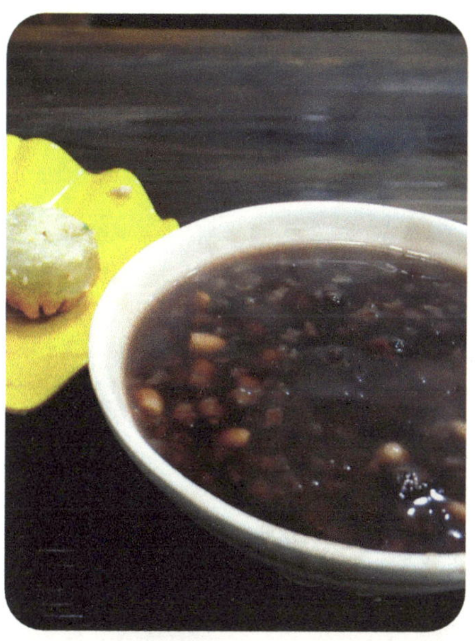

民间认为冬至日吃赤豆粥可以避邪。传说共工氏（中国古代神话中掌控洪水的水神）有不才子死于冬至这天，变为疫鬼，他畏惧赤豆，所以人们于冬至日做赤豆粥用以避瘟鬼。从医学角度而言，赤豆有清热解毒、消肿、通气、止吐等功效。

It is believed that eating red bean porridge during the Winter Solstice can dispel evil spirits. Legend has it that Gonggong (the ancient God of Water in Chinese mythology) had a son who died during the Winter Solstice and became a ghost spreading plagues everywhere. However, the son hated red beans, so people made red bean porridge during the Winter Solstice to keep him away. In terms of medical effects, red beans can clear heat and toxins from the body, prevent infection, enhance circulation, and help treat nausea.

例句：

根据传统，**赤豆粥**是人们于一年当中最短的一天（冬至）吃的食物。

Example Sentence:

According to old customs, red bean porridge is eaten on the shortest day of the year—the Winter Solstice.

冬至饺子 *Dongzhi jiaozi;* Winter Solstice dumplings

民间有“冬至大如年”之说，流传着丰富多彩的冬至饮食习俗。中国北方地区在冬至这一天有吃饺子的习惯。冬至饺子的习俗来源可参见词条“冬至节”。

A traditional food eaten during the Winter Solstice, popular in northern China. See the entry “Dongzhi Festival” for more.

例句：

民间素有“**冬至饺子**夏至面”的说法。冬至后，天气变得越来越冷，人们喜欢吃热气腾腾的饺子。

Example Sentence:

The custom of “eating dumplings at Winter Solstice and noodles at Summer Solstice” has a long history in China. People enjoy eating hot dumplings following the Winter Solstice as the weather gets colder and colder.

腊八节 *Laba Jie;* Laba Festival

中国民间传统节日。先秦时期就有，在十二月举行腊祭活动以祭祀祖先和神灵并祈求来年丰收吉祥的习俗。后来东汉时期佛教传入中国，十二月初八这天又是佛祖释迦牟尼成道之日，于是腊八节增添了新的内涵。吃“腊八粥”是腊八节最重要的习俗，沿袭至今。

A Chinese folk traditional festival, celebrated on the eighth day of the twelfth lunar month (*layue chuba*, or *laba* in short). Dating back to the Spring and Autumn Period and the Warring States Period, the festival was originally a time to offer sacrifices to ancestors and gods, and pray for a good harvest and good fortune in the coming new year. When Buddhism spread into China, the day was celebrated as the day Buddha became enlightened. This has given the Laba Festival new connotations. As the most important custom during the festival, having *laba* porridge is still popular today. See the entry "*laba* porridge" for more.

例句：

腊八节在南北朝时才有了固定的日期。

Example Sentence:

The Laba Festival did not become a celebration with a fixed date until the Southern and Northern Dynasties (420-589).

腊味 *la wei*; cured meat and fish

腊鱼、腊肉、腊肠、腊鸡等食品的总称，用中国独有的最原始的肉类深加工技术制成，可保存很长时间。每年冬季，一般是腊月，人们把鸡、鸭、鱼、肉等食品用盐腌后熏干或风干，存罐密封，数日后开启即可制成腊味食品。腊味在中国历史悠久，早在周朝就有相关记载。

The umbrella term for cured fish, bacon, sausage, and chicken. It is a unique traditional Chinese food made using the age-old meat-processing techniques, and thus can be preserved for a very long time. In the twelfth lunar month (the *la* month) every year, people salt chicken, duck, fish, meat, and other foods and then cure and season them. After being sealed for dozens of days, they will be made into cured foods. Cured meat and fish have a long history in China and can be found in historical records as early as the Zhou Dynasty (1046-256 BC).

例句：

粤菜有很多**腊味**菜肴。

Example Sentence:

Cantonese (Yue) cuisine has many dishes featuring cured meat and fish.

腊八粥 *laba zhou;* laba porridge

腊八节节令食品，用多种食材熬制的粥，亦称“七宝五味粥”。腊八粥的食材丰富多样，各地有所差异，一般有黄米、白米、江米、栗子、红江豆、去皮枣泥等。熬制腊八粥很有讲究，一般腊月初七晚上开始洗米、泡果、拨皮、去核，半夜时分开始用微火炖，一直炖到第二天清晨才算熬制好。腊八粥不仅好吃，还有丰富的营养价值，可以补血补铁、预防便秘、调理高血压、滋补五脏等。腊八节吃腊八粥习俗已有一千多年的历史，现在仍流行于中国大部分地区。

A porridge made from a variety of cereal and other ingredients normally eaten during the Laba Festival, also known as "porridge with seven ingredients and five flavors." The abundant ingredients of *laba* porridge vary from place to place, but it usually contains millet, white rice, glutinous rice, chestnuts, red beans, mashed and peeled jujubes, and other ingredients. Traditionally there are many steps in making the porridge. On the night before the festival, the rice is washed, the fruit is soaked, and the peels and kernels of the fruits are removed. Cooking the porridge begins at midnight over a low fire, and should be stewed until the next morning. *Laba* porridge is not only delicious, but also rich in nutrition. It can supplement blood and iron substances, prevent constipation, regulate blood pressure, and nourish internal organs. The custom of eating *laba* porridge has a history of more than a thousand years and is still popular in most parts of China.

例句：

受佛教影响，**腊八粥**也被称为“佛粥”，规模较大的寺庙一般会在腊八节向信徒提供腊八粥。

Example Sentence:

With the introduction of Buddhism in China, *laba* porridge is associated with the Enlightenment of Sakyamuni Buddha. *Laba* porridge is therefore also called *fo zhou* (Buddha porridge). Large Buddhist temples often offer *laba* porridge to Buddhist followers during the Laba Festival.

腊八豆腐 *laba doufu;* laba tofu

安徽黟县风味特产，也是腊八节的节令食品。每年在春节前夕的腊月初八，黟县家家户户都要晒制豆腐，民间将这种自然晒制的豆腐称作“腊八豆腐”。先用上等小黄豆做成豆腐并切成圆形或方形的块状，然后抹上盐水，在上部中间挖一小洞，放入适量食盐，经熬煮、滤渣、定型、压制、烘烤、晾晒六道工序纯手工制作而成。成品色泽黄润如玉，入口松软，咸中带甜，又香又鲜。“腊八豆腐”平时用草绳悬挂在通风处晾着，吃时摘取，一般可晾放三个月不变质、变味，既可单独吃，也可与肉类同炒、同炖。如今，腊八豆腐制作技艺已被列入黄山市市级非物质文化遗产名录。

A folk specialty of Yixian County, Anhui Province, normally eaten during the Laba Festival. The tofu is made with fine yellow soybeans and then cut it into round or square blocks and smeared with salt water. A small hole is dug in the middle of the upper part where a proper amount of salt is added. It is hand-made through six processes including cooking, slagging, shaping, pressing, baking, and drying. The color of the finished product is golden, and the texture is soft. It is salty and sweet, delicious, and fresh. *Laba* tofu is usually hung with straw ropes in a ventilated place where it can be taken off when cooking. It can be kept dried for three months without deteriorating or becoming sour. It can be eaten alone or fried and stewed with meat. Today, the technique of making *laba* tofu has been included into the municipal intangible cultural heritage list in Huangshan, Anhui Province.

例句：

腊八豆腐在晾晒过程中加入虾米等配料味道更佳。

Example Sentence:

Laba tofu tastes even better if it is flavored with dried sea shrimps and other seasonings while drying.

腊八蒜 laba suan; laba garlic

腊八节节令食品，冬季小菜，主要流行于中国北方，多腌制于腊月初八，故称“腊八蒜”。腌制腊八蒜的材料非常简单，即醋、大蒜瓣儿、密封器皿。腊八前后，将蒜剥皮后洗净晾干，挑选完整、饱满的蒜瓣放进干净的容器内，然后倒入醋，封口后静放在阴凉处，蒜瓣儿变成翠绿色即可食用。腊八蒜保存期长，口味偏酸微辣，脆嫩可口。

A winter seasonal dish of pickled garlic usually prepared during the Laba Festival, which is mainly popular in northern China. The ingredients of pickled garlic are vinegar and garlic cloves. During the festival, people wash, dry, and clean the garlic and select whole, well-formed, and unblemished garlic cloves. After rinsing, the garlic cloves are soaked in vinegar in a jar and then sealed and placed in the shade. The dish is done when the garlic turns emerald green. It tastes slightly sour, spicy, crisp, and delicious, and has a long shelf life.

例句：

腊八蒜蒜汁是一种很好的调料，风味独特。

Example Sentence:

Garlic sauce can serve as a seasoning with its unique flavor.

腊八面 *laba mian;* laba noodles

腊八节节令食品，地方传统面食，流行于陕西关中地区。以面和各种小菜为原料，将和好的面擀成薄片，切成菱形长条，待水烧开后，先把浸泡过的黄豆、小米、粉条、木耳、黄花菜等小菜一一放入，煮至快熟时把面片抻成长条放进去，面条煮熟后再把准备好的肉臊子放进去，加入盐、辣椒酱等调料，即做成美味的腊八面。

Customary noodles eaten during the Laba Festival, which is popular in central Shaanxi. Kneaded dough is rolled into thin slices and cut into rhombus strips. Soaked soybeans, millet, vermicelli, woodear mushrooms, daylilies, and other side dishes are then cooked, with the noodles added to the boiling soup. After the noodles are cooked, people usually add cooked diced meat, salt, pepper sauce, and other seasonings.

例句：

陕北人在腊八节时通常喜欢吃**腊八面**而不喝腊八粥。

Example Sentence:

People living in the northern part of Shaanxi Province generally prefer *laba* noodles over *laba* porridge during the Laba Festival.

泼水节 *Poshui Jie;* Water-Splashing Festival

傣族传统节日，也是傣历新年，流行于云南地区，一般在公历四月中旬举行，为期三到四天。布朗、德昂、阿昌等民族也庆

A traditional festival popular in Yunnan Province marking the new year of the Dai ethnic group. The festival usually lasts three or four days, and generally takes place from April 13-15 according to the

祝泼水节。一般认为，泼水节起源于印度，已经有七百余年的历史，泼水活动表示洗去身上过去一年的污秽，祝福新的一年幸福平安。节日期间还要举行放高升、丢包、跳孔雀舞等活动。2006 年 5 月 20 日，云南省西双版纳傣族自治州申报的傣族泼水节被列入第一批国家级非物质文化遗产名录。

Gregorian calendar. The Blang, De'ang, and Achang ethnic groups also celebrate this festival. It is generally believed that the Water-Splashing Festival originated from India and has a history of more than 700 years. Water splashing represents washing away all the filth from the past year and wishing for a happy and peaceful new year. During the Water-Splashing Festival there are many festive activities such as setting off *gaosheng* (a kind of fireworks), the bag-throwing game, and peacock dance performances. On May 20, 2006, the Water-Splashing Festival of the Dai Autonomous Prefecture of Xishuangbanna in Yunnan Province was included in the first batch of the National Intangible Cultural Heritage List.

例句：

泼水节展示了中国傣族的传统文化，东南亚许多民族也过泼水节。

Example Sentence:

The Water-Splashing Festival showcases the traditional culture of China's Dai ethnic group, and many other ethnic groups throughout southeast Asia share this festival.

丢包 *diu bao; bag-throwing game*

云南傣族节日风俗，年轻未婚小伙子与姑娘寻觅佳偶的游戏。“包”是象征爱情的信物，由女子用花布精心缝制，内裹木棉籽，四周镶花边，中间绣鸳鸯或孔雀。丢包时，未婚男女青年分成两排，相隔三四十步，向自己喜欢的人丢包，花包飞来飞去，最后感情交流到一定程度时双方悄悄退场去幽会。

A folk activity typically played during festivals among the Dai ethnic group of Yunnan Province, and also a courtship game for unmarried young people. The bag is a token of love, carefully stitched by women and contains kapok seeds which are surrounded by lace, with a peacock or mandarin ducks normally embroidered into the material. Young people are divided into two rows, about thirty or forty steps apart. Participants then throw the bags to the ones they like. After the game is over, both sides will sneak off the field and find a private place to date.

例句:

丢包是傣族节庆期间举行的一项体育活动，帮助青年男女寻求爱情。

Example Sentence:

Bag-throwing game is an event usually held during the festivals of the Dai ethnic group to help young people find love.

孔明灯 *Kongming deng;* Kongming lanterns

一种古老的中国手工艺品，用纸糊制的可以靠热空气上升到空中的灯笼。据传最初由诸葛孔明发明用于传递军事信息，因此而得名。入夜后，人们将灯烛点燃，放到纸灯内，灯即飞向天空。放孔明灯有祈愿、祝福之意，中国的许多地区都有这个节日习俗。

An old Chinese handicraft, which is a paper lantern that can fly into the sky in hot air. According to the legend, the Kongming lantern is named after Zhuge Kongming, a renowned military strategist during the Three Kingdoms Period (220-280), who designed such lanterns to pass secret messages regarding military intelligence. When night falls, people light candles and place them in these paper lanterns which then float into the sky. Lighting up the

Kongming lanterns signifies prayers and blessings for the coming new year, and is popular in many regions of China.

例句：

泼水节期间，燃放的**孔明灯**像星星一样照亮天空。

Example Sentence:

During the Water-Splashing Festival, Kongming lanterns are lit and light up the sky like stars.

放高升

fang gaosheng;
setting off fireworks on high-rising bamboo framework

云南傣族节日风俗，泼水节活动之一。高升是傣民用竹子和火药自制的一种大型爆竹，常在泼水节期间的夜晚燃放，寓意风调雨顺，五谷丰登，步步高升。爆竹置于竹子搭成的高升架上，接上引线燃放。每年泼水节都会举办“放高升”活动，以庆祝傣历新年。

One of the activities during the Water-Splashing Festival in which the Dai people set off large fireworks at night to pray for good weather and a bumper harvest. These fireworks are made by adding gunpowder into bamboo which enables them to go high up into the air. They are placed on a tall bamboo structure from which they are ignited and set off. The Dai people of Yunnan Province do this during the Water-Splashing Festival to celebrate the New Year.

例句：

傣家人欢度自己的新年时，总少不了**放高升**这一重要活动。

Example Sentence:

The Dai people always set off fireworks to celebrate their New Year.

孔雀舞 *kongque wu;* peacock dance

A thousand-year-old folk dance favored by the Dai ethnic group, which is particularly popular in parts of Yunnan Province where Dai people reside. Regarded as the "sacred bird" by the Dai people, peacock symbolises happiness and good fortune. When dancing, dancers wear costumes with patterns of peacock feathers. Dancers elegantly imitate a peacock's movements with the tempo of the elephant-foot drums and cymbals (*mangluo*). The Dai people create the elegant and unique dance to express their pursuit of beauty and wishes for a happy life.

有上千年历史的、最受傣族人民喜爱的民间舞蹈。广泛流传于云南傣族聚居区。孔雀是傣族人心目中的"圣鸟"，是幸福吉祥的象征。孔雀舞就是舞者身着饰有孔雀图案的衣裤或长裙随着象脚鼓、铓锣的节奏摹仿各种优美的孔雀动作的一种舞蹈，表达了傣族人民对美的追求和对幸福生活的向往。

例句：

相传1000多年前，傣族首领召麻栗杰数在舞蹈中模仿孔雀的姿态，后经历代民间舞蹈家加工创作形成了今天的**孔雀舞**。

Example Sentence:

Legend has it that more than a thousand years ago, Zhaomali Jieshu, the leader of the Dai ethnic group, imitated the elegant gestures of the peacock in a dance. Later generations of folk dancers improved the peacock dance and carried it into the present day.

那达慕大会

Nadamu Dahui;
Naadam Festival; Naadam Fair

中国蒙古族历史悠久的传统节日，是人们为了庆祝丰收而举行的文体娱乐大会。每年七、八月在草原上举行，为期三日左右。牧民从四面八方远道赶来参加大会，进行物资交流，品尝美食和佳酿，观看或参与赛马、摔跤、射箭活动。那达慕大会深受当地各族群众的喜爱，是蒙古族文化传统的重要载体，2006 年被列入第一批国家级非物质文化遗产名录。

A traditional festival of Mongolian people to celebrate bumper harvest, usually held as a grand event featuring recreational and sports activities. Naadam is generally a three-day festival, usually held out on the grasslands in July or August. People gather from great distances to attend the market and livestock fair to trade goods, eat and drink together, and enjoy the fair activities and events. Naadam is also the time for the three main competitions of horseback riding, wrestling, and archery. Favored by the local people, Naadam Festival is an important part of Mongolian culture. In 2006, it was included in the first batch of China's National Intangible Cultural Heritage List.

例句：

那达慕大会以赛马、摔跤、射箭三项比赛著称。

Example Sentence:

The Naadam Festival is famous for the competitions of horseback riding, wrestling, and archery.

蒙古式摔跤 *Menggushi shuaijiao;* Mongolian wrestling

蒙古族传统体育项目，那达慕大会主要活动之一。蒙古式摔跤有鲜明的民族特色。比赛在天然草原或土地上举行，采取单淘汰制，无时间限制，膝部以上任何部位触地即输掉比赛，一跤定胜负。摔跤手不受年龄、地区、体重限制。比赛前先推一位族中的长者对摔跤手进行编排和配对，担任裁判。摔跤手身着皮质短上衣，系腰带，穿肥大的裤子和高腰马靴，手舞足蹈跃入场内。该活动在蒙古族民间广为流传，历史悠久，2006年被列入第一批国家级非物质文化遗产名录。

A traditional sport of Mongolian people, and one of the main events of the Naadam Festival. The competition is usually held on a grassy field, with no weight or age restrictions. There is no time limit, and the wrestler who touches the ground with any part of the body above the knees loses the match. Victory or defeat is determined once and the loser is not allowed to compete again. Wrestlers enter the arena together with traditional singing and dancing, wearing traditional leather jackets, belts, fat pants, and high leather boots. A senior member of the tribe is selected to arrange and pair the wrestlers and to act as referee. The sport is widely popular among the Mongolian people and has a very long history. In 2006, it was included in the first batch of China's National Intangible Cultural Heritage List.

例句：

蒙古式摔跤在规则、方法、服装、场地等方面都有自己的特点。

Example Sentence:

Mongolian wrestling has its own characteristics in terms of rules, styles, clothing, and venues.

蒙古族射箭 *Mengguzu shejian;* Mongolian archery

蒙古族传统体育项目，那达慕大会主要活动之一。射箭主要分为静射和骑射。静射射手在规定距离处立于固定地点轮流发射，每人9支箭，分3轮射完，以中靶次数多少评定胜负。骑射即跑马射箭，射手策马急驰，瞄靶劲射。比赛跑道为4米宽、85米长、0.66米深的一条沟，共设3个靶位，分固定靶和活动靶，一般规定每人射9支箭，分3轮射完，以中靶的箭数来评定比赛结果。射箭运动深受蒙古族人民的喜爱。

A traditional sport of Mongolian people, and one of the main events of the Nadaam Festival. There are two major archery events: fixed target, and horseback. For fixed target archery, the archers aim at a fixed target from a fixed position. Each person shoots nine times in three rounds and the final outcome is evaluated by the total score. For horseback archery, archers ride on horses and shoot at targets while riding. The track is four meters wide, 85 meters long and 0.66 meters deep. Archers shoot at three different targets which are either fixed or moving. Each archer shoots 9 times in 3 rounds. The final outcome is evaluated by the total score. Archery is a favorite sport of the Mongolians.

例句:

壮观的草原风光，常吸引清帝与蒙古王公在此野宴，观看摔跤和**射箭**。

Example Sentence:

During the Qing Dynasty (1616-1911), emperors and Mongolian princes would often hold banquets out on the grasslands while viewing the wrestling and horseback archery competitions.

蒙古族赛马 *Mengguzu saima;* Mongolian horse race

蒙古族传统体育娱乐项目，是那达慕大会的主要活动之一。蒙古族的赛马方式多种多样，一般有奔马赛和走马赛。奔马赛一般为直线赛跑，比的是马的速度，先达终点者为胜。赛程一般为20、30、40公里，男女老少均可参加，年轻人较多。为了减轻马的负荷，不论老少，大都不备马鞍，不穿靴袜。走马赛技巧性很强，参赛骑手多为有经验的男性长者或中年人。参赛的走马必须经过严格训练，参赛时要备精美的鞍辔，既快又稳，姿势和谐、优美，并最先到达者为胜。

A traditional sports and entertainment activity of Mongolian people, and one of the main events during the Nadaam Festival. There are many forms of Mongolian horse race, among which are long-distance race and horseback competition. The former consists of a straight race usually from 20 to 40 kilometers. It is a long-distance race displaying the speed of the horse. Riders can be any age or gender, but most are young people. In order to be as light as possible, most participants don't ride with saddles or wear boots or extra clothing. The latter features the skills of the riders with their horses. The riders are mostly experienced adults who are trained for this event. The riders are dressed well and the horses should be equipped with fine saddles. The horses must endure extensive training to maintain a fast but stable speed as well as a harmonious and graceful gait during the race. The pair that reach the finish line first will be declared winner.

例句：

中国有五十六个民族，每个民族有自己独特的音乐，《赛马》便是一首著名的描绘**蒙古族赛马**场景的二胡曲。

Example Sentence:

Fifty-six ethnic groups in China have their own unique music. The song "Horse Racing" is a famous piece of music performed with the *erhu* depicting a Mongolian horse race.

白节 *Bai Jie;* Mongolian New Year

蒙古族一年中最大的节日，相当于汉族的春节，又称“查干萨日”，时间与汉族的春节一致。白节一般为期三天，有的持续好几个星期。蒙古族自古尚白，以白色为纯洁、吉祥、神圣之色，故称春节为“白节”。节日期间，有守岁、贴蒙古文对联、祭祖、探亲访友、到喇嘛寺祈年、寺院举行诵经仪式等习俗。这一传统节日起源于元代，一直延续至今，蒙古国也过此节。

A grand festival of the Mongolian ethnic group, also called the Tsagaan Sar in Mongolian (meaning "white moon"), and is widely celebrated in China's Inner Mongolia Autonomous Region. It is the Mongolian New Year based on the traditional lunisolar Mongolian calendar and falls on the same dates with the Spring Festival of the Han people, and many customs are similar to the Spring Festival. The festival generally lasts three days, though some may continue celebrating for many weeks. Mongolians consider the color white representing happiness, purity and holiness. Therefore the festival is called White Festival. During the festival, there are such customs as staying up late or all night on New Year's Eve, pasting Mongolian couplets on walls and doors, worshipping ancestors, visiting friends and relatives, praying in the lamasery for a good harvest, and performing chanting ceremonies in the temple. The traditional festival originated from the Yuan Dynasty (1206-1368) and has continued to this day. Mongolia also celebrates this festival.

例句：

蒙古族**白节**习俗和活动与汉族春节有许多相似之处。

Example Sentence:

The Mongolian New Year shares many similar customs and activities with the Spring Festival of the Han people.

查干萨日 *Chagansa Ri;* Tsagaan Sar

参见“白节”。

See *Bai Jie* (Mongolian New Year).

祭敖包 *ji Aobao;* worshipping at Aobao (sacred stone piles)

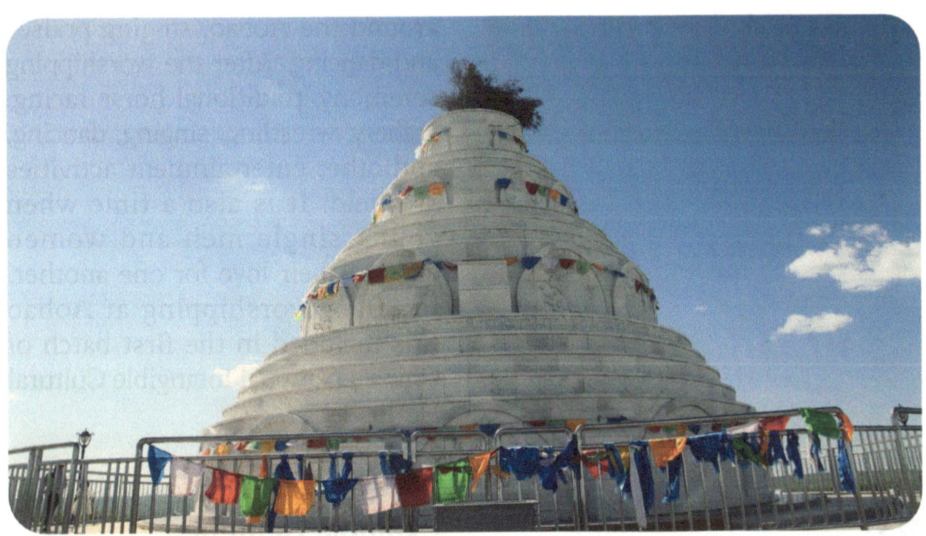

蒙古族传统祭祀活动。敖包是蒙古族的崇拜物，以石块堆积

Mongolian traditional worshipping activity. Aobao is a cone-shaped stone pile usually set up on the tops of hills or mountains. These stone

而成，通常建在山顶或丘陵之上，形状多为圆锥形，高低不等。这些敖包古时曾经作为地标帮助牧民辨认方位，后来逐渐带有宗教寓意。不同的部族建自己的敖包，象征祭祀祖先，并表达对自然和大地的敬重。每年五、六月祭敖包，以祈望风调雨顺，粮食丰收，牛羊健壮，国泰民安。祭敖包时，人们献上煮熟的牛、羊、猪肉等供品，并在敖包上洒白酒、奶酪等。牧民围绕敖包行跪拜礼，唱求神歌，跳吉祥舞。祭祀仪式结束后还举行传统的赛马、射箭、摔跤、唱歌、跳舞等娱乐活动，青年男女则在活动中互表爱慕之情。2006年被列入第一批国家级非物质文化遗产名录。

piles once served as landmarks to help herdsmen identify their locations in ancient times, but later came to carry more religious meanings. Different clans would construct their own Aobaos, which came to symbolize worship of their ancestors and also respect for nature and the land around them. Each year in May or June is the time when Mongolian people pray to these Aobaos for favorable weather and good crops, healthy cattle and sheep, and peace across the country. At the time of worship, people offer cooked beef, mutton, pork, and other offerings, and sprinkle white spirits and cheese on the Aobao. Herdsmen worship on bended knees around the Aobao, singing praises and dancing. After the worshipping ceremony, traditional horse racing, archery, wrestling, singing, dancing, and other entertainment activities are held. It is also a time when young single men and women express their love for one another. In 2006, worshipping at Aobao was included in the first batch of China's National Intangible Cultural Heritage List.

例句：

每年牧民们远道而来**祭敖包**，祈望风调雨顺，平安富足。

Example Sentence:

Each year, herdsmen travel great distances to worship at their clan's Aobao for good harvests, prosperity, and a peaceful life.

三月三 *San Yue San;* Song Festival Held on the Third Day of the Third Lunar Month

中华民族传统节日，在中国西南的壮族、苗族、瑶族等少数民族地区节日气氛尤为隆重和盛大。每年农历三月三，壮族青年男女在街上、河边或宴会上欢聚，举行对歌比赛。人们身着盛装携带五色糯米饭去赶歌圩、赴歌会，参加对歌比赛，还有抛绣球、放花炮、演壮戏等活动，场面十分壮观。歌圩旁摊贩云集，出售各种日用百货。三月三不仅是弘扬民族文化的盛会，亦是民族经济交流的盛会。

A traditional festival of China, which is most celebrated in the southwest regions where the Zhuang, Miao and Yao ethnic groups reside. Young men and women gather on the third day of the third lunar month each year in the streets, along the riversides or in banquets and sing songs to one another. It has since become a regular singing festival. People dress in traditional costumes and attend singing parties, bringing unique dishes such as five-colored glutinous rice. People throw embroidered balls, set off firecrackers, and perform dramas. Vendors gather and sell all kinds of daily goods. The festival is not only a grand party to celebrate unique customs, but also a grand gathering of ethnic cultural and economic exchange.

例句：

广西各地景区将举办丰富多彩的“**三月三歌节**”活动，展示广西各地美景和民俗风情。

Example Sentence:

The colorful “Song Festival on the Third Day of the Third Lunar Month” will be held in scenic spots in Guangxi Zhuang Autonomous Region to showcase the beauty and folk customs there.

藏历年 *Zangli Nian;* Tibetan New Year; Losar

藏族最重要的传统节日，藏历新年，又称"洛萨节"。进入藏历十二月人们便开始置办吃穿用玩等年货。节前几天家家户户扫尘，并在灶房正中的墙上用干面粉画上"八吉祥徽"。除夕晚上各家吃传统食物。初二开始，亲戚好友互相拜年。节日期间，人们跳弦子舞、锅庄舞或赛马、射箭、摔跤，孩子们燃放鞭炮，大家一起喝青稞酒、酥油茶，互相祝酒，尽情欢乐。藏历年于2011年列入第三批国家级非物质文化遗产名录。

The traditional Tibetan new year festival, the most important festival for the Tibetan ethnic group, also called Losar based on its Tibetan pronounciation. During the twelfth month of the lunisolar Tibetan calendar, people begin to prepare for the holiday by thoroughly cleaning the house and preparing festival clothing. Eight auspicious symbols are drawn on the house walls with white powder such as dry flour. On New Year's Eve, families eat traditional foods. On the second day of the new year, people visit friends and relatives. During the holiday, people participate in various festive events such as dancing, horse racing, archery, and wrestling while children set off firecrackers. Everyone drinks highland barley wine and buttered tea, toast each other, and have fun. In 2011, Losar was included in the third batch of China's National Intangible Cultural Heritage List.

例句：

藏戏是**藏历年**的重要组成部分。

Example Sentence:

Tibetan Opera is an important part of the Tibetan New Year celebrations.

林卡节 *Linka Jie;* Linka Festival

藏族传统节日，一般在每年藏历五月一日至五月十五日，节期不定。“林卡”在藏语中指绿意盎然的郊外公园或林地。“过林卡”是藏族人最普遍的休闲娱乐方式。节日期间，藏族人民身着盛装，带着青稞酒、酥油茶及各种美味食品涌向郊区的林卡，搭起帐篷，吃喝玩乐、唱歌跳舞，举办各种娱乐活动，如打藏牌、讲故事、看电影，或者举办射箭、摔跤等传统体育比赛项目。

A traditional Tibetan festival usually held from the first to the fifteenth day of the fifth month on the Tibetan calendar each year. "Linka" in Tibetan means a garden with flourishing trees and flowers in the suburbs. The Linka Festival is a time when friends and families meet together in parks or other such places for outdoor entertainment. People usually drink highland barley wine, buttered tea, and eat all kinds of delicious food. People put up tents where they eat, drink, sing, dance, play cards, tell stories, watch movies, etc. People also hold traditional sports events such as archery and wrestling competitions.

例句：

林卡节期间，藏族朋友和家人团聚， 在户外野餐，并进行其他户外娱乐活动。

Example Sentence:

The Tibetan Linka Festival is a time when Tibetan friends and families spend time together outdoors picnicking and enjoying fun outdoor activities.

雪顿节 *Xuedun Jie;* Xuedun Festival; Shoton Festival

藏族传统节日，每年藏历六月三十日开始，历时四至五天。“雪顿”在藏语中意为酸奶宴，因此雪顿节也称“酸奶节”；因为雪顿节期间有隆重、热烈的藏戏演出和规模盛大的晒佛仪式，所以有人也称之为“藏戏节”“展佛节”。雪顿节有三百多年的历史，据传佛教禁止喇嘛在藏历四月至六月期间离开寺庙，以防践踏随着天气变暖而复苏的昆虫和植物，六月底开禁后，老百姓会为他们酿酸奶，并举行郊游野宴和欢庆活动，主要包括展佛、藏戏表演、赛牦牛和马术表演等。节日期间，藏区全员放假，人们身着盛装在园内尽情宴饮，载歌载舞。雪顿节在西藏节日中隆重程度仅次于藏历新年。该节于2006年列入第一批国家级非物质文化遗产名录。

A traditional festival in Tibet, beginning on the thirtieth day in the sixth month of the Tibetan calendar and lasting four to five days. *Xuedun* (or Shoton) means a banquet of Yogurt, so the festival is also called the “Yogurt Festival”. It got other names such as “Tibetan Opera Festival” for its rich performance of Tibetan Opera, and “Sunning the Buddha Festival” for its spectacular ceremony of sunning the Buddha image. It dates back to over three hundred years ago when Buddhist monks were forbidden to leave the monastery from the fourth to the sixth month so as to avoid treading on any living creature, including insects or plants which just awoke to the warm climate. At the end of this period, local people would prepare yogurt as well as entertainment activities for them. Activities include Sunning the Buddha, Tibetan Opera performances, and yak and horse races. During the holiday, Tibetans dress in traditional clothing, picnic in the park, sing and dance. As one of the largest and grandest local festivals, the Shoton Festival showcases deep Tibetan traditions, ranking second only to the Tibetan New Year. In 2006, it was included in the first batch of China’s National

Intangible Cultural Heritage List.

例句：

作为**雪顿节**的序幕，晒佛是最令人瞩目的仪式，五彩丝绸织成的巨幅释迦牟尼唐卡可以覆盖整个山坡。

Example Sentence:

Sunning the Buddha, as the prelude of the Shoton Festival, is the most spectacular ceremony: A giant multi-colored silk Thangka (tapestry) bearing the image of the Buddha is unrolled in the sun, covering almost the entire hillside.

酸奶节 *Suannai Jie;* Yogurt Festival

参见“雪顿节”。

See *Xuedun Jie* (Xuedun Festival).

藏戏节 *Zangxi Jie:* Tibetan Opera Festival

参见“雪顿节”。

See *Xuedun Jie* (Xuedun Festival).

展佛节 *Zhanfo Jie;* Sunning the Buddha Festival

参见“雪顿节”。

See *Xuedun Jie* (Xuedun Festival).

古尔邦节 *Gu'erbang Jie;* Corban Festival; Eid al-Adha

伊斯兰教重要节日之一，又称“宰牲节”，时间在伊斯兰教历12月10日，是中国信仰伊斯兰教的回、维吾尔、哈萨克、东乡、柯尔克孜、撒拉、塔吉克、乌孜别克、保安、塔塔尔10个民族共同的节日。除会礼、宰牲奉祭外，人们还宴请亲友，有的地方还举行盛大的歌舞晚会。

One of the major Islamic festivals, also called the Festival of Sacrifice. It falls on the tenth day of the twelfth month of the Islamic calendar. In China, the Hui, Uygur, Kazak, Dongxiang, Kirgiz, Salar, Tajik, Uzbek, Bonan, and Tatar ethnic groups who profess Islam celebrate this festival. In addition to attending worshipping ceremonies and making animal sacrifices, people hold banquets for friends and family and at some places hold grand evening parties.

例句：

会礼是**古尔邦节**的核心内容之一，以诵读《古兰经》和纪念先知、赞美圣贤为主要内容。

Example Sentence:

Attending worshipping ceremonies is one of the important activities of the Corban Festival. At this ceremony, people recite passages from the Koran, commemorate the prophecy, and eulogize sages.

宰牲节 *Zaisheng Jie;* Festival of Sacrifice

参见“古尔邦节”。

See *Gu'er Bang Jie* (Corban Festival).

开斋节 *Kaizhai Jie;* Lesser Bairam; Kaizhai Festival

伊斯兰教重要节日之一，是中国信仰伊斯兰教的回、维吾尔、哈萨克、东乡、柯尔克孜、撒拉、塔吉克、乌孜别克、保安、塔塔尔10个民族共同的节日，中国新疆称之为“肉孜（Roza，波斯语，意为斋戒）节”。伊斯兰教规定，成年穆斯林在伊斯兰教历的每年九月封斋一个月，每日自黎明前至日落后禁绝饮食、房事和一切非礼行为。斋月始于九月初新月出现到十月初见到新月结束。开斋节即庆祝一个月的斋功圆满完成的日子，穆斯林在次日拂晓即吃食物，以示开斋，然后沐浴更衣前往清真寺参加会礼，济贫施舍，并互致节日问候。人们还会亲访友，互赠节日食品，并举办歌舞活动欢度节日。

A lavish and important Islamic festival celebrated by 10 Islamic ethnic groups in China, namely the Hui, Uygur, Kazak, Dongxiang, Kirgiz, Salar, Tajik, Uzbek, Bonan, and Tatar ethnic groups. In China's Xinjiang Uygur autonomous region it is called Roza (Rozah), which is a transliteration from Roza in Persian, which means "to fast." According to the tenets of the Islamic faith, every year in the ninth month of the Islamic calendar, adults need to fast for a month from sunrise to sunset. People must abstain from eating, drinking, sexual activities, and any impolite acts for the entirety of the day. After the last day of the fast, people celebrate having completed the month-long fast. This takes place on the day of the tenth month of the Islamic calendar. With the approach of dawn on this day, Muslims will eat again, bathe, change clothes, and then go to the mosque. There they will pray, give money to the poor, and send holiday greetings to one another. People will also visit relatives and friends, bring food as gifts, and sing and dance to celebrate the festival.

例句：

由于伊斯兰教历（中国称“回历”）为阴历，比公历每年约少 10 天，所以**开斋节**对应的公历时间每年均不相同，有可能出现在春夏秋冬任何一个季节。

Example Sentence:

Since the Islamic calendar is based on the moon, it is roughly ten days shorter than the Gregorian calendar every year. As a result, the corresponding date on the Gregorian calendar differs each year, and Lesser Bairam can fall on a date of any of the four seasons.

肉孜节 *Rouzi Jie;* Roza Festival; Rozah Festival

参见“开斋节”。

See *Kaizhai Jie* (Lesser Bairam).

火把节 *Huoba Jie;* Torch Festival

彝、白、傈僳、纳西、拉祜等少数民族的民间传统节日，被称为“东方狂欢节”。该节日起源于人们对火的自然崇拜，最初的目的是期望用火驱虫除害，保护庄稼生长。节日主要活动是燃火把绕村寨游行，到田边举行烧天虫仪式。节日期间，人们身着盛装，男女青年聚会歌舞，谈情说爱，还举行斗牛和其他娱乐活动。不同的民族举行火把节的时间不尽相同，大多是在农历的六月二十四日。

A traditional festival celebrated by such ethnic groups as the Yi, Bai, Lisu, Naxi, and Lahu. It has been called the "Eastern Carnival" and is derived from ancient fire worship ceremonies. Fire is employed during the festival with the original intent of expelling insects and ridding disasters in order to protect the crops. The principal activity involves parading a procession of torches around the village and down to the fields where a ceremony is held to burn away insects. During the festival, people wear rich attire and young folks gather together to sing and dance, perhaps even sparking future romances. Bullfighting and other activities are held as well. The time when the Torch Festival is held varies among different ethnic groups, but for the most part it is held on the twenty-fourth day of the sixth lunar month.

例句：

彝族**火把节**于每年农历六月二十四日举行，流行于云南、贵州、四川等彝族地区。

Example Sentence:

The Yi ethnic group Torch Festival is held every year during the twenty-fourth day of the sixth lunar month. It is popular throughout places Yi people reside, such as Yunnan, Guizhou, and Sichuan provinces.

东方狂欢节 *Dongfang Kuanghuan Jie;* Eastern Carnival

参见“火把节”。

See *Huoba Jie* (Torch Festival).

三月街 *Sanyue Jie;* Third Month Fair

云南省大理白族自治县白族民间传统集会。每年农历 3 月 15 日至 21 日在大理举行，已有 1000 多年历史。该节日最初带有宗教活动色彩，后来逐渐演变为一个盛大的物资交流会。节日期间除贸易外还举行赛马、射箭、赛龙舟和民间歌舞等活动。该节于 2008 年列入第二批国家级非物质文化遗产名录。

A traditional Bai ethnic group gathering in Dali Bai Autonomous Prefecture, Yunnan Province. Every year, from the fifteenth to the twenty-first day of the third lunar month, people converge on Dali. The festival originally had religious connotations dating back over 1,000 years, but over time it evolved into a grand meeting for exchanging supplies. Besides trade, the festival also features horse racing and archery. People also have dragon boat races and sing and dance. In 2008, it was included in the second batch of China's National Intangible Cultural Heritage List.

例句：

三月街不仅是大理白族人民的盛会，也吸引了附近其他民族和国内外慕名前来经商和观光旅游的客人。

Example Sentence:

The Third Month Fair is not only a vibrant gathering for the Bai ethnic group of Dali, but it also attracts people from other ethnic groups and from other parts of the country. People from other countries also converge on the site to do business and sightseeing.

人生仪礼

RITES OF PASSAGE

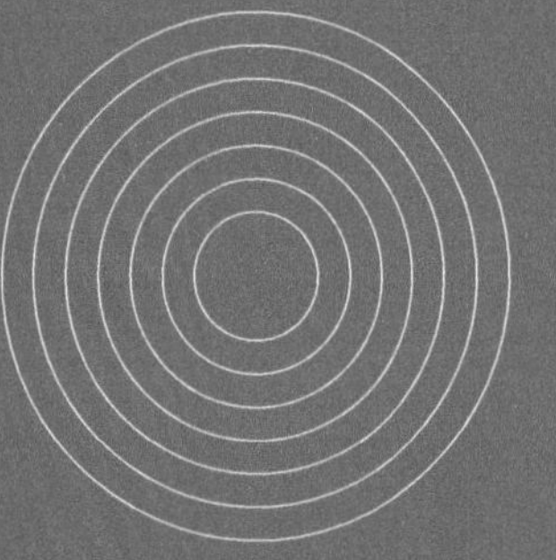

麒麟送子 *qilin song zi; qilin* sending a son

中国汉族民间祈子风俗。麒麟是民间传说中能带来祥瑞的仁兽。相传圣人伏羲、舜、孔子等降生时麒麟都曾出现，因此人们普遍认为求拜麒麟可以生育儿子且儿子大有出息。这一主题既见于图画、祝颂之辞，也见于儿童玩具、岁时活动，形成汉族独具一格的民俗文化事物。麒麟送子的图像多为童子手持莲花、如意骑在麒麟上，或仙女怀抱童子骑在麒麟上，多出现在年画、木刻、刺绣、陶瓷器、漆器等民间艺术作品中，表达人们对子孙满堂、多子多福的希冀。

A folk custom of the Han ethnic group to pray for sons. *Qilin*, an auspicious legendary animal in Chinese folklore, is said to have appeared when such ancient sages as Fuxi, Emperor Shun, and Confucius were born. Worshipping a *qilin* is thus generally believed to bring sons to the family and endow them with a bright future. The theme is often seen in pictures, blessings, toys, and festival activities. Pictures of "*qilin* sending a son" often depict a boy riding a *qilin* with a lotus and a *ruyi* (an S-shaped Chinese traditional ornamental object symbolizing good luck) in his hands, or a fairy on a *qilin* with a boy in her arms. They are often seen in New Year paintings, woodcuts, embroideries, porcelains, lacquer wares, and other folk artworks to express people's wishes for more descendants and greater happiness.

例句：

麒麟送子的传说在中国各地广为流传，且多出现在年画、刺绣等我国民间传统艺术作品中，宫廷用品则少见。

Example Sentence:

The story of "*qilin* sending a son" is very popular in China and the theme is often seen in New Year paintings, embroidery, and other traditional folk artworks, but it is seldom seen in imperial articles.

送子观音 *Songzi Guanyin;* Child-granting Guanyin; Child-bestowing Goddess of Mercy

中国民间崇拜的佛教神祇，俗称“送子娘娘”，是观音的化身之一。观音是佛教中救苦救难的菩萨，后与中国生育文化交融，逐渐形成了送子观音的专职形象，并成为中国民间观音信仰的主要功能之一。其形象多为观音怀抱一个婴儿或观音双手合十，前边站着一个童子。人们或到观音庙虔诚参拜或在家中供奉观音神像以求子，与之相关的宗教和民俗活动也非常丰富。

One form of Guanyin (Goddess of Mercy) who is believed to have child-bestowing abilities. Guanyin, the most widely beloved Buddhist bodhisattva in China for her infinite compassion and mercy, assumes the role of a fertility goddess after integrating with the Chinese childbearing culture. Child-granting Guanyin is generally portrayed as a young lady holding a baby or with her palms placed together devoutly with a boy in front. People pray to her in her temple or at home in front of her statue to bless them with sons to continue their family line. There are also variegated religious and folk activities related to this practice.

例句：

相传**送子观音**能保佑家庭和睦，婚姻美满，为妇女送子、助生，护佑小孩儿易养成人。

Example Sentence:

It is said that child-granting Guanyin blesses the family with harmony and marital happiness. She enables women to give birth to sons and serves as their patron during delivery and upbringing.

催生 *cui sheng;* heralding labor

中国民间生育习俗。生育在民间被视为传宗接代、家族繁衍的大事。妇女临近产期，娘家携带礼物前来探望，谓之“催生”。以往有面羊、面鹿催生之俗，如今北方不少地方尚有送催生馍的习惯。而南方则送鸡蛋等物，寄寓孕妇生孩子顺利。

A folk childbearing custom in China. To Chinese people, childbirth is vital to the continuation and prosperity of a family and a clan. When a pregnant woman is about to go into labor, her maiden family goes to visit her with specially prepared gifts. This practice is known as *cui sheng* (heralding labor). In the past, gifts sent on this occasion included lamb- and deer-shaped buns. Today, it is still customary in northern China to give buns to a woman before she goes into labor. In southern China, such gifts often include eggs. Such practices convey people's wishes for a smooth delivery.

例句：

催生这个习俗在中国由来已久，是一种比较简单的风俗，不同地域形式略有差异。

Example Sentence:

Heralding labor is an age-old Chinese tradition. It does not involve complicated procedures, and it varies slightly between different places.

添喜 *tian xi;* having a blessing; having a newborn baby

中国民间生育习俗用语，指婴儿降生。中国古代生男叫“弄璋之喜”，生女叫“弄瓦之喜”。今日有的地方仍称生男为“大喜”，生女为“小喜”。婴儿降生后，人们在产房或临街大门挂上红布等饰物，具有报喜和辟邪的意义。

A folk term in China to celebrate the birth of a newborn baby. In ancient China, having a boy was regarded as *nongzhang zhi xi* (joy of having a baby boy) and having a baby girl was regarded as *nongwa zhi xi* (joy of having a baby girl). Some regions in China refer to having a boy as "greater blessing," while having a girl is regarded as "lesser blessing." After a baby is born, the delivery room or the front door of the family's house is decorated with red cloth and other auspicious items to announce the good news and drive away evil spirits.

例句：

生育在中国民间被视为传宗接代、家族繁衍的大喜事，因此婴儿的降生被称为**“添喜”**。

Example Sentence:

To Chinese people, childbearing is vital to the continuation and prosperity of a family and a clan, so the birth of a baby is called *tian xi* (having a blessing).

弄璋之喜 *nongzhang zhi xi;* joy of having a baby boy

中国旧时民间生育习俗用语，指男婴降生，常用作贺词。"弄璋"源于男婴喜玩玉器的习俗，希望男婴长大后人品如玉璋那样高洁。

An ancient folk term in China used when a baby boy has been born. *Nongzhang* literally means "to play with a jade object." It comes from the early custom of giving a jade tablet to a baby boy to play with, expressing the wish for the boy to grow into a man as pure-minded and noble-minded as jade.

例句：

老张老来得子，大家都赶来恭贺他的**弄璋之喜。**

Example Sentence:

Lao Zhang had fathered a son at an old age. People congratulated him for his *nongzhang zhi xi* (joy of having a baby boy).

弄瓦之喜 *nongwa zhi xi;* joy of having a baby girl

中国旧时民间生育习俗用语，指女婴降生，常用作贺词。瓦是一种纺锤，弄瓦是希望女婴长大后勤俭持家，不辞辛苦。

An ancient folk term in China used when a baby girl has been born. *Nongwa* literally means "to play with a spindle." It comes from the custom of giving a spindle to a baby girl to play with, expressing the wish that the girl grow up into a hardworking, thrifty housewife.

例句：

恭喜霍少爷，夫人生了一个女孩儿，是**弄瓦之喜。**

Example Sentence:

Congratulations, Master Huo! Your wife gave birth to a baby girl. It is *nongwa zhi xi* (joy of having a baby girl).

坐月子 *zuo yuezi;* convalesce for a month following child delivery

中国民间生育习俗用语，指妇女产后用一个月的时间进行修养。坐月子是中国妇女产后既定的仪式性行为。由于产妇怀孕后期和分娩消耗了大量的体力，产后身体需要一定程度的恢复。"坐月子"就是在一个月内多卧床休息，并注意补充各种营养，如喝鸡汤、鱼汤等，以利产妇身体全面恢复和奶水充足。

A Chinese traditional postnatal practice. After delivery, the mother convalesces for one month to restore the tremendous amount of energy loss during the third trimester and delivery. During this month, she follows a special diet—including chicken soup and fish soup—and thoroughly rests to facilitate her full recovery and produce more milk for her baby.

例句：

旧时，**坐月子**有种种禁忌，例如月子期间不刷牙、不洗澡、不洗头，忌外出等，现在因为缺乏科学依据已经逐渐被摒弃。

Example Sentence:

According to traditional customs, during the month following child delivery, the mother is expected to refrain from brushing her teeth, taking a bath, washing her hair, and going out. These practices are seldom observed now due to lack of scientific evidence.

做三朝 *zuo sanzhao;* bathing on the third day

中国民间育儿旧俗，又称“洗三”。婴儿降生后第三天，接生婆在盛满用槐枝、艾叶熬成的汤水的大铜盆中为婴儿第一次洗浴，以祛除邪气。在给婴儿洗澡过程中及洗毕，都有一系列程序来祝愿孩子健康成长，福寿安康。

An old Chinese folk ceremony to celebrate childbirth, also referred to as the “third day cleaning.” Three days after a child was born, the midwife washed the baby in a big copper pot of water with scholar tree branches and mugwort. This would serve as the child’s first bath, which was believed to help dispel evil. Throughout the entire process, many ritual practices would be followed to wish the child good health and a long and peaceful life.

例句：

如今，婴儿通常是在出生后就洗澡了，因而民间一般不再举行**做三朝**的仪式了。

Example Sentence:

Nowadays, children are typically bathed right after birth. As a result, people no longer hold the ritual of bathing on the third day any more.

洗三 *xi san;* bathing on the third day

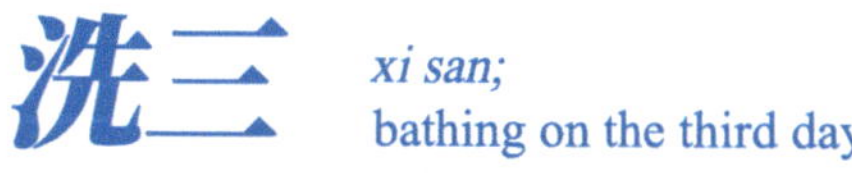

See *zuo sanzhao* (bathing on the third day).

添盆 *tian pen; filling the tub*

中国民间育儿旧俗。参加婴儿洗三仪式的亲友在婴儿洗浴前按照尊卑长幼顺序先往盆里添一勺清水，再往盆内放置钱币、喜蛋、枣等，接生婆根据亲友所投物品不同，口念不同的吉祥话，如若搁枣、栗子，就说“早立子”；若搁莲子，就说“连生贵子”。举行添盆仪式的目的是为了祝福婴儿。

An old Chinese folk ceremony to celebrate childbirth. In the past, a baby was given a bath three days after birth. The tub was filled with water one ladle at a time by the family and friends in the sequence of seniority, age and status. Next, they put coins, red-painted eggs, or dates into the tub. The midwife would speak lucky phrases according to the items they put in the tub with the intent of bestowing blessings upon the child. For example, if a person put in dates or chestnuts, the midwife would say “have a son soon” (with homophonic reference to the objects); if they brought lotus seeds, she would say “have one baby after another.”

例句:

添盆是做三朝仪式的一部分。

Example Sentence:

Filling the tub is a part of the ritual of bathing on the third day.

满月酒

manyue jiu;
celebration of a baby's first month

中国民间育儿习俗，即在婴儿满月时举行酒宴庆祝仪式。办满月酒，一是表示庆祝婴儿渡过人生第一个难关，二是让孩子与亲朋好友见面，接受大家的礼物，为孩子祈祷祝福。外婆会给宝宝肩膀上搭花线，脖颈上挂银质百家锁，寓意祝福外孙长命百岁，享受荣华富贵。请满月酒的主人需要提前告知亲朋，被邀请的亲朋需提前准备礼物，待满月酒当天送出。这一天，主人还会邀请理发师为孩子剃去胎毛，有人将婴儿胎毛制成毛笔留作纪念，此举预示孩子将来能"通文弄墨，才学出众"。

A Chinese childrearing ceremony in which parents hold a banquet to celebrate their baby turning one month old. During the party, the newborn baby is introduced to the extended family and friends for the first time. The celebration of a baby's first month is still practiced today. At the party, the new baby receives various gifts and blessings. The maternal grandmother puts colorful threads on the baby's shoulders and hangs a silver *baijia suo* (hundred-family padlock) on his or her neck as a blessing for the baby to live a long and prosperous life. Relatives and friends will also present gifts. The host will also invite a barber to shave the baby's fetal hair, which can be made into writing brushes, symbolizing the hope that the baby will be intelligent and talented in the future.

例句：

满月酒筵席上，亲朋好友一同举杯，庆祝家丁兴旺，预祝新生儿健康成长。

Example Sentence:

During the banquet for celebrating a baby's first month, friends and family raise their cups to wish the family prosperity and the newborn good health.

过百岁 *guo baisui;* celebrating the 100th day

中国民间育儿习俗，即在婴儿出生满一百天时举行庆祝活动，又称"过百日""百日礼"。在中国传统观念中，"百"是一个重要数目，有浓重的文化色彩，含有圆满、完全之意，因此，在婴儿出生一百天时，家长会邀请亲朋好友参加庆贺宴会，祝愿婴儿健康长寿。

A Chinese childrearing ceremony in which a celebratory banquet is held when an infant turns 100 days old. It is also known as "passing the 100th day (*guo bairi*)" or the "hundredth-day celebration (*bairi li*)."According to traditional Chinese notions,"100"is an important number which overflows with rich, important cultural implications of "consummation" and "completeness." Therefore, on an infant's 100th day, relatives and friends attend a celebratory banquet to wish the infant a long and healthy life.

例句：

潮汕地区**过百岁**时，亲友携食品、果蔬和小儿衣饰等礼品来贺，主人设宴款待。

Example Sentence:

In the Chaoshan region in east Guangdong Province, on the 100th day after an infant is born, the infant's parents would hold a banquet to entertain their relatives and friends who bring gifts for the baby such as food, fruits, vegetables, and baby clothes.

过百日 *guo bairi;* celebrating the 100th day

参见"过百岁"。但有些地方忌讳使用"过百日"，因为这

See *guo baisui* (celebrating the 100th day). But in some regions, this expression shall be used

个表述也可指人去世一百天，不吉利。

with caution as it can also refer to commemorating the 100th day after someone's death.

抓周 *zhuazhou;* item-grabbing test on the first birthday

中国民间传统育儿习俗，又称“试周”。在婴儿一周岁生日当天，父母会在婴儿面前摆放象征不同职业和才气的物件，如书、笔、算盘、弓箭、针线等，让婴儿选择。据说婴儿拿起的第一样东西会预示其性情爱好和未来有可能从事的职业。

A Chinese childrearing ceremony held on a child's first birthday, also called "testing on the first birthday." On that particular day, parents prepare some items which symbolize different occupations and talent, such as books, pens, abacus, bow and arrows, needles and threads. The baby is expected to choose from among those items. It is believed that the first item the baby picks up is indicative of his/her inclinations and hobbies as well as possible future careers.

例句：

现在**抓周**习俗仍然很盛行，但对很多家庭而言只是一种娱乐活动。

Example Sentence:

Nowadays, the item-grabbing test on a baby's first birthday is still prevalent, but mostly for fun.

添丁炮 *tianding pao;* firecrackers for newborns

中国江西客家人庆祝男性婴儿降生的民俗。添丁，预示着一家兴旺，历来是中国老百姓注重的大事。每年正月初二到元宵节期间，江西南部客家人聚集的村庄要约定好日子举行添丁炮民俗活动：村中最近一年中生了男孩儿的家庭大摆筵席，招待亲朋好友来喝添丁酒，客人前来祝贺时都要带来大盘鞭炮，燃放助兴。

A Hakka folk tradition in Jiangxi Province to celebrate a baby boy's birth. The birth of a baby boy has always been regarded as an important event by the Chinese people as it is seen as a sign that the family will become more prosperous. Between the 2nd and 15th day of the first lunar month, a folk event called *tianding pao* (firecrackers for newborns) is held on a chosen date. Families with newborn boys in the previous year hold grand banquets called *tianding jiu* (banquet for newborns) to treat their family and friends. The guests bring firecrackers as gifts and set them off to create a festive atmosphere.

例句：

燃放**添丁炮**是很热闹的场景。

Example Sentence:

Setting off firecrackers for newborns makes for a very lively scene.

长命锁 *changming suo;* longevity lock

中国传统育儿习俗。长命锁是用来祈求孩子健康成长、长命百岁的挂饰，也称“百家锁”。一般在新生儿满百日或周岁时挂在孩子脖子上，有的一直挂到十二岁或成年。其材质为金、银、铜、玉等，通常呈古锁状，寓意锁住生命，保佑平安。主流的长命锁以银质为主，锁正面一般刻有“长命富贵”“长命百岁”等吉祥祝语，另一面则有麒麟、老虎、金鱼、莲花、寿桃等吉祥图案，代表人们希望下一代健康平安成长的美好祝愿。民间认为长命锁由外婆、舅舅或干爹干妈送最好。

A pendant worn by newborns starting from the celebration of their hundredth-day or first birthday up to their 12th birthday or when they enter adulthood, as part of a Chinese folk custom about a child's growth. It is a symbol for health and longevity, and is often made of gold, silver, copper, or jade. Typically, it takes the form of an ancient lock, symbolizing a "locking" into life and embodying prayers for safety. Most of longevity locks convey auspicious wishes such as "a long life of abundance and decency" on the obverse and such lucky patterns as a *qilin*, tiger, goldfish, lotus, or peach on the reverse. It is said that it is best for the lock to be given by one's grandmother on the mother's side, maternal uncles, or nominally adoptive parents.

例句：

孩童脖子上挂的**长命锁**体现了长辈爱惜子孙、佑护生命的苦心。

Example Sentence:

A longevity lock is worn around a child's neck to symbolize protection and also the auspicious wishes for a bright future.

百家锁 *baijia suo;* families-blessed padlock; longevity lock

参见“长命锁”。古时百家锁为多家集银打造，民众认为集了百家银便可得到大家的保护，孩子容易养活。孩子戴上百家锁便是戴上了护身符，取牢锁不放之意，以祈求儿童长命百岁。

See *changming suo* (longevity lock). It was so named because in the old days, the materials for making the locks were donated by relatives and friends, symbolic of the belief that the baby who wore the pendant would be under the protection of all the donating families. This also hints at a wish for longevity. The lock is considered a protective talisman as it figuratively "locks" the child's life when it is worn.

例句：

麒麟送子是**百家锁**中最常见的图案。

Example Sentence:

One of the most common patterns on the families-blessed padlock is "*qilin* sending a son."

拴娃石 *shuanwa shi;* baby-fastening stone

中国民间习俗，是北方农民保护幼儿健康成长和镇宅避邪的物件。拴娃石是用石头雕刻而成的小石狮，因为主要放在炕头上，也叫“炕头石狮”，在陕西榆林、延安、渭北地区较为常见，在石匠众多的绥德县更为普遍。石狮最大的不过25厘米高，最小的仅3厘米。

A Chinese folk handicraft, also referred to as a stone lion on bed, as it is usually in the shape of a lion. It is a stone carving placed on the warmer end of a *kang* (a heatable brick bed), and can be 3 to 25 centimeters tall. In rural areas, when a baby starts to crawl, people will tie him or her to a stone lion with a red rope to prevent them from falling off the *kang*. A baby-fastening stone is

在农村，当婴儿学会爬行时，人们使用红绳将石狮与婴孩拴在一起，防止婴孩坠落炕下。特别是窑洞里的大炕与锅台是连在一起的，拴娃石可以防止小孩儿坠落到锅里，作用非常重要。“拴娃石狮”稚气、娇憨、顽皮的神态，如同孩子一样活泼可爱。拴娃石是孩子的伙伴，同时也有借助狮虎猛兽的神力镇宅避邪、保护婴孩健康成长的含义，还可作为室内陈设和装饰物。

extremely helpful in cave dwellings where the *kang* is connected to the kitchen top, as it prevents babies from falling into big woks. Stone lions are both childish and naughty in appearance, looking as lively and cute as a child. They are commonly used by farmers in northern China and seen in the cities of Yulin and Yan'an in Shaanxi Province as well as in the area north of the Weihe River, especially in Suide County, where many stonemasons reside. They are companions for children, and are also used as protection for the baby against evil and as ornaments for decorating rooms.

例句：

陕北的**拴娃石**一般从头顶到台座底部都刻有一些吉祥纹饰。这些纹饰代表着家人对新生命的关爱，也是一道孩童的护身符。

Example Sentence:

In the northern parts of Shaanxi Province, baby-fastening stones often have auspicious patterns at their bases. These patterns reflect the family's care and love for their children. In this sense, baby-fastening stones serve as protective talismans for children.

炕头石狮 *kangtou shishi;* stone lion on bed

参见“拴娃石”。

See *shuanwa shi* (baby-fastening stone).

小名 *xiaoming;* childhood name; nickname

中国民间习俗，又称“乳名”“奶名”。小名是父母给孩子起的昵称，与正式命名的大名相对；小名一般只在家庭内部和亲朋好友之间使用。旧时因医疗条件差，婴儿成活率低，为祈求孩子长大成人，起小名时往往采用卑贱的名字，如“阿牛”“阿狗”之类，盼望孩子平安成长。

A traditional folk custom, also known as *ruming* or *naiming*. A childhood name is a kind of nickname given to a child by the parents and is typically only used in the home by family members, relatives or close friends. In old times, the survival rate of infants was quite low due to poor medical conditions. As a result, people often chose humble childhood names such as “cow” or “dog” in hopes that their child would grow up safely.

例句：

汉武帝刘彻（前156年—前87年）**小名**刘彘，是汉朝的第五代皇帝。

Example Sentence:

Liu Che (156-87 BC), with the childhood name “Liu Zhi”, was the fifth Emperor of the Han Dynasty (206 BC-AD 220), and was known as “Emperor Wudi of Han.”

乳名 *ruming;* childhood name; nickname

参见“小名”。

See *xiaoming* (childhood name)

奶名 *naiming;* childhood name; nickname

参见“小名”。

See *xiaoming* (childhood name)

认干亲 *ren ganqin;* recognizing a nominally adoptive family

中国民间育儿习俗，指与没有血缘关系或婚姻关系的人结成类似亲属的关系。旧时民间生子生女后，或怕孩子娇贵，不好养活或是以前生子夭折，怕自己命中无子，往往借拜干亲来消灾免祸，保佑孩子健康成长。也有的是父母辈之间相处关系密切，希望通过认干亲来维系双方家庭之间的密切联系。认干亲时，孩子的父母一般会宴请宾客，备厚礼送给干亲家，孩子亦要跪拜叩头认干爹干娘；干爹干娘也会回赠礼物。认干亲使两家的关系自然地进入一种亲戚交往的序列之中。

A Chinese childrearing custom. It refers to forging a kinship between the child and those without a blood relationship or those not related via marriage. In former times, this custom was usually carried out after a baby was born to a couple who were afraid their child would be fragile, difficult to raise, or if they had already lost a son prematurely and feared this would happen again. In order to avoid such calamities and provide their child with the blessings to grow up in good health, they choose to forge a nominally adoptive kinship with another couple. It also happens to families that are on close terms with the hope that the children's generation will continue such friendship. The child's parents typically prepare lavish gifts for the adoptive parents, invite guests to a banquet to witness the occasion when the child kowtows before their nominally adoptive father and mother. In return, the nominally adoptive father and mother will present the child with gifts. After the adoption, the two families maintain close ties as if they were relatives.

例句：

宋代**认干亲**渐成习俗，直至民国末年，这一习俗仍然盛行。

Example Sentence:

In the Song Dynasty (960-1279), the custom of forging a nominally adoptive kinship family gradually took shape. It was still prevalent towards the end of the Republic of China period (1912-1949).

五子登科 *wuzi dengke;* Five Sons Passing the Imperial Examination

中国民间谚语。五子登科来源于一个民间故事。五代后周时期，燕山府（今北京）一个叫窦禹钧的人教子有方，五个儿子先后登科及第，故称“五子登科”。后来五子登科成为版画、雕塑等民间工艺品的主题，图案一般为五个活泼可爱的男童或小鸡，表达对孩童事业有成的期望。结婚时，在婚床上撒“五子（五种坚果）”的习俗也蕴含了早生贵子、五子登科的祝福。

A Chinese proverb derived from a folk tale. The story has it that in the Later Zhou Dynasty (951-960), a man named Dou Yujun from Yanshan Prefecture (present-day Beijing), brought up all of his five sons very well, and they all successfully passed the Imperial Examination. Later, the story became a popular theme in Chinese folk crafts such as in prints and sculptures in which images of five lively boys are depicted in scenes conveying the great expectations parents place on their children. Moreover, the wedding custom of sprinkling five kinds of nuts (referring to the five sons) on the wedding bed symbolizes a wish for the couple to quickly have children who will enjoy a bright future.

例句：

五子登科常用作结婚时的祝福词或吉祥语，寓意他们的孩子今后将学业有成、人生美满。

Example Sentence:

"Wishing your future children will be as successful as the Five Sons Passing the Imperial Examination" is a common greeting or auspicious wish said to a newly-married couple, displaying the hope that their future children will attain great success.

成丁 *cheng ding;* coming of age

中国旧时男子成年礼仪。男子通过一定的仪式或考验后即可成为社会的正式成员，可以成家立业，开始享有权利并履行义务。成丁礼一般在十五到二十岁间举行，一般有束发、加冠等形式，具体仪式内容因时代、民族而异。

A Chinese folk ceremony. After going through certain ceremonies or passing certain tests, a young man could be formally considered a member of society, and subsequently start a family or profession. From then on, he could enjoy certain adult rights, but would have obligations to fulfill as well. The ceremony was generally held when the young man was between the ages of fifteen and twenty, and typically involved such rituals as "Securing Hair" and "Capping." Ceremony specifics have varied over time and are different among ethnic groups.

例句：

据文献记载，周代已确立男子二十加冠和女子十五及笄的成人礼仪制度。而自晋代以来，十六岁多作为法定**成丁**年龄而为人们普遍接受。

Example Sentence:

According to ancient records, the coming of age rite was established during the Zhou Dynasty (1046-256 BC), in which 20 years old was the age for males (called *guanli*) and 15 years old was for females (called *jili*). However, after the Jin Dynasty (265-420), the age of 16 became the commonly accepted legal age of entering adulthood.

冠礼 *guanli;* capping ceremony

中国古代男性的成年礼，被称为“礼之始也”。冠礼一般在男子二十岁时举行，主要过程为：由主持仪式的正宾依次将三种适用于不同场合的冠加于将冠者，由卑到尊，暗示男子的德行与日俱增。行过冠礼后，男子将正式成为跨入社会的成年人，开始享有社交、婚姻，以及参与一些家族和社会大事的权利，开始践行相应的德行和责任，树立正确的人生观，形成是非判断能力，承担各种社会角色。有些地方还保留着相对独立的成年仪礼习俗，但传统意义的冠礼如今在民间大多已经与婚礼或幼子养育的习俗融为一体了。

A coming of age rite for young Chinese males in ancient times. It is also known as “the beginning of all rites” and was generally held for a young man at the age of twenty. As part of the ceremony, an honored guest invited to preside over the ceremony successively placed three different caps on the young man’s head. The three caps were arranged in an ascending order of status from meager to venerated, symbolizing that the young man’s virtue would grow with each passing day. The conclusion of the ceremony signified the young man’s formal admittance into society as an adult, enabling him to partake in certain social activities, marriage, and in family and social affairs while practicing corresponding virtues and committing to given obligations. As an adult, the young man is expected to establish an upright outlook on life, discern right from wrong, and strive to fulfill his social roles and duties. Some places have preserved relatively independent customs for coming of age ceremonies. However, the traditional capping ceremony has largely been merged with folk customs for weddings and parenting.

例句：

冠礼起源于氏族社会的成丁礼，在西周时演变为贵族男子的成人仪式，汉代以后，庶人也可举行冠礼。

Example Sentence:

The capping ceremony originated from the coming of age (*cheng ding*) ceremony in clan society and became a formal ceremony among the gentry during the Western Zhou Dynasty (1046-771 BC). Starting from the Han Dynasty (206 BC-AD 220), young men from ordinary families were also allowed to partake in such ceremonies.

笄礼 *jili;* hair-pinning ceremony

中国古代女性的成年礼。笄礼由女子的女性家长提出，约请女宾改变女子的幼年发式，具体做法为将女子头发绾成一个髻，然后用一块黑布将发髻包住，随即以簪（即笄）插定发髻。自周代起，规定贵族女子在订婚（许嫁）以后出嫁之前行笄礼，一般在十五岁举行；如果一直待嫁未许人，则年至二十也可行笄礼。由于中国传统社会是以男子为中心的，因此，古人对于冠礼的重视程度远远高于笄礼。

A coming of age rite for young Chinese females in ancient times, and a requirement for a girl before she could be married. The ceremony was initiated by the mother or female elder of the girl and performed by a female guest. The girl's hair was first put in a bun and then wrapped with a piece of black cloth. Finally, a hair stick was placed into the bun to hold it firmly. From the Zhou Dynasty (1046-256 BC), only girls from noble families, normally at the age of 15, were allowed to undergo the hair-pinning ceremony following their engagement and preceding the wedding. If a girl was still yet to be engaged, the hair-pinning ceremony was performed by the time she reached 20 at the latest. As the ancient Chinese society was male-centric, the "hair-pinning ceremony" was considered of much less importance than the "capping ceremony."

例句：

在古代中国，只有贵族的女子才举行**笄礼**仪式。

Example Sentence:

In ancient China, the hair-pinning ceremony was only held for girls from noble families.

定吉日

ding jiri;
finalizing an auspicious day for wedding

中国婚姻习俗，即确定结婚的吉利日期。旧时男女双方确定婚约后，双方父母会通过算命或占卜等方式选择宜于婚配的好日子将其定为结婚日期，然后向亲友发出婚宴请柬。接到请柬的人一般都会备好礼物或礼金前来道贺。现在仍有人遵循这一传统，只是一般由男女双方自己做主。

An ancient Chinese traditional marriage custom. When a marriage was agreed upon, parents of both families worked together to select a lucky day to hold the wedding by means of fortune-telling or divination. After the date was selected, wedding invitations were sent to relatives and friends. People who received invitations visited and congratulated the new couple with gifts or cash on the wedding day. This custom is still followed by some people, although the wedding day is typically chosen by the couple themselves instead of their parents.

例句：

古人结婚**定吉日**时非常慎重，忌讳颇多。

Example Sentence:

In ancient China, people were far more prudent with respect to selecting a wedding day, and there were many taboos to avoid.

终身大事 *zhongshen dashi;* the greatest event in life; the matter of lifelong importance; marriage

中国婚姻习俗用语，指男女婚姻大事。中国人的传统观念视婚姻为关系一辈子的大事情，男婚女嫁对个人、家庭和社会都具有重大意义。婚礼内容丰富，项目繁多，直到今天依然是中国民间最为隆重的人生仪礼活动。

A Chinese traditional term referring to hugely significant events in one's life but which mostly refers to marriage. In the traditional Chinese culture, marriage is considered a matter of vital importance to the couple involved, and has a significant bearing on their respective families and society at large. Rich in content and involving complicated rituals, marriage ceremonies to this day remain the most important rite of passage in the lives of Chinese people.

例句：

胡适创作的《**终身大事**》是中国现代文学中最早的话剧剧本之一，主要讨论婚姻自由问题。

Example Sentence:

Hu Shih's *The Greatest Event in Life* was one of the first dramas written in the style indicative of modern Chinese literature. It touches on the issue of freedom of marriage.

门当户对 *mendang-hudui;* marriage between families of equal social stature; a perfect match

中国婚姻缔结中的一种门第等级观念。中国旧时民居大都有门楼，官宦富贵人家的门楼一般修得比较高大，平民家的则比较矮小。一般认为只有当男女双方家庭的门楼（门第）相当，才适合缔结婚姻。婚姻的门第观念在西周时已经出现，在很长一段时间里一直是左右婚配的一条重要原则。在当代，门当户对仍是部分人择偶的标准，但考虑更多的是双方家庭背景、经济状况、宗教信仰、生活习惯等方面是否匹配。

A traditional notion that marriage should be arranged between families of equal social status. In the old days, Chinese residences had arches (*menlou*) over their gates. The arches of homes of gentry or the wealthy were often taller than those of common people. It was generally believed that only people with arches of a similar height (indicative of equal social status) could marry each other. Notions of hierarchy emerged during the Western Zhou Dynasty (1046-771 BC), and maintained a dominating principle of Chinese marriages for centuries. Nowadays, a great number of people still follow this notion when choosing their spouse; however, factors such as family background, economic conditions, religious beliefs, and habits are the main concerns in marriage decisions.

例句：

门当户对是中国古代封建宗法等级制度在婚姻观念形态中的反映。

Example Sentence:

The concept of marriage between families of equal social status is a reflection of the ancient hierarchal and patriarchal notions in the matter of marriage.

baoban hunyin;
arranged marriage; marriage based upon an arbitrary decision by a third party

中国嫁娶旧习俗。旧时人们认为婚姻大事应该唯父母之命、听媒妁之言，婚姻当事人自己不能过问，也不能发表意见。男女之间私自爱慕被认为是违背礼法的行为，会受到家族乃至社会的惩罚。包办婚姻以门当户对为基础，完全不考虑当事人的意愿，酿成了很多缺乏感情的婚姻悲剧。中华人民共和国成立后，国家明确规定禁止包办婚姻。

A traditional Chinese custom based on the belief that a person's marriage should be arranged according to the will of their parents and the advice of a matchmaker. Personal opinions by the couple concerned were not allowed to be voiced. Additionally, affection between a young man and woman without parental consent was regarded as a breach of social norms, prompting retributions from their families and society at large. The complete denial of one's rights in betrothal resulted in countless marriages devoid of love. Arranged marriages were forbidden following the founding of the People's Republic of China in 1949.

例句：

《中华人民共和国民法典》规定禁止**包办婚姻**、买卖婚姻和其他干涉婚姻自由的行为。

Example Sentence:

According to the Civil Code of the PRC, any marriage arranged by a third party, mercenary marriage, or any other act interfering with the freedom of marriage is prohibited.

指腹婚 *zhifu hun;* marriage based on prenatal betrothal

中国旧时一种特殊的包办婚姻形式，指男女双方尚在母腹中时，其婚姻关系就由双方父母确定下来。因为此时婚姻当事人尚未出生，因此双方父母一般约定，产后若为一男一女，则待长大后缔结婚姻。这种婚姻形式一般是朋友之间出于信义或世代交好的家族之间为了巩固关系而采取的一种措施，现已绝迹。

A special form of arranged marriage in ancient China. Prior to the birth of two children from two different families, the parents would arrange for their future marriage should they be born as a boy and a girl. Such practices were mostly performed between families with shared goodwill or friendship spanning multiple generations, with the intention to forge a stronger relationship between the two families. Such marriages have since been outlawed.

例句：

在中国，**指腹婚**的出现可以追溯到东汉。

Example Sentence:

In China, marriage based on prenatal betrothal can be traced back to the Eastern Han Dynasty (25-220).

童养婚 *tongyang hun;* marriage involving a child bride

中国旧时一种婚姻形式。一家生下男婴后（或生育子嗣前），抱养或买进别家幼女为养女，达到婚龄后与本家儿子成婚，使养女转为儿媳。若该家抱养

An ancient marriage custom in China wherein a girl was sold to or fostered in a family to be raised as their future daughter-in-law. After the birth of a baby boy, or sometimes even before the birth, the

幼女后始终没有诞下男婴，则将其作为养女出嫁。还有的人自己早已成年甚至已婚，但仍抱养幼女，待其长大与自己结婚。童养婚是把女子视为财产，进行买卖婚姻。中华人民共和国成立后，国家明确规定禁止买卖婚姻。

parents of the newborn would purchase a young girl to raise as an adopted daughter until the time she reached the age of marriage, in which she would then marry their son. If the family purchasing the girl did not give birth to a boy, they would raise the girl as an adopted daughter to marry off in the future. Sometimes adult men—even those who were already married—would also buy a child bride to raise as their own future wife. Such practice is essentially a form of mercenary marriage that treats girls as property, and has been prohibited by law since the founding of the PRC in 1949.

例句：

明清时期，**童养婚**现象遍及全国各地。

Example Sentence:

During the Ming (1368-1644) and Qing (1616-1911) dynasties, marriage practices involving child brides were popular throughout China.

入赘婚

ruzhui hun;
matrilocal marriage; uxorilocal marriage

中国旧时一种嫁娶方式，又称“倒插门”，指男子以自身为抵押（赘）入女家为婚。这种婚姻与汉族主流的男婚女嫁相反，多是女家无兄无弟，为了

A traditional form of marriage in pre-modern China, also called *dao chamen* (marrying into the wife's family). While a bride typically went to reside with her husband's family after marriage, the inverse is true of matrilocal marriages.

传宗接代招女婿上门，或父母爱其女不忍其出嫁远离。入赘男子多为家贫身壮、没有能力娶妻者，因此在社会上地位很低，备受歧视。入赘的婚姻仪式通常比较简单，不事铺张。入赘形式一般分为两种：一是终身上门，承嗣养老，婚生子女随女家姓；二是短期入赘，然后另立门户，带服役性质，部分子女可随父姓。现在男女平等，对这种婚姻形式的歧视已经基本消失。

An inability to continue the family line due to the absence of male offspring in a bride's family, or the parents' unwillingness to marry off their daughters to men far away were some of the motivations that led to matrilocal marriages. Usually, men in matrilocal marriages were of a lower social class than their brides, and were discriminated against on account of their humble origins and poverty that prevented them from getting a wife according to normal customs. There were two types of matrilocal marriages for men. The first involved a lifelong residence with the responsibility to support the wife's parents and use the mother's surname for their children. The second involved a short residence with the wife's family before the couple left to set up their own home. Some of their children would take the mother's surname while the father's was given to others. Nowadays, prejudice against such marriages has disappeared thanks to gender equality.

例句：

描写**入赘婚**是中国古代小说、戏曲中才子佳人故事的重要题材。

Example Sentence:

Portrayals of matrilocal marriages are an important theme in ancient Chinese novels and dramas, especially the love stories of gifted scholars and beautiful ladies.

倒插门 *dao chamen;* marrying into the wife's family

参见"入赘婚"。因为入赘婚这种形式与汉族主流的男婚女嫁形式完全相反，是女娶男嫁，因此称为"倒插门"，带有一定的贬义色彩。倒插门的男子被称为上门女婿。

See *ruzhui hun* (matrilocal marriage). A derogatory term used to describe a form of marriage in which a man of lower social and family status married into a woman's family, which was totally opposite to the mainstream form of marriage. Men in such a marriage were called *shangmen nüxu*, which meant "live-in son-in-law."

例句：

过去，**倒插门**是一个普通而又略带贬意的名词。现在上门女婿很多，也很常见，只不过是在女方家定居。

Example Sentence:

In the past, *dao chamen* was a commonly used, slightly derogatory term, but today it is quite common for a man to reside in his wife's house.

上门女婿 *shangmen nüxu;* live-in son-in-law

参见"倒插门"。中国民间对婚姻关系中入赘或倒插门到女方家庭的男子的称呼，过去略带贬意，男子在家庭和社会中的地位也比较低。现在男女平等，上门女婿很常见，也不再要求子女随女方姓，因此其贬义色彩已经基本消失。

See *dao chamen* (marrying into the wife's family). A slightly derogatory term in the past for a man of lower social and family status marrying into his bride's family. Nowadays, men in such marriages enjoy equality with their spouses and are no longer treated as inferior in the relationship. Their children will take either parent's family name.

例句：

这部小说讲述了一个**上门女婿**的奇特经历。

Example Sentence:

This novel tells the unusual story of a live-in son-in-law.

抛绣球 *pao xiuqiu;* throwing embroidered silk ball

中国的少数民族——壮族的传统体育项目和民间娱乐活动。绣球是姑娘们用手工做成的彩球，以圆形最为常见，也有椭圆形、方形、菱形等。绣球大如拳头，内装棉花籽、谷粟、谷壳等。作为一项体育运动，抛绣球的历史可追溯到2000多年前在作战和狩猎中甩投的用青铜铸造的古兵器——飞砣。随着社会的发展，这种武器逐渐退出历史舞台，人们用手工做成的彩球代替了兵器飞砣，在茶余饭后常互相抛接以娱乐身心，并发展成为一种需

A traditional sport as well as a form of entertainment of the Zhuang ethnic group in China. The ball is handmade by girls in colorful silk cloth, and is usually round, but there are other shapes such as oval, square, and rhombus. The ball is as big as a clenched fist, and is stuffed with cottonseeds, grain, or grain husks. As a sport, the activity can be traced back to 2,000 years ago when warriors and hunters threw cast-bronze projectiles called *feituo* (flying stone wheel) at their targets. Later these projectiles gradually disappeared and people used colorful embroidered silk balls to throw at each other in their leisure

要专门训练的体育项目。同时，抛接彩球的游戏在民间也逐渐演变成为壮族男女青年表达爱情的一种方式，并延续至今。

time. Later it develops into a sports game that requires special training. Meanwhile, the game has also served as a way for young men and women of the Zhuang ethnic group to express love for one another. This tradition is still prevalent among the Zhuang people.

例句：

抛绣球一般在每年春节及农历三月三歌节时举行，绣球内填放有谷物种子，寓意五谷丰登。

Example Sentence:

People usually play with the embroidered silk ball during the Spring Festival and the Singing Festival (the third day of the third month of the Chinese lunar year). The ball is filled with the seeds of grain symbolizing hopes for a bumper harvest.

三书六礼 *san shu liu li;* Three Letters and Six Rules of Etiquette

中国古代汉族传统婚姻习俗礼仪的总称。“三书”指结婚过程中所用的文书，是古人为保障婚姻所立的有效文字记录，包括聘书、礼书和迎书。“六礼”是指求婚至完婚过程中的六种礼仪，依次为纳采、问名、纳吉、纳征、请期、亲迎。六礼约始于周代，后世沿袭周礼，但名目和内容有所变化。三书

A summary of traditional marriage etiquette observed by the Han people in ancient China. “Three Letters” refer to three written documents used in the process towards a marriage, including the betrothal letter, the gift letter, and the wedding letter. These were written records made to certify that a marriage had come into effect. “Six Rules of Etiquette” refer to six steps that lead to an arranged marriage,

并非周礼，但后世常将三书和六礼搭配使用。实际上，正统的三书六礼主要流行于上层士绅之家，民间一般在其基础上变通取舍，化繁为简。

namely, *na cai* (proposing a marriage), *wen ming* (requesting birthday information to assess marriage compatibility), *na ji* (presenting betrothal gifts), *na zheng* (presenting a bride price), *qing qi* (making inquiries about the wedding date), and *qinying* (meeting and escorting the bride home for the wedding). The "Six Rules of Etiquette" began around the Zhou Dynasty and had been followed as part of the established "Zhou Rites," but specific names and practices varied at different times. The "Three Letters" were not part of the "Zhou Rites," but with the passage of time, the two came to be used together. Actually, the "Three Letters" and "Six Rules of Etiquette" were mainly prevalent among aristocratic families. Ordinary families typically practiced a much simplified procedure.

例句：

传统的**三书六礼**现在已不复存在了，只有部分内容，如纳征和亲迎保留了下来。

Example Sentence:

The traditional customs of the "Three Letters and Six Rules of Etiquette" no longer exist, although components of them are kept, such as *na zheng* (presenting a bride price) and *qinying* (meeting and escorting the bride home for the wedding).

聘书 *pinshu;* engagement letter; betrothal letter

中国传统婚姻习俗的三书之一。聘书是结婚过程中的纳吉（男女订立婚约）时男家交予女家的书柬，也是男女双方正式缔结婚约、保障婚姻的有效书面凭证。聘书内容一般包括对女方家世的赞扬、已确定的具体成婚时间及对婚姻美满的祝福等。

One of the "Three Letters (*san shu*)" of traditional Chinese marriage customs. It is a written document given by the groom's family to the bride's family in the process of confirming a betrothal (*na ji*). As a written record of a formal, confirmed betrothal, it is regarded as the proof and guarantee of a future marriage. The letter usually starts with a compliment of the bride's family and background, confirmation of the wedding date, and wishes for a happy marriage.

例句：

聘书是订婚的重要文书，是古代中国缔结婚约必需的礼仪。

Example Sentence:

The betrothal letter is an important written document of engagement and an essential rule of etiquette for confirming a betrothal in ancient China.

礼书 *lishu;* gift letter

中国传统婚姻习俗的三书之一。礼书是结婚过程中的纳征（过大礼）时使用的礼物清单，详列礼物种类及数量。所有礼金、礼饼、礼品等数量都为双数，寓意成双成对、幸福美满。

One of the "Three Letters (*san shu*)" of traditional Chinese marriage customs. It is a list detailing the wedding gifts presented from the bridegroom's family to the bride's family as part of the *na zheng* process, which specifies the types and quantities of the presents. The presents, whether in cash or in kind, are in even numbers, signifying that good things come in pairs, thereby expressing wishes for a happy marriage.

例句:

礼书是给女方家的聘礼清单，礼品数量及内容因各地风俗习惯及家庭贫富而异。

Example Sentence:

The gift letter is a list of betrothal gifts presented to the bride's family. The quantity and types of gifts vary in light of local customs and the financial conditions of the groom's family.

迎书 *yingshu;* wedding letter

中国传统婚姻习俗的三书之一，也称“迎亲书”。迎书是结婚当日迎娶新娘过门时男方送给女方的文书，也是婚书的雏形。

One of the "Three Letters (*san shu*)" of traditional Chinese marriage customs. It refers to the document which is prepared and presented to the bride's family on the day of the wedding to confirm and commemorate the formal acceptance of the bride into the bridegroom's family. It is considered the early form of the marriage certificate in China.

例句:

包括**迎书**在内的一些婚姻旧俗现在已经基本消失。

Example Sentence:

Some marriage customs from the olden days including the wedding letter have largely disappeared.

纳采 *na cai;* proposing a marriage; proposal of marriage

中国传统婚姻习俗的六礼之第一礼，议婚的第一个阶段，俗称“说媒”“提亲”。中国传统礼法中，青年男女的婚姻是由媒人说合、父母包办的。男子当婚时，男方家会请媒人去物色好的女方家说亲，得到应允后备礼向女方家正式求婚。早期通常以活雁和其他寓意吉祥的礼品，如合欢、鸳鸯、嘉禾等作礼，近代不再用雁，也有的用家鹅替代。

The first of the "Six Rules of Etiquette" in Chinese traditional marriage customs, more commonly known as *shuo mei* (acting as a matchmaker) and *ti qin* (making a marriage proposal). In ancient China, a marriage was typically proposed by a matchmaker and determined by the parents of both sides. When the parents of a young man find a girl whom they want their son to marry, they would usually engage a matchmaker to make a proposal to the girl's family. After obtaining the consent of the girl's parents, the man's family would present the girl's family with gifts as part of the engagement process. In the olden days, the common practice was to use wild geese (symbolizing loyal love) and other auspicious things like acacia, mandarin ducks, and strong crops as gifts. Later, wild geese were no longer used, and were replaced by domestic geese in some areas.

例句：

古代行**纳采**之礼，礼品中必须有雁，一种说法是雁失配偶，终生不再成双，象征忠贞的爱情。

Example Sentence:

According to ancient etiquette for *na cai* (proposing a marriage), the gifts presented to the girl's family must include wild geese. One interpretation is that wild geese represent true love as they are mated for life; once they lose their partner, they will stay alone for the rest of their lives.

说媒 *shuo mei;* proposing a marriage; acting as a matchmaker

"纳采"的俗称。参见"纳采"。

A colloquial expression of *na cai* (proposing a marriage). See *na cai.*

例句：

1900年，大教育家蔡元培的原配夫人因病去世。由于蔡元培学问高，社会地位又显赫，**说媒**者接踵而来。

Example Sentence:

Cai Yuanpei was a distinguished educator with high academic achievements and social status. When his first wife died of illness in 1900, matchmakers came one after another to introduce a new wife for him.

提亲 *ti qin;* proposing a marriage; making a marriage proposal

"纳采"的俗称。参见"纳采"。

A colloquial expression of *na cai* (proposing a marriage). See *na cai.*

例句：

他家里太穷，没有能力请媒人去**提亲**。

Example Sentence:

His family is too poor to engage a matchmaker to propose a marriage.

问名

wen ming;
requesting birth profile of the potential bride (to assess marriage compatibility); birthday matching

中国传统婚姻习俗的六礼之第二礼，议婚的第二个阶段，俗称“合八字”“请八字”。提亲后男家请媒人问女方的姓名及其生辰八字（出生年月日时），用来占卜吉凶，避免与男方生肖相克。后来，问名由问生辰八字逐步扩展到问门第、职位、财产，以及容貌、健康等许多方面。

The second of the “Six Rules of Etiquette” observed in Chinese traditional marriage customs, commonly known as *he bazi* (matching the eight-character birth profile), *qing bazi* (requesting for the eight-character birth profile). After the proposal was accepted, the matchmaker will visit the girl's family again on behalf of the man's family and ask for the full name and the *bazi* (eight-character birth profile) of the girl to determine whether it matches with that of the man. A conflict of the zodiac animals of the two are generally considered a bad match and should be avoided. Later, birthday matching was expanded to include aspects of social status, profession, property, and even facial features and health conditions.

例句：

广东许多地方常用槟榔作为**问名**携带的礼物。

Example Sentence:

In many places of Guangdong Province, people often used seeds of betel palms as gifts for the ritual of *wen ming* (birthday matching).

纳吉 *na ji;*

presenting betrothal gifts; confirming engagement; engagement gifts

中国传统婚姻习俗的六礼之第三礼，议婚的第三个阶段，又称“小聘”“过小礼”。问名之后，男方至宗庙进行占卜，预测婚姻是否吉顺；得到吉兆后，再备礼到女家告知结果并初步议定婚约。纳吉礼之后，婚约即正式确定。

The third of the “Six Rules of Etiquette” observed in Chinese traditional marriage customs, commonly known as *xiaopin* (presenting engagement gifts) and *guo xiaoli* (presenting moderate gifts). After obtaining the birth profile of the girl, the man's family performs divination in the ancestral temple to predict whether the proposed marriage is auspicious or problematic. If the result is favorable, the bridegroom's family will present betrothal gifts to the bride's family, and reaches a preliminary agreement on the proposed marriage. After this, the engagement is officially confirmed.

例句：

一旦双方的生辰相合，男方会安排媒人给女方送去聘礼，其中包括聘书，所谓**纳吉**。

Example Sentence:

Once the birth profiles of the two sides are confirmed to match well, the bridegroom's family will engage a matchmaker to present a bride price along with the betrothal letter to the bride's family. This is known as *na ji*.

纳征

na zheng;
presenting a bride price; paying bride wealth

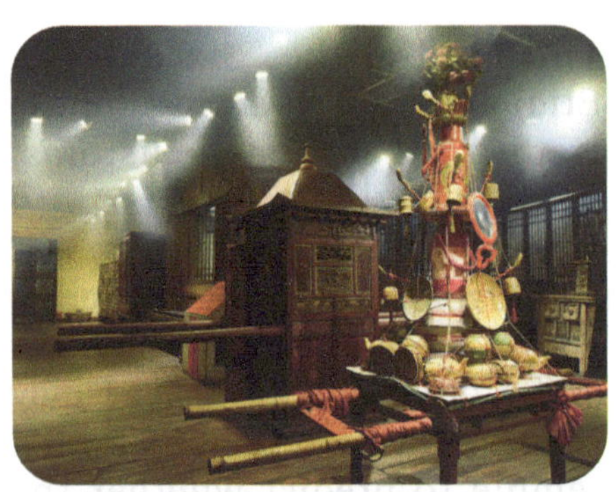

中国传统婚姻习俗的六礼之第四礼，成婚的第一个阶段，又称“纳币”，俗称“大聘”“过大礼”。男方在纳吉后向女方送聘礼，是订婚阶段的结束，是婚姻成立的主要标志之一。东周时人们通常用帛作为聘礼，后来增加了聘金，聘礼内容也日趋多样化，所纳之物多取吉祥如意之谐音双关语，而且喜双忌单。女方收到聘礼后一般会将聘礼的一部分加上其他礼物回送男方，称为回礼。纳征是古代六礼中唯一不用雁的仪式。

The fourth of the "Six Rules of Etiquette" observed in Chinese traditional marriage customs, also known as *na bi* (paying a bride price), commonly known as *dapin* (bride price), *guo dali* (presenting sumptuous gifts). After *na ji*, the bridegroom's family will present the bride's family with sumptuous bride price which marks the end of the engagement period and the formal establishment of the marriage bond. During the Eastern Zhou Dynasty (770-256 BC), people often used silk as bride price which was later supplemented with money. More and more items with auspicious and lucky connotations were added to the list of gifts, but wild geese were not among them, making *na zheng* the only one of the "Six Rules of Etiquette" that does not use wild geese as gifts. The gifts are often presented in even numbers, as this symbolizes couples and pairs. The bride's family usually sends return gifts which include a portion of the received gifts and some new items to the groom's family.

例句：

由于各地习惯不同和家庭贫富不等，**纳征**的内容和数量会有一定差异。

Example Sentence:

Owing to differences in local customs and a family's wealth, bride prices differ in content and quantity.

请期

qing qi;
making inquiries about the wedding date

中国传统婚姻习俗的六礼之第五礼，成婚的第二阶段，俗称“提日子”。男方通过占卜择定迎娶吉日后，须派媒人代表男方家人向女方家人请示婚期，表示谦虚不敢自专之意，故有“请期”之称。当女方家人一再推辞之后，媒人才将男方选定的日子告诉女方，双方确定迎娶的吉日良辰。

The fifth of the “Six Rules of Etiquette” observed in Chinese traditional marriage customs, commonly known as *ti rizi* (proposing a wedding date). The bridegroom’s family would select an auspicious date for the wedding through astrology and divination. However, they are expected to send the matchmaker to the bride’s family and ask them to propose a date for the wedding. This is a gesture of humility on the part of the groom’s family. When the bride’s family repeatedly declines to propose a date, which is what they are expected to do, the matchmaker would then inform them of the date chosen by the groom’s family. Both sides would then determine the exact date and time for the wedding.

例句：

请期的礼仪虽然没有纳征那样隆重，但其重要性仍不可忽视。

Example Sentence:

Although *qing qi* (making inquiries about the wedding date) does not involve formalities as grand as those of *na zheng* (presenting a bride price), it is still a crucial procedure.

提日子

ti rizi;
making inquiries about the wedding date

“请期”的俗称。参见“请期”。

A colloquial expression of *qing qi* (making inquiries concerning the wedding date). See *qing qi.*

亲迎 *qinying;* meeting and escorting the bride home for the wedding

中国传统婚姻习俗六礼的最后一礼，又称“迎亲”。成婚当日，男家派马车（后世改用轿子）去迎娶新娘，新郎骑马或乘轿亲自去女方家迎娶，称为“迎亲”。古时婚礼以昏为期，因此亲迎必在黄昏以后，甚至深夜进行。亲迎所用器物皆要偶数，以示夫妻成双成对。中国当代婚礼变化很大，但亲迎的形式依然在很多地方得以保存。

The last of the “Six Rules of Etiquette” observed in Chinese traditional marriage customs, also called *yingqin* (bringing the bride home for the wedding). On the wedding day, the groom—on horseback or in a sedan chair—will lead a party to meet the bride at her home and take her home by a horse-drawn carriage(to be replaced by a sedan chair later on) to the wedding. In ancient times, weddings were usually held at or after dusk, so the groom must meet and bring the bride home after dusk or even at midnight. The items used in this ritual should always be even-numbered to symbolize that the couple will always come in pairs. Marriage customs have changed a lot over the years, but this ritual has been kept in many places, albeit in simplified ways.

例句：

汉朝以后，皇太子成婚无**亲迎**礼。隋唐时期才恢复行亲迎礼。

Example Sentence:

The crown prince was not expected to follow the ritual of *qinying* (meeting and escorting the bride home for the wedding) during and after the Han Dynasty (206 BC-AD 220). But the custom was revived during the Sui and Tang dynasties (581-907) and was followed thereafter.

彩礼 *caili;* bride price; bride wealth

中国传统婚姻习俗，又称“聘礼”。男方在婚约初步达成时向女方赠送聘金、聘礼，其金额和数量与时代、地方风俗及家庭经济条件相关。彩礼本属贵族婚姻制度，自秦汉时期开始在普通民众中流行，至今仍在民间流行。

A traditional marriage custom in China, also called *pinli* in Chinese. It is a gift in the form of money, property or other valuable assets that the prospective husband would present to the bride's family when the marriage agreement is reached. The quantity and quality of the gift vary in light of local customs and a family's financial conditions. Initially as a rite of aristocratic marriages, the practice of bride price became popular among ordinary people around the Qin and Han dynasties (221 BC-AD 220). The custom still exists today.

例句：

婚前给**彩礼**在中国有些地方仍然盛行，成为一种约定俗成的习惯。

Example Sentence:

The custom of presenting bride price before wedding is still prevalent in some parts of China and is accepted as an established practice.

聘礼 *pinli;* bride price; bride wealth

参见“彩礼”。

See *caili* (bride price).

 八字

ba zi;
eight-character birth profile; eight-character birth data

中国民俗用语，即用中国传统的干支纪时法表达的人的生辰。因为出生年、月、日、时分别用天干、地支中各一字相配，加起来一共八个字，又称“生辰八字”。民间认为，根据八字可以推算一个人的命运。旧时议婚时须先交换男女双方的八字帖，推算他们是否相冲相克。如果八字相克就不宜婚配。现代婚姻已不再看八字。

A person's birth data according to traditional Chinese calendar using Heavenly Stems and Earthly Branches to record time. Each person's birthday data are recorded by using one of the 10 Heavenly Stems and one of the 12 Earthly Branches according to the year, month, day, and time they were born, thus producing eight characters, considered as one's astrological birth data. In ancient times, when considering a marriage, the man and woman would provide their eight characters to an astrologer to determine whether they would match well or conflict with one another. If they weren't considered a good match, then the marriage was deemed unsuitable. Modern marriages no longer factor in the eight characters during the decision-making process.

例句：

婚姻六礼中的问名就是问女方的生辰**八字**。

Example Sentence:

For the second rite (*wen ming*) of the “Six Rules of Etiquette” for traditional marriages, the bride is asked about her eight-character birth profile.

全福人 *quanfu ren;* person blessed in life

中国民间操办特定婚礼事项的人，指上有父母、下有儿女、夫妻恩爱、兄弟姐妹和睦相处的有福气的人，一般指女性，有时也指小孩儿。在中国民间传统婚俗中，很多婚礼事项必须由全福人来照料，以求新婚夫妇未来生活福气满满。在婚礼前一天，全福人要到新房中为新郎新娘扫床，边扫边念吉祥话或顺口溜，以求将好运带给新婚夫妇。在北方的大部分地区，全福人在新娘出嫁上轿之前做扫轿、熏轿、照轿的工作，营造祝福的氛围。

A person tasked with making certain arrangements during a wedding. A person blessed in life refers to one with loving parents/parents-in-law and children, a satisfactory marriage, and a harmonious relations with siblings. The term is usually applied to women or children. According to traditional Chinese customs, it is hoped that by partaking in certain marriage arrangements, this person can pass on his/her good fortune to the newlyweds. On the day before the marriage, the person goes to the bridal chamber to clean the bed while chanting auspicious words or certain phrases to help bring the couple good luck. In most parts of northern China, this person will clean the marriage sedan, perfume it, and check every corner with a mirror for any unpleasant or ill-boding objects before the bride gets in. This is done to instill an auspicious atmosphere.

例句：

古代迎亲时，选一个**全福人**家的小男孩儿乘一顶轿子前往女方家迎娶，称为压轿。

Example Sentence:

When the bridal sedan chair was ready to pick up the bride in ancient times, a boy of a blessed family rode in the sedan chair to the bride's house to greet her. This is called "holding down the sedan chair."

花轿 *huajiao;* bridal sedan; bridal sedan chair

中国传统婚礼上用来迎娶新娘的装饰华丽的轿子，又称“喜轿”。旧时婚嫁迎娶必用花轿，以示明媒正娶。花轿一般布置得华美喜庆，绣龙凤花鸟或百子吉祥图案。迎亲当天，新娘穿大红衣衫坐上喜轿，新郎骑马在轿子前引领，一路锣鼓唢呐喧天，热热闹闹地把新娘抬到新郎家举行拜天地等仪式。花轿通常由四人或八人扛抬，有的地方有牛拉花轿或驴驮花轿。如今花轿娶亲已被现代交通工具——汽车取代。

A beautifully decorated sedan chair used to take the bride to her wedding. It is also called a *xijiao* (wedding sedan). In ancient times, a sedan chair was required for a couple to be deemed officially wed. The bridal sedan chair is typically designed with ornate, festive patterns such as dragons, phoenixes, birds, flowers, or hundred-son auspicious images embroidered in the fabric. On the day the bride is escorted to the groom's house, the bride wears red clothes and gets in the sedan chair. The groom rides a horse to lead the sedan chair as a procession of gongs, drums, and *suona* horns ring through the air. Once they reach the groom's home, they hold such ceremonies as kneeling to worship heaven and earth. The bridal sedan chair is typically lifted and carried on the shoulders of four or eight people. In some places, an ox or donkey is tasked with carrying the bridal sedan chair. Today, this custom is rarely seen, as the bridal sedan chair has been replaced by modern motorcade processions.

例句：

花轿既是婚嫁礼仪中必备的仪仗，也是娶亲过程中的交通工具。

Example Sentence:

The bridal sedan is both an essential component of a marriage ceremony and vehicle for bringing the bride to the wedding.

嫁妆 *jiazhuang; dowry*

中国传统婚姻习俗。女儿出嫁，由娘家陪送的家具、被褥等日常用品称为“嫁妆”。丰盛的嫁妆往往是娘家社会地位和财产的显现，也为女儿出嫁后在婆家所处地位奠定良好的基础。有的地方还流行在嫁妆的枕头内装上筷子（谐音“快子”），在鞋内装上麸子（谐音“福子”），在被子内缝入枣子、花生（谐音“早生子”）等物，祝福女儿过门后早生贵子，儿女双全，生活幸福美满。种类繁多、琳琅满目的嫁妆往往成为当地民间艺术的展现。

A Chinese traditional wedding custom. A dowry refers to daily necessities, such as furniture and bedding, which the bride's family gives to newlyweds. A sumptuous dowry reflects the social status and wealth of a bride's family. It also helps strengthen the woman's position in her husband's home. In some places, it is customary to put special items in a dowry. For instance, chopsticks may be put in a pillow, bran in shoes, and jujubes and peanuts in quilts. This is a wish for the bride to give birth to a boy quickly and then have both sons and daughters, leading to a happy, content life. Local folk art is often reflected in the dowries of different locations.

例句：

四川洪雅山村的一支婚礼送亲队伍抬着箱柜家具等女方**嫁妆**送往男家。

Example Sentence:

In the rural, mountainous area of Hongya County, Sichuan Province, a bride's dowry, including trunks and cabinets, was carried to her husband's home.

奠雁礼 *dianyan li; goose-giving ceremony*

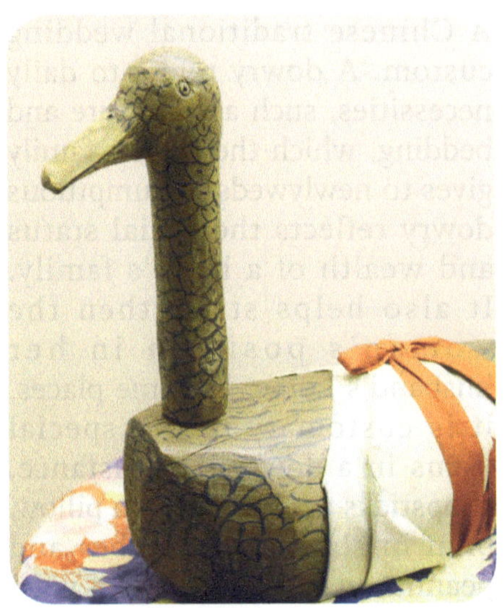

中国古代婚姻习俗中男方家赠与女方家礼品的仪式。早期礼品一般用活雁，雁是候鸟，随气候变化而迁徙，来去有时，表示儿女已是谈婚论嫁时；也有取大雁有信、终生只择一偶之意，因此这个仪式就被称为"奠雁礼"。近代不再用雁，也有的用家鹅或其他象征吉祥的礼物替代。

An ancient Chinese marriage custom wherein the groom's family ceremonially presents gifts to the bride's family. Early gifts typically involved migratory wild geese. These geese come and go at a certain time, and the gift symbolizes that the daughter and son have reached marriage age and will start their own family. It is also used because wild geese only pick one mate for life. Gifts of geese resulted in the name the "goose-giving ceremony." Wild geese were no longer used as marriage gifts in more recent past, and were replaced by domesticated geese or other auspicious items in some places.

例句：

传统朝鲜族的婚礼依然有**奠雁礼**，主要是由新郎将木雁送给女方家，并举行一系列的仪式。

Example Sentence:

Traditional Korean marriage customs still include the goose-giving ceremony. It mainly involves having the groom bring a wooden wild goose to the bride's family and a whole array of other rituals.

哭嫁 *ku jia;* weeping bride

中国传统婚姻习俗中新娘出嫁时告别娘家的哭唱仪式。该习俗源于古代掠夺婚时期，新娘往往在惊慌哭泣中出嫁。在中国封建社会，婚姻往往由父母包办，女子在迎亲前从未见过自己的丈夫，无法预知未来吉凶，只能以哭喊来表达对家人的不舍，对未来的忧虑与恐惧。后来哭嫁逐渐成为婚姻中的一种仪式。出嫁前，新娘哭得越厉害，反而预示未来生活越美好。

A traditional Chinese marriage custom wherein the bride ceremonially weeps good-bye to her family. The custom is derived from ancient times when women were kidnapped and forced to marry. In such situations, they often bitterly wept out of panic as they were married off. Also in Chinese feudal society, marriages were entirely arranged by parents. Before arriving at the groom's house, the woman typically had never seen her future husband before, making it impossible for her to predict whether her future held fortune or disaster. She could only weep to express her reluctance to part with her family, along with her worries and fear. Later, the custom gradually developed into part of the marriage ceremony in that the harder the bride wept before the wedding ceremony, the more fortune her future held.

例句：

有些地区**哭嫁**，哭的技巧要专门学习，且有陪哭烘托。

Example Sentence:

In areas where the weeping bride is still a custom, the skill of weeping needs to be specially practiced, and another person or a group of people often weep along with the bride.

别亲酒

bieqin jiu;
farewell banquet to loved ones; farewell banquet to one's family

中国传统婚姻习俗，又称“辞家宴”。女方父母在女儿出嫁前一天，要为嫁女备酒席。届时，椅披红垫，花烛齐燃，请嫁女首坐，平辈或晚辈之子女陪宴。在席上，新娘之母要斟酒，并对新娘说一些告诫的话。

A traditional Chinese marriage custom, also called *cijia yan*, (the home-leaving banquet). On the day before a woman gets married, her parents hold a banquet. Chairs are covered in red cloth and cushions, and wedding candles are lit. The daughter is the guest of honor and family members of her generation or younger accompany her. During the banquet, the bride's mother pours wine and gives advice to her.

例句：

别亲酒的习俗多流行于江浙一带。

Example Sentence:

The farewell banquet to loved ones is a custom that is mainly popular in Jiangsu and Zhejiang provinces.

辞家宴

cijia yan;
home-leaving banquet; farewell banquet to loved ones

参见“别亲酒”。

See *bieqin jiu* (farewell banquet to loved ones; farewell banquet to one's family).

喜堂 *xitang;* wedding hall

中国传统新婚仪式的举办场所。一般设在客厅或新房的外间屋，从大门到喜堂张灯结彩。喜堂门上挂一条刺绣的横幅，叫作“喜彩”，上面绣有和合二仙、福禄寿三星等。喜堂正中放围上绣花桌围的供桌，桌上摆龙凤花烛、香炉及各种供品，正中悬挂和合二仙像，两旁分挂红喜对联，四壁悬挂亲友送的喜帐，上书“天作之合、佳偶天成”之类的祝词。

The venue where a Chinese traditional wedding ceremony is held. A wedding hall is usually set up in the living room or in the room right outside of the bridal chamber. From the front gate to the wedding hall, decorations are everywhere. A silk banner called a *xicai* (wedding banner) is hung on the door of the wedding hall featuring embroidered images like the Immortals of Harmony and Reunion, as well as the three gods of Happiness, Prosperity, and Longevity. An altar table is set up in the middle of the hall wrapped in a piece of embroidered cloth. On the table, there will be an incense burner and also candles decorated with the patterns of a dragon, phoenix, and flowers. A picture of the Immortals of Harmony and Reunion is placed in the middle of the wall, with a pair of antithetical couplets extending good wishes hanging on the two sides. On the other walls, long red cloth or silk from friends and relatives can be displayed. Common words written on this cloth include "*tianzuo zhihe*" (a perfect match in heaven's will) and "*jia'ou tiancheng*" (a happy couple united by heaven).

例句：

现在农村变化很大，**喜堂**常常设在房间外面的院子里，临时搭好喜堂，或搭在戏台上，大红喜字一贴，气氛就出来了。

Example Sentence:

Today, rural China has changed in profound ways. Wedding halls are usually set up in a large, temporary tent or on a stage in a courtyard. Red Chinese character 喜 can be pasted up to create a festive atmosphere.

拜堂

bai tang;
paying traditional ceremonial obeisance in a wedding

中国传统婚姻礼仪，又称“拜天地”，即新婚夫妇在新郎家举行的参拜仪式。因古代婚礼的参拜礼都是在厅堂举

An important part of a traditional Chinese wedding ceremony. It is also known as *bai tiandi* (worshipping heaven and earth), and typically occurs at the groom's home. The phrase in Chinese literally means "worshipping the hall" as this ceremony was carried out in a family hall in ancient times. It is the most important part during traditional Chinese weddings. A typical traditional wedding ceremony includes burning incense and playing music in front of the ancestral memorial tablets in the front of the groom's family hall. Meanwhile the host of the wedding ceremony leads the newlyweds to kowtow towards earth and heaven, the groom's parents and to one another before they are taken to the bridal chamber. After this part of the ceremony, the new couple is officially considered husband and

行，因此称为“拜堂”，是中式传统婚礼中最重要的大礼。一般在男方家堂前设祖先牌位，燃喜烛，奏乐，由婚礼主持人引导新人先后跪拜天地、高堂（男方父母），然后夫妻对拜，最后将新人送入洞房。拜堂之后，新人即正式结为夫妻。现代婚礼中多不跪拜，改为对父母鞠躬，夫妻相对鞠躬，很少有人再拜天地。

wife. The majority of marriages today do not involve kowtowing. This custom has evolved into bowing to the parents and to one another. Today, many skip the part where they pay respects to earth and heaven.

例句：

古人**拜堂**的习俗体现出对天地神灵、对父母祖先和婚姻伴侣的尊重和承诺，婚姻本身也因此变得神圣、庄严。

Example Sentence:

The ancient custom of ceremonial obeisance in a wedding displays the bride and groom's respect and commitment toward the heaven and earth and the deities there, towards one's parents and ancestors, and towards each other. As a result, this imbued the wedding with a sacred, dignified quality.

拜天地

bai tiandi;
worshipping heaven and earth

参见“拜堂”。

See *bai tang* (paying traditional ceremonial obeisance in a wedding).

盖头 *gaitou;* bride veil

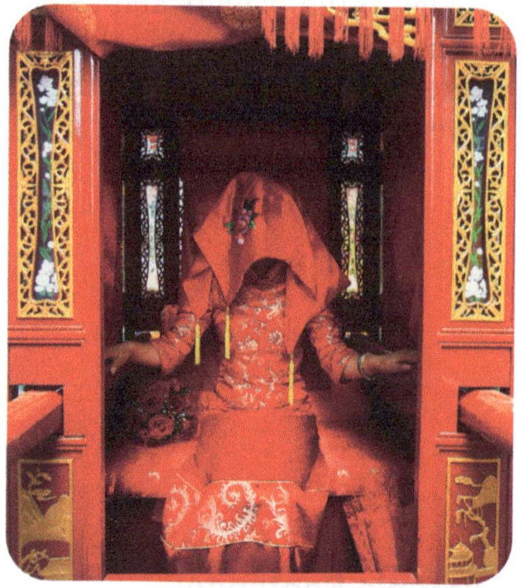

中国传统婚礼饰物，又称“盖巾”，指用来盖住新娘头面的红色纱或丝绸头巾。在传统婚礼上，新娘子通常会被蒙上盖头，待结婚仪式完毕进入洞房后由新郎揭开。戴盖头的习俗据说一是为新娘遮羞，二是为了辟邪。这一风俗已经不再流行。

A traditional Chinese marriage decoration, which is also called a head covering. The veil made of red cotton or silk was used to cover the face of the bride during traditional wedding ceremony, and it wasn't until the ceremony had finished and the newlyweds entered the bridal room that the groom could take it off. This custom is performed firstly to keep the bride from feeling shy and embarrassed and secondly to ward off evil spirits. Nowadays, only some people choose to follow this custom.

例句：

掀**盖头**是传统婚礼中最重要的环节之一，而红盖头也成为传统中式婚礼中新娘的标志性装饰。

Example Sentence:

Red veil was a symbolic adornment of brides in traditional Chinese wedding ceremonies and lifting the veil was one of the most important parts of the ceremony.

盖巾 *gaijin;* head covering for bride; bride veil

参见“盖头”。

See *gaitou* (bride veil).

交杯酒 *jiaobei jiu;* nuptial wine in crossed cups; drinking from crossed wine cups

中国传统婚姻习俗，又称“合卺”。在婚宴上，新婚夫妇要手臂相互交叉持杯饮酒，象征夫妇结为一体，相敬相爱。这种习俗在中国唐代已有记录，到宋代，盛行用彩丝将酒杯相联，绾成彩结，夫妻交杯共饮。该习俗在中国流传至今。

A traditional Chinese wedding custom. It is also referred to as "sharing the nuptial wine cups." At the wedding reception, the newlyweds interlock their arms to drink from each other's cup as a symbol of being united as one in love and respect. The custom was recorded as early as the Tang Dynasty (618-907), and during the Song Dynasty (960-1279) it was fashionable to perform the ritual by tying the two cups together into a knot with colorful silk threads and then having the newlyweds drink from crossed cups. This custom has been passed on to the present day.

例句：

在宋代，新婚夫妇饮完**交杯酒**后，将酒杯掷于床下，若一仰一合，即为吉兆，以示婚后百年好合。

Example Sentence:

In the Song Dynasty (960-1279), after the newlyweds finished drinking from crossed wine cups, they would throw the cups beneath the bed; if one cup was facing up and the other facing down, it would be considered an auspicious sign symbolizing a long and happy life together.

合卺

he jin;
share wine from ladles made of the same gourd;
share the nuptial wine cups

中国传统婚姻习俗。在古代交杯称“合卺”。卺俗称苦葫芦，是一种味苦不可食的匏瓜。合卺是将一只卺一分为二，用线将柄连在一起，新郎新娘各执装满酒的卺一饮而尽，寓意婚后两人将结为一体。

A traditional Chinese wedding custom. In ancient times, the ritual of drinking from crossed wine cups was referred to as *he jin*, i.e., sharing wine from ladles made of the same gourd. *Jin* is a type of bitter, inedible gourd. It was cut into two ladles with their handles linked with thread which were used as wine cups for the bride and groom. Drinking wine from the two ladles made of the same gourd was symbolic of the union of the husband and wife. See *jiaobei jiu*.

例句：

合卺酒异常苦涩，意味着今后夫妻两人要同甘共苦，患难与共。

Example Sentence:

The bitterness of the wine indicates that the husband and wife would go through thick and thin together from now on.

坐帐 *zuo zhang;* sitting behind the bed curtain

中国传统婚姻习俗，又称"坐床""坐福"。新婚夫妇拜完天地进入洞房后，并肩坐在洞房的炕沿或床边，寓意坐享幸福。有的地方只有新娘坐床，坐得越久表明新娘越贤惠端庄。有的地方新娘坐床时怀抱秤、瓶、箅（炊具）、筘（织具），象征公平、勤劳。

A Chinese wedding custom, also known as *zuo chuang* (sitting on the bed), or *zuo fu* (sitting for blessings). After the marriage ceremony is completed, the newlyweds enter the wedding chamber and sit side by side on the edge of the *kang* (heatable brick bed) or bed. This posture signifies their hope to enjoy future blessings. In some places, only the bride sits on the bed, and the longer she sits, the more virtuous and demure she is believed to be. In some places, she needs to hold four items — a steelyard balance, a bottle, a bamboo compartment used in a steamer, and a weaver's reed. These items signify fairness and diligence.

例句：

新婚夫妇入洞房前，先请两位全福人把床铺好，然后新娘入内盘膝**坐帐**。

Example Sentence:

Before the newlyweds enter their wedding chamber, two persons blessed in life will make the bed for them and then the bride sits cross-legged on the side of the bed.

踩四角 *cai sijiao;* stepping on the four corners (of the bed)

中国传统婚姻习俗。入洞房后，新郎挽新娘上炕。炕褥上放板栗、红枣等，由新郎拉着新娘上炕踩跳，翻找果物，寓意早生贵子。也有的地方是由新郎先入洞房，在新床的四角踩一踩，据说是为了检验床的安全，驱赶五毒。

A Chinese wedding custom. After entering the bed chamber, the groom helps the bride to sit on their *kang* (heatable brick bed). Within the sheets of the *kang* there will be chestnuts and jujubes (their pronunciations in Chinese sound similar to those of "having sons") . The groom will hold the bride's hand as they jump onto the bed and look for these items, known as stepping on the four corners. This expresses the wish for the couple to give birth to a son soon. Some places follow a different custom, in which the groom enters the chamber first and steps on the four corners of the bed. By doing so, he examines the quality of the bed and drives away *wudu* (five poisonous insects and animals).

例句：

踩四角这种极富地域特色的婚俗在陕北、山西一些地区非常盛行。

Example Sentence:

Stepping on the four corners is a wedding custom popular in regions such as northern Shaanxi Province and some places in Shanxi Province.

闹洞房 *nao dongfang;* teasing the newlyweds in the bridal chamber

中国民间婚姻习俗，又称“闹新房”“闹房”“暖房”。闹洞房是指新婚夜在新房内针对新婚夫妇开展的逗乐和戏谑活动，多带有开玩笑甚至恶作剧的性质。这一婚俗来历说法不一：一种说法认为闹洞房是人们性意识的外化；另一种说法认为闹洞房与古代婚制有关，因为封建社会的婚姻是父母之命、媒妁之言，婚前男女双方通常不认识，洞房花烛夜首次相见，闹洞房习俗有助于帮助消除两人之间的距离和陌生感，起到融洽感情的作用。这种习俗流行于中国各民族，最晚形成于汉代，至今仍盛行不衰。

A Chinese folk wedding custom, also known as *nao xinfang* (teasing the newlyweds in the wedding chamber), *nao fang* (teasing the newlyweds in the chamber) or *nuan fang* (warming up the chamber). This activity is held on the night of a wedding to amuse and tease the newlyweds, and usually involves playing a joke or prank on them. There are different stories as to how this marriage custom originated. Some people believe this is meant to hint playfully at the couples' future sexual relationship. Others believe this practice is related to the ancient marriage system. As feudal society marriages were arranged by parents through a matchmaker, the man and woman usually didn't know one another, and would see each other's face for the first time on their wedding night. Accordingly, this practice made it possible for them to become more familiar with each other and produce feelings of affection. This custom has become popular among all ethnic groups throughout the country. It emerged during the Han Dynasty (206 BC-AD 220), and it has remained prevalent ever since.

例句：

《中国青年报》社会调查中心的一项民意调查显示，79.2% 的受访者都曾经历过**闹洞房**，其中 45.4% 的人曾参与过闹洞房。

Example Sentence:

An opinion poll from the *China Youth Daily* survey center indicated that 79.2 percent of survey participants had witnessed the "teasing the newlyweds in the bridal room" practice, and 45.4 percent of them had participated in it in person.

守花烛

shou huazhu;
stay up late to watch the wedding candles

中国古代汉族婚礼习俗。作为中国旧式婚礼必备用品，婚礼中使用的蜡烛多半绘有龙凤彩饰，龙指新郎，凤指新娘，所以后世以花烛喻结婚。古人新婚之夜使用大红色的成对蜡烛，点燃于洞房之内，代表白头偕老，因此民间常言“洞房花烛夜”。两支花烛不可能同时熄灭，传说哪只花烛熄灭得早就预示着那个人以后会先死去，因而新婚之夜新郎新娘会通宵达旦守着花烛，等到一支熄灭了赶紧吹灭另一支，祈求白首同归。

A traditional Han Chinese folk wedding custom. Candles were essential items of old-style Chinese weddings and usually had dragons and phoenixes painted on them. The dragon was symbolic of the groom, and the phoenix, the bride. Thus, Chinese people use candles with such patterns (*huazhu*) as a metaphor for weddings. In ancient China, on the night of the wedding, a pair of big red candles were lit in the bridal chamber to indicate that the newlyweds would stay together till old age, hence people often use the expression of *dongfang huazhu ye* (the night with candles lit in the bridal chamber) to refer to the wedding night. The two candles were unlikely to go out at the same time. Whichever candle went out first was considered a prophecy as to which of the two newlyweds would be the first to pass away. As a result, the bride and groom would stay up late and keep an eye on the candles. As soon as one candle went out, they would quickly blow out the other, praying that when the time came, they would depart the world together.

例句：

如果新郎新娘不**守花烛**，则新人入睡后，伴娘须时时进房察看花烛有无异常，恐有不祥之兆。

Example Sentence:

If the newlyweds failed to stay awake to watch the candles in the bridal chamber, the bridesmaid would have to go into the chamber frequently after the newlyweds fell asleep and check on the candles to ensure that nothing went wrong.

百年好合

bainian haohe;
lifelong happiness in perfect harmony

中国婚礼祝福用语，用于祝贺新婚夫妇相亲相爱，白头到老。百合花在中国被认为寓意百年好合，因此适合作为婚礼上的礼物送给新人。

A congratulatory term used at weddings to wish the newlyweds a lifelong loving and caring relationship. In China, *baihe* (lily) which coincides with the first and last characters of the term, has been allegorically deemed indicative of a long and happy life together. As a result, it made an ideal gift for the newlyweds.

例句：

祝你们夫妻二人**百年好合**，永结同心！

Example Sentence:

May the two of you enjoy a lifelong happiness after tying the knot!

鸳鸯戏水 *yuanyang xi shui;* two mandarin ducks playing on water

A symbolic image of shared love and harmony between husband and wife in traditional Chinese culture. The birds always stay in pairs, one male (called *yuan*) and one female (called *yang*), whether resting on water or flying through the sky—and they hate to part from one another. As a result, they have always been used metaphorically to describe the fidelity and love between husband and wife.

中国传统文化中夫妻和睦相爱的美好象征。鸳鸯是一种水鸟，形似野鸭，鸳指雄鸟，鸯指雌鸟。这种鸟无论在水面休息还是在空中飞翔，总是成双入对、不离不弃，因此一直被用来比喻恋人、夫妻忠贞不渝，相亲相爱。

例句：

民俗文化中鸳鸯的形象无处不在，古人布置洞房时喜欢在门帘和窗帘上绣**鸳鸯戏水**图案，年画窗花也常以鸳鸯戏水作为题材。

Example Sentence:

The image of mandarin ducks is found in all forms of folk culture. Ancient Chinese people would decorate the bridal chambers with pictures or embroideries of mandarin ducks playing on water. Chinese New-Year paper-cuts often feature a pair of mandarin ducks playing on water as well.

早生贵子 *zaoshengguizi;* quickly give birth to a son

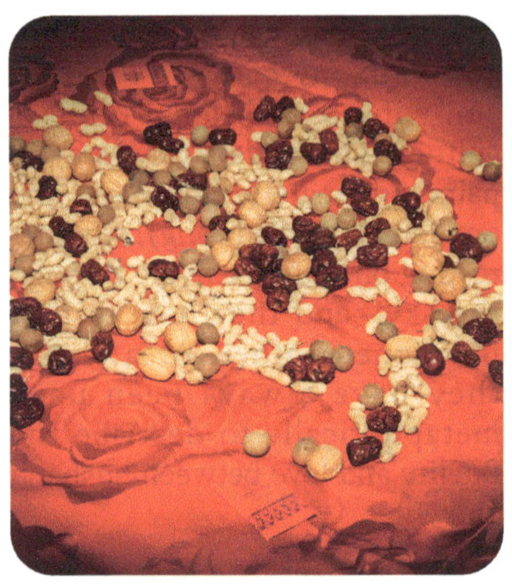

A Chinese phrase for wishing newlyweds well on their wedding day. On the day people get married, jujubes, peanuts, longan fruits, and melon seeds are placed on their bed or in the quilt. This is because the pronunciation of these four items is a homonym for the Chinese term, "quickly give birth to a son," which is considered a traditional way of wishing the couple to quickly have a child. This custom remains popular to this day in many rural areas.

中国婚礼祝福用语。新婚之日，人们会在新婚夫妇的床上或被子中放入枣、花生、桂圆、瓜子等，各取其中的一个字"枣、生、桂、子"，连起来组成谐音就是"早生贵子"，表达祝新婚夫妇早日生孩子的美好愿望。这一习俗至今在很多农村地区仍流行。

Example Sentence:

When Chinese people get married, wishes for them to "stay together until your hair turns white" and to "quickly give birth to a son" are the blessings they hear the most.

例句：

中国人结婚时听到的最多的祝福是白头偕老和**早生贵子**。

花馍

huamuo;
fancy steamed buns; steamed buns in fancy designs

中国黄河流域流传的民俗节令食品，又称“面花”“礼馍”“面塑”。花馍起源于中国民间祭祀活动中用面塑动物代替宰杀牛羊等动物的习俗，已有1000多年的历史。花馍以面粉为主料，手工塑造出各种飞禽走兽、水果蔬菜或人物花卉等形象，蒸成花式馒头，广泛用于各种节日、祭祀活动和婚丧嫁娶中，兼具食用、观赏、礼仪三大功能。花馍以加工精巧、内容丰富、造型生动、寓意深长而著称，被誉为可以食用的民间艺术品。

A traditional food for holidays in the Yellow River Basin area, also referred to as flowery rolls (*mianhua*), ceremonial buns (*limuo*), and sculpted buns (*miansu*). These rolls are derived from Chinese folk sacrificial customs wherein models of livestock were made to sacrifice to replace real livestock. This custom has a history of over 1,000 years. Fancy buns use flour as their main ingredient. They are sculpted by hand to look like birds, animals, fruits, vegetables, humans, flowers, etc. They are then steamed to form *mantous* (steamed buns). This type of food is used at all kinds of festivals and sacrificial ceremonies, and also during weddings and funerals. Fancy steamed buns are well known for their elaborate craftsmanship, rich designs, lively artwork, and deep cultural implications. They have been praised as an edible folk artwork.

例句：

婚礼中使用的**花馍**非常精美，比较常见的有龙凤礼馍、鸳鸯礼馍、金鱼礼馍等。

Example Sentence:

Fancy steamed buns used at wedding ceremonies are very delicately made. Typical designs include the patterns of dragons and phoenixes, mandarin ducks, and goldfish.

喜花 *xihua;* wedding paper-cuts

中国民间婚庆用的剪纸。喜花以红色纸剪成，婚庆时，用来装点各种器物用品和嫁妆。喜花的图案均以喜字为主，配有鸳鸯、蝴蝶、龙凤和喜鹊登梅等图案，寓意幸福美满、吉祥如意。

A Chinese folk decoration displayed during wedding celebrations. Wedding paper-cuts are made with red paper and are used to decorate wedding celebrations and also the dowry. The designs of these paper-cuts feature the Chinese character *xi* (喜, meaning happiness), supplemented with patterns of mandarin ducks, butterflies, dragons, phoenixes, and magpies perched on plum trees, and are symbolic of happiness and auspiciousness.

例句：

贴在墙和窗户上的**喜花**增强了喜庆气氛。

Example Sentence:

Wedding paper-cuts are pasted on walls and windows at wedding ceremonies to heighten the festive atmosphere.

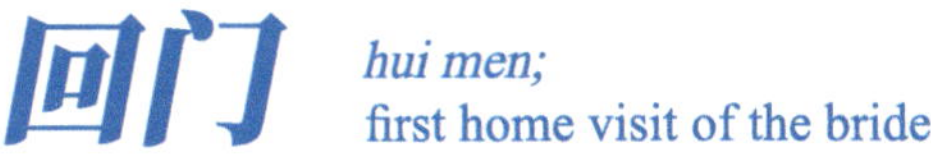

中国传统婚姻习俗。女子在出嫁后第三天携丈夫首次回娘家探亲，拜谒女方父母及亲属，向父母报平安，使他们内心安宁，因此又称“归宁”。归宁是女子同父母的正式告别，之后便不能随便回娘家了，除非父母发出邀请，或得到公婆、丈夫的批准。根据各地不同风俗，新女婿要献给岳父母回门礼、回门钱，娘家要设宴款待新婚夫妇。这一习俗流行至今，意指女儿成家后不忘父母养育之恩，女婿感谢岳父母恩德，也表示新婚夫妇婚后生活美满和睦。

A traditional Chinese marriage custom. On the third day after a woman is married, she and her husband return to her parents' home for the first time to visit her parents and relatives. This visit is meant to let her parents know that all is well in order to put their minds at ease, so it is also called "home visit to bring peace of mind" (*guining*). It also signifies that the woman is formally saying farewell to her parents. In the past, a married woman could not return to her parents' home whenever she liked. Only when her parents invited her or she received the approval of her husband or his parents could she return home. According to the customs in different localities, the husband should present his wife's parents with gifts and money on such an occasion, and the parents should host a banquet for them. This custom has remained prevalent to this day, showing that the daughter always remembers her parents for raising her, the son-in-law is appreciative to his wife's parents, and the newlyweds will enjoy a happy new life together.

例句：

按照中国传统婚俗习惯，**回门**是一种必不可少的礼节。

Example Sentence:

A fundamental custom of traditional Chinese marriages is for the bride to visit her home on the third day after her wedding.

归宁 *guining;* home visit to bring peace of mind

参见“回门”。

See *hui men* (first home visit of the bride).

住对月 *zhu duiyue;* month away

中国民间婚姻习俗。婚礼一个月后，娘家接新娘回家居住一段时间，新娘根据婆婆的吩咐住六、八、十日或者一个月都可以，之后新郎前往新娘家接回新娘。新娘返回婆家时往往要带些礼物，至此新人的婚礼全部结束。住对月最初是满族婚俗，后来山西、陕西、河南等地的汉族也都采用此婚俗。

A Chinese folk marriage custom. One month after a marriage, the bride's family invites her home to stay for some time. According to her mother-in-law's instruction, she may stay for six, eight, or ten days or even as long as a month. Afterwards, the groom goes to the bride's home to bring her back. When the bride returns to her husband's family, she typically brings some gifts for her in-laws. At this point, her ceremonial status as a "newlywed" ends. This custom was originally a Manchu marriage custom, but later it became prevalent among the Han people in Shanxi, Shaanxi, Henan, and other provinces.

例句：

现在，新媳妇回娘家**住对月**等传统风俗已逐渐消失。

Example Sentence:

Today, some folk customs including the "month away" have gradually disappeared.

做寿 *zuo shou;* celebrating a birthday (for the elderly)

中国民间为年长的人过生日而举行的庆祝活动。浙江绍兴民间有“生日年年有，寿诞六十首”的俗谚，意思是说人只有到60岁才有资格做寿。寿俗中还有一些不成文的习俗，例如做九不做十，男做九、女做十，逢五小寿小庆、逢十大寿大庆等。做寿这天寿星老人端坐于中，承受晚辈叩寿头。传说叩寿头是晚辈把自己的寿数用叩头的形式奉献给老人，所以叩头不会超过三个。

A Chinese folk celebration held on birthdays of the elderly. In Shaoxing, Zhejiang Province, there is a proverb that says while birthday comes each year, celebration of it starts at the age of 60. That is to say, people can only celebrate their birthdays when they reach 60 and over. Regarding the celebrations, there are also a few unwritten rules. Examples include "celebrating every ninth (birthday), not every tenth", "men celebrate every ninth, women every tenth", and "having a small celebration for every fifth and a big celebration for every tenth." On the day when a senior celebrates his/her birthday, he/she sits in a chair and the younger generations in the family kowtow before him/her. It is said that kowtowing to the elderly is a way in which the younger generation pass on some of the years they are predestined to be alive over to the elderly. So they do not kowtow more than three times.

例句：

按民俗，庆寿诞的时间可以提前到生日前，但不能延迟到生日后，过了生日当天就不能再**做寿**了。

Example Sentence:

According to popular customs, a birthday celebration for an elderly can be organized before the elderly's actual birth date, but not after. Celebration after the actual birth date is not acceptable.

bai shou;
congratulating an elderly on his/her birthday

中国传统庆寿礼仪，指在年长亲友生日时上门表示祝贺。旧时拜寿时，晚辈携礼物前往长辈家，向长辈行鞠躬礼或跪拜礼以表示敬贺。现在拜寿的礼节已经大大简化，一般以家庭寿宴的形式为老人贺寿。

Traditional Chinese etiquette for birthday celebration. It refers to visiting family elderly on their birthdays. In the past, one would bring gifts to visit a family elderly on his/her birthday, and bow or kowtow to him/her to show respect and congratulations. Nowadays, the ritual has been greatly simplified and people typically attend a family banquet to celebrate an elderly's birthday.

例句：

拜寿时，人们通常为老人献上寿桃、寿联，并吃寿面，恭祝老人健康长寿。

Example Sentence:

While congratulating an elderly on his/her birthday, people often present longevity peaches and couplets with congratulatory lines as gifts, and share longevity noodles to wish him/her a long and healthy life.

寿星 *shouxing;* God of Longevity; a person whose birthday is being celebrated

中国古代神话中的的长寿之神和道教中的一位神仙。寿星本为一个恒星的名字，后逐渐演变为仙人名称。在中国传统画像中，寿星为白须老翁，持杖，额部隆起，是长寿老人的象征，常衬托以鹿、鹤、仙桃等，象征长寿。民间常供奉寿星，以祈求健康长寿。现在该词也泛指过生日的人。

A god overseeing longevity in ancient Chinese mythology and a Daoist immortal. *Shouxing* (literally, longevity star) was originally the name of a fixed star, but over time it gradually evolved into the name of an immortal. In traditional Chinese portraits, *shouxing* is depicted as an old man with a white beard. He holds a cane and his forehead bulges out, symbolizing the aged. Also in the portraits are the deer, crane, and peach—symbols of longevity in Chinese culture. It is popular to make offerings to *shouxing* as a means of praying for a long and healthy life. Today, this word is also used to indicate a person who is celebrating a birthday.

例句：

明明和爷爷同一天过生日，每年家人都为这对小**寿星**和老寿星一起举办生日宴会。

Example Sentence:

Mingming and his grandfather have a birthday on the same day. Every year the family holds a birthday celebration for the little *shouxing* and the old *shouxing*.

寿桃 *shoutao;* longevity peach; birthday peach

原指中国神话中延年益寿的蟠桃，现多为用面粉做成的桃子形状的礼馍，作为馈赠中老年人的寿礼。中国古人认为桃树是神树仙木，其果实可以延年益寿。在神话传说中，王母娘娘做寿时设蟠桃会，用三千年一熟的蟠桃款待群仙。因此，民间常用桃来做庆寿的食品。

The legendary peach of immortality in Chinese mythology. Nowadays it often refers to the peach-shaped steamed bun which is made of wheat flour. It is presented to the elderly as a birthday gift. Ancient Chinese believed that the peach tree was divine, and that its fruits could promote longevity. Legend has it that when the Queen Mother of the West celebrated her birthday, a banquet of immortals was held. During the banquet, they were treated with longevity peaches which only became ripe once every 3,000 years. Therefore, it is popular to have peaches or peach-shaped steamed buns when celebrating birthdays for an elderly.

例句：

晚辈送**寿桃**给长辈是中国传统民俗之一，意在表达孝敬与祝福。

Example Sentence:

It is a Chinese tradition for the younger generation to present longevity peaches to their seniors as birthday gifts, which is a token of filial respect and blessings.

寿糕 *shougao;* birthday pastry

中国民间寿诞习俗糕点，常用作寿礼。寿糕多以面粉、糖等蒸制而成，并饰以云卷、如意或吉祥语等图案，糕上做出松鹤延年、老寿星等纹饰。

A kind of Chinese style pastry consumed when people celebrate their birthdays, and a popular birthday gift. It is made by steaming flour, wheat, sugar, and other ingredients. Patterns of clouds, ornamental scepters, or auspicious remarks are often added as decorations. Patterns of "pine and crane longevity" or the "God of Longevity" are also often seen.

例句：

中国江南地区的人们常用米粉蒸制**寿糕**，馈赠亲友，恭贺寿辰。

Example Sentence:

In the regions south of the Yangtze River, rice flour is usually used as the raw material of the birthday pastry. Such pastries are popular birthday gifts for family and friends.

寿面 *shoumian;* birthday noodles; longevity noodles

中国民间寿诞习俗食品，又称“长寿面”。在中国食品中，面条最为绵长，因而在寿日吃面象征着福寿绵长。吃寿面的习俗在中国南北方都很盛行。寿宴上，儿女等晚辈常向寿星长辈敬献长寿面。有的地方将团团面条摆放大盘中，叠成塔状，外套红色剪纸摆放在寿宴上以增添喜庆气氛。除为长者祝寿，吃长寿面庆生在各地也已成为普遍的习俗。

A kind of Chinese noodles eaten when people celebrate their birthday. Among various types of Chinese food, noodles are long and not easily broken. Therefore, eating noodles on one's birthday symbolizes that the person will enjoy a long and happy life. The custom of eating longevity noodles is popular in both southern and northern regions of the country. During the birthday banquets for seniors, the younger generations often present them with longevity noodles. In some places, noodles are piled up into a pyramid shape, which is then surrounded by red paper-cuts to add to the joyful atmosphere. Apart from being presented to the elderly, longevity noodles are also often eaten by the younger generation when they celebrate their birthdays, which has become a common practice in various parts of the country.

例句：

寿面是中国人过生日和祝寿时的常用食品，有福寿绵延之意。

Example Sentence:

Chinese people often eat birthday noodles when celebrating birthdays. This food symbolizes a long and happy life.

寿堂 *shoutang;* longevity hall

中国民间祝寿所设厅堂。为给年事已高之人祝寿，常在寿星府邸正屋设寿堂，堂内悬挂福禄寿三星画像、寿星像、八仙祝寿图或寿字画轴，旁配红纸金字寿联，多写“福如东海、寿比南山”等祝词。香案陈设寿桃、寿糕、寿面、八仙等，桌两旁摆万年青、长青藤或松柏之类的植物。寿堂上张灯结彩，点满写上寿字的寿烛，大红色寿烛表面配有龙凤图案，红烛高照，明灯闪耀，喜气盈门。寿翁寿婆端坐正中太师椅上，接受家人和来宾的拜贺。

A Chinese traditional venue used to celebrate birthdays of elderly people. In most cases, the longevity hall is set up in the main room at the elderly's home. Typically hanging in the hall are portraits of the three gods of Happiness, Prosperity, and Longevity, the eight immortals, and also calligraphy scrolls displaying the Chinese character for longevity. Couplets hanging on both sides were, written in golden letters on red paper with such phrases as “May Your Happiness Be as Immense as the East Sea” and “May You Live as Long as the Zhongnan Mountains.” Longevity peaches, cakes and noodles are set on the table along with incense and plants like evergreens, ivy, or cypress shrubs which are placed on either side of the table. The hall is decorated with lanterns, colored banners, and longevity candles carved with the character for “longevity” and also may feature the images of a dragon and phoenix. The red candles are very bright, producing a radiant light that fills the room with a festive atmosphere. The elderly person will usually sit in the ceremonial chair and accept birthday congratulations from guests.

例句：

有的**寿堂**的墙壁上还挂着一幅红纸金字寿屏，一般请当地名流书写，内容都是寿星的功德、业绩等。

Example Sentence:

Some people would hang a scroll of red paper written in golden characters on a wall of the longevity hall. Usually a famous local scholar will be asked to write this scroll. The content typically includes the achievements and merits of the birthday person.

寿幛 *shouzhang;* longevity scroll

中国民间祝寿专用刺绣品，是贵重耀眼的寿礼。寿幛以大幅红绸缎为料，上加刺绣，纹样多与画轴相同，有的刺绣寿字，或用百个寿字组成百寿图，或用寿字组成画面，富贵人家也有直接用金银缀成寿字的。寿幛有的做成刺绣挂屏装裱起来，有的装镜框作为寿礼赠送。

A traditional birthday gift for elderly people, considered a precious and dazzling birthday present. It is a large, beautiful piece of red fabric (usually silk or satin) with intricate embroidered designs featuring the Chinese character for longevity. The longevity scroll may have one large "longevity" character, one hundred small characters forming a hundred-longevity pattern, or the character is used to form an image. Wealthy families will even use real gold and silver to stitch the characters into the scroll. When presented as a birthday gift, the longevity scroll is either hung up or placed in a frame.

例句：

民国时期，用银元缀于**寿幛**比较常见，后来也有用大额钞票贴成寿字的寿幛。

Example Sentence:

During the Republic of China period (1912–1949), it was relatively common to have silver coins stitched into longevity scrolls. Later, high value bank notes were stuck onto the scroll to form the character for longevity.

寿匾 *shoubian;* longevity tablet

中国民间祝寿用横幅。匾是题字的横幅，一般为石刻或木刻，悬挂于门或墙的上部作为装饰，是中国古建筑的重要组成部分。匾上的文字

A tablet used to celebrate an elderly person's birthday. The tablet has calligraphy on its horizontal face made of carved stone or wood, and is then hung above a door or high on a wall as a decoration. This is an important component of ancient

体现了送匾者的文学修养、书法功底和审美情趣，是非常高雅的艺术品。因此古时人们爱匾、敬匾，刻匾、送匾之风盛行，送匾祝寿也由来已久。此风俗至今仍然在一些地方流行，但所送之匾大多为工厂定制，很少有亲自题写的了。

Chinese architecture. The writings on the tablet reflect the literary accomplishments, calligraphy skills, and artistry of the person who gives the tablet. It was a very elegant type of artwork, and was highly appreciated and treasured by ancient Chinese who were fond of creating such tablets and sending them as gifts, especially as birthday gifts for the elderly. The practice is still popular in some places, but the majority of these tablets today are made in factories and very few are made by hand.

例句：

寿匾中对长者的称呼和下面的落款都很有讲究，上款应对受匾者使用尊称，下款对自己使用谦称。

Example Sentence:

The way to address the elderly person and sign the sender's name on longevity tablets requires special attention. The artist must write the recepient's name with honorific titles on the upper part, and sign his own name with modesty on the lower part of the tablet.

长命百岁 *changming baisui;* long life to 100 years

中国民间祝福语。常在祝寿时用作贺辞，祝人长寿。古时由于战乱、瘟疫等影响，人的寿命普遍不长，因此能够活到百岁便是非常长寿了。现在随着医疗技术的进步和生活的安定，百岁老人已不鲜见了。

A Chinese way of wishing someone well on their birthday, especially an elderly person. Specifically, it wishes the elderly a long life. In ancient times the lifespan of people was generally very short, as their lives were often impacted by various wars and epidemics. As a result, living until 100 years old was indeed a great accomplishment. Today, with advances in medical technology and social stability, it is no longer rare to come across centenarians.

例句：

要想**长命百岁**，必须养成良好的生活习惯。

Example Sentence:

If one wants to live a long life of 100 years, he/she must develop good habits in life.

本命年 *benming nian;* birth sign year

与一个人出生之年同属相（生肖）的年份，俗称“属相年”。本命年按照中国传统农历计算，每十二年一个循环。民间认为本命年是一个不吉利的年份，需要跨过很多槛儿。因此，每到本命年，亲戚朋友会送红腰带给本命年的人系在腰上，或者送红背心、红裤衩给本命年的小孩儿穿上，俗称“扎红”，寄托人们祛邪、避灾、祈福的美好愿望。

The year with the same zodiac sign/animal as one's birth year according to the Chinese Zodiac, also referred to as a person's zodiac year (*shuxiang nian*). There are 12 years in one cycle, with each year corresponding to a zodiac animal. People believe that when their birth sign year arrives (at 12 years old, 24, 36, etc.), many ominous obstacles may occur. As a result, relatives and friends will give the person a red belt to wear during the year, while children are given red vests and red underpants. This is commonly referred to as "binding red," and it is intended to dispel evil spirits, avert disasters, and pray for good fortune.

例句：

中国人在**本命年**大多会系红腰带、穿红袜子以趋吉避凶，消灾免祸。

Example Sentence:

During a birth sign year, most Chinese people will wear a red belt and red socks to seek good luck and avert calamities and disasters.

属相年 *shuxiang nian;* zodiac year

参见“本命年”。

See *benming nian* (birth sign year).

麻姑献寿 *Magu xian shou;* Magu's birthday offerings

中国民俗画题材。麻姑是道教神话中有名的女寿仙，相传她曾经亲见东海三次变为桑田，因此被视为高寿的象征。又传说她曾用十三年时间用十三泉清水酿造成灵芝酒，在农历三月三日王母娘娘寿辰之时献酒祝寿，因此民间向女性祝寿时多绘麻姑像相送，称为“麻姑献寿”。

A popular theme for Chinese folk paintings. *Magu* is a famous female immortal of longevity in Daoist folklore. Legend tells that she lived so long that she personally witnessed three monumental changes of the landscape of the East Sea. As a result, she is regarded as a symbol of longevity. Another legend tells that she spent 13 years fermenting a "*lingzhi* wine" from the water of 13 different springs, and on the third day of the third month of the lunar calendar, she presented this gift to the Queen Mother of the West as a birthday present. Consequently, when people offer birthday congratulations to female elders, they often gift them portraits of *Magu*, which are called "*Magu*'s Birthday Offerings."

例句：

春节期间，有些地方有贴**麻姑献寿**年画的习俗。

Example Sentence:

In some places pictures of *Magu*'s Birthday Offerings are pasted on the walls during the Spring Festival.

事死如事生

shi si ru shi sheng;
serving the dead as if they were alive

中国古人的孝道传统，即对待死去的长辈和祖先应像其在世时一样，按照他们生前的喜好和要求来安排其葬礼和其后的祭祀活动，以便他们在阴间仍能够过上幸福的生活。“事死如事生”出自《礼记·中庸》。

A traditional Chinese custom of filial piety. This refers to treating one's deceased seniors and ancestors with the same respect as if they had not passed away, and abiding by their preferences and requests when arranging their funerals and, later, when offering sacrifices to them. This is done so that the deceased will be able to live happily in the netherworld. This notion is derived from the work *The Doctrine of Mean.*

例句：

举行祭祀活动就是为了怀念已故先祖，**事死如事生**。

Example Sentence:

People hold sacrificial ceremonies to cherish the memories of their ancestors, and during these ceremonies they should treat the deceased as if they were still alive.

寿终正寝

shouzhong-zhengqin;
passing away in one's home after a long life;
die a natural death

中国成语。寿终，指老年人自然死去。正寝，家宅的正房，人死后灵柩停放的地方。寿终正寝比喻人年老而安然死于家中，被视为喜丧。这

A Chinese idiom, the equivalent to "live to a ripe old age." After death, a person is laid in a coffin which is then placed in the central room of their house for the funeral. This idiom therefore metaphorically describes a person who has lived a long life and

个成语现在也用来喻指事物的自然消亡（含讽刺意味）。

was able to pass away peacefully at their home, which is regarded as a happy death. Today, this idiom is also used satirically to say that things die out naturally.

例句:

爷爷年过八十，他最大的心愿就是能回到故乡**寿终正寝**。

Example Sentence:

Grandfather is over 80 years old, and his greatest wish is to return to his ancestral home, live to an old age, and pass away naturally.

红白喜事 *hongbaixishi;* happy events in red and white; weddings and funerals

中国对婚丧的统称。男女结婚是喜事，用喜庆的红色；人高寿而自然去世也是喜事，用宁静的白色，二者统称红白喜事，后来泛指婚丧活动，这种说法反映了中国人对待死亡的达观态度。

A general term for marriage and death in China. The marriage of a man and woman is a happy event, and festive red is thus used for cloths and decorations. When a person lives to an old age and naturally passes away, this is also considered a happy event, and tranquil white is used. So the two together are called happy events in red and white. It was later extended to refer to all activities associated with weddings and funerals. This term reflects the positive attitude Chinese people have regarding death.

例句:

大户人家的**红白喜事**都很隆重。

Example Sentence:

Weddings and funerals of well-off families are usually ceremonious occasions.

喜丧 *xisang;* blessed funeral; happy funeral

中国民间对福寿双全、家族兴旺且自然老死的高龄老人的葬礼的称呼。中国人认为这种自然死亡是一件值得庆贺的事情，故称为"喜丧"。旧时老人去世后会停灵三至五日，家人大摆宴席招待亲朋好友，前来吊丧的人也会向家人道贺。

A term used to refer to a funeral of a senior person who is blessed with a fortunate and long life and a thriving family and who dies a natural death. Chinese people believe that this kind of natural death is one worth celebrating, and it is thus called a "blessed/happy funeral." In the past, relatives and friends would come to express condolences as well as congratulations before the coffin of the dead within three to five days after the death and the family of the diseased would treat the guests with banquets.

例句：

喜丧这种习俗反映了中国人对待死亡的乐观豁达的态度。

Example Sentence:

The concept of a happy funeral reflects the positive attitude Chinese people have regarding death.

送终 *song zhong;* pay one's last respect; arrange for a proper burial

中国民间葬礼习俗。指长辈在弥留之际，儿孙辈守在床前照料，送老人最后一程；也指安排长辈亲属的丧事。

A Chinese folk funeral custom. When a person is on the verge of death, their descendants are expected to keep close by their bed and attend upon them till their very last moment. The term can also mean arranging a proper burial for one's parents or other senior relatives.

例句：

一个人若是临死前，家人特别是子孙都能为其**送终**，就会被认为是有福之人。

Example Sentence:

If a person enjoys the company of his family, especially his children and grandchildren, at the last moment of his life, he/she is considered a fortunate person.

叫魂

jiao hun;
soul calling; calling back one's soul

中国旧时民间一种迷信习俗，又称"喊魂"，即召唤人的灵魂复归身体。中国古人认为人有疾病将死时魂魄离散，须招魂以复其精神，延其年寿。另一种情况是婴儿受惊吓会导致魂不附体，此时须叫魂收惊，使魂魄归来，除病消灾。叫魂的方式因地域而异。

An old superstitious Chinese folk custom, also called "calling souls" (*hanhun*). It refers to calling back a person's soul to their body. Ancient Chinese believed that when a person was about to die from some ailment, their soul would leave them, so people needed to call the soul back to their body to extend their life. People also believe that when an infant child is frightened their soul will leave their body, and at this moment people need to call the soul back to the body to avert a calamity. The specific practices of calling back a soul vary in different regions.

例句：

叫魂不能治好孩子的重病。

Example Sentence:

Soul calling cannot cure a child's serious disease.

喊魂

han hun;
calling souls

参见"叫魂"。

See *jiao hun* (soul calling).

招魂 *zhao hun;* soul summoning

中国古代丧葬习俗。亲属召唤死者灵魂回复身体，希望起死回生。挺尸之后行招魂礼，亲属挂上魂帛、魂幡，幡上串起与死者岁数相等的纸钱，持死者之衣登屋顶，北面三呼，召唤死者的灵魂返归于衣。

An ancient Chinese funeral custom. Relatives called out to the soul of the deceased, asking it to return to the body, hoping they can incite the deceased to come back to life again. The soul summoning ceremony began after rigor mortis had set in. One relative would raise a "soul-summoning banner" attached with paper money of an amount corresponding to the age of the deceased, climb to the roof with the clothing of the deceased at hands, and shout the name of the deceased for three times towards the north, to summon the soul to return to its clothing.

例句：

这个老太太宣称她能给死者**招魂**。

Example Sentence:

The old lady claims to be able to summon the souls for the deceased.

灵堂 *lingtang;* mourning hall; funeral hall

中国传统葬礼中吊唁逝者的场所，一般设在丧家的厅堂或在院子里搭灵棚。灵堂正中摆放灵柩，前面设牌位（现在是在灵堂上方高挂死者遗像），桌上摆供品，香炉、

The venue for offering condolences in a traditional Chinese funeral. In most cases, it is set up in the main hall or courtyard of the family of the deceased. The coffin is placed in the center of the mourning hall, in front of which is the memorial tablet (nowadays the photo of the deceased is hung on top

烛台和长明灯等，两边是鲜花与花篮，周围悬挂亲友赠送的挽联、祭幛。祭幛多为绸缎布料，上缀寄托哀思、一拜永别之类的悼词。灵堂前部边上是演奏哀乐的吹鼓手和守灵人。古人认为人的灵魂不死，设置灵堂是为了使死者灵魂在去阴间之前有个安息之处，也方便亲友前来吊丧。

of the wall instead) with an altar with offerings, candles, an incense burner, and a lamp that burns day and night. Flower baskets are placed on each side of the coffin. Elegiac couplets are hung in the hall alongside silk or satin scrolls inscribed with words of mourning such as "in profound grief" and "bowing to part forever." Musicians play somber music and people keep vigil in the front of the hall. Ancient Chinese people believe that a person's soul does not disappear after death, so a mourning hall (literally the soul's hall) is set up to offer a resting place for the soul of the deceased before it goes to the netherworld and make it convenient for relatives and friends to offer condolences.

例句：

现在城市里的丧事办理一般集中到殡仪馆进行，家中不再开设**灵堂**。

Example Sentence:

Today, funeral services in cities are typically carried out in funeral parlors. Mourning halls are no longer set up.

报丧

bao sang;
announcing the death

中国民间丧葬习俗。丧家将逝者逝世的消息通知已知或未知的亲友和村人。在汉族的观念里，报丧不仅是形式上的礼仪，更是

Chinese funeral ritual. The family informs relatives, friends and fellow countrymen of the death of a family member. It's not just a habitual ritual to be followed, but also an opportunity to seek emotional support from one's kinsfolk. This

和亲属家人一起分担悲痛的做法。报丧仪式早在周代便已形成，各地各民族的报丧方式各不相同。

practice had already taken shape during the Zhou Dynasty (1046-256 BC). The specific ways of announcing a passing away differ according to regional customs and ethnic traditions.

例句：

旧时办丧事有**报丧**、告祖、入殓、祭奠、出殡、送葬、居丧（即丁忧）等程序。

Example Sentence:

In ancient times, funeral arrangements included announcing the death, reporting to ancestors, putting the body in the coffin, giving offerings, holding the funeral procession, burying the dead, and observing the ritual mourning.

戴孝

dai xiao;
wearing mourning clothes; be in mourning

中国民间丧葬礼俗，也称“披麻戴孝”。葬礼期间，死者妻子儿孙及晚辈亲属需要穿戴白色或黑色孝服以表孝意和哀悼。孝服根据亲疏程度有不同长度和样式：直系子孙应全身披麻戴孝；关系较远的亲属头扎白巾或腰缠白布（有的胳膊上缠黑纱）。现在大多简化为臂带黑纱。

Chinese funeral ritual, also called “wearing gunny mourning clothes”. During the funeral, the wife, children, and other descendants of the deceased should dress in white or black mourning clothes to express their filial piety and grief. Mourning clothes are of different length and style according to how close one was in relation to the deceased. Children of the deceased should wear mourning clothes from head to foot; distant relatives only wrap a white cloth around their head or their waist, and some wrap a black band around their arms. Today, the custom has been greatly simplified, and most people simply wear a black armband.

例句:

这位**戴孝**的妇人在亲友的陪伴下蹒跚地走在路上。

Example Sentence:

Wearing mourning clothes, the woman trudges along the road, accompanied by friends and family members.

守灵

shou ling;
keep vigil beside the coffin; hold a wake

中国民间丧葬习俗，指死者配偶子女等守护、陪伴在灵床、灵柩或灵位边。孝男孝女为尽孝道，在葬礼期间日夜守在灵柩旁早晚烧纸，朝夕祭奠；男不剃头，女不梳头，寝苫枕块，啜粥吃素；逢亲友前来吊唁，守灵者须叩首感谢。演变到现在，守灵便是亲人们聚在一起悼念死者，抒发缅怀之情。

Chinese funeral custom. Sons and daughters as well as the spouse of the dead would keep vigil beside the death bed, coffin or memorial tablet. The children of the deceased would keep vigil day and night while burning paper money and making other sacrifices as a sign of filial piety. Men should not shave and women should not comb their hair. They sleep on a bed of straw with a pillow of clay, drink porridge and refrain from eating meat. Upon arriving, relatives offer condolences first, and the guardians of the coffin should kowtow to express thanks. The custom has changed over time, and it is now a time for kinsfolk to gather together to share their memories of the dead and console one another.

例句：

他们一家人希望能够遵照宗教习俗，为她净身后再**守灵**三夜。

Example Sentence:

The family wanted to adhere to the religious rituals of washing her body clean and holding a wake for three days.

守丧 *shou sang;* observing the conventions of mourning; be in mourning

中国传统丧葬习俗，又称居丧、守制、守孝、丁忧，指在父母或其他重要长辈去世后的一段时间（丧期）内为其服丧并遵循一定的行为规范，来表达对丧者的哀思。在封建社会，妻子也必须为丈夫守丧。守丧是儒家倡导的孝道的重要体现，在中国整个封建时期得到统治阶级的重视和倡导，并强制推行。守丧期间应谢绝应酬，不得应考、婚嫁，有官职的在丧期需要离职。古制一般要求父母去世后守丧三年。新中国成立以后，守丧的习俗逐渐消失。现在守丧常用来指守灵。参见“守灵”。

Traditional Chinese custom in honor of the dead, also called *jusang* (be in mourning), *shouzhi* (follow the etiquette for mourning), *shouxiao* (stay in mourning), *dingyou* (be in bereavement). It refers to the practice that people express sorrow over the loss of one's parent or a senior family member by observing certain conventions for a specified period of time. In the feudal society, a wife was also expected to stay in mourning after her husband's death. This practice is an important manifestation of the doctrine of filial piety advocated by the Confucian school, and had been promoted and institutionalized by feudal rulers in the past. People in mourning were expected to stay away from social activities, exams and marriages, and officials were expected to leave their positions and stay in bereavement at home. The old tradition required a period of three years in mourning

upon the death of one's parent. After 1949, the practice gradually disappeared. Nowadays, *shousang* is often used as a synonym of *shouling*. See *shouling* (keep vigil beside the coffin).

例句：

孔子认为，人出生三年后才离开父母的怀抱，因此应该以**守丧**三年来回报父母的恩情。

Example Sentence:

According to Confucius, children are mostly carried in the arms of their parents before they reach the age of three, therefore, they should be in mourning for their parents for three years to requite their love and care.

丁忧 *dingyou;* be in bereavement

原指遇到父母丧事。后多专指官员离职居丧。参见"守丧"。

Originally it meant the death of one's parent and related funeral arrangements, and later it refers specifically to officials who observe the conventions of mourning and leave their positions temporarily. See *shousang* (observing the conventions of mourning).

接三 *jie san;* receiving the returning soul on the third

中国民间丧葬旧俗，即在人死后第三天晚上举行超度祭奠仪式，满汉皆有，流行于东北、北京等地。旧俗认为人死后第三天亡灵会最后一次回望家中，所以丧者家中

An old Chinese funeral custom. It was a ritual to help the soul of the dead out of purgatory, observed on the evening of the third day after a person's death. The practice was popular in places such as northeast China

当日晚上要设灵堂，搭丧棚，迎亲朋吊唁，请亡灵回家享用祭品，称为接三；棚内设经台，请僧人道士做法事，并奏吹鼓乐，焚化纸糊车马等冥器，送亡灵上路，所以又称送三。

and Beijing among both the Manchu and Han ethnic groups. People in the past believed that on the third day after a person died, its soul would take a last look at its family. The grieving family therefore would set up a mourning hall or shed on that evening where relatives and friends could come and express their condolences and the soul of the dead could return to enjoy the offerings. Also on this occasion, monks or Daoist priests would be invited to perform rituals, drums and pipes would be played, and paper offerings such as paper chariots would be burned to bid farewell to the soul of the dead. Therefore, the ritual was also called *song san*, meaning “bidding farewell to the soul on the third.”

例句：

旧时葬礼，丧家延请僧、道做法事超度亡灵。法事以**接三**最为隆重。

Example Sentence:

At the funeral in the past, the grieving family would invite monks or Daoist priests over to hold religious rituals to pray for the soul of the dead out of purgatory. Of the rituals, receiving the returning soul on the third was most solemn.

song san;
bidding farewell to the soul on the third

参见“接三”。

See *jie san* (receiving the returning soul on the third).

吊丧 *diao sang;* (pay) a condolence visit

中国传统丧葬习俗，又称"吊孝"。吊丧是获悉亲戚朋友去世后到丧家进行吊唁慰问的活动，一般在停丧守灵期间举行。吊丧之礼自周代以来历代因袭。礼俗规定，吊丧者必须穿素服，馈赠奠仪，并烧香致奠。

A traditional Chinese funeral ritual, also called *diao xiao*. This refers to paying a condolence visit to the family of a relative or friend soon after their death, usually during the wake. According to the etiquette, the visitor typically wears white plain clothes, presents gifts as offerings and burns incense.

例句：

她丈夫死后的第二天，所有的妇女们都准备到她家**吊丧**以表哀悼。

Example Sentence:

The day after her husband's death, all the ladies prepared to visit her house and offer condolences and support.

吊孝 *diao xiao;* (pay) a condolence visit

参见"吊丧"。

See *diao sang* (pay a condolence visit).

谢孝 *xie xiao;* thank friends and relatives for offering condolences

中国传统丧葬习俗，指孝子等向前来吊唁的亲友行礼。礼俗规定，亲戚朋友来丧家吊唁时需向死者行礼，一般是平辈鞠躬，晚辈跪拜。死者亲属应对吊丧者行礼以示答谢，称谢孝。谢孝也指孝子在服满后拜谢曾来吊唁的亲友。

A Chinese funeral ritual in the past. It refers to the practice of sons and other family members of the deceased saluting visitors offering condolences. According to old etiquette, relatives and friends who came to offer condolences must salute the dead, either by bowing to (if they are of the same generation with the dead) or kneeling down (if they are junior) before the coffin. In return, members of the grieving family would salute the visitor to express appreciation, which is called "*xie xiao*" (thanking friends and relatives for offering condolences). This term is also used to refer to the custom where the son(s) visited relatives and friends to express appreciation for their presence at the funeral after the mourning period was over.

例句：

他以**谢孝**的名义邀请当地有影响的几位人物来商议一个秘密计划。

Example Sentence:

He invited a few influential figures in the locality to discuss a secret plan in the name of thanking them for their presence at his parent's funeral.

发丧

fa sang;
announce the death of a family member; arrange funeral affairs

中国丧葬用语，指丧家宣告某人去世，也指办理丧事。旧时举哀发丧时，多在家门前竖立招魂幡或挂魂帛。幡上缀一串纸钱，钱数与死者的岁数相同。有的地方有家人登屋顶呼唤死者亡魂归来的习俗。丧家门口贴出白纸以告白。房舍院内所有对联、画轴及镜子等都要用白纸遮挡严密。旧时葬礼丧家还要延请僧、道做法事，灵堂悬挂神像画轴，供桌设置法器，僧、道诵经，奉请神佛鬼魂及本家亡灵享祭。法事中夹杂乐班，吹奏哀乐和民间戏曲小调。

A term referring to the announcement of the death of a family member, or the entire funeral procedure in Chinese folk funeral customs. Upon the death of a family member, the family will erect a flag or silk sheet in front of the house for the purpose of guiding the soul of the deceased. A string with pieces of joss paper is attached to the flag, with the number of the pieces equaling the age of the deceased. In some areas, it is customary for family members to climb onto the house roof to call back the soul of the deceased. The family of the deceased announces the death through an obituary notice which is usually a piece of white paper posted on the house gate. All couplets, scrolls, and mirrors in the house are covered with white paper. Traditionally, the family of the deceased would invite monks and Daoist priests to perform religious rites. Hanging on the mourning hall walls are various scrolls, and instruments used for religious rites are placed on the altar. Monks and Daoist priests chant sutras and prayers inviting gods, the Buddha, ghosts, and the soul of the deceased to enjoy the offerings. Music troupes are also invited to play lamenting music and local opera songs.

例句:

他临死前嘱咐儿子，不要破财为他**发丧**，准备一个普通棺材就地掩埋就好。

Example Sentence:

On his deathbed, he told his son not to bankrupt himself for a funeral, and an ordinary coffin would suffice.

小殓 *xiaolian;* dress a dead body

旧时丧礼之一，指给死者沐浴，穿衣、覆衾等，一般在死后次日举行。也称“小敛”。

A Chinese funeral ritual in the past. It refers to the practice of cleaning and dressing the dead and covering it with quilt. It is usually held on the second day after death.

例句:

在古代，**小殓**在室内，殓毕移尸于堂。

Example Sentence:

In older times, the dead was dressed in a bedroom before it was moved to the mourning hall to be saluted.

大殓 *dalian;* enconffin

旧时丧礼之一，指移尸入棺，也称“入殓”，一般在人死后三日举行。旧时民间流行土葬，棺材被认为是死者最终永久的房舍，财力殷实的人家要用楠、梓等上等木料制作棺材，油漆多遍使其乌

A Chinese funeral ritual in the past, also called *ru lian*. It refers to the ritual of putting the body of the deceased into a coffin, which usually occurs three days after death. In older times, the practice of burying one in the ground was quite common, and the notion that the coffin constituted

黑发亮。入殓前亲属瞻仰死者遗容，向遗体告别，然后将棺材钉盖封口。

the deceased's final permanent residence took shape. Wealthy families had coffins made of premium materials such as *nanmu* and catalpa wood. Coffins usually have several layers of paint, giving them a lustrous black color. After mourners pay respects and bid farewell, the body is placed in the coffin which is sealed with nails.

例句：

大殓前，要举行向遗体告别仪式。

Example Sentence:

Before moving the body of the dead into the coffin, a farewell ceremony would be held.

 入殓 *ru lian;* enconffin

参见“大殓”。

See *dalian* (encoffin).

 出殡 *chu bin;* funeral procession

A Chinese folk funeral custom that refers to the procession that carries the coffin or cinerary casket to the cemetery or funeral home. According to traditional customs, on the day of a burial, musicians arrive at the home of the deceased as early as possible and play various kinds

中国丧葬旧俗，指移棺至墓葬地或殡仪馆舍。按照旧俗，出殡那天，乐队要早早来到丧家，吹奏乐曲。吊唁者陆续前来。吉时一到，丧家启灵，棺材抬出灵堂。一般八人或十六人抬棺，最多可达六十四人。司仪呼令，灵柩离地而起，此时孝子把瓦盆或瓷碗一下摔得粉碎，北方民间俗称“摔老盆”。出殡队伍前面为开路神、各色旗锣伞盖执事，后随铭旌、挽联、纸扎、乐队、影亭（内摆死者影像）、送殡众人、丧主、灵柩等。在哀乐和哭泣声中，出殡队伍缓缓向墓地行进。一路上出殡队伍抛撒纸钱，称为“买路钱”。

of music as mourners come to offer condolences. When the auspicious time arrives, the coffin is lifted up and prepared to be carried to the cemetery. As the coffin is lifted, the son of the deceased smashes a clay pot or porcelain bowl to pieces. This custom is referred to as "*shuai laopen*" (smash the old pot) in the north of China. The coffin is then carried to a cemetery; the number of people carrying the coffin is usually 8 or 16, but sometimes can be as many as 64. In the front of the funeral procession are people who hold symbols of gods along with various ceremonial flags, umbrellas, and gong strikers. The following person carries a flag bearing the identity of the deceased. Afterwards are people carrying elegiac couplets, paper burial items, a photo of the deceased, and the musicians. At the end of the procession are those attending the funeral, the family of the deceased, and finally the coffin. The procession marches slowly amidst the lamenting music and sounds of weeping. Paper money is scattered along the route, indicating that they are paying money for passage.

例句：

出殡途中，有的亲朋好友会摆桌设供举行路祭。

Example Sentence:

Relatives and friends may set up an altar to offer sacrifices at a halfway point on the funeral procession's path.

摔老盆 *shuai laopen;* breaking an old pot

中国民间丧葬旧俗。出殡当日起棺后，家中长子把瓦盆或瓷碗一下摔得粉碎，据说这样死者才能把盆或碗带到阴间使用。盆或碗摔得越碎越好，若未摔碎，忌摔第二次，由后面抬杠者将其踩碎。

A Chinese folk funeral custom in the past. On the day of a funeral, after the coffin is lifted up to be taken to the cemetery, the family's eldest son smashes either a tile pot or porcelain bowl. It is said that by doing this, the deceased can take it and use it in the netherworld. When breaking a pot, the more thoroughly it shatters, the better. If it does not shatter on the first attempt, it is inauspicious to try shattering it again; rather, the persons carrying the coffin should stamp the pot into pieces.

例句：

长子**摔老盆**时，如果亡者是父亲就用左手摔，如果亡者是母亲则用右手摔。

Example Sentence:

When the eldest son breaks an old pot during the funeral, he should use his left hand to break it if the deceased is his father, and use his right hand if the deceased is his mother.

纸扎 *zhizha;* paper offerings

中国民间丧葬用品，即旧时用纸扎成的用于祭奠的神像、人像、建筑物和各种器物用品，又称“纸活”。古人认为，人死后到了地下阴间依然要过生前那样的生活，因而逐渐形成了事死如事生的丧葬习俗。古代富贵人家建造高大的坟墓，在坟墓内埋放大量随葬物品。随着社会的发展，由早期人畜殉葬和实物陪葬，到后来用陶瓷、竹木做成的车马、房舍、冥器和泥制钱锭随葬。一千多年前已出现了焚化纸扎物品随葬的习俗。工匠以秫秸或竹篾扎成骨架，外糊彩纸，做成纸人、纸马、纸车、纸屋等。丧家出殡前将纸扎及焚烧用的纸钱和用金银纸做的元宝陈列门前，待到出殡下葬后，将其一同焚烧，供亡者在阴间使用。

Paper-made items in the shape of immortals, persons, buildings and household utensils of all kinds used as offerings at funerals in China in the past. It is also called "paper work." Ancient Chinese believed that after a person died they went to the netherworld which was similar to the living world. As a result, the notion of "treating the dead as if they were alive" became widespread. Affluent people usually built spacious tombs for the deceased, and buried a lot of items in the tomb, which included livestock and even people in early times, and miniature horses and carriages, houses, and other funerary items made of pottery, bamboo and wood as well as clay ingot later on as a result of social development. Over one thousand years ago, the custom of burning paper objects during burials took shape. Craftsmen used sorghum stalks or bamboo strips to make frames that they then covered with colorful paper to make figures resembling humans, horses, carriages, and houses. Before a burial ceremony, these miniature paper items were placed in front of the deceased's door along with joss paper, ingots made of gold and silver paper. They were then burned after the burial ceremony so the deceased could use them in the netherworld.

例句：

纸扎是将扎制、贴糊、剪纸、泥塑、彩绘等技艺融为一体的民间艺术。

Example Sentence:

Paper offerings draw on a combination of skills such as tying, pasting, paper-cutting, clay sculpture, and color painting to form a new folk art.

纸活 *zhihuo;* paper work

见"纸扎"。

See *zhizha* (paper offerings).

买路钱 *mai lu qian:* money for passing the road

中国民间丧葬习俗，指出殡时沿路抛撒的纸钱。人们认为这样一路上就不受鬼神阻挠，能够顺利通过。除汉族外，中国的侗族也有这一习俗。

A Chinese folk funeral custom. It refers to the practice of throwing replica paper money during the funeral procession. It is believed that by doing this, the deceased's path will not be obstructed by ghosts or spirits, allowing the deceased to smoothly pass. The Han and Dong ethnic groups both honor this custom.

例句：

出殡路上途经十字路口、过河、拐弯、过桥时，一律要撒**"买路钱"**，以免被鬼缠着迷了路。

Example Sentence:

When the funeral procession passes through an intersection, crosses a river, rounds a corner, or crosses a bridge, paper money must be scattered about without exception to prevent any trouble from ghosts.

祭坟 *ji fen;* offering sacrifices at the grave side

A Chinese funeral custom which refers to offering sacrifices to the deceased in front of their graves. It is also called *shang fen* or *sao mu* (sweeping the tomb). This was typically done on the third day after the burial, every seventh day for seven weeks after death, the 100th day and the anniversary after death. After that, during every Tomb Sweeping Day, Ghost Festival and Lunar New Year, family members will clean the grave site and reminisce over the deceased.

中国民间丧葬习俗，即到死者坟前祭奠，也称“上坟”“扫墓”。过去有在葬后第三天圆坟、死后第七天及其后的六个第七天烧七、死后一百天烧百日和一周年时烧周年等祭坟习俗。此后，每逢清明、中元和年节，家人均要上坟祭扫，以表缅怀之情。

Example Sentence:

Offering sacrifices at the grave side typically involves placing ceremonial objects and alcohol in front of the tomb and then burning paper money, lighting incense, pouring out alcohol, and saluting the deceased.

例句：

祭坟一般要在坟前摆放祭品、水酒，然后烧纸钱、焚香、奠酒、行礼。

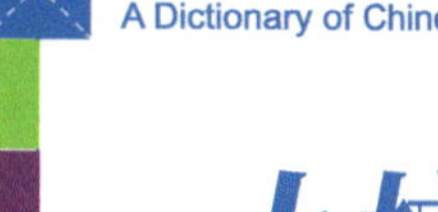

上坟 *shang fen;* offering sacrifices at the grave side

参见"祭坟"。

See *ji fen* (offering sacrifices at the grave side).

扫墓 *sao mu;* sweeping the tomb

参见"祭坟"。

See *ji fen* (offering sacrifices at the grave side).

圆坟 *yuan fen;* rounding the grave

中国某些地方的一种祭坟习俗，即死者亲属在死者葬后第三天，为新坟添土的习俗，也称"圆三"。

A custom in some Chinese regions where family members add soiling to the top of the grave three days after the burial. It is also called *yuan san* (rounding on the third).

例句：

圆坟后，丧礼基本结束。

Example Sentence:

Rounding the grave is considered as the last ritual for the funeral.

圆三 *yuan san;* rounding on the third

参见“圆坟”。

See *yuan fen* (rounding the grave).

做七 *zuo qi;* making offerings on the sevenths

中国民间丧葬旧俗，即从逝者去世之日起每隔七天祭奠一次，直到七七四十九天结束。因为祭奠期间会焚烧大量纸钱和纸扎，因此也称“烧七”。做七的习俗据说来源于佛教。佛教认为人死到投生转世之间有一个在阴间寻求生缘的中间阶段，以七日为一期；若七日终仍未寻到生缘，则可以更续七日，到第七个七日终一定会找到投生的所在。所以在这七七四十九天中，必须逢七举行超度、祭奠，助其早日投生。做七期间的具体礼仪繁多，各地做法不同，尤其是头七和满七的仪式比较隆重。现在不少地区依然流行此俗，但在仪式上已经大大简化。

A Chinese funeral custom. It refers to the ritual of holding a memorial ceremony on every seventh day for seven weeks after a person passes away. Since a great deal of replica paper money and paper items are burned as offerings, it is also called "burning paper offerings on the sevenths." The ritual is believed to be derived from Buddhism, which holds that an intermediate stage exists between a person's death and his reincarnation in which the deceased spends time in the netherworld looking for his next life. This period lasts for seven days each time. If their search is unsuccessful, they can continue for another seven days until the 49th day by which they must have found their new life. Thus, on every seventh day in the seven weeks, a ritual will be held and offerings be made to pray for the soul of the dead out of purgatory and help the soul find its destiny. Specific practices of the ceremonies are very complicated and differ from place to place, yet in general, the first on the 7th and the last on the 49th are particularly solemn. Today, this custom is still popular in many regions, but specifics of the ceremony have been greatly simplified.

例句：

死者安葬后，亲人在一定时期要举行表示追念的仪式，比较普遍的便是**做七**。

Example Sentence:

After the deceased is buried, close relatives will hold a remembrance ceremony within a certain period of time. Making offerings on the sevenths is a very common practice.

入土为安

rutuwei'an;
burial; interment

中国汉族传统丧葬观念，即将逝者土葬，使其灵魂得到安息。汉族发源地中原地区土地肥沃，人民世代以农耕为主，视土地为生命。另根据中国的创世神话，人类是始祖女娲用泥土造出来的，因此死后葬于土中，被认为是使灵魂得到安息的最好办法。

A traditional concept on death of the Han people. It is believed that the soul of the deceased will rest in peace once the body is buried into the ground. The Han people originally lived in the fertile Central Plains of China, where they had farmed for generations, and viewed the land as part of their life. According to China's creation mythology, human beings are created out of mud from the earth by Goddess Nüwa, so to be buried back to earth after death is considered the best way for the soul to be at ease.

例句：

现在中国虽然普遍推行火葬，但人们还是习惯于将骨灰盒埋入土中，**入土为安**。

Example Sentence:

Although cremation is nearly universal in China today, many people are still accustomed to burying a funerary casket in the ground in hopes that the departed may rest in peace.

FOOD, CLOTHING, SHELTER AND TRANSPORTATION

汉服 *hanfu;* Han clothing; traditional Han clothing

中国汉族的传统服饰，又称“华夏衣冠”“华服”。汉服是从黄帝即位到公元17世纪中叶（明末清初），在汉族的主要居住区，以华夏礼仪文化为中心，具有独特汉民族风貌、明显区别于其他民族的传统服装和配饰体系。古代汉服上衣下裳，衣领右衽的特点在商代已经基本确立。几经朝代更迭，汉服也在不断变化发展，春秋时期深衣出现，将以前各自独立的上衣下裳合二为一。汉服也体现了阶级差别，身份越高

Traditional clothing worn by the Han ethnic group, also known as “*huaxia yiguan*” or “*huafu*.” It is a unique form of ethnic clothing popular from the time of the legendary Yellow Emperor around 5,000 years ago to the middle of the 17th century (the late Ming and early Qing dynasties). The basic design of *hanfu* was developed during the Shang Dynasty (1600-1046 BC). Early *hanfu* consisted of a *yi*—a tunic tied with a sash—and an ankle-length skirt called a *chang*. The collar of the *yi* was crossed and tied to the right. However, the styles evolved through the ages. During the Spring and Autumn Period (770-476 BC), the *shenyi* (a deep robe) was invented, which was a combination of a tunic and a skirt. A person’s social status was reflected by more adornments, wider sleeves, and long gowns which indicated a higher social rank. Production of Han clothing required craftsmanship and skills in dyeing, weaving, and embroidery. A complete Han clothing set consisted of headwear, facial adornments, upper and lower garments, shoes, and more, and could be divided into formal and informal wear. It had a tremendous impact on East Asian culture as a whole. For

的人穿的汉服也愈加华美，贵族的衣服往往有宽袖长袍的特点。汉服承载了汉族的染、织、绣等杰出工艺和美学。汉服包括衣裳、首服、髮式、面饰、鞋履、配饰等一套完备的冠服体系。汉服可分为礼服和常服。汉服对整个东方世界产生了巨大影响，如日本和服、韩国韩服等均具有或借鉴汉服的特征。如今，随着中国传统文化的复兴，经过改良的现代汉服越来越受到人们的喜爱。

example, Japanese kimonos and Korean handboks both incorporate Han clothing features. Today as traditional Chinese culture grows in appeal, Han clothing, improved and modified with modern elements, enjoys increasing popularity.

例句：

传统**汉服**是汉族人民各类传统服饰的通称，拥有超过四千年的历史，据说始于黄帝的妃子嫘祖。

Example Sentence:

Traditional Han clothing or *hanfu* in Chinese is the term that refers to different styles of traditional clothing worn by Han people, the largest ethnic group in China. With a history that spans over four millennia, it was supposedly created by the Yellow Emperor's consort, Leizu.

华夏衣冠 *huaxia yiguan;* traditional Han clothing

参见“汉服”。

See *hanfu* (traditional Han clothing).

华服 *huafu;* traditional Han clothing

参见“汉服”。

See *hanfu* (traditional Han clothing).

唐装 *tangzhuang;* Tang suit

中国一种服饰，原指唐制汉服，为汉族服饰系统中的一种款式。现在流行的唐装是由清末的旗袍马褂演变而来，其款式结构有四大特点：立领、连袖、对襟和盘扣。传统唐装常以红、黄、绿、蓝为主色调。唐装多使用织锦缎面料，图案取材于中国文化中的吉祥物，如万寿花团、牡丹花、龙、凤等，象征吉祥长寿、龙凤呈祥。如今，唐装在吸收中国传统服饰独特文化韵味的基础上推陈出新，不断在世界时尚舞台展露中国特色。

例句：

在 2001 年上海 APEC 会议上，中国作为东道主请来参会的亚洲及太平洋经济体的领导人穿"**唐装**"，中国人由此兴起了一阵"唐装"热潮。

A type of Chinese attire, originally referring to the style of *hanfu* particularly popular during the Tang Dynasty (618-907). The "Tang suit" people wear today evolved from the mandarin jacket of the late Qing Dynasty (1616-1911). It has four main features, namely, a straight collar, set-in sleeves, a front opening, and coiled buttons. Traditional "Tang suits" are often red, yellow, green, and blue. They are usually made of brocade fabrics, and the motifs mainly come from symbolic images of traditional culture such as longevity flowers, peony flowers, and dragons and phoenixes. These images symbolize good luck, long life, and good fortune. Today, "Tang suits" represent the unique cultural features of traditional Chinese attire and showcase Chinese characteristics on the global fashion stage.

Example Sentence:

At the 2001 APEC summit in Shanghai, leaders who attended the event donned Tang suits, helping to create a new wave of popularity of *tangzhuang* among the Chinese people.

changpao;
long robe; long gown

中国清代及民国时期的流行服饰，不分上衣下裳，分为单袍、夹袍和棉袍。清朝时，着长袍者必在外面套马褂；辛亥革命后，长袍可单独穿用，在知识分子、商人和士绅中广为流行。长袍为右大襟式，一般左右两开衩，皇室则是四开衩。长袍在其流行过程中经历了较大的演变，从清初的肥大无领到清末的短瘦立领再到民国时期的口袋设计，不断满足人们的需求。颜色以蓝、灰为主，旧时人们会在重要节日及重大场合穿长袍以示体面。自 20 世纪 50 年代起，长袍开始被逐渐兴起的长仅及膝的小棉袍取代，销声匿迹。

A popular form of attire during the Qing Dynasty (1616-1911) and the Republic of China (1912-1949) period. These robes can be differentiated into unlined robes, lined robes, and cotton-padded robes. During the Qing Dynasty, people were required to wear robes with a *magua* (mandarin jacket) outside. After the Revolution of 1911, the robes could be worn without additional accessories and they became popular among scholars, businessmen, and gentries. A long robe has buttons on the right side, with slits usually on both the left and right sides. Imperial robes had four-slits. Long robes, which are typically blue and gray, have undergone great changes as they have grown in popularity. They evolved from wide collarless versions in the early Qing Dynasty to the short, thin, and straight collars of the later stage of the Qing Dynasty. Later, during the Republic of China, the pocket design emerged. In the past, people wore long robes on important festivals and occasions. Beginning in the 1950s, long robes began to be replaced by cotton-padded robes that only reach down to a person's knees.

例句：

长袍上下一体，从肩部一直延伸到脚面，最初为中国满族传统服装。

Example Sentence:

A *changpao* is a one-piece garment that extends from the shoulders all the way to the heels. It is a traditional type of clothing that was originally worn by the Chinese Manchu ethnic group.

大褂 *dagua;* unlined long gown

中国传统的中式单长衣，又称“长衫”。大褂上下相连、长及脚面，在长袍的基础上改制而成，清朝及民国时期颇受欢迎。大褂多为立领，左右开裾，衣身细瘦，窄袖，裁剪趋于贴身修长。皇家用黄色，民间多用青、蓝。面料可为布、绸缎等，因家庭经济状况而异。大褂同时还可以作为身份的象征，代表富裕的上层人士和文化人。

A traditional Chinese gown. Thin, long, and unlined, it is tailored to fit a person's body. It became popular during the Qing Dynasty (1616-1911) and Republic of China period (1912-1949). These long gowns have straight collars and slits on the left and right sides as well as very narrow sleeves. Imperial unlined gowns are yellow, while ordinary people wore green or blue. Such gowns were made of cloth, satin, or other materials depending on a person's financial conditions. Unlined long gowns also served as a symbol of class, representing the wealthy upper class and the literati.

例句：

大褂是西服在中国广泛流行前中国男士出席正式场合的着装。

Example Sentence:

A *dagua* was considered formal dress for men before Western-style suits became popular in China.

changshan; unlined long gown

参见“大褂”。

See *dagua* (unlined long gown).

马褂 *magua;* mandarin jacket; riding jacket

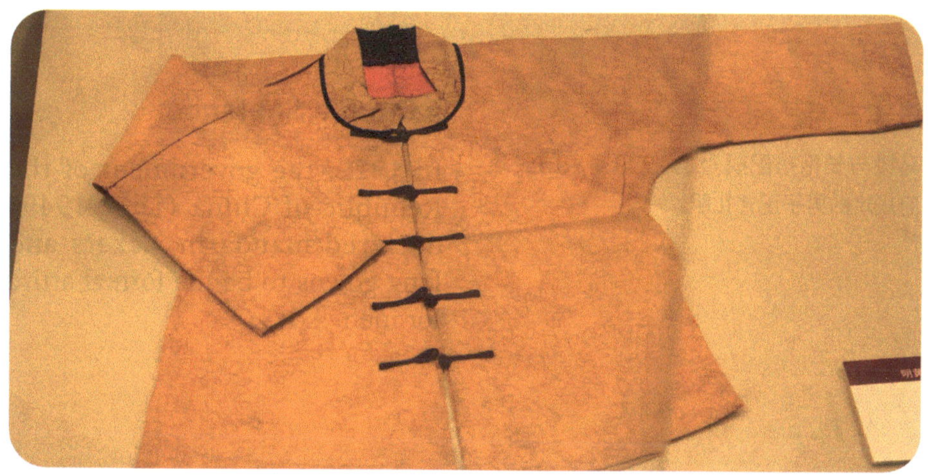

中国清代男子穿在长袍外面的对襟短褂，本为满族人骑马时的装束，故名“马褂”。马褂有对襟、大襟、别襟等式样，面料主要为纱或绸缎，一般长度到肚脐，袖子到肘部。马褂作为一种日常便服，深受官员和百姓欢迎，但特定式样如龙纹、蟒纹等则是皇家专用，不可僭越。民间

A short jacket with buttons down the front that was worn over a *changpao*, the long gown worn by Chinese men during the Qing Dynasty (1616-1911). Mandarin jackets, made of yarn or silk fabrics, come in two styles: front-opening (*duijin*) and right-side opening (*dajin*), and their sleeves extend to elbows. As a kind of everyday casual attire, mandarin jackets were popular among both officials and the public, but those with patterns such

较为流行的马褂多为天蓝色、黑色；黄马褂，又称“武功褂子”是皇帝用来赏赐随身侍卫或于国有功的臣下的特定官服，象征极高的政治殊荣。如今，国际上享有盛誉的唐装便是在马褂的基础上演变而来的。

as dragons could only be worn by the royal family. Among the public, sky blue and black jackets were popular. Yellow mandarin jackets, also known as "jackets reserved for people of great distinction," were a special kind of official attire granted by the emperor to his bodyguards or officials, symbolizing their high political status. Mandarin jackets eventually evolved into today's popular "Tang suit."

例句：

马褂与长袍搭配成为 1929 年南京国民政府规定的男子正式礼服。

Example Sentence:

In 1929, the government of the Republic of China (1912-1949) declared mandarin jackets and long gowns to be the formal attire for men.

坎肩 *kanjian;* sleeveless jacket

A Chinese sleeveless jacket that was popular in the Qing Dynasty (1616-1911). This collarless jacket came in a variety of styles such as front-opening, right-side opening, and a horizontal opening above the chest. In the early Qing Dynasty these sleeveless jackets were tight, small, and worn inside one's robes, but beginning in the late Qing Dynasty both men and women began wearing them over their robes or gowns. These sleeveless jackets were

中国无袖短上衣，盛行于清朝，有对襟、琵琶襟、大襟、一字襟和人字襟等式样，多无领。清初，坎肩窄小，一般穿在袍子里边，晚清开始将其穿于袍、衫之外，男女皆可穿着。坎肩面料多样，有棉坎肩、皮坎肩等以适应不同温度，保护肩部。清朝时还流行一种“巴图鲁（满语勇士）坎肩”，四周镶边，在正胸钉一横排十三粒钮扣，俗称“一字襟”或“十三太保”，最初仅内阁要员可穿着，又称“军机坎”，后扩展至普通人。坎肩因其美观、轻便、保暖等特性，至今仍经久不衰，为人们所喜爱。

available in a variety of fabrics such as cotton and leather that adapt to different temperatures and protect the shoulders. There was also a kind of Batulu (meaning "warriors" in Manchurian) sleeveless jacket prevalent in the Qing Dynasty. These had selvages that extended all around the attire and a horizontal row of thirteen buttons on the chest, giving rise to common names such as *"yizijin," "shisan taibao,"* or *"junjikan."* It was initially worn exclusively by key imperial court officials, but later common people began wearing them too. These sleeveless jackets have long been popular due to their nice appearance and convenience.

例句：

坎肩在各种季节都很好搭配，可套在夹衣、毛衣、薄棉衣外面搭配各种风格的服装，非常受时尚女性的青睐。

Example Sentence:

Sleeveless jackets can be worn in all seasons along with various lined garments, sweaters, and cotton-padded coats, and they also serve as a kind of popular lady wear.

中山装 *Zhongshanzhuang;* Chinese tunic suit; Sun Yat-sen suit

一种由孙中山先生在广泛吸收欧美服饰的基础上，综合了中式服装的特点而设计、提倡而得名的服装。上衣领子外翻，左右各有两个带盖子和扣子的明兜；下身是西式男裤。中山装具有中华民族的特点，穿着简便、舒适、挺括。曾一度被世界公认为中华人民共和国的“国服”。中山装做为中国人一度推崇的常式礼服，它同时也承载着一种文化，一种礼仪，一份民族自尊和自豪感。

A suit designed by Dr. Sun Yat-sen (1866-1925), who founded the Republic of China (1912-1949). This new suit combined the strengths of Western- and Chinese- style modern clothes. It features a classic collar and two patch pockets with a cover and a button on each side. It is often matched with Western-style trousers. The Chinese tunic suit became a symbol of the new Chinese nation as it was simple, comfortable, crisp and smooth. It was once recognized as the national clothing of the People's Republic of China. Often worn during official ceremonies, the suit represents Chinese culture, etiquette as well as national pride and self-respect.

例句：

中山装能适应老、中、青年穿着，不受社会地位的限制。

Example Sentence:

Regardless of social status, the Chinese tunic suit is suitable for young, middle-aged, and elderly people.

旗袍 *qipao*; cheongsam

妇女穿的一种长衣。原是清朝满族旗人妇女的服装。随着满族和汉族之间的融合逐渐增强，到了 20 世纪 20 年代初，汉族妇女也开始穿旗袍。旗袍直领，右开襟，上下呈直线。后来旗袍样式不断改进，款式变多，成为中国妇女的传统服式，成为中国文化的标志之一。2011 年 5 月 23 日，旗袍手工制作工艺成为中国国务院批准公布的第三批国家级非物质文化遗产之一。

A traditional dress that was originally worn by Manchu women during the Qing Dynasty (1616-1911). It became popular among Han women in the 1920s as a result of growing mutual influence between Manchu and Han ethnic groups. It entails a stand-up collar with buttons down the right side. Over the years it has seen many stylistic changes, but it gradually became the traditional dress worn by Chinese women and was later regarded as one of the cultural symbols of China. On May 23, 2011, the craftsmanship of *qipao* was included on China's National Intangible Cultural Heritage List.

例句：

旗袍主要由丝绸、锦缎等材质做成，色彩绚丽醒目，款式别致，能展现东方女性含蓄优雅之美。

Example Sentence:

Qipao is made of silk, brocade, or other materials. Brightly-colored with a unique style, it showcases the subtle elegance of Eastern women.

开裆裤

kaidangku;
open-seat pants; split pants or overalls

中国学龄前儿童穿的前后裤裆不缝合的裤子。过去给儿童穿开裆裤是为了便于孩子上厕所，并帮助孩子尽快学会自己上厕所。现在因其有不卫生、不安全、不保暖等缺点而较少使用了。

Pants for toddlers and young children that are not sewn together at the crotch. The pants date back to a child-rearing custom where parents had their children wear such pants so that their children could conveniently go to the bathroom, which people believed helped children quickly learn how to use the bathroom on their own. People have realized, however, that there are many drawbacks to wearing such pants such as they are unsanitary, unsafe, and not warm-keeping.

例句：

尽管人们认识到穿**开裆裤**有不少缺点，但满周岁儿童已经学会走路，而且大小便时不会自己穿脱衣裤，因此有些大人还习惯给孩子穿开裆裤。

Example Sentence:

Although people recognize the shortcomings of wearing open-seat pants, there are still many one-year-old children who can walk but can't take off their pants to go to the bathroom. As a result, some adults have their children wear these pants.

百家衣 *baijiayi; clothing of a hundred families*

中国传统婴儿服饰，为祈求儿童健康平安，长命百岁，家人集纳百家布料为婴幼儿缝制的衣服。百家的布料象征多人的力量和智慧保佑幼儿成长，百家衣上常饰有吉祥图案。目前这种习俗还存在于中国的部分地区。

Traditional Chinese folk clothing for babies which was made by stitching together patches of cloth from many families. Combining the patches signified the baby would have the protection of all the different families in the hope the child would grow up safe and healthy. For this purpose, auspicious patterns were often seen on such clothing. In some parts of China, people still make this kind of clothing for newborns.

例句：

制作**百家衣**时，刘、程姓家庭的布料最受欢迎，因为与“留”“成”谐音，有保佑孩子健康成长的寓意。

Example Sentence:

Patches from families surnamed Liu and Cheng were and continue to be particularly popular when making clothing of a hundred families because these surnames are homophonic with “to keep” and “grow up,” therefore eliciting good blessings.

老衣 *laoyi;* graveclothes; cerements

装殓死者的衣服，又称“寿衣”。老年人往往生前做好备用。中国古代重视丧葬礼仪，先小殓（换上寿衣），后大殓（入棺埋葬）。近代汉族寿衣包括衣5件（白布衬衫、衬裤、棉袍、袄或褂、裤各1件）、帽1顶、鞋1双，另有衾枕。寿衣颜色一般为蓝、褐色。

Traditional Chinese clothing worn by the deceased, also called *shouyi*. It is prepared by the soon-to-be deceased while they are still alive or by other elderly people. Ancient Chinese valued funeral rites and followed the rules from *xiaolian* (dressing the deceased in graveclothes) to *dalian* (putting the body into the coffin which is then buried). In modern China, the graveclothes used by the Han people include five pieces of clothing (white shirt, pants, cotton long gown, cotton jacket, and cotton trousers), a hat, a pair of shoes, and a quilt and pillow. Graveclothes are typically blue and brown.

例句：

现在少数乡村还沿用这类**老衣**，但多数农村和城市移风易俗，办丧事一般给死者穿整齐、干净的日常生活服装。

Example Sentence:

People in some rural areas still use such graveclothes today, but most rural and urban residents have changed their funeral customs. They dress the deceased in normal clothing which is clean and casual.

寿衣 *shouyi;* graveclothes

参见“老衣”。

See *laoyi* (cerements).

瓜皮帽

guapi mao;
skull cap; hemispherical cap

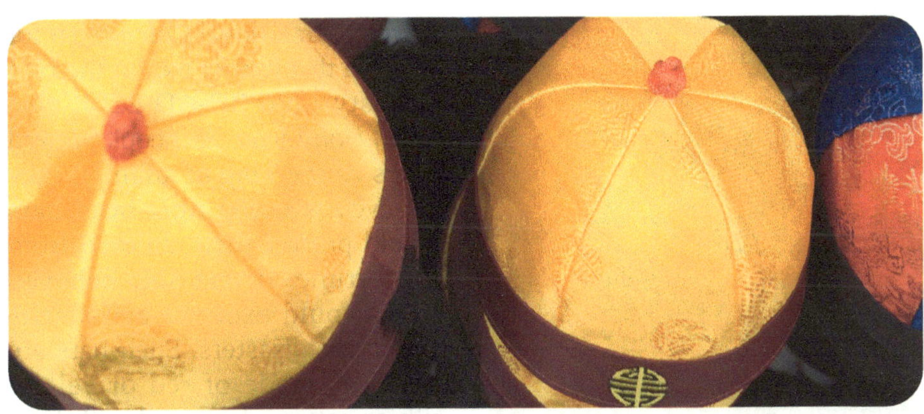

初现于明朝，流行于明、清、民国三代的一种男式帽子。分成六瓣，半圆形状如半个西瓜皮。无檐、窄檐或包有装饰窄边，多为黑色的绸、呢绒或纱制做。顶上饰有各种颜色和材料的疙瘩结。

A type of men's cap that appeared in the Ming Dynasty (1368-1644) and was popular during the Ming and Qing (1616-1911) dynasties as well as the Republic of China (1912-1949) period. It is divided into six equal parts and shaped like a semicircle, resembling a watermelon rind. It has no brim, has a narrow brim, or has a narrow hem. It is made of black silk, wool, or yarn. Its top is adorned with a lump knot that is made of many kinds of colorful materials.

例句：

瓜皮帽与清代男子辫发相配，看上去随意儒雅，广受欢迎。

Example Sentence:

During the Qing Dynasty the skull cap matched well with the plaits behind a man's head. It looked casual and erudite and was a popular head adornment.

虎头帽 *hutou mao;* tiger-head hat

中国民间儿童服饰中比较典型的一种童帽样式，又称“老虎帽”。最早出现于汉代。俗谓老虎可避鬼兵、驱瘟病；民间认为虎为兽中王，戴虎头帽可消灾避难、保护儿童健康成长，故多为少儿佩戴。虎头帽，一般是用红、黄色的丝绸或棉布做成帽筒，围以花边，绣上虎眉、虎眼、虎鼻、虎口、虎须，帽顶左右装饰两只毛皮耳朵，正中绣一“王”字。整个帽子的造型恰似一个虎头，各地的造型、刺绣纹样和用料各有不同。现在，虎头帽在农村仍然流行。

A type of traditional Chinese hat for children that had its root in the Han Dynasty (206 BC-AD 220), also called *laohu mao*. As people viewed tigers as the king of animals, they believed wearing tiger-head hats would protect their children from misfortune. It was also believed tigers could exorcise evil spirits and avoid disasters. Such hats are typically made of red or yellow silk or cotton, decorated with lace, and embroidered with the tiger's eyebrows, eyes, nose, mouth, and whiskers. The top of the hat is decorated with two fur ears, with the Chinese character 王 (king) embroidered in the middle. The embroidery and material of the hat vary in different localities. Today, tiger-head hats are still popular in rural areas.

例句：

虎头帽刺绣精致，一般由亲戚刺绣制作，送给家中刚出生的婴儿。

Example Sentence:

Tiger-head hats are known for their exquisite embroidery. They are typically made by relatives and given to newborn babies in the family.

草鞋 *cao xie;* straw shoes

用蒲草或玉米皮、麦草等天然草本植物编制而成的一种鞋，相传为黄帝的臣子不则所创造。有草拖鞋和草凉鞋等多种款式。草鞋在中国古代比较常见。据称，汉文帝刘恒也曾履草鞋见朝臣。自古以来，草鞋都是中国山区居民传统的劳动用鞋。随着物质生活水平的提高，草鞋已经少有人穿着。

Shoes made of natural herbs such as cat-tail stems, maize husks, or wheat straw. Straw shoes are said to have been created by Bu Ze, who was reportedly a minister under the Yellow Emperor. There are different kinds of straw shoes such as straw sandals and slippers. Straw shoes were a common footwear in China in ancient times. It is said that Liu Heng, an emperor during the Han Dynasty (206 BC-AD 220), once met his ministers in straw shoes. Since ancient times straw shoes have been worn by people in China's mountainous regions. As living standards have significantly improved, straw shoes are rarely seen these days.

例句：

20 世纪 30 年代中期，红军战士正是穿着**草鞋**走完两万五千里长征的。因此，“红军草鞋”成为中国艰苦奋斗的象征。

Example Sentence:

Because the Red Army wore straw shoes to complete the famous “Long March” (October 1934-1936), straw shoes have become the symbol of the hardship the soldiers endured.

兽鞋 *shou xie;* animal-shaped baby shoes

中国华北地区民间制作的带有兽形图案的童鞋。为新生儿制作并穿着兽鞋，是汉族的一种育儿风俗。孩子的女性亲属都会给孩子绣各种动物形象的鞋子。常见的兽形有虎、狮、龙、牛、豹、羊、兔、猫、狗等，都是生命力极强的动物。做鞋模仿这些动物的形状，希望孩子们消灾趋吉、健康成长。

A type of animal-shaped baby shoes common in north China. Making animal-shaped baby shoes is a custom of the Han ethnic group, usually made by women of the clan. The decorative patterns are usually vigorous animals such as tigers, lions, dragons, bulls, leopards, goats, rabbits, cats, and dogs. People hope that these animal-shaped baby shoes can help children avert misfortune and grow up to be strong and healthy.

例句：

兽鞋中最流行的是“虎头鞋”。在鞋前或鞋帮绣虎头，用形象逼真的虎头图案驱鬼辟邪，希望孩子们平安健康。

Example Sentence:

Tiger-head shoes are the most popular animal-shaped baby shoes. They are embroidered with a tiger's head which is believed to dispel evil spirits and bring good health.

虎头鞋 *hutou xie;* tiger-head shoes

Chinese traditional handmade shoes for children. Tiger-head shoes are named after the design of the shoe's front part, which resembles a tiger head. Such shoes are comfortable to wear and can also be appreciated and

一种中国传统民间手工艺制作的童鞋，因鞋头呈虎头模样而得名。它既有穿着舒适的实用价值，又有美观的观赏价值，还是一种可以用来辟邪的吉祥物。人们认为，虎是"百兽之王"，有了虎为小孩儿壮胆和保护，小孩儿就能像虎一样有生气，健康成长。通常小儿满周岁或生日时，要穿外婆新做的虎头鞋，除了辟邪，也有祝愿小孩儿长命百岁的意思。也有的地方用猪、鱼、兔子的形象来装饰小孩儿的鞋子，多半取其多子多福的意义。虎头鞋在中国各地都有，制作技艺已被列入非物质文化遗产。

collected as artwork. Moreover, they are often considered an auspicious object that can dispel evil spirits. Because Chinese people regard the tiger as the king of animals, it is believed that under the protection of tigers, children will grow up in good health. On birthdays — especially a child's first birthday — children wear new tiger-head shoes made by their maternal grandmothers. These shoes are meant to express hopes for longevity and also intended to dispel evil spirits. In some regions the images of pigs, fish, and rabbits are used to decorate children's shoes for auspicious purposes. Tiger-head shoes can be seen all over China. This type of craftsmanship has been listed as a form of China's intangible cultural heritage.

例句：

幼童一岁左右时，长辈们会给孩子穿**虎头鞋**。人们认为虎是百兽之王，穿上虎头鞋可以辟邪恶、保平安，护佑孩子健康成长。

Example Sentence:

When children turn one year old, they are given tiger-head shoes to wear, which suggests embodying hope for good health and also to deter evil spirits.

绣花鞋 *xiuhua xie;* embroidered shoes

一种以各色绸缎或帛为材料，用丝线在鞋面上绣有各种图案的女式布鞋，又称“绣鞋”“花鞋”。绣花鞋最初为王公贵族所穿，后来普及到民间，明清时绣花鞋最为流行，成为妇女钟爱的鞋式。如今，绣花鞋不仅是生活实用品，也是中华民族独创的手工艺品。中国历代妇女一代一代传承着古老的绣花鞋技艺，用一针一线述说着各个朝代的审美观念、文化传统、伦理道德与时尚价值。

A unique type of shoes worn by Chinese women. These shoes are made of silk or satin with a variety of silk patterns decorated on the surface. Initially, only aristocrats were allowed to wear embroidered shoes, but they gradually became permissible for the common people. During the Ming (1368-1644) and Qing (1616-1911) dynasties, embroidered shoes became quite popular among women. Now they are regarded as both a kind of footwear and a handicraft. The tradition of embroidering shoes has been handed down through generations ever since. Embroidered shoes reflect the aesthetic, cultural and ethical standards and fashion at different historical stages.

例句：

绣花鞋是中国鞋文化与刺绣艺术相结合的完美典范。

Example Sentence:

Embroidered shoes exemplify fashion and folk embroidery.

缠足 *chanzu;* foot binding; bound feet

中国古代的一种封建陋习，又称“裹足”。缠足在宋朝之前就已经出现，宋朝时期缠足人数增多，多出现在富裕的贵族家庭。到了明代，裹足之风进入兴盛时期，出现了“三寸金莲”之说，三寸相当于现在的10厘米。汉族女性须自三至五岁时以布紧缠双足，将除拇指外的脚趾向脚掌缠裹，使足骨变形，足形尖小，以此为美。缠足使女性行走极为不便，是对女性生理上和心理上的伤害。直至20世纪初，严重侵害女性权利的缠足陋习才逐渐被废除。

An ancient, feudal practice in old China, also called *guozu*. According to records, foot binding appeared before the Song Dynasty (960-1279), but during the Song period increasingly more girls of upper class families had their feet bound. It reached a peak during the Ming Dynasty (1368-1644) with the notion of the “three-inch golden lotus,” which refers to the Chinese inch (*cun*) that is about 10 centimeters long. It involved tightly wrapping a girl’s feet from the time she was three to five years old. The foot was wrapped tightly to bring the four smaller toes beneath the foot, deforming the foot into a small and bent triangular shape for aesthetic purposes. After many years, a girl’s feet became very small, making it difficult for her to walk. Foot binding deformed women’s feet and was also harmful psychologically. By the early 20th century, the practice of foot binding was banned due to its encroachment on the rights of women.

例句：

缠足美其名曰“三寸金莲”，让现代人无法理解。

Example Sentence:

Modern people are completely unable to understand the aesthetic appeal of “three-inch golden lotus” through the painful and dangerous process of foot binding.

三寸金莲 *sancun jinlian*; three-inch golden lotus; lotus feet

参见“缠足”。

A result of *chanzu* (foot binding). See *chanzu* (foot binding).

绣花鞋垫 *xiuhua xiedian*; embroidered shoe pads

一种中国民间手工艺品。绣花鞋垫距今已有三千多年的历史。相传这种用千针纳成的鞋垫为民间喜悦祥和之物，有消灾避难之效。绣花鞋垫制作精美细腻，纹样富贵吉祥，穿着舒适养生，更具一定的保健功能。绣花鞋垫都要经历做模子、打面浆、粘布板、描图、镶边和绣花等多道工序，然后根据不同

A Chinese folk handicraft. Embroidered shoe pads can be traced back over 3,000 years. It was believed that because of their beauty and elegance, shoe pads with intricate needlework could help protect the wearer from misfortune. Also, the embroidered patterns on the pad could help massage one's feet, which was beneficial to one's health. The process of making embroidered shoe pads involves several steps: molding, paste-making, pasting cloth patches together, drawing a pattern, sewing rims, and embroidering. Different patterns and designs can be embroidered on the pads specific to those who will receive them, such as lovers, friends, or relatives. Auspicious phrases such as "be as lucky as one wishes" and "be well-fed and well-clad" are often embroidered. Embroidered shoe pads are popular gifts to family and friends

赠予对象，一针一线绣上不同的几何图案和花鸟虫鱼等图像，绣上“吉祥如意”“丰衣足食”之类的吉词，分送情人、亲友和客人。绣花鞋垫具有很高的实用价值，又具有很高的收藏价值，更是馈赠亲友的上品。

on account of their artistic value and practicality.

例句：

在中国北方农村，姑娘在定亲之后，须得日夜赶绣鞋垫。婚礼上，亲友、来宾向新郎新娘馈赠贺金和礼物，新娘依俗要回赠**绣花鞋垫**等小礼品，一方面表达谢意，一方面向亲朋好友展示自己的手艺。

Example Sentence:

In the rural areas of northern China, women begin making shoe pads after getting engaged. During weddings, when guests give presents and money to the newly-married couples, brides give embroidered shoe pads in return. Shoe pads display the bride's embroidery skills and also convey the newlyweds' gratitude to their guests.

褡裢 *dalian; cloth bag*

A rectangular cloth bag commonly used by Chinese people in the old days. A precursor of the modern-day backpack, merchants and accountants used to wear a *dalian* over their shoulders to carry heavy loads when traveling. Two pockets are at both ends with an opening in the middle, and there are cords and buttons near the opening that are used to fasten it. A large *dalian* can be worn over the shoulder while a smaller

中国旧时民间长期使用的一种布口袋。过去的商人或账房先生外出时总是将它搭在肩上，以便空出两手，行动方便。褡裢为长方形，通常用很结实的布制成，开口在中央，两端各成一个口袋，口边留有绳扣，可以串连成锁，结实耐用。褡裢挂在肩上，一半在胸膛前，一半在背脊后。小的也可以挂在腰带上。褡裢颜色绚丽夺目，图案富有民族特色。

one can fit around the waist like a belt. They are usually brightly colored with ethnic patterns.

例句：

现在设计制作的小**褡裢**工艺精细，色彩艳丽，是难得的旅游纪念佳品。

Example Sentence:

The colorful, small *dalian* of today is exquisitely designed, making it a precious souvenir for tourists.

xiapei;
embroidered cloud shawl or cape

古代妇女礼服的一部分，类似披肩。由于其形美如彩霞，故得此名。霞帔是宫廷命妇的着装，平民女子只有出嫁时才可以穿。帔子是霞帔的前身，出现在南北朝时期，宋代时被列入礼服行列之中，明代时发展成了霞帔。

An accessory worn by Chinese women on formal occasions in ancient times. It was thus named because it was deemed as beautiful as a rosy cloud. It was often worn by the wife or mother of a senior official in the royal court. Ordinary women were only allowed to wear it during wedding ceremonies. Predecessor of the cloud shawl was the shawl, which appeared during the Southern and Northern Dynasties (420-589). In the Song Dynasty (960-1279), the shawl was regarded as a ceremonial type of clothing. It began to be called the cloud shawl during the Ming Dynasty (1368-1644).

例句:

霞帔是明清命妇礼服，是王室和官太太的象征。

Example Sentence:

The embroidered shawl was a type of ceremonial clothing worn by the wife or mother of a senior official and was regarded as a symbol of royalty.

汗巾 *hanjin;* sudarium

一种古代服装的附属物，主要以绸、缎、麻、布为原材料制成，规格也大小不等，有方形、长条形。本是用来擦汗的手巾，后变为束系内衣的腰带。

An accessory that was originally used to wipe one's sweat, but later became more commonly used as a waistband to hold up undergarments. It was mainly made of silk, satin, hemp, or cloth. *Hanjin* came in different sizes and were usually shaped in squares or rectangles.

例句:

汗巾的形状、系法各式各样，在古代既用来擦汗，也用来擦泪。

Example Sentence:

Hanjin come in different shapes and sizes and were used to wipe one's sweat or tears in old times.

簪子 *zanzi*; hairpin

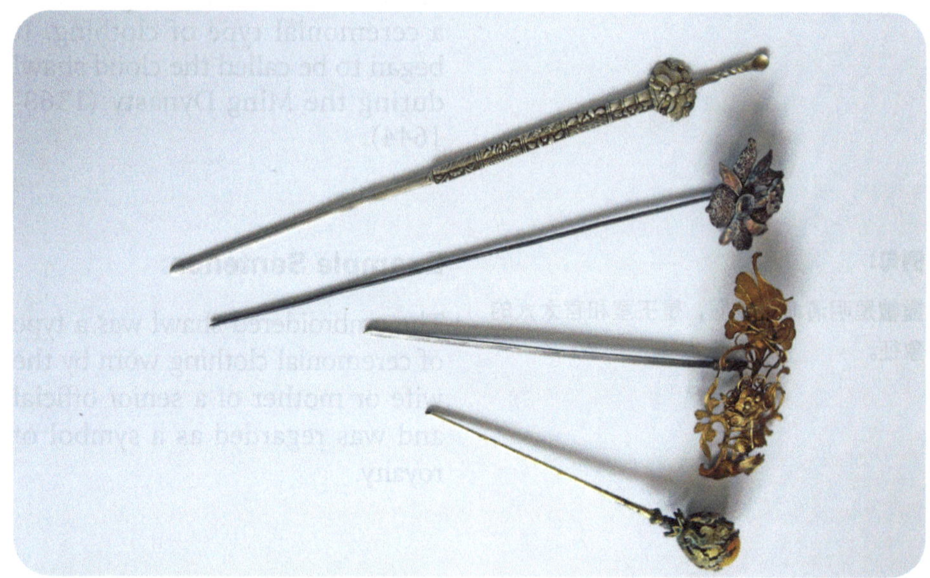

用来别住头发的一种首饰。先秦称“笄”。形状细长，一端尖锐，用竹、玉石、金属或骨头制成。女子用它固定发髻，男子用它将冠帽与头发相连，使不致脱落，兼具装饰作用。

An accessory used to clasp hair that dates back to the pre-Qin period (before 221BC). *Zanzi* was called *ji* in ancient times. It is slender in shape with one pointed end, and is made of bamboo, jade, metal, or bone. In ancient times, a woman used it to fix a hair bun in place, while a man used it to put his headgear and hair in place. It was regarded as an ornament.

例句：

唐宋时期是**簪子**流行的盛世。

Example Sentence:

During the Tang and Song dynasties(618-1279), the hairpin was a popular adornment in China.

枕顶 *zhending;* pillow end

中国旧时民间长柱形枕头的两端。中国旧时民间农家自制的枕头一般为长方形，内装小米、高粱、绿豆或荞麦皮。农家只置枕头而不铺枕巾，倘在枕头正面绣花易脏易破，故在枕头两端绣花。早晨收拾被褥时，人们将一个个枕头垒放在被褥一侧，枕顶便成炕床的装饰。枕顶上的刺绣称为枕顶绣，是中国民间刺绣的品种之一。枕顶绣上的刺绣图案内容丰富，题材广泛，是中国传统吉祥纹样的缩影。枕顶虽是两块方布片，但上面简单的刺绣图样可以反映一地风情。

The two ends of a handmade cuboid pillow used in the old days. Chinese pillows were traditionally made in the shape of a long cuboid filled with millet, sorghum, mung beans, or buckwheat husks. In rural households, pillow covers were rarely used, and the rectangular pillow faces on which people rested their heads wore out easily. Therefore, decorative patterns were usually embroidered on the two square-shaped ends of the pillow. When the bedding was folded in the morning, pillows would be placed on the side of the bedding, and the pillow-end designs would add luster to the *kang*—a brick or slab stone bed that could be heated. Pillow-end embroidery is a special type of folk embroidery, which is rich in design with many different themes. The embroidered, auspicious patterns reflect local customs and are miniatures of traditional, auspicious Chinese patterns.

例句：

枕顶图案多为黑底红花的花草虫鱼。新婚夫妇的枕头绣龙凤呈祥、鲤鱼穿莲、丹凤朝阳；老人的枕头多绣福寿双桃、喜鹊闹梅、猫蝶（耄耋）双寿；孩童的则绣狮虎一类的猛兽，借以驱邪保平安。

Example Sentence:

Pillow-end designs are typically flowers, plants, insects, and fish embroidered with red thread against a black background. Pillow-end designs for newlyweds usually include "prosperity brought by the dragon and the phoenix," "carp swimming across the lotus flowers," and "a red phoenix facing the morning sun." Designs for the elderly usually include peaches of happiness and longevity, magpies, plum blossoms, and cats and butterflies (a homophone for longevity in Chinese). Designs for children usually feature powerful animals such as lions or tigers, the images of which are thought to help protect children by warding off evil spirits.

枕顶绣

zhending xiu;
pillow end embroidery

枕顶上的刺绣，参见“枕顶”。

Also see *zhending* (pillow end). Decorative patterns usually embroidered on the two square-shaped ends of a pillow.

耳枕 erzhen; ear-friendly pillow

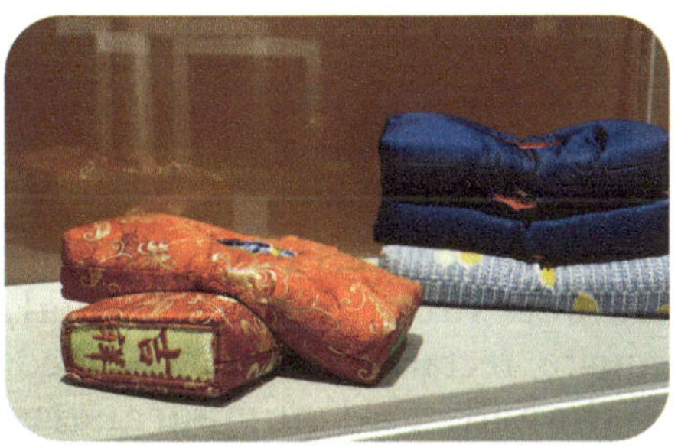

中国民间手工制作的保护耳朵的枕头，流行于陕西、甘肃黄土高原。因枕头中间挖去一块，空间大小正好使耳朵不受头挤压而得名。耳枕有利于缓解耳朵神经系统的压迫并能缓解疲劳，少生疾病。耳枕通常选用纯天然荞麦壳、野菊花、桂花等植物及中草药作为填充物，让人的身心在耳枕自然散发的芳香中彻底放松，较快进入良好的睡眠。

Chinese handmade pillow designed for ear protection. This type of pillow is popular on the Loess Plateau of Shaanxi and Gansu provinces. A hole is made in the middle of the pillow that prevents the head from applying too much pressure on the ear, which helps relieve fatigue and prevent minor illnesses. The pillow is often filled with special plants and Chinese herbal medicines such as pure buckwheat hulls, chrysanthemum, and osmanthus which emit a relaxing fragrance that helps people quickly fall into a good sleep.

例句:

耳枕上最常见的是鱼和蛙的形象，它们蕴含着繁衍子孙、多子多福的意思。

Example Sentence:

The most common designs on ear-friendly pillows are fish and frogs. Both of these designs have the cultural implications that there will be more blessings of offspring in the family.

荷包 *hebao; pouch*

中国民间用来装放零星物品或香料的小包，是用棉布、绸缎、皮革、五色丝线等材料缝制而成的。荷包的造型有圆形、椭圆形、方形、长方形、桃形、如意形、石榴形等。荷包的图案有繁有简，有花草、鸟兽、鱼虫、山水、人物等吉祥纹样，以及吉祥祝语、诗词文字等，适用于不同的人群。刺绣荷包的针法多样，配色典雅，装饰意味很浓。

A small bag for storing small articles or perfume, made with cotton, silk, satin, or leather, and it is then sewn with colorful threads. Pouches come in many shapes such as round, oval, square, rectangular, peach-shaped, S-shaped, and pomegranate-shaped. The embroidered patterns on a pouch can be simple or complicated. Common designs include flowers and plants, birds and beasts, fish and insects, landscapes, and human figures. Some also bear auspicious words or poems. Known for their exquisite needlework and elegant colors, embroidered pouches nowadays are more decorative than functional.

例句：

荷包虽小，但能显露出姑娘的心灵手巧。恋爱时，姑娘要将亲手绣的荷包作为信物送给心上人。荷包上常绣桃花、莲花、鸳鸯、凤凰和航船之类纹样，以表达相恋的心意。

Example Sentence:

Although small in size, pouches can reflect the clever mind and dexterity of the person who makes them. Women often make pouches for their lovers. With such designs as peach blossoms, a lotus, mandarin ducks, a phoenix, or ships, these pouches serve as a token of one's love to another.

围嘴 *weizui;* bib

中国民间围在儿童胸部的布。围嘴戴在幼儿脖子上，挡在胸前，以防止涎水和饮食流落时弄脏衣服。因这类围嘴可前后转动，故又称“转兜”。围嘴多为圆形，也有制成莲花、梅花瓣状的。围嘴或用蓝印花布，或用各种花布拼接，还有用单色布料刺绣、挑花而成。纹饰多为艾虎、龙、鲤鱼、蝴蝶和各种花卉，有的围嘴还绣上“福”“寿”“长命富贵”一类吉祥语。

A piece of cloth fastened around a baby's neck to prevent clothing from getting stained by drool or food. Bibs can be rotated, which is why bibs are also called *zhuandou* (rotatable bib). Bibs are usually round, but sometimes they are in the shape of lotus or plum petals. They are made with indigo-dyed cloth, split-joint colorfully-dyed cloth, or single-color cloth with embroidery or cross-stitch works. Common embroidery patterns include tigers, dragons, carp, butterflies, and various flowers. Chinese characters with auspicious meanings like happiness, longevity, and long and rich life can also be found on bibs.

例句：

随着商品种类的丰富，中国传统**围嘴**已不多见。

Example Sentence:

Traditional bibs are rarely seen nowadays as a greater variety of commodities have become available in China.

转兜 *zhuandou;* rotatable bib

参见“围嘴”。

See *weizui* (bib).

布腰带 *bu yaodai;* cloth belt

中国陕西农村地区的男性服饰。布腰带长约2米，在腰间能缠两到三圈，多为黑色或蓝色。这样的腰带除了能够保暖之外还有其他的实用功能，可以把零碎物品插在腰间，在田间、林间碰到野菜野果时，也可以放开腰带，将物品包起来，方便搬运。

An accessory worn by men in the rural areas of Shaanxi Province. The cloth belt is about two meters long and can be wrapped around the waist two to three times. It is usually black or blue. It not only keeps one warm, but also can be used to carry things such as wild fruit or vegetables. It can be loosened to wrap things inside it.

例句：

民间“三棉不如一缠”的俗语讲的就是**布腰带**的保暖功能。

Example Sentence:

The proverb “better to wear one cloth belt than three layers of cotton” refers to how the cloth belt can keep one warm.

遮裙带 *zhequn dai;* skirt belt

中国陕北妇女腰间的装饰物。它两端开孔或钉上钮扣，从腰后扣住围裙，以取代系结的两条长带。遮裙带只能婚后妇女自用，不可送人，它是已婚妇女的标志。遮裙带图案多样，陕北妇女常用鱼、石榴等图案表达她们对年年繁荣、子孙繁衍的愿望。她们在遮裙带上用虎形图案驱邪佑安，用凤凰图案祈求吉祥如意，具有浓郁的黄河流域民俗文化特色。

Ornamental accessory worn around the waist by women in China's northern Shaanxi Province. Apart from its ornamental functions, the skirt belt also serves as a replacement for apron laces. It is used to fasten an apron with a knot at one's back, and has holes or buttons on both ends. Skirt belts can only be kept by married women for themselves. Skirt belts can be made in various designs, depending on the purpose. For example, a fish and pomegranate design symbolizes a prosperous outlook and a flourishing family, a tiger design is meant to ward off evil spirits and keep one safe, and a phoenix acts as a prayer for auspiciousness. These designs all reflect distinct cultural features of those living in the Yellow River basin.

例句：

在陕北的一些地区，新婚女子出嫁前需在娘家做好一条**遮裙带**。

Example Sentence:

In some areas in northern Shaanxi Province, a bride is expected to make a skirt belt before the wedding.

针扎 *zhenzha;* needle cushion

中国北方妇女制作的藏针用的民间工艺品。北方妇女常将针扎垂挂胸前，以便在田间劳动小憩时随时穿针引线，纳鞋绣花。针扎既是实用物件也是装饰物品。民间妇女不但讲究针扎的形制，还要绣以美丽的纹样。姑娘出阁前要和姊妹们一起赶做大量的绣花针扎，作为婚嫁之日赠送亲友的见面礼。

Handmade folk handicraft used for storing sewing needles. This is popular with women in northern China, who often hang needle cushions in front of their chests. When taking a break from working in the fields, they take out their needles to work on shoe pads or embroidery. Beside its pragmatic functionality, a needle cushion is also a kind of ornament. When making needle cushions, women not only pay attention to their shapes, but also the patterns and designs embroidered on them. Usually a woman makes a large amount of needle cushions with her friends in preparation for her wedding. These cushions are given to relatives and friends as presents on the wedding day.

例句：

陕北姑娘爱绣花，她们以绣花**针扎**、荷包、鞋垫等工艺品或作为爱情信物送给心上人，或馈赠亲友，以显示自己的心灵手巧。

Example Sentence:

Women in northern Shaanxi Province love embroidery. They often display their needlework dexterity by making embroidered needle cushions, pouches, and shoe pads that they then give to lovers, family, and friends as gifts.

挑花 *tiaohua;* cross-stitch work

一种中国传统刺绣的针法，又称“十字花”“架子花”。挑花流行于湖北、湖南地区。农村妇女在自织的白色或青、蓝等色棉、麻布上，用绒线挑出一个一个十字花纹，并进而构成人物、鸟兽、花草、文字等丰富多彩的装饰图案。挑花色彩单纯沉着，质朴清雅。挑花纹样有团花、边花、填花、角花、花边等多种。挑花图案变化多端，有对称式、旋转式、向心式、放射式等，图案布局严谨，于对称中追求变化。

A form of sewing in Chinese traditional embroidery that is also known as *shizi hua* and *jiazi hua*. Cross-stitching is very popular in Hubei and Hunan provinces. In rural areas, women embroider white or blue cloth with such designs as human figures, birds and animals, flowers and plants, and Chinese characters. Cross-stitching is usually simple but elegant. The patterns include round flowers, side designs, corner designs, and decorative borders. The designs are well-organized but varied, following the styles of symmetry, rotation, centrality, and radiation.

例句：

挑花广泛应用于民众的生活之中。洞房花烛夜，人们将新娘挑绣的床单、被面、帐沿、门帘等张挂起来。亲友贺客闹新房，新娘须逐一回答绣品上的凤凰、鸳鸯、牡丹、莲花等所指何人何意。

Example Sentence:

Cross-stitching is actually a common part of people's daily lives. On a woman's wedding night, her cross-stitch designs on bed sheets, quilt covers, mosquito nets and curtains are hung up. These designs are in different patterns such as a phoenix, mandarin ducks, peonies, and lotus. When guests and relatives crowd into the bridal chamber to tease the new couple, the bride is required to say what her cross-stitched designs stand for.

蓝印花布 *lanyin huabu;* indigo-dyed cloth

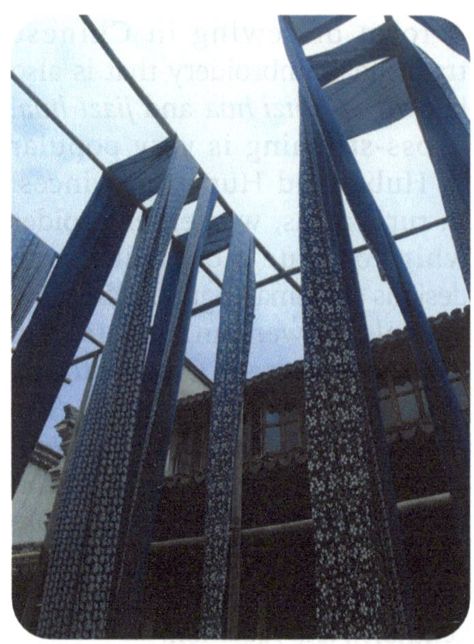

中国传统的手工艺印染品，将白色棉布用蓝靛染成蓝白图案。蓝印花布源于唐宋、盛于明清，从江南起源后流传至全国，距今已近千年历史。主产地包括江苏南通、山东沂蒙、浙江桐乡等。蓝印花布的印染工艺简便易行：匠师以油纸制成花版蒙在白布上，然后用石灰、豆粉和水调成的防染粉浆刮印，晒干后用蓝靛染色，晾干，刮去粉浆，花布便印染完成。印花布分蓝、白二色，质朴典雅，纹样多为花鸟、虫鱼及古钱等。

Traditional dyed Chinese product. Indigo-dyed cloth is made by dyeing indigo patterns onto a white cotton cloth. It dates back to the Tang (618-907) and Song (960-1279) dynasties, thriving during the Ming (1368-1644) and Qing (1616-1949) dynasties. It originates from the regions south of the Yangtze River, boasting a history of nearly a thousand years. It is mainly produced in Nantong, Jiangsu Province; Yimeng, Shandong Province and Tongxiang, Zhejiang Province. The process is easy. First, patterns are made into an oil-paper board which is then placed onto a white cotton cloth. The board is then painted with a dye-proof white paste made of lime, soybean powder, and water. The cloth is then hung until dry. After this, the white cloth is put into a dye vat and then dried in the open air. Once dry, the paste is scraped off and the work is done. Craftsmen could dye exquisite patterns onto clothing such as flowers, birds, insects, fish and coins. Although indigo-dyed cloth has only two colors — blue and white — its exquisite patterns make it very beautiful.

例句：

江苏南通是**蓝印花布**的重要产地。该地农村用蓝印花布制作的被面、被单、枕套、门帘、蚊帐、包裹皮等日用品遍及家家户户，很多家庭皆自制自用。

Example Sentence:

Nantong City, Jiangsu Province is an important production center for indigo-dyed cloth. Cloth made in rural Nantong is used for many daily necessities such as quilt covers, bed sheets, pillowcases, door curtains, mosquito nets, and wrapping cloths. Many families make these products for personal use.

彩印花布 *caiyin huabu;* colorfully-dyed cloth

中国传统的手工艺印染品，也称“花包袱”“包袱皮”。彩印花布是以不同颜色印染的布料。彩印花布和蓝印花布一样在民间广泛流行。彩印花布的工艺较为复杂，包括打版、制版、刻板、配色、印染等一系列步骤。复杂的作品需要100多张花版。老辈人穿的衣服、

Traditional dyed Chinese product. Colorfully-dyed cloth, also known as *hua baofu* or *baofu pi* (colorful wrapping cloth), is as popular as indigo-dyed cloth. As its name suggests, this kind of cloth is dyed with different colors. The dyeing process is therefore more complicated, including designing and working out a pattern, carving the pattern into the paper board, devising the color scheme, and dyeing. A complicated work may require over 100 carved boards. In the past, colorfully-dyed cloth was widely used for making clothes and door curtains, and it was also used for dowries and wrapping gifts and food. Bright colors such as red, green, pink, purple, and yellow are usually used. By combining some of these colors, the cloths take on magnificent features. The decorative patterns usually feature auspicious

日常用的门帘、闺女的嫁妆，以及走亲访友用于包装礼品和食品的包袱，大都是用彩印花布来做的。彩印花布主要以大红、翠绿、桃红、紫、黄等色套印，色彩富丽堂皇。图案装饰多以牡丹、凤凰、荷花、富贵、福寿及民间故事传说和历史故事传说为主。不同地区的彩印花布的图案设计和印染加工都各具特色。

themes such as peony, phoenix, lotus, or the Chinese characters for wealth, longevity, and good fortune. Sometimes the plots from folklore and historical stories are also depicted. The designs and dyeing processes vary from region to region.

例句：

彩印花布的图案寓意美好，用石榴、佛手、桃子组成寓意多子、多福、多寿的“三多”，或以音寓意的蝙蝠与寿字组合的“五福捧寿”等，表达出民众对美好生活的追求和向往，反映出他们的审美情趣。

Example Sentence:

The patterns on such colorfully-dyed cloths always carry auspicious meanings. For example, a combination of pomegranate, fingered citron, and peach symbolizes having many offspring, good fortune, and longevity. The pattern of bats (homophonic for *fu*, or good fortune in Chinese) surrounding the Chinese character for *shou* (longevity) symbolizes good fortune and longevity.

花包袱 *hua baofu*; colorfully-dyed cloth

参见“彩印花布”。

See *caiyin huabu* (colorfully-dyed cloth).

包袱皮 *baofu pi*; colorfully-dyed cloth

参见“彩印花布”。

See *caiyin huabu* (colorfully-dyed cloth).

羊皮披肩 *yangpi pijian;* sheepskin shawl

中国纳西族妇女的传统服饰。这种披肩源于纳西族先民的游牧生活。远古的时候，羊皮披肩是纳西族先民的主要御寒工具。羊皮披肩披在褂子外面，羊皮上端缝有两根白色长带，披时从肩搭过，在胸前交错又系在腰后。披肩上有两枚较大的绣花圆盘，象征日月，七枚较小的圆盘分别代表七颗星，象征纳西族妇女不辞辛劳。也有人认为羊皮披肩是蛙图腾崇拜在服饰上的反映，整个披肩看起来像一只匍匐着的青蛙。

A kind of traditional women's attire of China's Naxi ethnic group and representative of the Naxi ancient nomadic lifestyle. In ancient times, the sheepskin shawl was an important garment to keep warm. It is normally draped around a jacket, with two long white strings along the seams at either end. The shawl drapes around one's shoulders, and the string is tied together in front of the chest and placed around the waist. There are two large embroidered disks on both shoulders to symbolize the sun and the moon. There are seven smaller disks representing seven stars, which symbolize the hard-working Naxi women. The sheepskin shawl is also said to be a representation of ancient frog totem worship, and as a whole resembles a sitting frog.

例句：

纳西族的畜牧业有着悠久的传统，因而牛羊皮毛也就成为纳西族服饰的重要组成部分，其中纳西族妇女的**羊皮披肩**是其服饰中最具特色的一种。

Example Sentence:

Animal husbandry is an age-old tradition of the Naxi ethnic group, which is why leather and wool are widely used in Naxi clothing. Sheepskin shawls are signature clothing of Naxi women.

zangpao; Tibetan robe

中国藏族的特色服饰。基本特点是宽松、斜襟交领。藏族人平常穿藏袍只穿一只袖，而且是穿左袖，右袖空着，从后面拉到前面搭在右肩上。天热时，左袖也不穿，将两袖褪下来拉到前面，围系在腰间，这样穿法既有悠久历史，又有独特的原因，因藏族的主要聚居地青藏高原的昼夜温差较大，身着藏袍，方便他们在劳作时、炎热时将袖子褪下。藏袍有农、牧区之别。一般说来，农区藏袍讲究美观漂亮，牧区藏袍讲究实用温暖。

A distinctive type of Chinese Tibetan clothing, generally known for its loose-fitting and slanted collar. When Tibetans wear a Tibetan robe, often their left arm is in the sleeve while the right arm is not. When the day gets hot, both sleeves are wrapped around the waist. This style has a long history and is the result of the climate in the area which has a great shift in temperature between day and night on the Qinghai-Tibetan Plateau. Many people wear Tibetan robes as it is easy to take off the sleeves if they feel too hot while doing manual labor. The style of the Tibetan robe also differs slightly between agricultural and pastoral regions in that those worn in agricultural communities tend to be more aesthetically beautiful, while those in pastoral regions emphasize the practical use of the clothing of keeping people warm.

例句：

藏袍是对较长的藏族服饰的统称，可细分为多种不同式样，也有单、夹、棉、皮之分。

Example Sentence:

The Tibetan robe is the umbrella term for a relatively long type of Tibetan clothing. It can be further divided into a number of different styles such as unlined, lined, cotton, and animal hide.

哈达 *hada;* khata

中国蒙古族、藏族等民族表达敬意和祝贺的丝织品。哈达多为白色、蓝色，也有黄色等。此外还有五彩哈达，常在特定场合献给菩萨和近亲，是最珍贵的礼物。哈达的应用场合很多，包括拜佛、婚丧、节庆、拜访等。哈达越长，越显出敬献者的尊敬之情之深。哈达的制式、叠法，以及敬献的手法都要依据场合、对象等遵循特定的规矩。受赠的哈达需要珍藏起来，或者挂在屋中高处。献哈达是藏族人民优良的传统习惯，人们世世代代都把献哈达看成是至高无上的礼仪。哈达虽无黄金贵重，但却比黄金更加受到人们的崇敬，因为它象征着一片金子般的心，代表着最真诚的感

A traditional ceremonial silk fabric used by Mongolians and Tibetans as gifts to express respect or congratulations in China. A khata is typically white or blue, while yellow khatas are also occasionally seen. In addition, there are multi-colored khatas that include such colors as blue, white, yellow, green, and red. A multi-colored khata is the most precious gift, which is offered to Buddha or close family on certain occasions. There are many occasions for presenting a khata, such as worshipping the Buddha, weddings, funerals, holidays and festivals, and visiting friends. The longer a khata is, the more symbolic it becomes of the giver's respect. Khatas are made, folded, and presented according to specific rites that correspond to certain settings and recipients. Recipients of these khatas should store them carefully or hang them from the high point of a room. Giving khatas has a long tradition among Tibetan people, and over several generations people came to regard this as the greatest of all traditions. Although it is not as valuable as gold, it is nevertheless more respected than gold because the khata represents the sincerest forms of emotion, supports the finest of wishes, and represents the loftiest of aspirations. It also represents friendship, harmony, kind-

情，寄托着最美好的祝愿，标志着最崇高的敬意，能传达友谊、和谐、善良、安康等含义。

heartedness, and wishes for good health.

例句：

哈达已经成为藏、蒙等民族群众特有的礼仪往来必备之物，世代相传，在人们心中至高无上，是人们纯净的心灵与纯朴的情感具体的物化。

Example Sentence:

Giving a khata is a unique traditional custom among the Tibetan and Mongolian ethnic groups that has been passed down for generations. It is said to show the purest of good feelings from the giver to the receiver.

袷袢 *qiapan;* robe

中国塔吉克、维吾尔、柯尔克孜等族男子的传统服装。袷袢为对襟、宽袖长袍，男子一般内穿衬衣，外穿无领长外衣袷袢。

A traditional form of clothing worn by men of China's Tajik, Uygur, and Kyrgyz ethnic groups. The *qiapan* is a type of men's robe with loose sleeves and two sheets down the front. It does not have a collar, and a shirt is typically worn underneath it.

例句：

长袍是中国北方许多民族的传统服装，如蒙古袍、藏袍、**袷袢**等。

Example Sentence:

The men's robe (*changpao*) is a traditional form of clothing worn by people of many ethnic groups in northern China. There are therefore many different variations such as Mongolian and Tibetan robes, and the *qiapan*.

银腰带 *yin yaodai;* silver waistband

中国傣族妇女的系裙腰带和装饰品。傣族妇女一般喜欢穿窄袖短衣和筒裙，短袖衫和筒裙口处用一根银质腰带系紧，腰带上饰以孔雀、莲花等花型，一身装束显得婀娜多姿、潇洒飘逸。对傣族女性而言，银腰带是不可或缺之物，且越宽越美。按照傣族人的规矩，女孩在7岁以前腰上系布绳，7岁后则系上父母为其准备的银腰带，已婚妇女要把家中的钥匙挂在银腰带上作为标志，而腰带上没有挂钥匙的显然就是未婚的女子了。

A type of decorative waistband used by women of the Dai ethnic group in China. Dai women typically prefer narrow-sleeve jackets and straight skirts that are tightened by a silver waistband decorated with patterns of a peacock, a lotus, or other flowers. The outfit as a whole looks graceful and elegant. The silver waistband is indispensable to Dai women, and the wider ones are considered more beautiful. According to Dai customs, girls up to age seven should wear a cloth waistband, and after seven their parents have them wear a silver one. Married women should hook their keys on their silver waistband as a sign of marriage, and women without keys on their silver waistband are obviously single.

例句：

银腰带十分珍贵，由母亲代代相传，这也是一种信物，如果姑娘将银腰带交给哪个小伙子，就意味着她已爱上他了。

Example Sentence:

The silver waistband is a precious heirloom passed down from mother to daughter. A girl can also use it as a token of affection. To give it to a young man symbolizes that she has fallen in love with him.

凤凰装 *fenghuang zhuang;* phoenix dress

中国畲族女性的特色装扮。红头绳扎的长辫高盘于头顶，象征凤头；衣裳、围裙上用大红、杏黄及金银丝线镶绣出花边图案，色彩鲜艳，象征凤凰的颈项、腰身和羽毛；扎在腰后摇曳的金色腰带头，象征凤尾；佩于全身的银饰叮当作响，象征凤鸣。

A typical dressing style of women of the She ethnic group in China. She women coil their hair on top and tie it together with a thread of red wool, symbolizing the head of a phoenix. The colorful lace embroidery on their clothes and aprons is made with bright red, apricot yellow, silver, and golden silk thread, representing the phoenix's neck, body, and feathers. The golden waistband tied at the back flutters in the wind, symbolizing a phoenix's tail. The silver ornaments jingle, symbolizing the sound of a phoenix.

例句：

1989 年出版的《畲族风俗志》，首次使用了“**凤凰装**”这一名称。

Example Sentence:

The term "phoenix dress" first appeared in *Customs of the She Ethnic Group*, which was published in 1989.

鱼皮衣 *yupi yi;* fish skin clothing

中国赫哲族人特有的用鱼皮缝制的衣服。赫哲族缝制鱼皮衣已有上千年历史，这种鱼皮手工制作技艺散发着古代北方游猎民族独特的文化气息，赫哲族也因此被称为“鱼皮部落”。赫哲族鱼皮衣上都有云纹和鸟兽图案，纹饰内容包罗万象，有着深邃的内涵，反映赫哲族生产、生活、宗教信仰与生活习俗等各方面的内容。做鱼皮衣的材料也很有讲究，在长期的实践中，赫哲人逐步摸索出当地各种鱼皮的特点，并掌握了适合做不同衣物的材料。鱼皮衣是赫哲民族服饰中最具特色、最为显象性的

A type of special clothing of the Hezhen ethnic group. Their custom of making fish skin clothing has existed for over a thousand years, unique cultural heritage of ancient, northern nomads. As a result, the Hezhen ethnic group has often been called the "Tribe of Fish Skins." Fish skin clothing is embroidered with images of clouds, birds, plants, and beasts, all of which reflect the religious beliefs and general customs of the Hezhen people. The materials for making the clothing are carefully chosen. It was over a long period of time that various fish skins were examined to determine which were suitable for making clothes. Fish skin clothing marks the most distinctive example of Hezhen attire, and serves as an emblem of the Hezhen people. Such attire is light, warm, waterproof and suitable for people to make their living through hunting and fishing. However, as the Hezhen have developed new modernized ways of life, fish skin clothing has been gradually fading out.

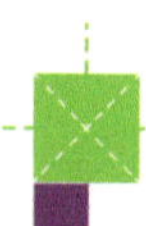

服饰，起着族徽的作用。鱼皮衣轻便、保暖、防潮、耐磨，适应了赫哲族人民渔猎生活的需要。如今，赫哲人的生活方式发生了巨大的变化，鱼皮衣已经很少见了。

例句：

鱼皮衣春秋季节穿上捕鱼不易透水，冬季穿着狩猎，结实耐磨。

Example Sentence:

Fish skin clothing is waterproof and good for spring and autumn fishing as well as winter hunting.

百岁毛 *baisuimao;* a hairstyle symbolizing longevity

中国小孩儿的一种发式。留百岁毛是汉族广为流传的一种育儿风俗，盛行于中国北方地区。每次给孩子理发时都要特意在脑后留一撮头发，称为“百岁毛”，直到十二周岁才剃掉，多见于男孩儿。

Hairstyle for Chinese children. Wearing a *baisuimao* is a common custom of the Han people, a custom especially popular in northern China. It refers to deliberately leaving a strand of hair on the back of a child's head and not cutting it until the child is 12 years old. This is most often seen on boys.

例句：

山西人认为留**百岁毛**可防止男孩儿特别是独子夭折。

Example Sentence:

People in Shanxi Province believe that wearing a *baisuimao* can bring longevity to a boy, especially if he is the only son in a family.

民以食为天

min yi shi wei tian;
People regard food as their prime want.

中国汉语成语，意即饮食为人们生存的根本，至关重要。这一说法源于《史记·郦生陆贾列传》："王者以民人为天，而民人以食为天"，意为统治者要深得民心，积极解决百姓最为关心的吃饭问题最为重要。受这一思想影响，中国形成了丰富多彩的饮食文化，八大菜系各有所长，地域特色鲜明。同时中国菜讲究色香味俱全，菜名追求雅致，彰显中国文化特色，且拥有源远流长的餐桌礼仪。时至今日，中国"民以食为天"的传统饮食文化依然广受欢迎。

A Chinese idiom which means "food is the paramount necessity of people." As written by Sima Qian in his *Records of the Grand Historian* (94 BC), "The king regards the people as heaven while the people take food as the first necessity." This shows that only through providing enough food for the people can a ruler win the support of his subjects. Under the influence of this thought, China has formed a rich and varied food culture with eight schools of cooking and distinctive regional characteristics and long-standing dining etiquette. Chinese cuisines have various dishes of differing colors, aromas, and tastes. The dishes have elegant names that reflect cultural connotations. This concept remains popular among people today.

例句：

中国有句古话：**"民以食为天"**。所以但凡中国人要在国外安家落户，一定会更青睐有正宗中餐的城市。

Example Sentence:

There is an old Chinese saying: "People regard food as their prime want." When settling down in a foreign country, Chinese people always like to live in a city with restaurants serving authentic Chinese dishes.

食物五性

shiwu wuxing;
five properties of food

中医认为食物有五性，平性、热性、温性、寒性、凉性。中国古人认为"药食同源"，根据食物的五性及身体需要合理搭配饮食、寒热适中方能增强体质，达到养生的目的。常见的食物中以平性食物居多，性质平和且最无伤害性，适合各种体质的人食用，如土豆、红萝卜等。热性及温性食物容易使身体发热，可增强人体活力，如辣椒、羊肉等，适用于体质偏寒者或冬天食用。寒性及凉性食物能清凉消热，祛火消炎，如绿豆、梨等，适用于热性病症者或夏天食用。

A traditional concept in Chinese medicine is that food has five properties: neutral, hot, warm, cold, and cool. In accordance with the view of "homology of medicine and food," ancient Chinese held that a balanced diet and appropriate intake of cold and hot food could enhance physical strength and maintain good health. Common foods such as potatoes and carrots are mostly neutral and suitable for people of various body constitutions. Hot and warm foods like chili and mutton are known to easily warm the body and enhance human vitality, preferably eaten in winter and by people with "cold" body constitutions. Cold and cool foods such as mung beans and pears can remove heat and diminish inflammation, appropriate for summer and people suffering from a fever.

例句：

如今，越来越多的养生专家呼吁人们要辨清**食物五性**，对症吃饭、科学养生。

Example Sentence:

Nowadays, more and more health experts are calling on people to have a clear understanding of the five properties of food so that they can maintain good health.

南甜北咸

nan tian bei xian;
sweet in the south and salty in the north

概括了中国饮食文化受地理环境影响、有地域差异的俗语。南甜：指苏州、无锡、上海等南方地区偏爱甜食。南方多雨，光热条件好，盛产甘蔗等糖类食物，养成了南方人喜吃甜食的习惯。"八大菜系"之一的苏菜就是"南甜"的代表。北咸：中国北方地处暖温带，冬季寒冷干燥，蔬菜难以过冬，北方人便把菜腌制起来慢慢"享用"，由此养成了北方人吃咸的习惯。其代表为"八大菜系"之一的鲁菜。

A common generalization of the different preferences of flavors in China based on geographical conditions. "Sweet in the south" refers to people's preference for sweet foods in Suzhou, Wuxi, Shanghai and other parts of southern China. Because of the rich rainfall, heat, and ample sunshine, southern China abounds with sugar cane and other sugary foods, thus making a tendency for people to prefer food with a sweet taste. Suzhou cuisine, one of China's "eight major schools of cooking," is typical of "sweet in the south." Northern China, however, is located in the warm temperate zone where the winter is cold and dry and thus hard for vegetables to survive. This has formed a preference for people to eat salted vegetables. Shandong cuisine is a typical example. It features a savory taste.

例句：

由于气候差异，中国的食物从北到南差异很大，口味也因地区不同而不同。"**南甜北咸**"是最好的概括。

Example Sentence:

Food in China varies from north to south because of climate differences. Tastes also differ regionally. One popular summary of Chinese food is "sweet in the south, salty in the north."

药补不如食补

yaobu buru shibu;
Diet cures more than the doctor's prescription.

中国食疗养生谚语，意指用食物来补养身体比药效更好。食物与药物都有治病疗疾的作用，但前者气味纯正、毒副作用小，对人体以滋养作用见长，宜用于养生；后者气味偏颇，毒副作用大，以攻邪作用为主，宜用于治病。从补益的角度看，食补优于药补。在调养过程中，先以食疗，食疗不愈，才以药治。中国人很早就在对各种食材的特性、搭配，不同季节的饮食等方面有深入的了解和研究，很多菜肴中会加入中药材，以达到饮食养生的目的。

A Chinese idiom for health and diet practices that means it is better to nourish the body with food than with medicine. Both food and medicine can treat diseases, but the former is more suitable for maintaining good health with its natural aroma, and low degree of undesirable side effect; the latter has a strong aroma and high side effects, making it more suitable for treating specific diseases. In the process of recuperation, a good diet should be the first choice, to be followed by medicine if needed. Chinese people have long understood the characteristics and nourishing properties of various ingredients, and their functions in different seasons. Certain medicinal herbs are added to Chinese dishes because of their health benefits.

例句：

从营养学角度出发，采用食物调养脾胃之气，遵循“**药补不如食补**”的饮食健康观，是中医的重要内容。

Example Sentence:

It is an important concept in traditional Chinese medicine that a healthy diet can help regulate one's *qi* in the spleen and stomach, which is an example of the dietary principle "Diet cures more than the doctor's prescription."

冬至饺子夏至面

dongzhi jiaozi xiazhi mian;
Eat dumplings at Winter Solstice and noodles at Summer Solstice

中国北方民俗。冬至和夏至是二十四节气中的两个节气，又是民间传统节日中的两个节日。冬至在公历12月22日左右，这一时段最主要标志就是天气严寒，因为饺子的形状酷似耳朵，民间才有“冬至吃饺子安耳朵”的说法和习俗。6月21日或22日为夏至。夏至日开始太阳几乎直射北回归线，北半球的白昼达到最长。民间传说，夏天吃热面有“避恶”之意，即驱除邪恶，用多出汗的方法祛除人体内滞留的潮气和暑气。

A folk custom in northern China. The Winter Solstice and Summer Solstice are two solar terms in the traditional lunar calendar, also celebrated as folk festivals. The Winter Solstice usually falls on December 22 of the Gregorian calendar and is marked by cold weather in northern China. A popular saying goes: “After having dumplings during the Winter Solstice, one’s ears will not suffer from frostbite no matter how cold it is.” The Summer Solstice falls on June 21 or 22 and is characterized by long days and hot weather. According to folklore, eating hot noodles in the summer can induce sweat to help get rid of heat and dampness in the body. It’s also said to help dispel undesirable elements in the body.

例句：

随着社会发展和历史变迁，民间的冬至节和夏至节都已算不上大节了，但在中国北方地区，“**冬至饺子夏至面**”的习俗传承千百年，至今未变。

Example Sentence:

Though the Winter and Summer Solstice are no longer very popular folk festivals, the custom of “eating dumplings at Winter Solstice and noodles at Summer Solstice” is still observed in northern China after thousands of years.

出门饺子回家面

chumen jiaozi huijia mian;
Eat dumplings at departure and noodles at arrival.

中国民间出行饮食习俗，流行于北方地区。意为亲人出远门时家人会做饺子为其送行，回家时家人会做面条为其接风洗尘。饺子形状酷似元宝，象征出行人“得财得利”；饺子捏起来的嘴则代表“祸从口出”，起“谨言慎行”的警示作用。面条细长的形状象征“长长久久”，面条质地顺滑，预示将归家人的不顺和委屈都驱赶走。该习俗表达家人对远行人的美好期望和祝福。

A folk dining custom for long journeys, popular in northern China. When a family member goes on a long journey, the family will make dumplings to see him or her off. Upon return, he or she will be greeted with a meal of noodles. The shape of dumplings resembles a gold ingot, thereby symbolizing wealth and good fortune on the long journey. The two pinched points of a dumpling symbolize taking great care during a journey and not talking too much to strangers. The phrase “out of the mouth comes evil” warns travelers to “be discreet in word and deed.” When a family member returns, they eat long noodles which symbolize the family’s hope that they will stay together at home for a long time. The slender and smooth texture of noodles also expresses the hope that any past troubles during the journey will be wiped away. The custom expresses the family’s good hopes and blessings to the traveling family member.

例句：

“**出门饺子回家面**”是具有很浓北方特色的中国饮食文化，人们通过食物表达自己对家人的祝福。

Example Sentence:

“*Chumen jiaozi huijia mian*” is part of the Chinese food culture popular in northern China in which people express their best wishes to traveling family members to have a safe journey or enjoy long happiness upon their safe return.

筷子 *kuaizi;* chopsticks

中国传统进食工具。是世界上常用餐具之一，中华饮食文化的标志之一，发明于中国，后传至亚洲其他国家。形状为竹、木、骨、金属等材料制作的两根等长的小棍，进食时用以夹菜和扒饭。在中国，筷子除了用来吃饭，在民间的婚、丧、喜庆等礼俗都有广泛运用。筷子不宜插入饭碗，只有在祭祀时才可将筷子插入贡品；女儿出嫁，嫁妆中必有筷子，取“早（快）生贵子”之意。

Traditional eating utensils of the Chinese people, chopsticks were invented in China and later introduced to other Asian countries. They consist of two sticks of equal length made of bamboo, wood, bone, or metal. There are also widely applied rules on how to use them at events such as wedding ceremonies and funerals. They should not be inserted into a rice bowl as this resembles incense burning during a sacrifice. When a girl is married, chopsticks are an indispensable part of her dowry because “chopsticks” in Chinese shares the same pronunciation with the characters meaning “fast” and “son,” symbolizing that she will give birth to a baby boy soon.

例句：

筷子是中国饮食文化的象征，在全世界广为人知。

Example Sentence:

Chopsticks are widely known as a symbol of Chinese food culture.

五谷 *wugu;* five grains

中国古代所称的五种谷物。古代五谷一般指黍、稷、麦、菽、稻。现代五谷指稻谷、麦子、大豆、玉米、薯类。五谷亦泛指粮食作物。谷类作为中国人的传统饮食，几千年来一直是老百姓餐桌上不可缺少的食物之一，在中国的膳食中占有重要的地位，被当作传统的主食。

Ancient Chinese collective term for the five types of grains. This typically includes broomcorn millet, millet, wheat, beans, and rice. In modern times, however, the five grains refer to rice, wheat, soybeans, corn, and tuber crops. For the past few thousand years, the five grains have constituted a major part of the traditional diet of Chinese people. These foodstuffs have played an important role in the Chinese diet and are regarded as the traditional staple foods.

例句:

民以食为天，中国的很多成语、俗语与**五谷**相关，例如：五谷杂粮、五谷丰登、五谷不分等。

Example Sentence:

Food is the life of the people. Many Chinese idioms and sayings are related to the five grains, such as "five grains and other crops," "bumper harvest of the five grains," and "unable to distinguish the five grains."

四大菜系 *si da caixi;* four best-known (Chinese) cuisines

参见“八大菜系”及各菜系词条。八大菜系中形成历史较早的四种地方菜肴，即鲁菜、川菜、苏菜、粤菜。

China's four popular regional cuisines, which are Shandong, Sichuan, Jiangsu, and Cantonese cuisines. Later, another four cuisines gained popularity, and togther, they are known as the eight best-known cuisines. See also *ba da caixi,* "eight best-known cuisines" and separate entries on each cuisine.

例句：

“**四大菜系**”成为清代初期最有影响的地方菜。

Example Sentence:

The four best-known cuisines were the most influential dishes during the early Qing Dynasty.

苏菜 *su cai;* Jiangsu cuisine; Su cuisine

八大菜系之一江苏菜系的简称。由淮扬菜、苏州菜、南京菜等组成。其特色是制作精细，因材施艺，四季有别，浓而不腻，味感清鲜，讲究造型。原料以水产为主，注重鲜活。代表菜品有淮扬狮子头、叫花鸡、松鼠鳜鱼、盐水鸭等。

One of the eight best-known Chinese cuisines which includes Huaiyang, Suzhou, and Nanjing cuisines in Jiangsu Province. It is characterized by its elaborate delicacy, refined methods of preparation and cooking, use of seasonal ingredients, fresh flavors that are strong but not oily, and exquisite presentation. The ingredients are mainly fresh aquatic products. Some of its most famous dishes are Huaiyang Meatballs, Beggar's Chicken, Sweet and Sour Mandarin Fish, and Boiled Salted Duck.

例句：

苏菜常用炖、焖、烤、煨等方法烹饪，口味平和而略带甜味。

Example Sentence:

Jiangsu cuisine is often prepared by stewing, braising, roasting, or simmering. It tastes mild and sweet.

粤菜

yue cai;
Cantonese (Guangdong) cuisine; Yue cuisine

八大菜系之一广东菜系的简称。主要由潮州菜和东江菜组成。其特色是选料广泛，讲究鲜、嫩、爽、滑、浓等。代表菜品有生蒸龙虾、脆皮乳猪、咕噜肉等。

One of the eight best-known Chinese cuisines consisting of typical Chaozhou and Dongjiang dishes that feature a wide variety of ingredients and fresh, tender, crisp, smooth, and rich flavors. Typical dishes are Steamed Lobster, Roasted Crispy Suckling Pig, Stewed Sweet and Sour Pork, and more.

例句：

粤菜常用烧、炆、煲、焗、软炸等方法烹饪，口味清淡鲜美。

Example Sentence:

Cantonese dishes are often cooked by braising, simmering, stewing, steaming, and soft frying. They taste fresh and delicious.

鲁菜 *lu cai;* Shandong cuisine; Lu cuisine

One of the eight best-known Chinese cuisines, mainly composed of poultry, vegetables, and seafood. It is characterized by meticulous choice of ingredients and fine cuts. Onions and ginger are often used for seasonings in addition to light or thick broth. Typical dishes of this cuisine include Fish in Sweet and Sour Sauce, Grilled Pork Hock, Stir-fried Lamb Slices with Scallions, and Stewed Tofu.

八大菜系之一山东菜系的简称。原料多选畜禽、海产、蔬菜。其特色是选料精细，刀法细腻，注重实惠，花色多样，善用葱姜蒜调味，以清汤、奶汤增鲜。代表菜品有糖醋鱼、锅烧肘子、葱爆羊肉、锅塌豆腐等。

例句：

鲁菜善用爆、熘、扒、烤、拔丝等方法烹饪，口味咸鲜比较明显。

Example Sentence:

Shandong cuisine is prepared by quick stir-frying, sautéing, braising, roasting and candying. It tastes savory and fresh.

川菜 *chuan cai;* Sichuan cuisine; Chuan cuisine

八大菜系之一四川菜系的简称。主要流行于长江上游。除四川外，还流行于云南、贵州和湖南、湖北等省。原料多选山珍、江鲜、野蔬和畜禽。其特色是讲究麻辣、鱼香等。代表菜品有东坡肘子、鱼香肉丝、麻婆豆腐、宫保鸡丁、夫妻肺片等。

A style of cuisine from Sichuan Province which is one of the eight best-known Chinese cuisines popular on the upper reaches of the Yangtze River. It is also popular in Yunnan, Guizhou, Hunan, and Hubei provinces. Its ingredients feature land and sea delicacies, wild vegetables, beef, pork, and poultry. It generally uses hot, spicy, and garlic sauce seasonings. Typical dishes include Dongpo Pork Hock, Sautéed Shredded Pork with Garlic Sauce, Spicy Tofu, Kung Pao Chicken, and Ox Tripe in Chili Sauce.

例句：

川菜善用小炒、干煸、干烧和泡、烩等方法烹饪。其味型较多，富于变化。

Example Sentence:

Sichuan cuisine has multiple flavors, featuring such cooking skills as stir-frying, sautéing, pickling, dry-braising, and braising.

八大菜系 *ba da caixi;* eight best-known cuisines

参见各个菜系词条。指八种自成体系的具有独特烹饪技艺和风味的地方菜肴，即鲁菜、川菜、苏菜、粤菜、闽菜、浙菜、湘菜、徽菜。

See also separate entries on each cuisine. China's eight cuisines which have their own distinct cooking methods and flavors. They are Shandong, Sichuan, Jiangsu, Cantonese, Fujian, Zhejiang, Hunan, and Anhui cuisines.

例句：

中国历史上一直以“**八大菜系**”代表中国东南西北各地风味。

Example Sentence:

The eight best-known cuisines represent the dishes from eastern, southern, western and northern China.

浙菜 *zhe cai;* Zhejiang cuisine; Zhe cuisine

One of the eight well-known Chinese cuisines. Zhejiang cuisine is represented by Hangzhou, Ningbo, Shaoxing, and Wenzhou dishes, among which Hangzhou cuisine is the most popular. Zhejiang cuisine is particular about every aspect of the dish from its color, aroma, and taste to the shape and tableware. The ingredients used are fresh and tender. Zhejiang cuisine chefs are adept at stir-frying, deep-frying, braising, sautéing, frying, and stewing. The taste is fresh and crisp, and the

中国八大菜系之一。浙菜有杭州菜、宁波菜、绍兴菜、温州菜四大流派，杭州菜则是主流。浙菜讲究色、香、味、形、器俱全，选料讲究“细、特、鲜、嫩”；烹调技法丰富，擅长炒、炸、烩、熘、烧；注重清鲜脆嫩，保持原料的本色和真味；菜品形态讲究，精巧细腻，清秀雅丽。浙菜代表有西湖醋鱼、东坡肉、荷叶粉蒸肉、龙井虾仁等；著名小吃有杭州的麻心汤圆、西湖藕粥，嘉兴的肉粽、蟹粉包，宁波的八宝饭、鲜肉馄饨，绍兴的五香豆腐干、松糕等。浙菜的代表菜多与文化名人、风景名胜有关。浙菜以其浓郁的文化特色享誉海内外。

dish preserves the original flavor of the ingredients. These dishes are known for being exquisite and delicate. Popular Zhe cuisine dishes include West Lake Vinegar Fish, Dongpo Pork, Steamed Pork with Rice Flour Wrapped in Lotus Leaf, and Shrimp Meat with Dragon Well Tea. Famous snacks include Tangyuan with Sesame Fillings and Lotus Root Porridge in Hangzhou, Meat Zongzi and Steamed Buns Stuffed with Crab Meat in Jiaxing, Eight Delicacies Rice and Meat Wonton in Ningbo, and Multi-Spiced Diced Tofu and Muffin in Shaoxing. These specialties are mostly associated with cultural luminaries and famous natural scenes. Zhejiang cuisine has garnered a worldwide reputation for its cultural value.

例句：

浙菜与苏菜相似，故经常合称为“江浙菜”。

Example Sentence:

Zhejiang cuisine shares many similarities with Jiangsu cuisine, so the two are collectively called Jiangzhe cuisine.

湘菜 *xiang cai;* Hunan cuisine; Xiang cuisine

中国八大菜系之一。早在汉朝就已经形成湘菜菜系。以湘江流域、洞庭湖区和湘西山区三种地方风味为主。湖南气候温和湿润，人们喜食辣椒，用以提神去湿，也喜用酸泡菜作调料，佐以辣椒烹制菜肴，成为湖南地区独具特色的饮食习俗。湘菜制作精细，用料广泛，口味多变，品种繁多，菜肴油重色浓，在品味上注重酸辣、香鲜、软嫩。湘菜在烹调方法上以煨、炖、蒸、炒为主，代表菜有东安子鸡、腊味合

One of the eight well-known Chinese cuisines. Hunan cuisine formed as early as the Han Dynasty (206 BC-AD 220). It mainly includes the flavors popular in the Xiangjiang River Valley, Dongting Lake, and the mountainous areas of western Hunan. Due to the region's mild and wet climate, Hunan people prefer eating peppers to refresh themselves and to get relief from humidity. They also like using sour-pickled vegetables as seasoning, which accompanies spicy chili dishes. Hunan cuisine is distinctive for its exquisite cooking techniques, extensive

蒸、油辣冬笋尖等。2017年湖南省质监局发布《湘菜系列地方标准》，对湘菜的原料产地、数量大小、制作要求、烹调方法甚至菜品摆盘等进行了精确要求。此标准旨在保留湘菜经典菜式的精髓与灵魂，是对当地饮食文化的保护与传承。

materials, variety of flavors, and diversity of styles. It pays close attention to the generous use of oil and bright colors, and in terms of taste it is a combination of sour, spicy, fresh, soft, and tender. Hunan cuisine cooking techniques include simmering, stewing, steaming, and stir-frying. Famous dishes include Dong'an Vinegar Chicken, Steamed Mixed Preserved Meat, and Spicy Bamboo Shoots. The Local Standards of Hunan Cuisine, published by the Bureau of Quality and Technical Supervision of Hunan Province, proposed strict requirements on Hunan cuisine's ingredients, quantity, cooking techniques, and even food presentation. The document aims to maintain the essence of Hunan cuisine dishes, which helps to protect and preserve local culinary traditions.

例句：

湘菜已走向国际，“湘菜香飘联合国”品鉴会2018年11月14日晚在纽约联合国总部举行，联合国官员及餐饮界代表等２００人出席活动。

Example Sentence:

The "Hunan Cuisine Comes to the UN" event was held at the UN headquarters in New York on November 14, 2018. Two hundred people including UN officials and members of the catering industry attended the event.

徽菜 *hui cai;* Anhui cuisine; Hui cuisine

中国八大菜系之一。徽菜由皖南、沿江和沿淮三种地方风味构成，皖南以徽州地区菜肴为代表，是徽菜的主流与渊源，经过漫长发展历程，徽菜已逐渐从徽州地区的山乡风味脱颖而出，汇集安徽各地的风味特色、名馔佳肴，成为一个雅俗共赏、南北咸宜、独具一格、自成一体的著名菜系。徽菜讲究火功，烹调方法以烧、焖、炖为主，重油重色，味道醇厚，保持原汁原味，还以烹制山珍海味闻名。徽菜代表菜有火腿炖甲鱼、符离集烧鸡、屯溪腌鲜鳜鱼等。

One of the eight well-known Chinese cuisines. Anhui cuisine comprises the culinary traditions of the southern Anhui region, the regions along the Yangtze River, and areas along the Huaihe River. As the representative cuisine of southern Anhui, Huizhou cuisine is considered the origin of Anhui cuisine. Anhui cuisine gradually stood out among the traditions of Huizhou and took on its own unique specialties and delicacies, forming into a distinctive cuisine appreciated throughout China. Chefs of Anhui cuisine pay particular attention to heat control, and are adept at braising and stewing. Important in the dishes are oil and color, and preserving nutrition and the original aroma of the food. Specialties include Stewed Soft-Shell Turtle with Ham, Fuliji Roast Chicken, and Tunxi Pickled Fresh Mandarin Fish.

例句：

徽商富甲天下且又偏爱家乡风味，其饮馔之丰盛、筵席之豪华对**徽菜**的发展起了推波助澜的作用，哪里有徽商哪里就有徽菜馆。

Example Sentence:

Though traditionally Anhui merchants were known to be wealthy and could afford to eat any kind of food, they preferred their local flavors. Their sumptuous dishes and banquets contributed to the development of Anhui cuisine. Wherever Anhui merchants went, Anhui cuisine restaurants quickly appeared.

闽菜

min cai;
Fujian cuisine; Min cuisine

中国八大菜系之一。闽菜包括福州、闽南、闽西三个流派，多以海鲜、山珍为原料，烹调方法以炒、熘、煎、煨为主，尤其以“糟”最有特色，菜肴特点是色彩美观，滋味清鲜。汤菜多是闽菜最大的特色，且“一汤百变”，即便普通百姓自己在家做汤也是每天换着花样，有清、有浓，有甜、有咸。闽菜还有一与众不同之处，因长期与南洋群岛人民交往，许多南洋食品和调味品传入福建，福建人将这些外来新品与本地原料结合，便产生了许多独一无二的美食。闽菜代表菜有佛跳墙、醉糟鸡、醉排骨等。

One of the eight well-known Chinese cuisines. Fujian cuisine comprises dishes from Fuzhou, southern Fujian, and western Fujian. The ingredients are mainly seafood and delicacies from the mountains. Fujian cuisine chefs are adept at stir-frying, sautéing, pan-frying, and simmering. They are also especially skilled in deriving flavors with pickled ingredients in distillers' grain alcohol or in wine. The dishes feature bright colors and a light and fresh taste. Different types of soups mark the most notable characteristics of this cuisine. Examples are clear soup, thick soup, sweet soup, and savory soup. Fujian cuisine is also unique in that many foods and condiments have been introduced to Fujian Province as a result of its long-term exchange with the people of the Malay Archipelago. Fujian people combined these foreign products with local ingredients to produce many unique delicacies. Specialties include Buddha Jumping Over the Wall, Chicken in Rice Wine, and Spare Ribs in Wine Sauce.

例句：

闽菜的生存、传播方式大体是跟着福建人走的，哪里有福建人聚居，哪里就有福建菜。

Example Sentence:

The spread of Fujian cuisine follows the Fujian people. Where there are Fujian people, there is Fujian cuisine.

沪菜

hu cai;
Shanghai cuisine; Hu cuisine

中国主要地方风味菜之一，又称“海派菜”。是江南一带的主要菜系，以上海地区传统菜肴为主，在与京、广、川、闽、徽、湘、杭、扬、苏、锡等著名烹调流派相互影响过程中发展起来，同时也吸收了西方菜肴的风味特点。沪菜选料注重活、生、鲜，烹调方法以红烧、生煸和煨法为多。沪菜调味擅长咸、甜、酸，注重原味，代表菜有椒盐排骨、水晶虾仁、芙蓉鸡片、肉丝黄豆汤等。

A Chinese culinary tradition that is also called "Haipai cuisine." It is popular in the south and consists mainly of traditional dishes of Shanghai. It integrated elements from other culinary traditions from Beijing, Guangdong, Sichuan, Fujian, Anhui, Hunan, Hangzhou, Yangzhou, Suzhou, and Wuxi. It even assimilated some features of Western cuisines. It uses live, fresh ingredients, and its chefs are adept at braising, sautéing, and stewing. The dishes highlight the original flavor of the ingredients and the tastes are savory, sweet, or sour. Specialties include Fried Spare Ribs with Spiced Salt, Sautéed Shrimp, Sautéed Sliced Chicken in Egg White, and Shredded Pork with Soybean Soup.

例句:

沪菜又称“本帮菜”，其热度并不亚于常见的川菜、粤菜等。

Example Sentence:

Hu cuisine is also called "Benbang cuisine," which is as popular as Sichuan cuisine, Cantonese cuisine and so on.

素菜 *su cai; vegetarian food; vegetarian dish*

中国菜肴流派之一。素菜是用蔬菜、豆制品、藻类和干鲜果品等植物性原料烹制的菜肴，其特点是以时鲜为主，清爽素净，花色繁多，制作考究，富含营养，有益健康。中国素菜历史悠久，产生于春秋战国时期，当时素菜主要用于祭祀和重大的典礼等活动。至魏晋南北朝时期，随着佛教传入，“吃素”理论逐渐形成，极大推动了素菜的发展，从此素菜就成为中国饮食文化的一个重要组成部分。中国素菜发展到现在，品种已达八千多种，主要分为寺院道观素菜、宫廷素菜和民间素菜。

A type of Chinese cuisine which is prepared with such ingredients as vegetables, soybean products, algae, and dry or fresh fruits. It is characterized by a fresh, light taste and a wide variety of seasonal vegetables. Chinese vegetarian food originated during the Spring and Autumn Period (770-476 BC) when it was mainly prepared for sacrificial and other important events. During the Wei (220-265), Jin (265-420) and Southern and Northern Dynasties (420-589) periods, Buddhism was introduced to China. As a result, vegetarianism gradually took root. Today, there are more than 8,000 vegetarian dishes. The cuisine is principally divided into monastic, royal court, and folk vegetarian traditions.

例句：

素菜营养丰富，别具风味，吃起来入口生津，有利于人体健康。

Example Sentence:

Vegetarian dishes provide an excellent source of nutrition with a unique flavor and lingering aftertaste. Vegetarian food is good for one's health.

药膳 *yaoshan;* medicated diet

指按一定配方将药材与某些食材配合使用制作成的、具有较高营养价值又可防病治病、保健强身的饭食。烹制药膳常以炖、煮、蒸为主，煎、炸、炒少，这样既有利于药物的有效成分析出，又有利于人体的吸收。

A highly specialized diet based on traditional Chinese medicine (TCM) made of Chinese medicinal ingredients and food. It has high nutritional value and is used to prevent and cure diseases and maintain one's health. It is mainly prepared by stewing, boiling, and steaming. It also occasionally involves some frying, deep-frying, and stir-frying. The cooking methods are conducive to achieving the positive medical effect of this diet.

例句：

食用**药膳**，有利于防病、健身和益寿延年。

Example Sentence:

The medicated diet is viewed as a more natural approach to curing and preventing diseases, improving health and ensuring long life.

仿膳 *fangshan;* fangshan cuisine

即仿制的清朝宫廷菜，是京菜中特有的一种。仿膳菜约有八百余种。它的特点是做工精细，形色美观，味道鲜醇，软嫩清淡，造型工巧，命名典雅。

A specific type of Chinese cuisine re-creating the imperial dishes of the Qing Dynasty (1616-1911). It includes more than 800 dishes that are characterized by their exquisite preparation, beautiful shapes and colors, and delicate flavors. The dishes are known for their freshness and succulence, artistic shapes, and elegant names.

例句：

仿膳最著名的菜肴当属“满汉全席”。

Example Sentence:

The Feast of Complete Manchu-Han Courses is the best example of dishes of fangshan cuisine.

涮羊肉

shuan yangrou;
instant-boiled mutton; hotpot, Mongolian style

又称“羊肉火锅”，是中国北方以羊肉为主料的火锅食品，在北京、天津、河北等地颇为流行。将细嫩羊肉切成大薄片，待火锅内鲜汤烧沸后，用筷子夹着羊肉片在锅内涮熟，蘸着芝麻酱、腐乳、韭菜花、卤虾油等搅成的调味汁吃。特点是肉质鲜嫩，不膻不腻。

A hotpot dish with mutton as the main ingredient, also called "mutton hotpot," popular in areas in north China like Beijing, Tianjin, and Hebei Province. It is prepared by dipping thinly-sliced mutton pieces into a pot of boiled water or flavored broth, cooking them a short time before being served. The cooked meat is served with a variety of sauces such as sesame, fermented tofu, chives, or shrimp sauces. Mutton cooked this way is fresh, tender, and not greasy. The meat does not have its normally strong smell.

例句：

涮羊肉里除了羊肉之外，还可以将蔬菜、豆腐等加入锅中涮食。

Example Sentence:

Vegetables, tofu and other food can also be boiled in the mutton hotpot in addition to mutton slices.

羊肉火锅

yangrou huoguo;
mutton hotpot; instant-boiled mutton

参见“涮羊肉”。

See *shuan yangrou* (instant-boiled mutton).

冰糖葫芦

bingtang hulu;
crystal sugar-coated haws on a stick

中国传统小吃，也叫“糖葫芦”，流行于北京等地。一般用竹签将山楂果或海棠果串成一串儿，蘸上熔化的冰糖或麦芽糖制成，造型美观，酸甜可口。据传冰糖葫芦早在宋朝就已出现，到清代其制作日趋精致，在民间社会广泛流行。现在它依然是中国人喜爱的传统小吃。

A traditional Chinese sweet snack made of haws or crab-apples skewered with a bamboo stick and then coated with crystal or malt sugar, giving it a sour and sweet taste. It is said that the snack dates back to the Song Dynasty (960-1279), but became more refined and popular during the Qing Dynasty (1616-1911). Today it is one of the favorite traditional snacks of Chinese people.

例句：

冰糖葫芦是一种既有益健康又具有观赏性的风味小吃。

Example Sentence:

Crystal sugar-coated haws on a bamboo stick are not only delicious, but also appealing to the eye and healthy to eat.

糖葫芦 *tang hulu;* crystal sugar-coated haws on a stick

参见“冰糖葫芦”。

See *bingtang hulu* (crystal sugar-coated haws on a stick).

炸酱面 *zhajiangmian;* noodles with soybean paste (Beijing Style)

富有北京特色的食物。炸酱用肉丁、葱、姜等及黄酱或甜面酱炸炒而成。面条煮熟后，浇上炸酱，拌以黄瓜、胡萝卜、豆芽等即可食用。有点类似意大利肉酱面的感觉，只是口感更清爽鲜香。

A specialty of Beijing cuisine. The soybean paste is made by stir-frying diced pork, spring onions and ginger together with salty fermented bean sauce. The boiled noodles are covered in the paste and topped with diced vegetables such as shredded cucumber, carrots, and bean sprouts. It is similar to spaghetti bolognese in form, but has a lighter and more refreshing taste.

例句：

炸酱面被称为中国的意大利面，风行于北京，每逢夏至，北京人都有吃面的习俗。

Example Sentence:

Nicknamed as “Chinese spaghetti,” the noodles with soybean paste have been popular throughout Beijing. At Summer Solstice, natives in Beijing have a tradition of eating noodles.

油条 *youtiao;* deep-fried twisted dough stick

一种日常中式面食，长条形外皮酥脆，内里绵软的油炸食品。把面粉揉制好后，放进油锅炸熟而成，多用作早点。有时人们会裹点白糖吃。

A daily snack usually eaten for breakfast in China. It resembles a non-sweet version of Western donuts. The dough is cut into long strips and deep-fried until light and crispy. Some are lightly flavored with sugar.

例句：

在上海，**油条**和大饼、豆浆、粢饭团并称上海传统早餐的“四大金刚”。

Example Sentence:

In Shanghai, the four typical foods of breakfast usually consist of deep-fried twisted dough sticks, big pancakes, soybean milk, and rice balls.

火锅 *huoguo;* hotpot

一种把肉片和蔬菜放入开水或汤料煮熟并用小料汁蘸食的中国美食。火锅烹饪用具由金属或陶瓷制成，加热可以用炭火，也可用电或天然气。传统的锅中央有炉膛，持续给汤加热。待汤沸腾后，便将肉片、蔬菜之类放进锅内的汤里，随煮随吃。吃时将肉片和蔬菜放在预先用麻酱、麻油、酱油、辣油、韭菜花、香菜、料酒、豆腐乳等佐料调好的小料里蘸食。

A Chinese dish in which sliced meat and vegetables are quickly boiled and served with different sauces. The cooking pot, which is made of metal or ceramic, is heated either by charcoal fire or a stove fueled by gas or electricity. Traditional copper hotpots have a central chimney which heats the surrounding soup. When the soup begins to boil, sliced meat and vegetables are added into the pot and cooked quickly. Then cooked meat and vegetables are dipped into a sauce that can be mixed with seasonings such as sesame sauce, sesame oil, soy sauce, chili oil, Chinese chives, cilantro, cooking wine, and pickled tofu.

例句：

火锅的肉片和蔬菜随煮随吃。

Example Sentence:

Sliced meat and vegetables are quickly boiled and then immediately served with a variety of sauces.

饸饹 *hele*; *hele* noodles

中国北方民间传统面食，山西、陕西常见，种类可达上百种。饸饹是将豌豆面、莜麦面、荞麦面或其他杂豆面和软，用饸饹床子（一种木制或铁制的有许多圆眼的工具），把面通过圆眼压出来，形成小圆条。饸饹比一般面条要粗些，但比面条劲道、质软，烹饪方式和面条差不多。饸饹味道鲜美，已成为北方人百吃不厌、独具特色的经典食物。2012 年无极饸饹制作技艺被列入河北省非物质文化遗产名录。

A kind of traditional noodles in northern China and popular in Shanxi and Shaanxi provinces where people make more than 100 types of noodles. *Hele* noodles are made by mixing together flour made of peas, oat, buckwheat or other beans, and then using a *hele chuangzi* (a tool made of wood or iron with many small round holes) to press out the noodles. Compared with other types of noodles, *hele* noodles are thicker, softer and thus chewier. Owing to its fresh taste, *hele* noodles have become a unique and classic food loved by people in northern China. In 2012, the skill for making Wuji *hele* noodles was included on the Intangible Cultural Heritage List of Hebei Province.

例句：

饸饹这种美味劲道的面条有着悠久的历史，早在 1500 多年前就是北方的一种大众化食品。

Example Sentence:

The tasty *hele* noodles are made with different types of flour and have been popular in northern China for more than 1,500 years.

东坡肉 *dongpo rou;* Braised Dongpo Pork

中国传统名菜之一。各地做法也有不同。最常见的做法是将五花肉煮到八分熟后切成方块，放入大砂锅或小陶罐内，加作料，开锅后改小火，煮、焖至酥烂，强调小火慢火。特点是薄皮嫩肉、色泽红亮、味醇汁浓、酥烂而形不碎，香糯而不腻口。传说此菜因北宋文学家苏东坡擅烹饪而得名。

A famous traditional Chinese dish of pork belly. There are many variations of preparation, but the most common method entails the pork belly being boiled until almost fully cooked, then cubed and put into a casserole or a small pot. Now seasonings are added. It is then brought to a boil again before being stewed at a low heat until tender. The result is a very tender meat with a shining color, rich flavor, and an appealing appearance. The dish is named after Su Dongpo, literati and poet of the Northern Song Dynasty (960-1127), who was said to be very skilled at cooking this dish.

例句：

东坡肉作为汉族佳肴，流行于江浙一带。

Example Sentence:

Braised Dongpo Pork, a dish of the Han ethnic group, is very popular in Jiangsu and Zhejiang provinces.

佛跳墙 *fotiaoqiang;* Buddha Jumping over the Wall

是集山珍海味于一体的闽菜传统名菜。选用鸡、鸭、干贝、鲍鱼、花菇等二十多种原料放入绍兴酒坛中，精心煨制而成。吃起来软嫩柔润、浓郁荤香、味中有味。

A famous Fujian dish which is elaborately cooked with more than 20 ingredients including chicken, duck, scallops, abalone, mushrooms, and many others. The ingredients are combined in a Shaoxing rice wine jar and simmered in a variety of seasonings for hours. It has a tender and soft texture with the rich and hearty aroma of cooked meat.

例句：

佛跳墙具有增强免疫力、调经润肠、美容养颜等功效。

Example Sentence:

The dish "Buddha Jumping over the Wall" can help improve the immune system, promote blood circulation, ease constipation and nourish the skin.

馕 *nang;* crusty pancake

古称为“胡饼”“炉饼”，在新疆地区有悠久的历史，是维吾尔族、哈萨克族人吃的一种面饼。馕以面粉为主，还可以放芝麻、洋葱、鸡蛋等原料。外皮为金黄色，大都呈圆形，中间薄，边沿略厚，中央戳有许多花纹。馕易于储存，是人们外出旅行的理想食品。

A large round, thin pancake baked by the Uygur and Kazak ethnic groups of China, also called “Hu pancake” or “Lu pancake” in ancient times. It has a long history in Xinjiang Uygur Autonomous Region. It is made from leavened flour with various ingredients such as sesame, onions, and eggs. It is usually round with a patterned middle and thicker edges, and baked until golden brown. It is a popular food for long journeys as it does not go bad over time.

例句：

最大的馕为“艾曼克”馕，直径足有 40 到 50 厘米，是馕中之王。

Example Sentence:

The largest crusty pancake is called aimanke *nang*, and has a diameter of 40 to 50 cm.

糌粑 *zanba;* roasted barley flour

藏族人的主食。“糌粑”为藏语音译，意即“炒面”。把青稞麦炒熟磨成面，吃时加上酥油茶或青稞拌合，再捏成小团儿入口。这种食品营养丰富，便于携带，适合于游牧生活，藏族人食用它已有一千多年历史。

A kind of Tibetan staple food. Zanba is transliterated from its Tibetan name meaning "stir-fried flour." It is essentially made from roasted barley flour and is often mixed with salty Tibetan butter tea when served. It is nutritious and easy to take along on journeys, and thus an ideal option for people who live a nomadic life. It has been a main food for the Tibetan people for over a thousand years.

例句：

糌粑热量高，很适合充饥御寒，还便于携带和储藏。

Example Sentence:

Roasted barley flour is high in calories and can keep one from hunger and cold. In addition, it is easy to carry and store.

杜康造酒 *du kang zao jiu;* Du Kang making alcohol

中国造酒传说。据说杜康是中国古代一个奴隶制王朝夏朝的第五代君主。少年杜康以放牧为生，常把带来的饭食挂在树上，后来杜康发现未吃掉的剩饭虽然变了味，但产生的汁水味道很好。杜康经反复研究思索之后，发现了自然发酵的原理，后来经其不断改进，形成了一套完整的酿酒工艺。这一发明奠定了杜康中国酿酒业开山鼻祖的地位，他所造的酒也被命名为“杜康酒”。后人为了纪念杜康，将他尊为酿酒始祖，现在“杜康”也成了酒的代名词。“杜康造酒”只是一个美丽的传说，中国酒的起源和发展经历了从自然酒到人工酒、从简单的自然发酵酒到蒸馏酒的过程。

A Chinese legend about making the first strong Chinese alcohol known as *baijiu* (strong liquor). Du Kang is believed to have been the fifth monarch of the Xia Dynasty (c. 2070-c.1600 BC). When he was young, Du would often hang his food in a tree during the day as he grazed livestock, and any uneaten food was left there. One day, he discovered that the leftover food in the tree had produced a pleasant-tasting juice. After research and contemplation, he discovered the principle of natural fermentation, and later, through continuous modification, developed a complete alcohol-producing process. This established Du Kang's position as the founder of China's alcohol industry, and the alcohol which he had produced earned the name Du Kang alcohol. In order to commemorate him, later generations honored him as the ancestor of alcohol production. "Du Kang" has become synonymous with Chinese strong alcohol. The story is just a beautiful legend, however, as the origin and development of Chinese strong alcohol has gone through a long process.

例句：

尽管杜康的生平及真实性有待考察，杜康仍因“**杜康造酒**”的传说被人们尊为酒神。

Example Sentence:

Although it is unknown where, when, or even if Du Kang actually lived, he still became deified as the "God of Alcohol" in China due to the legend of "Du Kang making alcohol."

琼浆玉液 *qiongjiang yuye;* mellow alcohol

古代中国神话传说中的美酒，中国美酒的代名词。“琼浆”指美玉制成的浆液，传说喝了它可以成仙；“玉液”指美玉般的酒或浆液。神话传说中，“琼浆玉液”是王母娘娘举办蟠桃盛会时引用的佳品。

A metaphor for a fine wine, alcohol, or luscious juice, based on ancient Chinese legends and tales. In mythology, *"qiongjiang yuye"* was an intoxicating alcoholic drink served at the peach banquet held by the Queen Mother. Legend has it that by drinking *qiongjiang*, a kind of syrup made from fine jade, one can gain immortality.

例句：

“琼浆玉液”在中国早有记载，是神仙、皇帝和王公贵族才能喝到的饮品。如今，“琼浆玉液”可用于指代上乘饮品。

Example Sentence:

In Chinese legends, *qiongjiang yuye* was a kind of mellow alcohol that can only be acquired by aristocrats and gods. Today the term is used to describe a very fine wine or drink.

白酒 *baijiu;* white wine; white spirits

中国特有的一种蒸馏酒，也叫“白干儿”“烧酒”，是以谷物及薯类等富含淀粉的作物为原料，经过发酵、蒸馏制成的酒。酒质无色（或微黄）透明，气味芳香纯正，一般酒精含量较高。著名的白酒有茅台、五粮液、汾酒、泸州老窖等。

A unique distilled alcohol made in China. It is fermented and distilled from grains, potatoes, and other starchy crops. Usually colorless, transparent, and fragrant, it contains a high percentage of alcohol. Famous brands include Moutai, Wuliangye, Fenjiu, and Luzhoulaojiao.

例句：

白酒是中国节日不可或缺的饮品。

Example Sentence:

Baijiu is usually served at every festive occasion in China.

黄酒 *huangjiu;* yellow wine

以大米、糯米、黄米等为原料，以酒曲为糖化发酵剂酿造而成的低度酒。色泽澄黄或呈琥珀色，清澈透明；含有丰富氨基酸，对人体保健有诸多功效。著名的黄酒有：绍兴黄酒、沉缸酒、丹阳封缸酒等。

A mild type of Chinese wine. Rice, glutinous rice, glutinous millet, and other ingredients are used as the raw material which is brewed with yeast to produce the transparent yellow or amber-colored wine with a low level of alcohol. With abundant amino acids, it is considered good for one's health. Famous yellow wines include Shaoxing Rice Wine, Chengang Wine, and Danyang Fenggang Wine.

例句：

黄酒是中国的汉族特产，属于酿造酒，与葡萄酒、啤酒并称世界三大古酒。

Example Sentence:

Yellow wine is a specialty of the Han ethnic group and is considered one of the world's three ancient alcohols along with grape wine and beer.

米酒 *mijiu;* rice wine

A wine made mainly from glutinous rice and millet. Unlike normal wine which is made by fermentation of naturally sweet grapes and other fruit, rice wine results from the fermentation of rice starch converted to sugar. It tastes sweet and has a low percentage of alcohol. Rice wine can stimulate digestion and promote appetite.

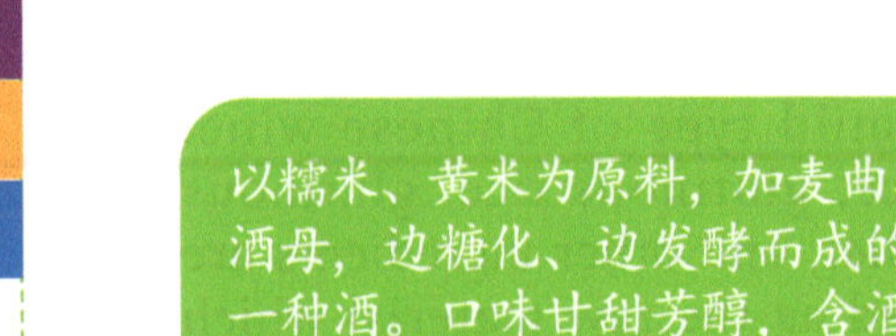
以糯米、黄米为原料，加麦曲、酒母，边糖化、边发酵而成的一种酒。口味甘甜芳醇，含酒精量极少，能刺激消化腺的分泌，增进食欲，有助消化。

例句：

现代**米酒**多采用工厂化生产，已成为人们日常饮用的一种饮品。

Example Sentence:

Modern rice wine is now processed in automated production assembly line, and has become a daily beverage for many Chinese people.

药酒 *yaojiu;* medicinal liquor

中国中医中的"酒剂"，一般由食用酒精、黄酒或葡萄酒等通过浸泡药材配制而成。药酒品种繁多，功效各异，分内服和外涂两种。中国用药酒治病历史悠久。其优势在于药借酒力、酒助药势，进而充分发挥其效力，提高疗效。

A kind of medicated liquor as part of traditional Chinese medicine. It is usually made by soaking medicinal materials in various kinds of alcohol such as edible alcohol, rice wine, and grape wine. Medicinal liquor comes in different varieties with varying therapeutic effects, and can be orally taken or applied externally. China has a long history of treating diseases with medicinal liquor. Medicinal liquor ensures that the medicine and alcohol mutually assist each other in the curative effects.

例句：

早在春秋战国时期，中国就已开始使用**药酒**。

Example Sentence:

Ancient Chinese began to use medicinal liquor as early as the Spring and Autumn and Warring States periods (770–221 BC).

jiuji; medicinal liquor

参见“药酒”。

See *yaojiu* (medicinal liquor).

女儿酒 *nü'er jiu;* daughter's wine

中国一种黄酒，源于浙江绍兴一个古老的酒俗：该地区的人家在生了女儿后会酿造几坛酒，用泥封口，埋入地下贮藏，待女儿出嫁时将其

A kind of Chinese yellow wine originating from an ancient custom in Shaoxing City, Zhejiang Province. After giving birth to a daughter, the parents will brew several jars of this wine, seal them with mud, bury them underground

作为嫁妆取出，或作为礼品赠予亲朋好友，这种酒即为“女儿酒”。女儿酒一般不用于婚礼上宴请亲朋好友，而是随着岁月久远，夫妻恩爱和睦，再启封饮用。女儿酒长期贮藏，开封时香气浓郁，满室芬芳，同时酒性柔和，有保健、调味等功能。

for storage, and eventually take them out as a dowry when their daughter gets married or give them as gifts to relatives and friends. Daughter's wine is usually not served at wedding banquets, but to be enjoyed by husband and wife over time as the couple live together in love and harmony. Because of its long-term storage, it has a rich aroma which is good for health and also seasoning food.

例句：

女儿酒又称花雕酒，一般在女孩子出生之后酿作。多为自己家酿，也有委托酒作坊代酿的。

Example Sentence:

Nü'er jiu or *huadiao jiu* is a wine usually home-brewed after the birth of a baby girl either by the newborn's family or a winery.

花雕酒 *huadiao jiu;* huadiao wine

参见“女儿酒”词条。盛装女儿酒的坛子颇有讲究，属专门特制，酒坛上雕有题词、龙凤呈祥、嫦娥奔月等图案式样，色泽鲜艳，古色古香，以象征白头偕老、吉祥如意。这种雕镂了精美花纹的酒坛被称为“花雕”，故女儿酒又称为“花雕酒”。如今，“花雕坛”作为一种传统的工艺品得到了珍视和发展。

Also see *nü'er jiu*; daughter's wine. Another name for a "daughter's wine." It is so called because the wine is kept in an exquisite and specially-made jar called a *huadiao*, or "flower carving." The jar is carved with inscriptions or patterns like "Prosperity brought by the dragon and the phoenix," "The Goddess Chang'e flying to the moon," and other auspicious sayings to symbolize a long life and good fortune. The "*huadiao* jar" has been cherished and developed as a traditional artwork.

例句：

花雕酒坛俗称“画花酒坛”，主要工艺是从古代的传统漆艺中分离出来的，制作工序繁杂，属手工制作的民间艺术品。

Example Sentence:

Commonly known as "flower-painted wine jar," the jar of *huadiao jiu* is made according to traditional lacquer art with sophisticated techniques.

屠苏酒 *tusu jiu;* Tusu wine

中国古代春节时饮用的酒品。“屠苏”是房屋名，据说此酒的发明者居住在名为“屠苏”的草庵中，“屠苏酒”由此得名。相传此酒有预防瘟疫、祛风散寒、避除疫疠之邪之功效。中国民间有在除夕或正月初一日饮用屠苏酒的习俗。饮酒时，合家按照先幼后长的顺序，逐人饮少许，“小者得岁，先酒贺之；老者失岁，故后饮酒。”直至清代，这一习俗仍不衰。今天人们已不再大规模践行此俗。

A kind of wine drunk during the Spring Festival in ancient China which was believed to have medicinal effects. Legend has it that the creator of Tusu wine was living in a thatched hut called *tusu*, hence the name. It is said that this wine could help prevent plague, colds, and epidemics. An ancient Chinese custom entails drinking Tusu wine on Chinese New Year's Eve or on the first day of the first lunar month. Each family member would drink a little according to age, starting with the youngest (to celebrate their coming years) to the oldest (to celebrate their longevity). The custom was popular until the Qing Dynasty (1616-1911), and is not widely observed today.

例句：

屠苏酒是中国古代流传下来的历史名酒和珍贵文化遗产，自东汉创制以来备受青睐。

Example Sentence:

Tusu wine was created during the Eastern Han Dynasty (25-220), and is regarded as precious cultural heritage handed down from ancient China.

jiaohua jiu; pepper flower wine

中国用椒花泡制成的酒。中国人有元宵节饮椒花酒的习俗，寓意吉祥、康宁、长寿。其饮酒礼节与屠苏酒相同：年岁小者得岁，先饮酒，年长者失岁，后饮酒。儿孙们须以椒花酒向长辈祝寿。

A kind of Chinese wine made with pepper flowers soaked in wine. The wine is believed to ensure auspiciousness, health, and longevity. It is customary to drink the wine during the Lantern Festival. Drinking etiquette is the same as that of drinking Tusu wine: young people should drink before their elders. It is also customary for young people to give pepper wine to older people on their birthday.

例句：

古代春节到来时，人们全家喝**椒花酒**、屠苏酒以防瘟疫，同祝安康。

Example Sentence:

Ancient Chinese believed drinking pepper flower wine and Tusu wine during the Spring Festival was good for the health and would help prevent the spread of diseases.

菖蒲酒 *changpu jiu:* calamus wine

中国端午节所饮之节令酒。菖蒲是生长于山涧泉流旁的一种名贵药材，具有开窍、祛痰、理气、活血、散风和去湿等功效。古人认为饮此酒可以避瘟气。明刘若愚《酌

A kind of Chinese wine with medicinal effects made from calamus known to grow beside mountains and creeks. It is believed that calamus has healing effects such as inducing resuscitation, removing phlegm, regulating *qi* energy, invigorating blood

中志》记载，宫中五月初五日午时，饮菖蒲酒。端午节时人们为了辟邪、除恶、解毒，一直保持着饮菖蒲酒的习俗。

circulation, dispelling cold and dampness, and preventing the spread of disease. Liu Ruoyu, a Ming Dynasty court historian, wrote that people in the imperial palace normally drank calamus wine on the fifth day of the fifth lunar month. It has been a custom to drink calamus wine during the Dragon Boat Festival to dispel evil spirits and relieve internal heat.

例句：

每逢端午，人们将菖蒲做成宝剑形的蒲剑悬于屋檐处，并饮**菖蒲酒**，以图逢凶化吉。

Example Sentence:

Chinese people have the custom of hanging calamus and drinking calamus wine during the Dragon Boat Festival in hope of having good luck.

菊花酒 *juhua jiu;* chrysanthemum wine

中国汉代出现，唐朝已广为普及。菊花酒有明目、治头昏、降血压等功效。古代每逢重阳节有饮菊花酒的习俗，象征吉祥，祛灾免祸。此酒用菊花与糯米、酒曲酿制而成。

A kind of Chinese wine which originated in the Han Dynasty (206 BC-AD 220) and was popular in the Tang Dynasty (618-907). The wine is said to have healing effects such as improving eyesight, alleviating headaches and reducing hypertension, all believed to contribute to longevity. Ancient Chinese had the custom of drinking chrysanthemum wine during the Double Ninth Festival (the 9th day of the 9th month on the lunar calendar, usually in late October), believed to help bring good luck and peace. The wine is brewed with chrysanthemums, glutinous rice, and distiller's yeast.

例句：

中国人会在重阳节赏菊和饮**菊花酒**，是因为菊花不仅象征长寿，同时也可以驱除昆虫和防寒。

Example Sentence:

The Chinese appreciate chrysanthemum flowers and drink chrysanthemum wine during the Double Ninth Festival. This is because chrysanthemum symbolizes longevity and helps repel insects and prevent chills during winter.

黄花酒

huanghua jiu;
chrysanthemum wine

参见“菊花酒”。

See *juhua jiu* (chrysanthemum wine).

接风酒

jiefeng jiu;
welcome banquet wine

中国酒俗，专为迎接刚从远道归来的人而摆设的酒席。接风酒主要表达人们对朋友到来的欢迎，并且也是希望

A Chinese custom of preparing a banquet to greet visitors, usually from afar. A welcome or reception banquet is held to express hospitality to friends who have

朋友旅途的疲惫可以减少一些，同时给朋友去除身上的厄运。接风酒也是希望自己的朋友在以后发展得更好，对朋友未来的一种祝愿。接风酒、送行酒等许多形式的白酒文化，从古代一直沿用到现在。

traveled from afar with the hope of relieving their fatigue after their long journey and wishing them success in the future. The drinking customs such as "welcome banquet" and "farewell banquet" have been observed since ancient times.

例句：

他们准备了**接风酒**来为公司首席执行官的归来接风洗尘。

Example Sentence:

They prepared a special welcome banquet to greet the Chief Executive Officer of the corporation.

饯行酒 *jianxing jiu;* farewell banquet

中国酒俗，送别亲友时特设的酒宴。现代人重视"接风酒"，而在古代，山高水长，交通不便，每次与亲友离别，都无法预知何年何月才能再相逢，因此古人更看重"饯行酒"，"饯行酒"的场面充满了离别的悲凉和哀愁，显得庄严和肃穆；朋友离别之后高山险阻，奔波劳顿，"饯行酒"也有祝愿一帆风顺和祈祷上天保佑之意。

A Chinese custom of holding a special banquet to see friends and relatives off before they began a journey. People nowadays often hold welcome banquet, while in ancient times, traveling on journeys was difficult and often dangerous. When embarking on journeys, relatives and friends would not know when they would meet again. Therefore, farewell banquets were often sad occasions, and they were held in a solemn and serene atmosphere to express good wishes for a smooth journey and blessings from Heaven.

例句：

亲朋好友临别饯酒，实际上意不在酒，而在于情意的交流与贮存，这便是**“饯行酒”**的真谛。

Example Sentence:

Friends and relatives hold a farewell banquet before long journeys to express their care and deep affection for one another.

jiu ling;
drinkers' wager game; drinking game

宴席上流行的一种民间风俗，一般是推举一人为令官，其他人听从令官号令开展各种活动。该风俗源于西周，开始是为了维持酒席秩序，而后用于助酒兴、活跃酒席气氛。令官要求人们轮流说诗词、联语或猜谜等，违令者或负者被罚饮酒。

A Chinese custom in which one drinker at a banquet or dinner is selected to determine the entertainment activities and games of all the drinkers. The custom originated in the Western Zhou Dynasty (1100–771 BC) for the purpose of maintaining order at a banquet. Games people enjoyed at the dinner table range from riddles to recitations of poetry or couplets. Normally the losers of such games will have to drink wine.

例句：

酒令的约束力很强，有“酒令如军令”之说。

Example Sentence:

The drinking game enjoys great authority over the banquet participants, and is likened to a military command.

划拳 *hua quan;* finger-guessing game

中国民间饮酒时一种助兴取乐的游戏。饮酒时两人同时伸出手指并各说一个数，谁说的数目跟双方所伸手指的总数相符，谁就算赢，输的人喝酒。如果双方猜的数字都对或都不对，划拳活动继续。

A traditional alcohol-drinking game. Two players simultaneously stick out a certain number of fingers on one hand, and each says aloud his guess of the total number of fingers of both players. If one guesses right, the other player must drink alcohol. If both players say the correct or wrong numbers, they will continue guessing.

例句：

划拳起源于汉代，是中国传统酒文化的内容之一。

Example Sentence:

The finger-guessing game, which dates back to the Han Dynasty (206 BC-AD 220), is part of traditional Chinese alcohol-drinking culture.

投壶 *touhu;* the game of throwing an arrow into a jug

A game played at banquets in ancient times, dating back to the Warring States Period (475-221 BC). Archery was considered an essential skill in ancient times which explains why archery was so often seen during ancient rituals and games. Because it was inconvenient and sometimes dangerous for guests to shoot

古代宴饮时的一种娱乐游戏，可追溯至战国时期。古时由于宴请时射箭既不方便也不安全，于是将射箭活动改为投壶。宾客依次把箭投入壶中，以投中多少决定胜负，负者须饮酒。

arrows at targets during a banquet, they would throw arrows into a jug instead as an entertaining competition. The person who threw the most arrows into the jug won, and the loser would have to drink alcohol.

例句：

投壶是从战国延续至清末的中国传统礼仪和宴饮游戏。

Example Sentence:

The game of throwing an arrow into a jug of alcohol was a traditional ritual as well as a game played at a banquet, which was popular from the Warring States Period until the late Qing Dynasty (1616-1911).

 敬酒 *jing jiu;* propose a toast

中国酒俗。敬酒又叫“劝酒”，通常要讲一些祝愿、祝福类的话，可以随时在饮酒的过

A Chinese custom to express good wishes and drink to one's health, happiness, and success during any time of a meal. The general

程中进行。一般情况下，敬酒应以年龄大小、职位高低、宾主身份为先后顺序，先敬长者或地位高的人。一般而言，拒绝接受敬酒是对敬酒人的不敬。中国人敬酒时都希望对方多喝酒，以表示自己的敬意。中国人的好客、人与人的感情交流往往在敬酒时得到升华。

protocol for toasting should occur in order of age, position, and status where the host, elders, and people of higher status should always be toasted first. It is considered impolite to refuse a drink if someone toasts you, and the amount you drink reflects the amount of respect you show to the one toasting you. Chinese people believe interpersonal relationships are promoted when toasting, and hope their guests and friends drink more so they can express their hospitality and enhance their friendship.

例句：

请大家将酒杯斟满，向远方的来客**敬酒**！

Example Sentence:

Please fill your glasses and drink a toast to the guests from afar!

quan jiu;
propose a toast

参见“敬酒”。

See *jing jiu* (propose a toast).

dai yin;
drink wine on somebody's behalf

中国酒俗。中国人宴请时，为表示热情好客，主人往往

A Chinese custom of drinking alcohol on behalf of someone else. It is customary for a Chinese host to repeatedly invite guests

会多次邀请客人喝酒，不擅饮酒或不方便饮酒的人便可以在征得大家同意的情况下找人代饮，这样既不失风度，又可回应主人的热情款待。

to drink. Those who are not good at drinking or feel uncomfortable can ask someone else to drink on their behalf so that they can still show respect to the host while declining to drink.

例句：

新郎酒量浅，新娘就**代饮**了几杯。

Example Sentence:

The groom is not a heavy drinker, so the bride drinks some wine on his behalf.

罚酒

fa jiu;
penalty drink

中国一种独特的敬酒方式。罚酒的理由五花八门，最为常见的可能是对酒席迟到者罚酒三杯。罚酒常常带点儿开玩笑的性质，主要是为了活跃气氛。

A humorous custom of having a guest drink more alcohol. There are many excuses and sayings to enact a penalty drink, the most common being to drink three cups as a punishment for being late for dinner. People are urged to take penalty drinks for reasons such as being late, saying something wrong or just for fun. This custom is mainly used to enliven the atmosphere at the dinner table.

例句：

大多数酒席迟到的人实际上都对**罚酒**欣然接受，如此一来他们就可以跟上大家的步调了。

Example Sentence:

Most latecomers actually enjoy the penalty drinks as it allows them to catch up with the rest of the people at the party.

感情深，一口闷

ganqing shen, yi kou men;
Drink it all down if we are good friends; good friends, bottoms up

中国劝酒词。喝酒是百姓生活的一部分，为了渲染喝酒气氛和增强感情，人们常说一些劝酒词来劝说对方和自己对饮，如"感情深，一口闷""感情浅，舔一舔"等。中国人在各类场合时有不同的劝酒词。这些劝酒词可以反映社情民意，更可以瞥见中国人的千古饮酒文化。

A Chinese saying used to urge people to drink alcohol at a party. Drinking alcohol has been a main part of Chinese culture throughout history. Chinese people believe that interpersonal relationships can be best promoted through drinking together. There are many interesting phrases used to urge people to drink such as "if we're really good friends, let's drink it all down" or "just take a sip if we're just casual acquaintances." These phrases can reveal ways of social interactions as well as reflect age-old Chinese drinking culture.

例句：

劝酒词"**感情深，一口闷**"把喝酒的多少与人的感情深浅联系到一起。

Example Sentence:

The saying "good friends, bottoms up" links the amount that you drink to your affection of the person you are drinking with.

先干为敬

xian gan wei jing;
I will finish my glass first to show my respect.

中国一种劝酒令，流行于全国各地的饮酒习俗，各地民间宴饮中的一种礼仪。为了劝客人饮酒．主人会说“我先干为敬，各位请随意”，而后一饮而尽，以此来表示对对方的敬意；主人饮过之后．客人亦须饮酒以回敬主人。

A Chinese saying to urge people to drink, popular in all parts of China. It is also a rule of etiquette at Chinese banquets. To urge his guests to drink more, the host will say, “I will finish my glass first to show my respect, but you can drink at your leisure.” The person being toasted is generally expected to at least take a sip of his drink to return the compliment.

例句：

敬您一杯，话在酒中，**先干为敬**！

Example Sentence:

I would like to propose a toast and finish my glass first to show my respect.

中国茶

zhongguo cha;
Chinese tea

中国出产的茶。中国是世界上最早发现并利用茶树的国家，早在两千多年以前，便开始茶树种植。随着制茶技艺逐渐完备，中国民间形成了饮茶的习俗，茶成为中国人的主要日常饮料。茶叶为茶树鲜嫩叶芽经加工的干燥制品，根据加工方法不同可分为红茶、绿茶、黑茶、青茶、白茶、黄茶六大类，亦可分为发酵茶、非发酵茶和半发酵茶三大类。各地茶叶品种繁多，浙江杭州龙井、江苏苏州碧螺春、湖南岳阳君山银针、福建安溪铁观音、云南普洱茶等均为茶中名品。茶，始于神农时代，与中华文化相伴已走过数千年的历史长河。中国茶是对人类健康的巨大贡献。

Tea produced in China. China is the first country in the world that discovered and used tea plants. Tea began to be cultivated in China over 2,000 years ago. The improvement of tea-making techniques helped propagate the custom of tea drinking, eventually making tea a major drink in the country. Tea leaves are the dry products after the tender leaf buds of tea plants are processed. Tea can be divided into six types based on the processing methods, namely, black, green, dark, Oolong, white, and yellow tea. Other types include fermented, non-fermented, and half-fermented tea. Types of tea vary from place to place; among the best-known are Hangzhou Longjing (Dragon Well) of Zhejiang Province, Suzhou Biluochun of Jiangsu Province, Yueyang Junshan Silver Needle of Hunan Province, Anxi Iron Guanyin of Fujian Province, and Pu'er of Yunnan Province. The health benefits of drinking tea were supposedly discovered by Shen Nong, a legendary figure in Chinese history who was believed to have lived some 6,000 years ago, and is regarded as the first to study and learn the health benefits of drinking tea.

例句：

中国茶文化是中华文化的一个重要组成部分。

Example Sentence:

Tea is an important part of Chinese culture.

茶道

chadao;
tea ceremony; the way of drinking tea

中国在饮茶、品茶过程中遵守的礼仪规范，也是一种生活艺术。茶道有一套严格煮茶、泡茶、品茶的程序。其精髓是将饮茶做为修身养性的文化活动，一方面展现茶艺，一方面休养精神。茶道已经超脱了传统饮食文化的范畴，更讲究精神层面上对情操的熏陶。茶道起源于古代中国，于唐朝时期形成完整体系，后传入日本，形成日本茶道。

The rules of etiquette observed in the process of drinking tea, which is also a life art. The tea ceremony includes a set of strict procedures in tea simmering, brewing, and drinking. The tea ceremony can help cultivate people's minds and develop character while showcasing the beauty and traditions of tea culture. It surpasses the scope of traditional food culture with more emphasis on cultivating the mind. It originated in China and developed into a complete system during the Tang Dynasty (618-907). It was later introduced to Japan where it evolved into the Japanese tea ceremony.

例句：

本质上，**茶道**是一种泡茶的正式方式，它能让茶汤具有最好的口感。

Example Sentence:

In essence, the tea ceremony is a formal way of brewing tea and bringing out its best taste.

茶艺 *chayi;* the art of tea

中国有关烹茶、饮茶及以茶待客的技艺。茶艺包括选茗、择水、烹茶技术、茶具艺术，环境的选择、创造等一系列内容。它在中国优秀文化的基础上又广泛吸收和借鉴了其它艺术形式，并扩展到文学、艺术等领域，形成了具有浓厚民族特色的中国茶文化，并为广大人民群众所喜爱。

The art imbedded in the Chinese ways of tea brewing, drinking, and serving guests. It includes tea selection, water selection, tea-brewing techniques, tea ware selection, and choosing the proper environment. Based on the most excellent characteristics within Chinese culture, it has borrowed from and extensively absorbed other arts, and has even impacted literature and other fields of arts, forming a Chinese tea culture with strong national characteristics and great popularity among Chinese people.

例句：

用中国古典乐器，如古筝、长笛等演奏的古典背景音乐也可以成为**茶艺**的一部分，让饮茶者享受传统美学和禅宗哲学。

Example Sentence:

Classical background music played with Chinese traditional instruments like the *guzheng* and flute is also a part of the art of tea. The music offers tea drinkers and tasters the joy of traditional Chinese aesthetics and imparts a Zen philosophy.

煎茶 *jian cha;* simmering tea

中国古代劳动人民发明的制茶工艺。古人饮茶用火煎煮，

A tea-making technique invented by people in ancient China who used fire to simmer tea leaves. Written records of this technique can be

故谓"煎茶"，该工艺文字记载可追溯到唐朝，唐代陆羽《茶经》始有详细记载。煎茶是制作食用茶的一道工序，即用水煮采集的嫩茶叶。后来煎茶逐渐被用来指代一个茶的品种，今天所说的煎茶就是以蒸汽杀青制造而成的绿茶。

traced back to the Tang Dynasty (618-907), and details can be found in *The Classic of Tea* written by Lu Yu of the Tang Dynasty. Simmering tea is a process of making edible tea, which used to refer to only boiled tender tea leaves. Nowadays, "simmering tea" refers to green tea after being steamed.

例句：

日本的**煎茶**道保留了中国煎茶道的精髓，并在此基础上发扬光大。

Example Sentence:

Japan has retained the essence of Chinese simmering tea art and has improved upon it.

吃茶 *chi cha; eating tea*

中国唐代及之前的一种饮茶方式。唐之前的茶以药材的形式存在，唐朝茶的吃法类似于现在的菜粥，先把生叶做成茶饼，焙干收藏，吃的时候再把茶饼碾成茶粉，放在锅中烹煮，并在汤中加盐调成咸味，"吃茶"由此而来。

A way of drinking tea in China popular before and during the Tang Dynasty (618-907). Prior to the Tang Dynasty, tea functioned as a medicinal ingredient, similar to vegetable porridge. Raw tea leaves were first made into tea cakes before they were baked and then stored for later usage. The tea cakes would be ground into tea powder when needed and then simmered with water. Then, the soup would be flavored with salt before being served.

例句：

古代**吃茶**是人们的日常生活，许多人会无茶不欢。

Example Sentence:

Eating tea was part of the daily diet for many ancient Chinese.

酒要满，茶要浅

jiu yao man, cha yao qian;
While serving guests wine, fill the wine glass to the brim; while serving guests tea, do not fill up the teacup.

中国宴席聚会中崇尚的社交原则。“酒要满”是指在宴席上主人为客人斟酒时倒至满溢以显示待客的诚挚；“茶要浅”是相对于“酒要满”而言的。浅茶同样是向对方表示敬意，与“酒要满”有异曲同工之妙。中国人饮酒与喝茶在氛围上有所不同，大口喝酒体现的是豪爽与干脆，喝茶体现的是细细品味。

The principle followed in banquets and other social gatherings in China. When serving guests wine, the host fills the wine glass to the brim to show his sincerity and hospitality. When serving guests tea, the host shows respect for his guests by not filling up the teacup. Chinese people treat the wine and tea cultures differently, namely, drinking wine shows an unrestrained and frank attitude, while drinking tea reflects the concept that people should savor the flavor a bit at a time.

例句：

“酒要满，茶要浅”是大多数中国人聚会时习惯遵循的一项传统。

Example Sentence:

“While serving guests wine, fill the wine glass to the brim; while serving guests tea, do not fill up the teacup” is a tradition that most Chinese people are likely to observe.

茶话会 *chahuahui;* tea party

中国一种备有茶及茶点的社会性集会形式，主要通过饮茶品茗达到交流思想的目的。人们借饮茶来展开话题，以达到促进交流、展望未来等目的。因此，古往今来，茶话会广泛地被运用于各种社交场合。

A type of social gathering in China for communication and exchange of ideas, usually accompanied with tea and pastries. Tea parties have been popular throughout the ages.

例句：

茶话会，顾名思义，是饮茶谈话之会。

Example Sentence:

A tea party, as the name suggests, is a social gathering for people to drink tea and talk.

功夫茶 *gongfu cha;* gongfu tea

中国广东、福建的饮茶习俗，起源于宋代。喝功夫茶非常讲究烧制过程、茶具、水质和待客礼仪，如今已经影响到全国各地。传统功夫茶所

A tea drinking custom popular in Guangdong and Fujian provinces which originated from the Song Dynasty (960-1279). The making of gongfu tea emphasizes the brewing process, the use of tea ware, the

用茶叶以乌龙茶为主，如今也扩展到普洱茶。喝功夫茶要按照一定的程序进行，而每一道程序都有很文雅的叫法，主要步骤包括：1. 白鹤沐浴；2. 投茶；3. 摇香醒茶；4. 高冲低泡；5. 凤凰三点头；6. 观赏汤色； 7. 关公巡城；8. 品啜甘霖。

quality of water, and the etiquette performed when serving guests. Today, the custom has spread to other parts of China. Traditionally, gongfu tea should be made using oolong tea, but today Pu'er tea is also popular. Strict procedures should be followed when making the tea, and each procedure has a name with rich cultural implications:

1. Snow Crane Takes Bath (The tea ware is rinsed with boiled water.)
2. Add Tea Leaves
3. Swirl Teacup to Release Aroma
4. Pour Hot Water and Steep
5. Phoenix Nods Three Times—pour out the infusion and gently shake the pot's spout three times.
6. Appreciate the Color
7. Guan Yu Patrols City (The infusion in the pitcher should be poured into the three cups quickly to ensure that it is well mixed.)
8. Taste Tea

例句：

各地饮茶习俗不同，广东、福建一带的**功夫茶**最有特色。功夫茶多用南方名茶乌龙茶泡制，器皿讲究，程序严谨，茶色清纯，茶香醇厚。

Example Sentence:

Different regions have different customs related to tea drinking. Of them, the most distinctive is the gongfu tea ceremony popular in Guangdong and Fujian provinces. Mainly using oolong tea, the ceremony emphasizes the use of tea ware and the procedures of tea brewing. A good cup of tea should be clear and bright in color with a long-lasting strong aroma.

盖碗茶

gaiwan cha;
tea in a lidded teacup

中国四川等地传统的饮茶风俗，因茶具而得名。茶具分为茶碗、茶盖、托盘（又称"茶船"）。茶盖既保茶水温度，又可搅动茶水，调匀茶味。隔着茶盖品茗，可免茶叶入口。茶船正中一个圆形凹坑，正好承托茶碗圈足，便于端放，又不烫手。四川人饮盖碗茶一般说来有五道程序：一是净具，二是置茶，三是沏茶，四是闻香，五是品饮。

A tea drinking custom popular in Sichuan and some other parts of China. It is named after the special tea set used. A set of such tea ware includes a teacup, a lid, and a saucer (or "tea boat"). The lid helps keep the tea hot, is used to stir the tea, and also helps filter the floating tea leaves when drinking. The tea saucer has a hollow part in its middle to help steady the teacup, making it easy for the tea drinker to hold the whole set of utensils and prevent the heat of the teacup from burning the drinker's hand. In Sichuan, the preparation of *gaiwan cha* involves five procedures: 1. Rinsing the tea ware; 2. Adding tea leaves; 3. Brewing the tea; 4. Appreciating the scent; 5. Tasting the tea.

例句：

盖碗茶盛行于清代，如今在四川成都、云南昆明等地已成为当地茶楼、茶馆等饮茶场所的一种传统饮茶方法。

Example Sentence:

Tea in a lidded teacup gained its popularity during the Qing Dynasty (1616-1911). It is a popular tea drinking custom often seen in tea houses throughout Chengdu of Sichuan Province, Kunming of Yunnan Province, and some other places as well.

砖茶 *zhuan cha;* brick tea; tea brick

一种以茶叶、茶茎，有时还配以茶末压制成的块状茶，也叫"紧压茶""茶砖"。毛茶经过甑蒸加工，放入模子或布袋，紧压定型成像砖一样的茶块。少数民族同胞最爱饮用砖茶。长期饮用砖茶能够帮助消化，有效促进调节人体新陈代谢，对人体起着一定的保健和病理预防作用。砖茶根据原料和制作工艺的不同可以分为青砖茶、米砖茶、黑砖茶、花砖茶、茯砖茶、康砖茶等几类。

A kind of Chinese tea, also known as compressed tea. It is made by steaming and refining raw tea leaves and tea stalks, putting them into molds or cloth bags, and then compressing them to form brick-like blocks. It is especially popular among ethnic minorities. Drinking brick tea can effectively improve digestion and metabolism and maintain good health. Since brick tea can be made by using different techniques and ingredients, there are a variety of brick teas such as green, rice, black, flower-patterned, *fu*, and *kang* brick tea.

例句：

在中国少数民族地区，由于肉、奶制品多而蔬菜少，**砖茶**已成为当地人生活中的必需品。因为茶既可消食去腻，又可补充人体所需微量元素。

Example Sentence:

Since meat and dairy products are abundant while vegetables are scarce in some areas inhabited by Chinese ethnic minorities, brick tea has become a daily necessity for many people there. Drinking brick tea can help improve one's digestion and provides many vitamins necessary for good health.

紧压茶 *jinya cha;* compressed tea; brick tea

参见“砖茶”。

See *zhuancha* (brick tea).

散茶 *san cha;* bulk tea

未压制成片或团的茶叶。散茶能在较短时间内与空气充分接触发生氧化反应，品饮效果较理想，能够保留更原始的茶性。但古时有些地方交通不便、路途遥远，而散茶占据很大空间，且若是生茶，茶香也易散去，这种情况下直接运输散茶就会造成损失，所以茶叶会被压制成茶饼、茶砖等运输。

A kind of tea that has not been compressed into pieces or lumps. Bulk tea can have an oxidizing reaction within a short period of time, which helps retain its original flavor. In ancient times, however, transporting tea was difficult as trade routes were often long and treacherous. Losses would be inevitable because bulk tea was packed loosely and occupied too much space (if it was raw, the aroma might easily disappear). To solve the problem, tea leaves were often pressed into cake or brick shapes for easy transportation.

例句：

茶从发酵工艺来分，可分为生茶和熟茶；按是否压制来分，可分为压制茶和**散茶**。

Example Sentence:

Tea can be divided into two kinds based on the fermentation/oxidation process: namely, raw tea and processed tea. It can also be divided into pressed and bulk tea depending on whether the tea has been pressed.

绿茶 *lü cha;* green tea

一种未经发酵的茶。它的特点是干茶和冲泡出来的茶汤色泽以绿色为主调。著名的品种有龙井、君山银针、毛峰、碧螺春等。

A non-fermented Chinese tea characterized by its green color both before and after brewing. Famous varieties include Longjing (Dragon Well), Silver Needle, Maofeng, and Biluochun.

例句：

常饮**绿茶**能降脂和减肥，吸烟者也可减轻其受到的尼古丁伤害。

Example Sentence:

Drinking green tea can help one lower lipid, lose weight and reduce the negative effects of nicotine for smokers.

红茶 *hong cha;* black tea

一种发酵茶。特点为干茶色泽和冲泡的茶汤以红色为主。经萎凋、揉捻、发酵、干燥等工序制成。萎凋和发酵是形成红茶品质特征的重要工序。品种有祁门红茶、滇红、闽红、川红等，尤以祁门红茶最为著名。

A type of fermented tea with reddish dried tea leaves which produces tea of the same shade. Black tea leaves are withered, twisted, fermented, and dried. There are many kinds of black tea in China, including Keemun (Anhui Province), Dianhong (Yunnan Province), Minhong (Fujian Province), and Chuanhong (Sichuan Province). Of all these, Keemun is the best-known black tea.

例句：

中国武夷山市的桐木关是**红茶**的重要产地之一。

Example Sentence:

Tongmuguan in the city of Wuyishan of Fujian Province is one of the major producers of China's black tea.

乌龙茶 *wulong cha;* oolong tea

中国特有的茶类，又称为“青茶”。乌龙茶经过部分发酵，绿叶红边，既有绿茶的鲜香浓郁，又有红茶的甜醇。著名品种有福建的铁观音和台湾的冻顶乌龙。

A type of Chinese tea, also known as *qingcha* (dark green tea). After having been partly fermented, the tea leaves become green with red edges, and have both the fresh and strong smell of green tea and the sweet flavor of black tea. Famous types of oolong tea include Tieguanyin (Iron Buddha) produced in Fujian and Frozen Peak Oolong produced in Taiwan.

例句：

在日本，乌龙茶又称为“美容茶”，具有分解脂肪、减肥健美的功效。

Example Sentence:

In Japan, oolong tea is also called beauty tea, and is considered effective in losing weight.

青茶 *qing cha;* dark green tea

参见“乌龙茶”。

See *wulong cha* (oolong tea).

白茶 *bai cha;* white tea

一种轻微发酵的中国名茶。它的特点是成品多为芽头，且满身披着雪白的茸毛，汤色黄绿清澈，滋味清淡回甘，具有清热退火的功效。主要产于福建。著名品种有白毫银针、白牡丹、寿眉等。

A famous type of Chinese tea with leaves slightly fermented and covered by fine silver-white hairs. The tea water looks yellow-green and clear, and tastes slightly sweet. White tea is said to be effective in relieving internal heat. There are many varieties of white tea, such as Silver Needle Tea, White Peony Tea, and Shoumei Tea. It is mainly produced in Fujian Province.

例句：

白茶经采摘后，无需杀青或揉捻，只经过晒或文火干燥后加工而成。

Example Sentence:

White tea can be made by drying the tea leaves under the sun or at low heat after harvesting them. It does not need baking or twisting.

黄茶 *huang cha; yellow tea*

黄茶属轻发酵茶类，加工工艺近似绿茶，杀青、闷黄、干燥、揉捻是黄茶必不可少的制作工艺。黄茶有“黄叶黄汤”的特点。湖南岳阳为中国黄茶之乡。

A lightly fermented tea. Its preparation process is similar to green tea. Roasting, oxidization, drying, and twisting are the indispensable skills required for making this tea. Compared with other tea, yellow tea leaves give the tea its yellow color. Yueyang in Hunan Province is home to yellow tea.

例句：

制作**黄茶**最重要的工序在于“闷黄”。

Example Sentence:

Oxidization is one of the most essential processes of producing yellow tea.

黑茶 *hei cha:* dark tea

黑茶属后发酵茶，茶叶的色泽为黑褐色，茶汤味道比较浓郁。著名黑茶有云南普洱茶、四川边茶、广西六堡散茶、湖南黑茶、湖北老黑茶、陕西茯茶等。黑茶能够助消化、抑制血压血糖升高、提高免疫功能，还有抗氧化、抗血凝、抗血栓的功效。

A type of post-fermented tea which is dark brown and has a strong taste when brewed. Some of the best-known dark teas are Yunnan Pu'er, Sichuan Bian Tea, Guangxi Liupu Tea, Hunan Dark Tea, Hubei Dark Tea, and Shaanxi Fu Tea. Dark tea facilitates digestion and can help lower blood pressure and blood sugar. It is conducive to boosting the immune system and has antioxidant, anticoagulant, and antithrombotic functions.

例句：

"中国**黑茶**之乡"是湖南省安化县，该县已将黑茶打造成全县首个百亿产业。

Example Sentence:

As the "hometown of Chinese dark tea," Anhua County, Hunan Province has turned its dark tea industry into a ten billion RMB yuan business, which is unprecedented in the county's history.

花茶 *hua cha;* scented tea

一种由精制茶与具有香气的鲜花如茉莉、玫瑰、桂花、玉兰等拌和加工而成的茶。它的特点是干茶和冲泡的茶汤芳香四溢。其工艺历史悠久，制作遍及全中国。

A kind of tea made by blending refined tea and fragrant fresh flowers such as jasmine, rose, osmanthus, and magnolia. Both its dried tea leaves and the liquid tea smell sweet and fragrant. This type of tea has a long history and is produced in all regions in China.

例句：

长期饮用**花茶**有排毒、养颜、调节内分泌等功效。

Example Sentence:

Drinking scented tea can help expel toxins, ensure skin care, and improve internal secretion.

奶茶(蒙古族)

nai cha;
milk tea (Mongolian)

中国北方游牧民族蒙古族人的日常饮品，用茶、牛奶、盐巴一道煮沸而成。奶茶多以青砖茶和黑砖茶为原料，煮沸茶砖，加入牛奶，在铁锅内烹煮，后加入适量盐巴。在牧区和高寒地区肉食较多，蔬菜很少，人们需要用奶茶来助消化；那里冬季寒冷，夏季干热，冬季大量饮奶茶可以迅速驱寒，夏季可以驱暑解渴。

A daily beverage of the Mongolians, a nomadic ethnic groups in northern China. They like to drink milk tea which is made by boiling tea, milk, and salt together. Bricks of green or dark tea are used as the raw material, which is first boiled in an iron pot before milk and salt are added. In pastoral regions and frigid zones, mutton and beef are the main food, which makes milk tea ideal to facilitate digestion. In cold winters and dry summers, drinking milk tea is also beneficial to helping quickly dispel colds or reduce heat.

例句：

蒙古高原是游牧民族的故乡，也是**奶茶**的发源地。

Example Sentence:

The Mongolian plateau is not only home of nomadic ethnic groups, but is also the birthplace of Chinese milk tea.

酥油茶

suyou cha;
buttered tea

蒙、藏等民族饮用的以茶和酥油制成的一种饮料。先将砖茶捣碎加水，煮开后滤出茶汤，再倒进预先放有酥油和盐的桶内用专门的打茶工具搅拌，使茶汤与油酥充分融合，然后放入置于炭火上的茶壶内，供随时饮用。酥油茶是蒙、藏族群众每日必备的饮品，它既可以治高原反应，又可以预防因天气干燥而嘴唇爆裂，还可以起到很好的御寒作用。

A type of drink made from tea and butter which is popular among Tibetan and Mongolian people. Bricks of tea are mashed and put into water which is then boiled. The tea is filtered before poured into a bucket with butter and salt, and then stirred with a special tool until it is fully blended with the butter. It is then poured into a teapot which is hung over a charcoal fire to keep the tea warm throughout the day. Buttered tea is considered a daily drink for Tibetan and Mongolian people, and it is said to help cure altitude sickness, prevent chapped lips due to dry weather, and combat cold.

例句：

酥油茶茶味芳香，能解渴，并产生较多的热量御寒。

Example Sentence:

Buttered tea has a mellow flavor and can alleviate thirst. In addition, it is high in calories which can help keep one warm in the cold winter.

茶馆 *cha guan;* teahouse

人们喝茶、交谈、休闲、做生意的场所，又称为“茶楼”“茶坊”“茶社”。茶馆的雏形出现在东晋时期，茶馆在唐代正式形成。现在茶馆是市民一个重要的活动场所。

A traditional place where people gather to drink tea and chat, conduct leisure activities, or do business, also called *cha lou* (tea building), *cha fang* (tea workshop) or *cha she* (tea community). Teahouses emerged during the Eastern Jin Dynasty (317-420) and took shape during the Tang Dynasty (618-907). It is still a popular place for common people to get together.

例句：

北京既有环境优雅的高档茶楼，又有大众化的街头**茶馆**。

Example Sentence:

In Beijing, there are various types of teahouses, from elegant places to popular street teahouses.

广东早茶 *guangdong zaocha;* Guangdong morning tea

中国岭南一种民间饮食风俗，在全国广为流传。每天一早都会有人坐在茶楼里，点上一壶茶，再点几样点心、菜肴，如叉烧包、虾饺、肠粉、豉汁排骨等，一边吃喝，一边谈论国事、家事，共度早间美好时光。

A breakfast tradition originally popular in southern China but having gained popularity across the whole country. People will go to a teahouse in the morning and order tea, snacks, or dishes such as steamed buns stuffed with grilled pork, shrimp dumplings, steamed vermicelli rolls, and steamed ribs in black bean sauce. It is also an occasion for people to chat with neighbors or friends.

例句：

广东人品茶大都一日早、中、晚三次，但**广东早茶**最为讲究，饮早茶的风气也最盛。

Example Sentence:

People in Guangdong often drink tea in the morning, at noon, and at night, but they attach great importance to morning tea.

紫砂壶 *zisha hu;* purple clay teapot; terra cotta teapot

中国特有的手工制造陶土工艺品。紫砂壶透气性能良好，能承受冷热急变而不至爆裂，又因传热慢而不烫手。用紫砂壶泡茶，茶汤色艳、清香、味醇。壶内壁的许多细小气泡具有较好的保温作用，贮茶不走味、不变色，盛夏泡茶隔日不馊。因此，紫砂壶为历代品茗者所珍视。

Unique clay handmade Chinese tea ware. A purple clay teapot is permeable, so it will not break even with a sudden temperature change from cold to hot. It will not burn the user's hand as it transmits heat slowly. When using a purple clay teapot to make tea, the tea will look clean, bright, and tastes aromatic and mellow. There are many tiny holes in the inner side of the pot that help sustain heat, maintain the scent and color of the tea, and prevent the tea from going sour, even after staying in the pot overnight during the summer. Thus, purple clay teapots have been favorite vessels for tea drinkers since ancient times.

例句：

江苏宜兴盛产**紫砂壶**，号称“陶都”。宜兴紫砂茶壶用当地紫砂泥烧制，质地细密，造型典雅。

Example Sentence:

Yixing in Jiangsu Province is a major producer of purple clay teapots, hence its nickname "the city of clay." Made of local clay, Yixing teapots boast fine composition and elegant appearance.

茶汤会 *chatang hui;* tea gathering

旧时民间活动，是佛教信徒组织施赠茶水的活动，用来招待施主和香客，一般于寺院宗教活动集会期间举行。该习俗可追溯到宋代。

Old folk custom in which Buddhist disciples treat benefactors and pilgrims with tea at monasteries. The gathering usually takes place during monastic religious activities. This custom can be traced back to the Song Dynasty (960-1279).

例句：

茶汤会有两种：一种是非正式茶汤会，另一种是正式茶汤会。

Example Sentence:

Tea gatherings can be both formal and casual.

茶祭 *cha ji;* tea sacrificial rites

中国旧时丧葬风俗。中国以茶进行祭祀活动最早可追溯到南北朝时期，茶祭一般有三种方式：以茶水为祭，放干茶为祭，只将茶壶、茶盅象征茶叶为祭。中国自古以来就有在死者手中放茶包、用茶叶随葬的习俗，希望逝者饮茶后在阴间保持明智而不受鬼役蒙骗，借助茶叶去除异味，保存遗体。

An old funeral custom in China which can be traced back to the Southern and Northern Dynasties (420-589). There are three ways to perform the tea sacrificial rites: with tea water, with dry tea leaves, and with teapots and handle-less teacups as symbols of tea leaves. It is believed that tea sacrificial rites can help the deceased remain sober to avoid being deceived by ghosts and better preserve their remains.

例句：

统治者遗骸旁精心随葬的茶叶，是茶叶受到重视的证据，**茶祭**在当时已十分流行。

Example Sentence:

Tea leaves deliberately buried alongside the dead ruler bear evidence that the value of tea was widely recognized and tea sacrificial rites were popular at that time.

四合院

siheyuan;
courtyard home; courtyard house; quadrangle house

中国一种传统的合院式建筑，格局为一个院子四面建有房屋，从四面将庭院合围在中间。四合院多见于中国北方，北京四合院是其中的代表。按照传统礼制，修建四合院以南北中轴线对称布置房屋和院落，院落有一进和多进，多为二进或三进。四合院大门多开在东南角上，门外设一对石鼓或石狮，严肃庄重，又含驱邪避灾之意。进门迎面为影壁，从影

A kind of courtyard building in China. The layout of a typical *siheyuan* centers around a courtyard which is surrounded by rooms on the four sides. *Siheyuan* are often seen in northern China with those in Beijing being the most representative. The layout of this kind of architecture reflects traditional values. Rooms and yard(s) are built in a symmetrical manner along a north-south axis. The compound may have one or more yards, but those with two or three yards are more common. The entrance gate is usually at the southeast corner of the compound. A pair of stone drums or stone lions are often placed outside the gate. The solemn and dignified stone sculptures are believed to have the power of warding off evil influences. Directly behind the gate is a screen wall. To the west of the screen wall there is a round gate known as the *yueliang men* (moon gate). The rooms facing the north are known as *daozuo* (opposite building) and were often used as servants'

壁前往西进月亮门是前院。南侧房屋称“倒座”，多为佣人住房。从前院经垂花门进入里院，为全宅的核心。北面三间正房，为大客厅和长辈住房。东西厢房各三间，长子住东厢，次子住西厢。正房、厢房之间有走廊相连。正房两侧附有耳房，并由小月亮门构成两个小跨院，安置厨房、杂屋和厕所。有的四合院正房后面还有一排后罩房，专供女眷居住。现在，一些四合院被列为文物保护单位。

living quarters. The inner yard is the core of a courtyard compound. The three rooms in the north are the main buildings, serving as the living room and bedrooms of the eldest members of the family. On the east and west sides, there are three wing rooms respectively. The eastern wing rooms are assigned to the eldest son, while the western ones are assigned to the second son. The main rooms and the wing rooms are connected with roofed pathways. There are also side rooms on the east and west sides of the main rooms. There are also two moon gates next to the side rooms, which connect the inner yard, where the kitchen, storeroom, and lavatory are located. In some courtyard compounds, there is a backyard behind the main buildings for the female members of the family. Now some *siheyuan* have been designated as sites to be protected for their historical and cultural value.

例句：

四合院是汉族地区最常见的民居建筑，充分体现了中华民族的传统观念。四合院四面封闭，房屋布局与家庭成员的住房都有严格的安排，体现传统家长制老幼尊卑有序的特点。

Example Sentence:

The *siheyuan* (courtyard house) is the most common style of residence of people of the Han ethnic group which fully demonstrates the traditional values of Chinese culture. A courtyard is surrounded by buildings on all four sides, with strict rules as to where a room should be and who should live in it, reflecting the rigid rankings of family members under the traditional patriarchal system.

倒座 *daozuo;* opposite building

参见"四合院"。
四合院中的南侧房屋。

See also *siheyuan* (courtyard house). The rooms facing the north in a courtyard house.

天井 *tianjing;* small yard; patio; sky well

宅院中房子和房子或房子和围墙围成的露天空地。"天井"最早产生于何时已无实迹可考，但这种建筑空间形态普遍存在于明清至今的中国传统民居中。天井的存在完善了建筑中的通风、采光、安防的功

An open-air space enclosed by houses and walls in a residential building. There are no records as to when this type of architecture first appeared, but it has been used in traditional Chinese residential housing since the Ming (1368-1644) and Qing (1616-1911) dynasties. The patio improves ventilation and lighting and ensures

能，并且在建筑中显天露地，起到天地合一的作用，使天、地、建筑在空间中融为一体，也体现了中国传统文化中天人合一的哲学思想。

safety. The sky and the earth are both visible, creating connectivity. By integrating the sky and the earth with the housing, this structure shows the Chinese philosophical notion of harmony between man and nature.

例句：

四合院的檐下回廊和**天井**是家族成员交流感情的场所。

Example Sentence:

Under the eaves of a *siheyuan* are winding corridors and a patio where family members can talk with each other outside their rooms.

yingbi;
screen wall

迎宅院大门而建、用作屏障的墙壁，又称"照壁"或"照墙"。影壁可建在大门内，也可建在大门外，前者称为"内影壁"，后者称为"外影壁"。影壁为中国建筑独有，是受信仰禁忌心理支配的产物，主要用来挡住"脉气"外走，防"三煞"，也避免外人直视院内景象。壁身多为正方形，中间或书"福"字，或绘吉祥图画。影壁是中国传统建筑不可分割的一部分，有着很高的建筑审美价值。

A structure constructed at the entrance to a residence that prevents people from seeing the inside. The screen wall is built just inside the main entrance to a house or just outside it; the former is called an inner screen wall while the latter an outer screen wall. The screen wall is a structure exclusive to Chinese architecture, and it is a product of beliefs and taboo. The owner of a residence mainly builds this to prevent *qi* from escaping the home and the "three demons" from getting in. It also prevents outsiders from looking directly into the residence. These walls are typically constructed like a square, and the Chinese character for "fortune" or an auspicious pattern is on the screen wall. This structure is an inseparable component of traditional Chinese architecture. Moreover, it has very high aesthetic values.

例句：

中国最大的一座**影壁**保存在山西大同市内，原为明太祖朱元璋的第十三子朱桂代王府前的一座照壁，长达45.5米，高8米，厚2.02米。壁上雕有九条七彩云龙，有的拨风弄雨，有的腾云欲飞，栩栩如生，各具姿态。

Example Sentence:

China's largest preserved screen wall is in Datong, Shanxi Province. It was the original screen wall in the palace of Zhu Guidai, the 13th son of Zhu Yuanzhang, founding emperor of the Ming Dynasty (1368-1644). It is 45.5 meters long, 8 meters tall, and 2.02 meters thick. Nine lifelike, multi-colored dragons are sculpted on the wall along with images of wind, rain and clouds.

垂花门 *chuihua men;* *chuihua* gate; ornamental inner gate

古代中国民居建筑院落内部的门。垂花门是四合院内的重要建筑，其檐柱不落地，垂吊在屋檐下，称为垂柱，柱头下端有一垂珠，通常彩绘为花瓣的形式，故称垂花门。垂花门位于整座宅院的中轴线上，界分内院外宅，建筑华丽，是全宅中最为醒目的地方。前院与内院用垂花门和院墙相隔。外院多用来接待客人，而内院则是自家人生活起居的地方，外人一般不得随便出入。凡垂花门都有两种功能：一是防卫，为此，在门向外一侧的两根柱间设有第一道门，厚重，与街门相仿，白天开启，供宅人通行，夜间关闭，有安全保卫作用；二是屏障，也是垂花门的主要功能，为保证内宅隐蔽。

Gate within a traditional Chinese courtyard house, and considered an important component of such residence. Its pillars extend out from the eaves but do not reach to the ground. They instead hang in the air, and are thus called hanging pillars. At the bottom of these pillars is a sphere, which is often adorned with paintings of petals. Accordingly, this structure literally means *chuihua* gate (the gate with hanging flowers). The *chuihua* gate is located along the central axis of the courtyard, separating an inner courtyard from an outer courtyard. It is an exquisite structure and the most striking part of the whole house. The outer courtyard is typically used for receiving guests while the inner courtyard is used for everyday living. Those who are not members of the family are typically not allowed to enter. The *chuihua* gate has two functions: first, it is used for keeping safety. Outwardly, this gate features two pillars and one entryway. It is similar to the street gate in that it is opened during the daytime so that members of the household can enter and exit the housing; at night it is firmly shut for their safety. Second, it serves as a privacy barrier, which is the primary function of the *chuihua* gate. It ensures that people cannot see into the house from the outside.

例句：

旧时人们常说的“大门不出，二门不迈”，“二门”就是指**垂花门**。

Example Sentence:

In the old days, people often used the expression of “not going beyond the main gate nor passing through the second gate” to refer to people who always stay at home. Here the “second gate” refers to the *chuihua* gate.

石库门 *shikumen*; *shikumen* residence; Shanghai-style courtyard house

上海最有代表性的民居建筑。上海石库门民居是一种立帖式砖木结构的建筑，是传统四合院与西方建筑艺术结合的产物。石库门民居外门选用石料做门框，多为砖木结构的二层楼房，坡形屋顶常常有老虎窗（凸在房

Shanghai’s unique style of residential housing. The Shanghai *shikumen* residence is known for its traditional Chinese-style brick and wood structures that combine traditional courtyard housing (*siheyuan*) with Western architectural art. The doorframes of *shikumen* houses are made with bricks, and for the most part they are two-story structures. Sloping roofs often have tiger windows (a small window built on a sloping part of the roof that allows light to enter the house), external walls of red bricks, and a traditional Chinese archway located at the entrance. In the early 1860s, *shikumen* residences first appeared in such famous Shanghai streets as Henan Road, Fuzhou Road, and Beijing Road, which was a central enclave of the city’s foreign concession district.

顶斜面的小窗，用以采光透气），红砖外墙，弄堂口有中国传统式牌楼。19世纪60年代初，第一批石库门出现在上海河南路、福州路、北京路一带，即租界的中心地区。如今，陕西南路、河南中路和新闸路的一些石库门民居被作为近代优秀建筑整组保存，充满浓厚的“上海味”。石库门通常被认为是上海近代都市文明的象征之一。

Today, some of the *shikumen* residences along Shaanxi South Road, Henan Middle Road, and Xinzha Road are protected as examples of modern architecture that teems with a rich Shanghai flavor, as these residences symbolize Shanghai's modern urban culture.

例句：

中西文化的碰撞使庭院式大家庭的传统生活模式被打破，取而代之的是适合单身移民和小家庭居住的**石库门**弄堂文化。

Example Sentence:

The integration of Chinese and Western cultures in Shanghai altered the traditional courtyard-style residential pattern, which was replaced by *shikumen* alley culture suitable for unmarried migrants and small families.

大宅院（晋陕豫）

dazhaiyuan;
residential compound with courtyards (in Shanxi, Shaanxi and Henan)

Large residential compounds in Shanxi, Shaanxi and Henan provinces. Such famous compounds include the Wang family compound and Qiao family compound in Shanxi, the residential compounds in Dangjia Village in Hancheng of Shaanxi Province, and the manor of Kang Baiwan in Gongyi of Henan Province. Most of the grand

中国山西、陕西、河南民间的大型宅第。著名的有山西的王家大院、乔家大院，陕西韩城的党家村，河南巩义市的康百万庄园等，大多为明清创造过辉煌的行帮富商创下的家业。这些大宅院形制与北京四合院相近，又别具特色。宅院院门开在大院的中轴线上，门外设置拴马柱和上马石。宅院多为两重院落。为避免西晒，院子狭窄修长。外院与里院之间用穿心过厅相连。内院正房是主人长辈的卧室和客厅，一般为三开间的二层楼房。楼上做成檐廊，所有梁头、雀替、栏杆等都有精美的雕饰。靠山地方的宅院还将正房做成窑洞形式，冬暖夏凉。左右厢房为晚辈居住，或三间或五间，厢房的屋顶多为单坡式，屋檐水流向院内，以“内水不外流”寓意敛财聚富。有的宅院旁建有侧院，多用作客房、厨房及仆人住房。侧院房屋低矮，多做成平顶，以示主次有别。大宅院保留了当地的民俗文化，其历史底蕴和文化传承受到人们的重视。

residential compounds were built by merchants who enjoyed great business success during the Ming (1368-1644) and Qing (1616-1911) dynasties. The layouts of these residential compounds are similar to the courtyard houses of Beijing, but show special local characteristics. The entrance gates are built on the axis line. There are stone hitching posts and horse mounting blocks outside the gate. The compounds usually have two yards. To avoid blazing sunshine, the yards are long and narrow. The outer yard and the inner yard are connected by a hall with open doors in the front and at the back. In the inner yard, the main building consists of the bedrooms and living room of the head of the family. It is usually a two-floor building with three rooms on each floor. There is a roofed pathway on the second floor. All beam ends, brackets, and railings are decorated with sophisticated carvings. In hilly areas, the main building is sometimes made in the style of a cave dwelling, which is warm in winter and cool in summer. The wing rooms on the left and right sides are assigned to the younger generations of the family, with three or five rooms on each side. Most of the wing rooms have a single-pitched roof, which ensures rainwater flows into the courtyard instead of outside, implying all wealth will come into the family. Some compounds have side yards, surrounding which are guest rooms, kitchens, and servants' quarters. The buildings in the side yards are all low with a flat roof to show the rank of those who dwell within. Such compounds carry on local folk art and tradition with well-acknowledged historical and cultural values.

例句：

大宅院的房屋布局和精雕细刻的营造无不渗透着华夏富裕百姓对子孙后代开创辉煌未来的希冀。

Example Sentence:

Wealthy merchants hoped the exquisite decorations of their grand mansions would inspire their descendants to also aspire to brilliant achievements.

平遥古城 *pingyao gucheng;* ancient city of Pingyao

中国保存最为完整的历史文化名城。位于山西平遥，始建于周宣王时期，明洪武三年（1370年）扩建。古城占地4.2平方千米，“四大街、八小街、七十二条蛐蜒巷”中分布着3700多处传统古民居，其中有400多处保存完整。除民居外，城中还有商业街、城隍庙、道观，以及衙门、寺院等，整体以南大街为轴线，呈对称格局。古民居都是四合院样式，有上马石、栓马桩，院落多用垂花门、花墙分割为二进院或三进院，院落多为南北长、东西窄的长方形。平遥成功的商人多，民居十分讲究，院落里诸多精美的石雕、砖雕和木雕，从装饰上处处体现儒家“三纲五常”“尊卑有序”的道德观念和礼制格局。1997年被列入世界文化遗产名录。

The best preserved ancient city in China revered for its historical and cultural value, located in Shanxi Province. The city walls of Pingyao were built between 827-782 BC and in 1370 it was expanded to its current size. The city covers an area of 42,000 square meters, consisting of 4 main roads, 8 streets and 72 winding alleys. There are more than 3,700 ancient residential houses, with over 400 still intact. There are also business streets, a temple to the City God, Daoist and Buddhist temples, and government buildings. All the buildings are aligned symmetrically along the south street. The residential houses are all in the style of courtyard homes. With horse-mounting blocks and stone hitching posts outside, a compound usually has two or three yards divided by ornamental inner gates and walls. Most of the courtyards run lengthwise from south to north. Pingyao used to be home to many successful merchants, so the houses were all very well-constructed. The sophisticated carvings on the stone, bricks, and wood reflect the moral values and etiquette of Confucianism, which stresses the three cardinal guides (ruler guides the subject, father guides the son, and husband guides the wife), five constant virtues (benevolence, righteousness, propriety, knowledge and sincerity), and the strict order of superiority and inferiority. Pingyao became a UNESCO World Heritage site in 1997.

例句：

平遥古城是中国古代城市在明清时期的杰出范例。

Example Sentence:

The ancient city of Pingyao is an outstanding example of the cities in the Ming and Qing dynasties (from the 14th to 20th centuries).

yaodong; cave dwelling

中国华北、西北黄土高原上的古老民居。在坡上横向挖掘或向下挖掘洞穴作为居室。此种居住方式多流行在黄土高原地区，即山西、宁夏、陕西等省。窑洞是黄土高原的产物，沉积了古老的黄土地深层文化。

A type of Chinese age-old residential house consisting of caves dug into a hillside or underground caves, popular on the Loess Plateau, namely in Shanxi and Shaanxi provinces and Ningxia Hui Autonomous Region. This type of dwelling is the result of local geographical conditions, which showcases the profound culture of the people living on the Loess Plateau.

例句：

窑洞所需建筑材料很少，施工简单，造价低，冬暖夏凉，故沿用至今。

Example Sentence:

Cave dwellings are built with few building materials, simple techniques, and low costs. Warm in winter and cool in summer, they are still used today.

靠山窑

kaoshanyao;
cliffside cave dwelling

中国陕北一种窑洞，又称“靠崖窑”。靠山窑是在背风向阳、避开沟壑的黄土山崖上掏挖出拱形窑洞，安上门窗而成。为防止泥土崩毁，有的还在洞内加砌砖或石块。

A kind of cave dwelling in north Shaanxi Province. Cliffside cave dwellings are built under a loess cliff, facing the sun on the lee side where there is no ravine nearby. The cliff is excavated to make an arched cave with doors and windows on the front side. To prevent cave-ins, some caves use bricks or rocks to reinforce the structure.

例句：

靠山窑是在山崖挖出的窑洞，为坚固起见，常在窑洞外面接一段石砌或砖砌的窑口。

Example Sentence:

Built on a cliff, a cliffside cave has its entrance built with rocks or bricks to ensure safety.

靠崖窑

kaoyayao;
cliffside cave dwelling

参见“靠山窑”。

See *kaoshanyao* (cliffside cave dwelling).

锢窑 *guyao; guyao cave dwelling*

中国陕北一种窑洞。锢窑是先在地面搭好木头模架，再用砖头或石块砌筑拱券顶和墙身，最后再往窑顶填上一两米厚的土层，夯实、碾平。锢窑可做单层，也可建双层楼式，还可以几座锢窑围成四合院。锢窑虽然费工费料，却建筑坚固，居住安全。

A kind of cave dwelling in north Shaanxi Province which is built on flat ground. After a wooden framework is built, bricks and rocks are used to build the arched roof and walls. The roof should be covered by mud one or two meters thick. Such a cave dwelling can have one or two stories. Several *guyao* cave dwellings can form a courtyard. Such dwellings may necessitate more money and manpower to build, but they are solid and safe.

例句：

锢窑由于顶上土层厚而冬暖夏凉。

Example Sentence:

Guyao cave dwellings, like other cave dwellings, are warm in winter and cool in summer, which is the result of the thick mud applied on top of the roof.

地坑院（河南）

dikengyuan;
underground cave dwellings (Henan)

中国河南民居。地坑院从地面向下挖出五米以上的深坑作为庭院，在坑壁上挖出窑洞，被称为中国北方的“地下四合院”。2011年“地坑院营造技艺”入选第三批国家级非物质文化遗产名录。

A type of cave dwelling in Henan Province. Most consist of an open central courtyard built down at least five meters into the earth connected on all sides to separate cave-type rooms. Underground cave dwellings are therefore also known as underground courtyard houses. In 2011, the construction skill of the underground cave dwellings was included in the third batch of China's national intangible cultural heritage list.

例句：

地坑院虽系农家小院，但受传统文化影响，建造还是十分讲究的。

Example Sentence:

Underground cave dwellings, found in rural areas, are exquisitely constructed, utilizing specialized local construction methods and skills.

蒙古包 Menggubao; Mongolian yurt

中国蒙古族牧民居住的帐篷式房子，便于拆卸和组装，适于牧业生产和游牧生活。蒙古包壁体由木枝条编成的骨架支撑，骨架可开可合，方便搬运，骨架外铺盖羊皮或者毛毡。蒙古包的平面多为圆形，下部为圆柱体，上部为圆锥体，包壁上仅有门，没有窗户，帐顶有天窗。天窗下方设炉灶。

Tent dwelling common of the Mongolian ethnic group. A Mongolian yurt is easy to assemble and dismantle, and is suitable for nomadic life. Its walls are comprised of a wooden framework covered with sheepskin or felt that supports the whole yurt. The wall of a Mongolian yurt is circular; the bottom is a cylinder and the top is cone-shaped. There is an entrance along the wall of the yurt, but no windows. There is an opening in the roof, with a stove situated beneath it.

例句：

蒙古包可大可小，小型的蒙古包直径为 4 至 6 米，内部无支撑，大型的蒙古包里面需要有 2 至 4 根柱子支撑。

Example Sentence:

Mongolian yurts come in a variety of sizes. Small ones have a diameter of four to six meters and have no interior support. Larger yurts need two to four pillars inside for support.

毡房 *zhan fang; yurt*

中国北方游牧民族居住的帐篷式房子，为木柱结构，多围以毛毡，因而得名"毡房"。毡房方便搬迁，可防风御寒，流行于中国藏、蒙古、哈萨克、塔吉克等民族。藏族和裕固族的毡房称"帐房"，蒙古族的毡房称"蒙古包"，各族的毡房在外观、构造、室内安排等方面都有一定差异。

A tent-like house inhabited by the northern Chinese nomadic ethnic groups. The main structure (*fang*) is made of wood and covered with felt (*zhan*); hence the name *zhan fang*. The yurt is easy to assemble and dismantle, allowing residents to relocate according to weather. They are popular among the Xizang (Tibetan), Mongolian, Kazak, Tajik, and other ethnic groups in China. The *zhan fang* varies greatly in terms of appearance, structure, and interior design.

例句：

在中国的青海、西藏等地，客人进入**毡房**时，主人会献上奶茶，以示欢迎。

Example Sentence:

In regions such as Qinghai Province and Xizang (Tibet) Autonomous Region, guests invited into the *zhan fang* are presented with milk tea as a sign of welcome.

仙人柱 *xianren zhu;* tent-like house

中国鄂伦春族、鄂温克族等民族居住的帐篷式房子，又称“斜仁柱”。仙人柱呈圆锥形，由木杆搭成棚架，顶端套柳条圈或芦苇等，帐身夏天围桦树皮，冬天围兽皮。

A type of dwelling of the nomadic Oroqen and Ewenki ethnic groups in northeast China. It is a tent-like house which can be easily built and dismantled at any time. It is cone-shaped, with a frame made of long wooden poles angled inwards and fastened together at the top of the cone with wicker or reed. It is generally covered with birch bark in summer. In winter, it may also be covered with animal hide.

例句：

仙人柱源自鄂伦春语的音译，仙人指木杆，柱指屋子，合起来是木杆搭起来的尖顶屋。

Example Sentence:

The term *xianren zhu* originates from the language of the Oroqen ethnic group. *Xianren* means “wooden poles,” and *zhu* means “house.” Put together, it means a cone-shaped house pitched with wooden poles.

干打垒草房（东北）

gandalei caofang;
adobe house;
house with walls of rammed earth (northeast China)

中国东北农村常见的夯土垒墙而盖成的简陋民居，多用谷草和泥垒起谷草墙，再盖上厚厚的山草屋顶，以防寒保暖。这种建筑结构严实，防寒性能好，暑天也不太热，适合居住，且施工简单，操作容易。特别是就地取材，随处可建。

A type of simple house with walls of rammed earth commonly seen in villages of the northeast China. The local residents build houses with walls of straw and mud and thick thatched roofs to keep warm. Owing to the tightly-knit structure, these houses are warm in winter and cool in summer. Moreover, they are easy to build since they are constructed with rammed earth.

例句：

20 世纪 60 年代，松辽大平原展开石油会战，在大庆临时修建了许多**干打垒草房**，用作石油工人的居住区和办公区。

Example Sentence:

In the 1960s, the exploitation of oil started in the Songliao Plain. Many makeshift adobe houses were built in Daqing, Heilongjiang Province as living quarters and offices for the oil workers.

地窨子（东北）

dijiaozi;
cellar dwelling (northeast China)

中国东北林区的一种临时住宅。在背风向阳的山坡上向地下挖出凹洞，周围垒上原

A type of makeshift dwelling in the forested areas of northeast China. People dug caves in leeward hillsides that faced the sun. They built the walls and

木为墙，上盖原木，埋泥为顶，内有灶台、火炕。地窨子建造简易，冬季能抵挡风雪严寒，但夏季阴暗潮湿闷热。20 世纪 50 年代后，地窨子逐渐被淘汰。

roofs with logs and covered roofs with mud. These cellar dwellings, which were equipped with a cooking bench and *kang* (heatable brick bed), are easy to build. They are warm in winter, but dark, humid, and hot in summer. After the 1950s, cellar dwellings gradually fell into disuse.

例句:

林区工人上山伐木，吃的是高粱米，住的是**地窨子**。

Example Sentence:

Forest laborers working in mountainous areas often eat sorghum and live in cellar dwellings.

水乡民居（江浙）

shuixiang minju;
waterside residence

中国传统民居建筑的重要组成部分。江南水乡民居以苏州、绍兴最具代表性，住宅外围墙壁高大，大多是较高的二层楼房。城镇沿河而设，民居前门临街开店，楼上住人，后门依水设置厨房，砌筑称为“河埠头”的通河石阶，为淘米、洗菜、浣衣之处，又是舟船停泊的码头。水路、街巷呈不规则的网状穿插于民居之中，白墙黑瓦，相映成趣，形成江南民居的独特风景。

A type of traditional residential dwelling in China. Suzhou in Jiangsu Province and Shaoxing in Zhejiang Province are home to the most representative traditional waterside residences. Most of these houses are two-story buildings with tall exterior walls. The towns are located along rivers, so local people open stores on the first floor of their residences, live on the second floor, and build kitchens in the back of their houses by the riverside. A stone stairway outside the house, known as a *hebutou* (river dock), leads to the river. Besides harboring boats, the dock can provide a space for local residents to wash rice, vegetables, and clothes. The zigzagging waterways and alleys form a network connecting residential buildings together. The white walls and gray-tiled roofs are picturesque and unique to the lower reaches of the Yangtze River.

例句：

一些**水乡民居**由水上过街楼相通。

Example Sentence:

There are roofed walkways over a river connecting waterside residences.

河埠头 *hebutou;* river dock

参见"水乡民居"。
水乡民居中的的通河石阶。

See also *shuixiang minju* (waterside residence). A stone stairway outside the waterside residence leading to the river.

徽州民居 *huizhou minju;* traditional residence in Huizhou

中国安徽徽州地区保存较好的明清时期的民居。徽州民居大多为对称的三合院或四合院，正房为三开间的二层楼，两侧为厢房。徽州民居立面造型丰富，正房两端山墙高出屋面，随屋顶斜坡面作阶梯状迭落。檐端翘起有如马头，俗称"马头墙"。

Well-preserved residences built during the Ming and Qing dynasties in Huizhou of Anhui Province. Most such residences consist of courtyard houses with buildings on three or four sides. The main building is a two-story structure with three rooms on each floor. There are wing rooms along the two sides of the main building. The facade and walls of traditional Anhui residences have

它既是封火墙，又是装饰物。墙头用青瓦筑成小山脊，角部微翘，轮廓清秀，古朴典雅。徽州民居正面檐墙多有精美的纹饰或砖刻。大门上部用满刻花纹的雕砖贴墙砌成各式门罩，梁枋椽檐俱全，椽檐口以上逐层挑出，盖以青瓦，飞檐翘脊，精丽华美。著名的徽州民居有宏村和西递的中心建筑群。

diverse designs. The gables of the main building are higher than the roof. They appear like a staircase, descending in steps instead of an even slope. These gables are also called a *matou qiang* (horse-head wall) because the upturned eaves look like horse heads. In addition to being a decorative element they can also help prevent the spread of fire. The eaves are built using gray up-turned tiles, looking simple but elegant. The front wall is usually decorated with elaborate carvings or built with beautifully carved bricks, and such bricks are also used to build multi-layered eaves over the entrance gate. A house has a great variety of beams, joists, rafters, and eaves, with the ends of rafters and eaves all turning upwards, which makes the house appear exquisite and gorgeous. Well known traditional residences in Huizhou can be seen in Hongcun and Xidi villages.

例句：

徽州民居建筑以堂屋为中心，文化气息浓厚，以牌匾字画、雕梁画栋和装饰屋顶、檐口见长。

Example Sentence:

The central room is the core of traditional residences in Huizhou. The room boasts the distinctive cultural taste of its residents, as it is always decorated with beautiful plaques, works of calligraphy and paintings, as well as elaborately-carved and painted beams, brackets, ceilings, and eaves.

宏村（安徽） *hongcun;* Hongcun Village

中国安徽省黟县古村落，始建于南宋，距今约有900年的历史。村落以半月形水塘月沼为中心，周边围以住宅和祠堂。宏村由水圳、月沼、南湖、水巷和民居“水院”组成水系网络，构成整体空间特色。宏村完整保存明清民居140余幢，有书院、祠堂、园林和许多住宅建筑，是徽州建筑的杰出代表。2000年，宏村被联合国教科文组织列入世界文化遗产名录。

An ancient village located in Yixian County, Anhui Province. Over 900 years old, it was originally built during the Southern Song Dynasty (1127-1279). The village stands around a half-moon shaped pond, and all residential buildings and ancestral halls are built around it. The village boasts a unique water network which consists of manmade ditches, Moon Lake, Nanhu Lake (Southern Lake), zigzagging natural waterways, and the private ponds in individual

households. There are more than 140 well-preserved traditional residence compounds built during the Ming (1368-1644) and Qing (1616-1911) dynasties here. There are also traditional schools, ancestral halls, and gardens. Together they constitute representations of traditional Huizhou architecture. In 2000, Hongcun Village was recognized as a UNESCO World Heritage Site.

例句：

宏村南湖书院位于安徽省黟县的南湖北畔，为明末宏村人修建的六所私塾。清嘉庆十九年（1814 年），六院合并，得名“南湖书院”。南湖书院是座具有传统徽派风格的古书院，占地约 6000 平方米。

Example Sentence:

Nanhu Shuyuan (Southern Lake Academy) is on the northern bank of Nanhu Lake (Southern Lake) in Hongcun Village, Yixian County, Anhui Province. It evolved from six private schools built by villagers in the late Ming Dynasty (1368-1644). In 1814, the six private schools were integrated and named the Southern Lake Academy. Covering 6,000 square meters, the compound boasts typical traditional Huizhou architectural style.

马头墙 *matouqiang;* horse-head wall

中国江南传统民居赣派和徽派古典建筑的重要特色，又称“防火墙”“封火墙”。特指高于两山墙屋面的墙垣，因形状酷似马头，故称“马头墙”。马头墙墙头都高于屋顶，轮廓呈阶梯状，脊檐长短随着房屋的进深而变化。江南传统民居建筑的墙体之所以采取这种形式，是因为古代房屋多用木材建造，在聚族而居的村落中，民居建筑密度较大，不利于防火，火势容易顺房蔓延，而高高的马头墙可以防火防风，隔断火源，故而马头墙又称为“封火墙”“防火墙”。

A style of architecture popular in areas south of the lower reaches of the Yangtze River, also called a fire prevention wall. It is the wall of a building which juts outwards from the roof along with two high gables, taking the shape of a "horse-head." It is taller than the roof, looking like a flight of steps. Ancient home structures were mostly built with wood, and when built closely together to form villages, these buildings became more susceptible to fire. This type of wall was created to prevent wind from spreading the fire, which is why it came to be known as a fire prevention wall.

例句：

马头墙错落有致，黑白辉映，蕴含着层次分明的韵律美。

Example Sentence:

Horse-head walls undulate between black and white, showing a distinctive, rhythmic beauty.

流坑村 *liukengcun;* Liukeng Village

中国江西抚州乐安的古代村落，始建于五代，历经千年，被专家誉为“千古第一村”。全村大多数人姓董，尊汉代大儒董仲舒为始祖。村中现有明清建筑260多处，其中有牌坊楼阁59座，古祠堂60多座。民居中留有丰富的文物资源，其中有各种木匾、楹联500多块（幅），为江西民居文化和古代宗族社会研究保留了一个典型的标本。流坑民居清一色的青砖黑瓦，朴实素雅。高峻的马头墙既可防风，又可防火。墙内民居为木制结构，上下两层，上层藏物，下层住人，有天井采光。敞开的厅堂，正面是供奉傩神和祖先的神案，左右是卧室，厅大房小，厅明房暗。

An ancient village located in Le'an County in central Jiangxi. Liukeng Village was originally built during the Five Dynasties (907-960) period. With a history of more than 1,000 years, it has been described as "the best village in history" by some scholars. Most residents in the village are surnamed Dong. They worship Dong Zhongshu, a great Confucian scholar of the Han Dynasty (206 BC-AD 220), as their ancestor. Today, there are more than 260 buildings of the Ming (1368-1644) and Qing (1616-1911) dynasties, including 59 memorial arches and pavilions and more than 60 ancestral halls. The residences boast a rich collection of cultural relics, including more than 500 wooden plaques and couplets, which are valuable in the study of folk residential culture and the history of ancient clans. The residences are characterized by the grayish green bricks and dark tiles, which look simple but tasteful. The tall horse-head walls can deter wind and fire. The buildings inside the walls are wood structures, with each building having two stories. While the upper floor rooms are used as storerooms, the first floor rooms are the living areas. In every compound, there is a patio which helps provide extra lighting in the buildings. The central room in the main building is always open. Inside the central room and directly opposite the gate is the altar to worship the Nuo god and ancestors. On the two sides of the central room are the bedrooms for family members, which are darker and smaller than the central room.

例句：

流坑村民居的门楣、房檐、墙壁、廊柱、天花板等多有雕刻彩绘，雕绘戏曲故事、山水人物、花鸟虫鱼、神魔鬼怪等，工艺精致。流坑村民居大多门上有匾，门旁有联，有的还装饰有面目狰狞的石雕或木雕吞口。

Example Sentence:

In the traditional residences of Liukeng Village, exquisite carvings and beautiful color drawings of traditional opera stories, landscapes, human figures, animals, plants, mythical figures, and other patterns can be found everywhere, such as on the door lintels, eaves, walls, columns, and ceilings. There are also many plaques above the door lintels and couplets on the two sides of the door. In some buildings, door lintels are decorated with stone or wooden sculptures of ferocious animals and monsters.

竹笆房 *zhubafang;* bamboo house

中国四川特有的传统民居。当地盛产竹，农家建房先用木头立起穿斗式房架，再将竹片编成竹笆，固定在房架之上，里外抹泥为墙，房顶架设檩条盖瓦或覆稻草。竹笆房造价低廉，修建快速。在炎热潮湿的夏天，竹笆房通风凉爽，居住宜人。竹笆房多为三间、五间。正中一间为堂屋，是吃饭、会客、谈天和从事竹编等劳作的处所。左右两侧分别为卧室、仓库和杂物间。卧室两侧再搭盖偏棚披屋，一侧作厨房，一侧为厕所、猪圈。

Characteristically traditional Sichuan residences as the province is abundant with bamboo. When building a bamboo house, builders should first establish a wooden framework in the pillars-and-transverse-tie-beams structure (or *chuandou*, also known as column-and-tie-beam construction). Then, bamboo strips should be used to make fences which will be tied onto the wooden framework. The bamboo fences will then be plastered with clay to make walls. The roof should be reinforced by purlins and covered by tiles or straw. Building bamboo houses is cost-efficient and time-efficient. Well-ventilated and cool, they are comfortable during hot and humid summer days. A bamboo house usually has three or five rooms. The room in the center is the central hall, where family members can dine, meet guests, chat, and do household chores like weaving bamboo ware. On the two sides of the central room are bedrooms, the storeroom and a utility room. Sometimes, there are sheds on each side of the bedrooms. One shed serves as the kitchen, and the other the lavatory and pigsty.

例句：

修建**竹笆房**时，先将竹笆固定在房架上，再里外抹泥为墙。

Example Sentence:

When building a bamboo house, builders should first attach bamboo strips onto the framework, and then plaster clay on each side of the strips to make walls.

夕佳山古民居（四川）

xijia shan gu minju; Xijiashan ancient residence

中国目前保存最完整的古代民居建筑群之一。夕佳山古民居位于四川省江安县坝上村，初建于明万历年间，至今已有400多年历史，有过几次较大的修缮。庄园有池塘、后花园、西花园、东花园。整个建筑布局严谨，主次分

One of the best-preserved ancient residential architectural complexes in China. The Xijiashan ancient residence is located in Bashang Village, Jiang'an County, Sichuan Province. Built during the Ming Dynasty (1368-1644), it has been standing for over 400 years, during which time it has undergone several

明，保留了古代民间追求人与自然和谐的建筑风格。夕佳山古民居以其优美的自然景观、精美的建筑艺术、丰富的文化内涵而闻名，现有珍贵的文物藏品2000多件。1996年被国务院批准为全国第四批重点文物保护单位。夕佳山古民居对研究中国民间建筑史、民间艺术史、民间风俗史和川南社会史都具有极高的价值。夕佳山古民居还是著名的影视拍摄基地，自20世纪80年代中期至今已有多部影视剧和专题纪录片在这里拍摄过。

major renovations. The residence includes a pond and gardens in the back, west, and east. Its design is carefully laid out, clearly delineating between major and minor components, and the ancient architectural style of seeking to produce harmony between man and nature has been preserved. The residence is famous for its elegant natural design, refined architectural aesthetics, and rich cultural connotations, and houses over 2,000 precious cultural relics. In 1996, through the approval of the State Council, the residence was listed as a key national cultural relic under protection. It has great value to studies of Chinese architecture and folk art, folk social customs, and sociology in southern Sichuan Province. It has also served as a famous site for film and television making since the 1980s.

例句：

夕佳山古民居的建筑结构仍保持着原汁原味，被誉为“中国民间建筑的活化石”。

Example Sentence:

Because the architectural structure of the Xijiashan ancient residence has maintained its original style, it has been deemed “a living fossil of Chinese folk architecture.”

一颗印（云南） *yikeyin;* seal-like compound

中国云南昆明一带的民居建筑。四面封闭无窗，外观方正，夯土而筑的外墙又厚又重，天井狭小，看上去就像一颗印章，因而得名"一颗印"。一颗印通常为三间两耳或三间四耳，即正房三间，左右耳房各一间或两间。正房较高，为两层楼房，一楼正中的堂屋是吃饭、待客、休憩之处，两侧房间堆放杂物。二楼正中明间是库房，两侧为卧室。左右耳房则分别为厨房和杂物间。

A type of residential structure often seen in the city of Kunming and adjacent areas in Yunnan Province. The compound is square and the yard is small, with no windows on the thick exterior walls which are made of rammed earth. The whole compound looks like a traditional Chinese seal, thus the name "seal-like compound." The compound usually has three main rooms with two or four side rooms. The main building is a two-story structure and is higher than the other buildings. The central room is in the middle of the first floor, and is where family members dine, meet guests, and rest. The rooms next to it are used to keep miscellaneous items. On the second floor is the open room in the middle which acts as the storeroom, while the rooms on the two sides are bedrooms. The side rooms on the left and right are the kitchen and utility rooms.

例句：

"一颗印"适宜山区、平坝、城镇、村寨各种地方，有单幢，也有联幢，有的豪华精致，有的简单朴素，千百年来是云南汉族地区最普遍、最温馨的平民住宅。

Example Sentence:

The seal-like compound is suitable for all kinds of environments such as hilly regions, level ground, urban areas and rural areas. It can be built as a single house or as row houses, and can be luxurious or plainly decorated. For centuries, seal-like compounds were the most popular and comfortable residences for common people in the Han-inhabited areas of Yunnan Province.

团山古村 *tuanshan gu cun;* Tuanshan Historical Village

A village with beautiful ancient houses in Yunnan Province, where the architectural style of the 19th century remains intact and the distinctive way of life has been preserved. The village began to take shape during the early Ming Dynasty(1368-1644) when Zhang Fu, a merchant from Poyang County of Jiangxi

中国云南精美的古民居群，位于云南建水县团山村，完整保存了19世纪风貌特色的原生态村落。明洪武年间，江西鄱阳县商人张福在此安家，繁衍子孙，成为巨族。团山村有21座保存完好的传统民居和古建筑，所有建筑一律坐西朝东，青瓦白墙，青砖墙裙。每座房屋都以天井为核心，大门多在主体建筑一侧。有一进院、二进院、三进院，平面布局包揽了云南传统民居中“四合五天井”“三坊一照壁”“跑马转角楼”等主要形式。团山宅院紧凑舒适，尤以屋檐窗棂间的精美木雕而为人称道。

Province, settled here and raised a large family. Today, there are 21 intact ancient Han-style residences and buildings, all of which face the east and feature gray-tiled roofs, whitewashed outer walls, and gray-brick dados. A yard is in the center of every compound, and an entrance gate is at one corner of the building. The residence can have one, two, or three yards. Common styles include courtyard houses with five yards, courtyard houses with a screen wall on one side and buildings on the other three sides, and corner-turning buildings. The residential buildings in Tuanshan are usually compact but very comfortable. They are particularly known for the exquisite carvings on the wooden eaves and window lattices.

例句：

团山古村保存较好的民居、庙宇、祠堂大多是19世纪或20世纪初建成的。

Example Sentence:

Most of the well-preserved residences, temples, and ancestral halls of Tuanshan Historical Village date back to the 19th and early 20th centuries.

四合五天井

sihewu tianjing;
courtyard house with five yards

中国白族传统民居，一种院落式住宅。由四坊房屋围合而成，中间是四方形的大院子，院落四角各建有耳房，耳房与主房之间形成小院（天井），称为“漏角天井”，四个小院加上中间四方形的大院，共五个庭院天井，故称“四合五天井”。各坊房屋多为三间两层，底层两侧为卧房，中间是客厅，楼上放粮草用具，也可当卧室。该民居吸收了中原文化，又根据本地环境特色创制而成，极具特色。

A type of traditional courtyard-style house of the Bai ethnic group in China. The house has a large square courtyard in the middle which is surrounded by four side rooms built separately in the four corners of the courtyard. Small yards (patios) are formed between side rooms and the main house, which are called the “yards at the corner.” There are five yards in the residence, including four small yards and a large square courtyard, thus called “courtyard house with five yards.” Most of the houses are two-story structures (each floor having three rooms), with a living room sandwiched between bedrooms on both sides on the first floor. Rooms on the second floor are used as bedrooms or to store grain, forage, and other things. This unique architectural style combines the culture of the Central Plains and the characteristics of the local environment.

例句：

大理人民街499号的**四合五天井**建于坡地，布局合理，采光好，是典型的白族传统民居。

Example Sentence:

The courtyard house with five yards at No. 499 Renmin Street in Dali, Yunnan Province, a typical traditional house of the Bai people, was built on a slope, with a rational design and ample sunshine.

三坊一照壁

sanfangyi zhaobi;
three houses with a screen wall

中国白族、纳西族的传统民居，由一面正房、两面厢房和一个照壁组成的封闭式院落。三面房屋一般是三间两层，中间为堂屋，两边是住房。照壁是正房对面的影壁，属于白族民居中最富民族特色的部分，其长度相当于三个开间。这种民居正房较高，两面厢房略低，主次分明，布局协调，融美学与力学于一体，大多建在山清水秀、树木苍翠的环境中，秀丽壮美，独具特色。现今仍是云南大理白族自治州和丽江纳西族自治县一带常见的民居形式。

A type of traditional house of the Bai and Naxi ethnic groups in China. It is a closed courtyard consisting of main rooms, two sets of wing rooms on each side, and a screen wall. The main rooms generally have two stories with a principal room situated between bedrooms on both sides. Endowed with unique ethnic features, the screen wall stands on the opposite side of the main rooms and is normally at least ten meters in length. With a clear distinction between the main and wing rooms, and a harmonious layout, this kind of residence features taller main rooms and slightly lower wing rooms on both sides, representing a perfect combination of aesthetics and architecture. Most of these houses are built in areas with beautiful mountains, clear waters, and green trees, and are commonly seen in Bai Autonomous Prefecture of Dali and Naxi Autonomous County of Lijiang, Yunnan Province.

例句：

丽江纳西族普遍的住宅为土木结构的瓦房，多为“**三坊一照壁**”，院落宽敞，阳光充足。

Example Sentence:

The homes common for the Naxi people in Lijiang are tile-roofed houses known as “three houses with a screen wall” with spacious courtyards and ample sunshine.

跑马转角楼

paoma zhuanjiaolou;
"corner-turning" building

中国传统民居。转角楼有两种表现形式：一种为在正房的左或右修建转角楼，一般为两层；另一种为左修转角楼，右修厢房，或右修转角楼，左修厢房。转角楼一般由正屋、偏屋、木楼三部分组成。其中正屋当中有一间称为堂屋，为敬祭祖先和迎接宾客之所；左右两间为火炕屋住人；两头称偏房，作灶房或磨房之用。紧接磨角处，一方或两边建起“转角楼”。这种建筑空间利用率高，可弥补封闭式院落房间采光的不足。

A type of Chinese traditional building. There are two layouts: one is to build a two-story "corner-turning" building on the left or right side of the main house; the other is to build a "corner-turning" building on the left side and the wing house on the right side, or vice versa. A "corner-turning" building is generally composed of three parts: the main rooms, the wing rooms, and the wooden "corner-turning" building. Among the main rooms one is known as the principal room for worshipping ancestors and receiving guests. The two rooms on the left and right sides of the main room serve as bedrooms. The rooms at the two ends of the main room are wing rooms, used as the kitchen or grinding mill. Next to the corner of the grinding mill, the "corner-turning" building is constructed on one side or both sides. With high-efficient space utilization, "corner-turning" buildings can allow ample sunshine for the enclosed courtyard buildings.

例句：

北京的四合院，山西、陕西的宅院，云南的“一颗印”，南方的**跑马转角楼**、吊脚楼等是中国南北各地具有代表性的民居。

Example Sentence:

Unique Chinese architecture styles include the *siheyuan* (courtyard homes) of Beijing, the *zhaiyuan* (residential compounds) of Shanxi and Shaanxi provinces, the *yikeyin* (seal-like compounds) of Yunnan Province, and the *paoma zhuanjiaolou* (corner-turning buildings) and *diaojiaolou* (stilt houses) of southern China.

竹楼 *zhulou;* bamboo stilt house

中国傣族标志性民居，是干栏式建筑的主要类型之一。房顶呈“人”字型，热带季风气候地区降雨量大，“人”

A type of house of the Dai ethnic group. One of the main types of stilt houses, its roof, made of the bamboo, takes the shape of the Chinese character 人 (people) for easy water drainage. This helps

字型房顶易于排水，不会出现积水问题。竹楼以竹子为主要建筑材料，一般为长方形，分上下两层：上层分为堂屋和卧室两部分，离地面二到三米，属居住生活区域；下层无墙开敞，用于饲养家禽和堆放杂物。这种民居通风良好，视野开阔，防潮散热，同时可防虫兽、地震，适合当地的自然环境。竹楼主要分布在中国云南的西双版纳和德宏州的傣族、景颇族、基诺族等民族地区。

avoid water accumulation in areas that have heavy precipitation because of a tropical monsoon climate. The bamboo stilt house is mainly constructed of bamboo and is generally rectangular-shaped with two stories. The upper-story housing the living area is composed of the hall and bedrooms two to three meters above the ground, while the lower floor is usually open without walls and mainly used for raising poultry and for storage. Such a house is well-ventilated, dry, and moisture-proof and provides good protection against insects, animals, and earthquakes. The bamboo stilt house fits well with the local natural environment. Such houses are mainly found in Dai Autonomous Prefecture of Xishuangbanna and Dai-Jingpo Autonomous Prefecture of Dehong, Yunnan Province where the Dai, Jingpo, and Jinuo ethnic groups live.

例句：

竹楼上的每一部分都有不同的含义，走进竹楼就好像走进主人家的历史和文化。

Example Sentence:

Each part of a bamboo stilt house has different implications. When you enter it, you will see the history and culture of the owner of the house.

吊脚楼 *diaojiaolou;* stilt house; stilted building

中国苗族、壮族、布依族、侗族、水族、土家族等少数民族的传统民居，又称“吊楼”“半边楼”。半干栏式建筑，一般依山靠河就势而建，适应山区的斜坡地，分上下两层：上层是正屋，即生活区域，内设卧室，外有堂屋，宽敞明亮，光线充足，建在实地上；下层用于饲养家禽和堆放杂物。这种民居通风良好，干燥防潮，又能防毒蛇、野兽，空间大，在渝东南及桂北、湘西、鄂西、黔东南地区很常见，有鲜明的民族特色。

A type of traditional building of the Miao, Zhuang, Bouyei, Dong, Tujia, Sui, and other ethnic minorities, also called “hanging building” or “half-side building.” *Diaojiaolou* is generally built along mountains and rivers and is well-suited for mountainous slopes. It typically has two stories, spacious and admitting adequate light with a solid foundation. The top floor houses the living room and bedrooms while the lower floor is used for raising poultry and for storage. The spacious *diaojiaolou* is well-ventilated and protected against snakes and other animals. With distinct ethnic characteristics, they are often seen in southeastern Chongqing, northern Guangxi, western Hunan, western Hubei, and southeastern Guizhou.

例句：

虽然现代修建的**吊脚楼**越来越少了，但是其建筑形式还是得到很多运用。

Example Sentence:

Although the number of *diaojiaolou* is small nowadays, its architectural style is still widely applied in many ways.

碉楼 *diaolou; watchtower*

中国传统建筑。平面呈矩形，楼高三至五层，大的高五至七层，最高可达九层。各层开有若干矩形窗，外观似碉堡，故称“碉楼”。碉楼有两种功能：一为防御侵略，若遇来犯者可在碉楼顶上燃起烟火通报紧急情况以求救援，也可利用碉楼上的枪眼进行自卫；二为居住及贮存粮食柴草。中国羌族的碉楼较为典型，碉楼的墙面由石片砌成，稳固牢靠，且冬暖夏凉，充分体现了当地高原山寨的特色。

A type of traditional building in China. The watchtower-like house is a rectangular flat structure ranging from three to nine stories. The building has a number of rectangular windows on each story, there are several rectangular windows, making the building look like a bunker, hence its name "watchtower." This has two functions. One is to resist aggression in that in case of an enemy attack, people can set a beacon fire from the top of the watchtower as an emergency call for reinforcements or use the embrasures to defend themselves. The other function is as a residence and storage of grain and firewood. The Qiang ethnic group is known for its watchtower, which has solid stone walls so that it is warm in winter and cool in summer, typical of mountain villages on the plateau.

例句：

一些古老的**碉楼**有400多年的历史，而最年轻的可以追溯到1948年。

Example Sentence:

Some age-old watchtowers have a history of more than 400 years, and the most recent ones can be traced back to 1948.

土楼（闽粤）

tulou;
earthen towers; *tulou* (in Fujian and Guangdong);
earthen houses

中国广东、福建客家人传统民居建筑，又称"围屋"。土楼主要有圆楼、方楼两种，多为三四层建筑。大环形土楼占地直径最大的达70米，可住50多户人家。土楼外墙以黏土、沙石及石灰为原料，内夹竹片、木条夯筑而成，异常坚固。楼内一层不开外窗，二、三、四层房间有朝外开设的窗口，可作为瞭望敌情、向外射击的枪孔。土楼大门坚固厚实，楼内挖

A type of traditional residence of the Hakka people in southeastern China's Guangdong and Fujian provinces. The earthen towers are typically round- or square-shaped and three or four stories high, of which the largest one has a diameter of 70 meters and can house over 50 families. The wall frames are built with wood and bamboo, which are then covered with clay, sandstone, and lime. Windows to the outside cannot be found on the first floor for defensive purposes. The well-

有水井，防卫严密，便于抵御匪敌进犯。土楼是世界上为数不多的大型民居形式，被称为中国传统民居的瑰宝。它是中国乃至东亚几次历史动荡和民众大迁徙的产物。其中分布最广、数量最多、品类最丰富、保存最完好的是福建土楼。2008 年 7 月 6 日，福建土楼被联合国教科文组织世界遗产委员会列入世界文化遗产名录。

defended earthen tower has a thick wall and strong gate, which helps protect residents from bandits and enemies. Inside the earthen tower are also wells to retrieve water. A unique style of residential housing in the world, the earthen tower is regarded as a treasure of traditional Chinese architecture. The formation of the earthen tower is the result of several waves of migration and turmoil in China and east Asia. Most earthen towers are found in Fujian Province, which are best preserved. On July 6, 2008, it was added to the UNESCO World Cultural Heritage List.

例句:

土楼是客家文化的象征，客家文化是土楼的灵魂。

Example Sentence:

The earthen tower is the symbol of the Hakka culture, and in turn, the Hakka culture is the soul of the earthen tower.

围屋 *weiwu; walled village*

参见“土楼”。

See *tulou* (earthen towers).

船形屋 *chuanxing wu;* boat-shaped hut

中国海南的古老民居，世代流传于海南黎族、苗族聚居区。黎族同胞为纪念渡海而来的黎族祖先，故以船的形状建造住屋。当地人就地取材，用茅草、稻草、泥土、竹子、藤条和木材等自然植物搭建成船形屋，长而阔，茅檐低矮，这样的建筑风格有利于防风防雨。所有的船形屋基本都是前后双开门。船形屋是海南省黎族祖先智慧的结晶，已列入国家级非物质文化遗产名录。

A type of old residence of the Li and Miao ethnic groups in Hainan Province. To cherish the memory of their ancestors who arrived by crossing the sea, the Li people built their homes in the shape of boats. They made use of local resources such as cogon grass, rice straw, soil, bamboo, rattan, wood, and other natural materials to build the homes. These houses are long and wide with eaves made of drooping reeds, protecting residents from wind and rain. They have an open door in both the front and the back. Such homes showcase the wisdom of the ancestors of the Li ethnic group. They have been included on China's Intangible Cultural Heritage List.

例句：

船形屋反映了古代黎族民居的营造技艺。

Example Sentence:

The boat-shaped huts of the ancient Li people showcase their ancient architectural skills.

祠堂 *citang;* ancestral temple; ancestral hall

中国祭祀祖先的场所。祠堂在中国传统民居建筑中占有重要地位。其址必择向阳背风、依山临水的上好处所，前面有池塘，后面是苍郁的风水林。祠堂供奉祖先牌位，逢年过节时合族家家备下三牲酒醴到祠堂祭祀祖先。族中每有兴学、修桥、铺路或订立族规民约之事，常在祠堂聚议。祠堂还是族中男婚女嫁、老人谢世时举办红白喜事的场所。祠堂建筑一般都比民宅规模大、质量好，越有权势和财势的家族，祠堂往往越讲究，高大的厅堂、精致的雕饰、上等的用材都是这个家族光宗耀祖的象征。

A place for offering sacrifices to ancestors. The ancestral temple is an important part of traditional Chinese architecture. The site should face the sun, built against a mountain at its back, and looks at the water. There should be a pond in the front and a forest behind. Within the temple, ancestors are consecrated on memorial tablets. During the Chinese New Year and other festivals, a family prepares offerings of meat and alcohol for their ancestors. Ancestral temples are also used for important meetings such as discussions of establishing schools, building bridges and roads, or formulating rules and other conventions. They are also places where weddings and funerals are held. Ancestral temples are larger and better constructed than traditional Chinese homes. The more powerful and wealthy an extended family or clan is, the more ornate their ancestral temple would be. A tall ancestral temple with delicate carvings and superior wood is considered a sign of honor to one's ancestors.

例句：

祠堂是族长行使族权的地方，违反族规的族人会在这里被教育和处罚，甚至被驱逐出宗祠。

Example Sentence:

The ancestral temple is the place where a patriarch exercises his authority over a clan. Any member of the family who violates its rules will be educated and punished here, or even expelled from the ancestral temple.

陈家祠堂

chen jia citang;
Chen Clan Ancestral Temple; Chen Clan Ancestral Hall; Chen Clan Academy

中国清代宗祠建筑，位于广东省广州市。陈家祠堂建于清代中叶，原为供同宗子弟读书或参加科举考试的书院，又是祭祖的宗祠。陈家

Built during the Qing Dynasty (1616-1911), the Chen Clan Ancestral Temple is located in Guangzhou, Guangdong Province. It used to be both an academy for sons of the same clan to study or prepare for the imperial

祠堂规模宏大，装饰华丽，是广东地区保存较完整的富有代表性的清末民间建筑。陈家祠堂占地面积1.32万平方米，祠堂内随处可见木雕、石雕、砖雕、陶塑、灰塑等传统建筑装饰及铁铸工艺。1988年中华人民共和国国务院批准为全国重点文物保护单位。

civil examination and also a place for offering sacrifices to the clan's ancestors. Large with exquisite decorations, it is one of the best-preserved buildings in Guangdong that is characteristic of late-Qing Dynasty architecture. The Chen Clan Ancestral Temple covers an area of 13,200 square meters. Throughout the complex, one can see carved wood, stone, brickwork, pottery, and other traditional decorations. There is also a great number of cast iron work. In 1998, with the approval of the State Council of China, it became a key historical and cultural site under national protection.

例句：

21世纪以来，**陈家祠堂**两度入选“新世纪羊城八景”，被誉为“广州文化名片”，成为广东地区最具文化艺术特色的博物馆。

Example Sentence:

In the 21st century, the Chen Clan Ancestral Temple has been included twice in the "Eight Sights of Yangcheng (Guangzhou) in the New Century," which is known as the "representative cultural site of Guangzhou."

会馆 *huiguan;* guild hall

中国明清时期都市中由同乡或同业组成的团体聚会场所。迄今所知最早的会馆是建于永乐年间的北京芜湖会馆。嘉靖、万历时期，会馆趋于兴盛，清代中期最多。会馆多为同乡或同业集资建造的宫庙式建筑，作为聚会、议事和接待的场所。馆内供奉乡梓神像，定期办会祭祀、演戏娱乐。会馆由大殿、东西厢房、后厢房、戏台、观戏楼等组成，结构雄伟，富丽堂皇。明清时期的会馆大体可分为三种：北京的大多数会馆主要为同乡官僚、缙绅和科举之士居停聚会之处，故又称为“试馆”；北京的少数会馆和苏州、汉口、上海等工商业城市的大多数会馆是以工商业者、行帮为主体的同乡会馆；四川的大多数会馆是入清以后由陕西、湖广、江西、福建、广东等省迁来的客民建立的同乡移民会馆。明清时期大量工商业会馆的出现，对于保护工商业者的自身利益有一定的积极意义。但会馆所代表的乡土观念也阻碍了商品交换的扩大和社会经济的发展。

Buildings constructed during the Ming and Qing dynasties (1368-1911) with the purpose of holding meetings for various groups of people. They were normally constructed by those of the same hometown or those working in the same trade within an area. The earliest known guild hall was the Wuhu Guild Hall in Beijing, constructed during the Ming Dynasty. The guild halls became increasingly popular, and reached a peak in number during the mid-Qing Dynasty. A guild hall was usually built like a temple or palace with funds donated by people from the same locality or in the same field. The hall provided a venue where people could gather to hold discussions, entertain guests, and worship local gods. Worshipping ceremonies, traditional operas, and other shows were also held regularly here. The compound of a guild hall was normally composed of the central hall, the eastern and western wing rooms, the rear rooms, the opera stage, an auditorium, and other rooms. Guild halls were known for their magnificent designs and grand architecture. During the Ming and Qing dynasties, guild halls could fall under three categories: the first was the Test Hall, which was popular in Beijing, mostly frequented by government officials from the same hometown, gentry, and participants of the imperial civil examinations. The second, Hometown Guild Hall, was also in Beijing, but not quite as popular. It appeared in other cities like Suzhou, Hankou, and Shanghai, and served as a place of convergence for people of the same trade and business. The third was most popular in Sichuan among people from the hometowns from Shaanxi, Hubei, Hunan, Jiangxi, Fujian, and Guangdong who had moved to Sichuan after the Qing Dynasty (1616-1911). During the Ming and Qing dynasties from the 14th to the early 20th centuries, a great number of business guild halls emerged, which clearly helped businessmen protect their interests. However, guild halls also created barriers to the exchange of goods and social and economic development as those who met there would tend to protect the interests of their own small groups.

例句：

会馆是旧时代科举制度和工商业活动的产物，也是各省在京各界人士政治和文化活动的中心。

Example Sentence:

Guild halls in Beijing came into being as a result of the imperial civil examination and commercial activities in ancient times. They served as centers of political and cultural activities for people from all walks of life who moved to Beijing from other provinces.

长窗 changchuang; long window

安装在上槛和下槛之间的落地窗户，又称“落地长窗”，在中国南方比较常见。长窗开启时是供人出入的门，关闭时又是可以采光、通风的窗。长窗上的装饰非常精美，人物故事、动植物图案内容丰富多彩。

A floor-to-ceiling window installed between the upper and lower sills of a house, commonly seen in southern China. When open, it can be used as a door for people to enter and exit and when closed it is used as a window for sunlight and ventilation. Long windows are exquisitely decorated with characters from literature and also patterns of animals and plants.

例句：

长窗的扇数随建筑开间大小而定，窗格明亮，便于采光，在苏州园林中极为常见。

Example Sentence:

The number of long windows to be installed depends on the size of the house. Long windows are very commonly seen in classical gardens of Suzhou.

华表

huabiao;
ornamental column; ornamental pillar

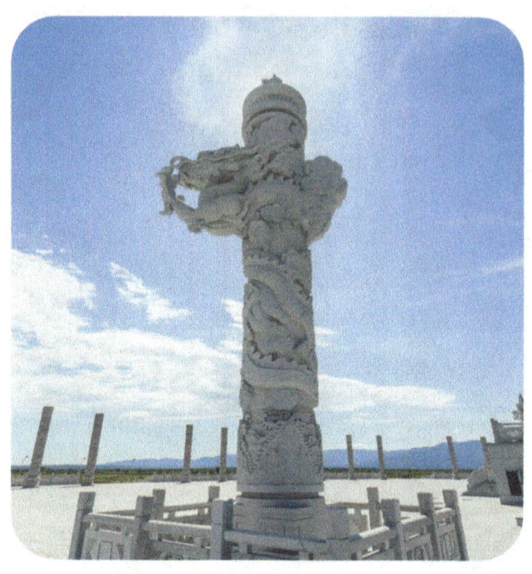

一种中国古代传统建筑形式，古代路口及宫殿、桥梁、陵墓等大型建筑前用的巨大成对立柱。元代之前的华表多为木制，明之后的华表多以石头或大理石制成。据传华表在古时既有道路标志的作用，又有供行人留言向王者纳谏的作用，是提醒古代帝王勤政为民的标志。华表的石柱上刻有龙凤等图案，上面还横插雕花石板。

A type of traditional architecture in ancient China, usually consisting of a pair of colossal pillars erected at crossroads and in front of palaces, bridges, tombs, and other large buildings. Before the Yuan Dynasty (1206–1368), most *huabiao* were made of wood, but since the Ming Dynasty (1368–1644) stone or marble *huabiao* became more common. It is believed that *huabiao* served as road signs and also places for people to leave messages to their rulers. This made *huabiao* symbols urge rulers to keep the interest of their people at heart. Patterns such as dragons and phoenixes are engraved on these pillars which also have carved stone slabs mounted on them.

例句：

天安门**华表**当推为中国所有华表之冠，它实际上已经和中华民族、和中国古老的文化紧密相连，可以说是中华民族的一种标志。

Example Sentence:

The ornamental columns in Tiananmen Square are the best in China. As symbols of the Chinese nation, ornamental columns have close associations with the Chinese nation and ancient Chinese culture.

牌坊 *paifang;* decorated archway; ornamental archway

中国传统建筑之一，是一种有柱门形构筑物，又称“牌楼”。牌坊主要有木、石、砖、琉璃几种。作为中华文化的一个象征，牌坊的历史源远流长，最早见于周朝，是用于旌表节孝的纪念物，后来在园林、寺观、宫苑、陵墓和街道均有建造。北京是中国牌楼最多的城市。牌楼曾作为多届世博会中国馆的门面建筑而吸引了世人的视线。

A type of unique structure that features traditional Chinese architecture and design. It is usually composed of two or four pillars topped with a brimmed arch and made of wood, stone, brick, or colored glaze. It is a symbol of Chinese civilization and has a long history, dating back as early as the Zhou Dynasty (1046-256 BC). Decorated archways are mostly found on city streets and in gardens, temples, royal palaces or tombs, and they were constructed to commend people who earnestly followed ethical rites in the old days. Beijing has the highest concentration of such decorated archways in China. They also served as façades for China's pavilions at several world expos where they attracted great attention of people from all over the world.

例句:

北京明十三陵入口处的石牌坊雕刻精美，是现存为数不多的**牌坊**代表作。

Example Sentence:

The decorated archway at the entrance of the Ming Tombs in Beijing was carved with exquisite patterns and is considered a fine example among the few remaining such structures.

牌楼

pailou;
decorated archway; ornamental archway

参见“牌坊”。

See *pailou* (decorated archway).

耳房

erfang;
side room

中国传统建筑中的一种房间。正房两端各有一间或两间较小的侧房，因位居正房

A kind of room in traditional Chinese architecture. It refers to the one or two smaller rooms located on both sides of the principal room. Because of this

两侧形似双耳而称之为“耳房”。耳房通常是大殿、城门、主厅进门前左右各一个的小房子。在过去，中间的正房是给长辈住的，耳房是小辈人住的，有地位的差别。现今，正房用来居住，耳房用来放东西。

configuration, it is also called *erfang* (ear room). Generally, the side room is located on both sides of the main hall, also the city gate, or the grand lobby. In the past, the principal rooms were allocated to elders and the side rooms were for the younger generation, reflecting family hierarchy. But now, side rooms are mainly used for storage.

例句：

四合院及云南一颗印民居中都常见**耳房**。

Example Sentence:

The side room is commonly seen in courtyard houses as well as in residential buildings known as seal-like compounds (*yikeyin*) in Yunnan.

厢房 *xiangfang; wing room*

中国传统建筑中的一种房间，多见于四合院式居所中，指位于正房两侧、左右相对的配房，规格大小仅次于正房。

A kind of room in traditional Chinese architecture. Commonly seen in courtyard houses, wing rooms are located on both sides of the principal room. They are opposite to each other and second in size only to the principal room.

例句：

四合院中，正房多由长辈居住，**厢房**由晚辈居住。

Example Sentence:

In courtyard houses, the principal room is for the elders and wing rooms are for the younger generation.

屏风 *pingfeng; screen*

中国古老的用来挡风或起障蔽作用的室内陈设。屏风在春秋时代已被使用，唐宋时制作日趋精美，上面雕刻各种图案花纹，富丽堂皇。至今屏风仍出现在豪华的楼堂馆所中，以作装饰之用。屏风是中国古代居室内重要的家具、装饰品，其形制、图案及文字均包含大量的文化信息，既能表现文人雅士的高雅情趣，也包含了人们祈福迎祥的深刻内涵。各式各样的屏风还凝聚着手工艺人富于创意的智慧和巧夺天工的技术。

A type of Chinese old indoor decoration which was used to shield wind and protect privacy. It first appeared during the Spring and Autumn Period (770-476 BC), and by the Tang Dynasty (618-907), the screens had become an art form, carved with various exquisite designs. Even today screens are still used in luxurious buildings and halls for decoration. They used to be an important piece of furniture or decoration exhibited in the living room. Their shape, pattern, and inscription on the surface conveyed significant cultural connotations such as the lofty spirit of scholars or auspicious blessings. All types of screens showcase the artisans' creative wisdom and their consummate craftsmanship.

例句：

东晋以来，许多著名书画家借**屏风**进行书法和绘画创作。

Example Sentence:

Beginning in the Eastern Jin Dynasty (317-420), many Chinese calligraphers and painters began to create their calligraphic works and paintings on screens.

八仙桌 *baxian zhuo; eight immortals' table*

一种中华民族传统家具。这种桌的桌面较宽，且四边长度相等，每边可坐二人，四边可围坐八人，犹如八仙，故民间雅称“八仙桌”。现今可考的八仙桌至少在辽金时代就已出现，明清盛行，

A traditional piece of Chinese furniture. It is a square table wide enough so that two people can be seated at each side, allowing a total of eight people to sit around the table, hence the name the "eight immortals' table." It is believed that this type of table existed as early as the Jin Dynasty (265-420). It became popular during the Ming (1368-1644) and Qing dynasties (1616-1911), especially during the Qing Dynasty, during which it was used by high-ranking officials as well as distinguished individuals and common people. Virtually everyone in China knows of this type of table, and it was often the only large piece of furniture in a home in the past. Even today the eight immortals' table is one of the most commonly

尤其是清代，无论达官显贵还是平头百姓，几乎家家都有八仙桌，八仙桌甚至成为很多家庭唯一的大型家具。现在，八仙桌是最常见的生活用具之一，用于吃饭、会客、读书。

seen pieces of everyday furniture, used for dining, receiving visitors, and studying.

例句：

石狮人素有“拜天公”的习俗，每逢正月初九，家家户户都会摆一张**八仙桌**，桌上摆满各式供品，非常丰盛。

Example Sentence:

People from the city of Shishi, Fujian province have always had the custom of “paying respects to heaven.” On the ninth day of the first lunar month, every household brings out an eight immortals’ table and covers it with all kinds of sumptuous offerings.

拔步床 *babu chuang; babu* bed

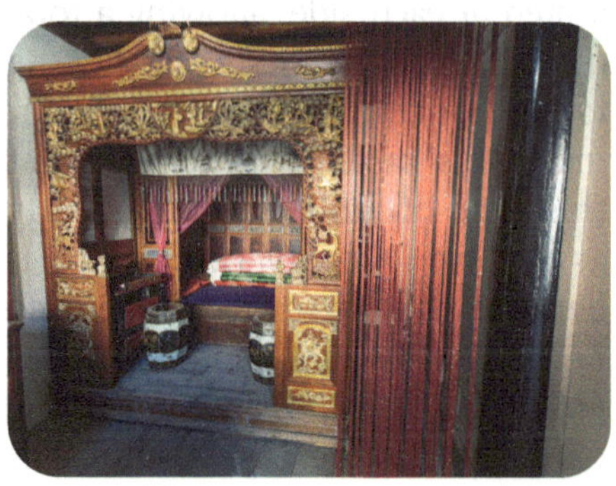

一种中国传统家具中体型最大的床。明晚期产生，在中国南方长江流域十分流行。拔步床整体配有精致的雕花和装饰，由架子床和前廊两

The largest of all Chinese beds and a type of traditional Chinese furniture. It first appeared in the late Ming Dynasty (1368-1644), and became especially popular in the Yangtze River Basin in southern China. The *babu* bed features exquisite carvings and decorations, combining the framework of a canopy bed and an archway. The space created within the alcove is quite spacious, and small furniture can be placed inside such as a bench, chamber pot, lantern, and dressing table. This type of bed is essentially a small room

部分组成，床前廊内活动空间充裕，可放置桌凳、便桶、灯盏、梳妆台等小型家具，如此，拔步床本身就是一个小房间。由于拔步床体型庞大、结构精巧、雕工繁复，造价相当高昂，旧时几乎只有富豪大户才用得起这种床，所以拔步床逐渐演变成一种社会地位和家族财富的象征。

and is quite expensive given its large dimensions, elaborate composition, and complicated woodcarving work. Mostly owned by rich and powerful individuals, they became a symbol of social status and family wealth.

例句：

进入民国后，**拔步床**仍然在江南一带的富庶家中使用，所饰多为吉祥图案及历史典故。

Example Sentence:

After the Republic of China (1912-1949) was founded, *babu* beds remained widely used among affluent families in areas south of the Yangtze River. They were decorated with auspicious patterns and classical stories.

土炕 *tukang; earthen kang*

A type of brick bed that uses fire to keep warm, also called a *kang*. It is made from adobe or brick with bedding placed on top. There is a space below for the heat to enter. One side of the bed is connected to a kitchen stove. When this stove is lit, heat passes through the space to warm the *kang*'s surface. The smoke exits via an exhaust space at the other side of the bed. A variety of patterns are carved into the *kang*, some of which are made

一种可用火取暖的土床，又称“火炕”。炕体用土坯或砖头砌成，上面铺席，下面炕内有烟道，一端与灶台相接，灶生火，余热可顺烟道烤热炕面，烟气由烟道末端入烟囱排出。炕围上面配有多种图案，常请民间艺人绘制。土炕的雏形最早出现于早期铁器时代（公元前1世纪）。明清时期，土炕采暖普遍盛行于中国北方的城镇和农村，除睡觉外，平常休息、用餐也皆在其上。土炕至今仍是北方村镇的主要取暖方式。

by folk artists. The earliest form of earthen *kang* appeared as early as the iron age (about 1000 BC), and during the Ming (1368-1644) and Qing (1616-1911) dynasties these types of beds were commonly used in urban and rural areas of northern China. People often sleep, relax and dine on *kang* beds. Fire *kangs* still remain one of the principal ways of heating in rural areas of northern China.

例句：

8至10世纪，女真人已有与现代形制相同的火炕；12世纪后半期，**土炕**成为女真人住房的必备设施。

Example Sentence:

Between the eighth and tenth centuries, the Nüzhen people already had fire *kangs* that are similar in design to modern *kangs*. By the late 12th century, the earthen *kang* had already become an essential component of Nüzhen homes.

 砖雕 *zhuandiao; brick engravings*

Artwork on engraved, blue-tinted bricks. Brick engraving refers to a type of engraving process on blue-tinted bricks that feature mountain scenery, flowers, plants, figures, and other designs. It is an important ancient architectural carving method. Brick engravings are decorations added

一种用青砖雕刻的艺术品，指在青砖上雕出山水、花卉、人物等图案，是古建筑雕刻中很重要的一种艺术形式。砖雕大多作为建筑构件或大门、照壁、墙面的装饰。在艺术上，砖雕远近均可观赏，具有完整的效果。在题材上，砖雕以龙凤呈祥、三阳开泰、麒麟送子、松柏、兰花、竹、鲤鱼等寓意吉祥和人们所喜闻乐见的内容为主。民间砖雕从实用和观赏的角度出发，形象简练，风格浑厚，不盲目追求精巧和纤细，以保持建筑构件的坚固，能经受日晒和雨淋。

to architectural structures, large gates, screen walls, and the surfaces of walls. Brick engraving designs are such that they can be admired closely or far away, allowing for a comprehensive viewing experience. In terms of subject matter, the designs are centered around auspicious moral stories and images such as dragon and phoenix figures, a *qilin* (a Chinese mythical spirit animal) delivering a son, pine and cypresses, orchids, bamboo, and carp. The artistry is succinct and unsophisticated, choosing not to blindly pursue an elaborate and ornate style, but rather a solid architectural design that can withstand sunshine and rainstorms alike.

例句：

砖雕通常保留砖的本色，不另行染色，但也有少量砖雕进行彩绘处理。

Example Sentence:

Brick engravings typically retain the original color of the raw material, but there are a small number of such engravings that are colored.

拴马石 *shuanma shi; hitching post*

A unique stone carving artwork in northern China, also called *shuanma zhuang*, which is popular in Shaanxi Province. In the past, decorative hitching posts were used by rich families

中国北方独有的一种民间石刻艺术品，也称“拴马桩”，在陕西省使用尤为广泛。拴马石是旧时殷实富裕家庭拴系骡马的雕刻实用条石，以坚固耐磨的整块青石雕凿而成，常立于住宅大门的两侧，既有装点建筑的作用，同时还被赋予了避邪镇宅的意义。拴马石雕刻在整体上综合运用圆雕、浮雕、线刻手法，具有浓厚的地方特色。在陕西所见到的拴马石是北方农耕文化的产物和缩影。栓马石是中国古代人民文化艺术的产物和智慧的结晶，对考古和文化艺术研究具有重要意义。

to tie up horses and dispel evil spirits. They were made of solid and durable blue stones, and usually placed on both sides of house gates. Stone carving skills include circular, relief, and line carving, and have peculiar local characteristics. The hitching posts in Shaanxi Province reflect northern farming culture, and are invaluable in the studies of Chinese archeology, culture, and arts.

例句：

关中民俗博物院藏有 8600 多根**拴马石**。

Example Sentence:

The Guanzhong Folk Art Museum houses over 8,600 hitching posts.

乌篷船

wupeng chuan;
black-awning boat

中国浙江绍兴独特的水上交通工具。船身窄、船篷低，船体轻盈，船篷用竹蔑编织而成，呈拱形，中间夹着竹箬，既可遮阳又可挡雨，牢固耐用，制成后用烟煤粉和桐油拌搅涂于船篷。乌篷船由此得名。其动力是靠船老大（船夫）用脚踏桨，船的航向用手划桨来控制。

A unique type of boat in Shaoxing, Zhejiang Province. The black-awning boat has a narrow and light hull. The low awning is arch-shaped and made of interweaving bamboo strips and leaves, which can shelter people from sunshine and rain. The durable awning is then covered with soot and tung oil, giving it a black appearance, hence the name "black-awning boat." It is powered by a boatman paddling with both feet and hands and his hands steer the boat by paddling.

例句：

浙江绍兴水乡的村民下田干活，串亲访友，老人寿诞，出殡送葬，全得用**乌篷船**。

Example Sentence:

Black-awning boats are commonly seen in Shaoxing, a waterside city in Zhejiang Province. Living in a city with abundant waterways, people often travel by such boats to farm in the fields, visit their friends, and even celebrate birthdays or have funeral processions.

轿子 *jiao zi;* sedan chair

A means of transport in the old days. It typically consists of two long poles with a box-type enclosed seat attached in the middle, and is carried by people or animals. Sedan chairs originated in the Eastern Zhou Dynasty

中国旧时靠人或畜扛载而行、供人乘坐的一种交通工具。基本样式是两根长杆、中置箱式座位，通常用人肩扛手抬。中国的轿子最早出现于东周时期，历代统治阶级都曾制定过轿子的形制等级，体现在轿子的大小、帷帐用料质地的好坏和轿夫的人数等方面。现代轿子仅用于婚庆接送新娘，并在旅游景点保留。

(770-256 BC). There were specific rules regarding the status of passengers and the type of sedan chair which could be used, with the rank of the passenger reflected in the size of the chair, the quality of the drapery, and the number of bearers. Later, sedan chairs became more common, and were used often in wedding ceremonies to carry the bride to her wedding. Nowadays, sedan chairs are mostly used at tourist attractions.

例句：

中国民间有用**轿子**迎接新娘的习惯。

Example Sentence:

Sedan chairs are used to bring brides to their weddings in some parts of China.

马帮

mabang;
caravan; a train of horses carrying goods

A group of horse-riding people and their mule and horse teams that transport goods and are organized according to folk rules. The caravan was a special means of transport in southwestern China along the Ancient Tea Horse Road. Professional caravans were normally privately operated as long-term businesses, while non-professional caravans were usually short-term business ventures often consisting of two

按民间约定俗成的方式组织起来的一群赶马人及其骡马队，又称“马队”。马帮是大西南地区特有的一种交通运输方式，也是茶马古道主要的运载手段。马帮分专业帮和拼伙帮，专业帮多指单独的私家长期经营的马帮，拼伙帮由两个以上不大的马帮合伙组成，短期经营。最小的马帮有十几匹马，大的马帮有百匹马以上。马帮行动灵活、方便，驮运里程可近可远，适宜在崎岖不平的山路运输，旧时常见于云南、贵州等地。马帮约始于东晋时期，发展到清代，已形成滇东、滇西、滇南三条马帮运输干线，成为云南地区的主要运输方式，促进了云南经济贸易的发展。后随着交通运输条件的改善，马帮逐渐消失。

or more small caravan partners. The smallest caravan could consist of a dozen horses, while larger ones could have well over a hundred. Caravans were flexible and convenient, able to provide both short-range and long-range services, suitable for traversing rugged mountain roads, and very popular in Yunnan and Guizhou provinces in ancient times. Caravans started operating during the Eastern Jin Dynasty (317-420). During the Qing Dynasty (1616-1911), they operated the three transport routes of east, west, and south Yunnan and were the main means of transport in the province, promoting economic and trade. With better transportation conditions today, caravans have gradually disappeared.

例句：

近代云南**马帮**兴起，解决了普洱茶外运的问题。

Example Sentence:

The caravan in Yunnan Province in modern history made it much easier to transport Pu'er tea.

madui;
caravan; a train of horses carrying goods

参见“马帮”。

See *mabang* (caravan).

廊桥 *lang qiao;* covered bridge; roofed bridge

一种有顶的长廊式桥梁，又称“虹桥”，在浙江南部及福建北部较为常见。廊桥均为木石结构，坚固耐久。因其有顶而可供行人遮风避雨、纳凉、休憩乃至交流聚会。

Covered bridges mostly found in southern Zhejiang and northern Fujian provinces, also called rainbow bridges. Such bridges are usually made of wood and (or) stone, making them sturdy and durable. The roof makes the bridge an ideal place to shade from the hot summer sun, take some rest or even meet friends.

例句:

有的**廊桥**有供人暂居的房间。

Example Sentence:

Some roofed bridges have rooms for temporary lodging.

虹桥 *hong qiao;* rainbow bridge; covered bridge

参见“廊桥”。

See *lang qiao* (covered bridge).

风雨桥 *fengyu qiao;* wind-and-rain-proof bridge

中国侗族地区特有的一种廊桥，因可遮风避雨而得名"风雨桥"。其显著特点为桥梁的整体结构除青石垒砌的桥墩外，桥梁、桥柱及桥面建筑全用杉木凿榫衔接，不用一钉。

A type of covered bridge unique to China's Dong ethnic group. It gained its name because it could shelter travelers from wind and rain. Except for the stone piers, the bridge is built of fir timber without a single nail, using mortise-and-tenon joints.

例句：

过去，**风雨桥**上还设有神台祭坛，人们可在祭坛上祈求神灵保佑。

Example Sentence:

In the past, there were altars in the pavilions of some wind-and-rain-proof bridges where people would pray for protection and blessings from gods and spirits.

信仰崇拜
BELIEFS
AND WORSHIP

天公 *Tiangong;* Lord of Heaven; Emperor of Heaven

中国民间信仰中主宰自然界的最高神，俗称“老天爷”。祭拜苍天的礼仪在中国源远流长。周朝时天被神化，称为“天公”，统御天、地、人三界，代表至高无上的权力和天道公平。随着道教的兴盛，道教的主神玉皇大帝逐渐与天公融合，被称作天帝。民间认为农历正月初九是天公的生日，由衍生出了多种相关民俗活动，最为典型的是福建人大年初九举行的拜天公仪式（行祭拜礼、上香膜拜、敬献供品等），表达了人们祛邪避灾、迎祥纳福的美好愿望。现如今“天公”一词也可引申为命运。

The supreme deity who dominates the natural world according to Chinese folk beliefs, also called *Laotianye*. Worshipping Heaven has a long history in China. During the Zhou Dynasty (1046–256 BC), the Heaven was deified as Tiangong (Lord of Heaven). *Tiangong* is the sovereign ruler of heaven, the secular world, and the underworld, representing supreme power and justice. Along with the rise of Daoism, images of *Tiangong* and the Jade Emperor (the supreme deity of Daoism) were gradually merged into the image of the Emperor of Heaven. It is believed that the ninth day of the first lunar month is the birthday of *Tiangong*. There are many folk activities during this time, such as ceremonies worshipping *Tiangong* held in Fujian Province. Rituals include prostrating, burning incense, and offering sacrificial food with the intention to bring good fortune and avert calamities. Nowadays, the term *Tiangong* can also be used to indicate an unpredictable fate.

例句：

民间将**天公**奉为正义的化身顶礼膜拜，但当人们遭遇不公或冤屈时也会抱怨老天爷“不开眼”，以此表达自己失望、愤怒的情绪。

Example Sentence:

Tiangong (Lord of Heaven) is worshipped as the embodiment of justice, but it is also blamed for being “blind” when one is unfairly treated or done wrong as a way of expressing his/her disappointment and anger.

老天爷 *Laotianye;* the Lord

参见“天公”。

See *Tiangong* (Lord of Heaven).

后土娘娘 *Houtu Niangniang;* Goddess of the Earth; Mother Earth

中国道教中司掌土地的神祇，又称“大地之母”。后土信仰源于中国古代对土地的崇拜，认为后土掌管阴阳，孕育万物，主宰大地山川。古人以天为阳，地为阴，后土形象经历了由男性神到女性神的转变。汉代时将土地祭祀列入皇朝祀典，汉武帝专门建立后土祠亲自祭祀，此后帝王代代沿袭。后土娘娘同时还作为生育之神和丰收之神广受人们尊敬与崇拜。

The Daoist Goddess of the Earth, also called Dadi Zhimu (Mother Earth). She is in charge of yin and yang, gives birth to all things, and governs mountains and rivers. She originated from the worship of the earth in ancient China. Her image changed from a male god to a female goddess as ancient Chinese came to consider heaven as the embodiment of yang (male) and the earth of yin (female). During the Han Dynasty (206 BC-AD 220), sacrifices to Mother Earth were included in royal ceremonies. Emperor Wudi of the Han Dynasty had special Houtu temples built to worship Mother Earth, and emperors throughout the ages continued these ceremonies. Meanwhile, Houtu Niangniang is also widely revered and worshipped as the goddess of birth and good harvest.

例句：

中国民间常将**后土娘娘**与玉皇大帝合称“天公地母”。

Example Sentence:

Mother Earth and the Jade Emperor are often known collectively as “*Tiangong Dimu*” (Lord of Heaven and Mother Earth).

大地之母 *Dadi Zhimu;* Mother Earth

参见“后土娘娘”。

See *Houtu Niangniang* (Goddess of the Earth).

玉皇大帝 *Yuhuang Dadi;* Jade Emperor

中国道教信奉的天神，四御（四大天帝）之首，简称玉皇、玉帝。玉皇的信仰在唐代逐渐流行，北宋真宗、徽宗又相继加封尊号，将中国古代历朝帝王的"昊天上帝"崇拜与"玉皇大帝"合为一体，玉皇信仰因此大盛，民间流传犹广。玉皇大帝成为总执天道之神，在道教众神中地位最高。他除了统领所有的天神外，还管理宇宙万物的兴隆衰败。

The supreme deity in Chinese Daoism and head of the Four Celestial Sovereigns, also called *Yuhuang* and *Yudi* in short. Belief in the Jade Emperor gradually spread during the Tang Dynasty (618-907), and this mythical emperor was given honorific titles by Emperor Zhenzong and Emperor Huizong of the Northern Song Dynasty (960-1127). Thereafter, the Clear Sky Emperor worshipped by Chinese emperors of past dynasties merged with the Jade Emperor to be the one and only emperor in heaven, and belief in the Jade Emperor flourished among common people. Daoists believed the Jade Emperor to be the god in charge of the heavenly realm and was therefore deemed the most important of all the gods. In addition to commanding all the gods, the Jade Emperor is in charge of the rise and fall of all things in the universe.

例句：

中国古人认为**玉皇大帝**是神圣且万能的，在生活中无论遇到任何事都会求玉皇大帝保佑。

Example Sentence:

Ancient Chinese people believed that the Jade Emperor was a divine, omnipotent being and would pray to the Jade Emperor for blessings and protection.

玉皇 *Yuhuang;* Jade Emperor

参见"玉皇大帝"。

See *Yuhuang Dadi* (Jade Emperor).

玉帝 *Yudi;* Jade Emperor

参见"玉皇大帝"。

See *Yuhuang Dadi* (Jade Emperor).

西王母 *Xi Wangmu;* Queen Mother of the West

中国古代广泛流传的神话人物，天界所有女神的领袖，天宫里地位最高的女神，又称“王母”“王母娘娘”。据说西王母掌管的蟠桃园里种有三千年一熟的桃子，吃后能使人长生不老；西王母过生日的时候会举办蟠桃盛会，用仙桃宴请群仙。在嫦娥奔月神话中，嫦娥吞下的长生不老仙丹就是后羿从西王母处请来的。这些神话故事的广泛传播使西王母的神性进一步扩大，在民间她被视为长寿和平安之神，掌管婚姻、送子之神，影响广泛。

Popular mythical figure in ancient China who was considered the leader of all the female gods in the heavenly realm and the highest ranking goddess in heaven. This figure is also known as the "*Wangmu* (Queen Mother)" and the "*Wangmu Niangniang* (Queen Mother Goddess)." It is said that the Queen Mother of the West is in charge of a peach orchard where peaches ripen once every 3,000 years and grant immortality. During her birthday, the Queen Mother of the West holds immortality peach banquets, wherein groups of celestials dine on her peaches. In the legend of Chang'e running to the moon, the immortality elixir that Chang'e takes was obtained by her husband Houyi from the Queen Mother. These widely spread mythical stories consolidated the status of the Queen Mother as a divine being. In Chinese folk beliefs, she became not only the goddess to whom one prays for longevity and peace, but also the goddess in charge of marriage and childbirth.

例句：

《山海经》中记载的**西王母**是一个居住在洞穴里的半人半兽凶神，带有野蛮时代的氏族神特点。

Example Sentence:

In the famous Chinese book *The Classic of Mountains and Seas*, the Queen Mother of the West is portrayed as a half-human, half-beast demon that lives in a cave, typical of primitive tribal spirits from ancient times.

王母 *Wangmu;* Queen Mother

参见“西王母”。

See *Xi Wangmu* (Queen Mother of the West).

王母娘娘 *Wangmu Niangniang;* Queen Mother Goddess

参见“西王母”。

See *Xi Wangmu* (Queen Mother of the West).

星相学 *xingxiang xue;* astrology; horoscope

通过观测星体的大小、明暗、位置移动等来预测人世间各种事物的一种方术，又称占星术。星相学来源于古代的星辰崇拜。古时候人们无法破解星辰的自然属性，便将其神化并赋以神秘力量加以崇拜，认为天体，尤其是行星和星座，都以某种因果性或非偶然性的方式预示人间万物的变化。早期占星术多用来占卜国家大事如战争胜负、社会动乱，后来逐渐扩展到预测个人命运及生活琐事。

Chinese astrology: the technique of observing the size, brightness, movement and other features of the stars for divination and predictions. Stars were deified with mysterious powers and worshipped by ancient Chinese who did not understand the law of their movements and thus believed that the celestial objects—especially the planets and constellations—appear in the sky in certain ways that would foretell events on earth in a predictable manner. Ancient

Chinese used astrology to predict important state affairs such as the outcomes of wars and periods of social unrest. Later, astrology was also used to tell personal fortunes and trivial matters.

例句：

古时候**星相学**认为星辰的陨落代表人间生命的消亡。

Example Sentence:

Ancient astrological theories believe that the falling of a star implies the death of a person.

扫帚星

saozhou xing;
broom star; comet; jinx

中国古代民间对彗星的俗称，因其形同扫帚而得名。古人缺乏对彗星的科学认识，认为它是不吉利的灾星，其出现会带来饥荒、瘟疫、战争等天灾人祸。传说中扫帚星的人物原型是神魔小说《封神演义》中姜子牙的妻子马氏，她因嫌贫爱富而背弃了姜子牙。

Ancient Chinese folk name for comets due to their likeness to brooms in terms of their shape. In ancient times, people regarded comets as evil omens and believed that comets would bring such natural calamities and man-made misfortunes as famine, plague, and war. In the novel *The Investiture of the Gods*, the character of Jiang Ziya (a famous chancellor of the Zhou Dynasty) granted his former wife the title of *saozhou xing* (broom star, which later came to mean "jinx") on account of her snobbishness and betrayal.

例句：

扫帚星现在主要是骂人的说法，指会带来灾难或厄运的人。

Example Sentence:

Nowadays, *saozhou xing* is an insulting expression used to blame people for causing misfortune or disaster.

兄弟参商

xiongdi shenshang;
animosity between two brothers; sibling rivalry

中国古代成语，比喻兄弟之间互动干戈，不和睦。这个成语源于一个神话故事。传说上古时期部落首领帝喾的两个儿子阏伯和实沈不和，为了缓和兄弟矛盾，帝喾派阏伯主祀辰星（即商星），住在东方；派实沈主祀参星，住在西方。参商二星此出则彼没，永不相见。

An ancient Chinese idiom used to describe animosity between brothers. It originates from a mythical story that tells of disharmony between Yan Bo and Shi Shen, the two sons of Emperor Ku (one of the legendary "Three Sovereigns and Five Emperors" in ancient Chinese folklore). Emperor Ku eases tensions by sending Yan Bo to govern the Shang Star (Antares) in the east and Shi Shen to govern the Shen Star (Orion) in the west. As one star disappears when the other appears, the two brothers would never come across each other.

例句：

中国历代文学作品中，**兄弟参商**的题材并不少见。

Example Sentence:

The *xiongdi shenshang* (animosity between brothers) theme has been quite common in Chinese literary works throughout the ages.

雷公 *Leigong;* Lord of Thunder

中国古代神话中主管打雷的神，又称“雷神”。雷神信仰起源于中国古人对雷电的自然崇拜。相传雷神生于古雷泽（故址在今山东菏泽），龙身人头，鼓其腹则雷。道教神话记载了不同级别的雷神，其中“普化天尊”级别最高。自春秋战国以来，雷公被赋予了代天行罚、惩恶扬善、主持正义的社会职能，民间传说做了坏事或违背誓言的人会遭雷击而死。雷神又是行雨之神，人们在求雨活动中常常祭祀雷公。中国民间把雷神生日定在农历六月二十四，这一天要举行祭祀仪式，寄托人们祛邪、避灾、祈福的美好愿望。

The deity in charge of thunder in Chinese folk mythology, also called *Leishen* (God of Thunder). Belief in the God of Thunder comes from the worship of the power of thunder and lightning practiced by ancient Chinese. Legend has it that the God of Thunder was born in ancient Leize (in present-day Heze, Shandong Province) and has a dragon's body, a human's head, and the ability to produce thunder by drumming on his belly. Daoist mythology actually records different levels of Gods of Thunder, and *Puhua Tianzun* was ranked at the top. Since the Spring and Autumn and Warring States periods (770-221 BC), the God of Thunder has become the representative of justice by inflicting strikes of lightning on those who behave poorly or fail to keep their promises. As he is also said to possess the power to incite rainfall, he is often worshipped while praying for rain. It is believed that the God of Thunder was born on the 24th day of the sixth month according to the lunar calendar. On this day people would offer sacrifice to him and pray for his blessings and protection from calamities and evil forces.

例句：

传说中，**雷公**用鼓和槌来打雷，以凿子来惩罚恶人。

Example Sentence:

According to mythology, the Lord of Thunder carries a drum and mallet to produce thunder and a chisel to punish evildoers.

雷神 *Leishen;* God of Thunder

参见“雷公”。

See *Leigong* (Lord of Thunder).

电母 *Dianmu;* Goddess of Lightning

中国古代神话中主管闪电的女神，又称“闪电娘娘”。电母常被认为是雷神的妻子，有“雷公电母”之称。传说电母为双手各拿一面镜子的女神，因雷公视力不好，他需要电母先用镜子照清世间善恶后再打雷，以避免误伤。据说雷公电母吵架时天上会雷电交加。从前人们还常在房顶塑雷公电母像，祈求防火防灾。雷公电母原来只是管理雷电，但是自先秦两汉起，民众就赋予雷电以惩恶扬善、伸张正义的意义。

The goddess in charge of lightning in Chinese folk mythology, also called *Shandian Niangniang* (Lady Lightning). She is known as the wife of the God of Thunder. She carries a pair of mirrors on her hands because the God of Thunder has poor vision and must first look at her mirrors before he casts a bolt of lightning. By doing this, he can differentiate between good and evil and avoid striking someone innocent. It is also said that thunder and lightning appears when the God of Thunder and the Goddess of Lightning quarrel. In ancient times, people often worshipped statues of the God of Thunder and the Goddess of Lightning, which they placed on their roofs to avert fires and disasters. Originally, the two deities only had the power to produce thunder and lightning, but since about 4,000 years ago, people began to believe they also possessed the power to punish the evil and uphold justice.

例句：

中国古代许多神魔小说中都出现了**电母**这一形象，如《西游记》。

Example Sentence:

The Goddess of Lightning is often seen in ancient Chinese mythology novels, such as *Journey to the West*.

闪电娘娘 *Shandian Niangniang;* Lady Lightning

参见“电母”。

See *Dianmu* (Goddess of Lightning).

风伯 *Fengbo;* God of Wind; Earl of Wind

中国古代神话中主管风的神，又称“风师”。传说中的风神形象不一，或为星宿或为飞禽，唐宋以后逐渐发展为人形。后世流传最广的是男性风神“风伯”，须发皆白，左手持轮，右手执扇，掌八风消息，通五运气候。风伯主要配合雨神和雷神调节气候、滋养万物生长。风伯形象常见于历代文字记载、口头传说及壁画等艺术作品中。

The deity in charge of wind in Chinese folk mythology, also called *Fengshi* (Master of Wind). The God of Wind's appearance varies according to different legends, depicted as either a star or a bird before the Tang (618-907) and Song (960-1279) dynasties, but afterwards began to take the shape of a person. The most common image of the Master of Wind is *Fengbo* (Earl of Wind), an old, white-haired man with a wheel in his left hand and a fan in his right hand. Keeping informed of the eight signs of wind and the five harbingers of climate, he assists the God of Rain and the God of Thunder with regulating the climate and nourishing things in the world. Images of the God of Wind have often appeared in historical books, oral traditions, and murals throughout the ages.

例句：

祭祀**风伯**的传统在秦汉时期已经被列入国家祀典。

Example Sentence:

Worshipping the God of Wind was listed as a national sacrificial rite as early as the Qin (221-206 BC) and Han (206 BC-AD 220) dynasties.

风师

Fengshi;
Master of Wind

参见“风伯”。

See *Fengbo* (God of Wind).

雨师

Yushi;
Master of Rain; God of Rain; Rain Spirit

中国古代神话中主管雨的神。关于雨师的中国神话传说最早来自对雨水的自然崇拜。雨水对古代农业社会至关重要，雨神便成为民间及官方最常祭拜的神灵之一。人们祭拜雨师以祈求风调雨顺，五谷丰登。关于雨神的形象众说纷纭，殷商时雨神是女神名“媚”，西周时称“雨师”，西汉之后，奉仙人赤松子为雨师。求雨祭神，一般用奏乐、歌舞的仪式，也有用柴燃烧供物的献祭。自秦汉以来，雨师主要被用于国家祀典，民间则普遍流行拜龙王求雨的习俗。

The deity in charge of rain in ancient Chinese mythology. The legend of the Master of Rain originated from the worship of rainwater. Because rainwater was of vital importance to ancient agricultural societies, the God of Rain became one of the most frequently worshipped gods by both the general public and officials who prayed to the God of Rain for favorable weather and a good harvest. Visual depictions of the God of Rain have been numerous, depicted as the Goddess Mei during the Shang Dynasty (1600-1046 BC), the Master of Rain during the Western Zhou Dynasty (1046-771 BC) and the immortal Chisongzi during the Western Han Dynasty (206 BC-AD 25). People worshipped the God of Rain by playing music, singing, dancing, and burning sacrificial offerings to pray for rain. Beginning in the Qin (221-

206 BC) and Han dynasties (206 BC-AD 220), worship of the God of Rain was a sacrifice carried out by the state, while the general public worshipped Longwang (the Dragon King) to pray for rain.

例句：

据传说，**雨师**和风伯在蚩尤与黄帝的大战中曾帮过蚩尤，但没能成功。

Example Sentence:

It was said that the Master of Rain and the God of Wind joined Chiyou in his fight against the Yellow Emperor, but were defeated.

海神 *Haishen;* Sea God

中国古代神话中掌管海事的神。海神崇拜源于人们对大海的神秘力量的敬畏与恐惧，试

The deity in charge of the sea in ancient Chinese mythology. The worship of the Sea God stems from people's awe and fear of the vast sea, which they believed to have mystical powers and for which they sought spiritual support. Belief in the Sea God in China has evolved over time. Initially, the Sea God was depicted with a human face with a bird's body, but this notion changed with the development of the Sea God of the Four Seas, the Sea Dragon King, Mazu, and other incarnations of the god. In ancient times, people believed that immortals resided in the sea. Since the Song and Yuan dynasties

图由此寻求精神庇护。中国的海神信仰大致经历了从人面鸟身的早期海神到四海海神、海龙王、妈祖、地方海神和专业海神的发展演化。古时候人们常认为海洋为神仙居所，宋元以来，随着海运及海上贸易的繁荣发展，官方及民间都会举行日益隆重的海神祭祀仪式，以祈求航行平安。

(960-1368), along with the development of sea transportation and marine trade, officials and the general public began holding grand sacrificial ceremonies for the Sea God, praying for safe navigation.

例句：

妈祖是中国民间信仰中著名的**海神**之一，流行于中国东南沿海地区。

Example Sentence:

Mazu is a famous sea goddess in Chinese folk beliefs, popular in coastal areas of southeastern China.

河伯

Hebo;
River God; Earl of the Yellow River

中国古代神话中的黄河水神，原名冯夷。传说他过河时被淹死，之后便被天帝任命为河伯管理河川。传说中的河伯鱼尾人身，头发是银白色的，眼睛和鳞片是流光溢彩的琉璃色。由于黄河经常泛滥，人们对河伯充满敬畏，将其奉为神灵进行祭祀，以祈求远离水患，风调雨顺。祭祀河伯主要用“沉”和“浮”，即将牛羊等祭品沉入河底或

The deity in charge of the Yellow River in Chinese mythology, whose human name was Feng Yi. Legend has it that Feng Yi drowned when he was fording the Yellow River. The Emperor of Heaven took pity on him and appointed him Hebo (Earl of the River). The River God was said to have a human body with a fish tail, silvery white hair, and glittering eyes and fish scales. Fearful of the frequent floods of the Yellow River, people revered Hebo and deified him. They prayed to him for favorable weather and to

漂浮于水上。殷商时期盛行人祭，后来演变成将少女沉入河中给河伯做妻子，“河伯娶妻”的传说在民间广为流传。

avert floods. People drowned cows and sheep in the river as sacrifices to the River God. During the Shang Dynasty (1600-1046 BC), human sacrifices became prevalent, leading to the widespread story of “Hebo’s Bride” which tells of a bride drifting down the river on a raft as an offering to the River God and how a wise local governor puts an end to the practice.

例句：

作为黄河的化身，**河伯**一方面代表善良仁慈，另一方面又象征着贪婪、多变及危险。

Example Sentence:

As the embodiment of the Yellow River, Hebo, the River God, symbolizes benevolence and kindness as well as greed, unpredictability, and danger.

Shanshen; Mountain God

中国民间原始信仰中掌管某个山岳的神。中国是一个多山的国家，山神崇拜自古以来便较为盛行，敬奉“五岳”（东岳泰山、西岳华山、南岳衡山，北岳恒山，中岳嵩山）的习俗由来已久。历代君王封禅祭天地时都会大祭山神，祈求神明护佑，国泰民安。祭山时大多用玉石和玉器埋于地下，也有用“投”和“悬”的祭法，即

The deity in charge of various mountains in Chinese folk beliefs. Because of China’s many mountains, worshipping mountain gods has been a long-standing tradition in China ever since ancient times. The Five Great Mountains are: East Great Mountain (Taishan Mountain in Shandong Province), West Great Mountain (Huashan Mountain in Shaanxi Province), South Great Mountain (Hengshan Mountain in Hunan Province),

将祭品鸡、羊、猪或玉石投入山谷或悬在树梢。民间求拜山神既为祈福禳灾、祛病驱邪，求长生长寿，又为祈求风调雨顺，丰衣足食。

North Great Mountain (Hengshan Mountain in Shanxi Province) and Center Great Mountain (Songshan Mountain in Henan Province). These mountains have been famous ritual sites for imperial worship and sacrifice. Throughout history, almost all emperors would hold grand sacrificial ceremonies to worship the Mountain God when worshipping Heaven and Earth, so as to pray for peace and prosperity of the country and its people. Sacrifices to the Mountain God mainly consisted of burying jade in the ground or throwing sacrificial offerings such as chicken, sheep, pigs, or jade into valleys or hanging them from trees. People believed that praying to the Mountain God could bring great fortune, good health, longevity, favorable weather, and a prosperous life.

例句：

在中国民间信仰中，每座山不论大小都有**山神**。

Example Sentence:

According to Chinese folk beliefs, each mountain—large or small—has its god.

东岳大帝 *Dongyue Dadi;* Emperor of the East Great Mountain; God of Taishan Mountain

中国民间信仰中最有名的山神，又称“泰山神”。东岳泰山是五岳之首，群山之祖，古人认为这里是太阳升起的地方，也是万物发祥之地，还是人与天相通的神地所在，对泰山特别崇拜敬畏，因此尊泰山之神为“东岳大帝”，执掌人间赏罚和生死大事。历代帝王对泰山尊崇有加，许多皇帝曾到泰山封禅，祭告天地，祈求国泰民安。每年农历三月二十八为东岳大帝圣诞，各地东岳庙纷纷开庙祭奉东岳大帝，以求延年益寿，富贵荣华，子孙繁荣，并由此形成了一系列相关的民俗活动，在民间广受欢迎且流传至今。

The deity in charge of the Taishan Mountain in Shandong Province. Also called *Taishan Shen* (God of Taishan Mountain), it is the most famous Mountain God in Chinese folk beliefs. Taishan Mountain is regarded as the most sacred of the Five Great Mountains as well as the ancestor of all mountains. It is regarded by ancient Chinese as the place where the sun rises, the birthplace of all things, and the connection between Heaven and the mortal world. The deity was thus revered and respected as the Emperor of the East Great Mountain who controls worldly rewards and punishments as well as life and death. Many ancient emperors offered sacrifices to Heaven and Earth on Taishan Mountain to pray for peace and prosperity of the state. A series of special folk activities take place on the twenty-eighth day of the third lunar month every year at Dongyue temples all over the country to celebrate the birthday of the God of Taishan Mountain. This event has remained widely popular up to the present day. It is believed that worshipping the god can bring longevity, great fortune, and family prosperity.

例句：

岱庙是**东岳大帝**之庙，是中国各地东岳庙的祖庙，也是古代举行祭祀大典的地方。

Example Sentence:

Daimiao Temple, a temple for the Emperor of the East Great Mountain located in Shandong Province, is the ancestral temple of all Dongyue temples in China and the place where ancient sacrificial ceremonies were held.

泰山神 *Taishan Shen;* God of Taishan Mountain

参见“东岳大帝”。

See *Dongyue Dadi* (Emperor of the East Great Mountain).

碧霞元君 *Bixia Yuanjun;* Goddess of Taishan Mountain

A Daoist goddess in charge of fertility and childbirth in China, also called *Taishan Niangniang* (Lady Taishan) and *Taishan Laomu* (Mother Taishan). She is one of the most influential goddesses in Chinese history, though opinions differ concerning her origin. According to some legends, she is the daughter of the Emperor of East Great Mountain. The magnificent Bixia Yuanjun Temple still stands on the top of Taishan Mountain today. It is said that the birthday of the goddess falls on the eighteenth day of the fourth lunar month. On this day, those

中国道教信奉的生育、送子女神，又称“泰山娘娘”“泰山老母”。作为中国历史上影响最大的女神之一，其来历众说纷纭，民间流传最广的说法是她为泰山神之女，至今泰山顶上仍保存有规模宏大的碧霞元君祠。传说农历四月十八是碧霞元君的生日，在此日前往碧霞元君祠烧香可祈福祛灾，护佑儿童。也有传说认为碧霞元君信仰始于宋真宗封禅泰山时发现的玉女石像，此后，其司职范围不断扩大。至明清时期，碧霞元君在民间的影响已大大超过了泰山主神东岳大帝，即其父亲。碧霞元君在人们心目中更为神通广大，能保佑农耕、经商、旅行、婚姻，能治病救人，尤其能使妇女生子，儿童无恙。

who come to the Bixia Yuanjun Temple burn joss sticks and pray for blessings for their children. Another legend has it that the belief in *Bixia Yuanjun* stems from a stone statue of a maiden discovered by Emperor Zhenzong of the Song Dynasty (960-1279) when he offered sacrifices to Heaven and Earth on Taishan Mountain. During the Ming and Qing dynasties, the goddess gained greater popularity than her father—the Emperor of East Great Mountain. People believe that she has omnipotent powers and can bring blessings to farming, business, travel, marriage and health in addition to delivering babies to women and safeguarding children.

例句：

民间传说中，**碧霞元君**有求必应，护佑众生，尤其护佑妇女和儿童。

Example Sentence:

In Chinese folk mythology, the Goddess of Taishan Mountain grants whatever is requested and blesses all living creatures, especially women and children.

泰山娘娘 *Taishan Niangniang;* Lady Taishan

参见“碧霞元君”。

See Bixia Yuanjun (Goddess of Taishan Mountain).

泰山老母 *Taishan Laomu;* Mother Taishan

参见“碧霞元君”。

See Bixia Yuanjun (Goddess of Taishan Mountain).

社林 *shelin;* woods around land god temples

中国乡村土地庙四周的树林，古代为祭祀场所。在先民的原始自然崇拜中，因林木具有同山川相似的神性而成为人们祭祀的对象，并把它们当作有灵的神来崇拜。上古不论天子、诸侯、大夫、百姓，必各自立社以奉神，社的标志即是社树，社林。作为土地神的象征，社林在上古社会中具有崇高的地位。

The woods surrounding land god temples in the countryside, which serve as sacrificial sites in ancient China. According to this primitive form of nature worship, forests also possess divine quality similar to mountains and rivers, and could thus be deified and worshipped as gods. In ancient times, people of all social classes would set up their respective *she* (land god temples) for worship which were typically surrounded by trees. As the symbol of the local Land God, *shelin* was highly revered in ancient Chinese society.

例句：

“社”在先秦时指土地神，也指祭祀土地神的的场所。**社林**指社庙周边的丛林。

Example Sentence:

She refers to the Land God or the sacrificial site where the Land God was worshipped before the Qin Dynasty China. *Shelin* (*lin* means woods in Chinese) refers to the woods around the land god temple.

十二花神 *Shi'er Huashen;* the twelve flower goddesses

中国民间信仰中司花的神，每一种花都有花神。十二花神是根据岁时花信的自然规律，按每年十二个月冠以花名而形成的。常见的说法为：一月梅花神、二月杏花神、三月桃花神、四月牡丹花神、五月石榴花神、六月莲花神、七月玉簪花神、八月桂花神、九月菊花神、十月兰花神、十一月山茶花神、十二月水仙花神。十二花神多由中国历史上出名的美人担任，如二月花神杨玉环、六月花神西施、十月花神貂蝉、十一月花神王昭君等。花神节一般于农历二月初二、二月十二或二月十五举行。节日期间，人们结伴到郊外游览赏花，称为踏青；姑娘们剪五色彩纸粘在花枝上，称为赏红。花神题材较常见于戏曲、瓷器等艺术创作中。

Nature deities in charge of flowers in Chinese folk beliefs. There is a flower goddess for every flower. The twelve flower goddesses of the twelve months correspond with the blossoms in each month of the year, namely, the Plum Blossom Goddess in January, Apricot Blossom Goddess in February, Peach Blossom Goddess in March, Peony Goddess in April, Pomegranate Flower Goddess in May, Lotus Goddess in June, Hosta Goddess in July, Osmanthus Goddess in August, Chrysanthemum Goddess in September, Orchid Goddess in October, Camellia Goddess in November, and Narcissus Goddess in December. The flower goddesses are usually represented by famous beauties in Chinese history, such as Yang Yuhuan, Xi Shi, Diao Chan, Wang Zhaojun and others. The Flower Festival falls on the second, twelfth or fifteenth day of the second lunar month. During the festival, people often go to the countryside to see the beautiful flowers, which is called outing; while girls put colorful papers onto flowering branches, which is called appreciating colors. The flower goddesses are often depicted in Chinese operas, on porcelain, and in other artistic creations.

例句:

中国著名戏曲《牡丹亭》对**十二花神**进行了生动的描述。

Example Sentence:

The twelve flower goddesses of the twelve months are depicted vividly in *The Peony Pavilion*, a famous Kunqu Opera.

岁寒三友

suihan sanyou;
three companions of winter; three cold weather friends

中国文人对松、竹、梅三种植物的雅称。松、竹经冬不凋，梅凌寒绽放，故称"岁寒三友"。这三种植物常作为吉祥图案在国画、年画、剪纸、刺绣、文具、建筑装饰等艺术作品中出现。历代文人墨客多借物咏志，以岁寒三友象征冰清玉洁、坚贞不屈的君子品格，至今仍为人们所喜爱。

The term given by Chinese intellectuals for pine trees, bamboo, and plums. These three plants do not wither when winter arrives, so they have been collectively called the "three cold weather friends." This theme is frequently seen in Chinese artwork, such as New Year paintings, paper-cutting, embroidery, stationery, and architectural decorations. Throughout the ages, men of letters have used the "three companions of winter" metaphorically to refer to men of moral integrity who are noble, tenacious, and resilient.

例句:

岁寒三友常被用来喻指忠贞不渝的友谊，寄托对于孤傲高洁人格的崇尚和向往。

Example Sentence:

Suihan sanyou (three companions of winter) is often used to refer to loyal and strong friendship and also represents the fine qualities of high-mindedness and proud aloofness.

梧桐栖凤

wutong qifeng;
a phoenix selects Chinese parasol tree to perch in; a talented person chooses a patron of integrity

源于中国古老的民间传说的一句习语，意思是作为百鸟之王的凤凰非梧桐不栖。凤凰是中国传说中的神鸟，其形象为鸡头、蛇颈、燕颔、龟背、五彩色，集诸多动物为一身，因“凤凰涅槃”的神话传说而被视为吉祥和永生的象征。梧桐是树中之王，被看作“灵树”，具有应验时事、知时知令之能，传说梧桐的灵性能引来凤凰。凤凰择木而栖，后比喻贤才择主而侍。

A proverb derived from a Chinese ancient folk tale, meaning the king of birds rest only in the king of trees. The phoenix is a mythological bird believed to reign over all other birds, and can obtain new life by rising from the ashes of its former life. It is a five-colored animal with the head of a chicken, the neck of a snake, the chin of a swallow, and the back of a tortoise. It symbolizes immortality and auspiciousness. The Chinese parasol tree is regarded as the king of trees, as well as a “holy tree” which provides prophesies and signals the turning of seasons. Because of this, the folk tale says that a Chinese parasol tree is the best choice for a phoenix to perch in. Later, the phrase has come to be interpreted as “a prudent bird chooses the right tree to nestle in as a wise man selects the correct leader to follow.”

例句：

民间传说“**梧桐栖凤**”，如今亦指“良禽择木而栖”。

Example Sentence:

The folk tale *wutong qifeng* tells of the phoenix perching in a Chinese parasol tree. It is now used as a metaphor to mean “a wise bird selects the right tree to perch in.”

四灵崇拜 *siling chongbai; worship of the four spirit animals*

中国民间信仰中对四种祥兽的崇拜。四灵是指龙、凤凰、麒麟、龟。前三灵都为想象中的神秘动物，龟则因为长寿，被人们认为能知人情、知吉凶而受到崇拜。四灵的出现被认为是祥瑞的先兆。

Four spirit animals worshipped by Chinese people in ancient times. In ancient China, the dragon, phoenix, *qilin*, and tortoise were regarded as the four most revered animals. The first three are imaginary, while the tortoise was revered because of its ability to live a very long life and was thus considered capable of understanding human feelings and foreseeing good or bad luck. The appearance of these four revered animals in Chinese folklore was always regarded as an auspicious event.

例句：

四灵崇拜反应了人们对自然界的敬畏及对于美好生活的向往。

Example Sentence:

Ancient Chinese worshipped the four spirit animals, which reflected their awe of nature and their yearning for a better life.

龙 *long;* dragon

中国古代传说中的灵兽，与凤凰、龟、麒麟合称为四灵。据说黄帝统一中原后从各部落图腾中各取一部分组成了一个新的动物形象，取名为"龙"，龙成为中原地区各部落统一的图腾，因而近代中国人自称是"龙的传人"。龙的形象是多种动物的混合：蛇身，有鳞、角、足和爪，有的还有翼，能在水中游、天上飞，并能呼风唤雨，被尊为"龙神""龙王"。汉代以来，封建帝王自称"真龙天子"，于是与帝王有关的事物均冠以"龙"字。中国大

Ancient Chinese mythical spirit animal. It is one of the four spirit animals, along with the phoenix, tortoise, and *qilin*. It is said that after the Yellow Emperor unified the Central Plains, elements from every tribe's totems were adopted to form a new animal image, which was called a "dragon." This became the unified totem of all the tribes in the Central Plains. As a result, modern Chinese people call themselves the "descendants of the dragon." The image of the dragon is a mixture of multiple animals: it has the body of a snake with scales, horns, feet, talons, and some dragons even have wings. It swims in water, flies in the sky, and can summon wind and rain. It has been honored as the "dragon spirit" and "dragon king." Ever since the Han Dynasty (206 BC-AD 220), each feudal ruler proclaimed himself the "son of Heaven and reincarnation of the Divine Dragon." As a result, objects related to the emperor often include some form of the character "dragon." The majority of Chinese ethnic groups worship the dragon, and events and folklore related to the dragon abound, forming a culture that has lasted for over a millennium.

多数民族都崇拜龙，与龙有关的民俗活动和神话传说丰富多彩，形成了延续千年的龙文化。今天，龙已经成为中华民族的象征。

Today, the dragon is a symbol of the Chinese nation.

例句：

在中国古代，与**龙**相关的符号、图案等为皇家垄断专用，只有帝王才能使用。

Example Sentence:

In ancient China, symbols and designs related to dragons were exclusive only to the royal family, and only the emperor could use them.

麒麟 *qilin;* kylin

中国古代传说中的灵兽、神兽，与龙、凤凰、龟合称为四灵。雄为麒，雌为麟，形状为麇身、牛尾、狼蹄、独角，全身有鳞角，口能吐火，声音如雷。传说中麒麟虽然形象威武却有仁爱之心，行走中不踩踏虫、

Ancient mythical Chinese spirit animal. It is considered one of the four spirit animals, along with the dragon, phoenix, and tortoise. Its male version is called a *qi*, and its female version is called a *lin*. It has the body of a moose, tail of an ox, hooves of a wolf, a single horn, and is covered with scales. It can spit fire and its voice is like thunder. According to legend, although *qilin* is mighty in appearance, it has a benevolent heart. When walking, it will not step on insects or grass, and as a result it is considered a benevolent animal. People believe that the appearance of a *qilin* can bring good fortune, prosperity, and longevity. It is said that one day before Confucius

草，因此被视为一种仁兽，人们认为麒麟出现能带给人类福禄、丰年和长寿。据称孔子出生前一日即有麒麟出现，因此民间自古将麒麟当作贤明君主、杰出将帅的象征，并延伸出麒麟送子的信仰。麒麟信仰主要流行于中国汉族、纳西族等民族聚居地区，以及汉文化圈的日本等国。

was born, a *qilin* appeared. As a result, since time immemorial people have considered the *qilin* to be a symbol of sagacious rulers and outstanding leaders. This notion has even been extended to the belief that *qilins* can bless people with baby boys. Belief in *qilins* is primarily popular in regions inhabited by Han and Naxi ethnic groups in China, as well as other countries influenced by Han culture, such as Japan.

例句：

麒麟图案常用于服装配饰，也常出现在中国建筑装饰图案中。

Example Sentence:

Qilin designs are frequently used on clothes and ornaments, and they also often appear in patterns on buildings.

凤凰

fenghuang;
phoenix

Multicolored mythical bird from Chinese antiquity. It is considered one of the four spirit animals along with the dragon, tortoise, and *qilin*, and is revered as the ruler of all birds. The phoenix is an amalgamation of the characteristics of many different kinds of birds and animals. It has a rooster's head, snake's neck, swallow's chin, and tortoise's back. It is a symbol of luck and harmony, and an important component of Chinese culture.

中国古代传说中的五彩神鸟，与龙、龟、麒麟合称四灵，又称“丹凤”，被誉为百鸟之王。凤凰集多种鸟禽形象特征于一身：鸡头、蛇颈、燕蛉、龟背，象征吉祥和谐，是中国文化的重要元素。中国古人认为，每逢太平盛世就有凤凰飞来，象征天下太平，大吉大利。龙与凤在古代常并称，并与王权相关联：龙标志帝王，凤标志帝后。凤凰图案出现在中国衣食住行各个方面，穿戴的凤冠、凤鞋，住的凤楼，出行的凤辇等。

Ancient Chinese people believed that whenever a phoenix takes to the sky, people would enjoy a period of peace and prosperity. In ancient times, the dragon and phoenix were often jointly mentioned and associated with imperial power where the dragon symbolized the ruler and the phoenix indicated the empress. Phoenix designs appear in all aspects of Chinese life, such as a "phoenix hat" and "phoenix shoes." People might live in a "phoenix building" and travel in a "phoenix carriage."

例句：

凤凰本来是一对神鸟，雄的叫“凤”，雌的叫“凰”，后来被雌性化，与龙并列作为帝后的象征。

Example Sentence:

The phoenix (*fenghuang*) is a mythological bird. Originally the term referred to both sexes, with the male phoenix called a *feng* and the female called a *huang*. The animal was later feminized and made to stand beside the dragon, and was deemed a symbol of the empress.

丹凤 *danfeng;* phoenix

参见“凤凰”。

See *fenghuang* (phoenix).

龟 *gui;* tortoise

一种爬行动物，因长寿而成为中国文化中的瑞兽，并与凤凰、麒麟、龙合称“四灵”。古代帝王的皇宫、宅院和陵墓里常有石雕或铜铸的神龟，象征“万古长存”。古人认为龟背的纹理蕴藏天意，因此常用龟甲占卜来判断人事吉凶，因此，龟被称为“神龟”“灵龟”；占卜的结果记录在龟甲和兽骨上，成为中国最古老的文字“甲骨文”。

One of the four spirit animals of China along with the phoenix, *qilin*, and dragon because it lives for a very long time. In ancient imperial palaces, residences, and tombs there are often stone or copper statues of mythical tortoises, symbolizing they will “exist forever.” Ancient people believed the patterns on a tortoise's shell contained celestial meanings; consequently, tortoise shells were often used in divination to determine human affairs. This led to the tortoise being known as the “divine tortoise” or “spirit tortoise.” The result of divination was usually carved into tortoise shells or animal bones, leading to the Chinese language's oldest form of script—the oracle bone script.

例句：

中国民间传说中，**龟**是一种忠厚善良的动物，象征坚毅不朽。

Example Sentence:

In Chinese folk legends, the tortoise is an honest and kind-hearted animal that symbolizes perseverance and immortality.

wu da xian;
the five great fairy animals

旧时中国汉族民间对五种动物的合称，一般指狐狸、黄鼠狼、刺猬、蛇、老鼠，认为它们有灵性。北方民间也将前四种动物合称“四大门”；一些地方将虎、鳖、兔等凑成另五大仙。民间认为五大仙属亦妖亦仙的灵异，侵犯它们的人会受到其不同程度的惩罚，供奉它们则会得到其庇佑。民间对狐仙（狐狸）、黄仙（黄鼠狼）和白仙（刺猬）尤为敬畏，有人专设密室为五大仙绘图像或立牌位，夜深人静之时跪敬礼拜奉祀。现在对五大仙的信仰已基本消亡。

The term used by the Han people to refer to five intelligent animals, which usually refer to the fox, yellow weasel, hedgehog, snake, and mouse. The first four animals are also collectively called “the four great fairy animals” (*si da men*) in northern China. In some localities, the “five great fairy animals” are a tiger, a turtle, a rabbit, and others. People believed that these fairies punished those who displeased them and blessed those who worshipped them. Among the five, the fox, yellow weasel, and hedgehog were most widely revered. People used to place portraits or tablets of these animals in a special room and offered sacrifices and kowtowed before them late in the night. Belief in the five great fairy animals has since greatly diminished.

例句：

古人认为，家道生业盛衰、个人命运凶吉全系于这**五大仙**的意志。

Example Sentence:

Ancient Chinese believed that the rise and fall of a family and the fate of an individual were at the mercy of the five great fairy animals.

狐仙 *huxian;* fox fairy; fox spirit

中国民间传说中修炼成仙的狐狸，为五大仙之一。民间认为狐狸有灵性，能修炼成精，幻化成人，通晓世事，并能给人带来福气或灾难。五千多年前，中国民间就有大禹治水时曾娶九尾白狐为妻生下夏代第一位君主启的传说故事。崇信狐仙之俗在秦汉时就已形成。旧时一些地区专为狐神立庙供奉，祈求平安。

A fox which becomes a fairy through rigorous self-cultivation according to Chinese folk legend. As one of the five great fairy animals, the fox fairy is depicted as a worldly and wise spirit that possesses magical power, and can take the shape of a human and bring happiness or misfortune to people. In ancient mythology, Yu the Great encountered a white nine-tailed fox who married him and later gave birth to Qi, the first monarch of the Xia Dynasty (2070-1600 BC). Fox worship came into being during the Qin and Han dynasties (221 BC-AD 220). In the past, people in some localities even set up fox fairy temples to pray for safety.

例句：

清代小说《聊斋志异》中塑造了一批**狐仙**形象，它们集人类全部美德于一身，忠贞爱情，尊重友谊，比人类更可爱。

Example Sentence:

The novel *Strange Tales from a Lonely Studio*, which was written in the Qing Dynasty (1616-1911), conjured up images of a group of fox fairies that combined all the virtues of human beings. Their loyalty to love and respect for friendship rendered them even more lovable than human beings.

狐狸精 *hulijing;* fox spirit; seductress

参见“狐仙”词条。因狐狸乖巧伶俐，聪明狡诈，旧时民间传说或文人墨客多用“狐狸精”指年轻貌美、对异性富有诱惑力的女子，带有贬义色彩。

See *huxian* (fox fairy). As foxes are perceived as lovely, shrewd, intelligent and cunning creatures in Chinese folklore, men of letters in ancient times often used the derogatory term "*hulijing* (seductress)" to refer to beautiful and beguiling young women who seduce men.

例句：

狐狸精(九尾狐)一说源自于中国神话故事，常见于东亚地区神话传说之中。

Example Sentence:

The fox spirit or the nine-tailed fox—a common motif in East Asian mythology—is a mythical fox entity originating from Chinese mythology.

蛇仙

shexian;
snake fairy; snake spirit

中国民间传说中修炼成仙的蛇，为五大仙之一。蛇仙信仰主要流行于南方多蛇地区。传说伏羲和女娲都是人首蛇身的神人。民间传说蛇能作祟祸害人，故而将之奉为仙，目的是祈求它远离自己，以求平安。蛇还被认为是龙的化身，古人认为龙为蛇所生育，亦有人认为蛇脱皮后会变成龙，以上认

A snake that has become a fairy through rigorous self-cultivation according to Chinese folk legend, and is one of the five great fairy animals. Snake worship is mainly popular in southern China where there is an abundance of snakes. In Chinese mythology, the two ancient gods Fuxi and Nüwa who are said to have created the human race have the head of a human being and the body

知赋予蛇更多的神秘感和威力。对蛇的称谓因地区而不同，如北京地区称之为“小龙”，浙江一代称之为“大仙天龙”，江西地区称之为“祖宗蛇”，山西民间称之为“神蛇”或“神龙”，并奉蛇为山神或财神。

of a serpent. Since snakes are generally depicted as scourges in folklore, people worshipped them in the hope that they would stay away and stop making trouble. The snake is also considered to be the incarnation of the dragon, for ancient Chinese believed that the dragon was born as a snake, and it will transform into a dragon after shedding its skin. Such notions infuse the snake with greater mystery and power. The names for snakes vary from place to place. It is called “small dragon” in Beijing, “great immortal celestial dragon” in Zhejiang Province, “ancestor snake” in Jiangxi Province, and “divine snake” or “divine dragon” in Shanxi Province, to name a few. In the folklore of Shanxi Province, the snake is also revered as the Mountain God or the God of Wealth.

例句：

民间传说《白蛇传》中的白娘子和小青代表了善良可爱的**蛇仙**形象。

Example Sentence:

The popular folk tale *The Legend of the White Snake* depicts its two protagonists—the white snake and the green snake—as kind-hearted, lovely snake fairies.

四大门

si da men;
the four great fairy animals

中国北方民间对狐狸（“胡门”）、黄鼠狼（“黄门”）、刺猬（“白门”）和蛇（“柳门”）四种动物的总称，也有的地方加上鼠（“灰门”）称为“五大门”或“五大仙”。四大门信仰源于远古时的动物崇拜，认为这四种灵性动物能够通过修行吸收天地之精气，从而具有特别的神力，能影响人的前途命运和兴衰祸福，因此常将他们供奉于家中，或者避免打扰他们。

The term used in northern China to refer to four spirit animals, namely: the fox (*humen*), the yellow weasel (*huangmen*), the hedgehog (*baimen*), and the snake (*liumen*). In some localities, the mouse (*huimen*) is also added to the list, thus becoming the five great fairy animals. Worship of the four great fairy animals (*si da men*) originated from ancient animal worship. It was believed these four animals could absorb the essence of Heaven and Earth through practice, imbuing them with divine powers. In this way, they were able to affect the fates of people. These animals were therefore often worshipped at home or left undisturbed.

例句：

旧时人们认为“**四大门**”通过“附体”于人而发挥神力，那些被附体之人被称为“大仙”。

Example Sentence:

In the past, the four great fairy animals were said to exert their magic power by possessing the bodies of human beings. Those people were thus regarded as agents of the corresponding animals and were addressed as “great immortals.”

喜鹊报喜 *xique baoxi;* the magpies forecast good news

中国民间迷信说法。鹊本为常见鸟类，多飞集于房屋旁边的树上，其毛色及叫声令人愉悦，故被视为吉祥之鸟，名之“喜鹊”。人们认为喜鹊的叫声预示着会有喜事降临。该说法源于唐代一个鸟鹊报恩的故事：一只喜鹊去狱中看望曾有恩于它、被诬告入狱的主人，似在传语；三日后，主人获释。至今人们仍愿意相信“喜鹊报喜”的说法。

A superstitious folk saying in China. The magpie is a commonly-seen bird that flocks and perches in trees next to houses. The bird is considered adorable and its chirp is pleasant to the ear. Many people consider it auspicious and a harbinger of joy, hence the name *xique* (happy magpie). The saying is derived from a widespread legend about the magpie in the Tang Dynasty (618-907). According to the story, a magpie joyfully chirped when it went to prison to visit its owner, who had been jailed on a groundless charge and to whom the magpie was indebted. Three days later, the man was set free. People still believe the saying today.

例句：

中国最早的撰于春秋时代的鸟类专著《禽经》中就已提到**喜鹊报喜**的说法。

Example Sentence:

The saying *xique baoxi* (the magpies forecast good news) first appeared in *The Book of Birds*, a work written by ornithologists during the Spring and Autumn Period (770-476 BC).

乌鸦报丧 *wuya baosang;* the crows foreshadow misfortune

中国民间迷信说法。乌鸦嗅觉灵敏，喜食腐肉，颈部似有白圈，羽毛多为黑色，好像穿戴孝服，而且叫声喑哑，如同报丧，因此民间多将其视为不祥之物，认为在路上遇乌鸦迎面飞来或居家时有乌鸦集于屋顶鸣叫是大凶之兆，有可能预示家破人亡。

A superstitious folk saying in China. The crow has a keen sense of smell and enjoys carrion. It has a white circle plume on its nape and black plumage (as if being in mourning), and a raucous mourning call. These qualities have made crows ominous and a sign of misfortune. People believe that seeing a flock of crows hovering overhead or chirping on roofs are bad omens of a possible family disaster or even devastating misfortune.

例句：

类似于“**乌鸦报丧**”的说法在其他文化里面也有出现。

Example Sentence:

The belief that *wuya baosang* (the crows foreshadow misfortune) can be found in other cultures as well.

松鹤延年 *songhe yannian;* pine and crane as blessings for longevity

中国民间常用的表示吉祥、长寿的祝福语。在道教神话中，松是长青不朽的象征，又称“不老松”，也是长寿和有志有节的象征。鹤是一种长寿

A commonly used auspicious idiom in China. *Song*, or pine tree, which is also known as the “evergreen pine,” is a symbol of immortality and noble aspirations in Daoist mythology. Cranes are long-living animals that

的禽类，又称"仙鹤"，道教认为鹤为修炼升天成仙者的坐骑，有"驾鹤成仙"之说，于是鹤被视作吉祥、长寿的象征。两种仙物结合在一起即是祝人如松鹤般高洁、长寿。

are depicted as celestial beings in Daoism. Coupled with the mythology claiming that the crane can carry immortals to the Heaven, cranes are subsequently regarded as a symbol of longevity and auspiciousness. Therefore, the phrase *songhe yannian* includes a reference to both pine trees and cranes and is used as a blessing for longevity and a noble and unsullied aspiration.

例句：

"**松鹤延年**"旧时常写于寿幛上，作为祝贺老人寿辰的礼物。

Example Sentence:

"Pine and crane as blessings for longevity" is a commonly used auspicious phrase and a motif on a *shouzhang*, which is a large, oblong sheet of red silk with inscriptions that are presented to an elderly person as a birthday gift.

游蛇灯 *you shedeng;* snake lantern parade

中国民俗活动，在福建省闽江边的樟湖镇最为流行。"游蛇灯"活动在每年元宵节前后举行，从正月初六到廿一历时16天，其间正月十七、十八、十九三天最为热闹。蛇

A Chinese folk event popular in the town of Zhanghu in Fujian Province. The snake lantern parade takes place around the Lantern Festival, from the 6th to the 21st day of the first lunar month, during which the celebration from the 17th to the

灯由蛇头、蛇身、蛇尾三部分组成。节日前，具有威望的老人聚集祠堂，用木板和竹篾扎制蛇头和蛇尾。蛇身分由各家各户制作，每家在一块长约2米、宽约0.2米的木板上装三盏纸灯制成一段蛇身。太阳落山，人们集合在各自的祠堂前，将蛇灯板板板相连，再与蛇头蛇尾相接，成为一支一二公里长浩浩荡荡的蛇阵。在鞭炮声中，蛇阵绕镇而行，各家各户出来迎接，祈求神灵带来吉祥。农历廿一深夜，游灯结束，村民将“蛇头”“蛇尾”送进蛇王庙焚化，祈祝蛇王升天，护佑全境水陆平安。此习俗由来已久，源于闽越先民的蛇崇拜文化。樟湖镇中建于明代的蛇王庙至今依然完好。

19th is the grandest. The huge snake is comprised of the head, body, and tail. The snake head and tail are made by the revered elderly of the town, who gather in the ancestral halls to make the head and tail with wooden boards and bamboo strips. The body is divided into equal sections made of a flat wooden board two meters long and 20 centimeters wide, with three lanterns placed on top, to be made by each family in their own homes. At sunset on the 6th day, all the people gather in front of their ancestral halls and join the lantern boards, and then the head and tail, forming a long winding “snake” about 1-2 kilometers long. Amid the sound of firecrackers, the snake parade down the streets. Every family comes out to welcome the parade and pray for auspiciousness and good fortune. This continues until the 21st day when the festival draws to a conclusion. At that time, the head and tail of the snake are burned in the Temple of the Snake King, signifying the rise of the Snake King to heaven, from where he will protect the land and waters of the town. This custom has a long history, dating back to primitive times when snake worship was practiced in Fujian. The Temple of the Snake King in Zhanghu Town, built during the Ming Dynasty, is still kept intact.

例句：

游蛇灯队伍在旗幡鼓乐的引导下，如游蛇一般走街串巷，缓缓行进。

Example Sentence:

Led by flags and drums, the snake lantern parade wriggles through the town like a winding snake.

祭祖 *jizu;* ancestor worship

祭祀祖先的传统。古代中国宗法社会以血缘为纽带，人们祭祀代代相传的宗祖，奉祀家族祖先及家庭先人，增进家族观念，表达缅怀、感恩之情，祈求保佑后代子孙。国有太庙，族有宗祠，家有祖龛，这些是国家、家族和家庭最重要的礼仪活动场所。中国人非常重视家族，因此宗祠拜祖在民间比较盛行，大多将祖先牌位依次摆在祠堂正厅，陈列丰盛的供品，然后祭拜者按长幼顺序上香跪拜。

The Chinese tradition of offering sacrifices to one's ancestors. Ancient Chinese patriarchal society was based on family bloodlines, and people worshipped clan and family ancestors to maintain strong bonds, express gratitude to ancestors, and pray for blessings on their offspring. The Imperial Ancestral Temple, clan ancestral halls, and shrines in homes are considered important worship sites for the state, clans, and families respectively. Chinese people attach great importance to clan relations, and clan ancestral worship is very popular. Most people place their ancestral memorial tablets in their front halls amongst a rich display of offerings. Here, they line up to pray according to seniority, and then kowtow with lit incense sticks one after another before the shrines.

例句：

年节**祭祖**是人们缅怀先辈、抒发不忘故土和思亲寻根深情的民间盛典。

Example Sentence:

Ancestor worship is a grand occasion during the Spring Festival and other festivals to cherish the memories of ancestors and express deep affection for hometowns and family root.

人祖庙会

Renzu Miaohui;
Creator Temple Fair; *Taihao Fuxi* Temple Fair

地方传统民俗文化盛会。"人祖庙"是河南淮阳城北太昊伏羲陵的俗称，传说这是埋葬人类始祖伏羲、女娲头骨之处。每年农历二月二至三月三，当地举行盛大的"人祖庙会"，其间每天数以万计群众前来进香朝拜。香客从家乡带来泥土，进香后把土撒于伏羲陵墓上，祈祷祖宗香火不断，子孙兴旺。传说女娲是创造人类的女神。当地传说伏羲、女娲抟土为人，使男女交合，生儿育女，繁衍后代，被民众尊为"神媒"，奉为婚姻之神。

A Chinese traditional temple fair in Henan Province. The Creator Temple refers to the Tomb of Fuxi in northern Huaiyang County, Henan Province. Legend has it that the skulls of Fuxi and Nüwa—the creators of humanity—are buried here. Every year from the second day of the second lunar month to the third day of the third lunar month, local people hold this grand fair. Every day, tens of thousands of people come to burn incense and worship. Worshippers carry soil from their hometowns with them, and after they burn incense they sprinkle it on Fuxi's tomb, praying for continuance of their bloodlines and plenty of offspring. Legend says that Nüwa was the goddess who created humanity. Local people believe that Fuxi and Nüwa together created people from the mud of the earth, made man and woman copulate, bear and raise children, and multiply. Nüwa has been revered as the *shenmei* (matchmaker goddess) and is considered the goddess of marriage.

例句：

人祖庙会期间，竹马、旱船、舞狮子、耍龙灯等 60 余种传统的民间游艺登台亮相，各种物资汇聚成一个商贸大集市，是一场热闹的大众文化节。

Example Sentence:

The Creator Temple Fair is a lively cultural event with a huge market of goods of all kinds, and over 60 kinds of traditional folk performances like bamboo horses, land boats, lion dance, and dragon lanterns.

三皇 *Sanhuang;* Three Sovereigns

中国神话传说中三位上古帝王的统称，其说法源于战国时期。最初有天皇、地皇、泰皇（人皇）的“三皇”之说，后来演变为人间帝王的“三皇五帝”说。“三皇”是传说中在“五帝”之前出现的三位知名部落首领，但具体所指众说纷纭，至汉代才基本确定为伏羲、神农和黄帝，并将人类生存技术的进步，如捕猎、原始农业、人工取火等归功于他们。之后的朝代开始立庙奉祀三皇，在三皇诞辰之日举行隆重的祭奠

An umbrella term for three legendary Chinese sovereigns of antiquity. The term originally appeared during the Warring States Period (475-221 BC) to refer to the Emperor of Heaven, Emperor of the Earth, and Emperor of Tai (Humanity). Later, the term evolved into the “Three Sovereigns and Five Emperors” where the “Three Sovereigns” were the three famous tribal leaders who preceded the “Five Emperors.” However, it wasn’t until the Han Dynasty (206 BC- AD 220) that a general consensus was reached that the

活动。元代时三皇也被奉为医家先圣先师，因此三皇庙也称“先医庙”。三皇五帝崇拜是一种祖先崇拜，是在母系氏族社会向父系氏族社会的发展过程中形成的。

“Three Sovereigns” referred to Fuxi, Shennong, and the Yellow Emperor, who are said to have bolstered humanity's ability to survive by teaching them how to hunt, farm, and make fire. People of subsequent dynasties began building shrines in their names, and grand memorial ceremonies are held on their birthdays to honor them. During the Yuan Dynasty (1206-1368), the Three Sovereigns were revered as sagely masters of medicine. As a result, shrines to the Three Sovereigns are also called “shrines of medical sages.” Worship of the Three Sovereigns and Five Emperors is a form of ancestor worship that developed during the shift from a matriarchal to a patriarchal society.

例句：

“**三皇**五帝”原为传说中中国远古时代的氏族部落或部落联盟的领袖，后用“三皇五帝时代”借指远古传说时代。

Example Sentence:

The “Three Sovereigns and Five Emperors” originally referred to the mythical leaders of unified clans or tribes in ancient China. Later, the term “the age of the Three Sovereigns and Five Emperors” was used to refer to this legendary period in remote antiquity in Chinese history.

五帝 *Wudi;* Five Emperors

中国神话传说中五位最知名的古帝王的统称。战国秦汉时代对天帝的崇拜已发展为“天有五帝”之说，即白帝、青帝、黄帝、赤帝（炎帝）、黑帝。后来从天帝演变为上古时代中国传说中的五位部落首领或部落联盟首领，但不同史料记载中五帝具体所指有几种不同的说法。汉代以后，少昊、颛顼、帝喾、尧、舜为五帝说逐渐成为定制。

The umbrella term referring to the five most famous mythological rulers of ancient China. *Wudi* (five emperors) is the name coined as early as the Warring States Period (475-221 BC) and refer to the five celestial rulers, namely, the White Emperor, the Green Emperor, the Yellow Emperor, the Red Emperor and the Black Emperor. The identities of the Five Emperors later evolved from these celestial rulers to the five legendary tribal leaders. However, there are several different accounts of Five Emperors in different historical records. Following the Han Dynasty (206 BC-AD 220), the dispute was eventually settled, and the five emperors were identified as Shaohao, Zhuanxu, Emperor Ku, Emperor Yao, and Emperor Shun.

例句：

几千年来，中国一直流传着“三皇**五帝**”的传说。

Example Sentence:

The popular legend of “Three Sovereigns and Five Emperors” spans several thousand years.

伏羲 *Fuxi;* Fuxi

中国神话传说中的上古三皇之一，中华民族人文始祖，又称“太昊伏羲”。相传伏羲是华胥氏踩了雷泽中雷神的足印生出的儿子，龙身，牛耳，虎鼻，大眼睛，长九尺一寸；但汉代画像石刻中的伏羲是人面蛇身，下半部与同样人面蛇身的女娲绞结在一起。传说中的伏羲对中华文明贡献卓越：他发明了八卦，成为中国古代占卜术的典型代表；他与女娲创立婚姻制度，保证人类繁衍；他发明了工具，教会人们耕种和渔猎；他引导人们走出了蒙昧

One of the “Three Sovereigns” and co-creator of the Chinese nation, also referred to as *Taihao Fuxi*. Legend has it that Fuxi was born of Lady Huaxu after she stepped on the footprints of the Thunder God, that he has a dragon's body, cow's ears, tiger's nose, big eyes, and is over three meters tall. However, stone carvings from the Han Dynasty (206 BC-AD 220) depict Fuxi as a god with a human face and a snake's tail which intertwines with the tail of Nüwa, the goddess of creation in Chinese mythology who also has a human face. Legend says Fuxi made remarkable contributions to Chinese civilization. He became a preeminent

的原始生活，奠定了几千年中华文明昌盛的根基。为了纪念和彰显伏羲的功绩，后人修建了伏羲庙并进行一年一度的祭祀活动。至今在河南淮阳地区有一座相当规模的“伏羲陵”，被当地人尊称为“人祖庙”。人们经常到此烧香祈拜，除祈求农事丰收之外，也向他表达得子的愿望。

figure in ancient Chinese divination culture by inventing the Eight Trigrams. He also established the marriage system with Nüwa to ensure human reproduction, invented tools and imparted knowledge to people which allowed them to farm, fish, and hunt. In short, Fuxi led humanity out of their ignorant, primitive lives and laid a solid foundation for the development of Chinese civilization. To commemorate and highlight Fuxi's achievements, people built temples to Fuxi where there are annual sacrificial activities to worship him. The Fuxi Temple in Huaiyang, Henan Province is respectfully called the Creator Temple by the local people and is still used today where worshippers go to burn incense and pray for good harvests and sons to continue the family line.

例句：

据《山海经》记载，**伏羲**和女娲是居住在昆仑山中的始祖神。

Example Sentence:

According to *The Classic of Mountains and Seas*, Fuxi and Nüwa, who lived on the mythical Kunlun Mountain, were the creators of the human race.

太昊伏羲 *Taihao Fuxi;* Taihao Fuxi

参见“伏羲”。

See *Fuxi* (Fuxi).

女娲 *Nüwa;* Nüwa

中国上古神话中的创世女神，中华民族的共同人文始祖。女娲是原始社会母系氏族时期流传下来的一位伟大的女神形象，传说她用黄泥仿照自己的样子创造了人，开创人类社会并建立婚姻制度。女娲还是创造万物的自然之神，每天至少能创造出七十样东西，被称为大地之母。后来自然界发生了大灾难，天塌地陷，洪水泛滥，恶禽猛兽出来残害人类。女娲熔炼五色石修补苍天，并斩断鳌足代替天柱，树立在大地的四方，将天撑起来。在中国西

The mother goddess of creation in ancient Chinese mythology, said to be the co-creator of the Chinese nation, also referred to as "*Wahuang* (Empress Wa)." Her legend can be traced back to China's primitive matriarchal society. Legend says that she used yellow clay to create the first humans in her image. She gave them life, and the ability to have children, and is thus credited for establishing the marriage system. She is also credited for creating the spirits of all things in nature, said to have produced at least seventy types of things per day, and is called Mother of the Earth. According to legend, there were great disasters in the natural world, and the sky collapsed, the earth caved in, flood waters burst forth, and evil pests and beasts emerged, all of which devastated humanity. Nüwa smelted five-colored stones to repair the sky, and chopped the four legs from a mythical sea turtle to use as pillars to support the sky. According to folklore by Miao and Yao ethnic groups, Nüwa and her brother Fuxi hid inside a gourd during a great flood. They were the only survivors and later became husband and wife, becoming the ancestors for a new generation of human beings.

南苗族和瑶族的传说中，伏羲与女娲原为兄妹，在一场大洪水中他们藏身于葫芦中，成为仅有的幸存者；后结为夫妻，成为人类再生的先祖。

例句：

女娲补天的传说所反映的应该是母系氏族社会时人类治水和抵御其他自然灾害的历史。

Example Sentence:

The legend of Nüwa mending the sky is a reflection of early humans attempting to contain floods or battle other natural disasters during ancient matriarchal society.

炎帝 *Yandi;* Emperor Yan; Flame Emperor

A mythological pre-dynastic figure credited as being one of the ancient Three Sovereigns, also known as Shennong (literally Deity Farmer). His mythical reign pre-dates even the Xia Dynasty (2070-1600 BC). Legend says he knew how to use fire for agricultural purposes and became the head of the Jiang tribe, thus earning the name Emperor Yan (Flame Emperor). He is said to have taught ancient people how to till the soil for grain, which boosted the development of agricultural productivity. He

中国传说中上古时期姜姓部落的首领，战国时期炎帝与原始农业发明者神农氏合并，被奉为上古三皇之一。传说姜姓部落的首领由于懂得用火而得到王位，所以称为“炎帝”。相传炎帝教百姓耕种五谷，促进了农业生产的发展；他遍尝百草，了解其功能，奠定了中医学的基础；他分辨昼、夜、日、月，确定一个月有三十天；他开创了以物换物的市场，是中国货币、商业的起源；他领导部落人民制造饮食用的陶器和炊具，使人们可以加工食物等等。代表原始农耕文明的炎帝神农氏与开启华夏文明的黄帝轩辕氏浓缩了中华文明孕育过程的漫长历史，因此炎帝和黄帝被共同尊奉为中华民族的始祖。

is also known for learning the properties of plants and herbs, establishing the foundations of traditional Chinese medicine. He also distinguished between day and night, and days and months, confirming that there were 30 days in a month. He created the marketplace and established the trade and barter system, the origination of Chinese currency and commerce. He also taught the tribe to make pottery and cooking utensils for eating and drinking, allowing people to process food. In the records of the Warring States Period (475-221 BC), the ancient figures of Emperor Yan and Shennong were the same figure. The legendary stories of Emperor Yan representing China's agricultural tradition and the Yellow Emperor as the pioneer of Chinese civilization are reflections of the birth and early development of the Chinese civilization. As a result, Emperor Yan and the Yellow Emperor are jointly revered as the ancient ancestors of all Chinese people.

例句：

炎帝陵位于湖南省株洲市炎陵县，常年接待前来谒祖、参观的公众。

Example Sentence:

Emperor Yan's tomb is located in Yanling County in Zhuzhou, Hunan Province. People come from all across China and the world to pay tribute to this ancient ancestor.

黄帝 *Huangdi;* Yellow Emperor

中国传说中上古时期华夏部落联盟首领，上古三皇之一，后被尊为中华民族的"人文初祖"。黄帝发展农业，整饬军队，经过多场战争统一了当时黄河流域的各个部落，成为天下第一个共主。据文献记载，黄帝时代有许多发明创造，这些发明创造加速了中华民族的文明进程，一般认为黄帝时代为距今五千多年前，所以有中国"五千年文明"之说。

One of the ancient Three Sovereigns who served as the first leader of the Huaxia tribe and was later revered as the father of Chinese civilization. The Yellow Emperor is credited with agriculture and military development and attributed to unifying the tribes of the Yellow River basin, thereby forming the first centralized Chinese nation. Relevant documents recorded that the era of the Yellow Emperor was filled with many inventions and innovations that sped up the course of Chinese civilization. Since it is typically believed that the Yellow Emperor's time occurred nearly 5,000 years ago, people often note China's "5,000 years of civilization."

例句:

自唐代以来，陕西黄陵县的桥山**黄帝**陵成为举行祭祀黄帝活动的场所。

Example Sentence:

Since the Tang Dynasty (618-907), the tomb of the Yellow Emperor on Qiaoshan Mountain in Huangling County, Shaanxi Province has served as the site for sacrifices to the Yellow Emperor.

炎黄子孙

yanhuang zisun;
descendants of the Flame Emperor and the Yellow Emperor; the Chinese nation

中华民族的自称。“炎黄”是指炎帝神农氏和黄帝轩辕氏，是中国上古传说中的两个部落首领。后来两个部落逐渐融合成为华夏部落。在当时中原地区的民族和部落中，华夏部落比较强大，文明程度较高，最终统一了中原地区，因而成为中原文化的代表。炎帝和黄帝也是中国文化、技术的始祖，传说他们及他们的臣子、后代创造了上古几乎所有重要的发明。中国人把炎帝和黄帝尊为中华民族的始祖。

A term used by the Chinese people to address themselves as well as people of Chinese origin. Yan-Huang refers to the Flame Emperor (Yandi) and the Yellow Emperor (Huangdi), two tribal leaders in ancient Chinese mythology. The two tribes later merged into the Huaxia tribe, which became a fairly strong tribe with advanced civilization among the ethnic groups and tribes in the Central Plains. Ultimately the Huaxia tribe unified the entire region and came to represent the culture in the Central Plains. The Flame Emperor and the Yellow Emperor are known as the earliest ancestors of Chinese culture and technology. According to legend, virtually all of the most important inventions during the remote ages were attributed to them, their subordinates and descendants. The Chinese people have revered these two emperors as the forefathers of the Chinese nation.

例句：

中国丰富的非物质文化遗产承载了数千年来**炎黄子孙**的情感与智慧。

Example Sentence:

China's rich intangible cultural heritage embodies thousands of years of attachment and wisdom of the Chinese people.

祠堂 *citang;* ancestral temple/hall

中国大家族的族人祭祀祖先或先贤的场所。祠堂多建于家族的聚居地或其附近，其内存放有家谱和祖先牌位等，旧时称为"祠庙"或"家庙"。除祭祀祖先外，祠堂也是各房子孙办理婚、丧、寿、喜等的场所，族亲们商议族内重要事务之地。祠堂也可指旧时社会公众或某个阶层为共同祭祀某个人物而建立的庙堂，如成都有祭祀诸葛亮的武侯祠，上海有祭祀黄道婆的黄母祠等。作为地方民俗文化的重要组成部

A sacred place dedicated to worshipping the ancestors of a large family or a clan. Ancestral temples are usually built within or close to the family residential quarters, with a record of the family tree and tablets of deceased ancestors enshrined in it. They can also be used for other family- and clan-related matters such as weddings, birthdays, funerals, and important family meetings. The term can also refer to a memorial temple set up by the public or certain groups to enshrine a certain figure, such as the Wuhou Memorial Temple in Chengdu to honor the famous military strategist Zhuge Liang, and the Huangmu Memorial Temple in Shanghai to worship the great inventor of weaving and spinning techniques Huang Daopo. The practice emerged during the Xia, Shang, and Zhou dynasties (c. 2070-256 BC), became relatively established during the Song Dynasty (960-1279), and matured in the Ming (1368-1644) and Qing (1616-1911) dynasties. Nowadays, some rural areas still retain the tradition of worshipping their ancestors at their ancestral halls during the Spring Festival and

分，祠堂文化从夏、商、周朝开始兴起，到宋代形成了比较完备的体系，明、清时代发展到高峰。现在一些农村地区还保留着逢年过节到祠堂祭祖的传统。

other traditional festivals.

例句：

祠堂的形成与儒家文化及其对孝道的提倡息息相关。

Example Sentence:

The culture of worshipping ancestral temples is closely linked to Confucian culture and its advocacy for filial piety.

祠庙 *cimiao;* ancestral temple

参见“祠堂”。

See *citang* (ancestral temple).

家庙 *jiamiao;* family temple

参见“祠堂”。

See *citang* (ancestral temple).

娘娘庙 *niangniang miao;* goddess temple

中国民间对供奉女神的庙宇的统称，也可指具体的庙宇。各地娘娘庙所供主神有所不同，北方多供奉碧霞元君，沿海地区多供奉海神妈祖，大多为保佑合家安康，送子送福。因为中国人非常重视生育儿子以延续家族血脉，因此各地的娘娘庙是中国民间香火最为旺盛的寺庙。拜娘娘庙的大多是妇女，她们的主要心愿是求子，保护儿童，赐福免灾。

A general term used for temples dedicated to Chinese goddesses such as *Bixia Yuanjun*, who is mostly worshipped in northern China, and the sea goddess Mazu who is mostly worshipped in coastal regions. The goddesses are believed to bring peace, blessings and offspring to families. Because of the importance of fertility and reproduction in Chinese ancient culture, worshipping in goddess temples became very popular, mostly attended by women praying for the birth of healthy sons, for the protection of their children, for good fortune, and for the avoidance of disasters.

例句：

娘娘庙所供主神，各庙有所不同。

Example Sentence:

A wide variety of goddesses are enshrined in different goddess temples.

子孙窑 *zisun yao;* Offspring Hole; Hole for Beseeching Offspring

河南省太昊伏羲陵的一块青石台基上有一圆孔，游人香客称之为“窑”，相传求子之人用手摸一摸就可以多子多孙，故称“子孙窑”，又名“求子石”。此说法源于古代女性生殖崇拜。“子孙窑”谐音“子孙要”，就是要子孙之意，因此当地百姓认为其寓意多子多孙。每年农历二月二至三月三，太昊陵人祖庙会都会迎来数万五湖四海的游客来此地拜祭人祖太昊伏羲氏。其中想要求子之人，尤其是女性，都要用手摸一摸这子孙窑，以求得子。

The name given to a small hole at the Taihao Fuxi Tomb (Creator Temple) in Huaiyang County, Henan Province where people—mainly women—go to pray for having offspring. It is also called the “*qiuzi shi* (Stone for Requesting Offspring).” *Zisun* is the Chinese word for “offspring” and *yao* is the Chinese word for “hole”, which is a homonym for “want.” As a result, *zisun yao* sounds like “I want offspring” when said aloud. Every year from the second day of the second lunar month to the third day of the third lunar month, tens of thousands of visitors from all over the country flock to the temple to worship Fuxi, believed to be the co-creator of humanity. Visitors, especially female visitors wishing to have children, will rub their hands inside the hole.

例句：

民间相传，摸着**子孙窑**逆时针转三圈代表男孩，顺时针转三圈代表女孩，如果左右各转三圈，将来一定生一对龙凤双胞胎。

Example Sentence:

It is believed that rubbing the Offspring Hole in three counterclockwise circles will bring a baby boy, while three clockwise circles will bring a baby girl. If a person rubs three circles in each direction, they will probably end up with having a twin of a boy and a girl.

求子石 *qiuzi shi;* Stone for Beseeching Offspring

参见“子孙窑”。

See *zisun yao* (Offspring Hole).

偷瓜送子 *tou gua song zi;* stealing melons to pray for sons

中国旧时民间求子风俗，又称“送瓜”“送瓜崽”。该风俗流行于湖南、贵州一带，迷信色彩浓重。如有妇女婚后数年不育，其亲友就会于中秋节前几日，从人丁兴旺的人家瓜园里偷得一瓜，给瓜穿上新衣，画上眉目，装扮成婴儿模样，选一个小孩子抱着，乘轿骑马，鼓乐鸣奏，送至不育妇女家中，放在床上，并唱诵吉祥之语。夜晚，不孕妇女伴瓜而眠，翌日将瓜煮熟吃掉，认为这样便可怀孕生子。

An old, superstitious custom to help a woman bear a child, prevalent throughout Hunan and Guizhou provinces. If a woman failed to get pregnant after several years in a marriage, her relatives or friends would help her by stealing a melon from the garden of a family with many children several days before the Mid-Autumn Festival. They would then dress the melon up with clothing and make-up to make it look like a baby. Then a child would ride a horse or a sedan chair to the woman's house with the melon in hand and loud music in drums, and place the melon on her bed while chanting auspicious words. The woman would sleep with the melon the whole night. The next day, the woman would cook the melon and eat it, believing that this would help her become pregnant.

例句：

除汉族外，中国的仡佬族也有“**偷瓜送子**”的习俗。

Example Sentence:

Besides the Han ethnic group, the custom of “stealing melons to pray for sons” was also practiced by the Gelao ethnic group in Guizhou Province.

行业神

hangye shen;
patron saint of a trade; god of a particular trade

各行各业的人们供奉的用来保佑自己和本行业吉利、兴旺的神灵。这些神灵多为历史上的能工巧匠，被认为对某种行业有开创发明之功，所以又被称作行业“祖师爷”，如建筑业奉祀鲁班，酒坊奉祀杜康，医药业奉祀扁鹊、孙思邈，纺织业奉祀黄道婆等。每逢祖师诞辰，业内人必烧香礼供，举行大集会。旧时纸马香烛店都有雕印的祖师神马供应。神马图像大多是神龛式，中间为主神，两侧有童子或侍从。人们信奉行业神以求保佑本行业兴旺发达，并以此团结约束从业人员，共同维护行业利益。

Deities worshipped by persons of the same trades. Chinese people believe each trade has a deity who protects both the trade and the practitioners and brings them prosperity and good fortune. They are mostly master craftsmen and craftswomen in history who were deified by later generations as founders of their respective trades, so they are also called *zushiye* (founding father) of a particular trade. Famous deities include Lu Ban (patron saint of architecture), Du Kang (patron saint of breweries), Bian Que and Sun Simiao (patron saints of medicine), Huang Daopo (patron saint of weaving). Upon the birthdays of the founding fathers, practitioners of the corresponding trade would gather together to burn incense and make offerings. In ancient times, paper incense stores provided prints of images of these deities which were mostly used to hang in home shrines. Most of these images feature the deity in the middle, with a boy or an attendant on each side. People believe that a common deity for the trade would not only ensure long-term prosperity for the trade as a whole, but also help to build solidarity among practitioners and protect their collective interests.

例句：

佛教、道教以及小说戏曲、神话传说，对某些**行业神**的形成有一定影响。

Example Sentence:

To some extent, Buddhism, Daoism, novels, plays and legends have contributed to the formation of the patron saints of some trades.

药王 *Yaowang;* Patron Saint of Medicine

The deity in charge of medicine, also known as *Yaowangye* (Lord of Medicine). Originally worshipped by the general public, it was later adopted as a Daoist deity. Different places and different ages have enshrined different patron saints of medicine, usually famous doctors in Chinese history or legend who are deified by later generations. There are many figures in Chinese history and mythology who have made great contributions to the development of Chinese medicine

中国民间供奉的司掌医药之神，俗称“药王爷”，后成为道教俗神。药王一般由中国古代历史上或传说中的名医演化而来，因此不同地方、不同时代供奉的药王也有所不同。传说中遍尝百草之神农氏、战国时期名医扁鹊和唐代著名医学家和药学家孙思邈等人都被奉为药王，他们都是对中国医药发展做出过卓越贡献的人物。中国各地均建有药王庙，河北安国药王庙、陕西耀县药王庙等地还有盛大庙会。

such as Shennong who tried hundreds of herbs, Bian Que who was a famous doctor during the Warring States Period (475-221 BC), and Sun Simiao who was a famous doctor and an expert on Chinese herbal medicine in the Tang Dynasty (618-907). They were all deified as patron saints of medicine, and different temples in honor of them can be found across the country. Grand temple fairs are held in such temples, such as the ones in Anguo County, Hebei Province, and Yaoxian County, Shaanxi Province.

例句：

旧时中药店中多奉祀孙思邈。常于农历四月二十八举行**药王**会，以表崇敬。

Example Sentence:

In earlier times, Sun Simiao was worshipped as the Patron Saint of Medicine in most Chinese pharmacies. On the twenty-eighth day of the fourth lunar month, a celebration would be held to honor him.

药王爷 *Yaowangye;* Lord of Medicine

参见“药王”。

See *Yaowang* (Patron Saint of Medicine).

匠神 *Jiangshen;* Patron Saint of Artisans

中国民间信仰中木匠、泥瓦匠及石匠等手工建造行业的保护神，一般特指鲁班。鲁班是春秋时著名工匠和发明家，善造云梯及各种工具，技能超群，称绝一时，是中国名声最大、影响最久的行业神。近代木匠、泥水匠十分信奉鲁班，凡拜师授徒、造屋上梁、营造桥梁佛塔或举行行会庆典等活动，都要祭祀鲁班。香港鲁班节在农历六月十六举行，届时泥瓦匠、木匠和搭棚工都要放假一天，白天到鲁班庙参拜，夜晚开怀

The patron saint worshipped by Chinese carpenters, masons, stonemasons, and the like. This figure is often personified as Lu Ban, China's most prestigious and influential inventor, engineer, and carpenter, and by far the most well-known and influential patron saint of any trade. He is credited with several great inventions such as the cloud ladder (a mobile, counter-weighted siege ladder). Modern carpenters and masons revere Lu Ban, and he is worshipped during ceremonies when new apprentices

畅饮。据说，在这天饮了祖师爷的寿酒，可以保施工平安。在福建，造船业也把鲁班供奉为祖师。造船者在开工建造新船以前都先要用果品茶酒敬拜鲁班，以求祖师保佑造船顺利。

are accepted and ceremonies celebrating the building of a house, a bridge, a Buddhist pagoda or events honoring the industry. The Lu Ban Festival in Hong Kong is on the sixteenth day of the sixth lunar month. On that day, masons, carpenters, and shed builders are given a day off to visit the Lu Ban Temple and have a drink at night. It is said that people drink Lu Ban's wine on that day to ensure safety throughout the course of their construction project. Lu Ban is also revered by the shipbuilding industry in Fujian Province where shipbuilders worship him with fruit, tea, and wine prior to building ships, hoping for a smooth construction.

例句：

北方**匠神**祭祀一般只祭鲁班，南方有些地方祠庙则同时供奉鲁班、张班。张班是由鲁班引出的建筑业保护神，出现很晚，在民间影响远不如鲁班。

Example Sentence:

Only Lu Ban is revered in northern China while both Lu Ban and Zhang Ban are revered in some temples in southern China. As a patron saint of construction, Zhang Ban is far less influential than Lu Ban.

蚕神 *Canshen;* Patron Saint of Sericulture

中国民间信仰中司蚕的神。商周时已开始祭祀蚕神。蚕神的姓名、来历说法不一，但最广为流传的蚕神是黄帝的正妃嫘祖。传说她最早发明养蚕抽丝技术，促进了中国蚕桑业乃至纺织业的发展，因此被尊为“蚕神”。直至明清，蚕神均列入国家祀典，始终享受着国家级祭祀。中国民间的蚕神信仰主要集中在江南浙江嘉兴和湖州等养蚕地区，主要祭祀马头娘、青衣神和蚕姑等地域性蚕神。

The deity who oversees sericulture according to Chinese folk beliefs, worshipped since the Shang and Zhou dynasties (c. 1600 -256 BC). There are several different figures and origins of the Patron Saint of Sericulture, among whom Leizu (wife of the Yellow Emperor) is the most widely worshipped. Legend has it that Leizu initiated silkworm-raising and silk-drawing techniques, and promoted the development of China's sericulture and textile industry. Until the Ming and Qing dynasties (1368-1911), worship to the Patron Saint of Sericulture had been officially recognized as a state sacrificial rite. The general public, especially those in silkworm-raising areas in southern China such as the cities of Jiaxing and Huzhou in Zhejiang Province, worshipped local patron saints of sericulture such as *Matou Niang* (Lady with a Horse-Head), *Qingyi Shen* (Goddess in Cyan), and *Can Gu* (Aunt Silkworm).

例句：

由于种桑养蚕在中国古代农耕经济中有重要地位，所以**蚕神**信仰产生很早。

Example Sentence:

Belief in the Patron Saint of Sericulture started very early due to the dominant position of mulberry-planting and silkworm-raising in ancient China's agricultural economy.

茶神 *Chashen;* Patron Saint of Tea; Tea God

The deity in charge of tea production in Chinese folk beliefs. Lu Yu, a tea master who lived in the Tang Dynasty (618-907), is widely considered to be the Tea God on account of his great contributions to the creation and refinement of the Chinese tea ceremony. He was skilled at water identification, cultivation and breeding of tea plants, and processing of tea leaves. He also penned his monumental book *The Classic of Tea*, which is the world's first monograph on tea. He is honored as *Chaxian* (Immortal of Tea) and *Chasheng* (Saint of Tea).

中国民间信仰中司茶的神。俗传此神为唐代著名茶学家陆羽，他精于茶道，善于鉴别煮茶之水，熟悉茶树栽培、育种和加工技术，并擅长品茗。他撰写的《茶经》三卷，成为世界上第一部茶叶专著，他也被誉为“茶仙”“茶圣”。

例句：

茶神陆羽所著的《茶经》最有历史价值的内容可能是第七章，主要汇辑了从传说时代到唐朝千年间有关茶叶的掌故及药效。

Example Sentence:

Lu Yu is regarded as the Patron Saint of Tea. Perhaps Chapter 7 of Lu Yu's *The Classic of Tea* holds the most historical value regarding tea. It records stories of tea and the effects of tea over a thousand years, from legendary times to the Tang Dynasty.

酒神

Jiushen;
Patron Saint of Wine; Wine God

中国古代传说中的酿酒始祖，一般公认为仪狄和杜康，也称“酒祖”。仪狄传说是夏禹的一位祭司，是最早见诸史书的酿酒专家，据说他将当时民间各种造酒的方法归纳总结出来，使之流传于后世。杜康传说为夏朝第五代君主姒少康，他发现了食物发酵现象，从而发明了一整套酿酒术。由于杜康酒非常美味，“杜康”后来成为酒的代名词。中国人的酒文化源远流长，但中国民间并未形成祭酒神的礼俗。

The deity responsible for liquor and wine production in ancient Chinese mythology, also called *Jiuzu* (Father of Wine). Yi Di and Du Kang are generally recognized as wine gods. Legend has it that Yi Di was a priest of Yu the Great, the legendary founder of the Xia Dynasty (c. 2070-1600 BC). Yi Di is said to have summarized the methods for making wines at the time and passed them down to later generations. Du Kang is perhaps China's most famous wine maker. As a monarch also living during the Xia Dynasty in Chinese legend, Du Kang is said to have discovered the quality of fermented food and therefore invented an alcoholic beverage, which was an outstanding contribution to the ancient Chinese wine industry. As a result, Du Kang's name later became synonymous with wine. China has a long history of rich wine culture, but worship of the Wine God has not become a ritualized practice in Chinese folklore.

例句：

中国没有**酒神**崇拜文化，可能与夏禹及后代一些帝王禁酒有关。

Example Sentence:

There is no worship of the Wine God in China, which may be attributed to the prohibition of alcohol imposed by Yu the Great (the legendary founder of the Xia Dynasty) and some other emperors of later dynasties.

酒祖 *Jiuzu;* Father of Wine

参见"酒神"。

See *Jiushen* (Patron Saint of Wine).

梨园神 *Liyuan Shen;* Patron Saint of Opera; God of the Pear Orchard

中国戏剧界所奉之神，一般认为是唐玄宗李隆基。梨园是中国唐代设置的培训宫廷歌舞人员的机构，精通音律的唐玄宗在宫内大兴梨园，在长安和洛阳还办有别院和新院，共有艺人多达几千人，都被称为"皇帝梨园弟子"。梨园培养出了大批优秀的音乐舞蹈表演人才，在中国音乐史上产生了深远影响。因此，后世戏曲班社多以"梨园"为代称，戏曲艺人亦称"梨园弟子"，唐玄宗也被后世尊为"梨园神"。梨园神像多为白脸男子，面容俊美，身披黄袍。

Deity worshipped by Chinese opera circles. Emperor Xuanzong (712–755) of the Tang Dynasty is generally considered the Patron Saint of Opera. The Pear Orchard (*Liyuan*) was the first known royal singing and dancing academy in China founded by Emperor Xuanzong in his palace in Chang'an (present-day Xi'an), with branches in Chang'an and Luoyang, teaching music, dancing and acting. The Pear Orchard trained several thousand outstanding performers of music and dance, and left a lasting mark on the history of Chinese music. The Pear Orchard, named after the pear trees planted throughout the academy, was an acting school established to produce a form of drama that was primarily musical. Thereafter, the term "Pear Orchard" has been used to refer to opera groups, and the performing artists were known as "Disciples of the Pear Orchard." The statue of the Patron Saint of Opera generally features a man with a white, handsome face and a yellow robe.

例句:

在唐朝，想进入戏班学艺的人必须先拜祭**梨园神**，求祖师爷保佑。

Example Sentence:

In the Tang Dynasty (618-907), if anyone wanted to enter a theatrical troupe to study opera, they first needed to worship the Patron Saint of Opera and ask for his blessings.

观音菩萨 *Guanyin Pusa;* Guanyin Bodhisattva; Goddess of Mercy

中国佛教四大菩萨之一，全称“观世音菩萨”。观音菩萨以宽广的慈悲胸怀救济众生，能够完全自在、毫无障碍地观察俗世，寻声救苦，随心所欲，因此又被称为“观自在菩萨”“大

One of the four great bodhisattvas of Chinese Buddhism. The full name of this bodhisattva is "*Guanshiyin Pusa* (bodhisattva who perceives the world's lamentations)." According to Chinese Buddhism, Guanyin uses her immense compassion to save all sentient beings. She is able to observe the secular world without any hindrance. She seeks to save those who suffer and does as her heart desires. As a result, she is also called the *Guanzizai Pusa* (Bodhisattva of Contemplation) and *Dabei Pusa* (Bodhisattva of Great Compassion). Depictions of Guanyin in a female form are popular in China. She possesses a motherly kind of tenderness and is a very popular and influential Buddhist deity in China. The Guanyin Bodhisattva is said to take on many forms, and the most popular include the white-

悲菩萨”。观音在中国流行为女相，具有母性般的温柔慈祥，在民间影响非常大，信仰者众。观音救渡世人有种种化身，以白衣观音、千手观音、送子观音最为常见。各地普遍建有白衣庵、观音寺，一般佛寺也都有观音殿，香火极盛。

clothes Guanyin, thousand-hands Guanyin, and son-delivering Guanyin. White-cloth nunneries and Guanyin monasteries are common throughout China, and most Buddhist monasteries include Guanyin halls that attract many followers and pilgrims.

例句：

观音菩萨的道场相传在浙江普陀山，每逢农历二月十九、六月十九、九月十九分别是观音菩萨诞辰、出家、得道三大香会期，全山人山人海，寺院香烟缭绕，一派海天佛国景象。

Example Sentence:

It is believed that the Guanyin Bodhisattva's site of practice is in the Putuo Mountain, Zhejiang Province. On the nineteenth day of the second lunar month, the nineteenth day of the sixth lunar month, and the nineteenth day of the ninth lunar month, three festivals are held commemorating Guanyin's birth, joining of the Sangha, and attainment of enlightenment. During these three days, the whole mountain is filled with people, a thick cloud of incense smoke wafts through the air, and a bustling sight of Buddhist activities adds luster to the seaside landscape.

关圣帝君 *Guansheng Dijun;* Holy Emperor Guan; Saint Emperor Guan

中国民间信仰俗神，即三国名将关羽，又称“关帝”“关公”，俗称“关老爷”。关羽能征善战，智勇双全，忠于蜀汉，忠义千秋。关羽自宋以后屡受皇帝敕封，明万历间被封为“三界伏魔大帝神威远镇天尊关圣帝君”，列入国家祀典，由“万世人杰”成为“神中之神”。民间奉关羽为武圣人，与文圣人孔子并列。民间相信关羽司驱邪除祟，赏善罚恶，又能聚财赐福，庇护商贾，乃至抗旱祷雨皆求祀于关圣。

The deified name of Guan Yu, also called *Guandi* (Emperor Guan), *Guangong* (Lord Guan), *Guan Laoye* (Master Guan). Guan Yu is a seasoned, valiant general during the Three Kingdoms period (220-280) who is mostly known for his loyalty to the Kingdom of Shu. For many generations, he has been praised as the epitome of loyalty and righteousness, and since the Song Dynasty (960-1279) he has been conferred with many titles by emperors. During the Ming Dynasty (1368-1644), Emperor Wanli bestowed Guan Yu the title "Holy Emperor Guan, the Great God Who Subdues Demons in the Three Worlds and Whose Awe Spreads Far and Moves Heaven" and honored him with a national sacrificial ceremony. Common people regard Guan Yu as the "Saint of War," which is of the same rank as Confucius, who was known as the "Saint of Culture." People believe that he can drive out evil spirits, reward the virtuous and punish the wicked. He is also worshipped by business people because he is believed to be helpful in the course of accumulating wealth and bestowing blessings. Sometimes, people even pray to Guan Yu to combat drought and grant rain.

例句：

随着中国近现代工商业的繁盛，**“关圣帝君”**又被尊为“武财神”，被工商业者尊为保护神。

Example Sentence:

With the development of commerce and industry in contemporary and modern China, Guan Yu has become revered as the Martial God of Wealth. People pray to him as a patron saint.

妈祖 *Mazu;* Mazu

中国沿海地区声名显赫的海神。相传妈祖为宋代福建莆田湄洲岛人，原名林默。她聪慧、善良，学得踏海不沉的法术，常在海上为渔民指引航向，救援遇难渔民。妈祖死后被渔民船户尊为海神，宋朝以后历代

A sea goddess widely worshipped in China's coastal areas, also known as "*Tianfei* (Princess of Heaven)," "*Tianhou* (Queen of Heaven)." She is purported to have been a woman named Lin Mo who was born in Putian on Meizhou Island, Fujian Province during the Song Dynasty (960-1279). She was said to be smart and kind-hearted, and could walk on sea water. She often charted the course for fishermen and saved them from danger. After her death, Mazu was deified as the goddess of the sea. During the Ming (1368-1644) and Qing (1616-1911) dynasties, she was even more highly esteemed than the Dragon King. Her good deeds of saving fishermen from disasters spread far and wide. Temples for the "Queen

帝王对其进行褒奖和册封。明清时妈祖作为海神超越了龙王的地位，民间广泛流传遇险渔民得到海神娘娘营救的故事。从渔村到城镇，乃至北京、天津、南京等大都市都建有奉祀妈祖的天后宫、天妃宫，香火甚盛。清康熙封她为天后，列入国家祀典。妈祖的职司也逐渐由航海之神扩大为漕运之神，民众祈雨、驱疫、求子也往往祈求妈祖神佑。

of Heaven" or "Princess of Heaven" can be found almost everywhere, from fishing villages and towns to big cities such as Beijing, Tianjin, and Nanjing. Her temples attract large swaths of worshippers. As time went by, the duty of Mazu gradually extended from protecting marine transportation to protecting waterborne transportation. People pray to Mazu for rainfall, to repel plagues, and help with fertility.

例句：

相传农历三月二十三为妈祖生日，很多地方都会举行隆重的**妈祖**祭典。

Example Sentence:

It is said that Mazu was born on the twenty-third day of the third lunar month. On that day, sacrificial ceremonies are held solemnly in many places.

月老 *Yuelao;* God of Marriage

中国汉族民间传说中主管天下婚姻之神。传说世间姻缘是命中注定的，都记录在一大本婚姻簿中。唐朝一位叫韦固的人在一个月夜看见一位老人在翻看婚姻簿，准备为有情人牵线，于是这位神仙就被称为“月下老人”。月老手持红绳，将婚姻簿上的每对男女的脚用红绳系在一起，这样他们无论距离远近、地位高下，都会走到一起结为夫妻。现在“月老”也被用来指称婚姻介绍人、婚姻介绍所、媒人等。有些地方，如北京市门头沟区的妙峰山，仍有月老神像供人参拜。

The deity in charge of marriage in Chinese Han folklore. Legend has it that all marriages are predestined, written in a marriage book by *Yuelao*, an old man who sits in the moonlight matching up future lovers. The lovers are believed to be bound by a red rope by *Yuelao*, and will be married regardless of distance or social status. Today, *Yuelao* also refers to matchmakers or matchmaking agencies. People still worship the statue of *Yuelao* in some places, such as Miaofeng Mountain in Mentougou District of Beijing.

例句：

俗语“千里姻缘一线牵”就是源于**月老**的传说，其中的“线”就是指月老的红绳。

Example Sentence:

The proverb "A marriage is made by a single thread connecting the couple who may be a thousand miles apart" comes from the legend of *Yuelao*, and the "thread" refers to the red rope which connects lovers.

和合二仙 *Hehe Erxian;* Immortals of Harmony and Union

The gods in charge of harmonious relationships according to Chinese folklore, also called the "Twin Saints." Generally, they are portrayed as two lively, lovely children with shoulder-length hair. One holds a lotus while the other holds a round plate. These items sound like the words "harmony" and "union" in Chinese, symbolizing a harmonious relationship between couples, friends, and family.

民间传说中主婚姻和合的神，也作"和合二圣"。其形象一般为两个活泼可爱、长发披肩的孩子，一个手持荷花，一个手捧圆盒。"荷"与"和"、"盒"与"合"谐音，"和合"意为"和（荷）谐合（盒）好"，寓意夫妻、朋友、家人和谐美好之意。

Example Sentence:

Images of the Immortals of Harmony and Union are often hung at weddings as a hope that the newlyweds can stay together until old age and be of one heart and one mind.

例句：

民间婚礼上常挂**和合二仙**的画像，祝愿新婚夫妻白头偕老，永结同心。

八仙 *Baxian;* Eight Immortals

中国民间流传的八位仙人，即铁拐李、钟离权（又称汉钟离）、吕洞宾、张果老、曹国舅、韩湘子、蓝采和、何仙姑。八仙人物出处不一，时代也不同，道教将他们组合成为一组神仙后，八仙故事逐渐广泛流传，内容日益丰富。因八仙的法术各异，民间有“八仙过海，各显神通”的说法。民间传说、说唱中有不少关于他们的故事，讲述他们得道成仙的经过和种种离奇的经历。民间工艺美术中也有很多八仙形象，以八仙庆寿、八仙过海故事流传最广。

A group of eight legendary immortals in Chinese mythology. They are composed of Li Tieguai (Iron Crutch Li), Zhongli Quan (also known as Zhongli of the Han Dynasty), Lü Dongbin, Zhang Guolao, Cao Guojiu (Royal Uncle Cao), Han Xiangzi, Lan Caihe, and He Xiangu. According to early records, the Eight Immortals lived in different times and had achieved immortality through different means. After they were grouped together as the Eight Immortals by Daoism, their stories became popular and enriched. The magical power of each immortal is different. Derived from their stories, the Chinese saying “the Eight Immortals cross the sea, each revealing their divine power” indicates a situation where everyone is able to tap their full potential and achieve a common goal. The Eight Immortals are revered in Chinese society. Their stories are told in various literary and folk tales, and they are depicted in folk artworks. The most popular stories about them are “The Eight Immortals Offering Birthday Blessings” and “The Eight Immortals Crossing the Sea.”

例句：

传说蓬莱是**八仙**居住的地方，也是他们过海的地方。

Example Sentence:

Penglai is said to be where the Eight Immortals have resided before setting out on their trip across the sea.

黄大仙 *Huang Daxian;* Immortal Huang

中国民间和道教信仰的神仙，又称“赤松大仙”。相传晋代道士黄初平（号赤松子）在浙江金华山洞中修炼成仙，因此当地人在金华山中建祠供奉。据传他擅长法术，曾“叱石成羊”。黄大仙的信仰在东南沿海一带比较盛行，后来随着华侨外出谋生，黄大仙信仰逐渐传至海外。

A Chinese Daoist deity invested with the power to heal, also called the Chisong Daxian (Red Pine Immortal). Huang Daxian was born in Jinhua, Zhejiang Province under the name Huang Chuping during the Jin Dynasty (265-420). Huang Chuping began practicing Daoism and became an immortal on Jinhua Mountain. Legend has it that he was able to transform stones into sheep. In ancient times, there was a widespread belief in this immortal throughout the coastal regions in southeastern China. People there spread his legend abroad as they migrated to Southeast Asian countries, where he is also known as Wong Tai Sin based on his name's Cantonese pronunciation.

例句：

现今数香港的**黄大仙**祠最为著名，终年进香朝拜者甚众。

Example Sentence:

Today, the Wong Tai Sin (Huang Daxian) Temple in Hong Kong is the most well-known shrine for Immortal Huang and many pilgrims come to worship him throughout the year.

灶神 *Zaoshen;* Kitchen God

中国民间广泛信奉的神祇之一，又称"灶君""灶王爷"。灶神最初的职责是执掌灶火，管理饮食，后来扩大为考察人间善恶，以降福祸。据说灶王爷每年年末要上天向玉皇大帝汇报人间一年的功过，因此民间盛行在腊月二十三或二十四举行祭灶仪式，请灶王爷"上天言好事，下界保平安"。传统的祭灶仪式由男子主持，妇女一般不参与。1949年以前，中国大部分家庭都在厨房供奉灶王爷的神像，有的神像只画灶王爷一人，有的还画上了他的妻子"灶王奶奶"。现在部分乡村仍有腊月祭灶习俗。

One of the most widely worshipped gods among Chinese people. The Kitchen God—also known as *Zao Jun or Zao Wangye*—was known to watch over the domestic affairs of a family, and later also known to investigate the good and evil deeds of human beings. It is believed that just before Chinese New Year, the Kitchen God returns to Heaven to report the activities of every household over the past year to the Jade Emperor. Traditionally, on the twenty-third or twenty-fourth day of the twelfth lunar month, each household holds a ceremony to ask the Kitchen God to report the good deeds of the family in Heaven and bring peace to the secular world. Such a ceremony was participated by male members only. Before 1949, most households in China had a painting of the Kitchen God, sometimes along with his wife, hanging in the kitchen. Nowadays, this tradition is still popular in some rural areas in China.

例句：

传说新年来临之际，**灶神**将带着玉帝旨意回到人间，人们会在除夕晚上架柴火迎接灶神。

Example Sentence:

According to legend, as the New Year approaches, the Kitchen God returns to earth with the orders of the Jade Emperor. People would set out firewood to welcome the Kitchen God on the Chinese New Year's Eve.

土地神 *Tudi Shen;* Village Land God; local land god

中国民间传说中的村社守护神，俗称“土地爷”“土地公公”等。中国古代就有奉土祭社的礼俗，以感谢土地生养万物之恩。土地神的出处很多，因时代、地域不同而有不同的故事。东晋以后，民间多将生前行善或廉正之官吏奉为本地土地神。明清以后民间又多以名人作为各方土地神。民间对土地神的信仰十分广泛，1949年以前，几乎每个村落都有土地庙。一般认为土地神为地方行政神，保护乡里安宁平静；也有学者认为土地神是地府的行政神，掌管乡里死者的户籍；很多地方的土地神还兼有财神的性质。每年农历二月初二为土地神诞辰之日，家家作祭，为土地公公祝寿。土地神信仰寄托了人民祈福、求财、保平安、保农业收成的美好愿望。

The guardian god of village communities according to Chinese folklore, commonly known as "*Tudi Ye* (Lord of the Village)" or "*Tudi Gonggong* (Lord of the Village)." In ancient China, land worship ceremonies were held to thank the land for raising and nourishing all things. The origins of the Village Land God vary in different times and regions. After the Eastern Jin Dynasty (317-420), the local land god was believed to have been a local official who had performed good deeds and shown integrity. After the Ming (1368-1644) and Qing (1616-1911) dynasties, folk people mostly worshipped prominent figures as the Village Land God. Before 1949, nearly all villages had altars to their land gods in temples of various sizes scattered throughout rural areas. People generally believe that the land god is the local administrative god who ensures peace and order in the community. Some scholars believe that the land god is the administrative god of hell who is in charge of the residence records of the deceased. In many places the land god also assumes the responsibilities of the god of wealth. Every year on the second day of the second lunar month, every household offers sacrifices to celebrate the birthday of the Village Land God. People pray to him for blessings, wealth, peace, and good harvests.

例句：

土地神形象多为须发皓然、慈祥和蔼、神态可掬的老者。

Example Sentence:

Village land gods are typically depicted as benign-looking old men with gray hair and white beard.

三星神 *Sanxing Shen;* Gods of the Three Stars; Three Stellar Gods

中国民间传说和道教神系中的“福星”“禄星”和“寿星”的合称，象征幸福、吉利、长寿。“福星”又称“福神”，掌管人间福气的分配。“禄星”是读书人的保护神，掌管人间功名利禄，自科举制度形成之后在民间开始备受尊崇。“寿星”是长寿之神，其独特形象为额头大，手中握寿桃，象征长生不老。福、禄、寿三星是民间最受欢迎的三个福神和吉祥如意的象征，是中国传统绘画的常见题材。

A collective term for trio stellar gods: the gods of *fu* (happiness), *lu* (prosperity), and *shou* (longevity) in Chinese folklore and Daoist beliefs. The star of *fu* was believed to be in charge of the distribution of blessings to people. The star of *lu* blessed those who took exams and competed for the highest paying jobs, and it had been highly respected ever since the formation of the imperial civil examination system. The star of *shou* is the star god of longevity. He is recognized by his high, domed forehead and the peach which he carries as a symbol of immortality. Gods of *fu*, *lu*, and *shou* are the most popular gods among the Chinese, and they are also a common subject of traditional Chinese paintings.

例句：

中国民间祝寿时，常在正屋墙上悬挂福、禄、寿**三星神**的画像，两侧寿联一般为“福如东海、寿比南山”。

Example Sentence:

When Chinese people celebrate their birthdays, they often hang a picture of the Gods of the Three Stars on the wall. The couplet on either side generally reads “May your happiness be as immense as the East Sea and may you live as long as the Zhongnan Mountains.”

福星 *Fuxing;* Star of Happiness; God of Happiness

中国民间信仰的三星神之一，又称“福神”。福星原为主管农业的岁星（即木星）；唐朝时，人们将唐道州刺史阳城尊为福神，因为他敢于上书皇帝，废除了将当地侏儒作为玩物进贡朝廷的陋习。侏儒们为感激阳城的善行，为他树立雕像，并祭拜。从此以后，阳城成为“福星”的化身。宋元以后，道教的赐福天官逐渐取代阳城成为民间普遍接受的福星。福星一般为头戴官帽、手持玉如意或手捧小孩儿的官员形象，深受老百姓尊敬和爱戴。每至新春佳节或吉日，人们便在家里贴福神像，希冀福降家门，福运绵长。

One of the Gods of the Three Stars in Chinese mythology, known in Chinese as *Fuxing* and *Fushen* (God of Happiness). The star, believed to be Jupiter, was originally in charge of agriculture. During the Tang Dynasty (618-907), a governor named Yang Cheng risked his life by writing a letter to the emperor imploring him to save the lives of dwarves who had been pressed into service as personal servants and court entertainers. Grateful for Yang's actions, the dwarves erected images of their benefactor and offered sacrifices to him. Yang Cheng became immortalized as *Fuxing*. After the Song (960-1279) and Yuan (1206-1368) dynasties, the Daoist Heavenly Official for bestowing happiness gradually replaced Yang Cheng as the Star of Happiness. *Fuxing* is generally depicted as an official wearing an official hat and holding a jade Ruyi scepter or a child in his hands. He is deeply respected and loved by the people. Every year during the Spring Festival, people paste images of the God of Happiness to their doors to pray for enduring good fortune.

例句：

福星、禄星和寿星是中国民间信仰中极受欢迎的三位神仙。有中国人的地方就能看到这三位神仙的形象。

Example Sentence:

The Three Gods of Happiness, Prosperity, and Longevity are three very popular deities that can be found virtually wherever there are Chinese communities.

福星高照

fuxing gaozhao;
having one's lucky star in the ascendant; full of blessings

祝福他人幸运和有福气的成语，又称"吉星高照"。福星是中国民间信仰中象征幸福的神仙。福星高照意指在福星庇佑下人们能逢凶化吉，安康如意。多用于小辈对长辈，也可用于平辈亲属友人之间祈愿福运相伴，一路坦途。

An auspicious expression used to congratulate one over their good luck and happiness. It is also said as "*jixing gaozhao* (having one's fortune star shining high)." The Star of Happiness is a symbol of happiness according to Chinese folk beliefs. Having one's lucky star in the ascendant indicates blessings, luck, and peace. It is often used by people to give best wishes to people of an older generation, and it is also used between peers, relatives, and friends to bless the arrival of lucky things.

例句：

一个人如果并不是生来就**福星高照**的话，他就得发奋努力去获得他想要得到的东西。

Example Sentence:

If one doesn't have a lucky star in the ascendant upon birth, then he has to work harder to get what he wants.

五福临门

wufu linmen;
may the five blessings descend upon this home

中国民间常见祝福语，指长寿、富贵、康宁、好德、善终五种人生的福气一起降临。五福临门是中国古人关于幸福观的五条标准:“长寿”指福寿绵长；“富贵”指富足尊贵；“康宁”指健康安宁;“好德”指仁善宽厚;“善终”安详离世。后世也有把“福禄寿喜财”作为五福的。民间认为“五福”俱全才能构成幸福美满的人生。

A blessing and auspicious expression said among Chinese people. *Wufu* (the five blessings) refers to longevity, wealth, health, virtue, and a natural death in ancient China. The saying *wufu linmen* means “the five blessings have descended upon the house,” and is one of many auspicious expressions used during the Chinese New Year. *Wufu* actually provides the five criteria deemed indicative of happiness by ancient Chinese people. They believe a happy and perfect life should include elements of the five blessings. Later, another interpretation of the five blessings appears, namely, happiness, prosperity, longevity, joy, and wealth. People believe that these five blessings constitute a happy life.

例句：

五福临门是中国新年期间使用的许多吉祥语之一。

Example Sentence:

Wufu linmen (The five blessings have descended upon the house) is one of many auspicious expressions said during the Chinese New Year.

天官赐福

tianguan cifu;
heavenly blessings;
May the Heavenly Official bestow happiness.

旧时用来祈福消灾的吉利语。天官为道教神仙天、地、水三官之一，道教中有天官赐福、地官赦罪、水官解厄的说法，因此民间一般认为天官是福神。传说正月十五（上元节）是天官诞辰，每年这一天天官会下凡人间，赐福于民。“天官赐福”的吉祥图或年画很常见，画上天官或手执写着“天官赐福”四个大字的横幅，或抱着象征吉祥的如意，或抱着手捧吉祥物的五个童子，背靠花团锦簇的“福”字，象征着吉祥富贵。民间戏班开场前必演《天官赐福》，表示天官将赐福来看戏的所有人。

An auspicious saying said as a prayer to extricate oneself from misfortune. *Tianguan* is one of the three officials in Daoism. *Tianguan*, the Heavenly Official, bestows happiness while *Diguan*, the Earthly Official, forgives sins, and *Shuiguan*, the Water Official, averts misfortune. Legend has it that the fifteenth day of the first lunar month (Shangyuan Festival) is the birthday of *Tianguan*, and that every year on this day the Heavenly Official will descend to the world and bless the people. The auspicious picture of "*tianguan cifu*" and the four characters on a banner are a common sight during this time. *Tianguan* often holds a scepter (*ruyi*, the symbol of good luck) or five boys with mascots symbolizing good fortune and wealth while the background depicts many flowers surrounding the character *fu* (happiness). Before beginning their programs, Chinese folk theatres needed to play "The Heavenly Official Brings Happiness," symbolizing that *Tianguan* will bless the audience.

例句：

每逢春节，中国人会在门上贴**天官赐福**对联或年画以表吉祥之意，期望上天降福人间。

Example Sentence:

Every Spring Festival, the Chinese people paste couplets including the expression "*tianguan cifu*" (heavenly blessings) on their doors or other New Year pictures that symbolize wishes for auspiciousness and blessings.

福到(倒) *fu dao*; the character *fu* is upside down (good fortune is drawing near)

中国传统年俗，即把“福”字倒着贴，寓意“福到”。每逢新春佳节，家家户户在屋门、墙壁上贴上大大小小的“福”字，有正贴和倒贴两种贴法。春节倒贴“福”字寄托了人们对幸福生活的向往，也是对美好未来的祝愿。

A Chinese traditional custom during the Lunar New Year. The character *fu* (meaning happiness) is pasted upside down (*dao*, which is pronounced the same as the word meaning arriving), meaning “blessings are coming.” During the Spring Festival, virtually every household has *fu* characters pasted on their doors and walls as they are or upside down. The custom of placing the character *fu* upside down during the Spring Festival symbolizes hopes for a happy life and wishes for a better future.

例句：

“福到（倒）”是民间贴“福”字的风俗，与清朝皇帝农历新年赐“福”字的惯例有关。

Example Sentence:

The Chinese folk custom of placing the character *fu* upside down is related to the practice of granting calligraphy work of the character *fu* by the emperors of the Qing Dynasty (1616-1911) to their subordinates during the Lunar New Year.

禄星 *Luxing;* Star of Prosperity; God of Prosperity

中国民间信仰的三星神之一，主司功名利禄之神，又称“禄神”。隋唐科举制度产生后，禄星逐渐成为掌管士人命运的主宰神，天下学子莫不对之顶礼膜拜。禄神常常和福神、寿神一起接受祭祀，不少地方建有三星庙。

One of the Gods of the Three Stars in Chinese mythology, also known as *Lushen* (God of Prosperity). The Star of Prosperity oversees promotions and salary increase. The word *lu* specifically refers to the salary of a government official. In ancient times, a career as an official was believed to lead to wealth and fortune. As such, the *lu* god is the god of prosperity, rank, and influence. Accordingly, people pray to the God of Prosperity, hoping to enjoy a prosperous career. God of Prosperity is often seen together with the God of Happiness and the God of Longevity. Some places have temples of the trio gods.

例句：

封建时代，做官和科举有着密不可分的联系，掌管文运之神往往就是**禄星**神。

Example Sentence:

The Star of Prosperity was worshipped as the deity who dictates one's success in the imperial civil examinations, which can lead to success in one's political career and prosperity.

禄神 *Lushen;* God of Prosperity

参见“禄星”。

See *Luxing* (Star of Prosperity).

文曲星 *Wenqu Xing;* God of Literature; Star of Literature

中国古代民间信仰中主管人间功名利禄的神，也指重要文职官员及文才盖世之人，也称“文昌星”“文星”。文曲星本为星名，是北斗第四星，古代星相学家将文昌星解释为主大贵的吉星。道教兴起后将其尊为主宰功名利禄之神，也称“文昌帝君”。隋唐科举制度产生以后，文人学子在读书、科举考试时供奉、膜拜文曲星。现在文曲星常用来指极有文采的人。

The god in charge of riches and successes in official careers according to ancient Chinese folk beliefs, also called *Wenchang Xing* or *Wen Xing*. This is the god who oversees important civilian officials and men of literary talent. *Wenqu Xing* was originally the name of a star in the Big Dipper, and is regarded as a lucky star in charge of great wealth and splendor. After the rise of Daoism, the star was also referred to as *Wenchang Dijun* (Imperial Sovereign Wenchang). After the establishment of the Imperial Examination System in the Sui (581-618) and Tang (618-907) dynasties, the literati and students worshipped *Wenqu Xing* while preparing for and taking part in imperial examinations. Nowadays, *Wenqu Xing* is used to refer to people with exceptional literary talents.

例句:

最广为人知的**文曲星**的化身是周代圣人张亚子，据说他可预测未来他死后，为了纪念他，人们就把他当成神加以崇拜。

Example Sentence:

The human personification of *Wenqu Xing* is regarded as Zhang Yazi, a saint of the Zhou Dynasty (1046-256 BC) who was said to be able to predict the future. After his death, he was worshipped as the God of Literature.

寿星 *Shouxing;* Star of Longevity; God of Longevity

中国民间信仰的三星神之一，掌管福寿之神，又称“南极老人星”。民间将其绘成老人形象，慈眉善目，白须持杖，头部长而隆起，常衬托以鹿、鹤、仙桃等，象征长寿。秦汉时已有寿星祠和老人庙。自东汉起祭祀寿星与敬老活动相结合，历代皆列入国家祀典，至明初始罢。作为长寿和尊老的象征，寿星在民间流传甚广，人们对其顶礼叩拜，以求延寿、多福。

One of the Gods of the Three Stars in Chinese mythology, along with *fu* and *lu*. *Shouxing* is in charge of longevity, also called *Nanji Laoren Xing* (the Old Man of the South Pole). He is often depicted as a benign old man with a long white beard and domed forehead. He is holding a stick and surrounded by symbols of longevity such as deer, crane, and peach. Temples to worship the God of Longevity had appeared during the Qin (221-206 BC) and Han (206 BC-AD 220) dynasties, and in the Eastern Han Dynasty (25-220) people worshipped the God of Longevity and held activities to honor elderly people. From this time on, all dynasties incorporated this custom into their national rituals, up to the beginning of the Ming Dynasty (1368-1644). As a symbol of longevity and respect for elderly people, *Shouxing* is widely recognized, and sacrifices are made to him to pray for good health, longevity, and blessings.

例句：

人们相信**寿星**可以给人延长生命。民间勾绘的寿星形象都是他手里拿着一颗寿桃。很多中国人在生日那天会通过吃桃子来表达延年益寿的愿望。

Example Sentence:

God of Longevity is said to be the god who grants longevity. He is always portrayed as an old man holding the peach of immortality in his hand. This famous peach has inspired many Chinese people to eat peaches on their birthdays, hoping for longevity.

福禄双全

fu lu shuang quan;
May you enjoy both happiness and prosperity.

用来祝福的吉利语。“福”指福气，“禄”指官吏的俸给，“双全”指二者齐备，多祝颂人命运好。古人常以蝙蝠、鹿、葫芦等组成“福禄双全”吉祥图案。取“蝠”与“福”同音，“鹿”与“禄”同音，“葫芦”与“福禄”谐音之意。

An auspicious saying in Chinese culture, meant to impart good wishes. *Fu* refers to blessings and *lu* refers to the salary of an official. Ancient Chinese often used bats, deer, gourds, and other objects to reference the auspicious term *fu lu shuang quan*, as these words are homophones: bat is pronounced *fu*, blessing is also pronounced *fu*, deer is pronounced *lu*, and salary is also pronounced *lu*. In addition, gourd is pronounced *hulu*, which is similar to the pronunciation of “blessing and high salary” (*fu lu*).

例句：

让温馨的祝愿在新年来到你身边，伴你左右，祝你**福禄双全**。

Example Sentence:

May the warmest wishes, happy thoughts, and friendly greetings come during New Year and stay with you all through the year. May you enjoy both happiness (*fu*) and prosperity (*lu*).

福如东海，寿比南山

fu ru donghai, shou bi nanshan;
May you enjoy happiness as immense as the East Sea, and live as long as the Zhongnan Mountains.

中国祝寿用语，也作“福如东海长流水，寿比南山不老松”。“东海”指现在的渤海，古有“海纳百川”之说。古代中国的经济中心在黄土高原、华北平原，毗邻渤海，所以古人认为渤海是最大的海，因此以“福如东海”比喻福气自四方云集，像东海的水一样绵绵不尽。“南山”指终南山，即位于陕西省西安市南边的秦岭山脉中段，亦作“中南山”或“太乙山”，素有天下第一福地之称。“寿比南山”比喻人的寿命如终南山一般长久。

An auspicious greeting spoken on a person's birthday. The "east sea" refers to the Bohai Sea, which was once thought to be the largest in the world, with thousands of rivers flowing into it. It borders the Loess Plateau and the North China Plain, which was the economic center of China in ancient times. In Chinese, *fu ru donghai* is used to signify that endless blessings will come from near and far, just like the waters flowing to the east sea. The Zhongnan Mountains—also known as the Southern Mountains—are the main artery of the Qinling Mountains and located to the south of Xi'an, Shaanxi Province. They were regarded as the first land to be blessed in the world, and therefore the oldest. The greeting imparts the wish that one's life span will be as long as the Zhongnan Mountains.

例句：

奶奶过生日那天，大家举杯祝福：“祝您**福如东海，寿比南山**。”

Example Sentence:

At the birthday party held for my grandmother, everyone proposed this toast, "May you enjoy happiness as immense as the East Sea and live as long as the Zhongnan Mountains!"

财神 *Caishen;* God of Wealth

中国民间信仰中主宰人世间金钱财运之神。财神信仰起源于人们希冀发财致富的共同心理，在宋代以后广为流传。财神的来源比较多元，民间大多供奉秦朝终南山人赵公明，但也有些地方区分文财神和武财神，其属下又有利市仙官、招财使者等。旧时民间财神信仰最普遍，尤其体现在春节期间：农历除夕有人执财神画像挨家挨户送财神，正月初二家家设供接财神，正月初五商店开市必鸣放鞭炮向财神焚香礼拜，以祈求生意兴隆。各地皆有财神庙。

The deity of wealth in Chinese mythology. Aspirations for wealth and prosperity resulted in the worship of the God of Wealth. There are many types of this god, such as the Civil God of Wealth, Martial God of Wealth, and Goddess of Wealth. They also have many subordinates, such as *Lishi Xianguan* (Immortal Official of Profitability) and *Zhaocai Shizhe* (Envoy of Attracting Wealth). In the past, ceremonies related to the God of Wealth are more frequent than those for other deities, especially during the Spring Festival. On the eve of the Lunar New Year, people used to go door to door selling ceremonial pictures of the God of Wealth. On the second day of the first lunar month, households offer sacrifices to welcome the God of Wealth. On the fifth day of the first lunar month, shops reopen after being closed for the New Year, and shopkeepers burn joss sticks and set off firecrackers to pay their respects to the god and pray for a thriving business. Temples and shrines dedicated to the God of Wealth can be found almost everywhere.

例句：

正月初二是出嫁女儿回娘家的日子，也是迎**财神**的日子。

Example Sentence:

The second day of the first lunar month is the time for married women to return to their parents' homes. It is also the day to greet the God of Wealth.

Wen Caishen; Civil God of Wealth

来源于文官的财神，相传为商朝忠臣比干和春秋战国时的范蠡。比干为商朝末代暴君纣王的叔叔，也是丞相，为人公正无私，敢于直谏，被后人奉为文财神。范蠡是春秋时期越王勾践手下的大臣，曾帮助越王成就霸业。他料到君王可以“共患难而不能共富贵”，事成后便隐姓埋名，理财致富（号陶朱公），被商界奉为文财神。

A form of the god of wealth derived from the image of civil officials. According to Chinese folk legend, the Civil God of Wealth can be traced back to Bi Gan, a loyal minister of the Shang Dynasty (1600-1046 BC), and Fan Li of the Spring and Autumn and the Warring States periods (770-221 BC). Bi Gan, the Prime Minister, was the uncle of the tyrant King Zhou, the last ruler of the Shang Dynasty. Bi Gan was fair, selfless, and often advised the ruler to rectify his corrupt nature. Later generations regarded him as the Civil God of Wealth. Fan Li was a minister under King Yue Goujian during the Spring and Autumn Period. He helped the king build a powerful state, but predicted that the king would render him a threat when their country was strong and powerful despite his contributions. After completing his service to the king he chose to live a secluded life, and became rich on account of his business management. He was later referred to as Tao Zhugong, and became honored as the Civil God of Wealth.

例句：

文财神比干被誉为“亘古忠臣”，受到历代帝王的尊崇。

Example Sentence:

Bi Gan, Civil God of Wealth, was honored as an honest official and revered by emperors throughout the ages.

武财神 *Wu Caishen;* Martial God of Wealth

来源于武官的财神，相传为赵公明和关羽（也称“关公”）。相传赵公明为秦朝人，在终南山修行得道，被奉为道教四大元帅之一，为中国正财神，司掌世间财源。关羽是三国时期蜀国国主刘备的结拜兄弟、心腹大将，他对刘备忠贞不二。概因关羽极重义气而被合伙经商者奉为武财神。

A form of the god of wealth derived from the image of military officers. Zhao Gongming and Guan Yu were believed to be Martial Gods of Wealth. According to legend, Zhao Gongming was a practitioner of Daoism during the Qin Dynasty (221-206 BC), and was enshrined as one of the four supreme commanders of Daoism after attaining “the Way” at Zhongnan Mountains. He was regarded as the God of wealth in China, who is in charge of all wealth. Guan Yu (also known as Lord Guan) was a confidant and loyal military general of Liu Bei, the king of the Shu Kingdom during the Three Kingdoms period (220-280). Because of his loyalty, he was regarded as a Martial God of Wealth by business communities.

例句：

武财神关公成为海外华人最为看重的精神护身符。

Example Sentence:

Guan Gong, the Martial God of Wealth, has long become the most important spiritual protector for many overseas Chinese.

jie caishen;
(the ceremony of) welcoming the God of Wealth

中国旧时民间岁时习俗。旧俗在农历正月初二或初五早晨摆出各种供品，燃放爆竹迎接财神降临，以祈发财致富。后来接财神逐渐发展成流行于中国很多地区的商业风俗。每年农历正月初五，浙江宁波地区各商店均设五色茶点来恭迎第一位顾客登门，称其为“财神”且给予优惠。上海民间初四夜和初五有接财神之俗，合家老小跪拜祈求今年财神爷送财降福，各商铺店肆也都在这时举行仪式迎接“财神”。

A Chinese folk custom held on the second or fifth day of the first lunar month. During this time, families make offerings and set off firecrackers to invite the God of Wealth to their homes in the early morning, hoping to make a fortune in the coming year. The custom later spread into business circles and became particularly popular in many places in China. On the fifth day of the first lunar month, many store owners in Ningbo of Zhejiang Province prepare colorful refreshments to welcome their first customer. They refer to this customer as the “God of Wealth” and give him/her a discount. On the evening of the fourth and fifth day of the first lunar month, folk communities in Shanghai also observe this custom. Every family member will worship the God of Wealth, hoping to receive blessings and make a fortune, and many stores also hold various rituals to welcome the God of Wealth.

例句:

旧时人们相信**接财神**会令他们在新的一年里发财致富。

Example Sentence:

In the past, people believe that welcoming the God of Wealth will bring them prosperity for the new year.

门神 *Menshen;* Door God

中国民间信仰中司门之神，人们把神像或挂或贴在门上使妖魔不敢入内，以保佑全家一年平安。最早的门神是神荼、郁垒，传说他们两人十分威猛，奉命把守鬼门。据传唐代大将秦叔宝和尉迟敬德，他们两人戎装立在唐太宗门外，唐太宗晚上即不再做噩梦，于是唐太宗命画工画两人形象悬于宫门之上，后世民间沿袭下来，称二人为门神。

Gods who guard gates and doorways in Chinese folk beliefs. Traditionally, people placed portraits of the Door Gods on doors to ward off evil forces and offer blessings. The earliest door gods were known as Shen Shu and Yu Lu. It is said that the two of them were very mighty and were ordered to guard the gates of hell. It is said that the generals Qin Shubao (also known as Qin Qiong) and Yuchi Jingde (also known as Yuchi Gong) were stationed outside the palace of Emperor Taizong of the Tang Dynasty (618-907), after which he no longer had nightmares. The emperor therefore gave orders to have their portraits hung on the palace gate. The general public then followed suit. From then on, the portraits of the two generals were addressed as Door Gods.

例句：

《西游记》第十章对**门神**起源介绍得很详细。

Example Sentence:

Chapter 10 of the Chinese novel *Journey to the West* records the story about the origins of the door gods.

文官门神 *Wenguan Menshen;* Civil Door God

中国旧时民间信仰中的文官形象的门神，也称“祈福门神”，其代表有天官、状元、福禄寿星、和合二仙、财神等。他们一般戴纱帽，穿一品绣鹤朝服。商人一般供奉招财童子。文官门神专为祈福而用，而非保护者，一般贴在堂屋及厢房门上。这些门神的出现寄托了人们祈望升官发财、延年益寿的愿望。

A form of the door god in Chinese mythology focusing less on warding off evil and more on blessing the residents with promotions, prosperity and longevity, also called *Qifu Menshen* (the Door God of Blessings). They are represented by civil officials such as *Tianguan* (Heavenly Officials), *Zhuangyuan* (the number one scholar of an imperial examination to select officials in feudal China), *Fu Lu Shou Xing* (the Gods of Three Stars), and *Hehe Erxian* (Immortals of Harmony and Union), and the God of Wealth. They usually wear silk hats and court robes with a pair of embroidered cranes. In addition, merchants generally worship *Zhaocai Tongzi* (the Immortal Child of Wealth). The Door Gods are often pasted on the doors of living halls and wing rooms.

例句：

文官门神大多是在文官或历代文人形象基础上描绘出来的。

Example Sentence:

Depictions of the Civil Door Gods are mostly based on famous civil officials from Chinese history.

祈福门神 *Qifu Menshen;* Door God of Blessings

参见“文官门神”。

See *Wenguan Menshen* (Civil Door God).

武将门神

Wujiang Menshen;
Martial Door God; Military Door God

中国旧时民间信仰中的武将形象的门神。武将门神多取自中国古典名著中的英雄好汉，唐代将军秦琼和尉迟恭是流传最广、至今沿袭的武将门神形象。武将门神通常贴在临街的大门上，多手持兵器，或立或坐，形象英武勇猛，负责镇住恶魔或灾星从大门外进入屋宅，保护家人平安。

A form of the door god whose images are based upon heroic military officers. Tang Dynasty generals Qin Qiong and Yuchi Gong are the two most widely recognized figures for martial door gods. Prints of the martial door gods are usually pasted on the front door of a house. Either standing or sitting, they are armed with weapons and appear both heroic and imposing. They are intended to keep demons and evil spirits from entering a home in order to protect the family inside.

例句：

武将门神通常成对贴在大门上，使人们在心理上产生一些安全感。

Example Sentence:

Martial door gods are placed in pairs to make people living in the residence feel they are well protected.

钟馗 *Zhong Kui;* Zhong Kui

中国知名门神之一，后被道教纳入其神仙体系。相传钟馗是唐朝时期的终南山人，他才华出众，刚正不阿，却因相貌丑陋在殿试中落第，愤而撞柱而死。之后他托梦给唐明皇，发誓要灭天下妖孽。唐明皇醒后命画工吴道子绘其图像，并昭告天下，要求家家户户在门上悬挂钟馗画像以镇妖驱邪。从此钟馗作为捉鬼之神的地位就确定了下来，成为最有名的门神之一。钟馗门神画像怒目圆睁，一手持剑一手捉妖，很有震慑力。

A famous Chinese door god included in the Daoist immortal system. Legend has it that Zhong Kui was born in the Zhongnan Mountain near the city of Xi'an during the Tang Dynasty (618-907). He was very talented and honest, but also very ugly. Upon taking the Imperial Martial Examinations, he was not allowed to pass because of his ugly appearance. Filled with regret over losing the chance to serve his country, Zhong Kui committed suicide. One night, Tang Dynasty Emperor Tang Xuanzong (685-762) had a dream of a man named Zhong Kui who vowed to wipe out all demons. When the emperor woke, he ordered images of Zhong Kui to be made, and made an announcement that every family should hang a portrait of Zhong Kui on their doors to keep out evil spirits. Zhong Kui's status as a ghost-hunting god was established, and he became one of the most famous door gods in China. Depictions of Zhong Kui have glaring, round eyes, and he powerfully, aggressively wields a sword with which he vanquishes demons.

例句：

相传**钟馗**在殿试中考了第一，但由于相貌丑陋，被皇上剥夺了“状元”头衔。

Example Sentence:

Though Zhong Kui ranked first in the final Imperial Examination, his rightful title of "*Zhuangyuan*" (top-scorer) was stripped away from him by the emperor because of his disfigured and ugly appearance.

阴曹地府

yincao difu;
netherworld; the Kingdom of the Underworld

中国民间信仰中认为人死后所去的地方，又称“阴间”，与人所生活的“阳间”对应。中国古代有三界之说，即天上、人间和地狱，人在死后先要到阴曹地府去报到，在那里接受阎罗王的审判：在阳间积德好善的人会得道成仙升到天上；普通人要投胎转世再做人；坏人、恶人要打入地狱接受不同程度的惩罚。中国古代神话和佛教、道教典籍中都有阴曹地府的记载，那里有阎罗王、判官、小鬼等各个级别的众多神职人员，等级森严。

In Chinese folk beliefs, the place where people go after death to receive judgment. It is also known as *yinjian*, the underworld or the world of the dead as opposed to *yangjian*, the world of the living. Ancient Chinese believed in three worlds: Heaven, Earth, and Hell. After death, it was believed the souls of people first went to *yincao difu*, where they were given a sentence by the King of Hell based on the lives they lived on earth. Those who were good rose to Heaven, common people were reincarnated and returned to Earth, and those who were evil were sent to Hell to accept their appropriate degree of punishment. Ancient Chinese mythology and Buddhist and Daoist classics all contain writings regarding *yincao difu*. There is a hierarchy of gods and officials, such as the King of Hell, judges, and devils.

例句：

阴曹地府是神话、佛教和道教中的鬼域世界，用来向世人宣扬轮回报应的思想。

Example Sentence:

Yincao difu is a world of ghosts in Chinese mythology, Buddhism and Daoism, which is used to advocate the idea of karma.

阎王 *Yanwang;* Yama; King of Hell; King of the Underworld

中国民间传说中阴间的主宰神，又称"阎罗王"。原为古印度神话传说中主宰地狱的一位冥神，随着佛教传入中国而成为民间广泛信仰的众鬼之王，负责审判人生前的行为并给予相应的惩罚。旧时常有信众在阎王庙为死去的亲人超度亡灵或做祈福活动。

The supreme god of the underworld according to Chinese folklore, also known as *Yanluo Wang*. He was originally the god who dominated the underworld according to ancient Indian mythology. As Buddhism was introduced to China, people believed him to be king of all ghosts and responsible for imparting judgment to each soul upon death, inflicting a corresponding punishment or reward for their actions during life. In olden days, there were often believers who prayed for dead souls or prayed inside the Temple of Yama.

例句：

四川"鬼城"丰都的天子殿正中有一尊极具威严的**阎王**坐像，殿外设有东、西地狱，展示恶人受刑的凄惨场面，以警戒人们生前不要作恶。

Example Sentence:

In the middle of the Tianzi Hall in Fengdu County, Sichuan Province, there is a statue of the majestic Yama and a "West Hell" and an "East Hell" outside the temple to show miserable scenes of punishments inflicted upon the wicked as a warning to prevent people from evildoings.

城隍爷 *Chenghuangye;* City God

中国民间敬奉的地方保护神和冥界的一城之主，简称"城隍"。古人认为城隍可以保护一个地方的安全并主管当地的水旱疾疫和冥籍，是阴间的地方最高神灵。唐代奉祀城隍已比较盛行，明代以后城隍庙遍及各地城镇。人们把生前"正直"或被认为有功于当地的人奉为城隍爷，因此各地城隍爷都不相同。旧时中国各地分别在清明、农历七月半、十月初一举行盛大的城隍出巡活动。

Local land god who protects cities of the living and of the dead in Chinese mythology, known as Chenghuang in short. Ancient Chinese believed that the city god could protect the safety of a place, control floods and plagues, and manage the underworld household registration system. In the Tang Dynasty (618-907), worship of the City God was quite popular and after the Ming Dynasty (1368-1644), City God temples spread throughout China. Later, people who were regarded as "righteous" during their lifetime or who were considered to have contributed to their local communities were also regarded as city gods. As a result, the city gods of different places vary. In olden days, grand tours of city gods were held during the Qingming Festival, on the fifteenth day of the seventh lunar month, and the first day of the tenth lunar month.

例句：

中国有很多为**城隍爷**修建的庙宇。中国人和古印度人、古希腊人一样，相信城镇保护神能够庇护他们所在的城市。

Example Sentence:

There are temples dedicated to local city gods (*Chenghuangye*) in many cities throughout China. Similar to ancient Indians and Greeks, the Chinese traditionally believed that city gods watched over cities.

十八层地狱

Shibaceng Diyu;
18 Levels of Hell; the Hell

中国民间信仰中的阴间监狱和刑场，用于囚禁和惩罚罪孽深重的亡魂。相传人死后其灵魂将进入阴间也即冥界，而生前作恶者死后其灵魂将会到地狱受审，接受折磨和惩罚。十八层地狱，是以受罪时间的长短与罪行等级轻重而排列的，而不是空间上的层级。被打入十八层地狱，即意味着终生受苦，永世不得翻身。

The afterlife prison and place where souls receive everlasting punishment according to Chinese folk beliefs. Legend has it that after one dies their soul enters the underworld where they will be judged by the King of Hell to ascend to rewards in Heaven, return to earth to be reincarnated, or descend into Hell to be punished. The 18 Levels of Hell are arranged according to the length and severity of the punishment given to the soul according to their crimes while alive on earth. Being plunged into the 18th level of Hell means that one will suffer for the rest of eternity and never return to the world.

例句：

阎王为地狱之首，属下的十八位判官分别主管**十八层地狱**。

Example Sentence:

Yama is the supreme ruler of Hell, and the 18 judges under him are in charge of the 18 Levels of Hell.

牛头马面 *Niu Tou Ma Mian*; Bull-Headed and Horse-Faced Hell Guards

中国民间流传的地狱中的两名狱卒，一个牛头人身，一个马头人身，在地府里负责巡逻和搜捕逃跑的罪鬼。民间传说中，牛头马面是阎王、判官的下属，有时爱占点小便宜，有时干点违法乱纪的事，有时又很有同情心，这也是封建时代人间差役的形象。现在人们用牛头马面来比喻各种各样的丑恶人物或帮凶。

Two jailers in hell, according to Chinese folklore. One has the head of a bull and the other, the face of a horse. They are responsible for patrolling in Hell and searching for fugitive souls. In folklore, *Niu Tou* and *Ma Mian* are two subordinates of the King of Hell and the judges of Hell. They sometimes are very compassionate while sometimes they take advantage of others and violate rules, which are actions typical of bailiffs during feudal times. Now people use *Niu Tou Ma Mian* as a metaphor for all kinds of evildoers or accomplices.

例句：

牛头马面虽然源于佛教，但在佛寺很少见到，倒是常见于道教的城隍庙、东岳庙、阎王庙等。

Example Sentence:

Although *Niu Tou Ma Mian* is said to be originated from Buddhism, they are rarely seen in Buddhist temples; rather, they are commonly seen in Daoist temples, such as the City God Temple, the Dongyue Temple, and the Yama Temple.

黑白无常

Heibai Wuchang;
Black and White Impermanence; Guard in White and Guard in Black

中国道教神话中的一对勾魂使者，简称“无常”。他们专职缉拿鬼魂，协助赏善罚恶。民间认为人将死时会有无常鬼来勾魂。据说生前作恶之人会遇见黑无常，生前良善之人会遇见白无常。民间认为黑白无常为阎罗王、城隍、东岳大帝等冥界神明的部将。白无常头戴白帽，身穿白袍，手拿一把芭蕉扇；黑无常头戴黑帽，身穿黑袍，手执铁索。

A pair of ghosts from Chinese Daoist mythology who bring souls of the dead to the King of Hell for judgment. They are referred to as *wuchang* (Impermanence) for short. They are dedicated to catching souls and providing assistance at rewarding good and punishing evil. People believe that when a person dies, Impermanence will come and take their soul. It is also believed that people who did evil during their life will encounter Black Impermanence while those who did good will encounter White Impermanence. They are often viewed as the officers of such gods as Yama, the city gods, and the Emperor of East Great Mountain. *Baiwuchang* (White Impermanence) wears a white hat and white robe, holding a palm-leaf fan in his hand, while *Heiwuchang* (Black Impermanence) wears a black hat, a black robe, and holds an iron rope.

例句：

黑白无常是地狱的守卫，他们的职责是引导鬼魂进入阴间。

Example Sentence:

Black and White Impermanence are the guards of the hell, whose job is to guide the souls from the world of the living into the realm of the dead.

无常 *Wuchang;* Impermanence; guards of the Hell

参见“黑白无常”。

See *Heibai Wuchang* (Black and White Impermanence).

鬼城 *guicheng;* (Fengdu) ghost town/city

指四川历史文化古城丰都县城，又称“鬼都”。关于鬼城来历的说法很多，流传最广的版本是阴长生和王方平二人舍弃荣华富贵在丰都修道，成仙升天，阴、王二仙的故事后被世人误读为“阴王”，丰都就成了鬼都。在后来的两千多年历史中，丰都不断受到儒家、佛家、道家的文化影响，产生了种种神话传说，逐渐成为有名的鬼城，成为人类亡灵的归宿之地。它不仅是传说中的鬼城，还是集儒、道、佛为一体的民俗文化艺术宝库，是长江黄金旅游线上最著名的人文景观之一。

A reference to the historical and cultural city of Fengdu in Fengdu County, Sichuan Province, also called the "*guidu* (ghost city)." There are different stories regarding how Fengdu becomes the ghost town. The most told is about immortalization of Yin Changsheng and Wang Fangping. These two men came to Fengdu to practice Daoist teaching, leaving behind wealth and political career. They became immortals. Later people misnamed them Yinwang by combining their family names. Yinwang means the King of Hell. Therefore, Fengdu ghost town gained its name. Over the following two thousand years, Fengdu became influenced by Confucianism, Buddhism, and Daoism, producing various netherworld-related myths and legends. The place has gradually become known as China's most famous "ghost" town and the earthly location of the door to *yincao difu* (the netherworld/Hell) for souls. The city is a treasure trove of folk culture and art that integrates Confucianism, Daoism, and Buddhism. It is one of the most famous cultural destinations on the Yangtze River tourist route.

例句：

鬼城内有高楼、建筑、实景模型及与地狱相关的鬼怪雕塑。

Example Sentence:

The Fengdu ghost town consists of a variety of buildings, structures, dioramas, and statues related to the netherworld, and Hell.

guidu;
ghost city

参见“鬼城”。

See *guicheng* (ghost town/city).

纸钱

zhiqian;
joss paper; ghost money

中国民间信仰中送给死者在阴间使用的钱币。一般用白、黄色纸仿铜钱状剪制而成，抑或用木槌将钱模形状打在纸上，近代也有仿纸币印制而成的纸钱。一般在祭祀死人或神明时抛撒于野外墓坑，或者焚化给死者。纸钱源于汉代随葬钱币，到唐朝时抛洒或焚化纸钱的习俗逐渐在民间盛行，后世，在汉族地区和不少少数民族地区，撒纸、化纸已成了葬仪祭祀中不可缺少的一环，许多地区至今沿习。

In Chinese folklore, paper used to symbolize currency which is used by the deceased in the netherworld. Joss paper was cut from white and yellow paper and made into the shape of copper coins. In modern times, joss paper is made with an appearance similar to banknotes. It is usually thrown into graves or burned so that the deceased can use it in the netherworld. During the Han Dynasty (206 BC-AD 220), people were often buried with coins, believed to help the deceased pay

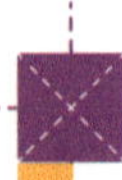

for things in the netherworld. Later, paper was used to replace and symbolize the coins. Over the centuries, the practice of throwing or burning joss paper became an indispensable part of funeral rituals in regions inhabited by Han people and certain ethnic groups. The practice is still prevalent in many parts of China.

例句：

纸钱一般由粗糙的竹纸制成。

Example Sentence:

Joss paper is traditionally made from coarse bamboo paper.

纸马

zhima;
paper horse print; ceremonial print of a god or an immortal

旧时民间祭祀活动中供奉或焚烧的神祇画像，又称“神马”“甲马”。马在古代是重要的交通工具，因此被古人想象为天地交通的灵物，因此这类祭神类木版画就被称为“纸马”。纸马多为木版刻印，风格古朴，刀法粗犷。纸马集宗教、艺术、民俗于一体，旨在追求天、地、人的抱合和神、人、鬼的互通。神马种类繁多，除用于节日供奉外，还用于婚丧寿诞及祛病驱邪等民俗活动中。

Woodblock prints of deities which is burned as an offering in worship, also known as *shenma* (divine horse print), *jiama* (armored horse print). When the portrait is burned or worshipped, the spirits of the deities “ride” to the netherworld on this virtual “horse,” as horse is an important means of transportation in ancient times. Most such ceremonial portraits were produced through woodblock print. The images of the portraits are simple and unadorned, and the woodworking is coarse, incorporating religious, artistic, and popular folk customs into one style. There are different kinds of ceremonial prints of gods which are used as offerings and for a variety of folk customs during weddings, funerals, birthdays, prayers to drive away illnesses, and exorcising evil spirits.

例句：

纸马自唐代出现以来伴随着宗教民俗的发展而广为流布，成为各地民间信仰活动中最常见的俗信物品。

Example Sentence:

Burning *zhima* was established in the Tang Dynasty (618-907), and has spread widely throughout China through various folk religions and beliefs, becoming one of the most widely seen activities during folk rituals.

shenma;
divine horse print

参见“纸马”。

See *zhima* (paper horse print).

甲马

jiama;
armored horse print

参见“纸马”。

See *zhima* (paper horse print).

巫术 *wushu;* witchcraft; shamanism

一种企图借助超自然的神秘力量而对人、事、物施加影响以达到某种目的的手段。远古时代社会发展水平低下，先民往往将许多无法解释的自然现象归结为不可知的神秘力量的控制，因此产生了巫术这种初级信仰。巫术具有神秘性和仪式性，曾广泛用于祭祀、祈福、辟邪等方面，体现了人们寻求保护、避免灾害的愿望。进入文明社会以后，民间巫术与佛教、道教等人为宗教和鬼神信仰结合起来，延续至今。巫师在从事民俗宗教活动的同时还参与民间娱乐活动。民间巫术很多，常见的有“招魂巫术”“驱鬼巫术”“放蛊巫术”“神判巫术”等，不少民间艺术活动和艺术品成为巫术的工具和手段。

In ancient folk beliefs, an alleged method of using supernatural and mystical powers to influence people, affairs, or things in order to achieve some objective. During ancient society, when the level of development was low, people often attributed all manner of unexplainable natural phenomena to the realm of the supernatural. This produced primitive beliefs in witchcraft, which are mystical and ceremonial in nature. It uses all forms of offerings, prayers, and admonitions to gain protection from and prevent disasters. As society developed, folk witchcraft beliefs were combined with other religious and supernatural beliefs like Buddhism and Daoism. Some of these beliefs have lasted to the present day, and are used in folk religious activities as well as recreational events. There are many forms of witchcraft; some of the most common include “summoning the soul,” “expelling ghosts,” “releasing poisons,” and “mystical divination.” Many pieces of folk art are used as tools and means for such witchcraft.

例句：

巫术的实施通常要选择场所、占卜日期，巫师要穿戴法衣，有的地区还要戴面具，准备法器，严格按照特定程序来进行。

Example Sentence:

When performing witchcraft, a public arena and divination date typically need to be selected. Practitioners usually wear religious clothes, and in some regions they also wear masks. Ritual instruments are prepared for the event, which must rigorously conform to specific rules.

巫舞 *wuwu;* witch dance; wizard dance

原始祭祀舞蹈。原始社会生产力低下，图腾崇拜与鬼神迷信观念十分兴盛，逐渐产生了沟通人神之间的"巫"。巫舞是祭祀时伴随巫术仪式而进行的各类舞蹈，被认为是巫与超自然神灵通话的语言，是巫术中的一种重要活动。巫舞的特点是动作硬直、多棱角，幅度大，带有浓厚的神秘色彩。但后期经过人们加工整理，许多巫舞已被改造成民俗性节日中的舞蹈，具有很高的审美价值。

A primitive form of worship dance combined with superstitious beliefs. In ancient times, people often attributed unknown conditions or events to the supernatural; therefore, totem worship and superstitions regarding ghosts and gods were widespread. This gradually led to the notion of a village "witch" who "communicated" between gods and human beings. The witch dance was accompanied by witchcraft rituals usually held during sacrifices. It was considered the way of communication between witches and supernatural gods, and was an important activity in witchcraft culture. The witch dance was a mystical ritual characterized by stiff, straight, and exaggerated movements involving a variety of different angles. Thousands of years later, witch dances have become adapted into dances that are performed during folk festivals, and have high aesthetic, historical, and cultural value.

例句：

巫舞表演让观众一览这种古老而又神秘的文化。

Example Sentence:

During a witch dance show, audiences can get a glimpse of this ancient and mysterious folk art.

巫觋

wuxi;
witch; sorcerer and sorceress

人类早期信仰中据信能与鬼神沟通、代表鬼神说话、实现鬼神意愿的人，“巫”即女巫师，“觋”即男巫师。当时的人们认为巫觋掌握着沟通天地人神的特殊能力，具有亦人亦神的双重身份。

People who were believed to possess the magical power to communicate with ghosts and spirits, speak on their behalf, and realize their wishes in ancient times. *Wu* refers to a sorceress and *xi* refers to a sorcerer. They were said to have the special ability to facilitate communication between humans and deities, and would act as both a person and a spirit.

例句：

祭祀活动中，**巫觋**以卜筮、巫词、咒语及歌舞等手段制造气氛，沟通人神之间的“联系”，其中尤以舞蹈为重要手段。

Example Sentence:

During sacrificial ceremonies, witches used divination, shamanic terms, magical words, and even songs and dances to create a special atmosphere that allowed them to connect the celestial and human realms. Dances were an especially important method employed during such activities.

傩 *Nuo*; *nuo* sacrificial ceremony

中国古代驱除疫鬼的一种巫术活动，是原始宗教信仰的产物，也称“傩祭”。早在三千多年以前的商周时期，傩祭已成为举国重视的大典。早期的傩祭一般由头戴面具、手持兵器的巫师带队到各处搜寻疫鬼。后来傩的宗教祭祀功能逐渐淡化，向傩舞、傩戏演变，成为娱神与娱人相结合的歌舞、戏剧形式。一般认为，傩最初产生于中原地区，后逐渐与各地区、各民族文化融合，产生了不同形式的傩戏，主要流传于长江流域、黄河流域和西南地区的多个民族。现今的傩祭活动大多穿插在傩戏演出中，目的在于驱鬼逐疫，招祥纳吉。傩是中国最古老、传统文化意蕴最深厚也是最具生命力的活态非物质文化遗产。

Originally a shamanic activity in ancient China believed to exorcise ghosts spreading pestilence, also called *nuoji* (*nuo* sacrifice). As early as 3,000 years ago during the Shang (c. 1600-1100 BC) and Zhou dynasties (c. 1100-256 BC), *nuoji* was known all across ancient China. Shamans with masks and weapons would lead teams of people to search for demons. Later, the religious sacrificial functions of *nuoji* faded out, and it evolved into a dance and opera form to entertain the gods and also people. These first performances are generally believed to have originated in Central China, and then integrated with different cultures in various regions and ethnic groups. As a result, different types of *nuo* performances emerged, mainly gaining popularity in the Yangtze and Yellow river valleys as well as among some ethnic minorities in China's southwestern areas. Today, most *nuoji* are included in *nuo* operas, which aim to ward off disease and pray for good luck. *Nuo* sacrificial ceremony marks China's oldest living intangible cultural heritage, and has a profound traditional culture which is still vital today.

例句：

2018年5月1日在贵阳花溪举办了首届傩文化艺术节，首次集中向游客展示了“**傩**”这一特殊文化。

Example Sentence:

The First *Nuo* Culture and Art Festival, which was held on May 1st, 2018 in Guiyang, Guizhou Province introduced the unique *nuo* culture to tourists for the first time.

傩祭 *nuoji; nuo* sacrifice

参见“傩”。

See *nuo* (*nuo* sacrificial ceremony).

傩面具 *nuo mianju; nuo* masks

傩祭、傩舞、傩戏中使用的驱邪和表演用面具，俗称“脸子”“鬼脸”。在原始宗教信仰中，面具被视为神的化身，请神就是请面具。面具一般以木材、兽皮、丝麻、泥和纸浆等为原料，经雕塑、彩绘而成。举行傩祭时，巫师用面具装饰自己，身披兽皮而舞，以示能通鬼神。早期巫师的面具多为动物形象，是原始宗教与图腾崇拜的产物，后来改成了人面具。面具初次使用时要举行开光仪式，据说这样面具才有神的灵验。

Traditional masks used in *nuo* exorcisms and performances, commonly known as *lianzi* (face) or *guilian* (face of a ghost). In primitive religious beliefs, masks were considered the incarnation of gods. They are made of wood, hides, silk linen, clay, and paper pulp and then carved and painted. During *nuoji*, shamans would dance with masks and wear hides, showing that they could communicate with gods and ghosts. The early masks took the form of animals, integrating primitive religions and totem worship. Later, they were changed into human faces. It is said that in order to make the masks effective, they needed to be consecrated before first use.

例句：

宋代以后傩祭逐渐消失，但**傩面具**在傩戏、傩舞中得到广泛应用，一直流传至今。

Example Sentence:

Nuoji (*nuo* rites and ceremonies) gradually disappeared after the Song Dynasty (960-1279), but *nuo* masks have been widely used in *nuo* operas and *nuo* dances until today.

傩戏 *nuoxi; nuo* opera

一种从原始傩祭活动中发展出来的戏剧形式。它是宗教文化与戏剧文化相结合的产物，在各个历史时期不断融入当时的宗教文化和民间戏曲艺术。明代中期以后，傩戏演出已经相当普遍。不同民族和不同地区的傩戏名称不一，但多与源于傩祭驱逐疫鬼的仪式有关。在其发展过程中，祭祀的功能逐渐淡化，娱乐内容和歌舞方面的内容越来越突出。

A traditional folk drama derived from primitive *nuoji* which integrates various religious and dramatic concepts into folk opera, and developed during various historical periods in Chinese history. *Nuo* operas became quite popular after the mid-Ming Dynasty (1368-1644) and developed into different plays in different regions and among different ethnic groups, but their origins can be tracked back thousands of years to ancient *nuo* ceremonial rituals meant to dispel ghosts and exorcise demons. The religious aspect of *nuo* rituals has faded over the years, and stories, singing, and dancing have been added to make it more entertaining.

例句：

傩戏是研究中国古代舞蹈和戏剧艺术发展的“活化石”。

Example Sentence:

Nuo opera is considered a “living fossil” for studying the development of Chinese ancient dance and drama.

南丰跳傩 *Nanfeng Tiaonuo;* Nanfeng *nuo* dance

流行于江西省南丰县的一种傩舞，源于汉代，沿袭古代驱鬼逐疫的仪式“驱傩”。南丰傩仪沿袭古礼，结构复杂，舞蹈形态多样，面具造型各异，所用法器道具非常多。鼎盛时期，南丰县有傩班160多个，2000多名艺人，传承着完整的傩仪和丰富多彩的傩舞形式，被誉为“中国古代舞蹈的活化石”。每逢春节，初一“起傩”，傩班艺人走村串户，举行驱鬼逐疫仪式，祈祷五谷丰登、人畜兴旺；元宵后“收傩”。其中最有代表性的是石邮村跳傩。石邮村跳傩在每年春节期间从

A derivative dance of traditional folk dancing seen in *nuo* performances, emerging during the Han Dynasty (206 BC-AD 220) and gaining popularity in Nanfeng County of Jiangxi Province. The dance evolved from *qu nuo,* an ancient ceremony believed to exorcise ghosts spreading pestilence. It has a complex structure, numerous dance forms, as well as various masks and instruments. During its golden age, over 160 *nuo* troupes and 2,000 performers in Nanfeng County performed the complete *nuoyi* and diverse *nuo* dance, making it a “living fossil of Chinese ancient dance.” During the Spring Festival, performances of

初一到十七持续不断，有起傩、跳傩、搜傩、圆傩等一整套仪式过程。跳傩演出有开山、纸钱、雷公、傩公傩婆等节目。始建于清代的傩神庙是跳傩活动中心。2006年，南丰跳傩被列入首批国家级非物质文化遗产项目名录。

the *nuo* dance would last from the first day until the Lantern Festival. Performers would travel from door to door, holding ceremonies to exorcise demons, dispel diseases, and pray for a good harvest and a rich life for the inhabitants. The *nuo* dance in Shiyou Village would last from the first day to the seventeenth day of the Spring Festival, during which time people would see a set of rituals including the opening ceremony, the *nuo* dance, exorcising ghosts, and closing ceremony. The Nanfeng *nuo* dances include Splitting the Mountain, Joss Money, the God of Thunder, the God and Goddess of *Nuo*, and other performances. The Temple of *Nuo* Gods built in the Qing Dynasty (1616-1911) is where the *nuo* dance is now performed. In 2006, the Nanfeng *nuo* dance was among the first group to be included on China's Intangible Cultural Heritage List.

例句：

经过一千多年的发展，到明清时期，**南丰跳傩**吸收了戏曲、木偶、灯彩、武术等多种表演技艺，变得更加世俗化、娱乐化。

Example Sentence:

By the Ming and Qing dynasties, through over 1,000 years of development, the Nanfeng *nuo* dance had assimilated drama, puppeteering, lanterns, martial arts, and other performance skills, making it more secular and entertaining.

池州傩戏 *Chizhou nuoxi;* Chizhou *nuo* opera

流行于安徽省贵池、青阳、石台等地的一种傩戏。池州傩戏是以宗族为演出单位、以请神敬祖和驱邪纳福为目的、以戴木制面具为表演特征的古老艺术形式。它既无职业班社也无专职艺人，靠各宗族“口传心授”世代沿袭，至今保持着古朴、粗犷的原始风貌。池州傩戏每年农历正月初七至十五进行，其主要表现形式兼有傩仪、傩舞和傩戏，保存有完整的请神、送神、祭祖的仪式。傩舞是正戏演出前后的舞蹈，情节简单，内容多是驱灾逐疫、祈求丰收、平安吉祥的吉利语，舞时大多用锣鼓伴奏，配合身段，节奏明快，动作性强，粗犷有力。傩戏有唱有白，有完整的故事情节。池州傩面具吸收和融汇了儒、释、道、巫的宗教意识，以及民俗、雕刻、绘画等内容，是中国民间艺术的精华。

A type of traditional *nuo* performance popular in Guichi, Qingyang, Shitai, and other places in Anhui Province. It is similar to other *nuo* operas in that it aims to worship gods and ancestors, exorcise devils and pray for good luck. It is different, however, in that it is organized by clans and it is performed by practitioners who are not professional performers. It has been passed down through generations by oral teaching and self-understanding, enabling it to maintain a quaint and rough style. Chizhou *nuo* operas last from the seventh day to the fifteenth day of the first lunar month, and mainly maintain the same forms of *nuoyi*, *nuo* dance and *nuo* operas. Ceremonies for receiving the gods, seeing off the gods, and offering sacrifices to the ancestors are included in the performances. The *nuo* dance is performed before and after the *nuo* opera. The dancing, based on simple plots, expresses the wish to drive off diseases and disasters, to pray for a good harvest, peace, and good luck. The performers usually dance in powerful movements with gongs and drums, making the whole performance lively and vigorous. *Nuo* operas tell a story with singing and narration. Chizhou *nuo* masks reflect the religious ideologies of Confucianism, Buddhism, Daoism, and shamanic beliefs. They also showcase ethnic customs and carving and painting skills, making them the essence of Chinese folk arts.

例句：

池州傩戏是中国一种古老的地方戏曲剧种，被誉为“戏曲活化石”，以古朴淳厚的魅力打动人心。

Example Sentence:

Chizhou *nuo* opera is a unique Chinese folk art form, which has been called a “living fossil of drama.” They possess an unsophisticated and yet deep charm that touches a chord with audiences.

安顺地戏 *Anshun Dixi;* Anshun opera

流行于贵州省贵阳市郊和安顺市一带的一种地方戏，当地俗称“跳神”，也称“军傩”。地戏的产生与明初来自安徽、江苏、江西、河南等地的安顺屯军有关，是古代军队在岁末或誓师祭祀仪式中戴面具的群队傩舞，兼具祭祀、实战训练和娱乐的功能。地戏多在空旷平地演出，剧目描述南征北战的英雄人物，其显著特点是演出者头蒙青巾，腰围战裙，脸上戴着面具，手执戈矛刀戟之类的武器，随口而唱，应声而舞。同时，地戏也富有巫术内容，被当地群众称为“跳神”。在饰演中又加进了许多青面獠牙的人物，以加强驱邪逐祟的气氛。当地每年上演两次地戏，一次在春节其间，称为“玩新春”，另一次在农历七月，称为“跳米花神”。2006年，安顺地戏被列入首批国家级非物质文化遗产项目名录。

A traditional Chinese folk drama derived from traditional *nuo* operas, popular in Anshun and the suburbs of Guiyang in Guizhou Province. It is also known as *tiaoshen* (sorcerer's dance) and *jun nuo* (military *nuo* opera). The origins of this form of *nuo* opera date back to the Ming Dynasty (1368-1644), when soldiers from Anhui, Jiangsu, Jiangxi, and Henan were stationed at the Anshun garrison. Soldiers performed the ancient *nuo* dance at the end of the year or in a mass pledge or sacrificial ceremony. It had multiple functions of worship, combat training, and entertainment, telling stories about the heroes on the battlefield. The performers sing and dance with musical accompaniment, wearing green head scarves, war skirts, masks and holding spears, swords, or halberds. The drama is also a shamanic activity, and many terrifying characters have been added to the drama to strengthen the atmosphere of warding off evil and worshipping gods. The local drama is first performed during Spring Festival to celebrate the New Year, and in the 7th lunar month, the Mihua God dance is performed. In 2006, Anshun opera was listed among the first group on China's Intangible Cultural Heritage List.

例句：

安顺地戏是研究戏剧发生学、人类学、宗教学、民俗学等学科不可多得的活材料。

Example Sentence:

Anshun opera is a rare living source of material on China's ancient religions, anthropology, folklore, and other subjects.

跳神

tiaoshen;
sorcerer's dance

参见“安顺地戏”。

See *Anshun Dixi* (Anshun opera).

军傩

jun nuo;
military *nuo* opera

参见“安顺地戏”。

See *Anshun Dixi* (Anshun opera).

打黄鬼 *da huanggui;* hunting the yellow devil

中国民间古老的大型社火活动，每年元宵节期间在河北省武安市固义村举行。黄鬼既是洪涝、虫害、疫病等灾异的人格形象，又是人间忤逆不孝等邪恶势力的代表。活动在半夜开始，“黄鬼”藏在村外的野地坟堆里，经过搜索，“大鬼”“二鬼”和“跳鬼”在黎明前捉住“黄鬼”后，押回村中游街示众；下午，“黄鬼”被押解到新搭建的审判台前，经过“判官”“阎王”两轮审议，最后判处极刑。这一系列仪式表达了人们期盼战胜自然灾异，确保风调雨顺、五谷丰登、人畜平安的美好愿望。

A large scale traditional *shehuo* performance held every year during the Lantern Festival in the village of Guyi, Hebei Province. The "Yellow Devil" is a personification of disasters like floods, pests, and plagues; it also represents evil people such as those who disobey their parents and bully the weak. At midnight, the "Yellow Devil," who is played by a veteran performer, hides himself in the graveyard outside the village. Villagers, dressed as the "Elder Spirit," "Younger Spirit," and "Leaping Spirit" search for and chase the "Yellow Devil," catching him before dawn. The "Yellow Devil" is then shackled and led in a parade through in the streets. In the afternoon, after a trial is conducted by the "King of Hell" and the "Justice Official of Hell," the "Yellow Devil" is sentenced to death and "executed" by being "cut up" on the riverbank. The performance conveys the desire of people to defeat disasters and enjoy bountiful harvests, a harmonious family, and a peaceful life.

例句：

“打黄鬼”中的各种人物角色大都以脸谱和面具为扮相。

Example Sentence:

Most of the actors involved in "Hunting the Yellow Devil" are dressed in elaborate costumes and masks.

符咒 *fuzhou;* magic spell; charm

中国道教用以传道修持的主要手段之一。“符”是用朱笔或墨笔所画的点线组合的神秘图形，有的外用佩戴或贴挂，有的烧灰服用；“咒”是反复诵唱、带有神秘色彩的口诀，内容大多为向鬼神祈求或命令。一般情况下，画符、用符都有咒语配合。民间用“符咒”祈福消灾或召驱鬼神，以达到平安吉祥的目的。符咒现仍没有在民间消失。

Daoist magic spells, charms, and incantations in a written form used for protection and punishment. *Fu* (magic symbols) would be drawn in mysterious graphs of dots and lines with red or black ink. It can be carried with, hung up or pasted up. Some are supposed to be burnt and swallowed. *Zhou* is a verbal charm or spell spoken repeatedly with special tones. Generally, *fu* is drawn and used simultaneously with *zhou*. People used *fuzhou* to pray for good fortune, ward off disasters, and to exorcise ghosts and deities with the hope of gaining a peaceful and happy life.

例句：

符咒源于巫觋，后被早期道教吸收并规范化。

Example Sentence:

Casting spells and charms (*fuzhou*) originated from sorcery and was incorporated and standardized by early Daoism.

吞口 *tunkou;* door faces; gate masks

中国南方部分地区悬挂在民宅大门门楣上的木雕或石刻的辟邪兽头。按照传统的风水理论，民居有凶宅和吉宅两类，那些因各种条件限制无法辨别、选择的民宅，要借助守护神的威力来驱邪止煞，逢凶化吉。“吞口”多绘成变形的虎头，也有的绘上阴阳太极及八卦图像，其造型来源于驱鬼活动的面具。常见的木雕吞口大多圆眼外鼓，獠牙龇嘴，面目狰狞。挂在内房门口的虎头模板面具多怒目阔口。石雕吞口则常常和石刻门匾连成一体。

Wood or stone carvings of animal faces hanging on the gates or doors of private residences meant to deter evil spirits, found in some parts of southern China. According to feng shui theory, houses are generally divided into two categories: lucky houses and unlucky ones. When a home owner is unable to determine or select a good location for their house, they often resort to using guardian spirits to exorcise evil and demons, effectively turning misfortune into fortune. The door face usually takes the design of a tiger head, and it is sometimes painted with such symbols as *taiji* and the eight trigrams. The designs originate from masks used in exorcism. These faces usually have ferocious facial expressions with round, protruding eyes and long, sharp teeth. Masks that are hung at doors usually bear the design of a tiger head with glaring eyes and a big mouth. Masks are often integrated into horizontal stone boards with inscriptions in them that are placed above gates.

例句：

吞口以凶神恶煞的形象吓唬鬼魔，为人们守护大门。

Example Sentence:

Gate masks with ferocious facial expressions are believed to guard the home by deterring demons and ghosts.

八卦

bagua;
trigram; eight trigrams formerly used in divination

中国古代的一套含有象征意义的符号。由符号“-”和“--”每三个一组组合成八种不同的形式，其中“-”代表阳，“--”代表阴，这八种不同形式的符号组合即被称为“八卦”。八卦的名称是：乾、兑、离、震、巽、坎、艮、坤。古人认为，每一卦形都有其一定的象征意义，乾卦象征天，坤卦象征地，坎卦象征水，离卦象征火，震卦象征雷，艮卦象征山，巽卦象征风，兑卦象征沼泽。人们借由八卦的象征意义及其相互演变规律来解释自然与社会的发展变化。根据史料记载，八卦的形成源于河图和洛书，相传由伏羲和周文王所创，伏羲所创称之为“先天八卦”，周文王所创称之为“后天八卦”。八卦出自《易经》，是中国文化的基本哲学概念。

A deep and rich philosophical concept used in ancient China for divination and to help deduce the relationship between various phenomena in nature. It consists of eight combinations of three broken (--) or unbroken (-) lines, representing yin or yang. *Bagua* and their symbolic meanings are *qian* for heaven, *dui* for marsh, *li* for fire, *zhen* for thunder, *xun* for wind, *kan* for water, *gen* for mountain, and *kun* for earth. The symbolic meaning of *bagua* and their interchanging rules are used to interpret and even forecast the developments of nature and society. According to records, *bagua* originated from *Hetu* and *Luoshu,* and the concept was created by Fuxi and King Wen (1152 -1056 BC) of the Zhou Dynasty. Recorded in the monumental work *The Book of Changes, bagua* is a basic philosophical concept of Chinese culture.

例句：

据《汉书·艺文志》记载，伏羲画**八卦**，周文王演为六十四卦。

Example Sentence:

According to the *Book of Han,* Fuxi first drew the eight trigrams and King Wen of the Zhou Dynasty is credited with having formed the sixty-four hexagrams.

占卜 *zhanbu;* divination

人类推断吉凶祸福的手法。中国古代很早就出现了占卜活动，“占”指观察，“卜”指烧灼龟壳，占卜最初是指将动物龟甲或骨头钻孔，用火烧烤，通过其呈现出的裂纹走向来判断福祸。早期的占卜多用于战争、农事等集体活动中，后来也可通过占卜预测个人的吉凶福祸，判断其才华。据史料记载，三皇五帝的传说时代已出现占卜活动，周朝出现了占卜的典籍《周易》，形成一套以八卦为理论依据的预测、占卜理论，之后发展为用各种手段和方式试图预测事物的发展变化。占卜术到唐宋时达到鼎盛。明清以后，随着自然科学知识的普及，占卜逐渐走向衰落。

The practice of predicting the future or using superstitious methods to gain understanding of natural phenomena or worldly events in ancient China. One of the earliest methods was to carve symbols into a tortoise shell or the bones of animals, and then place them in raging flames; predictions could supposedly be made by the directions in which cracks appeared. Approaching battles or agricultural concerns were the most likely reason for divination, but the custom later became used to predict individual fortunes. According to historical records, the superstition first appeared in the legendary era of the Three Sovereigns and Five Emperors. Later, a detailed methodology of divination based on eight trigrams was laid out in *The Book of Changes*, composed in the Zhou Dynasty (c.1100-256 BC), which later became a method used to predict unknown future developments. After the Ming (1368-1644) and Qing (1616-1911) dynasties, this form of divination became less popular with the development of science and technology.

Example Sentence:

There are many types of divination

例句：

中国的**占卜**方法很多，但影响最大、流传最广的还是以八卦为理论依据的筮占法及由此衍生出的各种方法。

methods in China, but divination based on the *bagua* theory (found in *The Book of Changes*) and other various methods derived from *bagua* are the most popular and influential forms of divination.

占星术 *zhanxingshu;* astrology

通过观测天象来预卜人间事务的一种占卜术。占星术源于古人对于超自然力量的崇拜。占星术最晚在西周已出现，常用于国运、战争及个人性格命运的预测。秦汉时占星术已经十分兴盛，之后出现了与占星术相关的书籍。

A means of divining information about human affairs by studying the movements and relative positions of celestial objects. Chinese astrology originated from ancient worship of supernatural forces, appearing in China in the late Western Zhou Dynasty (c. 1100-771 BC). Chinese astrology was mainly used to predict state affairs, wars, and the futures and characteristics of people. In the Qin (221-206 BC) and Han (206 BC-AD 220) dynasties, works on astrology had already become popular and widespread throughout society.

例句：

占星术牵强地把天象与人事联系在一起，是非科学的。但占星术对古代天文学的发展有一定促进作用。

Example Sentence:

Astrology observes the relationships between astronomical phenomena and human affairs in a non-scientific way. However, astrology did advance the study of astronomy, to some degree, in ancient times.

qiuqian;
pray and draw divination sticks at temple

中国民间占卜的一种方法。迷信的人通过抽签方式来占卜吉凶。求签多在寺庙、道观进行，每一竹签所刻内容不同，分上、中、下三类，上为吉，中为平，下为凶。求签者先向神像虔诚地跪拜、磕头祷告，诉说欲求何事，然后从签筒中任抽一签，根据所抽取的竹签内容判断吉凶祸福。

A form of Chinese folk divination believed to foretell fortunes by drawing divinatory sticks. Monasteries and Daoist temples would have divinatory sticks (籤筒 *qiantong*) placed in divinatory stick holders (籤條 *qiantiao*). The sticks are usually made of bamboo and engraved with different contents in top, middle and low categories where the top is auspicious, the middle is normal, and the low is ominous. People would first kowtow and pray to the deities regarding what is desired, and then draw a divinatory stick from the holder and read the result.

例句：

庙里也有管姻缘的神，女人们会在那里**求签**问其未来的姻缘。

Example Sentence:

In temples which also have a god that oversees marriage, women often pray and draw divinatory sticks to learn about their future spouses.

风水

fengshui;
feng shui; Chinese geomancy

中国历史悠久的一门玄术，也叫"堪舆"，源于中国古代天人合一的哲学思想。"风"指元气和场能，"水"指流动和变化。风水本为相地之术，指住宅基地、坟地等的地理形势，是一种研究环境与宇宙规律的哲学。迷信的人认为风水好坏可影响住家或葬者家庭的盛衰吉凶，因此民间有请风水先生看风水的习俗。而从科学的角度来说，风水理论实际上是地球物理学、水文地质学、建筑学、生态学，以及人体生命信息学等多种学科综合一体的一门自然科学。

Feng shui is a geomancy theory in China that has a long history and is also known as *kanyu*. It focuses on achieving harmony between humans and their environment. *Feng* refers to vital and field energy, while *shui* refers to flow and change. Feng shui involves the geographic conditions of residences or graveyards, which is a philosophy about the environment and laws of the universe. Some superstitious people believe that good or bad feng shui can affect the fortunes of families that occupy a house, and the feng shui of a tomb can influence the fortunes of the deceased's offspring. As a result, people have the custom of inviting a feng shui master to come and inspect the feng shui of a site. From a scientific perspective, feng shui can be viewed as a natural science combining geophysics, hydrography, architecture, ecology, and life information science.

例句：

信**风水**的人认为，住在一个风水好的住宅里的人，各种运势都会好。

Example Sentence:

People who believe in feng shui think that those living in a home with good feng shui will have good fortune.

冲喜 *chongxi;* arrange a wedding to counteract bad luck

中国民间借婚娶转凶为吉的封建婚俗。冲喜分为两种。一种是给病人冲喜。男子身患重病，医治无望，便筹办婚礼，娶女子过门，希望能借喜气消除病魔。另一种是为家人冲喜。家中长辈身患重病时安排家中适龄男子娶亲，以期通过喜气冲走不祥之气，使病人病情好转，转危为安。旧时中国很多地区盛行冲喜，这种愚昧荒唐的做法使很多女子一过门就守寡，凄惨一生。1949年后，冲喜的做法基本上消失了。

A Chinese folk marriage custom involving using a wedding to turn bad luck into good luck. There are two forms of *chongxi*. If a man suffers from a serious illness and shows no sign of recovery, he will marry a woman through a wedding arrangement by his family with the hope that the wedding will help cure his illness. The second form is when an elder in a family suffers from a serious illness, a man of marriageable age in the family will have a wedding arranged with the hope that it will ward off evil spirits and in turn improve the elder's physical condition. The custom was prevalent in many parts of China, causing many women to become widowed and lead a miserable life. The custom was banned after the founding of the People's Republic of China in 1949.

例句：

他今年时运不佳，需要冲**冲喜**才好。

Example Sentence:

He'd better arrange a wedding to counteract his bad luck this year.

黄道吉日

huangdao jiri;
auspicious date; lucky date

迷信的人认为的中国传统历法黄历中诸事皆顺的好日子，简称"黄道日"。在中国传统习俗中，人生中的重要事情如婚嫁、盖房、乔迁新居等都需要选择吉日进行，以避凶险。中国古代以星象来推断吉凶，认为黄道十二星神中的青龙、明堂、金匮、天德、玉堂、司命六辰为吉神，他们值日之时会事事顺利，不避凶忌，即为"黄道吉日"；另外六位黑道凶神当值时就会诸事皆忌。人们会专门挑选黄道吉日做重要的事情，以求大吉大利，这种做法在中国乡村依旧很流行。

An auspicious day for a certain event according to the Chinese traditional lunar calendar. It is called "*huangdao ri*" for short. In traditional Chinese culture, important activities such as weddings, building a house, moving into a new house, are carried out on auspicious days to avoid danger. Chinese astrology was consulted to ascertain the good days for certain events. Among the 12 gods of the zodiac, the six auspicious gods are Qinglong, Mingtang, Jinkui, Tiande, Yutang, and Siming. Therefore, days when the six auspicious gods were "on duty" were deemed auspicious days. People undoubtedly avoid doing important things on days when the other six ominous gods were on duty. As a result, people specifically selected these days for important activities, with the hopes of bringing good luck. This custom is still observed in China's countryside.

例句：

现在**黄道吉日**一般泛指比较吉利的日子，例如带 8（与"发"谐音）的日期。

Example Sentence:

Nowadays, auspicious dates are calculated more simply, such as days related to the number eight—*ba* in Chinese, which rhymes with *fa* meaning "prosperity."

避讳 *bihui;* taboo; practice of placing a taboo on certain words

一种语言禁忌。中国古代对帝王、圣贤和尊长不能直呼其名，书写时或用同音字、同义字代替，或以缺笔、不写来避免，这就叫作“避讳”。“避讳”分为国讳（帝王名字必须避讳），圣讳（孔圣人的名字必须避讳）和家讳（不能直接称呼父母长辈的名字），最初是一种古老的语言禁忌，后来发展成为统治阶级维护其封建等级制度的工具。“避讳”又是一种修辞格，对犯忌的事物通过委婉语表述其本意，该修辞手法就是“避讳”。

The ban on speaking or writing a certain word, words or name. For example, in ancient China, people were not allowed to directly say the names of emperors, sages, or elders. When writing, they would use homophones or synonyms as substitutes for their names or avoid them altogether by intentionally missing a stroke or component. Linguistic taboos can be differentiated as a state taboo (names of emperors must be avoided), a sage taboo (names of sages such as Confucius must be avoided), and private taboos (names of parents or elders in a family should not be referred to directly). This ancient form of banning communicating words and names later became a tool for the ruling class to uphold its feudal hierarchy and power. This resulted in a figure of speech where people speak indirectly about things in order to refer to them so as to avoid directly saying the taboo word. Hence, it became known as *bihui*.

例句：

现在看来，这种**避讳**的行为令人啼笑皆非，但是在古代，这种避讳之风确实深刻地影响着人们的生活。

Example Sentence:

Nowadays, the practice of placing a taboo on certain words is considered absurd. But in ancient times, this practice produced a profound impact on people’s lives.

太岁头上动土

taisui toushang dongtu;
challenge sb. far superior in power or strength; beard the lion in his den

中国俗语，比喻触犯强者，自找霉运。“太岁”是中国古代民间对木星的别称，木星每12年围绕太阳转一圈，每年换一个位置，民间迷信认为地下相对应的方位就有一个太岁的化身。传说建筑房屋时屋门不能正对着太岁在天上的星位，否则地上的太岁化身就会动怒，引发灾难。于是逐渐形成了“太岁头上不能动土”的说法。

A Chinese proverb. It is a metaphor for offending the strong and asking for trouble. *Taisui* was an ancient Chinese nickname for Jupiter, which revolves around the sun every 12 years and changes its position every year. Folk superstition believed there was an opposing incarnation of Jupiter which existed in the underground world. Therefore, when building a house, the door cannot face the position of Jupiter in the sky, otherwise the incarnation of Jupiter in the underground world would become angry and cause a disaster. The phrase has come to be interpreted as “don’t provoke someone far superior in power or strength.”

例句：

他说一个身份不明的男子打电话给他，并警告他“不要在**太岁头上动土**”。

Example Sentence:

He said an unidentified man called him and warned him not to beard the lion in his den.

三长两短

sanchang liangduan;
unexpected misfortune; unforeseen disasters or accidents (usually refers to death)

中国俗语，比喻意外的变故、灾祸，特指人的死亡。这一说法与棺材有关。棺材一般由六片木材拼凑而成，上下左右四块长，两头短。由于上面的棺盖在尸体入棺后才盖上，所以在装殓尸体时只有三长两短五块木板，故而“三长两短”成为遇难、死亡的隐语、讳词。人人认为用餐时筷子长短不齐地放在桌子上会不吉利，有“三长两短”的意思，预示灾祸或者死亡。在日常生活中，人们也经常使用“三长两短”意指各种危及人生命的风险。

A Chinese idiom, directly translated as “three long ones and two short ones,” which has come to be a metaphor for unexpected changes or disasters, especially death. The saying is related to a coffin, which is made of four long pieces—the bottom, top, and two sides—and two short pieces at the head and foot. When a dead body is placed inside the coffin, there are only three long and two short pieces of wood as the top piece will only be used after that. Therefore, the expression “three long ones and two short ones” becomes a euphemism for death and disaster. In the same way, a pair of chopsticks of uneven length on the table is also considered inauspicious and an indication of disaster or death. In daily life, people often use this expression to refer to the many risks that endangers one’s life.

例句：

你要是有个**三长两短**，我也就活不成了。

Example Sentence:

I wouldn’t be able to live if anything happened to you!

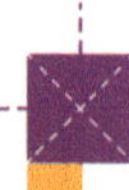

六六大顺

liuliu dashun;
lucky double six; double six makes for good luck

中国人常用的祝福语，寓意事事顺利，吉祥如意。中国人认为“六”是吉祥数字，因为其谐音为“（有）路”，表示办事顺利，两个“六”自然就是“路路大顺”了。还有一种说法来自《易经》：六为阴爻，代表阴柔；六六为至柔至顺之卦，而柔能克刚，因此代表顺利。

A Chinese greeting meaning that everything will proceed smoothly. In Chinese, it is pronounced *liuliu da shun*, directly translated as “six six very smooth.” It is deemed lucky because the Chinese word for “six” (*liu*) sounds like the word for “road” (*lu*), which has the meaning that “all roads ahead are smooth.” Another explanation originates from *The Book of Changes*, where six is the female trigram and represents the feminine. Six-six is the most gentle and soft trigram. As the soft can overcome the hard, it represents “smoothness.”

例句：

数字“六”在中国人看来是个最吉祥不过的数字了，中国有句俗语叫“**六六大顺**”，这充分说明了数字“六”的吉祥之意。

Example Sentence:

The number “six” in Chinese is considered the most auspicious number. The Chinese saying “double six makes for good luck” fully reveals the auspicious implications of the number “six.”

好事成双

haoshi chengshuang;
Good things come in pairs.

成语比喻两件好事同时到来，时来运到。中国人认为双数吉利，单数不祥，所以喜欢好事成双，现在可用做祝福语。

A Chinese idiom. It is a general belief in Chinese culture that even numbers are auspicious while odd numbers are ominous. Therefore, it is believed that a good thing will not happen singularly, but will be accompanied by another good thing. Nowadays it can be used as a greeting.

例句：

中国人讲究**好事成双**，所以送礼时要尽量挑选双份。

Example Sentence:

Chinese people believe that good things come in pairs, so gifts in pairs are always welcome.

寡妇年

guafu nian;
widow year

中国农历年中没有“立春”节气的年份，又名“盲年”或“哑年”。中国的历法是一种阴阳合历，一年按太阳的运行分为二十四节气，按月亮的运行分为十二个月，并用增设闰月的办法来解决阴历与阳历之间的时间差问题。于是就会出现某

A Chinese lunar year without the solar term “Beginning of Spring” as a result of the discrepancy between the solar and lunar calendars, also called *mangnian* (blind year) or *yanian* (dumb year). The solar calendar is based on the earth's orbit around the sun, and dates are basically fixed, with days in the year set at 365.24. The lunar calendar is based on cycles

些阴（农）历年份有十三个月的情形。这样，阳历年的立春节气就有可能出现在上一阴历年的腊月，或者下一阴历年的正月，从而出现无春年和双春年。民间认为立春是春天的起始，一年之中无"立春"即无阳气来临，对于女人即无男人相配，自然就是寡妇，所以称无春年为"寡妇年"。民间认为在"寡妇年"结婚不吉利，丈夫会早死。

of the moon in one month, which average out to about 29 days per month, resulting in a year with 354 days. Traditional Chinese calendar is a combination of the solar and lunar calendars. There is a method of adding a lunar month to make up for the difference, resulting sometimes in years with 13 lunar months. As a result, the "Beginning of Spring" solar term in a solar calendar may appear in the twelfth month of a lunar year and the first lunar month of the lunar year that follows, thus leading to a year without "spring" or one with "double spring." The Chinese people believe that springtime is associated with the yang male characteristic. Therefore, if there is no "Beginning of Spring" then there is no yang energy. For people, it means a year without a male partner, hence a "widow's year." It is believed that getting married during a widow year is ominous and may cause the husband to die prematurely.

例句：

寡妇年不宜结婚的说法根本没有科学依据，但民间仍有不少人相信。

Example Sentence:

There is no scientific basis for the saying that it is inauspicious to marry during a widow year, but many Chinese people still choose to believe it.

左眼跳财，右眼跳灾

zuoyan tiao cai, youyan tiao zai;
twitching left eye foretells fortune, twitching right eye foretells disaster

中国民间迷信说法。中国人认为眼皮的跳动会预示吉凶。中国人认为事物都有两面性，一阴一阳，一好一坏，于是将人的左右眼皮不由自主的跳动也分出吉凶，认为左眼皮跳是吉利的预兆，右眼皮跳则是不祥的预示。

A Chinese folk superstitious phrase not based on scientific fact. Some Chinese people believe a twitching eyelid foretells events to come. Chinese traditionally believe that two opposite things—such as left and right, top and bottom—are associated with yin and yang and therefore one must be negative while the other is positive. The involuntary movements of the two eyelids are no exception, with twitching of the left eye foretelling fortune (yang) and that of the right eye forecasting imminent disaster (yin).

例句：

左眼跳财，右眼跳灾的说法纯属迷信，事实上，眼皮跳和人的身体健康状况是息息相关的。

Example Sentence:

It is a superstitious saying that a twitching eyelid is a forecast of good or bad things to come. In fact, a twitching eyelid is closely related to one's health.

附录一

Appendix I:

中国历史年代简表

A Brief Chronology of Chinese History

<table>
<tr><td colspan="3">夏 Xia Dynasty</td><td>c. 2070-1600 BC</td></tr>
<tr><td colspan="3">商 Shang Dynasty</td><td>1600-1046 BC</td></tr>
<tr><td rowspan="3">周
Zhou Dynasty①</td><td colspan="2">西周 Western Zhou Dynasty</td><td>1046-771 BC</td></tr>
<tr><td rowspan="2">东周
Eastern Zhou Dynasty</td><td>春秋
Spring and Autumn Period</td><td>770-476 BC</td></tr>
<tr><td>战国
Warring States Period</td><td>475-221 BC</td></tr>
<tr><td colspan="3">秦 Qin Dynasty</td><td>221-206 BC</td></tr>
<tr><td rowspan="2">汉
Han Dynasty</td><td colspan="2">西汉 Western Han</td><td>206 BC-AD 25</td></tr>
<tr><td colspan="2">东汉 Eastern Han</td><td>25-220</td></tr>
<tr><td rowspan="3">三国
Three Kingdoms Period</td><td colspan="2">魏 Wei</td><td>220-265</td></tr>
<tr><td colspan="2">蜀 Shu</td><td>221-263</td></tr>
<tr><td colspan="2">吴 Wu</td><td>222-280</td></tr>
</table>

注释 Note:
①战国时期公元前256年，秦国战胜周朝最后一任君王周赧王，周朝结束。秦国于公元前221年统一中国，建立秦朝。
The Zhou Dynasty (1046-256 BC) ended in 256 BC when its last emperor Nan was defeated by the State of Qin during the Warring States Period. Qin unified China in 221 BC and the Qin Dynasty began.

<table>
<tr><td rowspan="2">晋 Jin Dynasty</td><td colspan="2">西晋 Western Jin</td><td>265-317</td></tr>
<tr><td colspan="2">东晋 Eastern Jin</td><td>317-420</td></tr>
<tr><td rowspan="9">南北朝
Southern and Northern Dynasties</td><td rowspan="4">南朝
Southern Dynasties</td><td>宋 Song</td><td>420-479</td></tr>
<tr><td>齐 Qi</td><td>479-502</td></tr>
<tr><td>梁 Liang</td><td>502-557</td></tr>
<tr><td>陈 Chen</td><td>557-589</td></tr>
<tr><td rowspan="5">北朝
Northern Dynasties</td><td>北魏
Northern Wei</td><td>386-534</td></tr>
<tr><td>东魏
Eastern Wei</td><td>534-550</td></tr>
<tr><td>北齐
Northern Qi</td><td>550-577</td></tr>
<tr><td>西魏
Western Wei</td><td>535-556</td></tr>
<tr><td>北周
Northern Zhou</td><td>557-581</td></tr>
<tr><td colspan="3">隋朝 Sui Dynasty</td><td>581-618</td></tr>
<tr><td colspan="3">唐朝 Tang Dynasty</td><td>618-907</td></tr>
</table>

<table>
<tr><td rowspan="16">五代十国
Five Dynasties and Ten States Period</td><td rowspan="5">五代
Five Dynasties</td><td>后梁
Later Liang</td><td>907-923</td></tr>
<tr><td>后唐
Later Tang</td><td>923-936</td></tr>
<tr><td>后晋
Later Jin</td><td>936-947</td></tr>
<tr><td>后汉
Later Han</td><td>947-950</td></tr>
<tr><td>后周
Later Zhou</td><td>951-960</td></tr>
<tr><td rowspan="11">十国
Ten States</td><td>北汉
Northern Han</td><td>951-979</td></tr>
<tr><td>吴 Wu</td><td>902-937</td></tr>
<tr><td>吴越 Wuyue</td><td>907-978</td></tr>
<tr><td>闽 Min</td><td>909-945</td></tr>
<tr><td>南汉
Southern Han</td><td>917-971</td></tr>
<tr><td>荆南
(又称“南平”)
Jingnan
(Also Nanping)</td><td>924-963</td></tr>
<tr><td>楚 Chu</td><td>927-951</td></tr>
<tr><td>南唐
Southern Tang</td><td>937-975</td></tr>
<tr><td>前蜀
Former Shu</td><td>907-925</td></tr>
<tr><td>后蜀
Later Shu</td><td>934-965</td></tr>
</table>

宋朝 Song Dynasty	北宋 Northern Song	960-1127
	南宋 Southern Song	1127-1279
辽 Liao		907-1125
金 Jin		1115-1234
西夏 Xixia		1038-1227
元 Yuan Dynasty		1206-1368
明 Ming Dynasty		1368-1644
清 Qing Dynasty		1616-1911
中华民国 Republic of China		1912-1949
中华人民共和国 People's Republic of China		1949-

附录二

Appendix II:

中国各民族

Ethnic Groups in China

（按汉语拼音排序）

(Arranged in Pinyin alphabetical order)

中文 In Chinese	英文 In English	主要分布地区 Main Distribution Areas
阿昌族	Achang	云南 Yunnan
白族	Bai	云南、贵州、湖南 Yunnan, Guizhou, Hunan
保安族	Bonan	甘肃 Gansu
布朗族	Blang	云南 Yunnan
布依族	Bouyei	贵州 Guizhou
朝鲜族	Korean	辽宁、吉林、黑龙江 Liaoning, Jilin, Heilongjiang
达斡尔族	Daur	内蒙古、黑龙江 Inner Mongolia, Heilongjiang
傣族	Dai	云南 Yunnan
德昂族	De'ang	云南 Yunnan
东乡族	Dongxiang	甘肃、新疆 Gansu, Xinjiang
侗族	Dong	贵州、湖南、广西 Guizhou, Hunan, Guangxi
独龙族	Derung	云南 Yunnan

中文 In Chinese	英文 In English	主要分布地区 Main Distribution Areas
俄罗斯族	Russian	新疆、黑龙江 Xinjiang, Heilongjiang
鄂伦春族	Oroqen	黑龙江、内蒙古 Heilongjiang, Inner Mongolia
鄂温克族	Ewenki	内蒙古 Inner Mongolia
高山族	Gaoshan	台湾、福建 Taiwan, Fujian
仡佬族	Gelao	贵州 Guizhou
哈尼族	Hani	云南 Yunnan
哈萨克族	Kazak	新疆 Xinjiang
汉族	Han	分布全国 all over China
赫哲族	Hezhen	黑龙江 Heilongjiang
回族	Hui	宁夏、甘肃、河南、新疆、青海、云南、河北、山东、安徽、辽宁、北京、内蒙古、天津、黑龙江、陕西、贵州、吉林、江苏、四川 Ningxia, Gansu, Henan, Xinjiang, Qinghai, Yunnan, Hebei, Shandong, Anhui, Liaoning, Beijing, Inner Mongolia, Tianjin, Heilongjiang, Shaanxi, Guizhou, Jilin, Jiangsu, Sichuan
基诺族	Jino	云南 Yunnan
京族	Gin	广西 Guangxi
景颇族	Jingpo	云南 Yunnan
柯尔克孜族	Kirgiz	新疆 Xinjiang

中文 In Chinese	英文 In English	主要分布地区 Main Distribution Areas
拉祜族	Lahu	云南 Yunnan
黎族	Li	海南 Hainan
傈僳族	Lisu	云南、四川 Yunnan, Sichuan
珞巴族	Lhoba	西藏 Xizang
满族	Manchu	辽宁、河北、黑龙江、吉林、内蒙古、北京 Liaoning, Hebei, Heilongjiang, Jilin, Inner Mongolia, Beijing
毛南族	Maonan	广西 Guangxi
门巴族	Monba	西藏 Xizang
蒙古族	Mongol	内蒙古、辽宁、吉林、河北、黑龙江、新疆 Inner Mongolia, Liaoning, Jilin, Hebei, Heilongjiang, Xinjiang
苗族	Miao	贵州、湖南、云南、广西、重庆、湖北、四川 Guizhou, Hunan, Yunnan, Guangxi, Chongqing, Hubei, Sichuan
仫佬族	Mulam	广西 Guangxi
纳西族	Naxi	云南 Yunnan
怒族	Nu	云南 Yunnan
普米族	Primi	云南 Yunnan
羌族	Qiang	四川 Sichuan

中文 In Chinese	英文 In English	主要分布地区 Main Distribution Areas
撒拉族	Salar	青海 Qinghai
畲族	She	福建、浙江、江西、广东 Fujian, Zhejiang, Jiangxi, Guangdong
水族	Sui	贵州、广西 Guizhou, Guangxi
塔吉克族	Tajik	新疆 Xinjiang
塔塔尔族	Tartar	新疆 Xinjiang
土族	Tu	青海、甘肃 Qinghai, Gansu
土家族	Tujia	湖南、湖北、重庆、贵州 Hunan, Hubei, Chongqing, Guizhou
佤族	Va	云南 Yunnan
维吾尔族	Uygur	新疆 Xinjiang
乌孜别克族	Uzbek	新疆 Xinjiang
锡伯族	Xibe	辽宁、新疆 Liaoning, Xinjiang
瑶族	Yao	广西、湖南、云南、广东 Guangxi, Hunan, Yunnan, Guangdong
彝族	Yi	四川、云南、贵州、广西 Sichuan, Yunnan, Guizhou, Guangxi
裕固族	Yugur	甘肃 Gansu
藏族	Tibetan	西藏、四川、青海、甘肃、云南 Xizang, Sichuan, Qinghai, Gansu, Yunnan
壮族	Zhuang	广西、云南、广东 Guangxi, Yunnan, Guangdong

附录三

Appendix III:

中国主要传统节日

Main Traditional Festivals in China

春节	Spring Festival (first of the first lunar month)
元宵节	Lantern Festival (fifteenth of the first lunar month, marking the end of the Spring Festival)
清明节	Qingming Festival (around the fifth day of April, a festival in commemoration of the dead and a time for outings)
端午节	Dragon Boat Festival (fifth of the fifth lunar month, celebrated by eating *zongzi* and holding dragon boat races)
七夕节	Qixi Festival (seventh of the seventh lunar month, considered Chinese Valentine's Day)
中秋节	Mid-Autumn Festival (fifteenth day of the eighth lunar month, celebrated by eating moon cakes and enjoying the full moon)
重阳节	Double Ninth Festival (ninth day of the ninth lunar month, on which people ascend heights to ask for blessings)
除夕	Spring Festival Eve

附录四

Appendix IV：

二十四节气

The Twenty-four Solar Terms

季节 Season	节气名称 Name of Solar Term	日期 Date on Gregorian Calendar
春季 Spring	立春 Beginning of Spring 雨水 Rain Water 惊蛰 Insects Awakening 春分 Spring Equinox 清明 Pure Brightness 谷雨 Grain Rain	February 3, 4, or 5 February 18,19, or 20 March 5, 6, or 7 March 20 or 21 April 4, 5, or 6 April 19, 20, or 21
夏季 Summer	立夏 Beginning of Summer 小满 Grain Full 芒种 Grain in Ear 夏至 Summer Solstice 小暑 Lesser Heat 大暑 Greater Heat	May 5, 6, or 7 May 20, 21, or 22 June 5, 6, or 7 June 21 or 22 July 6, 7, or 8 July 22, 23, or 24
秋季 Autumn	立秋 Beginning of Autumn 处暑 Limit of Heat 白露 White Dew 秋分 Autumn Equinox 寒露 Cold Dew 霜降 First Frost	August 7, 8, or 9 August 22, 23, or 24 September 7, 8, or 9 September 22, 23, or 24 October 8 or 9 October 23 or 24
冬季 Winter	立冬 Beginning of Winter 小雪 Light Snow 大雪 Heavy Snow 冬至 Winter Solstice 小寒 Lesser Cold 大寒 Greater Cold	November 7 or 8 November 22 or 23 December 6, 7, or 8 December 21, 22, or 23 January 5, 6, or 7 January 20 or 21

拼音索引
Pinyin Index

A

B

C

		(of the bed)	
彩礼	*caili*	bride price; bride wealth	265
财神	*Caishen*	God of Wealth	610
彩印花布	*caiyin huabu*	colorfully-dyed cloth	367
蚕神	*Canshen*	Patron Saint of Sericulture	584
草鞋	*cao xie*	straw shoes	347
草编	*caobian*	straw figure; straw plaited article	086
茶馆	*cha guan*	teahouse	448
茶祭	*cha ji*	tea sacrificial rites	451
插茱萸	*cha zhuyu*	picking and wearing cornel	181
茶道	*chadao*	tea ceremony; the way of drinking tea	430
查干萨日	*Chagansa Ri*	Tsagaan Sar	209
茶话会	*chahuahui*	tea party	434
插柳	*chaliu*	planting soft willow branches	124
缠百索	*chan baisuo*	tying a multi-colored thread braid	143
蟾宫	*Chan Gong*	Toad Palace	170
长窗	*changchuang*	long window	501
嫦娥奔月	*Chang'e Benyue*	Chang' e Flying to the Moon	174
长命百岁	*changming baisui*	long life to 100 years	301
长命缕	*changming lü*	longevity thread braid	130
长命锁	*changming suo*	longevity lock	236
长袍	*changpao*	long robe; long gown	335
菖蒲酒	*changpu jiu*	calamus wine	418
长衫	*changshan*	unlined long gown	337
长寿线	*changshou xian*	longevity threads	144
缠足	*chanzu*	foot binding; bound feet	351
茶神	*Chashen*	Patron Saint of Tea; Tea God	585
茶汤会	*chatang hui*	tea gathering	451
茶艺	*chayi*	the art of tea	431
陈家祠堂	*chen jia citang*	Chen Clan Ancestral Temple; Chen Clan Ancestral Hall;	497

辞家宴	*cijia yan*	home-leaving banquet; farewell banquet to loved ones	272
祠庙	*cimiao*	ancestral temple	575
祠堂（衣食住行）	*citang*	ancestral temple; ancestral hall	496
祠堂（信仰崇拜）	*citang*	ancestral temple/hall	574
催生	*cui sheng*	heralding labor	226
蹴鞠	*cuju*	kick the ball	120

D

打黄鬼	*da huanggui*	hunting the yellow devil	641
大地之母	*Dadi Zhimu*	Mother Earth	523
大褂	*dagua*	unlined long gown	336
大寒	*Dahan*	Greater Cold	047
戴香包	*dai xiangbao*	wearing a perfume pouch	142
代饮	*dai yin*	drink wine on somebody's behalf	425
戴柳	*dailiu*	wearing soft willow branches	125
戴孝	*dai xiao*	wearing mourning clothes; be in mourning	311
褡裢	*dalian*	cloth bag	353
大殓	*dalian*	enconffin	319
丹凤	*danfeng*	phoenix	550
荡秋千	*dang qiuqian*	playing on a swing	119
大年初一	*danian chuyi*	Chinese New Year's Day	075
倒插门	*dao chamen*	marrying into the wife's family	252
倒座	*daozuo*	opposite building	454
大暑	*Dashu*	Greater Heat	034
大雪	*Daxue*	Heavy Snow	043
大宅院（晋陕豫）	*dazhaiyuan*	residential compound with courtyards (in Shanxi, Shaanxi and Henan)	459

E

F

G

盖碗茶	*gaiwan cha*	tea in a lidded teacup	436
干打垒草房（东北）	*gandalei caofang*	adobe house; house with walls of rammed earth (northeast China)	470
感情深，一口闷	*ganqing shen, yi kou men*	Drink it all down if we are good friends; good friends, bottoms up	427
干支	*ganzhi*	stems and branches	018
功夫茶	*gongfu cha*	gongfu tea	434
古尔邦节	*Gu'erbang Jie*	Corban Festival; Eid al-Adha	216
挂艾叶	*gua ai'ye*	hanging mugwort leaves	139
寡妇年	*guafu nian*	widow year	655
广东早茶	*guangdong zaocha*	Guangdong morning tea	449
广寒宫	*Guanghan Gong*	Guanghan Palace	169
冠礼	*guanli*	capping ceremony	243
关圣帝君	*Guansheng Dijun*	Holy Emperor Guan; Saint Emperor Guan	590
观音菩萨	*Guanyin Pusa*	Guanyin Bodhisattva; Goddess of Mercy	588
瓜皮帽	*guapi mao*	skull cap; hemispherical cap	345
姑姑节	*Gugu Jie*	Married Daughter's Home Visit Day	146
龟	*gui*	tortoise	551
鬼城	*guicheng*	(Fengdu) ghost town/city	624
鬼都	*guidu*	ghost city	625
鬼节	*Guijie*	Ghost Festival; Hungry Ghosts Festival	158
归宁	*guining*	home visit to bring peace of mind	290
过百日	*guo bairi*	celebrating the 100th day	233
过百岁	*guo baisui*	celebrating the 100th day	233
过小年	*guo Xiaonian*	celebrating Xiaonian (Minor Chinese New Year)	052
锢窑	*guyao*	*guyao* cave dwelling	465
谷雨	*Guyu*	Grain Rain	027

H

J

接姑奶奶	*jie gunainai*	welcoming a married daughter back for a visit	113
节	*jie*	festival; solar term	003
接风酒	*jiefeng jiu*	welcome banquet wine	420
接三	*jie san*	receiving the returning soul on the third	314
祭坟	*ji fen*	offering sacrifices at the grave side	325
笄礼	*jili*	hair-pinning ceremony	244
敬酒	*jing jiu*	propose a toast	424
惊蛰	*Jingzhe*	Insects Awakening	023
紧压茶	*jinya cha*	compressed tea; brick tea	438
九九消寒图	*jiu jiu xiaohan tu*	The 9 Nines Drawing for Winter	188
酒令	*jiu ling*	drinkers' wager game; drinking game	422
酒要满，茶要浅	*jiu yao man, cha yao qian*	While serving guests wine, fill the wine glass to the brim; while serving guests tea, do not fill up the teacup.	433
酒剂	*jiuji*	medicinal liquor	415
旧历	*jiuli*	the Old Calendar	010
酒神	*Jiushen*	Patron Saint of Wine; Wine God	586
酒祖	*Jiuzu*	Father of Wine	587
祭月	*jiyue*	moon worship	171
祭灶	*ji zao*	worshipping the Kitchen God	053
祭祖（岁时节令）	*jizu*	worshiping one's ancestors; ancestor worship	160
祭祖（信仰崇拜）	*jizu*	ancestor worship	562
菊花酒	*juhua jiu*	chrysanthemum wine	419
军傩	*jun nuo*	military *nuo* opera	640

K

开裆裤	*kaidangku*	open-seat pants; split pants or overalls	342
开市	*kaishi*	resuming business	080
开斋节	*Kaizhai Jie*	Lesser Bairam; Kaizhai Festival	217
炕头石狮	*kangtou shishi*	stone lion on bed	238
坎肩	*kanjian*	sleeveless jacket	338
靠山窑	*kaoshanyao*	cliffside cave dwelling	464
靠崖窑	*kaoyayao*	cliffside cave dwelling	464
孔明灯	*Kongming deng*	Kongming lanterns	201
孔雀舞	*kongque wu*	peacock dance	203
筷子	*kuaizi*	chopsticks	383
哭嫁	*ku jia*	weeping bride	271

L

腊味	*la wei*	cured meat and fish	192
腊八豆腐	*laba doufu*	laba tofu	195
腊八节	*Laba Jie*	Laba Festival	191
腊八面	*laba mian*	laba noodles	197
腊八蒜	*laba suan*	laba garlic	196
腊八粥	*laba zhou*	laba porridge	193
腊祭	*Laji*	Winter Sacrifice	050
廊桥	*lang qiao*	covered bridge; roofed bridge	516
蓝印花布	*lanyin huabu*	indigo-dyed cloth	366
老鼠嫁女	*Laoshu Jia Nü*	Mouse Marries Off His Daughter	087
老天爷	*Laotianye*	the Lord	521
老衣	*laoyi*	graveclothes; cerements	344
腊月忙年	*layue mangnian*	preparation for the coming Chinese New Year during the twelfth lunar month	051
雷公	*Leigong*	Lord of Thunder	530

M

N

纳吉	*na ji*	presenting betrothal gifts; confirming engagement; engagement gifts	261
南甜北咸	*nan tian bei xian*	sweet in the south and salty in the north	379
馕	*nang*	crusty pancake	408
南丰跳傩	*Nanfeng Tiaonuo*	Nanfeng *nuo* dance	635
闹洞房	*nao dongfang*	teasing the newlyweds in the bridal chamber	281
闹元宵	*nao yuanxiao*	celebrating the Lantern Festival	092
纳征	*na zheng*	presenting a bride price; paying bride wealth	262
年糕	*niangao*	Chinese New Year cake; Spring Festival cake	071
娘娘庙	*niangniang miao*	goddess temple	576
年画	*nianhua*	New Year picture; Spring Festival painting	066
年夜饭	*nianye fan*	New Year's Eve dinner; Chinese New Year reunion dinner	070
牛头马面	*Niu Tou Ma Mian*	Bull-Headed and Horse-Faced Hell Guards	622
农历	*nongli*	the Chinese calendar	009
弄瓦之喜	*nongwa zhi xi*	joy of having a baby girl	228
弄璋之喜	*nongzhang zhi xi*	joy of having a baby boy	228
女儿节	*Nü'er Jie*	Girl's Festival	149
女儿酒	*nü'er jiu*	daughter's wine	415
傩面具	*nuo mianju*	*nuo* masks	632
傩	*Nuo*	*nuo* sacrificial ceremony	631
傩祭	*nuoji*	*nuo* sacrifice	632
傩戏	*nuoxi*	*nuo* opera	634
女娲	*Nüwa*	Nüwa	569

P

牌坊	*paifang*	decorated archway; ornamental archway	503
牌楼	*pailou*	decorated archway; ornamental archway	504
抛绣球	*pao xiuqiu*	throwing embroidered silk ball	253
跑马转角楼	*paoma zhuanjiaolou*	“corner-turning” building	488
屏风	*pingfeng*	screen	506
平遥古城	*pingyao gucheng*	ancient city of Pingyao	461
聘礼	*pinli*	bride price; bride wealth	265
聘书	*pinshu*	engagement letter; betrothal letter	256
皮影戏	*piying xi*	Chinese shadow puppetry	099
泼水节	*Poshui Jie*	Water-Splashing Festival	198
破五	*powu*	lifting prohibitions on the fifth of the first lunar month	079

Q

抢孤	*qianggu*	offerings-grabbing competition	165
巧果	*qiaoguo*	fried thin pastry	154
袷袢	*qiapan*	robe	372
祈福门神	*Qifu Menshen*	Door God of Blessings	615
麒麟送子	*qilin song zi*	*qilin* sending a son	224
麒麟	*qilin*	kylin	548
青茶	*qing cha*	dark green tea	441
清明节	*Qingming Jie*	Qingming Festival; Tomb-Sweeping Day	114
清明柳	*Qingming liu*	Qingming willow; pure brightness willow	123
清明	*Qingming*	Pure Brightness; Fresh Green	026

R

S

赏月	*shangyue*	appreciating the moon	172
山神	*Shanshen*	Mountain God	537
烧包衣	*shao baoyi*	burning joss paper and paper clothing for the deceased	164
烧纸钱	*shao zhiqian*	burning joss paper	184
社火	*shehuo*	festival entertainment	094
社林	*shelin*	woods around land god temples	542
神马	*shenma*	divine horse print	627
蛇仙	*shexian*	snake fairy; snake spirit	555
时	*shi*	two-hour time span; season	002
十二花神	*Shi'er Huashen*	the twelve flower goddesses	543
十二生肖	*shi'er shengxiao*	twelve zodiac animals	014
十二支	*shi'erzhi*	twelve branches	017
十八层地狱	*Shibaceng Diyu*	18 Levels of Hell; the Hell	621
十干	*shigan*	ten stems	016
石库门	*shikumen*	*shikumen* residence; Shanghai-style courtyard house	458
事死如事生	*shi si ru shi sheng*	serving the dead as if they were alive	305
食物五性	*shiwu wuxing*	five properties of food	378
守花烛	*shou huazhu*	stay up late to watch the wedding candles	282
兽鞋	*shou xie*	animal-shaped baby shoes	348
寿匾	*shoubian*	longevity tablet	299
寿糕	*shougao*	birthday pastry	295
守灵	*shou ling*	keep vigil beside the coffin; hold a wake	312
寿面	*shoumian*	birthday noodles; longevity noodles	296
守丧	*shou sang*	observing the conventions of mourning; be in mourning	313
守岁	*shousui*	staying up all night on	075

		Chinese New Year's Eve	
寿堂	*shoutang*	longevity hall	297
寿桃	*shoutao*	longevity peach; birthday peach	294
寿星（人生仪礼）	*shouxing*	God of Longevity; a person whose birthday is being celebrated	293
寿星（信仰崇拜）	*Shouxing*	Star of Longevity; God of Longevity	607
寿衣	*shouyi*	graveclothes	344
寿幛	*shouzhang*	longevity scroll	298
寿终正寝	*shouzhong-zhengqin*	passing away in one's home after a long life; die a natural death	305
数九歌	*Shu Jiu Ge*	the "Nines of Winter Song"; "9 Nines Song"	187
摔老盆	*shuai laopen*	breaking an old pot	322
拴马石	*shuanma shi*	hitching post	511
涮羊肉	*shuan yangrou*	instant-boiled mutton; hotpot, Mongolian style	400
霜降	*Shuangjiang*	First Frost	040
拴娃石	*shuanwa shi*	baby-fastening stone	237
水乡民居（江浙）	*shuixiang minju*	waterside residence	471
说媒	*shuo mei*	proposing a marriage; acting as a matchmaker	259
属相年	*shuxiang nian*	zodiac year	303
属相	*shuxiang*	birth sign	016
四大菜系	*si da caixi*	four best-known (Chinese) cuisines	385
四大门	*si da men*	the four great fairy animals	557
四合五天井	*sihewu tianjing*	courtyard house with five yards	486
四合院	*siheyuan*	courtyard home; courtyard house; quadrangle house	452

T

汤圆	*tangyuan*	glutinous rice ball (southern style)	091
唐装	*tangzhuang*	Tang suit	334
桃花坞年画	*taohuawu nianhua*	Taohuawu New Year picture	067
踏青	*taqing*	a nature walk; spring outing	118
提日子	*ti rizi*	making inquiries about the wedding date	263
填仓节	*Tiancang Jie*	Tiancang Festival; Granary-Filling Festival	110
天穿节	*Tianchuan Jie*	Tianchuan Festival; Sky-Patching Festival	109
添丁炮	*tianding pao*	firecrackers for newborns	235
天干	*Tiangan*	Heavenly Stems	016
天公	*Tiangong*	Lord of Heaven; Emperor of Heaven	520
天官赐福	*tianguan cifu*	heavenly blessings; May the Heavenly Official bestow happiness.	603
天井	*tianjing*	small yard; patio; sky well	454
添盆	*tian pen*	filling the tub	231
添喜	*tian xi*	having a blessing; having a newborn baby	227
挑花	*tiaohua*	cross-stitch work	365
跳神	*tiaoshen*	sorcerer's dance	640
贴福字	*tie fu zi*	mounting character *fu* (blessings)	065
提亲	*ti qin*	proposing a marriage; making a marriage proposal	259
童养婚	*tongyang hun*	marriage involving a child bride	249
偷瓜送子	*tou gua song zi*	stealing melons to pray for sons	578
投壶	*touhu*	the game of throwing an arrow into a jug	423

兔儿爷	*Tu'r Ye*	Rabbit God	170
团山古村	*tuanshan gu cun*	Tuanshan Historical Village	484
团圆饼	*tuanyuan bing*	tuanyuan cake; family reunion cake	178
土地神	*Tudi Shen*	Village Land God; local land god	598
土炕	*tukang*	earthen *kang*	509
土楼 （闽粤）	*tulou*	earthen towers; *tulou* (in Fujian and Guangdong); earthen houses	493
吞口	*tunkou*	door faces; gate masks	643
屠苏酒	*tusu jiu*	Tusu wine	417

W

王母娘娘	*Wangmu Niangniang*	Queen Mother Goddess	527
王母	*Wangmu*	Queen Mother	527
万年历	*wannianli*	perpetual calendar	011
为牛庆生	*wei niu qingsheng*	celebrating the birthday of the ox	153
围屋	*weiwu*	walled village	494
围嘴	*weizui*	bib	361
文财神	*Wen Caishen*	Civil God of Wealth	611
文官门神	*Wenguan Menshen*	Civil Door God	615
问名	*wen ming*	requesting birth profile of the potential bride (to assess marriage compatibility); birthday matching	260
文曲星	*Wenqu Xing*	God of Literature; Star of Literature	606
武财神	*Wu Caishen*	Martial God of Wealth	612
五大仙	*wu da xian*	the five great fairy animals	552
吴刚伐桂	*Wu Gang fa gui*	Wu Gang chopping the osmanthus tree	176

X

		show my respect.	
湘菜	*xiang cai*	Hunan cuisine; Xiang cuisine	391
厢房	*xiangfang*	wing room	505
仙人柱	*xianren zhu*	tent-like house	469
小寒	*Xiaohan*	Lesser Cold	046
小殓	*xiaolian*	dress a dead body	319
小满	*Xiaoman*	Grain Full	029
小名	*xiaoming*	childhood name; nickname	239
小暑	*Xiaoshu*	Lesser Heat	033
小雪	*Xiaoxue*	Light Snow	042
霞帔	*xiapei*	embroidered cloud shawl or cape	354
夏至	*Xiazhi*	Summer Solstice	032
谢孝	*xie xiao*	thank friends and relatives for offering condolences	317
喜花	*xihua*	wedding paper-cuts	288
夕佳山古民居（四川）	*xijia shan gu minju*	Xijiashan ancient residence	481
星相学	*xingxiang xue*	astrology; horoscope	527
兄弟参商	*xiongdi shenshang*	animosity between two brothers; sibling rivalry	529
雄黄酒	*xionghuang jiu*	realgar wine	141
喜鹊报喜	*xique baoxi*	the magpies forecast good news	558
喜丧	*xisang*	blessed funeral; happy funeral	307
喜堂	*xitang*	wedding hall	273
绣花鞋	*xiuhua xie*	embroidered shoes	350
绣花鞋垫	*xiuhua xiedian*	embroidered shoe pads	352
悬菖蒲	*xuan changpu*	hanging calamus	140
雪顿节	*Xuedun Jie*	Xuedun Festival; Shoton Festival	214
熏花	*xunhua*	soot-blackened flower	064
熏烟剪纸	*xunyan jianzhi*	soot-blackened paper-cut	064

Y

油条	*youtiao*	deep-fried twisted dough stick	403
圆坟	*yuan fen*	rounding the grave	326
圆三	*yuan san*	rounding on the third	327
元宵节	*Yuanxiao Jie*	Yuanxiao Festival; Lantern Festival	088
元宵	*yuanxiao*	glutinous rice ball (northern style)	090
鸳鸯戏水	*yuanyang xi shui*	two mandarin ducks playing on water	285
玉帝	*Yudi*	Jade Emperor	525
粤菜	*yue cai*	Cantonese (Guangdong) cuisine; Yue cuisine	386
月老	*Yuelao*	God of Marriage	592
月饼	*yuebing*	moon cake	177
月宫	*Yuegong*	Moon Palace	168
玉皇大帝	*Yuhuang Dadi*	Jade Emperor	523
玉皇	*Yuhuang*	Jade Emperor	525
盂兰盆节	*Yulanpen Jie*	Ullambana; Yulanpen Festival	159
鱼皮衣	*yupi yi*	fish skin clothing	375
雨师	*Yushi*	Master of Rain; God of Rain; Rain Spirit	534
雨水	*Yushui*	Rain Water	022

X

宰牲节	*Zaisheng Jie*	Festival of Sacrifice	216
簪榴花	*zan liuhua*	wearing pomegranate blossoms with hairpins	145
糌粑	*zanba*	roasted barley flour	409
藏历年	*Zangli Nian*	Tibetan New Year; Losar	212
藏袍	*zangpao*	Tibetan robe	370
藏戏节	*Zangxi Jie*	Tibetan Opera Festival	215
簪子	*zanzi*	hairpin	356

灶神	*Zaoshen*	Kitchen God	597
早生贵子	*zaoshengguizi*	quickly give birth to a son	286
赠扇	*zengshan*	giving fans; granting fans	144
炸酱面	*zhajiangmian*	noodles with soybean paste (Beijing Style)	402
毡房	*zhan fang*	yurt	468
占卜	*zhanbu*	divination	645
展佛节	*Zhanfo Jie*	Sunning the Buddha Festival	215
占星术	*zhanxingshu*	astrology	646
招魂	*zhao hun*	soul summoning	309
浙菜	*zhe cai*	Zhejiang cuisine; Zhe cuisine	389
折柳赠别	*zheliu zengbie*	picking up willow branches as departure gifts	125
枕顶绣	*zhending xiu*	pillow end embroidery	358
枕顶	*zhending*	pillow end	357
针扎	*zhenzha*	needle cushion	364
遮裙带	*zhequn dai*	skirt belt	363
指腹婚	*zhifu hun*	marriage based on prenatal betrothal	249
纸活	*zhihuo*	paper work	324
纸马	*zhima*	paper horse print; ceremonial print of a god or an immortal	626
纸钱	*zhiqian*	joss paper; ghost money	625
纸塑窗花	*zhisu chuanghua*	embossed window paper-cut	062
纸扎	*zhizha*	paper offerings	323
钟馗	*Zhong Kui*	Zhong Kui	617
中国茶	*zhongguo cha*	Chinese tea	428
中秋节	*Zhongqiu Jie*	Mid-Autumn Festival; Moon Festival	167
中山装	*zhongshanzhuang*	Chinese tunic suit; Sun Yat-sen suit	340
终身大事	*zhongshen dashi*	the greatest event in life;	246

		the matter of lifelong importance; marriage	
中元节	*Zhongyuan Jie*	Zhongyuan Festival; Ghost Festival	157
住对月	*zhu duiyue*	month away	290
砖茶	*zhuan cha*	brick tea; tea brick	437
砖雕	*zhuandiao*	brick engravings	510
转兜	*zhuandou*	rotatable bib	362
抓周	*zhuazhou*	item-grabbing test on the first birthday	234
竹笆房	*zhubafang*	bamboo house	480
竹楼	*zhulou*	bamboo stilt house	489
紫砂壶	*zisha hu*	purple clay teapot; terra cotta teapot	450
子孙窑	*zisun yao*	Offspring Hole; Hole for Beseeching Offspring	577
鬃人	*zongren*	bristle figure	085
粽子	*zongzi*	sticky rice dumpling	135
做三朝	*zuo sanzhao*	bathing on the third day	230
坐月子	*zuo yuezi*	convalesce for a month following child delivery	229
坐帐	*zuo zhang*	sitting behind the bed curtain	279
做七	*zuo qi*	making offerings on the sevenths	327
做寿	*zuoshou*	celebrating a birthday (for the elderly)	291
左眼跳财，右眼跳灾	*zuoyan tiao cai, youyan tiao zai*	twitching left eye foretells fortune, twitching right eye foretells disaster	657

出　　版　　人： 王君校
责 任 编 辑： 吴爱俊　张　乐
英 文 编 辑： 薛彧威
封面版式设计： 智玖拾（成都）文化传媒有限公司
印 刷 监 制： 汪　洋

图书在版编目（CIP）数据

中国民俗文化词典：插图本：汉英对照 /《中国民俗文化词典》编写组著 . -- 北京：华语教学出版社，2023.9
ISBN 978-7-5138-2457-6

Ⅰ . ①中… Ⅱ . ①中… Ⅲ . ①风俗习惯－中国－汉、英 Ⅳ . ① K892

中国国家版本馆 CIP 数据核字 (2023) 第 133956 号

中国民俗文化词典·插图本（汉英对照）
《中国民俗文化词典》编写组 著
*

华语教学出版社有限责任公司出版
（中国北京百万庄大街 24 号　邮政编码 100037）
电话：（86）10-68320585　68997826
传真：（86）10-68997826　68326333
网址：www.sinolingua.com.cn
电子信箱：hyjx@sinolingua.com.cn
北京中科印刷有限公司印刷
2023年（16开）第 1 版
2024 年第 1 版第 2 次印刷
（汉英）
ISBN 978-7-5138-2457-6
059900